Statement	Description (page in text)	
FUNCTION	Declares the start of a function subprogram (p. 346)	INTEGER FUNCTION ...
GO TO k	Transfer execution to the statement beginning with label k (p. 110)	GO TO 10
IMPLICIT NONE	Cancels default typing (an extension to FORTRAN 77) (p. 60)	IMPLICIT NONE
INQUIRE	Used to learn information about a file either by name or logical unit (p. 440)	INQUIRE (NAME='X', EXIST=FLAG)
INTEGER	Declares variables, parameters, or arrays of type INTEGER (p. 34)	INTEGER I, J, K
INTRINSIC	Specifies names of specific intrinsic functions that may be passed as command line arguments (p. 358)	INTRINSIC EXP
LOGICAL	Declares variables, parameters, or arrays of type LOGICAL (p. 34)	LOGICAL LTEST1, LTEST2

Logical Block IF	Structure to decide whether or not to execute particular blocks of statements, depending on whether one or more logical expressions are true or false (p. 91)	IF (X .GT. 0.) THEN
		    RES = SQRT(X)
		ELSE IF (X .EQ. 0.) THEN
		    RES = 0.
		ELSE
		    RES = SQRT(-X)
		END IF

Logical IF	Executes or skips a statement, depending on whether a logical expression is true or false (p. 108)	IF (X .LT. 0.) X = -X
OPEN	Opens a file (pp. 196, 432)	OPEN (UNIT=10,FILE='X',STATUS='OLD')
PARAMETER	Defines parameters (named constants) (pp. 35, 236)	PARAMETER (PI = 3.141592) PARAMETER (MAXSIZ = 1000)
PROGRAM	Defines the start of a program, and gives it a name (p. 25)	PROGRAM MYPROG
READ	Read in data (pp. 54, 445)	READ (12,100) RATE, TIME READ (LU,'(I6)') COUNT READ (*,*) NVALS
REAL	Declares variables, parameters, or arrays of type REAL (p. 34)	REAL COEF1, COEF2, COEF3
RETURN	Returns control from a subprogram to the calling routine (p. 298)	RETURN
REWIND	Position file pointer at first record in a file (pp. 205, 449)	REWIND (LU) REWIND 11
SAVE	Preserve local variables in a subprogram between calls to the subprogram (p. 329)	SAVE NCALLS, ISEED SAVE
STOP	Stop program execution (pp. 26, 619)	STOP STOP 'bad data'
SUBROUTINE	Declares the start of a subroutine (p. 298)	SUBROUTINE SORT (DATA1, NVALS)
WRITE	Write out data (pp. 55, 448)	WRITE (12,100) RATE, TIME WRITE (LU,'(1X,I6)') COUNT WRITE (*,*) NVALS

FORTRAN 77 FOR ENGINEERS AND SCIENTISTS

With an Introduction to FORTRAN 90

FORTRAN 77 FOR ENGINEERS AND SCIENTISTS

With an Introduction to FORTRAN 90

STEPHEN J. CHAPMAN

University of Maryland

HarperCollins*CollegePublishers*

**This book is dedicated to my wife, Rosa, the great love of my life
and the mother of our seven wonderful children.**

Sponsoring Editor: John Lenchek
Developmental Editor: Nicholas Murray
Project Editor: Cathy Wacaser
Design Administrator: Jess Schaal
Text and Cover Design: Lesiak/Crampton Design Inc: Cindy Crampton
Cover Photo: Dominique Sarraute/The Image Bank
Production Administrator: Randee Wire
Compositor: Interactive Composition Corporation
Printer and Binder: R.R. Donnelley & Sons Company
Cover Printer: The Lehigh Press, Inc.

FORTRAN 77 for Engineers and Scientists With an Introduction to FORTRAN 90
Copyright © 1995 by HarperCollins College Publishers

Library of Congress Cataloging-in-Publication Data

Chapman, Stephen J.
    FORTRAN 77 for engineers and scientists: with an introduction to Fortran 90/
Stephen J. Chapman.
      p. cm.
    Includes index.
    ISBN 0-06-500068-4
    1. FORTRAN 77 (Computer program language)   2. FORTRAN 90 (Computer
program language)   I. Title.
QA76.73.F25C47   1994
005. 13' 3—dc20

                                                    94-27331
                                                       CIP

94 95 96 97 9 8 7 6 5 4 3 2 1

Contents

Preface

This book was conceived as a result of my experience in writing and maintaining large FORTRAN programs in both the defense and the geophysical fields. During my time in industry, it became obvious that the strategies and techniques required to write large, *maintainable* FORTRAN programs were quite different from what new engineers were learning in their FORTRAN programming classes at school. The incredible cost of maintaining and modifying large programs once they are placed into service absolutely demands that they be written to be easily understood and modified by people other than their original programmers. My goal for this book is to teach simultaneously both the fundamentals of the FORTRAN language and a programming style that results in good, maintainable programs. In addition, it is intended to serve as a reference once the students graduate and begin working in industry.

It is a challenge to teach undergraduates the importance of taking extra effort during the early stages of the program design process in order to make their programs more maintainable. Class programming assignments must by their very nature be simple enough for one person to complete in a short period of time, and they do not have to be maintained for years. Because the projects are simple, a student can often "wing it" and still produce working code. A student can take a course, perform all of the programming assignments, pass all of the tests, and still not learn the habits that are really needed when working on large projects in industry.

From the very beginning, this book attempts to teach FORTRAN in a style suitable for use on large projects.

- It emphasizes the importance of going through a detailed design process before any code is written, using a top-down design technique to break the program up into logical portions that can be implemented separately.
- It stresses the use of subprograms to implement those individual portions, and the importance of unit testing before the subprograms are combined into a finished product.
- Finally, it emphasizes the importance of exhaustively testing the finished program with many different input data sets before it is released for use.

In addition, this book teaches FORTRAN as it is actually encountered by engineers and scientists working in industry and in laboratories. Two facts of life are common in all programming environments: large amounts of old legacy code that have to be maintained, and the existence of subroutine libraries to make some programming tasks easier. The legacy code at a particular site may have been originally written in FORTRAN IV (or an even earlier version!), and it may use programming constructs that are no longer common today. For example, such code may use arithmetic **IF** statements, or computed or assigned **GO TO** statements.

Practical approaches to these features of the FORTRAN programming environment are presented in two chapters:

- Chapter 11 prepares the student to use FORTRAN libraries. It teaches the student about the types of libraries available, and about how to select and interface with a particular routine from a library. A small library called BOOKLIB is shipped with the Instructor's Manual that accompanies this book, and the routine descriptions for the BOOKLIB library are included in Appendix D. This library is used in Chapter 11 to teach the student to use library indexes, to read manual pages, and to interface with library routines.
- Chapter 12 is devoted to those older features of the language that are no longer commonly used, but that are encountered in legacy code. The chapter emphasizes that these features should *never* be used in a new program, but also prepares students to handle them when they encounter them.

FEATURES OF THE PRACTICAL APPROACH

Many features of this book are designed to emphasize the proper way to write reliable FORTRAN programs. These features should serve a student well as he or she is first learning FORTRAN, and should also be useful to the practitioner on the job.

Emphasis on Top-Down Design Methodology

The book introduces a top-down design methodology in Chapter 3, and then uses it consistently throughout the rest of the book. This methodology encourages a student to think about the proper design of a program *before* beginning to code. It emphasizes the importance of clearly defining the problem to be solved and the required inputs and outputs before any other work is begun. Once the problem is properly defined, it teaches the student to employ stepwise refinement to break the task down into successively smaller subtasks, and to implement the subtasks as separate subroutines or functions. Finally, it teaches the importance of testing at all stages of the process, both unit testing of the component routines and exhaustive testing of the final product. Several examples are given of programs that work properly for some data sets, and then fail for others.

The formal design process taught throughout the book may be summarized as follows:

1. *Clearly state the problem that you are trying to solve.*
2. *Define the inputs required by the program and the outputs to be produced by the program.*
3. *Describe the algorithm that you intend to implement in the program.* This step involves top-down design and stepwise decomposition, using pseudocode or flow charts.
4. *Turn the algorithm into FORTRAN statements.*

5. *Test the FORTRAN program.* This step includes unit testing of specific subprograms, and also exhaustive testing of the final program with many different data sets.

Emphasis on Subroutines and Functions

The book emphasizes the use of subroutines and functions to logically decompose tasks into smaller subtasks. It teaches the advantages of subprograms for data hiding. It also emphasizes the importance of unit-testing subprograms before they are combined into the final program. In addition, the book informs students about the common mistakes made with subprograms, and how to avoid them (argument-type mismatches, array-length mismatches, etc.).

Emphasis on Strong Typing

The **IMPLICIT NONE** statement is used consistently throughout the book to force the explicit typing of every variable used in the program, and to catch common typographical errors at compilation time. The book emphasizes that the **IMPLICIT NONE** statement is an extension to FORTRAN 77, but a very common one. If it is available on a particular compiler, it should be used. In conjunction with the explicit declaration of every variable in a program, the book emphasizes the importance of creating a variable dictionary that describes the purpose of each variable in a routine.

Emphasis on Portability and Standard FORTRAN 77

The book stresses the importance of writing portable FORTRAN code so a program can easily be moved from one computer to another one. It teaches students to use only standard FORTRAN 77 statements in their programs (with the exception of the **IMPLICIT NONE** statement) so they will be as portable as possible. FORTRAN 77 extensions that are found in some compilers and not in others, or that are implemented differently in different compilers, are avoided. Thus, for example, the **NAMELIST** statement is never mentioned in the sections of the book dealing with I/O statements.

The book also teaches students to isolate machine-dependent code into a few specific subroutines and functions, so only those subroutines and functions will have to be rewritten when a program is ported between computers.

Emphasis on the Limits of Computer Mathematics

Chapters 9 and 10 introduce problems associated with the limited precision of computer mathematics, and discuss ways to avoid them. In the discussion of the **DOUBLE PRECISION** data type in Chapter 9, the book introduces ill-conditioned systems of equations and shows how the limited precision of computer math can lead to incorrect answers even though the algorithm being used is correct. It then provides guidelines for using the **DOUBLE PRECISION** data type to avoid these problems.

Chapter 10 is an introduction to numerical methods. It expands on the material in Chapter 9 to discuss truncation and rounding errors, errors due to the subtraction of nearly equal numbers, cascading errors, and errors due to incorrect models. The examples in the chapter include higher order least squares fits, numerical integration, and finding the roots of equations. Examples of numerical methods from other chapters include statistical subroutines, sorting, solving simultaneous equations, and taking derivatives.

Comprehensive Coverage

The book endeavors to be a complete reference to the FORTRAN 77 language, so that a practitioner can locate any required information quickly. Special attention has been paid to the index to make features easy to find. A special effort has also been made to cover such obscure and little-understood features as passing subprogram names by reference, and defaulting values in list-directed input statements. This comprehensive coverage will make the book valuable as a reference work for years after graduation.

Introduction to FORTRAN 90

Chapter 13 contains an introduction to the FORTRAN 90 language, which was approved as an ISO Standard in 1991 and an ANSI Standard in 1992. FORTRAN 90 is a superset of FORTRAN 77 that has been extensively enhanced. While it is not possible to discuss all the new features of FORTRAN 90 in a single chapter, the book presents the major new features and attempts to give the feel of the language through many examples.

FEATURES TO AID LEARNING

The book includes several features designed to aid student comprehension.

Examples

Numerous detailed examples appear throughout the text that show students how to put concepts into practice.

Quizzes

A total of 25 quizzes appear scattered throughout the chapters. Answers to all quiz questions appear in Appendix E. These quizzes can serve as useful self-tests of comprehension.

Exercises

In addition, there are approximately 270 end-of-chapter exercises. The answers to selected exercises appear in Appendix F.

"Good Programming Practice" and "Programming Pitfalls"

Good programming practices are highlighted as a boxed feature in all chapters to reinforce their importance. Likewise, boxes are used to highlight common errors in programming to help students avoid them. Examples of these features are shown below.

■ GOOD PROGRAMMING PRACTICE

Always indent the body of an **IF** structure by two or more spaces to improve the readability of the code.

PROGRAMMING PITFALLS

Beware of integer arithmetic. Integer division often gives unexpected results.

Chapter Review

End-of-chapter materials include summaries of good programming practice, lists of key terms, and summaries of FORTRAN statements and structures.

The BOOKLIB Library

An important pedagogical feature of this text is the BOOKLIB library, a small library of subroutines supplied on a diskette with the Instructor's Solution Manual. The instructor can compile and install the BOOKLIB library on whatever computer is being used to teach FORTRAN, and students can use it to learn how to choose and link to library subroutines.

■ SUPPLEMENTARY MATERIALS

Instructor's Solution Manual

The Instructor's Solution Manual contains solutions to all end-of-chapter exercises. It also contains a diskette with the BOOKLIB library and the source code for all examples in the book, as well as for the end-of-chapter programming exercises.

Test Bank and Transparency Masters

The Test Bank and Transparency Masters includes a test bank of more than 250 questions, and 100 transparency masters.

LAHEY PERSONAL FORTRAN 77

Included with this book is a coupon for a discounted copy of Lahey Personal FOR-TRAN 77 and all associated development tools. This coupon entitles the purchaser of the book to buy a copy of Lahey Personal FORTRAN 77 for only $59. Lahey FORTRAN 77 is an outstanding implementation of the language, and it comes with a complete suite of development tools, including an excellent source-code debugger. I strongly encourage anyone who does not have access to another compiler to purchase Lahey Personal FORTRAN 77 as a learning tool. With the discount coupon, you can purchase both this book and the compiler for the price of the compiler alone.

A FINAL NOTE TO THE USER

No matter how hard I try to proofread a document like this book, it is inevitable that a few typographical errors will slip through and appear in print. If you should spot any such errors, please drop me a note via the publisher, and I will do my best to get them eliminated from subsequent printings and editions. Thank you very much for your help in this matter.

ACKNOWLEDGMENTS

I am grateful to the reviewers listed below for their constructive critiques of the manuscript as it was being developed. Special thanks are due to Betty Barr, whose comments were unusually thorough and helpful.

Betty Barr, *University of Houston*
Tony Connor, *Clemson University*
Georges M. Fadel, *Georgia Institute of Technology*
Donald Fitzwater, *University of Wisconsin-Madison*
Billy W. Friar, *Wright State University*
D. D. Hearn, *University of Illinois at Urbana-Champaign*
Daniel D. Ludwig, *Virginia Polytechnic Institute and State University*
Mary Lynch, *University of Florida*
Robert Madison, *Purdue University*
G. Paskusz, *University of Houston*
Lawrence Petersen, *Texas A & M University*
Frederick H. Reardon, *California State University-Sacramento*
Michael J. Rider, *Ohio Northern University*
Barbara Schreur, *Texas A & M University*
Timothy D. Thomasma, *University of Michigan-Dearborn*

I would like to thank Paul Breem of Lahey Computer Systems, Inc., for providing me with copies of Lahey's F77L FORTRAN 77 compiler and a beta version of Lahey's new FORTRAN 90 compiler to use while developing this book. The FORTRAN 90 compiler was essential to verify that the examples given in Chapter 13 were correct. Lahey was also kind enough to allow the readers of this book to purchase their excellent Personal FORTRAN compiler at a discount. I would also like to thank Microsoft Corporation for providing me with a copy of Microsoft FORTRAN 5.1 to use while developing this book.

I would like to thank John Lenchek, my sponsoring editor; Sandy Cubelic, his assistant; and Nick Murray, developmental editor; for their support and encouragement during the development of this text, as well as the rest of the staff at Harper-Collins who contributed to its publication.

Finally, I would like to thank my wife, Rosa, and our children, Avi, David, Rachel, Aaron, Sarah, Naomi, and Shira, for putting up with me during the writing of this book. Sometimes it seemed that it would never end. Maybe we'll see more of each other now!

Stephen J. Chapman

FORTRAN 77 FOR ENGINEERS AND SCIENTISTS

With an Introduction to FORTRAN 90

Introduction to Computers and the FORTRAN Language

The computer is the most important invention of the twentieth century. It affects our lives profoundly in many ways. When we go to the grocery store, the scanners that check out our groceries are run by computers. Our bank balances are maintained by computers, and the automatic teller machines that allow us to make banking transactions at any time of the day or night are run by more computers. Computers control our telephone and electric power systems, run our microwave ovens and other appliances, and even control the engines in our cars. Almost any business in the United States would collapse overnight if it were suddenly deprived of its computers. Considering their importance in our lives, it is almost impossible to believe that the first electronic computers were invented only 50 years ago.

Just what is this device that has had such an impact on all of our lives? A **computer** is a special type of machine that stores information, and can perform mathematical calculations on that information at speeds much faster than human beings can think. A **program,** which is stored in the computer's memory, tells the computer what sequence of calculations are required, and which information to perform the calculations on. Most computers are very flexible. For example, the computer on which I write these words can also balance my checkbook, if I just load it with a different program.

Computers can store huge amounts of information, and with proper programming, they can make that information instantly available when it is needed. For example, a bank's computer can hold the complete list of all the checks and deposits made by every one of its customers. On a larger scale, credit companies use their computers to hold the credit histories of every person in the United States—literally billions of pieces of information. When requested, they can search through those billions of pieces of information to recover the credit records of any single person, and present those records to the user in a matter of seconds.

It is important to realize that *computers do not think as we understand thinking.* They merely follow the steps contained in their programs. When a computer appears to be doing something clever, it is because a clever person has written the program that it is executing. That is where we humans come into the act. It is our collective creativity that allows the computer to perform its seeming miracles. This book will help teach you how to write programs of your own, so that the computer will do what *you* want it to do.

1.1   THE COMPUTER

A block diagram of a typical computer is shown in Figure 1-1. The major components of the computer are the **central processing unit (CPU)**, **main memory, secondary memory,** and **input** and **output devices.** These components are described in the paragraphs below.

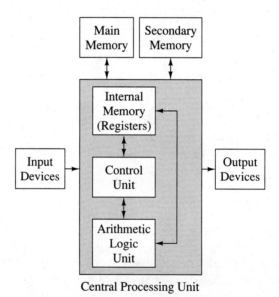

Central Processing Unit

FIGURE 1-1   A block diagram of a typical computer.

1.1.1   The CPU

The CPU is the heart of any computer. It is divided into a *control unit,* an *arithmetic logic unit (ALU),* and internal memory. The control unit within the CPU controls all of the other parts of the computer, while the ALU performs the actual mathematical calculations. The internal memory within a CPU consists of a series of *memory registers* used for the temporary storage of intermediate results during calculations.

The control unit of the CPU interprets the instructions of the computer program. It also fetches data values from input devices or main memory and stores them in the memory registers, and sends data values from memory registers to output devices or main memory. For example, if a program says to multiply two numbers together and save the result, the control unit fetches the two numbers from main memory and stores them in registers. Then, it will present the numbers in the registers to the ALU along with directions to multiply them and store the results in another register. Finally, after the ALU multiplies the numbers, the control unit takes the result from the destination register and stores it back into main memory.

FIGURE 1-2   A typical personal computer. *(Courtesy of Gateway 2000 Inc.)*

1.1.2 Main and Secondary Memory

The memory of a computer is divided into two major types of memory: *main* or *primary memory,* and *secondary memory*. Main memory usually consists of semiconductor chips. It is very fast, and relatively expensive. Data that is stored in main memory can be fetched for use in 100 nanoseconds[1] or less (sometimes *much* less) on a modern computer. Because it is so fast, main memory is used to temporarily store the program currently being executed by the computer, as well as the data that the program requires.

---

[1] A nanosecond is 0.000000001, or 10^{-9} second.

Main memory is not used for the permanent storage of programs or data. Most main memory is **volatile,** meaning that it is erased whenever the computer's power is turned off. Besides, main memory is expensive, so we only buy enough to hold the largest programs actually being executed at any given time.

Secondary memory consists of devices that are slower and cheaper than main memory. They can store much more information for much less money than main memory can. In addition, most secondary memory devices are **nonvolatile,** meaning that they retain the programs and data stored in them whenever the computer's power is turned off. Typical secondary memory devices are **hard disks, floppy disks,** and tape drives. Secondary storage devices are normally used to store programs and data that are not needed at the moment, but which may be needed some time in the future.

1.1.3   Input and Output Devices

Data is entered into a computer through an input device, and is output through an output device. The most common input device on a modern computer is a keyboard. Using a keyboard, we can type programs or data into a computer. Other types of input devices found on some computers are scanners and microphones.

Output devices permit us to use the data stored in a computer. The most common output devices on today's computers are cathode ray tube (CRT) screens and printers. Other types of output devices include plotters and speakers.

1.2   DATA REPRESENTATION IN A COMPUTER

Computer memories are composed of millions of individual switches, each of which can be ON or OFF, but not at a state in between. Each switch represents 1 **binary digit** (also called a **bit**); the ON state is interpreted as a binary 1, and the OFF state is interpreted as a binary 0. Taken by itself, a single switch can only represent the numbers 0 and 1. Since we obviously need to work with numbers other than 0 and 1, a number of bits are grouped together to represent each number that we use in a computer. When several bits are grouped together, they can be used to represent numbers in the *binary* (base 2) *number system.*

The smallest common grouping of bits is called a **byte.** *A byte is a group of 8 bits that are used together to represent a binary number.* The byte is the fundamental unit used to measure the capacity of a computer's memory. For example, the personal computer on which I am writing these words has a main memory of 4 megabytes (4,000,000 bytes), and a secondary memory (disk drive) with a storage of 200 megabytes.

The next larger grouping of bits in a computer is called a **word.** A word consists of 2, 4, or more consecutive bytes which are used to represent a single number in memory. The size of a word varies from computer to computer, so words are not a particularly good way to judge the size of computer memories. Word sizes for a few common computers are shown in Table 1-1.

TABLE 1-1 Word Size for Some Common Types of Computers

Computer	Bytes	Bits
DEC PDP-11	2	16
DEC VAX	4	32
Sun Sparcstation	4	32
486-based PC	4	32
Cray supercomputer	8	64

1.2.1 The Binary Number System

In the familiar base 10 number system, the smallest (rightmost) digit of a number is the ones place (10^0). The next digit is in the tens place (10^1), and the next one is the hundreds place (10^2), etc. Thus, the number 122_{10} is really $(1 \times 10^2) + (2 \times 10^1) + (2 \times 10^0)$. Each digit is worth a power of 10 more than the digit to the right of it in the base 10 system (see Figure 1-3(a)).

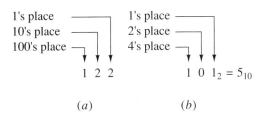

(a)   (b)

FIGURE 1-3 (a) The base 10 number 122 is really $(1 \times 10^2) + (2 \times 10^1) + (2 \times 10^0)$. ($b$) Similarly, the base 2 number 101_2 is really $(1 \times 2^2) + (0 \times 2^1) + (1 \times 2^0)$.

Similarly, in the binary number system, the smallest (rightmost) digit is the ones place (2^0). The next digit is in the twos place (2^1), and the next one is in the fours place (2^2), etc. Each digit is worth a power of 2 more than the digit to the right of it in the base 2 system. For example, the binary number 101_2 is really $(1 \times 2^2) + (0 \times 2^1) + (1 \times 2^0) = 5$, and the binary number $111_2 = 7$ (see Figure 1-3(b)).

Note that three binary digits can be used to represent eight possible values: $0 (= 000_2)$ to $7 (= 111_2)$. In general, *if n bits are grouped together to form a binary number, then they can represent 2^n possible values.* Thus a group of 8 bits

Two's Complement Arithmetic

The most common way to represent negative numbers in the binary number system is the two's complement representation. What is two's complement, and what is so special about it? Let's find out.

The Two's Complement Representation of Negative Numbers

In the two's complement representation, the leftmost bit of a number is the *sign bit*. If that bit is 0, then the number is positive; if it is 1, then the number is negative. To change a positive number into the corresponding negative number in the two's complement system, we perform two steps:

1. Complement the number (change all 1s to 0 and all 0s to 1).
2. Add 1 to the complemented number.

Let's illustrate the process using simple 8-bit integers. As we already know, the 8-bit binary representation of the number 3 would be 00000011. The two's complement representation of the number −3 would be found as follows:

1. Complement the positive number: 11111100
2. Add 1 to the complemented number: 11111100 + 1 = 11111101

The exact same process is used to convert negative numbers back to positive numbers. To convert the number −3 (11111101) back to a positive 3, we would:

1. Complement the negative number: 00000010
2. Add 1 to the complemented number: 00000010 + 1 = 00000011

Two's Complement Arithmetic

Now we know how to convert a positive number to a negative number in the two's complement representation. The special secret of the two's complement

(1 byte) can represent 256 possible values, a group of 16 bits (2 bytes) can be used to represent 65,536 possible values, and a group of 32 bits (4 bytes) can be used to represent 4,294,967,296 possible values.

In a typical implementation, half of all possible values are reserved for representing negative numbers, and half of the values are reserved for representing positive numbers. Thus, a group of 8 bits (1 byte) is usually used to represent numbers

numbers is that *positive and negative numbers may be added together according to the rules of ordinary addition without regard to the sign, and the resulting answer will be correct, including the proper sign.* Because of this, a computer may add any two integers together without checking to see what the signs of the two integers are. This simplifies the design of computer circuits.

Let's do a few examples to illustrate this point.

1. Add 3 + 4 in two's complement arithmetic.

3	00000011
+ 4	00000100
7	00000111

2. Add (−3) + (−4) in two's complement arithmetic.

−3	11111101
+ −4	11111100
−7	111111001

    In a case like this, we ignore the extra ninth bit resulting from the sum, and the answer is 11111001. The two's complement of 11111001 is 00000111 or 7, so the result of the addition was −7!

3. Add 3 + (−4) in two's complement arithmetic.

3	00000011
+ −4	11111100
−1	11111111

    The answer is 11111111. The two's complement of 11111111 is 00000001 or 1, so the result of the addition is −1!

With two's complement numbers, binary addition comes up with the correct answer regardless of whether the numbers being added are both positive, both negative, or mixed.

between −128 and +127, inclusive, and a group of 16 bits (2 bytes) is usually used to represent numbers between −32768 and +32767, inclusive.[2]

---

[2]There are several different schemes for representing negative numbers in a computer's memory. They are described in any good computer engineering textbook. The most common scheme is the so-called *two's complement* representation, which is described in the note above.

1.2.2   Octal and Hexadecimal Representations of Binary Numbers

Computers work in the binary number system, but people think in the decimal number system. Fortunately, we can program the computer to accept inputs and give its outputs in the decimal system, converting them internally to binary form for processing. Most of the time, the fact that computers work with binary numbers is irrelevant to the programmer.

However, there are some cases in which an engineer has to work directly with the binary representations coded into the computer. For example, individual bits or groups of bits within a word might contain status information about the operation of some machine. If so, the programmer will have to consider the individual bits of the word, and work in the binary number system.

An engineer who has to work in the binary number system immediately faces the problem that binary numbers are unwieldy. For example, a number like 1100_{10} in the decimal system is 010001001100_2 in the binary system. It is easy to get lost working with such a number! To avoid this problem, we customarily break binary numbers down into groups of 3 or 4 bits, and represent those bits by a single base 8 (octal) or base 16 (hexadecimal) number.

To understand this idea, note that a group of 3 bits can represent any number between 0 ($=000_2$) and 7 ($=111_2$). These are the numbers found in an **octal** or base 8 arithmetic system. An octal number system has 8 digits: 0–7. We can break a binary number up into groups of 3 bits, and substitute the appropriate octal digit for each group. Let's use the number 010001001100_2 as an example. Breaking the number into groups of three digits yields $010 \mid 001 \mid 001 \mid 100_2$. If each group of 3 bits is replaced by the appropriate octal number, the value can be written as 2114_8. The octal number represents exactly the same pattern of bits as the binary number, but it is more compact.

Similarly, a group of 4 bits can represent any number between 0 ($=0000_2$) and 15 ($=1111_2$). These are the numbers found in an **hexadecimal** or base 16 arithmetic system. A hexadecimal number system has 16 digits: 0 through 9 and A through F. Since the hexadecimal system needs 16 digits, we use 0 through 9 for the first 10 of them, and then A through F for the remaining 6. Thus, $9_{16} = 9_{10}$, $A_{16} = 10_{10}$, $B_{16} = 11_{10}$, and so forth. We can break a binary number up into groups of 4 bits, and substitute the appropriate hexadecimal digit for each group. Let's use the number 010001001100_2 again as an example. Breaking the number into groups of four digits yields $0100 \mid 0100 \mid 1100_2$. If each group of 4 bits is replaced by the appropriate hexadecimal number, the value can be written as $44C_{16}$. The hexadecimal number represents exactly the same pattern of bits as the binary number, but more compactly.

Some computer vendors prefer to use octal numbers to represent bit patterns, while other computer vendors prefer to use hexadecimal numbers to represent bit patterns. Both representations are equivalent, in that they represent the pattern of bits in a compact form.

TABLE 1-2   Table of Decimal, Binary, Octal, and Hexadecimal Numbers

Decimal	Binary	Octal	Hexadecimal
0	0000	0	0
1	0001	1	1
2	0010	2	2
3	0011	3	3
4	0100	4	4
5	0101	5	5
6	0110	6	6
7	0111	7	7
8	1000	10	8
9	1001	11	9
10	1010	12	A
11	1011	13	B
12	1100	14	C
13	1101	15	D
14	1110	16	E
15	1111	17	F

1.2.3 Types of Data Stored in Memory

Three common types of data are stored in a computer's memory: **character data, integer data,** and **real data** (numbers with a decimal point). Each type of data has different characteristics, and takes up a different amount of memory in the computer.

Character Data

The **character data** type consists of characters and symbols. A typical system for representing character data must include the following symbols:

1. The 26 uppercase letters **A** through **Z**
2. The 26 lowercase letters **a** through **z**
3. The 10 digits **0** through **9**
4. Miscellaneous common symbols, such as: " , ( ) { } [ ] ! ~ @ # $ % ^ & *, etc.

Since the total number of characters and symbols required to write any Western language is less than 256, *it is customary to use 1 byte of memory to store each character*. Therefore, 10,000 characters would occupy 10,000 bytes of the computer's memory.

The particular bit values corresponding to each letter or symbol may vary from computer to computer, depending on the coding system used for the characters. There are two common systems in use. The most important coding system is ASCII, which stands for the American Standard Code for Information Interchange. The ASCII coding system is used by most of the computer manufacturers in the world.[3] The other common system is EBCDIC, which stands for Extended Binary Coded Decimal Interchange Code. EBCDIC is used by IBM on its mainframe computers. The 8-bit codes corresponding to each letter and number in each of the above coding systems are given in Appendix A.

Integer Data

The **integer data** type consists of the positive integers, the negative integers, and zero. The amount of memory devoted to storing an integer will vary from computer to computer, but is usually 1, 2, 4, or 8 bytes. Four-byte integers are the most common type in modern computers.

Since a finite number of bits are used to store each value, only integers that fall within a certain range can be represented on a computer. Usually, the smallest number that can be stored in an n-bit integer is

$$\text{Smallest Integer Value} = -2^{n-1} \qquad \textbf{(1-1)}$$

and the largest number that can be stored in an n-bit integer is

$$\text{Largest Integer Value} = 2^{n-1} - 1 \qquad \textbf{(1-2)}$$

For a 4-byte integer, the smallest and largest possible values are $-2,147,483,648$ and $2,147,483,647$, respectively. Attempts to use an integer larger than the largest possible value or smaller than the smallest possible value result in an error called an *overflow condition*.[4]

---

[3]The ASCII character set includes all of the characters needed to write English, but does not include all of the special characters needed to write some other European languages (à, ô, ñ, etc.). These extra characters are included in a superset of ASCII called Extended ASCII. Most computer vendors actually implement the Extended ASCII character set so that they can sell their computers in as many countries as possible.

[4]When an overflow condition occurs, most computers will abort the program causing the overflow condition. However, this behavior varies among different types of computers.

Real Data

The integer data type has two fundamental limitations:

1. It is not possible to represent numbers with fractional parts (0.25, 1.5, 3.14159, etc.) as integer data.
2. It is not possible to represent very large positive integers or very small negative integers, because there are not enough bits available to represent the value. The largest and smallest possible integers that can be stored in a given memory location are given by Equations (1-1) and (1-2).

To get around these limitations, computers include a **real** or **floating-point** data type.

The real data type stores numbers in a type of scientific notation. We all know that very large or very small numbers can be most conveniently written in scientific notation. For example, the speed of light in a vacuum is about 299,800,000 m/s. This number is easier to work with in scientific notation: 2.998×10^8 m/s. The two parts of a number expressed in scientific notation are called the **mantissa** and the **exponent.** The mantissa of the number above is 2.998, and the exponent (in the base 10 system) is 8.

The real numbers in a computer are similar to the scientific notation above, except that a computer works in the base 2 system instead of the base 10 system. Real numbers usually occupy 32 bits (4 bytes) of computer memory, divided into two components: a 24-bit mantissa and an 8-bit exponent.[5] The mantissa contains a number between −1.0 and 1.0, and the exponent contains the power of 2 required to scale the number to its actual value.

Real numbers are characterized by two quantities: **precision** and **range**. *Precision* is the number of significant digits that can be preserved in a number, and *range* is the difference between the largest and smallest positive numbers that can be represented. The precision of a real number depends on the number of bits in its mantissa,

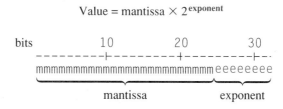

FIGURE 1-4   This floating-point number includes a 24-bit mantissa and an 8-bit exponent.

---

[5]This discussion is based on the IEEE standard for floating-point numbers, which is representative of most modern computers. Some computers use a slightly different division of bits (e.g., a 23-bit mantissa and a 9-bit exponent), but the basic principles are the same in either case.

while the range of the number depends on the number of bits in its exponent. A 24-bit mantissa can represent approximately $\pm 2^{23}$ numbers, or about seven significant decimal digits, so the precision of real numbers is about seven significant digits. An 8-bit exponent can represent multipliers between 2^{-128} and 2^{127}, so the range of real numbers is from about 10^{-38} to 10^{38}. Note that the real data type can represent numbers much larger or much smaller than integers can, but only with seven significant digits of precision.

When a value with more than seven digits of precision is stored in a real variable, *only the most significant 7 bits of the number are preserved.* The remaining information is lost forever. For example, if the value 12345678.9 is stored in a real variable on an IBM PC, it is rounded off to 12345680.0. This difference between the original value and the number stored in the computer is known as **roundoff error**.

You will use the real data type in many places throughout this book and in your programs after you finish this course. It is quite useful, but you must always remember the limitations associated with roundoff error, or your programs might give you an unpleasant surprise. For example, if your program must be able to distinguish between the numbers 1,000,000.0 and 1,000,000.1, then you cannot use the real data type.[6] It simply does not have enough precision to tell the difference between these two numbers!

PROGRAMMING PITFALLS

Always remember the precision and range of the data types that you are working with. Failure to do so can result in subtle programming errors that are very hard to find.

Quiz 1-1

This quiz provides a quick check to see if you have understood the concepts introduced in Section 1.2. If you have trouble with the quiz, reread the section, ask your instructor, or discuss the material with a fellow student. The answers to this quiz are found in the back of the book.

1.   Express the following decimal numbers as their binary equivalents:
   (*a*) 27_{10}
   (*b*) 11_{10}
   (*c*) 35_{10}
   (*d*) 127_{10}

---

[6]We will learn how to use high-precision floating-point numbers in Chapter 9.

2. Express the following binary numbers as their decimal equivalents:
   (*a*) 1110_2
   (*b*) 01010101_2
   (*c*) 1001_2
3. Express the following binary numbers as octal and hexadecimal numbers:
   (*a*) 1110010110101101_2
   (*b*) 1110111101_2
   (*c*) 1001011100111111_2
4. Is the fourth bit of the number 131_{10} a 1 or a 0?
5. Assume that the following numbers are the contents of a character variable. Find the character corresponding to each number according to the ASCII and EBCDIC encoding schemes:
   (*a*) 77_{10}
   (*b*) 01111011_2
   (*c*) 249_{10}
6. Find the maximum and minimum values that can be stored in a 2-byte integer variable.
7. Can a 4-byte variable of the real data type be used to store larger numbers than a 4-byte variable of the integer data type? Why or why not? If it can, what is given up by the real variable to make this possible?

1.3   COMPUTER LANGUAGES

When a computer executes a program, it executes a string of very simple operations such as load, store, add, subtract, multiply, and so on. Each such operation has a unique binary pattern called an *operation code* (*op code*) to specify it. The program that a computer executes is just a string of op codes (and the data associated with the op codes[7]) in the order necessary to achieve a purpose. Op codes are collectively called **machine language,** since they are the actual language that a computer recognizes and executes.

Unfortunately, we humans find machine language very hard to work with. We prefer to work with English-like statements and algebraic equations that are expressed in forms familiar to us, instead of arbitrary patterns of zeros and 1s. We like to program computers with **high-level languages**. We write out our instructions in a high-level language, and then use special programs called **compilers** and **linkers** to convert the instructions into the machine language that the computer understands.

There are many different high-level languages, with different characteristics. Some of them are designed to work well for business problems, while others are designed for general scientific use. Still others are especially suited for applications like operating systems programming. It is important to pick a proper language to match the problem that you are trying to solve.

---

[7]The data associated with op codes are called *operands*.

Some common high-level computer languages today include Ada, Basic, C, COBOL, FORTRAN, and Pascal. Of these languages, FORTRAN is the preeminent language for general scientific computations. Everything from computer models of nuclear power plants to aircraft design programs to seismic signal processing systems has been implemented in FORTRAN, including some projects requiring literally millions of lines of code.

1.4   THE HISTORY OF THE FORTRAN LANGUAGE

FORTRAN is the grandfather of all scientific computer languages. The first version of the FORTRAN language was developed during the years 1954–1957 by IBM for use with its Type 704 computer (see Figure 1-5). Before that time, essentially all computer programs were generated by hand in machine language, which was a slow, tedious, and error-prone process. FORTRAN was a truly revolutionary product. For the first time, a programmer could write a desired algorithm as a series of standard algebraic equations, and the FORTRAN compiler would convert the statements into the machine language that the computer could recognize and execute.

FORTRAN was a wonderful idea! People began using it as soon as it was available because it made programming so much easier than machine language did. The language was officially released in April 1957, and by the fall of 1958 more than half of all IBM 704 computer programs were being written in FORTRAN.

The original FORTRAN language was very small compared to our modern versions of FORTRAN. It contained only a limited number of statement types, and sup-

FIGURE 1-5   The IBM Type 704 computer. *(Courtesy of IBM Archives)*

The IBM Type 704 Computer

The IBM Type 704 computer was the first computer ever to use the FOR-TRAN language. It was released in 1954, and was widely used from then until about 1960, when it was replaced by the Model 709. As you can see from Figure 1-5, the computer occupied a whole room.

What could a computer like that do in 1954? Not much, by today's standards. Any PC sitting on a desktop can run rings around it. The 704 could perform about 4000 integer multiplications and divisions per second, and an average of about 8000 floating-point operations per second. It could read data from magnetic drums (the equivalent of a disk drive) into memory at a rate of about 50,000 bytes/s. The amount of data storage available on a magnetic drum was also very small, so most programs that were not currently in use were stored as decks of punched cards.

By comparison, a typical modern PC (circa 1992) performs more than 20,000,000 integer multiplications and divisions per second, and millions of floating-point operations per second. Some of today's workstations are small enough to sit on a desktop, and yet can perform more than 100,000,000 floating-point operations per second! Reads from disk into memory occur at rates greater than 10,000,000 bytes/s, and a typical PC disk drive can store more than 200,000,000 bytes of data.

The limited resources available in the 704 and other machines of that generation placed a great premium on efficient programming. The structured programming techniques that we use today were simply not possible, because there was not enough speed or memory to support them. The earliest versions of FORTRAN were designed with those limitations in mind, which is why we find many archaic features preserved as living fossils in modern versions of FORTRAN.

ported only the integer and real data types. There were also no subroutines in the first FORTRAN. It was a first effort at writing a high-level computer language, and naturally many deficiencies were found as people started using the language regularly. IBM addressed those problems, releasing FORTRAN II in the spring of 1958.

Further developments continued through 1962, when FORTRAN IV was released. FORTRAN IV was a great improvement, and it became the standard version of FORTRAN for the next 15 years. In 1966, FORTRAN IV was adopted as an American National Standards Institute (ANSI) standard, and it came to be known as FORTRAN 66.

(a)

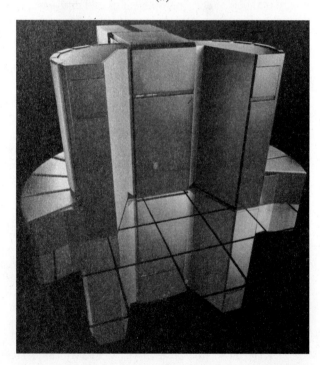

(b)

FIGURE 1-6 Two pictures illustrating the wide range of computers that run FORTRAN 77: (a) The original IBM PC *(Courtesy of IBM Corporation)*. (b) The Cray Y-MP/832 Supercomputer. *(Courtesy of Cray Research, Inc.)*

The FORTRAN language received another major update in 1977. FORTRAN 77 included many new features designed to make structured programs easier to write and maintain, and it quickly became "the" FORTRAN. Today, FORTRAN 77 runs on all sizes and types of computers, from the original IBM PC up to the largest Cray supercomputers.

The designers of FORTRAN 77 were careful to make the language backward compatible with earlier versions of FORTRAN. Because of this backward compatibility, most of the millions of programs written in earlier versions of FORTRAN also worked with FORTRAN 77. Unfortunately, being backward compatible with earlier versions of FORTRAN required that FORTRAN 77 retain some archaic features that should never be used in any modern program. *In this book, we learn to program in FORTRAN 77 using only its modern features.* The archaic features that are retained for backward compatibility are relegated to Chapter 12 of this book. They are described there in case you run into any of them in old programs, but they should never be used in any new program.

1.5   FORTRAN 90

A major new revision of FORTRAN was approved as an ANSI standard in 1992. FORTRAN 90 includes all of FORTRAN 77 as a subset, and extends the language in many important new directions. At the time I am writing this, FORTRAN 90 compilers are still rare, but they will become more and more common over the next few years.

This book will teach you how to write good structured programs using the FORTRAN 77 language, but with an eye to the future emergence of FORTRAN 90. Many of the features of FORTRAN 90 are already common as vendor-supplied extensions to the FORTRAN 77 language. These features are described whenever we come to them, but they are clearly labeled as *extensions* to FORTRAN 77. You may use these extensions in your programs if your particular FORTRAN compiler supports them, and be assured that the programs will still run when you switch over to FORTRAN 90 in the future.

However, if your programs must run on several different computers now, *do not use any of the FORTRAN 90 extensions.* If you do, you will limit the portability of your code, since not all extensions will be present on all FORTRAN 77 compilers.

FORTRAN 90 Extension
All of the common FORTRAN 77 extensions that are discussed in this book are part of the FORTRAN 90 standard. They will be marked by boxes like this one.

PROGRAMMING PITFALLS

It is possible to use the FORTRAN 90 extensions present in your FORTRAN 77 compiler with confidence that the programs will continue to work after you upgrade to FORTRAN 90. However, FORTRAN 90 extensions will make your code less portable among FORTRAN 77 compilers. If your code must work with many FORTRAN 77 compilers, do not use any extensions in your programs.

1.6   SUMMARY

A computer is a special type of machine that stores information, and can perform mathematical calculations on that information at speeds much faster than human beings can think. A program, which is stored in the computer's memory, tells the computer what sequence of calculations are required, and which information to perform the calculations on.

The major components of a computer are the CPU, main memory, secondary memory, and input and output devices. The CPU performs all of the control and calculation functions of the computer. Main memory is fast, relatively expensive memory that is used to store the program being executed, and its associated data. Main memory is volatile, meaning that its contents are lost whenever power is turned off. Secondary memory is slower and cheaper than main memory. It is nonvolatile. Hard disks are common secondary memory devices. Input and output devices are used to read data into the computer and to output data from the computer. The most common input device is a keyboard, and the most common output device is a printer.

Computer memories are composed of millions of individual switches, each of which can be ON or OFF, but not at a state in between. These individual switches are binary devices called *bits*. Eight bits are grouped together to form a *byte* of memory, and 2 or more bytes (depending on the computer) are grouped together to form a *word* of memory.

Computer memories can be used to store *character, integer,* or *real* data. Each character in a character data set occupies 1 byte of memory. The 256 possible values in the byte allow for 256 possible character codes. Integer values occupy 1, 2, 4, or 8 bytes of memory, and store integer quantities. Real values store numbers in a kind of scientific notation. They usually occupy 4 bytes of memory. The bits are divided into a separate mantissa and exponent. The *precision* of the number depends on the number of bits in the mantissa, and the *range* of the number depends on the number of bits in the exponent.

The earliest computers were programmed in *machine language*. This process was slow, cumbersome, and error-prone. High-level languages began to appear in about 1954, and they quickly replaced machine language coding. FORTRAN was one of the first high-level languages ever created.

The FORTRAN computer language and compiler were originally developed in 1954–1957. They have since gone through many revisions. This book teaches good programming practices using the FORTRAN 77 version of the language. FORTRAN 90 has recently been released, and is described briefly in this book. FORTRAN 90 features that are usable in many FORTRAN 77 compilers are flagged with blue shading throughout this textbook.

CHAPTER 1 KEY WORDS

bit (binary digit)	machine language
byte	main memory
central processing unit (CPU)	mantissa
character data	nonvolatile
compiler	octal (base 8) numbers
computer	precision
exponent	printer
floppy disk	program
hard disk	range
hexadecimal (base 10) numbers	real (or floating-point) data
high-level language	roundoff error
input and output devices	secondary memory
integer data	volatile
linker	word

CHAPTER 1 EXERCISES

1. Express the following decimal numbers as their binary equivalents:
   (a) 10_{10}
   (b) 32_{10}
   (c) 77_{10}
   (d) 63_{10}
2. Express the following binary numbers as their decimal equivalents:
   (a) 01001000_2
   (b) 10001001_2
   (c) 11111111_2
   (d) 0101_2
3. Express the following numbers in both octal and hexadecimal forms:
   (a) 1010111011110001_2
   (b) 330_{10}
   (c) 111_{10}
   (d) 11111101101_2

4. Express the following numbers in binary and decimal forms:
   (*a*) 377_8
   (*b*) $1A8_{16}$
   (*c*) 111_8
   (*d*) $1FF_{16}$

5. Some computers (such as IBM mainframes) implement the real data using a 23-bit mantissa and a 9-bit exponent. What precision and range can we expect from real data on these machines?

6. Cray supercomputers support 46-bit and 64-bit integer data types. What are the maximum and minimum values that we could express in a 46-bit integer? in a 64-bit integer?

7. Find the 16-bit two's complement representation of the following decimal numbers:
   (*a*) 55_{10}
   (*b*) -5_{10}
   (*c*) 1024_{10}
   (*d*) -1024_{10}

8. Add the two's complement numbers 0010010010010010_2 and 1111110011111100_2 using binary arithmetic. Convert the two numbers to decimal form, and add them as decimals. Do the two answers agree?

9. The largest possible 8-bit two's complement number is 01111111_2, and the smallest possible 8-bit two's complement number is 10000000_2. Convert these numbers to decimal form. How do they compare to the results of Equations (1-1) and (1-2)?

10. The FORTRAN language includes a second type of floating-point data known as **DOUBLE PRECISION**. A double precision number occupies 8 bytes (64 bits), instead of the 4 bytes occupied by a real number. In the most common implementation, 53 bits are used for the mantissa and 11 bits are used for the exponent. How many significant digits does a double precision value have? What is the range of double precision numbers?

2 Basic Elements of FORTRAN

2.1 INTRODUCTION

As engineers and scientists, we write and execute computer programs to accomplish a goal. The goal typically involves technical calculations that would be too difficult or would take too long to be performed by hand. FORTRAN is one of the computer languages most commonly used for these technical calculations.

This chapter introduces the basic elements of the FORTRAN language. By the end of the chapter, we will be able to write simple but functional FORTRAN programs.

2.2 THE FORTRAN CHARACTER SET

Every language, whether it is a natural language such as English, or a computer language such as FORTRAN, Pascal, or C, has its own special alphabet. Only the characters in this alphabet may be used with the language.

The special alphabet used with the FORTRAN 77 language is known as the FORTRAN *character set*. It consists of the 50 symbols shown in Table 2-1.[1]

TABLE 2-1 The FORTRAN 77 Character Set

26	Letters of the alphabet: **A** − **Z**
10	Digits: **0** − **9**
5	Arithmetic symbols: + − * / **
9	Miscellaneous symbols: ( ) . = , ' $: **blank**

---

[1]The FORTRAN 90 character set also includes the underscore character (_) and the lowercase letters **a** through **z**. In FORTRAN 90, the lowercase letters **a** through **z** are explicitly defined as equivalent to the uppercase letters **A** through **Z**.

21

Note that only the uppercase letters of the alphabet are included in the FOR-TRAN character set. The lowercase letters are not defined in the FORTRAN 77 standard. However, for all modern FORTRAN compilers, lowercase letters are equivalent to the corresponding uppercase ones. (For example, the uppercase letter **A** is equivalent to the lowercase letter **a**.) In other words, FORTRAN is *case-insensitive*. This behavior is in contrast with such case-sensitive languages as C, in which **A** and **a** are two totally different things.

2.3   THE STRUCTURE OF A FORTRAN STATEMENT

A FORTRAN program consists of a series of *statements* put together to accomplish the goal of the programmer. There are two basic types of statements: **executable statements** and **nonexecutable** statements. Executable statements describe the actions taken by the program when it is executed (additions, subtractions, multiplications, divisions, etc.), while nonexecutable statements provide information necessary for the proper operation of the program. We will see many examples of each type of statement as we learn more about the FORTRAN language.

As we mentioned in Chapter 1, FORTRAN was one of the first major computer languages to be developed. It originated in the days before terminals and keyboards, when the punched card was the major form of input to the computer. Each punched card had a fixed length of 80 columns, and one character, number, or symbol could be typed in each column. The structure of a FORTRAN statement still reflects this fixed limitation of 80 characters per line. Figure 2-1 shows the use of these 80 columns in a FORTRAN statement.

Columns 1–5 are reserved for statement labels. A **statement label** is a number between 1 and 99,999. It is the "name" of a FORTRAN statement, and may be used to refer to the statement in other parts of the program. Note that a statement label has no significance other than as a "name" for the statement. It is *not* a line number, and it tells nothing about the order in which statements are executed. For example, one line of a program could be labeled 9999, and the very next line of the program could be labeled 1. The two lines would be executed in the same order regardless of the specific label assigned to each statement.

The statement label is optional, and most FORTRAN statements do not have labels attached to them. If a statement label is used, it must be unique within a given program segment. For example, if 100 is used as a statement label on a line, it cannot be used again as a statement label on any other line in the same program segment.

A statement label may be located anywhere within columns 1 through 5, with either leading or trailing blanks. For example, the label 100 could be placed in columns 1–3, 2–4, or 3–5, and it would still be the same label.

A letter **C** or an asterisk (*****) placed in column 1 indicates that the statement is a **comment.** The FORTRAN compiler completely ignores any statement beginning with these characters. As we will see, comment statements help us to properly document the operation of FORTRAN programs.

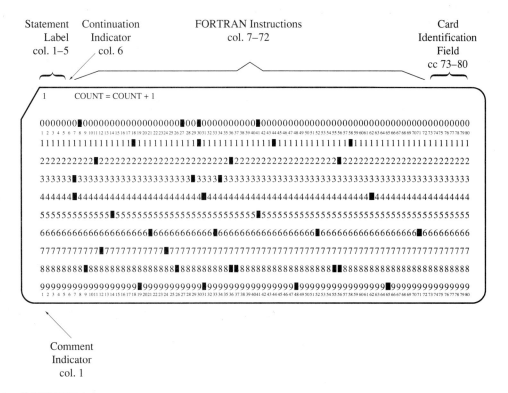

FIGURE 2-1   The structure of a FORTRAN statement.

Column 6 is normally blank. If any character other than a blank or a zero is placed in that column, then the statement is interpreted as a continuation of the statement immediately preceding it. Up to 20 continuation lines may be used with a FORTRAN statement, which permits us to write extremely long FORTRAN instructions, if necessary.

Columns 7–72 contain the FORTRAN instructions that are interpreted by the compiler. The instructions may be freely placed anywhere within this area. Programmers typically take advantage of this freedom to indent certain instructions (loops and branches) to make their code more readable.

Columns 73–80 are sometimes called the **card identification field.** This field is totally ignored by the compiler, and may be used by the programmer for any desired purpose. In the days when programs were saved on decks of punched cards, this field was used to number the cards in consecutive order. If someone accidentally dropped a numbered card deck, it was possible to reconstruct the order of the statements in the program from the numbers on the cards. Today these columns are usually blank.

2.4   THE STRUCTURE OF A FORTRAN PROGRAM

Each FORTRAN program consists of a mixture of executable and nonexecutable statements, which must occur in a specific order. An example of a simple FORTRAN program is shown in Figure 2-2. This program reads in two numbers, multiplies them together, and prints out the result. We will now point out the significant features of this program.

```
     5    10   15   20   25   30   35   40   45   50   55   60   65   70
----|----|----|----|----|----|----|----|----|----|----|----|----|----|
      PROGRAM FIRST
C
C  Purpose:
C    To illustrate some of the basic features of a FORTRAN program.
C
C     (This is a comment line, since it has a "C" in column 1.)
*     (This is a comment line, since it has a "*" in column 1.)
C
C
C  Declare the variables used in this program.
C
      INTEGER I, J, K
C
C  Get the variables to multiply together.
C
      WRITE (*,*) ' Enter the numbers to multiply: '
      READ  (*,*) I, J
C
C  Multiply the numbers together.
C
      K = I * J
C
C  Write out the result.
C
      WRITE (*,*) ' Result = ', K
C
C  Finish up.
C
      STOP
      END
----|----|----|----|----|----|----|----|----|----|----|----|----|----|
     5    10   15   20   25   30   35   40   45   50   55   60   65   70
```

FIGURE 2-2   A simple FORTRAN program.

This FORTRAN program, like all FORTRAN programs, is divided into three sections:

1. *The declaration section.* This section consists of a group of nonexecutable statements at the beginning of the program which define the name of the program and the number and types of variables referenced in the program.

2. *The execution section.* This section consists of one or more statements describing the actions to be performed by the program.

3. *The termination section.* This section consists of statement(s) stopping the execution of the program and telling the compiler that the program is complete.

Note that comment statements may be inserted freely anywhere between the **PROGRAM** statement and the **END** statement.

2.4.1 The Declaration Section

The declaration section consists of the nonexecutable statements at the beginning of the program which define the name of the program and the number and types of variables referenced in the program.

The first statement in this section is the **PROGRAM** statement. It is a nonexecutable statement that specifies the name of the program to the FORTRAN compiler. A program name may consist of up to six alphanumeric characters, but the first character in the name must always be alphabetic. The **PROGRAM** statement must be placed at the beginning of the program. In this example, the program has been named FIRST. Note that the word **PROGRAM** in this example begins in column 7, which is the first column of the FORTRAN instruction field. This statement would have worked just as well in any other column as long as the characters **PROGRAM FIRST** fit between columns 7 and 72.

If the **PROGRAM** statement is left out of a program, some compilers assign a default name to the program, while other compilers generate an error. At any rate, it is good practice to always include a **PROGRAM** statement to name any program that you write.

The next several lines in the program are comment statements. These comments describe the purpose of the program, and illustrate the two forms that the comment statement can take.

Next comes the **INTEGER** type declaration statement. This nonexecutable statement is described later in this chapter. Here, it declares that three integer variables called I, J, and K will be used in the program.

2.4.2 The Execution Section

The execution section consists of one or more executable statements describing the actions to be performed by the program.

The first executable statement in this program is the **WRITE** statement, which writes a message prompting the user to enter the two numbers to be multiplied together. The next line is a **READ** statement, which reads in the two integers supplied by the user. The next executable statement instructs the computer to multiply the two numbers I and J together, and to store the result in variable K. The final **WRITE** statement prints out the result for the user to see.

All of these statements are explained in detail later in this chapter.

2.4.3   The Termination Section

The termination section consists of the **STOP** and **END** statements. The **STOP** statement is an executable statement which tells the computer to stop running the program. The **END** statement is a nonexecutable statement that tells the compiler that there are no more statements to be compiled in the program segment.

When the **STOP** statement immediately precedes the **END** statement as in this example, it is optional. The compiler automatically generates a **STOP** command when the **END** statement is reached.

2.4.4   Compiling and Executing the FORTRAN Program

Before the sample program can be run, it must be compiled into object code, and then linked with the system libraries to produce the executable program. The details of compiling and linking are different for every compiler and operating system, so you should ask your instructor or consult the appropriate manuals to determine the proper procedure for your system.

Depending on the computer and operating system being used, FORTRAN programs may be compiled, linked, and run in either **batch mode** or **interactive mode**. In *batch mode,* the commands required to compile, link, and run the program are written into a file together with any data required by the program. This file is then submitted to the *batch processor,* which compiles, links, and executes the program without user intervention. In *interactive mode,* the program is compiled, linked, and executed by commands entered by a user at a terminal or keyboard. A program that is executed in interactive mode can prompt the user for input while it is running. Programs under development are usually run in interactive mode, so that the programmer can immediately see whether or not it is working right.

NOTE: The following paragraphs show the compiling, linking, and loading process for one particular compiler on a PC-compatible computer. The paragraphs are provided to illustrate the general idea of compiling, linking and loading with a specific example. *This is probably not how compiling, linking, and loading will work on your particular computer system.* The process will be different for every compiler and operating system, so you must ask your instructor or consult the appropriate manuals to determine the proper procedure for your computer system.

A typical example of the compiling, linking, and running process for an interactive computer system is shown in Figure 2-3. Figure 2-3 is the listing resulting when the sample program is compiled, linked, and run using Microsoft FORTRAN 77 on a PC-compatible. The sample program was in a file called FIG23.FOR, and the executable program was created in a file called FIG23.EXE.

```
C:\BOOK\FORT>dir

 Volume in drive C is VOL_C
 Directory of C:\BOOK\FORT

.            <DIR>    07-05-90   1:32a
..           <DIR>    07-05-90   1:32a
FIG23   FOR      617 07-05-90   8:27p
     3 file(s)        617 bytes
               45309952 bytes free
```

```
C:\BOOK\FORT>fl /FsCON fig23.for
Microsoft (R) FORTRAN Optimizing Compiler Version 5.00
Copyright (c) Microsoft Corp 1982-1989. All rights reserved.

fig23.for
                                                            PAGE   1
                                                            07-05-90
                                                            20:28:18


Line#  Source Line   Microsoft FORTRAN Optimizing Compiler Version 5.00

    1        PROGRAM FIRST
    2   C
    3   C  Purpose:
    4   C    To illustrate some of the basic features of a FORTRAN program.
    5   C
    6   C    (This is a comment line, since it has a "C" in column 1.)
    7   *    (This is a comment line, since it has a "*" in column 1.)
    8   C
    9   C
   10   C  Declare the variables used in this program.
   11   C
   12        INTEGER I, J, K
   13   C
   14   C  Get the variables to multiply together.
   15   C
   16        WRITE (*,*) ' Enter the numbers to multiply: '
   17        READ  (*,*) I, J
   18   C
   19   C  Multiply the numbers together.
   20   C
   21        K = I * J
   22   C
   23   C  Write out the result.
   24   C
   25        WRITE (*,*) ' Result = ', K
   26   C
   27   C  Finish up.
   28   C
   29        STOP
   30        END

main   Local Symbols

Name                      Class  Type        Size  Offset

I . . . . . . . . . . . . local  INTEGER*4      4  0002
J . . . . . . . . . . . . local  INTEGER*4      4  0006
K . . . . . . . . . . . . local  INTEGER*4      4  000a


Global Symbols

Name                      Class  Type        Size  Offset

main. . . . . . . . . . . FSUBRT ***          ***  0000
```

```
Code size = 0113 (275)
Data size = 0048 (72)
Bss size  = 000e (14)

No errors detected

Microsoft (R) Segmented-Executable Linker  Version 5.03
Copyright (C) Microsoft Corp 1984-1989. All rights reserved.

Object Modules [.OBJ]: FIG23.OBJ
Run File [FIG23.EXE]: FIG23.EXE
List File [NUL.MAP]: NUL
Libraries [.LIB]:
Definitions File [NUL.DEF]: ;

C:\BOOK\FORT>fig23
 Enter the numbers to multiply:
3  5
 Result =           15
Stop - Program terminated.


C:\BOOK\FORT>dir

 Volume in drive C is VOL_C
 Directory of C:\BOOK\FORT

.               <DIR>     07-05-90   1:32a
..              <DIR>     07-05-90   1:32a
FIG23    FOR      617 07-05-90   8:27p
FIG23    OBJ      892 07-05-90   8:27p
FIG23    EXE    21559 07-05-90   8:28p
        3 file(s)          617 bytes
                   45277184 bytes free
```

FIGURE 2-3 A sample dialog showing how to compile, link, and run a FORTRAN program using Microsoft FORTRAN on a PC-compatible computer. (User inputs are shown in boldface.)

Let's examine Figure 2-3 more closely. The first directory listing shows that only the source file FIG23.FOR was present on the disk before running the FOR-TRAN compiler. The compiler compiled the program to produce the object file FIG23.OBJ, and the linker linked it with the system libraries to produce an executable file called FIG23.EXE.

Notice that there are several sections in the compiler listing. The first section of the listing displays the source code being compiled. If any errors had occurred, they would have appeared in the listing intermingled with the source code. The source code is followed by a listing of the local and global symbols used in the program, and a summary of the size of the compiled program.

When FIG23 is run, the program writes out the message, **Enter the Numbers to Multiply:**, and then reads the two numbers entered by the user. When the numbers are entered, it multiplies them together and prints out the result. In the example shown, the numbers 3 and 5 are multiplied to get 15, which is obviously the correct answer.

2.5   Constants and Variables

A **FORTRAN constant** is a quantity that is defined before a program is executed, and that does not change value during the execution of the program. When a FORTRAN compiler encounters a constant, it places the value of the constant in a known location in memory, and then references that memory location whenever the constant is used in the program.

A **FORTRAN variable** is a quantity that can change value during the execution of a program. (A FORTRAN variable may or may not be defined before a program is executed.) When a FORTRAN compiler encounters a variable, it reserves a known location in memory for the variable, and then references that memory location whenever the variable is used in the program.

Each FORTRAN variable in a program must have a unique name. FORTRAN variable names may be up to six characters long and contain both alphabetic characters and digits. However, the first character in a name must be alphabetical. The following examples are valid variable names:

```
TIME
A1
Z12345
BUTTON
```

The following examples are invalid variable names:

```
HOMEWORK     Name is too long.
3X           First character is a number.
A$           $ is an illegal character.
MY-HLP       - is an illegal character.
```

When writing a program, it is important to pick meaningful names for the variables. Meaningful names make a program *much* easier to read and to maintain. Names such as DAY, MONTH, and YEAR are clear even to a person seeing the program for the first time. With the six-character limit imposed by FORTRAN, it is sometimes necessary to be creative in selecting variable names. For example, *exchange rate* might become XCHGRT.

■ **GOOD PROGRAMMING PRACTICE**

Use meaningful variable names whenever possible.

> ***FORTRAN 90 Extension (common in FORTRAN 77)***
> In FORTRAN 90 (and in most modern FORTRAN 77 compilers), variable names may be up to 31 characters long, and may include the underscore character. Thus an exchange rate could be named EXCHANGE_RATE.

It is also important to include a **variable dictionary** in the header of any program that you write. A variable dictionary lists each variable used in a program and defines it. A variable dictionary may seem unnecessary while the program is being written, but it is invaluable when you or another person has to go back and modify the program at a later time.

■ **GOOD PROGRAMMING PRACTICE**

Create a variable dictionary for each program to make program maintenance easier.

There are six types of FORTRAN constants and variables. Four of them are numerical (types **INTEGER, REAL, DOUBLE PRECISION,** and **COMPLEX**), one is logical (type **LOGICAL**), and one consists of strings of characters (type **CHARACTER**). Types **INTEGER, REAL, CHARACTER,** and **LOGICAL** will be discussed now, while a discussion of the other data types will be postponed to Chapter 9.

2.5.1 Integer Constants and Variables

An **integer constant** is any number that does not contain a decimal point. These constants can be positive, negative, or zero. If a constant is positive, it may be written either with or without a + sign. No commas may be embedded within an integer constant. The following examples are valid integer constants:

```
        0
     -999
123456789
      +17
```

The following examples are *not* valid integer constants:

```
1,000,000    Embedded commas are illegal.
    -100.    If it has a decimal point, it is not an integer constant!
```

The integer data type was previously described in Chapter 1.

An **integer variable** is a variable containing a value of the integer data type.

Constant and variables of the integer data type are usually stored in a single word on a computer. Since the length of a word varies from 16 to 64 bits on different computers, the largest integer which can be stored in the computer also varies. Table 2-2 shows the maximum number of decimal digits for integers on several common computers. (The maximum number of decimal digits can be determined from the results of Equations (1-1) and (1-2).)

TABLE 2-2   Maximum Number of Decimal Digits for Integers on Several Computers

Computer	*Number of Bits*	*Maximum Number of Decimal Digits*
VAX	32	10
IBM 370	32	10
PC	32 (or 16)*	10 (or 5)*
Cray	46 (or 64)*	14 (or 19)*

*Indicates optional lengths. The default length is given first.

2.5.2   Real Constants and Variables

A **real constant** is any number with a decimal point. These numbers can be written with or without an exponent, and they can be positive, negative, or zero. If a constant is positive, it may be written either with or without a + sign. No commas may be embedded within a real constant. The real data type corresponds to the floating-point number described in Chapter 1.

Real constants may be written with or without an exponent. If used, an exponent consists of the letter E followed by a positive or negative integer which corresponds to the power of 10 used when the number is written in scientific notation. If the exponent is positive, the + sign may be omitted. The mantissa of the number (the part of the number that precedes the exponent) should contain a decimal point. The following examples are valid real constants:

```
      10.
    -999.9
   3.141593
      1.0E-3     = 1.0 × 10⁻³, or 0.001
  123.45E20      = 123.45 × 10²⁰, or 1.2345 × 10²²
    0.12E + 1    = 0.12 × 10¹, or 1.2
```

The following examples are *not* valid real constants:

`1,000,000.`	Embedded commas are illegal.
`111E3`	A decimal point is required in the mantissa.
`-12.0E1.5`	Decimal points are not allowed in exponents.

A real constant corresponds to the real or floating-point data type described in Chapter 1. It is stored in the computer in two parts: the mantissa and the exponent. The number of bits allocated to the mantissa determines the *precision* of the constant (i.e., the number of significant digits to which the constant is known), while the number of bits allocated to the exponent determines the *range* of the constant (that is, the largest and the smallest values that can be represented). For a given word size, the more precise a real number is, the smaller its range is, and vice versa, as described in the previous chapter.

A **real variable** is a variable containing a value of the real data type.

Table 2-3 shows the precision and the range of real constants and variables on several different computers.

TABLE 2-3 Precision and Range of REAL Numbers on Several Computers

Computer	Total Number of Bits	Number of Bits in Mantissa	Precision in Decimal Digits	Number of Bits in Exponent	Exponent Range
VAX	32	24	7	8	10^{-38}–10^{38}
IBM 370	32	23	6	9	10^{-77}–10^{76}
PC	32	24	7	8	10^{-38}–10^{38}
Cray	64	49	14	15	10^{-2465}–10^{2465}

2.5.3 Character Constants and Variables

A **character constant** is a string of characters enclosed in single quotes. The minimum number of characters in a string is 1, while the maximum number of characters in a string varies from compiler to compiler. The maximum number of characters is at least 256, and is often as large as 32,767.

The following are valid character constants:

`'This is a test!'`	
`' '`	A single blank
`'3.141593'`	Note that this is a character string, *not* a number.

The following are not valid character constants:

```
This is a test!        No single quotes
"Try this one.'        Unbalanced single quotes
```

If a character string must include an apostrophe, then that apostrophe should be represented by two consecutive single quotes. For example, the string "Man's best friend" would be written in a character constant as

```
'Man''s best friend'
```

Character constants are most often used to print descriptive information using the **WRITE** statement. For example, the string 'RESULT = ' in Figure 2-2 is a valid character constant:

```
WRITE (*,*) ' Result = ', K
```

A **character variable** is a variable containing a value of the character data type.

2.5.4 Logical Constants and Variables

A **logical constant** is a constant that can take on one of two possible values: TRUE or FALSE (note that periods are required on either side of these values to distinguish them from variable names).

The following are valid logical constants:

```
.TRUE.
.FALSE.
```

The following are not valid logical constants:

```
TRUE       No periods—this is a variable name
.FALSE     Unbalanced periods
```

Logical constants are rarely used, but logical expressions and variables are commonly used to control program execution, as we will see in Chapter 3.

2.5.5 Default and Explicit Variable Typing

When we look at a constant, it is easy to see whether it is an integer, real, character, or logical constant. If a number does not have a decimal point, it is of type integer; if it has a decimal point, it is of type real. If the constant is enclosed in single quotes, it is of type character. If it is TRUE or FALSE, it is of type logical. With variables, the situation is not so clear. How do we (or the compiler) know if the variable JUNK contains an integer, real, character, or logical value?

There are two possible ways in which the type of a variable can be defined: **default typing** and **explicit typing.** If the type of a variable is not explicitly specified in the program, then default typing is used. By default:

NOTE: Any variable names beginning with the letters I, J, K, L, M, or N are assumed to be of type **INTEGER**. Any variable names starting with another letter are assumed to be of type **REAL**.

Therefore, a variable called INC is assumed to be of type integer by default, while a variable called BIG is assumed to be of type real by default. This default typing convention goes all the way back to the original FORTRAN I in 1954. Note that no variable names are of type character or logical by default, because these data types didn't exist in FORTRAN I!

The type of a variable may also be explicitly defined in the declaration section at the beginning of a program. The following FORTRAN statements can be used to specify the type of variables:

```
INTEGER var1, var2, var3, . . .
REAL    var1, var2, var3, . . .
LOGICAL var1, var2, var3, . . .
```

These nonexecutable statements are called **type specification statements**. They should be placed after the **PROGRAM** statement and before the first executable statement in the program, as shown in the example below.

```
PROGRAM EXAMPL
INTEGER DAY, MONTH, YEAR
REAL    SECOND
LOGICAL TEST1, TEST2
(Executable statements)
```

There are no default names associated with the character data type, so all character variables must be explicitly typed using the **CHARACTER** type specification statement. This statement is a bit more complicated than the previous ones, since character variables may be of different lengths. Its form is

```
CHARACTER*<len>  var1, var2, var3, . . .
```

where <len> is the number of characters in the variables. For example, the type specification statements

```
CHARACTER*10 FIRST, LAST
CHARACTER*1  INITL
```

define two 10-character variables called FIRST and LAST, and a one-character variable called INITL. These variables could also be declared in a single statement in one of the following forms:

```
CHARACTER FIRST*10, LAST*10, INITL*1
```

or

```
CHARACTER*10 FIRST, LAST, INITL*1
```

2.5.6 Keeping Constants Consistent in a Program

It is important to always keep your physical constants consistent throughout a program. For example, do not use the value 3.14 for π at one point in a program, and 3.141593 at another point in the program. Also, you should always write your constants with at least as much precision as your computer will accept. If the real data type on your computer has seven significant digits of precision, then π should be written as 3.141593, *not* as 3.14!

The best way to achieve consistency and precision throughout a program is to *assign a name to a constant, and then to use that name to refer to the constant throughout the program.* If we assign the name PI to the constant 3.141593, then we can refer to PI by name throughout the program, and be certain that we are getting the same value everywhere. Furthermore, assigning meaningful names to constants improves the overall readability of our programs, because a programmer can tell at a glance just what the constant represents.

Names are assigned constants using the **PARAMETER** statement. The form of a **PARAMETER** statement is

```
PARAMETER ( name = value )
```

where *name* is the name assigned to constant *value*. The data type of *name* must match the data type of the supplied value. The type of the name may be declared explicitly with a type specification statement, or it may be defaulted according to the standard FORTRAN 77 rules (I-N is integer, everything else is real). **PARAMETER** statements appear in the declaration section of a program together with the type specification statements. For example, the following statements assign the name PI to the constant 3.141593.

```
REAL PI
PARAMETER ( PI = 3.141593 )
```

■ GOOD PROGRAMMING PRACTICE

Keep your physical constants consistent and precise throughout a program. To improve the consistency and understandability of your code, assign a name to any important constants, and refer to them by name in the program.

Quiz 2-1

This quiz provides a quick check to see if you have understood the concepts introduced in Section 2.5. If you have trouble with the quiz, reread the section, ask your instructor, or discuss the material with a fellow student. The answers to this quiz are found in the back of the book.

Questions 1–14 contain a list of valid and invalid constants. State whether or not each constant is valid. If the constant is valid, specify its type. If it is invalid, say why it is invalid.

1. `10.0`
2. `-100,000`
3. `123E-5`
4. `'That's ok!'`
5. `-32768`
6. `'OLD/1'`
7. `3.14159`
8. `.TRUE.`
9. `'3.14159'`
10. `'Distance =`
11. `2.718281828459`
12. `17.877E+6`
13. `FALSE.`
14. `6.02E23`

Questions 15–18 contain two real constants each. Tell whether or not the two constants represent the same value within the computer:

15. `4650.; 4.65E+3`
16. `-12.71; -1.27E1`
17. `0.0001; 1.0E4`
18. `3.14159E0; 314.159E-3`

Questions 19–21 contain a list of valid and invalid FORTRAN 77 program names. State whether or not each program name is valid. If it is invalid, say why it is invalid.

19. `PROGRAM MYPROG`
20. `PROGRAM NEWPROG`
21. `PROGRAM 3RD`

Questions 22–28 contain a list of valid and invalid FORTRAN 77 variable names. State whether or not each variable name is valid. If the variable name is valid, specify its type (assume default typing). If it is invalid, say why it is invalid.

22. `LENGTH`
23. `DISTANCE`
24. `T_1`
25. `1PROB`
26. `HELP`
27. `TIME1`
28. `ABORT0`

*Are the following **PARAMETER** statements correct or incorrect? Assume default typing for the parameter names. If a statement is incorrect, state why it is invalid.*

29. `PARAMETER BEGIN = -30`
30. `PARAMETER ( NAME = 'STEVE' )`
31. `PARAMETER ( TIMEO = 0.000001 )`

2.6   Assignment Statements and Arithmetic Calculations

Calculations are specified in FORTRAN with the **assignment statement,** whose general form is

```
variable name = expression
```

The assignment statement calculates the value of the expression to the right of the equal sign, and *assigns* that value to the variable named to the left of the equal sign. Notice that here the equal sign does not mean equality in the usual sense of the word. Instead, it means: *store the value of* **expression** *in location* **variable name.** For this reason, the equal sign is called the **assignment operator.** A statement like

```
I = I + 1
```

is complete nonsense in ordinary algebra, but makes perfect sense in FORTRAN. In FORTRAN, it means: Take the current value stored in variable I, add one to it, and store the result back into variable I.

The expression to the right of the assignment operator can consist of any valid combination of constants, variables, and standard arithmetic operators. The standard arithmetic operators included in FORTRAN are

+	Addition
-	Subtraction
*	Multiplication
/	Division
**	Exponentiation

Notice that the symbols for multiplication (*), division (/), and exponentiation (**) are not the ones used in ordinary mathematical expressions. These special symbols were chosen because they were available in 1950s-era computer character sets, and because they were different from the characters being used in variable names.

The five arithmetic operators described above are **binary operators,** which means that they should occur between and apply to two variables or constants, as shown:

```
A + B
A - B
A * B
A / B
A ** B
```

In addition, the $+$ and $-$ symbols can occur as **unary operators,** which mean that they apply to one variable or constant, as shown:

```
+23

-A
```

There are certain rules that must be followed when using FORTRAN arithmetic operators:

1. No two operators may occur side by side. Thus the expression A * -B is illegal. In FORTRAN, it must be written as A * (-B). Similarly, A ** -2 is illegal, and should be written as A ** (-2).
2. Implied multiplication is illegal in FORTRAN. An expression like $x(y + z)$ means that we should add y and z, and then multiply the result by x. The implied multiplication must be written explicitly in FORTRAN as X * (Y + Z).
3. Parentheses may be used to group terms whenever desired. When parentheses are used, the expressions inside the parentheses are evaluated before the expressions outside parentheses. For example, the expression 2 ** ((8 + 2)/5) is evaluated as shown below

```
2 ** ((8+2)/5) = 2 ** (10/5)
               = 2 ** 2
               = 4
```

2.6.1 Integer Arithmetic

Integer arithmetic is arithmetic involving only integer constants and variables. Integer arithmetic always produces a result that is an integer. This is especially important to remember when the expression involves division, since there can be no fractional components in the answer. If the division of two integers is not itself an integer, the computer automatically truncates the fractional part of the answer. This behavior can lead to surprising and unexpected answers. For example, integer arithmetic produces the following strange results:

$$\frac{3}{4} = 0 \qquad \frac{4}{4} = 1 \qquad \frac{5}{4} = 1 \qquad \frac{6}{4} = 1$$

$$\frac{7}{4} = 1 \qquad \frac{8}{4} = 2 \qquad \frac{9}{4} = 2$$

Because of this behavior, integers should never be used to calculate real-world quantities that vary continuously, such as distance, speed, time, etc. They should only be used for things that are intrinsically integer in nature, such as counters and indices.

PROGRAMMING PITFALLS

Beware of integer arithmetic. Integer division often gives unexpected results.

2.6.2   Real Arithmetic

Real arithmetic is arithmetic involving real constants and variables. Real arithmetic always produces a result that is real. The results of calculations with real numbers are essentially what we would expect. For example, real arithmetic produces the following results:

$$\frac{3.}{4.} = 0.75 \qquad \frac{4.}{4.} = 1. \qquad \frac{5.}{4.} = 1.25 \qquad \frac{6.}{4.} = 1.50$$

$$\frac{7.}{4.} = 1.75 \qquad \frac{8.}{4.} = 2. \qquad \frac{9.}{4.} = 2.25 \qquad \frac{1.}{3.} = 0.3333333$$

However, real numbers do have peculiarities of their own. Because of the finite word length of a computer, some real numbers cannot be represented exactly. For example, the number 1/3 is equal to 0.33333333333 ... , but since the numbers stored in the computer have limited precision, the representation of 1/3 in the computer might be 0.3333333. As a result of this limitation in precision, some quantities that are theoretically equal will not be equal when evaluated by the computer. For example

$$3. * (1. / 3.) \neq 1.,$$

but

$$2. * (1. / 2.) = 1.$$

Tests for equality must be performed very cautiously when working with real numbers.

PROGRAMMING PITFALLS

Beware of real arithmetic: Due to limited precision, two theoretically identical expressions often give different results.

2.6.3   Hierarchy of Operations

Often, many arithmetic operations are combined into a single expression. For example, consider the equation for the distance traveled by an object starting from rest and subjected to a constant acceleration:

```
DIST = 0.5 * ACCEL * TIME ** 2
```

In this expression, there are two multiplications and an exponentiation. In such an expression, it is important to know the order in which the operations are evaluated. If exponentiation is evaluated before multiplication, this expression is equivalent to

$$\text{distance} = 0.5\ a(t^2)$$

But if multiplication is evaluated before exponentiation, this expression is equivalent to

$$\text{distance} = (0.5\ at)^2$$

These two equations have different results, and we must be able to unambiguously distinguish between them.

To make the evaluation of expressions unambiguous, FORTRAN has established a series of rules governing the hierarchy or order in which operations are evaluated within an expression. The FORTRAN rules generally follow the normal rules of algebra. The order in which the arithmetic operations in an expression are evaluated is:

1. The contents of all parentheses are evaluated first, starting from the innermost parentheses and working outward.
2. All exponentials are evaluated, working from right to left.
3. All multiplications and divisions are evaluated, working from left to right.
4. All additions and subtractions are evaluated, working from left to right.

Following these rules, we see that the first of our two possible interpretations is correct—time is squared before the multiplications are performed.

EXAMPLE 2-1

Variables A, B, C, D, E, F, and G have been initialized to the following values:

```
A = 3.    B = 2.    C = 5.    D = 4.
E = 10.   F = 2.    G = 3.
```

Evaluate the following FORTRAN assignment statements:

(*a*) OUTPUT = A*B+C*D+E/F**G

(*b*) OUTPUT = A*(B+C)*D+(E/F)**G

(*c*) OUTPUT = A*(B+C)*(D+E)/F**G

SOLUTION

(*a*) Expression to evaluate: OUTPUT = A*B+C*D+E/F**G
Fill in numbers: OUTPUT = 3.*2.+5.*4.+10./2.**3.
First, evaluate 2.**3.:   OUTPUT = 3.*2.+5.*4.+10./8.

Now, evaluate multiplications
and divisions from left to
right:

```
OUTPUT = 6.    +5.*4.+10./8.
OUTPUT = 6.    +20.  +10./8.
OUTPUT = 6.    +20.  + 1.25
```

Now evaluate additions:

```
OUTPUT = 27.25
```

(**b**) Expression to evaluate:

```
OUTPUT = A*(B+C)*D+(E/F)**G
```

Fill in numbers:

```
OUTPUT = 3.*(2.+5.)*4.+(10./2.)**3.
```

First, evaluate parentheses:

```
OUTPUT = 3.*7.*4.+5.**3.
```

Now, evaluate exponents:

```
OUTPUT = 3.*7.*4.+125.
```

Evaluate multiplications
and divisions from left to
right:

```
OUTPUT = 21.*4.+125.
OUTPUT = 84. +125.
```

Evaluate additions:

```
OUTPUT = 209.
```

(**c**) Expression to evaluate:

```
OUTPUT = A*(B+C)*(D+E)/F**G
```

Fill in numbers:

```
OUTPUT = 3.*(2.+5.)*(4.+10.)/2.**3.
```

First, evaluate parentheses:

```
OUTPUT = 3.*7.*14./2.**3.
```

Now, evaluate exponents:

```
OUTPUT = 3.*7.*14./8.
```

Evaluate multiplications
and divisions from left to
right:

```
OUTPUT = 21.*14./8.
OUTPUT = 294./8.
OUTPUT = 36.75  ●
```

As we see in the above example, the order in which operations are performed has a major effect on the final result of an algebraic expression.

EXAMPLE 2-2

Variables A, B, and C have been initialized to the following values:

$$A = 3. \quad B = 2. \quad C = 3.$$

Evaluate the following FORTRAN assignment statements:

(**a**) `OUTPUT = A**(B**C)`

(**b**) `OUTPUT = (A**B)**C`

(**c**) `OUTPUT = A**B**C`

SOLUTION

(**a**) Expression to evaluate: `OUTPUT = A**(B**C)`

Fill in numbers: `OUTPUT = 3.**(2.**3.)`

Evaluate expression in parentheses: `OUTPUT = 3.**8.`

Evaluate remaining expression: `OUTPUT = 6561.`

(**b**) Expression to evaluate: `OUTPUT = (A**B)**C`
     Fill in numbers: `OUTPUT = (3.**2.)**3.`
     Evaluate expression in parentheses: `OUTPUT = 9.**3.`
     Evaluate remaining expression: `OUTPUT = 729.`

(**c**) Expression to evaluate: `OUTPUT = A**B**C`
     Fill in numbers: `OUTPUT = 3.**2.**3.`
     First, evaluate rightmost exponent: `OUTPUT = 3.**8.`
     Now, evaluate remaining exponent: `OUTPUT = 6561.` ●

The results of (*a*) and (*c*) are identical, but the expression in (*a*) is easier to understand and less ambiguous than the expression in (*c*).

It is important that every expression in a program be made as clear as possible. Any program of value must not only be written but also be maintained and modified when necessary. You should always ask yourself: "Will I easily understand this expression if I come back to it in 6 months? Can another programmer look at my code and easily understand what I am doing?" If there is any doubt in your mind, use extra parentheses in the expression to make it as clear as possible.

■ **GOOD PROGRAMMING PRACTICE**

Use parentheses as necessary to make your equations clear and easy to understand.

If parentheses are used within an expression, then the parentheses must be balanced. That is, there must be an equal number of open parentheses and closed parentheses within the expression. It is an error to have more of one type than the other. Errors of this sort are usually typographical, and they are caught by the FORTRAN compiler. For example, the expression

```
(2.+4.) / 2.
```

is legal and evaluates to 3.0, while the expression

```
(2.+4.) / 2.)
```

produces an error during compilation because of the mismatched parentheses.

2.6.4 Mixed-Mode Arithmetic

When an arithmetic operation is performed using two real numbers, its immediate result is of type **REAL**. Similarly, when an arithmetic operation is performed using two integers, the result is of type **INTEGER**. In general, arithmetic operations are only defined between numbers of the same type. For example, the addition of two real numbers is a valid operation, and the addition of two integers is a valid operation, but the addition of a real number and an integer is *not* a valid operation. This is true because real numbers and integers are stored in completely different forms in the computer.

What happens if an operation is between a real number and an integer? Expressions containing both real numbers and integers are called **mixed-mode expressions,** and arithmetic involving both real numbers and integers is called *mixed-mode arithmetic.* In the case of an operation between a real number and an integer, the integer is converted by the computer into a real number, and real arithmetic is used on the numbers. The result is of type real. For example, consider the following equations:

Integer expression:	$\dfrac{3}{2}$	is evaluated to be 1	Integer result
Real expression:	$\dfrac{3.}{2.}$	is evaluated to be 1.5	Real result
Mixed-mode expression:	$\dfrac{3.}{2}$	is evaluated to be 1.5	Real result

The rules governing mixed-mode arithmetic can be very confusing to beginning programmers, and even experienced programmers may trip up on them from time to time. This is especially true when the mixed-mode expression involves division. Consider the following expressions:

	Expression	**Result**
1.	1 + 1 / 4	1
2.	1. + 1 / 4	1.
3.	1 + 1. / 4	1.25

Expression 1 contains only integers, so it is evaluated by integer arithmetic. In integer arithmetic, 1 / 4 = 0, and 1 + 0 = 1, so the final result is 1 (an integer). Expression 2 is a mixed-mode expression containing both real numbers and integers. However, the first operation to be performed is a division, since division comes before addition in the hierarchy of operations. The division is between integers, so the result is 1 / 4 = 0. Next comes an addition between a floating-point 1. and an integer 0, so the compiler converts the integer 0 into a real number, and then performs the addition. The resulting number is 1. (a real number). Expression 3 is also a mixed-mode expression containing both real numbers and integers. The first operation to be performed is a division between a real number and an integer, so the compiler converts the integer 4 into a real number, and then performs the division. The result is a real 0.25. The next operation to be performed is an addition between an integer 1 and a real 0.25, so the compiler converts the integer 1 into a real number, and then performs the addition. The resulting number is 1.25 (a real number).

To summarize:

1. An operation involving an integer and a real number is called a mixed-mode operation, and an expression containing one or more such operations is called a mixed-mode expression.

2. When a mixed-mode operation is encountered, FORTRAN converts the integer into a real number, and then performs the operation to get a real result.

3. Note that the automatic mode conversion does not occur until a real number and an integer both appear in the *same* operation. Therefore, it is possible for a portion of an expression to be evaluated in integer arithmetic, followed by another portion evaluated in real arithmetic (as in (2) above).

Automatic-type conversion also occurs when the variable to which the expression is assigned is of a different type than the result of the expression. For example, consider the following assignment statement:

```
N = 1.25 + 9 / 4
```

where N is an integer. The expression to the right of the equal sign evaluates to 3.25, which is a real number. Since N is an integer, the 3.25 is automatically converted into the integer number 3 before being stored in N.

Now consider the following assignment statement:

```
AVE = (N1 + N2) / 2
```

where N1 and N2 are integers, and AVE is a real number. The expression to the right of the equal sign will be performed in integer arithmetic, but since AVE is a real variable, the result will be converted to real form before being stored in AVE.

PROGRAMMING PITFALLS

Mixed-mode expressions are dangerous because they are hard to understand and may produce misleading results. Avoid them whenever possible.

Later in this chapter, we will learn about a pair of functions called type conversion functions which can be used to force a variable of one type to be converted into a variable of the other type. We will see how to use them to make our equations clearer.

2.6.5 Mixed-Mode Arithmetic and Exponentiation

As a general rule, mixed-mode arithmetic operations are undesirable because they are hard to understand and can sometimes lead to unexpected results. However, there is one exception to this rule: exponentiation. For exponentiation, mixed-mode operation is actually *desirable*.

To understand why this is so, consider the assignment statement

```
RESULT = Y ** N
```

where RESULT and Y are real, and N is an integer. The expression Y ** N is shorthand for "multiply Y by itself N times," and that is exactly what the computer does when it encounters this expression. Since Y is a real number and the computer is multiplying Y by itself, the computer is really doing real arithmetic and not mixed-mode arithmetic!

Now consider the assignment statement

```
RESULT = Y ** X
```

where RESULT, Y, and X are real. The expression Y ** X is shorthand for "multiply Y by itself X times," but this time X is not an integer. Instead, X might be a number like 2.5. It is not physically possible to multiply a number by itself 2.5 times, so we have to rely on indirect methods to calculate Y ** X when necessary. The most common approach is to use the standard algebraic formula which says that

$$y^x = e^{x \ln y}$$ (2-1)

Using this equation, we can evaluate Y ** X by taking the natural logarithm of Y, multiplying by X, and then calculating e to the resulting power. While this technique certainly works, it takes longer to perform and is less accurate than an ordinary series of multiplications. Therefore, if given a choice, we should try to raise real numbers to integer powers instead of real powers.

■ **GOOD PROGRAMMING PRACTICE**

Use integer exponents instead of real exponents whenever possible.

Also, note that *it is not possible to raise a negative number to a power when using real exponents.* Raising a negative number to an integer power is a perfectly legal operation. For example, (-2.0)**2 = 4. However, raising a negative number to a real power does not work, since the natural logarithm of a negative number is undefined. Therefore, the expression (-2.0)**2.0 will produce a run-time error.

PROGRAMMING PITFALLS

Never raise a negative number to a real power.

Quiz 2-2

This quiz provides a quick check to see if you have understood the concepts introduced in Section 2.6. If you have trouble with the quiz, reread the section, ask your instructor, or discuss the material with a fellow student. The answers to this quiz are found in the back of the book.

1. In what order are the arithmetic and logical operations evaluated if they appear within an arithmetic expression? How do parentheses modify this order?

2. Are the following expressions legal or illegal? If they are legal, what is their result? If they are illegal, what is wrong with them?
   (*a*) 37 / 3
   (*b*) 37 + 17 / 3
   (*c*) 28 / 3 / 4
   (*d*) (28 / 3) / 4
   (*e*) 28 / (3 / 4)
   (*f*) 3. ** 4. / 2.
   (*g*) 4. ** -3

3. Evaluate the following expressions:
   (*a*) 2 * 13 / 3
   (*b*) 2 * (13 / 3)
   (*c*) (2 * 13) / 3
   (*d*) 2. * 13 / 3
   (*e*) 2.* (13 / 3)
   (*f*) (2 * 13) / 3.

4. Evaluate the following expressions:
   (*a*) 2 + 5 * 2 - 5
   (*b*) (2 + 5) * (2 - 5)
   (*c*) 2 + (5 * 2) - 5
   (*d*) (2 + 5) * 2 - 5
   (*e*) 2 + 5 * (2 - 5)

5. Are the following expressions legal or illegal? If they are legal, what is their result? If they are illegal, what is wrong with them?
   (*a*) 2. ** 2. ** 3.
   (*b*) 2. ** (-2.)
   (*c*) (-2) ** 2
   (*d*) (-2.) ** 2.

6. Are the following statements legal or illegal? If they are legal, what is their result? If they are illegal, what is wrong with them?

```
INTEGER I, J, K
PARAMETER ( K = 4)
I = K ** 2
J = I / K
K = I + J
```

7. What value is stored in RESULT after the following statements are executed?

```
REAL A, B, C, RESULT
A = 10.
B = 1.5
C = 5.
RESULT = A / B + B * C ** 2
```

8. What values are stored in A and N after the following statements are executed?

```
REAL A
INTEGER N, I, J
I = 10.
J = 3
N = I / J
A = I / J
```

2.7 ASSIGNMENT STATEMENTS AND LOGICAL CALCULATIONS

Like arithmetic calculations, logical calculations are specified with an assignment statement, whose form is

Logical Variable Name = Logical Expression

The assignment statement calculates the value of the expression to the right of the equal sign, and assigns that value to the variable named to the left of the equal sign.

The expression to the right of the equal sign can consist of any valid logical constant, logical variable, or logical operation. A **logical operation** is an operation on numerical or logical data that yields a logical result. There are two basic types of logical operations: **relational logic operations** and **combinational logic operations.**

2.7.1 Relational Logic Operations

Relational logic operations are operations on two numerical or character values which yield a logical result. The result depends upon the *relationship* between the two values being compared, so these operations are called relational. The general form of a relational logic operation is

a_1 .op. a_2

where a_1 and a_2 are arithmetic expressions, variables, constants, or character strings, and .op. is one of the following relational logic operators (Table 2-4):

TABLE 2-4   Relational Logic Operators

Operation	*Meaning*
.EQ.	Equal to
.NE.	Not equal to
.GT.	Greater than
.GE.	Greater than or equal to
.LT.	Less than
.LE.	Less than or equal to

The periods are a part of the operator and must always be present. If the relationship between a_1 and a_2 expressed by the operator is true, then the operation returns a value of TRUE; otherwise, the operation returns a value of FALSE.

Some relational logic operations and their results are given below:

Operation	Result
3 .LT. 4	.TRUE.
3 .LE. 4	.TRUE.
3 .EQ. 4	.FALSE.
3 .GT. 4	.FALSE.
3 .GE. 4	.FALSE.
4 .LT. 4	.FALSE.
4 .LE. 4	.TRUE.
'A' .LT. 'B'	.TRUE.

The last logical expression is TRUE because characters are evaluated in alphabetical order.

In the hierarchy of operations, relational operators are evaluated after all arithmetic operations have been completed. Therefore, the following two expressions are equivalent (both are TRUE).

```
7 + 3  .LT.  2 + 11
(7 + 3) .LT. (2 + 11)
```

If the comparison is between real and integer values, then the integer value is converted to a real value before the comparison is performed. Comparisons between numerical data and character data are illegal and will cause a compile-time error:

```
4 .EQ. 4.     .TRUE.   Integer is converted to real and comparison is made.
4 .LE. 'A'    Illegal—produces a compile-time error
```

2.7.2 Combinational Logic Operations

Combinational logic operations are operations on logical values that yield a logical result. There are four binary operators, **.AND., .OR., .EQV.,** and **.NEQV.,** and one unary operator, **.NOT.**. The general form of a binary combinational logic operation is

$$l_1 \text{ .op. } l_2$$

where l_1 and l_2 are logical expressions, variables, or constants, and .op. is one of the following combinational operators (Table 2-5):

TABLE 2-5 Combinational Logic Operators

Operator	Function	Definition
l_1 .AND. l_2	Logical AND	Result is TRUE if both l_1 and l_2 are TRUE; otherwise, it is FALSE
l_1 .OR. l_2	Logical OR	Result is TRUE, if either or both l_1 and l_2 are TRUE; otherwise, it is FALSE
l_1 .EQV. l_2	Logical equivalence	Result is TRUE, if either l_1 is the same as l_2 (either both TRUE or both FALSE); otherwise, it is FALSE
l_1 .NEQV. l_2	Logical non-equivalence	Result is TRUE, if one of l_1 and l_2 is TRUE and the other one is FALSE; otherwise, it is FALSE
.NOT. l_1	Logical NOT	Result is TRUE, if either l_1 is FALSE; otherwise, it is FALSE

The periods are a part of the operator and must always be present. If the relationship between l_1 and l_2 expressed by the operator is true, then the operation returns a value of TRUE; otherwise, the operation returns a value of FALSE.

The results of the combinational logic operations are summarized in the following **truth tables** (Tables 2-6(a) and (b)), which show the result of each operation for all possible combinations of l_1 and l_2.

TABLE 2-6(a) Truth Tables for Binary Combinational Logic Operators

l_1	l_2	l_1 .AND. l_2	l_1 .OR. l_2	l_1 .EQV. l_2	l_1 .NEQV. l_2
.FALSE.	.FALSE.	.FALSE.	.FALSE.	.TRUE.	.FALSE.
.FALSE.	.TRUE.	.FALSE.	.TRUE.	.FALSE.	.TRUE.
.TRUE.	.FALSE.	.FALSE.	.TRUE.	.FALSE.	.TRUE.
.TRUE.	.TRUE.	.TRUE.	.TRUE.	.TRUE.	.FALSE.

TABLE 2-6(b) *Truth Table for .NOT. Operator*

l_1	.NOT. l_1
.FALSE.	.TRUE.
.TRUE.	.FALSE.

In the hierarchy of operations, combinational logic operators are evaluated *after all arithmetic operations and all relational operators have been evaluated*. The order in which the logic operators in an expression are evaluated is:

1. All relational operators (**.EQ., .NE., .GT., .GE., .LT., .LE.**) are evaluated, working from left to right.
2. All **.NOT.** operators are evaluated.
3. All **.AND.** operators are evaluated, working from left to right.
4. All **.OR.** operators are evaluated, working from left to right.
5. All **.EQV.** and **.NEQV.** operators are evaluated, working from left to right.

As with arithmetic operations, parentheses can be used to change the default order of evaluation.

Examples of some combinational logic operations and their results are given below:

EXAMPLE 2-3

Assume that the following variables are initialized with the values shown, and calculate the result of the specified operations:

```
L1 = .TRUE.
L2 = .TRUE.
L3 = .FALSE.
```

Logical Expression	Result
(*a*) .NOT. L1	.FALSE.
(*b*) L1 .OR. L3	.TRUE.
(*c*) L1 .AND. L3	.FALSE.
(*d*) L1 .EQV. L2	.TRUE.
(*e*) L2 .NEQV. L3	.TRUE.
(*f*) L1 .AND. L2 .OR. L3	.TRUE.
(*g*) L1 .OR. L2 .AND. L3	.FALSE.
(*h*) .NOT. (L1 .EQV. L2)	.FALSE. ●

Combinational logical operations are evaluated after all relational logic operations, and the **.NOT.** operation is evaluated before other combinational logic operations. Therefore, the parentheses in part (*h*) of the above example were required. If they had been absent, the expression in part (*h*) would have been evaluated in the order (**.NOT. L1) .EQV. L2**.

In the FORTRAN 77 standard, combinational logic operations involving numerical or character data are illegal and will cause a compile-time error:

```
4 .AND. 3          Error
```

Some FORTRAN compilers permit combinational logical operations to be used with integer or real data as an extension to FORTRAN 77. *Do not use this feature.* It is nonstandard, and it makes your programs nonportable.

2.7.3 The Significance of Logical Variables and Expressions

Logical variables and expressions are rarely the final product of a FORTRAN program. Nevertheless, they are absolutely essential to the proper operation of most programs. As we will see in Chapter 3, the major branching and looping structures of FORTRAN are all controlled by logical values, so we will have to be able to read and write logical expressions to understand and use FORTRAN control statements.

2.8 INTRINSIC FUNCTIONS

Scientific and technical calculations usually require functions which are more complex than the simple addition, subtraction, multiplication, division, and exponentiation operations that we have discussed so far. Some of these functions are common, and are used in many different technical disciplines. Others are rarer and specific to a single problem or a small number of problems. Examples of very common functions used in scientific calculations are the trigonometric functions, logarithms, and square roots. Examples of rarer functions include the hyperbolic functions, Bessel functions, and so forth.

The FORTRAN 77 language has mechanisms to support both the very common functions and the less common ones. Many of the most common functions (such as trigonometric functions) are built directly into the FORTRAN language. They are called **intrinsic functions.** Less common functions are not included in the FORTRAN language, but any function needed to solve a particular problem may be supplied by the user as an **external function.** External functions are described in Chapter 6.

A FORTRAN function takes one or more input values, and calculates a *single* output value from them. The input values to the function are known as **arguments;** they appear in parentheses immediately after the function name. The output of a function is a single number, which can be used together with other functions, constants, and variables in arithmetic expressions.

A list of some common intrinsic functions is given in Table 2-7, and a complete list of FORTRAN 77 intrinsic functions is given in Appendix B, along with a brief description of each one.

TABLE 2-7   Some Common Intrinsic Functions

Function Name and Argument	Function Value	Argument Type	Result Type	Comments
SQRT(X)	$\sqrt{x}$	REAL	REAL	Square root of x for $x \geq 0$
ABS(X)	$\lvert x \rvert$	*	*	Absolute value of x
SIN(X)	$\sin(x)$	REAL	REAL	Sine of x (x must be in *radians*)
COS(X)	$\cos(x)$	REAL	REAL	Cosine of x (x must be in *radians*)
TAN(X)	$\tan(x)$	REAL	REAL	Tangent of x (x must be in *radians*)
EXP(X)	e^x	REAL	REAL	e raised to the xth Power
LOG(X)	$\log_e(x)$	REAL	REAL	Natural logarithm of x for $x > 0$
LOG10(X)	$\log_{10}(x)$	REAL	REAL	Base-10 logarithm of x for $x > 0$
INT(X)		REAL	INTEGER	Integer part of x (x is truncated)
NINT(X)		REAL	INTEGER	Nearest integer to x (x is rounded)
REAL(I)		INTEGER	REAL	Converts integer value to real
MOD(I, J)		*	*	Remainder or modulo function
MAX(I, J)		*	*	Picks the larger of I and J
MIN(I, J)		*	*	Picks the smaller of I and J
ASIN(X)	$\sin^{-1}(x)$	REAL	REAL	Inverse sine of x (results in *radians*)
ACOS(X)	$\cos^{-1}(x)$	REAL	REAL	Inverse cosine of x (results in *radians*)
ATAN(X)	$\tan^{-1}(x)$	REAL	REAL	Inverse tangent of x (results in *radians*)

*If argument(s) are REAL, the result is REAL, and if argument(s) are INTEGER, the result is INTEGER.

FORTRAN functions are used much like the mathematical functions they are based on. For example, the intrinsic function SIN can be used to calculate the sine of a number. Its form is

```
Y = SIN(THETA)
```

where THETA is the argument of the function SIN. After this statement is executed, the variable Y contains the sine of the value stored in variable THETA. Note from Table 2-7 that the trigonometric functions expect their arguments to be in radians. If the variable THETA is in degrees, then we must convert degrees to radians ($180° = \pi$ radians) before computing the sine. This conversion can be done in the same statement as the sine calculation:

```
Y = SIN (THETA*(3.141593/180.))
```

The inner set of parentheses is not really required, but it is used to emphasize that 3.141593/180. is a conversion factor. This is an example of using extra parentheses for clarity.

The REAL, INT, and NINT functions may be used to avoid undesirable mixed-mode expressions by explicitly converting variable types from one form to another. The REAL function converts an integer into a real number, and the INT and NINT functions convert real numbers into integers. The INT function truncates the real number, while the NINT function rounds it. To understand the distinction between these two operations, consider the real number 2.9995. The result of INT(2.9995) is 2, while the result of NINT(2.9995) is 3. The NINT function is very useful when converting back from real to integer form, since the small roundoff errors occurring in real calculations will not affect the resulting integer value.

The argument of a function can be a constant, a variable, an expression, or even the result of another function. All of the following statements are legal:

```
Y = SIN(3.141593)      Argument is a constant.
Y = SIN(X)             Argument is a variable.
Y = SIN(PI*X)          Argument is an expression.
Y = SIN(SQRT(X))       Argument is the result of another function.
```

Functions may be used in expressions anywhere that a constant or variable may be used. However, functions may never appear on the left side of the assignment operator (equal sign), since they are not memory locations, and nothing can be stored in them.

The type of argument required by a function and the type of value returned by it are specified in Table 2-7 for the intrinsic functions listed there. Some of these intrinsic functions are **generic functions,** which means that they can use more than one type of input data. The absolute value function ABS is a generic function. If X is a real number, then the type of ABS(X) is real. If X is an integer, then the type of ABS(X) is integer. Some functions are called **specific functions,** because they can use only one specific type of input data, and produce only one specific type of output value. For example, the function IABS requires an integer argument and returns an integer result. A complete list of all intrinsic functions (both generic and specific) is provided in Appendix B.

2.9 List-Directed Input and Output Statements

An **input statement** reads one or more values from an input device and stores them into variables specified by the user. The input device could be a keyboard in an interactive environment, or an input disk file in a batch environment. An **output statement** writes out one or more values to an output device. The output device could be a CRT screen in an interactive environment, or an output listing file in a batch environment.

We have already seen input and output statements in PROGRAM FIRST, which was shown in Figure 2-2. The input statement in the figure was of the form

```
READ (*,*) list
```

where *list* is the list of variables in which the values being read in are to be placed. If there is more than one variable in the list, they should be separated by commas. The parentheses (*,*) in the statement contains control information for the read. The first field in the parentheses specifies the *logical unit* from which the data is to be read (the concept of a logical unit is explained in Chapter 4). An asterisk in this field means that the data is to be read from the standard input device for the computer. The standard input device is usually the keyboard when running in interactive mode, and the input file when running in batch mode. The second field in the parentheses specifies the format in which the data is to be read (formats also are explained in Chapter 4). An asterisk in this field means that **list-directed input** is to be used.

The term *list-directed input* means that *the types of the variables in the variable list determine the required format of the input data.* For example, consider the following statements:

```
PROGRAM IN
INTEGER I, J
REAL A
CHARACTER*12 CHARS
READ (*,*) I, J, A, CHARS
END
```

The input data supplied to PROGRAM IN must consist of two integers, a real number, and a character string. Furthermore, they must be in that order. The values may be all on one line separated by commas or blanks, or they may be on separate lines. The list-directed READ statement will continue to read input data until values have been found for all of the variables in the list. If the input data supplied to the program at execution time is

```
1, 2, 3.,'This one.'
```

then the variable I will be filled with a 1, the variable J will be filled with a 2, the variable A will be filled with a 3.0, and the variable CHARS with be filled with 'THIS ONE.   '. Note that the input character string is only 9 characters long, while the variable CHARS has room for 12 characters. The string is *left-justified* in the character variable, and three blanks are automatically added at the end of it to fill out the remainder of CHARS. Also note that for list-directed reads, input character strings must be enclosed in single quotes.

When using list-directed input, the values to be read must match the variables in the input list both in order and type. If the input data had been

```
1, 2, 'This one.', 3.
```

then a run-time error would have occurred when the program tried to read the data.

Each READ statement in a program begins reading from an new line of input data. If any data was left over on the previous input line, that data is discarded. For example, consider the following program:

```
PROGRAM IN1
INTEGER I, J, K, L
READ (*,*) I, J
READ (*,*) K, L
END
```

If the input data to this program is

```
1, 2, 3, 4
5, 6, 7, 8
```

then after the READ statements, I will contain a 1, J will contain a 2, K will contain a 5, and L will contain a 6.

It is a good idea to always *echo* any value that you read into a program from a keyboard. Echoing a value means displaying the value with a WRITE statement after it has been read in. If you do not do so, a typing error in the input data might cause a wrong answer, and the user of the program would never know that anything was wrong. You may echo the data either immediately after it is read in or somewhere further down in the program output, but *every single input variable should be echoed somewhere in the program's output.*

■   **GOOD PROGRAMMING PRACTICE**

Always echo any variables that a user enters into a program from a keyboard, so that the user can be certain that they were typed and processed correctly.

The *list-directed output statement* is of the form

```
WRITE (*,*) list
```

where *list* is the list of variables, constants, and expressions which are to be written. If there is more than one item in the list, then the items should be separated by commas. The parentheses (*,*) in the statement contains control information for the write. The first field in parentheses specifies the logical unit to which the data is to be written. An asterisk in this field means that the data is to be written to the standard output device for the computer. The standard output device is usually the CRT screen when running in interactive mode, and the output listing file when running in batch mode. The second field in the parentheses specifies the format in which the data is to be written (see Chapter 4). An asterisk in this field means that *list-directed output* is to be used.

The term list-directed output means that *the types of the values in the list of the write statement determine the format of the output data.* For example, consider the following statements:

```
PROGRAM OUT
INTEGER IX
LOGICAL TEST
REAL THETA
IX = 1
THETA = 3.141593
TEST = .TRUE.
WRITE (*,*) ' IX =                   ', IX
WRITE (*,*) ' THETA =                ', THETA
WRITE (*,*) ' COS(THETA) =           ', COS(THETA)
WRITE (*,*) ' IX - COS(THETA) = ', (REAL(IX) - COS(THETA))
WRITE (*,*) ' TEST =                 ', TEST
WRITE (*,*) REAL(IX), NINT(THETA)
END
```

The output resulting from these statements is:

```
IX =                   1
THETA =                3.141593
COS(THETA) =           -1.000000
IX - COS(THETA) =      2.000000
TEST =              T
        1.000000       3
```

This example illustrates several points about the list-directed write statement:

1. The output list may contain constants ('I = ' is a constant), variables, functions, and expressions. In each case, the value of the constant, variable, function, or expression is output to the standard output device.
2. Note that the format of the output data matches the type of the value being output. For example, even though THETA is of type real, NINT(THETA) is of type integer. Therefore, the sixth write statement produces an output of 3 (the nearest integer to 3.141593). Also note that when a logical value is included in a WRITE statement, a single T or F (as appropriate) is written out.
3. The output of list-directed write statements is not very pretty. The values printed out do not line up in neat columns, and there is no way to control the number of significant digits displayed for real numbers. We will learn how to produce neatly formatted output in Chapter 4.

Quiz 2-3

This quiz provides a quick check to see if you have understood the concepts introduced in Sections 2.6, 2.7, 2.8, and 2.9. If you have trouble with the quiz, reread the sections, ask your instructor, or discuss the material with a fellow student. The answers to this quiz are found in the back of the book.

Convert the following algebraic equations into FORTRAN assignment statements:

1. The equivalent resistance R_{eq} of four resistors R_1, R_2, R_3, and R_4 connected in series:

$$R_{eq} = R_1 + R_2 + R_3 + R_4$$

2. The equivalent resistance R_{eq} of four resistors R_1, R_2, R_3, and R_4 connected in parallel:

$$R_{eq} = \frac{1}{\dfrac{1}{R_1} + \dfrac{1}{R_2} + \dfrac{1}{R_3} + \dfrac{1}{R_4}}$$

3. The period T of an oscillating pendulum:

$$T = 2\pi \sqrt{\frac{L}{g}}$$

where L is the length of the pendulum, and g is the acceleration due to gravity.

4. The equation for damped sinusoidal oscillation:

$$v(t) = V_M e^{-\alpha t} \cos\omega t$$

where:

V_M is the maximum value of the oscillation
α is the exponential damping factor
ω is the angular velocity of the oscillation

Convert the following FORTRAN assignment statements into algebraic equations:

5. The motion of an object in a constant gravitational field:

```
DIST = 0.5 * ACCEL * T**2 + V0 * T + X0
```

6. The oscillating frequency of a damped RLC (resistor-inductors-capictor) circuit:

```
FREQ = 1. / (2. * PI * SQRT(L * C))
```

where PI is π (3.141592 . . .).

7. Energy storage in an inductor:

```
ENERGY = 1.0 / 2.0 * L * I**2
```

8. What values will be printed out when the following statements are executed?

```
PROGRAM QUIZ1
INTEGER I
LOGICAL L
REAL A
A = 0.05
I = NINT ( 2. * 3.141493 / A)
L = I .GT. 100
A = A * (5 / 3)
WRITE (*,*) I, A, L
END
```

9. Suppose that the real variables A, B, and C contain the values −10., 0.1, and 2.1, respectively, and that the logical variable L1, L2, and L3 contain the values TRUE, FALSE, and TRUE, respectively. Is each of the following expressions legal or illegal? If an expression is legal, what will its result be?

(*a*) `A .GT. B .OR. B .GT. C`
(*b*) `(.NOT. A) .OR. L1`
(*c*) `L1 .AND. .NOT. L2`
(*d*) `A .LT. B .EQV. B .LT. C`
(*e*) `L1 .OR. L2 .AND. L3`
(*f*) `L1 .OR. (L2 .AND. L3)`
(*g*) `(L1 .OR. L2) .AND. L3`
(*h*) `A .OR. B .AND. L1`

10. If the input data is as shown, what will be printed out by the following program?

```
PROGRAM QUIZ2
INTEGER I, J, K
REAL A, B, C
READ (*,*) I, J, A
READ (*,*) B, K
C = SIN ((3.141493 / 180) * A)
WRITE (*,*) I, J, K, A, B, C
END
```

The input data is

```
1, 3
2, 45., 17.
30., 180, 6.
```

2.10 INITIALIZATION OF VARIABLES

Consider the following program:

```
PROGRAM INIT
INTEGER I
WRITE (*,*) I
END
```

What is the value stored in the variable I? What will be printed out by the **WRITE** statement? The answer is: We don't know!

The variable I is an example of an **uninitialized variable.** It has been defined by the **INTEGER I** statement, but no value has been placed into it yet. The value of an uninitialized variable is not defined by the FORTRAN 77 standard. Some compilers automatically set uninitialized variables to zero, and some set them to different arbitrary patterns. Other compilers leave in memory whatever values previously existed in the computer's memory at the location of the variables. Some compilers even produce a run-time error if a variable is used without first being initialized.

Uninitialized variables can present a serious problem. Since they are handled differently on different machines, a program that works fine on one computer may fail when transported to another one. On other machines, the same program could work sometimes and fail sometimes, depending on the data left behind by the previous program occupying the same memory. Such a situation is totally unacceptable, and we must avoid it by always initializing all of the variables in our programs.

■ **GOOD PROGRAMMING PRACTICE**

Always initialize all variables in a program before using them.

There are three basic techniques available to initialize variables in a FORTRAN program: assignment statements, **READ** statements, and **DATA** statements. An assignment statement assigns the value of the expression to the right of the equal sign into the variable that appears to the left of the equal sign. In the following code, the variable I is initialized to 1, and we know that a 1 will be printed out by the **WRITE** statement.

```
PROGRAM INIT1
INTEGER I
I = 1
WRITE (*,*) I
END
```

A **READ** statement may be used to initialize variables with values input by the user. In the following code, the variable I is initialized by the **READ** statement, and we know that whatever value was read in by the **READ** statement will be printed out by the **WRITE** statement.

```
PROGRAM INIT2
INTEGER I
READ (*,*) I
WRITE (*,*) I
END
```

The third technique available to initialize variables in a FORTRAN program is the **DATA** statement. A **DATA** statement is a nonexecutable specification statement. It should be located in the declaration section of the program after all type specification statements (**INTEGER, REAL, CHARACTER**, etc.), and before the first executable statement. A **DATA** statement specifies that *a value should be preloaded into a variable during the compilation and linking process*. Note the fundamental difference between a **DATA** statement and an assignment statement: a **DATA** statement initializes the variable before the program begins to run, while an assignment statement initializes the variable during execution.

The general form of the **DATA** statement is

```
DATA list of variable names / list of constants /
```

The number of constants must match the number of variables in the list of variable names, and the types of the constants must match the types of the corresponding variables. An example of a **DATA** statement used to initialize a series of variables is

```
REAL    TIME, DIST
INTEGER LOOP
LOGICAL DONE
DATA    TIME, DIST, LOOP, DONE / 0.0, 5128., 10, .FALSE. /
```

Before program execution, TIME is initialized to 0.0, DIST is initialized to 5128., LOOP is initialized to 10, and DONE is initialized to FALSE.

If a number of the constants in the list are identical, it is not necessary to write each one out separately. Instead, an integer constant followed by an asterisk can be used to indicate repetition. For example, real variables A, B, C, D, and E can all be initialized to 3.141593 by the following statement:

```
DATA A, B, C, D, E / 5*3.141593 /
```

In the following code, the variable I is initialized by the **DATA** statement, so we know that when execution starts, the variable I will contain the value 1. Therefore, the **WRITE** statement will print out a 1.

```
PROGRAM INIT3
INTEGER I
DATA I /1/
WRITE (*,*) I
END
```

2.11 THE **IMPLICIT NONE** STATEMENT[2]

There is another nonexecutable type specification statement that we should deal with: the **IMPLICIT NONE** statement. When it is used, the **IMPLICIT NONE** statement disables the default typing provisions of FORTRAN. Recall that if no type specification statements are used, FORTRAN automatically assigns any variable beginning with the letters I through N as type integer, and any other variables as type real. When the **IMPLICIT NONE** statement is included in a program, *any variable that does not appear in an explicit type specification statement is considered an error*. The **IMPLICIT NONE** statement should appear after the **PROGRAM** statement and before any type specification statements.

If the **IMPLICIT NONE** statement is included in a program, then the programmer must explicitly declare the type of every variable in the program. On first thought, this might seem to be a disadvantage, since the programmer must do more work when he or she first writes a program. This initial impression couldn't be more wrong. In fact, there are several advantages to using the statement.

---

[2]The **IMPLICIT NONE** statement is a common extension to the FORTRAN 77 standard that is a part of the FORTRAN 90 standard.

The majority of programming errors are simple typographical errors. The **IM-PLICIT NONE** statement catches these errors at compilation time, before they can produce subtle errors during execution. For example, consider the following simple program:

```
PROGRAM TEST1
REAL TIME
TIME = 10.0
WRITE (*,*) 'TIME = ', TMIE
END
```

In this program, the variable TIME is misspelled TMIE at one point. When this program is compiled with the Microsoft FORTRAN compiler and run on a PC-compatible, the output is 'TIME = 0.000000', which is the wrong answer! By contrast, consider the same program with the **IMPLICIT NONE** statement present:

```
PROGRAM TEST2
IMPLICIT NONE
REAL TIME
TIME = 10.0
WRITE (*,*) 'TIME = ', TMIE
END
```

When compiled with the same compiler, this program produces the following compile-time error:

```
Line# Source Line            Microsoft FORTRAN Optimizing Compiler Version 5.00
     1        PROGRAM TEST2
     2        IMPLICIT NONE
     3        REAL TIME
     4        TIME = 10.0
     5        WRITE (*,*) 'TIME = ',  TMIE
***** implicit.for(5) : error F2347: TMIE : missing type
     6        END
1 errors detected
```

Instead of having a wrong answer in an otherwise-working piece of code, we have an explicit error message flagging the problem at compilation time. This is an enormous advantage when working with longer programs containing many variables.

Another advantage of the **IMPLICIT NONE** statement is that it makes the code more maintainable. Any program using the statement must have a complete list of all variables included in the declaration section of the program. If the program must be modified, a programmer can check the list to avoid using variable names which are already defined in the program. This checking helps to eliminate a common error, in which the modifications to the program inadvertently change the values of some variables used elsewhere in the program.

In general, the use of the **IMPLICIT NONE** statement becomes more and more advantageous as the size of a programming project increases.

FORTRAN 90 Extension (common in FORTRAN 77)
The IMPLICIT NONE statement is an extension to FORTRAN 77 that is a part of the FORTRAN 90 standard. It is a common extension to FORTRAN 77, but it may not be available on all compilers.

The **IMPLICIT NONE** *statement is an extension to standard* FORTRAN 77. As such, it may not be available in all compilers. However, it is available in the compilers for almost all popular computers, including IBM mainframes, VAX, Hewlett-Packard (HP), Cray, Sun, and PC-compatible computers. Furthermore, it is a part of the FORTRAN 90 standard. The use of **IMPLICIT NONE** is so important to the writing of good programs that we will use it consistently everywhere throughout this book. It is the only FORTRAN 90 extension that is integrated into the main body and examples of this text.

If the compiler that you are using does not support the **IMPLICIT NONE** statement, you may still run all of the examples in the book. Simply comment out or delete the **IMPLICIT NONE** statement, and recompile the example.

■
GOOD PROGRAMMING PRACTICE

Always explicitly define every variable in your programs, and use the **IMPLICIT NONE** statement to help you spot and correct typographical errors before they become program execution errors.

2.12   Program Examples

In Chapter 2, we have presented the fundamental concepts required to write simple but functional FORTRAN programs. We will now present a few example problems in which these concepts are used.

■
EXAMPLE 2-4 *Temperature Conversion*   Write a FORTRAN program which reads an input temperature in degrees Fahrenheit, converts it to an absolute temperature in kelvins, and writes out the result.

Solution The relationship between temperature in degrees Fahrenheit (°F) and temperature in kelvins (K) can be found in any physics textbook. It is

$$T \text{ (in kelvins)} = \frac{5}{9}\left(T \text{ (in °F)} - 32.0\right) + 273.15 \qquad \text{(2-2)}$$

The physics books also give us sample values on both temperature scales, which we can use to check the operation of our program. Two such values are:

The boiling point of water	212° F	373.15 K
The sublimation point of dry ice	-110° F	194.26 K

Our program must perform the following steps:

1. Prompt the user to enter an input temperature in °F.
2. Read the input temperature.
3. Calculate the temperature in kelvins from Equation (2-2).
4. Write out the result, and stop.

The resulting code is shown below.

```
        5    10   15   20   25   30   35   40   45   50   55   60   65   70   75   80
----|----|----|----|----|----|----|----|----|----|----|----|----|----|----|----|
      PROGRAM TEMP
C
C  Purpose:
C     To convert an input temperature from degrees Fahrenheit to
C     an output temperature in kelvins.
C
C  Record of revisions:
C      Date       Programmer        Description of change
C      ====       ==========        =====================
C     02/02/91   S. J. Chapman      Original code
C
C  List of variables:
C     TEMPF -- Temperature in degrees Fahrenheit
C     TEMPK -- Temperature in kelvins
C
        IMPLICIT NONE
C
C  Declare the variables used in this program.
C
        REAL TEMPF, TEMPK
C
C  Prompt the user for the input temperature.
C
        WRITE (*,*) ' Enter the temperature in degrees Fahrenheit: '
        READ  (*,*) TEMPF
C
C  Convert to kelvins.
C
        TEMPK = (5. / 9.) * (TEMPF - 32.) + 273.15
C
C  Write out the result.
C
        WRITE (*,*) TEMPF, ' degrees Fahrenheit = ', TEMPK, ' kelvins'
C
C  Finish up.
C
        STOP
        END
----|----|----|----|----|----|----|----|----|----|----|----|----|----|----|----|
        5    10   15   20   25   30   35   40   45   50   55   60   65   70   75   80
```

To test the completed program, we will run it with the known input values given above:

```
C:\BOOK\FORT>temp
 Enter the temperature in degrees Fahrenheit:
212.
    212.000000 degrees Fahrenheit =            373.150000 kelvins
Stop - Program terminated.

C:\BOOK\FORT>temp
 Enter the temperature in degrees Fahrenheit:
-110.
    -110.000000 degrees Fahrenheit =           194.261100 kelvins
Stop - Program terminated.
```

Notice that the results of the program match the values from the physics book for these input values. ●

In the above program, we echoed the input values and printed the output values together with their units. The results of this program only make sense if the units (degrees Fahrenheit and kelvins) are included together with their values. As a general rule, the units associated with any input value should always be printed along with the prompt that requests the value, and the units associated with any output value should always be printed along with that value.

GOOD PROGRAMMING PRACTICE

Always include the appropriate units with any values that you read in or print out in a program.

The above program exhibits many of the good programming practices that we have described in this chapter. It uses the **IMPLICIT NONE** statement to force the explicit typing of all variables in the program. It includes a variable dictionary defining the uses of all of the variables in the program. It also uses descriptive variable names. The variable TEMPF is initialized by a **READ** statement before it is used. All input values are echoed, and appropriate units are attached to all printed values.

EXAMPLE 2-5 *Electrical Engineering: Calculating Real, Reactive, and Apparent Power* Figure 2-4 shows a sinusoidal alternative current (AC) voltage source with voltage V supplying a load of impedance $Z \angle \theta$ Ω. From simple circuit theory, the rms current I, the real power P, reactive power Q, apparent power S, and power factor PF supplied to the load are given by the equations

$$I = \frac{V}{Z} \tag{2-3}$$

$$P = VI \cos \theta \tag{2-4}$$

$$Q = VI \sin \theta \tag{2-5}$$

$$S = VI \tag{2-6}$$

$$PF = \cos \theta \tag{2-7}$$

where V is the root-mean-square (rms) voltage of the power source in units of volts (V). The units of current are amperes (A), of real power are watts (W), of reactive power are volt-amperes-reactive (VAR), and of apparent power are volt-amperes (VA). The power factor has no units associated with it.

Given the rms voltage of the power source and the magnitude and angle of the impedance Z, calculate the rms current I, the real power P, reactive power Q, apparent power S, and power factor PF of the load (Figure 2-4).

SOLUTION In this program, we need to read in the rms voltage V of the voltage source and the magnitude Z and angle θ of the impedance. The input voltage source is measured in volts, the magnitude of the impedance Z is measured in ohms, and the angle of the impedance θ is measured in degrees. Once the data is read into the program, we must convert the angle θ into radians for use with the FORTRAN trigono-

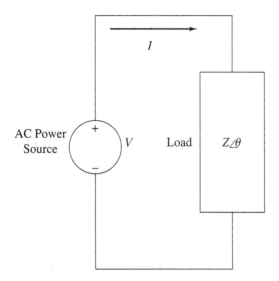

FIGURE 2-4 A sinusoidal ac voltage source with voltage V supplying a load of impedance $Z \angle \theta \ \Omega$.

metric functions. Next, the desired values must be calculated, and the results must be printed out.

The program must perform the following steps:

1. Prompt the user to enter the source voltage in volts.
2. Read the source voltage.
3. Prompt the user to enter the magnitude and angle of the impedance in ohms and degrees.
4. Read the magnitude and angle of the impedance.
5. Calculate the current I from Equation (2-3).
6. Calculate the real power P from Equation (2-4).
7. Calculate the reactive power Q from Equation (2-5).
8. Calculate the apparent power S from Equation (2-6).
9. Calculate the power factor PF from Equation (2-7).
10. Write out the results, and stop.

The final FORTRAN program is shown below.

```
     5   10   15   20   25   30   35   40   45   50   55   60   65   70   75   80
----|----|----|----|----|----|----|----|----|----|----|----|----|----|----|----|
      PROGRAM POWER
C
C  Purpose:
C    To calculate the current, real, reactive, and apparent power,
C    and the power factor supplied to a load.
C
C  Record of revisions:
C      Date      Programmer         Description of change
C      ====      ==========         =====================
C    02/02/91  S. J. Chapman      Original code
C
C  List of variables:
C    AMPS  -- Current in the load
C    CONV  -- Conversion factor to convert degrees to radians
C    P     -- Real Power of the load
C    PF    -- Power factor of the load
C    Q     -- Reactive power of the load
C    S     -- Apparent power of the load
C    THETA -- Impedance angle of the load
C    VOLTS -- Rms voltage of the power source
C    Z     -- Magnitude of the impedance of the load
C
      IMPLICIT NONE
C
C  Declare the variables used in this program.
C
      REAL AMPS
      REAL CONV
      REAL P
      REAL PF
      REAL Q
      REAL S
```

```
      REAL THETA
      REAL VOLTS
      REAL Z
C
C  Define constant CONV with the degrees-to-radians conversion factor:
C      PI radians = 180 degrees == >0.01745329 radians / degree
C
      PARAMETER ( CONV = 0.01745329 )
C
C  Prompt the user for the rms voltage.
C
      WRITE (*,*) ' Enter the rms voltage of the source: '
      READ  (*,*) VOLTS
C
C  Prompt the user for the magnitude and angle of the impedance.
C
      WRITE (*,*) ' Enter the magnitude and angle of the impedance '
      WRITE (*,*) ' in ohms and degrees: '
      READ  (*,*) Z, THETA
C
C  Calculate the rms current in the load.
C
      AMPS = VOLTS / Z
C
C  Calculate the real power of the load.
C
      P = VOLTS * AMPS * COS (THETA * CONV)
C
C  Calculate the reactive power of the load.
C
      Q = VOLTS * AMPS * SIN (THETA * CONV)
C
C  Calculate the apparent power of the load.
C
      S = VOLTS * AMPS
C
C  Calculate the power factor of the load.
C
      PF =  COS (THETA * CONV)
C
C  Write out the result.
C
      WRITE (*,*) ' Voltage         = ', VOLTS, ' volts'
      WRITE (*,*) ' Impedance       = ', Z, ' ohms at ', THETA,' degrees'
      WRITE (*,*) ' Current         = ', AMPS, ' amps'
      WRITE (*,*) ' Real Power      = ', P, ' watts'
      WRITE (*,*) ' Reactive Power  = ', Q, ' VAR'
      WRITE (*,*) ' Apparent Power  = ', S, ' VA'
      WRITE (*,*) ' Power Factor    = ', PF
C
C  Finish up.
C
      STOP
      END
----|----|----|----|----|----|----|----|----|----|----|----|----|----|----|----|
    5   10   15   20   25   30   35   40   45   50   55   60   65   70   75   80
```

This program also exhibits many of the good programming practices that we have described in this chapter. It uses the **IMPLICIT NONE** statement to force the explicit typing of all variables in the program. It includes a variable dictionary defining the uses of all of the variables in the program. It also uses descriptive variable names (although some of the variable names are short, P, Q, S, and PF are the standard accepted abbreviations for the corresponding quantities). All variables are initialized before they are used. The program makes use of a **PARAMETER** statement to name the degrees-to-radians conversion factor, and then uses that name everywhere throughout the program that the conversion factor was required. All input values are echoed, and appropriate units are attached to all printed values.

To verify the operation of program POWER, we will do a sample calculation by hand and compare the results with the output of the program for the same input data. If the rms voltage V is 120 V, the magnitude of the impedance Z is 5 Ω, and the angle θ is 30°, then the values are

$$I = \frac{V}{Z} \tag{2-3}$$

$$I = \frac{120 \text{ V}}{5 \ \Omega} = 24 \text{ A}$$

$$P = VI \cos \theta \tag{2-4}$$

$$P = (120 \text{ V})(24 \text{ A}) \cos 30° = 2494 \text{ W}$$

$$Q = VI \sin \theta \tag{2-5}$$

$$Q = (120 \text{ V})(24 \text{ A}) \sin 30° = 1440 \text{ VAR}$$

$$S = VI \tag{2-6}$$

$$S = (120 \text{ V})(24 \text{ A}) = 2880 \text{ VA}$$

$$PF = \cos \theta \tag{2-7}$$

$$PF = \cos 30° = 0.86603$$

When we run program POWER with the specified input data, the results are identical with our hand calculations:

```
C:\BOOK\FORT>power
 Enter the rms voltage of the source:
120.
 Enter the magnitude and angle of the impedance
 in ohms and degrees:
5., 30.
 Voltage        =      120.000000 volts
 Impedance      =        5.000000 ohms at     30.000000 degrees
 Current        =       24.000000 amps
 Real Power     =     2494.153000 watts
 Reactive Power =     1440.000000 VAR
 Apparent Power =     2880.000000 VA
 Power Factor   =     8.660254E-01  ●
```

■
EXAMPLE 2-6 *Carbon 14 Dating* A radioactive isotope of an element is a form of the element that is not stable. Instead, it spontaneously decays into another element over a period of time. Radioactive decay is an exponential process. If Q_o is the initial quantity of a radioactive substance at time $t = 0$, then the amount of that substance which will be present at any time t in the future is given by

$$Q(t) = Q_o e^{-\lambda t} \tag{2-8}$$

where λ is the radioactive decay constant (Figure 2-5).

Because radioactive decay occurs at a known rate, it can be used as a clock to measure the time since the decay started. If we know the initial amount of the radioactive material Q_o present in a sample, and the amount of the material Q left at the current time, we can solve for t in Equation (2-8) to determine how long the decay has been going on. The resulting equation is

$$t_{decay} = -\frac{1}{\lambda} \log \frac{Q}{Q_o}. \tag{2-9}$$

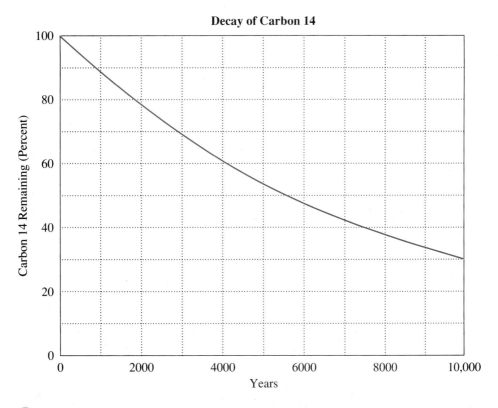

FIGURE 2-5 The radioactive decay of carbon 14 as a function of time. Notice that 50% of the original carbon 14 is left after about 5730 years have elapsed.

Equation (2-9) has practical applications in many areas of science. For example, archaeologists use a radioactive clock based on carbon 14 to determine the time that has passed since a once-living thing died. Carbon 14 is continually taken into the body while a plant or animal is living, so the amount of it present in the body at the time of death is assumed to be known. The decay constant of carbon 14 is well known to be 0.00012097/year, so if the amount of carbon 14 remaining now can be accurately measured, then Equation (2-9) can be used to determine how long ago the living thing died.

Write a program that reads in the percentage of carbon 14 remaining in a sample, calculates the age of the sample from it, and prints out the result with proper units.

SOLUTION   Our program must perform the following steps:

1. Prompt the user to enter the percentage of carbon 14 remaining in the sample.
2. Read in the percentage.
3. Convert the percentage into the fraction $\frac{Q}{Q_0}$.
4. Calculate the age of the sample in years using Equation (2-9). (The units of λ are years^{-1}.)
5. Write out the result, and stop.

The resulting code is shown below:

```
      5    10   15   20   25   30   35   40   45   50   55   60   65   70   75   80
----|----|----|----|----|----|----|----|----|----|----|----|----|----|----|----|
      PROGRAM C14DAT
C
C  Purpose:
C    To calculate the age of an organic sample from the percentage
C    of the original carbon 14 remaining in the sample.
C
C  Record of revisions:
C      Date       Programmer        Description of change
C      ====       ==========        =====================
C    02/03/91   S. J. Chapman      Original code
C
C  List of variables:
C    AGE    -- The age of the sample in years.
C    LAMBDA -- The radioactive decay constant of carbon 14, in
C              units of reciprocal years.
C    PERCNT -- The percentage of carbon 14 remaining at the time of
C              the measurement.
C    RATIO  -- The ratio of the carbon 14 remaining at the time of
C              the measurement to the original amount of carbon 14.
C
```

```
      IMPLICIT NONE
C
C Declare the variables used in this program.
C
      REAL AGE, LAMBDA, PERCNT, RATIO
C
C Assign a name to the decay constant LAMBDA for Carbon 14:
C     LAMBDA = 0.00012097 per year
C
      PARAMETER ( LAMBDA = 0.00012097 )
C
C     Prompt the user for the percentage of C-14 remaining.
C
      WRITE (*,*) ' Enter the percentage of carbon 14 remaining:'
      READ  (*,*) PERCNT
C
C     Echo the user's input value.
C
      WRITE (*,*) ' The remaining carbon 14 = ', PERCNT, ' %.'
C
C     Convert the percentage into a fractional ratio.
C
      RATIO = PERCNT / 100.
C
C     Calculate the age of the sample, in years.
C
      AGE = (-1.0 / LAMBDA) * LOG ( RATIO )
C
C     Tell the user about the age of the sample.
C
      WRITE (*,*) ' The age of the sample is  ', AGE, ' years.'
C
C     Finish up.
C
      STOP
      END
----|----|----|----|----|----|----|----|----|----|----|----|----|----|----|----|
    5   10   15   20   25   30   35   40   45   50   55   60   65   70   75   80
```

To test the completed program, we will calculate the time it takes for half of the carbon 14 to disappear. This time is known as the *half-life* of carbon 14.

```
C:\BOOK\FORT>c14dat
Enter the percentage of carbon 14 remaining:
50.
 The remaining carbon 14 =      50.000000 %.
 The age of the sample is     5729.910000 years.
```

The *Handbook of Chemistry and Physics* (CRC Press, 1993) states that the half-life of carbon 14 is 5730 years, so output of the program agrees with the reference book to the four significant digits given in the book. ●

2.13 DEBUGGING FORTRAN PROGRAMS

There is an old saying that the only sure things in life are death and taxes. We can add one more certainty to that list: If you write a program of any significant size, it won't work the first time you try it! Errors in programs are known as **bugs,** and the process of locating and eliminating them is known as **debugging.** Given that we have written a program and it is not working, how do we debug it?

Three types of errors are found in FORTRAN programs. The first type of error is a **syntax error.** Syntax errors are errors in the FORTRAN statement itself, such as spelling errors or punctuation errors. These errors are detected by the compiler during compilation. The second type of error is the **run-time error.** A run-time error occurs when an illegal mathematical operation is attempted during program execution (e.g., attempting to divide by 0). These errors cause the program to abort during execution. The third type of error is a **logical error.** Logical errors occur when the program compiles and runs successfully but produces the wrong answer.

The most common mistakes made during programming are *typographical errors.* Some typographical errors create invalid FORTRAN statements. These errors produce syntax errors which are caught by the compiler. Other typographical errors occur in variable names. For example, the letters in some variable names might have been transposed. If you have used the **IMPLICIT NONE** statement, then most of these errors will also be caught by the compiler. However, if one legal variable name is substituted for another legal variable name, the compiler cannot detect the error. This sort of substitution might occur if you have two similar variable names. For example, if variables VEL1 and VEL2 are both used for velocities in the program, then one of them might be inadvertently used instead of the other one at some point. This sort of typographical error will produce a *logical error.* You must check for that sort of error by manually inspecting the code, since the compiler cannot catch it.

Sometimes is it possible to successfully compile and link the program, but there are run-time errors or logical errors when the program is executed. In this case, there is either something wrong with the input data or something wrong with the logical structure of the program. The first step in locating this sort of bug should be to *check the input data to the program.* Your program should have been designed to *echo* its input data. If not, go back and add **WRITE** statements to verify that the input values are what you expect them to be.

If the variable names seem to be correct and the input data is correct, then you are probably dealing with a logical error. You should check each of your assignment statements.

1. If an assignment statement is very long, break it into several smaller assignment statements. Smaller statements are easier to verify than larger ones.
2. Check the placement of parentheses in your assignment statements. It is a very common error to have the operations in an assignment statement evaluated in

the wrong order. If you have any doubts as to the order in which the variables are being evaluated, add extra sets of parentheses to make your intentions clear.
3. Make sure that you have initialized all of your variables properly.
4. Be sure that any functions you use are in the correct units. For example, the input to trigonometric functions must be in units of radians, not degrees.
5. Check for possible errors due to integer or mixed-mode arithmetic.

If you are still getting the wrong answer, add **WRITE** statements at various points in your program to see the results of intermediate calculations. If you can locate the point where the calculations go bad, then you know just where to look for the problem, which is 90% of the battle.

If you still cannot find the problem after all of the above steps, explain what you are doing to another student or to your instructor, and let them look at the code. It is very common for a person to see just what he or she expects to see when they look at their own code. Another person can often quickly spot an error that you have overlooked time after time.

GOOD PROGRAMMING PRACTICE

To reduce your debugging effort, make sure that during your program design you:

1. Use the **IMPLICIT NONE** statement.
2. Echo all input values.
3. Initialize all variables.
4. Use parentheses to make the functions of assignment statements clear.

Many computers have special debugging tools called *symbolic debuggers*. A symbolic debugger is a tool that allows you to walk through the execution of your program one statement at a time, and to examine the values of any variables at each step along the way. Symbolic debuggers allow you to see all of the intermediate results without having to insert a lot of **WRITE** statements into your code. They are powerful and flexible, but unfortunately they are different on every type of computer. If you will be using a symbolic debugger in your class, your instructor will introduce you to the one appropriate for your computer.

2.14   SUMMARY

In Chapter 2 we have presented many of the fundamental concepts required to write functional FORTRAN programs. We described the basic structure of FORTRAN programs, and introduced four types of FORTRAN constants and variables: integer, real, logical, and character. We introduced the assignment statement, arithmetic calculations, intrinsic functions, and list-directed input/output statements. Throughout the chapter, we have emphasized those features of the language that are important for writing understandable and maintainable FORTRAN code.

The FORTRAN statements introduced in this chapter must appear in a specific order within a FORTRAN program. The proper order is summarized in Table 2-8.

TABLE 2-8   The Order of FORTRAN Statements in a Program

1. **PROGRAM** statement
2. **IMPLICIT NONE** statement
3. **Type specification statements:**
   REAL statement(s)
   INTEGER statement(s)
   LOGICAL statement(s)   Any number in any order
   CHARACTER statement(s)
   PARAMETER statement(s)[3]
4. **DATA** statement(s)
5. **Executable statements:**
   Assignment statement(s)
   READ statement(s)   Any number in the order
   WRITE statement(s)   required to accomplish the
   STOP statement(s)   desired task
6. **END** statement

The order in which operations are evaluated in FORTRAN expressions follows a fixed hierarchy, with operations at a higher level evaluated before operations at lower levels. The order in which expressions are evaluated is summarized in Table 2-9.

The FORTRAN language includes a number of built-in functions to help us solve problems. These functions are called *intrinsic functions,* since they are intrinsic to the FORTRAN language itself. Some common intrinsic functions are summarized in Table 2-7, and a complete listing of intrinsic functions is contained in Appendix B.

[3]**PARAMETER** statements may be mixed with type specification statements in any order. However, if **IMPLICIT NONE** is used, the name defined in the **PARAMETER** statement must have already been declared in a preceding type specification statement before it is used in a **PARAMETER** statement. For example
```
REAL SQRT2
PARAMETER ( SQRT2 = 1.41421356 )
```

There are two varieties of intrinsic functions: specific functions and generic functions. Specific functions require that their input data be of a specific type; if data of the wrong type is supplied to a specific function, the result will be meaningless. By contrast, generic functions can accept input data of more than one type and produce correct results.

TABLE 2-9 FORTRAN Hierarchy of Operations

1. Operations within parentheses are evaluated first, starting with the innermost parentheses and working outward.
2. All exponential operations are evaluated next, working from *right* to *left*.
3. All multiplications and divisions are evaluated, working from left to right.
4. All additions and subtractions are evaluated, working from left to right.
5. All relational operators (**.EQ., .NE., .GT., .GE., .LT., .LE.**) are evaluated, working from left to right.
6. All **.NOT.** operators are evaluated.
7. All **.AND.** operators are evaluated, working from left to right.
8. All **.OR.** operators are evaluated, working from left to right.
9. All **.EQV.** and **.NEQV.** operators are evaluated, working from left to right.

2.14.1 Summary of Good Programming Practice

Every FORTRAN program should be written so that another person who is familiar with FORTRAN can easily understand it. This is very important, since a good program may be used for a long period of time. Over that time, conditions change, and the program will need to be modified to reflect the changing conditions. The program modifications may be done by someone other than the original programmer. The programmer making the modifications must understand the original program well before attempting to change it.

It is much harder to write clear, understandable, and maintainable programs than it is to simply write programs. To do so, a programmer must develop the discipline to properly document his or her work. In addition, the programmer must be careful to avoid known pitfalls along the path to good programs. The following guidelines will help you to develop good programs:

1. Use meaningful variable names whenever possible. Use names that can be understood at a glance, like DAY, MONTH, and YEAR, and not incomprehensible names like D, M, and Y.
2. Create a variable dictionary in each program that you write. The variable dictionary should name and define each variable in the program. Be sure to include the physical units associated with the variable, if applicable.
3. Use a consistent number of significant digits in constants. For example, do not use 3.14 for π in one part of your program, and 3.141593 in another part of the program. To ensure consistency, the constant may be named with a **PARAMETER** statement, and that constant may be referenced by name wherever it is needed.

4. Be sure to specify all constants with as much precision as your computer will support. For example, specify π as 3.141593, *not* 3.14.

5. Do not use integer arithmetic to calculate continuously varying real-world quantities such as distance, time, etc. Use integer arithmetic only for things that are intrinsically integral, such as counters.

6. Avoid mixed-mode arithmetic except for exponentiation. If it is necessary to mix integer and real variables in a single expression, use the intrinsic functions REAL, INT, and NINT to make the type conversions explicit.

7. Use extra parentheses whenever necessary to improve the readability of your expressions.

8. Always echo any variables that you enter into a program from a keyboard to make sure that they were typed and processed correctly.

9. Always use the **IMPLICIT NONE** statement to catch typographical errors in your program at compilation time.

10. Always initialize all variables in a program before using them. The variables may be initialized with assignment statements, with **READ** statements, or with **DATA** statements.

11. Always print the physical units associated with any value being written out. The units are important for the proper interpretation of a program's results.

CHAPTER 2 KEY WORDS

Argument	Intrinsic function
Assignment operator	List-directed input
Assignment statement	List-directed output
Batch mode	Logical error
Binary operation	Logical operation
Bug	Logical unit
Card identification field	Mixed-mode expression
Combinational logic operation	Nonexecutable statement
Comment	Output statement
Constant	Real arithmetic
Debugging	Real constant
Default typing	Relational logic operation
Executable statement	Run-time error
Explicit typing	Statement label
External function	Syntax error
FORTRAN constant	Truth tables
FORTRAN variable	Type specification statement
Generic function	Unary operation
Input statement	Uninitialized variable
Integer arithmetic	Variable
Integer constant	Variable dictionary
Interactive mode	

CHAPTER 2 SUMMARY OF FORTRAN STATEMENTS

The following summary describes the FORTRAN statements introduced in this chapter.

Assignment Statement:

```
variable = expression
```

Examples:

```
PI = 3.141593
DIST = 0.5 * ACCEL * TIME ** 2
SIDE = HYPOT * COS(THETA)
```

Description: The left side of the assignment statement must be a variable name. The right side of the assignment statement can be any constant, variable, function, or expression. The value of the quantity on the right-hand side of the equal sign is stored into the variable named on the left-hand side of the equal sign.

CHARACTER Statement:

```
CHARACTER*<len> variable name(, variable name)
CHARACTER variable name*<len>
```

Examples:

```
CHARACTER*10 FIRST, LAST, MIDDLE
CHARACTER YES*3, NO*2, INITL*1
CHARACTER*10 FIRST, LAST, INITIAL*1
```

Description: The **CHARACTER** statement is a type specification statement that declares variables of the character data type. The length of each variable is specified by the *<len> either appended to the word **CHARACTER** or appended to the individual variable names. If *<len> is appended to both the word **CHARACTER** and to a variable name, then the length specified on the variable name overrides the length specified on the word **CHARACTER**.

DATA Statement:

```
DATA variable name / constant /
```

Example:

```
DATA I / 10 /
DATA A, B, C, L / 3*10.0, 10 /
DATA START / 0.0 /, ENDTIM / 1000.0 /
```

Description: The **DATA** statement is a specification statement which defines the initial values of variables. Note that the values specified in the **DATA** statement are loaded into the variables during the compilation and linking process; they are already present before program execution begins.

END Statement:

```
END
```

Description: The **END** statement must be the last statement in a FORTRAN program segment. It tells the compiler that there are no further statements to process. Program execution is stopped when the **END** statement is reached.

IMPLICIT NONE Statement:

```
IMPLICIT NONE
```

Description: The **IMPLICIT NONE** statement turns off default typing in FORTRAN. If it is used in a program, then every variable in the program must be explicitly declared in a type specification statement. This statement is an extension to the FORTRAN 77 standard, but is included in the FORTRAN 90 standard.

INTEGER Statement:

```
INTEGER variable name(, variable name, etc.)
```

Example:
```
INTEGER I, J, COUNT
```

Description: The **INTEGER** statement is a type specification statement that declares variables of the integer data type. This statement overrides the default typing specified in FORTRAN.

LOGICAL Statement:

```
LOGICAL variable name(, variable name, etc.)
```

Example:
```
LOGICAL INIT, DEBUG
```

Description: The **LOGICAL** statement is a type specification statement that declares variables of the logical data type.

PARAMETER Statement:

```
PARAMETER ( name1 = con1, name2 = con2, ... )
```

Examples:
```
PARAMETER ( PI = 3.141593 )
PARAMETER ( ISTART = 1, IEND = 100 )
```

Description: The **PARAMETER** statement is a specification statement that assigns a name *name1* to a constant *con1*. Once a name has been assigned to a constant, the name may be used in place of the constant anywhere within a program unit.

The names in **PARAMETER** statements follow the standard rules for naming FORTRAN variables: they may be up to six characters long, and must begin with a letter. If default typing is used, the type of a name also follows the standard typing convention.

PROGRAM Statement:

```
PROGRAM program name
```

Example:
```
PROGRAM MYPROG
```

Description: The **PROGRAM** statement specifies the name of a FORTRAN program. It must be the first statement in a FORTRAN program. The name must be unique, and cannot be used as a variable name within the program. A program name may consist of one to six alphanumeric characters, but the first character in the program name *must* be alphabetical.

READ Statement (List-Directed READ):

```
READ (*,*) variable name (,variable name, etc.)
```

Examples:
```
READ (*,*) STRESS
READ (*,*) DIST, TIME
```

Description: The list-directed **READ** statement reads one or more values from the standard input device and loads them into the variables in the list. The values are stored in the order in which the variables are listed. Data values must be separated by blanks or by commas. As many lines as necessary will be read. Each **READ** statement begins searching for values with a new line.

REAL Statement:

```
REAL variable name(, variable name, etc.)
```

Examples:
```
REAL STRESS
REAL DIST, TIME
```

Description: The **REAL** statement is a type specification statement that declares variables of the real data type. This statement overrides the default typing specified in FORTRAN.

STOP Statement:

```
STOP
```

Description: The **STOP** statement stops the execution of a FORTRAN program. There may be more than one **STOP** statement within a program. A **STOP** statement that immediately precedes an **END** statement may be omitted, since execution is also stopped when the **END** statement is reached.

WRITE Statement (List-Directed WRITE):

```
WRITE (*,*) expression (,expression, etc.)
```

Examples:
```
WRITE (*,*) STRESS
WRITE (*,*) DIST, TIME
WRITE (*,*) ' SIN(THETA) = ', SIN(THETA)
```

Description: The list-directed **WRITE** statement writes the values of one or more expressions to the standard output device. The values are written in the order in which the expressions are listed.

CHAPTER 2 EXERCISES

1. State whether or not each of the following FORTRAN 77 constants is valid. If valid, state what type of constant it is. If not, state why it is invalid.
    - (*a*) 3.14159
    - (*b*) '.TRUE.'
    - (*c*) -123,456.789
    - (*d*) +1E-12
    - (*e*) 'Who's coming for dinner?'
    - (*f*) .FALSE
    - (*g*) +256
    - (*h*) 256.E0

2. For each of the following pairs of numbers, state whether they represent the same value or different values within the computer.
    - (*a*) 123.E+0; 123
    - (*b*) 1234.E-3; 1.234E3
    - (*c*) 1.41421, 1.41421E0
    - (*d*) 0.000005E+6; 5.

3. State whether each of the following program names is valid or not. If not, state why the name is invalid.
    - (*a*) JUNK
    - (*b*) NEW_1
    - (*c*) 3RD
    - (*d*) FINDROOT

4. Are the following FORTRAN 77 variable names valid or invalid? If a variable name is valid, state the type of the variable. Assume default typing is used. If it is invalid, say why it is invalid.
    - (*a*) NEWDATA
    - (*b*) TST1_1

    (c)   `3RDRT`

    (d)   `FIRST`

    (e)   `INDEX3`

    (f)   `TIME_TO_INTERCEPT`

5. Which of the variable names in exercise 4 would be valid in FORTRAN 90?

6. Which of the following expressions are legal in FORTRAN 77? If an expression is legal, evaluate it.

    (a)   `2.**3 / 3**2`

    (b)   `2 * 6 + 6 **· 2 / 2`

    (c)   `2 * 10.**-3.`

    (d)   `2 / 10. ** 3.`

    (e)   `2 * 10 / -7.`

    (f)   `(23 / 4) / 8`

    (g)   `23 / (4 / 8)`

7. Which of the following expressions are legal in FORTRAN 77? If an expression is legal, evaluate it.

    (a)   `((58/4)*(4/58))`

    (b)   `((58/4)*(4/58.))`

    (c)   `((58./4)*(4/58.))`

    (d)   `((58./4*(4/58.))`

8. Evaluate each of the following expressions.

    (a)   `13 / 5 * 6`

    (b)   `(13 / 5) * 6`

    (c)   `13 / (5 * 6)`

    (d)   `13. / 5 * 6`

    (e)   `13 / 5 * 6.`

    (f)   `(13 / 5) * 6.`

    (g)   `13. / (5 * 6)`

    (h)   `INT(13. / 5) * 6`

    (i)   `NINT(13. / 5) * 6`

    (j)   `13 / 5 * REAL(6)`

9. Evaluate each of the following expressions.

    (a)   `4 ** 3 ** 3`

    (b)   `(4 ** 3) ** 3`

    (c)   `4 ** (3 ** 3)`

10. What values will be output from the following program?

```
PROGRAM SAMP1
INTEGER I1, I2, I3
REAL A1, A2
A1 = 2.4
I1 = A1
I2 = INT ( A1 * I1 )
I3 = NINT ( A1 * I1 )
A2 = A1**I1
WRITE (*,*) I1, I2, I3, A1, A2
END
```

11. Which of the following expressions are legal in FORTRAN 77? If an expression is legal, evaluate it.

(**a**) `5.5 .GE. 5`
(**b**) `20 .GT. 20`
(**c**) `5 .GE. 5`
(**d**) `.NOT. 6 .GT. 5`
(**e**) `15 .LE. 'A'`
(**f**) `.TRUE. .GT. .FALSE.`
(**g**) `35 / 17. .GT. 35 / 17`
(**h**) `6. .GT. 5 .AND. 7 .LE. 7`
(**i**) `7 .LE. 8 .EQV. 3 / 2 .EQ. 1`
(**j**) `17.5 .AND. (3.3 .GT. 2.)`
(**k**) `.FALSE. .OR. 17 + 7 .GT. 23 .AND. .NOT. 6 .EQ. 7`

12. Figure 2-6 shows a right triangle with a hypotenuse of length C and angle θ. From elementary trigonometry, the length of sides A and B are given by

$$A = C \cos \theta$$
$$B = C \sin \theta$$

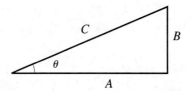

FIGURE 2-6   The right triangle of Example 2-12.

The following program is intended to calculate the lengths of sides A and B given the hypotenuse C and angle θ. Will this program run? Will it produce the correct result? Why or why not?

```
PROGRAM TRINGL
REAL A, B, C, THETA
WRITE (*,*) ' Enter the length of the hypotenuse C:'
READ (*,*) C
WRITE (*,*) ' Enter the angle THETA in degrees:'
READ (*,*) THETA
A = C * COS ( THETA )
B = C * SIN ( THETA )
WRITE (*,*) ' The length of the adjacent side is ', A
WRITE (*,*) ' The length of the opposite side is ', B
STOP
END
```

13. What output will be produced by the following program?

```
PROGRAM EXAMPL
REAL A, B, C
INTEGER K, L, M
READ (*,*) A, B, C, K
READ (*,*) L, M
WRITE (*,*) A, B, C, K, L, M
STOP
END
```

The input data to the program is:

```
-3.141592
100, 200., 300, 400
-100, -200, -300
-400
```

14. Write a FORTRAN program that calculates an hourly employee's weekly pay. The program should ask the user for the person's pay rate and the number of hours worked during the week. It should then calculate the total pay from the formula

    Total Pay = Hourly Pay Rate × Hours Worked

    Finally, it should display the total weekly pay. Check your program by computing the weekly pay for a person earning $5.50/hour and working for 39 hours.

15. The potential energy of an object due to its height above the surface of the Earth is given by the equation

    $$PE = mgh \qquad \text{(2-10)}$$

    where m is the mass of the object, g is the acceleration due to gravity, and h is the height above the surface of the Earth. The kinetic energy of a moving object is given by the equation

    $$KE = \frac{1}{2}mv^2 \qquad \text{(2-11)}$$

    where m is the mass of the object and v is the velocity of the object. Write a FORTRAN equation for the total energy (potential plus kinetic) possessed by an object in the earth's gravitational field.

16. If a stationary ball is released at a height h above the surface of the Earth, the velocity of the ball v when it hits the earth is given by the equation

    $$v = \sqrt{2gh} \qquad \text{(2-12)}$$

    where g is the acceleration due to gravity, and h is the height above the surface of the Earth (assuming no air friction). Write a FORTRAN equation for the velocity of the ball when it hits the Earth.

17. Write a program to calculate the diameter, circumference, and area of a circle of radius r. Use good programming practices in your program.

18. The period of an oscillating pendulum T (in seconds) is given by the equation

$$T = 2\pi \sqrt{\frac{L}{g}} \qquad (2\text{-}13)$$

where L is the length of the pendulum in meters, and g is the acceleration due to gravity in meters per second squared. Write a FORTRAN program to calculate the period of a pendulum of length L. The length of the pendulum will be specified by the user when the program is run. Use good programming practices in your program. (The acceleration due to gravity at the Earth's surface is 9.8 m/sec^2.)

19. Write a program to calculate the hypotenuse of a right triangle, given the lengths of its two sides. Use good programming practices in your program.

20. Write a program using the **IMPLICIT NONE** statement, and do not declare one of the variables in the program. What sort of error message is generated by your compiler?

21. The distance between two points $(x1, y1)$ and $(x2, y2)$ on a Cartesian coordinate plane is given by the equation

$$d = \sqrt{(x1 - x2)^2 + (y1 - y2)^2} \qquad (2\text{-}14)$$

Write a FORTRAN program to calculate the distance between any two points $(x1, y1)$ and $(x2, y2)$ specified by the user. Use good programming practices in your program. Use the program to calculate the distance between the points $(2, 3)$ and $(8, -5)$ (Figure 2-7).

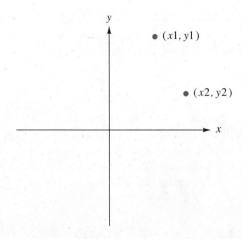

FIGURE 2-7   Two points in a cartesian coordinate system.

22. Engineers often measure the ratio of two power measurements in *decibels*, or dB. The equation for the ratio of two power measurements in decibels is

$$dB = 10 \ \log_{10} \frac{P_2}{P_1}$$

where P_2 is the power level being measured, and P_1 is some reference power level. Assume that the reference power level P_1 is 1 mW, and write a program that accepts an input power P_2 and converts it into dB with respect to the 1-mW reference level.

23. The hyperbolic cosine function is defined by the equation

$$\cosh x = \frac{e^x + e^{-x}}{2}$$

Write a FORTRAN program to calculate the hyperbolic cosine of a user-supplied value X. Use the program to calculate the hyperbolic cosine of 3.0. Compare the answer that your program produces to the answer produced by the FORTRAN intrinsic function **COSH(X)**.

Control Structures and Program Design

In the previous chapter, we developed several complete working FORTRAN programs. However, all of the programs were very simple, consisting of a series of FORTRAN statements which were executed one after another in a fixed order. Such programs are called *sequential* programs. They read in input data, process it to produce a desired answer, print out the answer, and quit. There is no way to repeat sections of the program more than once, and there is no way to selectively execute only certain portions of the program depending on values of the input data.

In this chapter, we introduce a number of FORTRAN statements that allow us to control the order in which statements are executed in a program. There are two broad categories of control statements: **branches,** which select specific sections of the code to execute, and **loops,** which cause specific sections of the code to be repeated.

With the introduction of branches and loops, our programs are going to become more complex, and it will get easier and easier to make mistakes. To help avoid programming errors, we will introduce a formal program design procedure based on the technique known as top-down design. We will also introduce two common algorithm development tools, flowcharts and pseudocode.

3.1 INTRODUCTION TO TOP-DOWN DESIGN TECHNIQUES

Suppose that you are an engineer working in industry, and that you need to write a FORTRAN program to solve some problem. How do you begin?

When given a new problem, there is a natural tendency to sit down at a terminal and start programming without "wasting" a lot of time thinking about it first. It is often possible to get away with this "on the fly" approach to programming for small problems, such as many of the examples in this book. In the real world, however, problems are larger, and a programmer attempting this approach will become hopelessly bogged down. For larger problems, it pays to completely think out the problem and the approach you are going to take to it before writing a single line of code.

We will introduce a formal program design process in this section, and then apply that process to every major application developed in the remainder of the book. For some of the simple examples that we will be doing, the design process will seem like overkill. However, as the problems that we solve get bigger and bigger, the process becomes more and more essential to successful programming.

When I was an undergraduate, one of my professors was fond of saying, "Programming is easy. It's knowing what to program that's hard." His point was forcefully driven home to me after I left college and began working in industry on larger-scale software projects. I found that the most difficult part of my job was to *understand the problem* I was trying to solve. Once I really understood the problem, it became easy to break the problem apart into smaller, more easily manageable pieces with well-defined functions, and then to tackle those pieces one at a time.

Top-down design is the process of starting with a large task and breaking it down into smaller, more easily understandable pieces (subtasks) which perform a portion of the desired task. Each subtask may in turn be subdivided into smaller subtasks if necessary. Once the program is divided into small pieces, each piece can be coded and tested independently. We do not attempt to combine the subtasks into a complete task until each of the subtasks has been verified to work properly by itself.

The concept of top-down design is the basis of our formal program design process. We will now introduce the details of the process. The steps involved are:

1.   Clearly state the problem that you are trying to solve.
Programs are usually written to fill some perceived need, but that need may not be articulated clearly by the person requesting the program. For example, a user may ask for a program to solve a system of simultaneous linear equations. This request is not clear enough to allow a programmer to design a program to meet the need; he or she must first know much more about the problem to be solved. Is the system of equations to be solved real or complex? What is the maximum number of equations and unknowns that the program must handle? Are there any symmetries in the equations which might be exploited to make the task easier? The program designer will have to talk with the user requesting the program, and the two of them will have to come up with a clear statement of exactly what they are trying to accomplish. A clear statement of the problem will prevent misunderstandings, and it will also help the program designer to properly organize his or her thoughts. In the example we were describing, a proper statement of the problem might have been:

> Write a program to solve a system of simultaneous linear equations having real coefficients and with up to 20 equations in 20 unknowns.

2.   Define the inputs required by the program and the outputs to be produced by the program.
The inputs to the program and the outputs produced by the program must be specified so that the new program will properly fit into the overall processing scheme. In the above example, the coefficients of the equations to be solved are probably in some preexisting order, and our new program needs to be able to read them in that order. Similarly, it needs to produce the answers required by the programs which may follow it in the overall processing scheme, and to write out those answers in the format needed by the programs following it.

3. Describe the algorithm that you intend to implement in the program.

An **algorithm** is a step-by-step procedure for finding the solution to a problem. It is at this stage in the process that top-down design techniques come into play. The designer looks for logical divisions within the problem, and divides it up into subtasks along those lines. This process is called *decomposition*. If the subtasks are themselves large, the designer can break them up into even smaller subsubtasks. This process continues until the problem has been divided into many small pieces, each of which does a simple, clearly understandable job.

After the problem has been broken down into small pieces, each piece is further refined through a process called *stepwise refinement*. In stepwise refinement, a designer starts with a general description of what the piece of code should do, and then defines the functions of the piece in greater and greater detail until they are specific enough to be turned into FORTRAN statements. Stepwise refinement is usually done with **pseudocode,** which will be described in the next section.

It is often helpful to solve a simple example of the problem by hand during the algorithm development process. If the designer understands the steps which he or she went through in solving the problem by hand, the designer will be better able to apply decomposition and stepwise refinement to the problem.

4. Turn the algorithm into FORTRAN statements.

If the decomposition and refinement process was carried out properly, this step is very simple. All the programmer has to do is to replace pseudocode with the corresponding FORTRAN statements on a one-for-one basis.

5. Test the resulting FORTRAN program.

This step is the real killer. The components of the program must first be tested individually, if possible, and then the program as a whole must be tested. When testing a program, we must verify that it works correctly for *all legal input data sets*. It is very common for a program to be written, tested with some standard data set, and released for use, only to find that it produces the wrong answers (or crashes) with a different input data set. If the algorithm implemented in a program includes different branches, we must test all of the possible branches to confirm that the program operates correctly under every possible circumstance.

Large programs typically go through a series of tests before they are released for general use. The first stage of testing is sometimes called *unit testing*. During unit testing, the individual subtasks of the program are tested separately to confirm that they work correctly. After the unit testing is completed, the program goes through a series of *builds* during which the individual subtasks are combined to produce the final program. The first build of the program typically includes only a few of the subtasks. It is used to check the interaction between those subtasks and the functions performed by the combinations of the subtasks. In successive builds, more and more subtasks are added, until the entire program is complete. Testing is performed on each build, and any errors (bugs) which are detected are corrected before moving on to the next build.

Testing continues even after the program is complete. The first complete version of the program is usually called the **alpha release.** It is exercised by the programmers and others very close to them in as many different ways as possible, and the bugs discovered during the testing are corrected. When the most serious bugs have been removed from the program, a new version called the **beta release** is prepared. The beta release is normally given to "friendly" outside users who have a need for the program in their normal day-to-day jobs. These users put the program through its paces under many different conditions and with many different input data sets, and they report any bugs which they find to the programmers. When those bugs have been corrected, the program is ready to be released for general use.

Because the programs in this book are fairly small, we will not go through the sort of extensive testing described above. However, we follow the basic principles in testing all of our programs.

The program design process may be summarized as follows:

1. Clearly state the problem that you are trying to solve.
2. Define the inputs required by the program and the outputs to be produced by the program.
3. Describe the algorithm that you intend to implement in the program.
4. Turn the algorithm into FORTRAN statements.
5. Test the FORTRAN program.

■ **GOOD PROGRAMMING PRACTICE**

Follow the steps of the program design process to produce reliable, understandable FORTRAN programs.

In a large programming project, the time actually spent programming is surprisingly small. In his book *The Mythical Man-Month (Addison-Wesley, 1974)*, Frederick P. Brooks, Jr. suggests that in a typical large software project, 1/3 of the time is spent planning what to do (steps 1 through 3), 1/6 of the time is spent writing the program (step 4), and fully 1/2 of the time is spent in testing and debugging the program! Clearly, anything that we can do to reduce the testing and debugging time is very helpful. We can best reduce the testing and debugging time by doing a very careful job in the planning phase, and by using good programming practices. Good programming practices reduce the number of bugs in the program, and make the ones that do creep in easier to find.

3.2   USE OF PSEUDOCODE AND FLOWCHARTS

As a part of the formal design process, it is necessary to describe the algorithm that you intend to implement. The description of the algorithm should be in a standard form which is easy for both you and other people to understand, and the description should aid you in turning your concept into FORTRAN code. The standard forms that we use to describe algorithms are called **structures,** and an algorithm described using these structures is called a structured algorithm. When the algorithm is implemented in a FORTRAN program, the resulting program is called a **structured program.**

The structures used to build algorithms can be described in two different ways: pseudocode and flowcharts. *Pseudocode* is a hybrid mixture of FORTRAN and English. It is structured like FORTRAN, with a separate line for each distinct idea or segment of code, but the descriptions on each line are in English. Each line of the pseudocode should describe its idea in plain, easily understandable English. Pseudocode is useful for developing algorithms, since it is flexible and easy to modify. It is especially useful since pseudocode can be written and modified on the same computer terminal used to write the FORTRAN program—no special graphical capabilities are required.

For example, the pseudocode for the algorithm in Example 2-4 is

```
Prompt user to enter temperature in degrees Fahrenheit
Read temperature in degrees Fahrenheit (TEMPF)
TEMP in kelvins ← (5./9.) * (TEMPF - 32) + 273.15
Write temperature in kelvins
```

Notice that a left arrow ($\leftarrow$) is used instead of an equal sign ($=$) to indicate that a value is stored in a variable, since this avoids any confusion between assignment and equality. Pseudocode is intended to aid you in organizing your thoughts before converting them into FORTRAN code.

Flowcharts are a way to describe algorithms graphically. In a flowchart, different graphical symbols represent the different operations in the algorithm, and our standard structures are made up of collections of one or more of these symbols. Flowcharts are useful for describing the algorithm implemented in a program after it is completed. However, since they are graphical, flowcharts tend to be cumbersome to modify, and they are not very useful during the preliminary stages of algorithm definition when rapid changes are occurring. The most common graphical symbols used in flowcharts are shown in Figure 3-1, and the flowchart for the algorithm in Example 2-4 is shown in Figure 3-2 on page 92.

Throughout the examples in this book, we will illustrate the use of both pseudocode and flowcharts. You are welcome to use whichever one of these tools gives you the best results in your own programming projects.

3.3 CONTROL STRUCTURES: BRANCHES

Branches are FORTRAN statements that permit us to select and execute specific sections of code (called *blocks*) while skipping other sections of code. They are all variations of the **IF** statement.

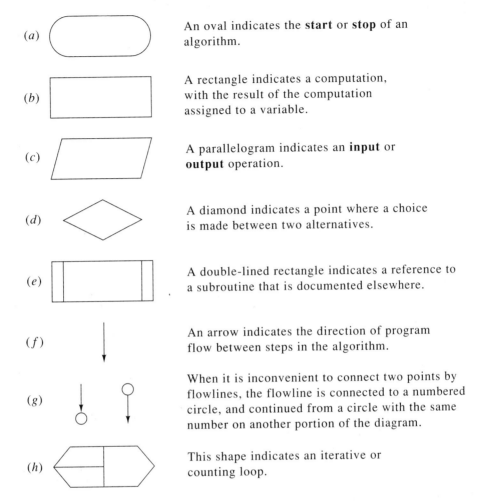

(a) An oval indicates the **start** or **stop** of an algorithm.

(b) A rectangle indicates a computation, with the result of the computation assigned to a variable.

(c) A parallelogram indicates an **input** or **output** operation.

(d) A diamond indicates a point where a choice is made between two alternatives.

(e) A double-lined rectangle indicates a reference to a subroutine that is documented elsewhere.

(f) An arrow indicates the direction of program flow between steps in the algorithm.

(g) When it is inconvenient to connect two points by flowlines, the flowline is connected to a numbered circle, and continued from a circle with the same number on another portion of the diagram.

(h) This shape indicates an iterative or counting loop.

FIGURE 3-1   Common symbols used in flowcharts.

3.3.1 The Logical Block IF Structure

This simplest form of the **IF** statement is the logical block **IF** structure. This structure specifies that a block of code will be executed if and only if a certain logical expression is TRUE. The logical block **IF** structure has the form

```
IF (logical expression) THEN
      Statement 1
      Statement 2
      Statement 3    Block 1
      ...
      Statement n
END IF
```

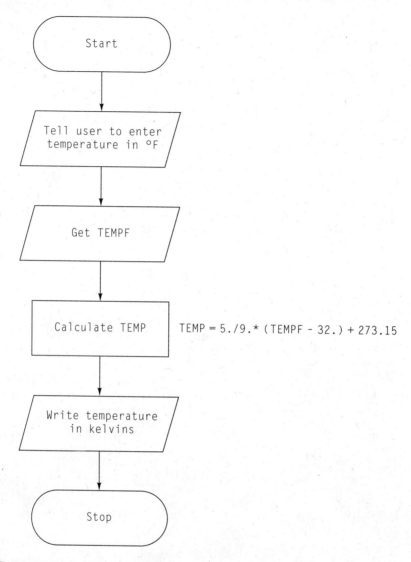

FIGURE 3-2 Flowchart for the algorithm in Example 2-4.

If the logical expression is TRUE, the program executes the statements in the block between the **IF** and **END IF** statements. If the logical expression is FALSE, the program skips all of the statements in the block between the **IF** and **END IF** statements, and executes the next statement after the **END IF.** The flowchart for a logical block **IF** structure is shown in Figure 3-3.

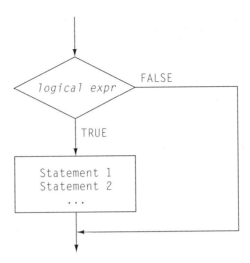

FIGURE 3-3   Flowchart for a simple Logical Block **IF** Structure.

The **IF (...) THEN** is a single FORTRAN statement which must be written to-gether on the same line, and the statements to be executed must occupy separate lines below the **IF (...) THEN** statement. An **END IF** statement must follow them on a separate line. There should not be a statement number on the line containing the **END IF** statement. For readability, the block of code between the **IF** and **END IF** statements is usually indented by two or three spaces, but this is not actually re-quired.

■ GOOD PROGRAMMING PRACTICE

Always indent the body of an **IF** structure by two or more spaces to improve the readability of the code.

As an example of an **IF** statement, consider the solution of a quadratic equation of the form

$$ax^2 + bx + c = 0 \tag{3-1}$$

The solution to this equation is

$$x = \frac{-b \pm \sqrt{b^2 - 4ac}}{2a} \tag{3-2}$$

The term $b^2 - 4ac$ is known as the *discriminant* of the equation. If $b^2 - 4ac > 0$, then there are two distinct real roots to the quadratic equation. If $b^2 - 4ac = 0$, then there is a single repeated root to the equation, and if $b^2 - 4ac < 0$, then there are two com-plex roots to the quadratic equation.

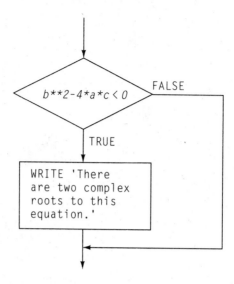

FIGURE 3-4   Flowchart showing structure to determine if a quadratic equation has two complex roots.

Suppose that we wanted to examine the discriminant of the quadratic equation and tell a user if the equation has complex roots. In pseudocode, the logical block **IF** structure to do this would take the form:

```
IF (B**2 - 4.*A*C) < 0. THEN
     Write message that equation has two complex roots.
END IF
```

In FORTRAN, the logical block **IF** statement is

```
IF ( (B**2 - 4.*A*C) .LT. 0.) THEN
     WRITE (*,*) 'There are two complex roots to this equation.'
END IF
```

The flowchart for this structure is shown in Figure 3-4.

3.3.2   The ELSE Clause

In the simple block **IF** structure, a block of code is executed if the controlling logical expression is TRUE. If the controlling logical expression is FALSE, all of the statements in the structure are skipped.

Sometimes we want to execute one set of statements if an expression is TRUE, and a different set of statements if the expression is FALSE. An **ELSE** clause may be added to the logical block **IF** structure for this purpose. The logical block **IF** structure with an **ELSE** clause has the form

```
IF (logical expression) THEN
      Statement 1 ⎫
      Statement 2 ⎪
      Statement 3 ⎬ Block 1
      ...          ⎪
      Statement n ⎭
ELSE
      Statement 1 ⎫
      Statement 2 ⎪
      Statement 3 ⎬ Block 2
      ...          ⎪
      Statement n ⎭
END IF
```

If the logical expression is TRUE, the program executes the statements in Block 1. Otherwise, the program executes the statements in Block 2.

Like the **IF (...) THEN** and **END IF** statements, the **ELSE** statement must occupy a line by itself. There should not be a statement number on the line containing the **ELSE** statement.

To illustrate the use of this structure, let's reconsider the quadratic equation. Suppose that we wanted to examine the discriminant of the quadratic equation and to tell a user whether the equation has complex roots or real roots. In pseudocode, the structure to do this would take the form

```
IF (B**2 - 4.*A*C) < 0. THEN
      Write message that equation has two complex roots.
ELSE
      Write message that equation has real roots.
END IF
```

The corresponding FORTRAN statements are

```
IF ( (B**2 - 4.*A*C) .LT. 0.) THEN
      WRITE (*,*) 'This equation has complex roots.'
ELSE
      WRITE (*,*) 'This equation has real roots.'
END IF
```

The flowchart for this structure is shown in Figure 3-5 on page 96.

3.3.3   The ELSE IF (...) THEN Clause

Sometimes the decisions required to implement a particular algorithm are too complex to represent by a simple either/or test. Instead, we might have to consider three or more options. The **ELSE IF (...) THEN** clause is designed to accommodate those cases. A logical block **IF** structure with an **ELSE IF (...) THEN** clause has the form

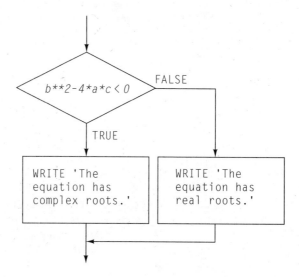

FIGURE 3-5   Flowchart showing structure to determine if a quadratic equation has complex roots or real roots.

```
IF (logical expression 1) THEN
        Statement 1 ⎫
        Statement 2 ⎪
        Statement 3 ⎬ Block 1
        ...         ⎪
        Statement n ⎭
ELSE IF (logical expression 2) THEN
        Statement 1 ⎫
        Statement 2 ⎪
        Statement 3 ⎬ Block 2
        ...         ⎪
        Statement n ⎭
END IF
```

If logical expression 1 is TRUE, then the program executes the statements in Block 1, and skips to the first executable statement following the **END IF.** Otherwise, the program checks for the status of logical expression 2. If logical expression 2 is TRUE, then the program executes the statements in Block 2, and skips to the first executable statement following the **END IF.** If both logical expressions are FALSE, then the program skips all of these statements and continues executing at the first executable statement following the **END IF.**

There can be any number of **ELSE IF** clauses in an **IF** structure. The logical expression in each clause will be tested only if the logical expressions in every clause above it are FALSE. Once one of the expressions proves to be TRUE and the corresponding code block is executed, the program skips to the first executable statement following the **END IF.** It is also possible to have an **ELSE** clause, which is executed if all of the logical expressions are FALSE.

The flowcharts for logical block **IF** structures with **ELSE IF** and/or **ELSE** clauses are shown in Figure 3-6.

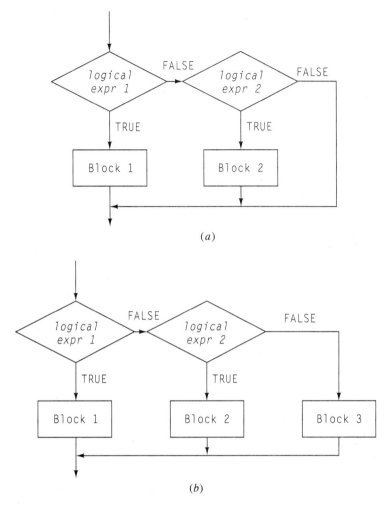

FIGURE 3-6 (*a*) Flowchart for a Logical Block **IF** Structure with an **ELSE IF** (**...**) **THEN** clause. (*b*) Flowchart for a Logical Block **IF** Structure with an **ELSE IF** (**...**) **THEN** clause and an **ELSE** clause.

To illustrate the use of the **ELSE IF** clause, let's reconsider the quadratic equation once more. Suppose that we wanted to examine the discriminant of a quadratic equation and to tell a user whether the equation has two complex roots, two identical real roots, or two distinct real roots. In pseudocode, this structure would take the form

```
IF (B**2 - 4.*A*C) < 0. THEN
      Write message that equation has two complex roots.
ELSE IF (B**2 - 4.*A*C) = 0. THEN
      Write message that equation has two identical real roots.
ELSE
      Write message that equation has two distinct real roots.
END IF
```

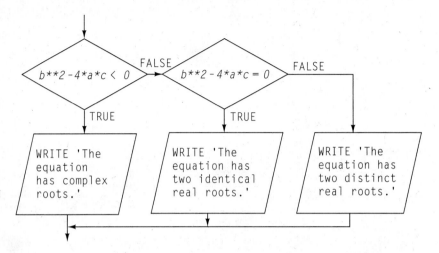

FIGURE 3-7   Flowchart showing structure to determine whether a quadratic equation has two complex roots, two identical real roots, or two distinct real roots.

The FORTRAN statements to do this are

```
IF ( (B**2 - 4.*A*C) .LT. 0. ) THEN
      WRITE (*,*) 'This equation has two complex roots.'
ELSE IF ( (B**2 - 4.*A*C) .EQ. 0. ) THEN
      WRITE (*,*) 'This equation has two identical real roots.'
ELSE
      WRITE (*,*) 'This equation has two distinct real roots.'
END IF
```

The flowchart for this structure is shown in Figure 3-7.

3.3.4   Examples Using Logical Block IF Structures

We will now look at two examples that illustrate the use of logical **IF** structures.

EXAMPLE 3-1   *The Quadratic Equation*   Write a general program to solve for the roots of a quadratic equation, regardless of type.

SOLUTION   In solving this problem, we will follow the design steps outlined earlier in the chapter:

1. Clearly state the problem that you are trying to solve.
2. Define the inputs required by the program and the outputs to be produced by the program.
3. Describe the algorithm that you intend to implement in the program.
4. Turn the algorithm into FORTRAN statements.
5. Test the FORTRAN program.

1. State the problem.

The problem statement for this example is simple. We want to write a program that will solve for the roots of a quadratic equation, whether they are distinct real roots, repeated real roots, or complex roots.

2. Define the inputs and outputs.

The inputs required by this program are the coefficients a, b, and c of the quadratic equation

$$ax^2 + bx + c = 0 \qquad \text{(3-1)}$$

The output from the program will be the roots of the quadratic equation, whether they are distinct real roots, repeated real roots, or complex roots.

3. Describe the algorithm.

This task can be broken down into three major sections, whose functions are input, processing, and output:

```
Read the input data
Calculate the roots
Write out the roots
```

We will now break each of the above major sections into smaller, more detailed pieces. There are three possible ways to calculate the roots, depending on the value of the discriminant, so it is logical to implement this algorithm with a three-branched **IF** statement. The resulting pseudocode is

```
Prompt the user for the coefficients A, B, and C.
Read A, B, and C
Echo the input coefficients
DISCR ← B**2 - 4. * A * C
IF DISCR > 0 THEN
    X1 ← ( -B + SQRT(DISCR) ) / ( 2. * A )
    X2 ← ( -B - SQRT(DISCR) ) / ( 2. * A )
    Write message that equation has two distinct real roots.
    Write out the two roots.
ELSE IF DISCR = 0 THEN
    X1 ← -B / ( 2. * A )
    Write message that equation has two identical real roots.
    Write out the repeated root.
ELSE
    RE ← -B / ( 2. * A )
    IM ← SQRT ( ABS ( DISCR ) ) / ( 2. * A )
    Write message that equation has two complex roots.
    Write out the two roots.
END IF
```

The flowchart for this program is shown in Figure 3-8.

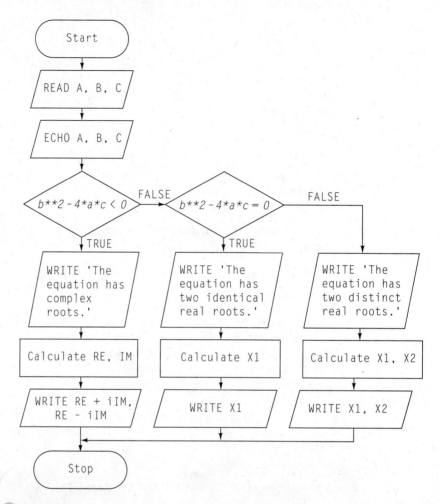

FIGURE 3-8   Flowchart of program ROOTS.

4. Turn the algorithm into FORTRAN statements.
The final FORTRAN code is shown in Figure 3-9.

```
      PROGRAM ROOTS
C
C  Purpose:
C    This program solves for the roots of a quadratic equation of the form
C    A * X**2 + B * X + C = 0.  It calculates the answers regardless of the
C    type of roots that the equation possesses.
C
C  Record of revisions:
C     Date        Programmer        Description of change
C     ====        ==========        =====================
C    12/24/90  S. J. Chapman        Original code
C
```

```
C   List of variables:
C     A      -- Coefficient of X**2 term of equation
C     B      -- Coefficient of X term of equation
C     C      -- Constant term of equation
C     DISCR -- Discriminant of the equation
C     IM     -- Imaginary part of equation (for complex roots)
C     RE     -- Real part of equation (for complex roots)
C     X1     -- First solution of equation (for real roots)
C     X2     -- Second solution of equation (for real roots)
C
      IMPLICIT NONE
C
C   Declare the variables used in this program.
C
      REAL A, B, C
      REAL DISCR
      REAL RE, IM
      REAL X1, X2
C
C   Prompt the user for the coefficients of the equation
C
      WRITE (*,*) ' This program solves for the roots of a quadratic '
      WRITE (*,*) ' equation of the form A * X**2 + B * X + C = 0. '
      WRITE (*,*) ' Enter the coefficients A, B, and C:'
      READ  (*,*) A, B, C
C
C   Calculate discriminant
C
      DISCR = B**2 - 4. * A * C
C
C   Echo back A, B, and C.
C
      WRITE (*,*) 'The coefficients A, B, and C are: ', A, B, C
C
C   Solve for the roots, depending upon the value of the discriminant
C
      IF ( DISCR .GT. 0. ) THEN
         X1 = ( -B + SQRT(DISCR) ) / ( 2. * A )
         X2 = ( -B - SQRT(DISCR) ) / ( 2. * A )
         WRITE (*,*) 'This equation has two real roots:'
         WRITE (*,*) 'X1 = ', X1
         WRITE (*,*) 'X2 = ', X2
      ELSE IF ( DISCR .EQ. 0. ) THEN
         X1 = ( -B ) / ( 2. * A )
         WRITE (*,*) 'This equation has two identical real roots:'
         WRITE (*,*) 'X1 = X2 = ', X1
      ELSE
         RE = ( -B ) / ( 2. * A )
         IM = SQRT ( ABS ( DISCR ) ) / ( 2. * A )
         WRITE (*,*) 'This equation has complex roots:'
         WRITE (*,*) 'X1 = ', RE, ' +i ', IM
         WRITE (*,*) 'X1 = ', RE, ' -i ', IM
      END IF
C
C   Finish up.
C
      END
```

FIGURE 3-9   Program ROOTS from Example 3-1.

5. Test the program.

Next we must test the program using real input data. Since there are three possible paths through the program, we must test all three paths before we can be certain that the program is working properly. From Equation (3-2), it is possible to verify the solutions to the equations given below:

$$x^2 + 5x + 6 = 0 \qquad x = -2, \text{ and } x = -3$$
$$x^2 + 4x + 4 = 0 \qquad x = -2$$
$$x^2 + 2x + 5 = 0 \qquad x = -1 \pm i2$$

If this program is compiled, and then run three times with the above coefficients, the results are:

```
C:\BOOK\FORT>ROOTS
This program solves for the roots of a quadratic
equation of the form A * X**2 + B * X + C = 0.
Enter the coefficients A, B, and C:
1,5,6
The coefficients A, B, and C are:        1.000000      5.000000
        6.000000
This equation has two real roots:
X1 =          -2.000000
X2 =          -3.000000

C:\BOOK\FORT>ROOTS
This program solves for the roots of a quadratic
equation of the form A * X**2 + B * X + C = 0.
Enter the coefficients A, B, and C:
1 4 4
The coefficients A, B, and C are:        1.000000      4.000000
        4.000000
This equation has two identical real roots:
X1 = X2 =          -2.000000

C:\BOOK\FORT>ROOTS
This program solves for the roots of a quadratic
equation of the form A * X**2 + B * X + C = 0.
Enter the coefficients A, B, and C:
1,2,5
The coefficients A, B, and C are:        1.000000      2.000000
        5.000000
This equation has complex roots:
X1 =        -1.000000 +i        2.000000
X1 =        -1.000000 -i        2.000000
```

The program gives the correct answers for our test data in all three possible cases.●

EXAMPLE 3-2 *Evaluating a Function of Two Variables* Write a FORTRAN program to evaluate a function $f(x, y)$ for any two user-specified values x and y. The function $f(x, y)$ is defined as follows.

$$f(x, y) = \begin{cases} x + y & x \geq 0 \text{ and } y \geq 0 \\ x + y^2 & x \geq 0 \text{ and } y < 0 \\ x^2 + y & x < 0 \text{ and } y \geq 0 \\ x^2 + y^2 & x < 0 \text{ and } y < 0 \end{cases}$$

SOLUTION   The function $f(x,y)$ is evaluated differently depending on the signs of the two independent variables x and y. To determine the proper equation to apply, it is necessary to check for the signs of the x and y values supplied by the user.

1.   State the problem.

This problem statement is simple: Evaluate the function $f(x, y)$ for any user-supplied values of x and y.

2.   Define the inputs and outputs.

The inputs required by this program are the values of the independent variables x and y. The output from the program will be the value of the function $f(x, y)$.

3.   Describe the algorithm.

This task can be broken down into three major sections, whose functions are input, processing, and output:

```
Read the input values x and y
Calculate f(x,y)
Write out f(x,y)
```

We now break each of the above major sections into smaller, more detailed pieces. There are four possible ways to calculate the function $f(x, y)$, depending on the values of x and y, so it is logical to implement this algorithm with a four-branched **IF** statement. The resulting pseudocode is:

```
Prompt the user for the values X and Y.
Read X and Y
Echo the input coefficients
IF X ≥ 0 and Y ≥ 0 THEN
    F ← X + Y
ELSE IF X < 0 and Y ≥ 0 THEN
    F ← X**2 + Y
ELSE IF X ≥ 0 and Y < 0 THEN
    F ← X + Y**2
ELSE
    F ← X**2 + Y**2
END IF
Write out F(X,Y)
```

The flowchart for this program is shown in Figure 3-10.

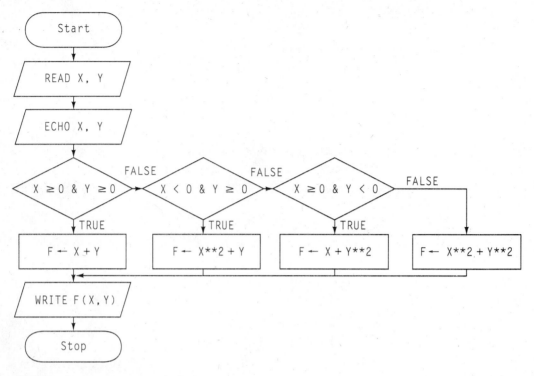

FIGURE 3-10   Flowchart of program **FUNXY**.

4. Turn the algorithm into FORTRAN statements.
The final FORTRAN code is shown in Figure 3-11.

```
      PROGRAM FUNXY
C
C  Purpose:
C    This program solves the function f(x,y) for a user-specified x and y,
C    where f(x,y) is defined as:
C
C             _
C            |   X + Y              X >= 0  and Y >= 0
C            |   X**2 + Y           X <  0  and Y >= 0
C  F(X,Y) =  |   X + Y**2           X >= 0  and Y <  0
C            |   X**2 + Y**2        X <  0  and Y <  0
C            |_
C
C  Record of revisions:
C      Date        Programmer          Description of change
C      ====        ==========          =====================
C    07/08/93    S. J. Chapman         Original code
C
C  List of variables:
C    X        -- First independent variable
C    Y        -- Second independent variable
C    FUN      -- Resulting function
C
```

```
      IMPLICIT NONE
C
C Declare the variables used in this program.
C
      REAL X, Y, FUN
C
C Prompt the user for the values X and Y
C
      WRITE (*,*) 'Enter the coefficients X and Y:'
      READ  (*,*) X, Y
C
C Write the coefficients of X and Y.
C
      WRITE (*,*) 'The coefficients X and Y are: ', X, Y
C
C Calculate the function f(x,y) based upon the signs of X and Y.
C
      IF ( ( X .GE. 0. ) .AND. ( Y .GE. 0. ) ) THEN
         FUN = X + Y
      ELSE IF ( ( X .LT. 0. ) .AND. ( Y .GE. 0. ) ) THEN
         FUN = X**2 + Y
      ELSE IF ( ( X .GE. 0. ) .AND. ( Y .LT. 0. ) ) THEN
         FUN = X + Y**2
      ELSE
         FUN = X**2 + Y**2
      END IF
C
C Write the value of the function.
C
      WRITE (*,*) 'The value of the function is: ', FUN
C
C Finish up.
C
      END
```

FIGURE 3-11   Program FUNXY from Example 3-2.

5. Test the program.

Next we must test the program using real input data. Since there are four possible paths through the program, we must test all four paths before we can be certain that the program is working properly. To test all four possible paths, we execute the program with the four set of input values $(x, y) = (2, 3), (-2, 3), (2, -3),$ and $(-2, -3)$. Calculating by hand, we see that

$$f(2, 3) = 2 + 3 = 5$$
$$f(-2, 3) = (-2)^2 + 3 = 7$$
$$f(2, -3) = 2 + (-3)^2 = 11$$
$$f(-2, 3) = (-2)^2 + (-3)^2 = 13$$

If this program is compiled, and then run four times with the above values, the results are

```
C:\BOOK\FORT>funxy
Enter the coefficients X and Y:
2. 3.
The coefficients X and Y are:      2.000000      3.000000
The value of the function is:      5.000000
```

```
C:\BOOK\FORT>funxy
Enter the coefficients X and Y:
-2. 3.
The coefficients X and Y are:      -2.000000      3.000000
The value of the function is:       7.000000

C:\BOOK\FORT>funxy
Enter the coefficients X and Y:
2. -3.
The coefficients X and Y are:       2.000000     -3.000000
The value of the function is:       11.000000

C:\BOOK\FORT>funxy
Enter the coefficients X and Y:
-2. -3.
The coefficients X and Y are:      -2.000000     -3.000000
The value of the function is:       13.000000
```

The program gives the correct answers for our test values in all four possible cases.

●

3.3.5 Notes Concerning the Use of Logical IF Structures

The Logical Block **IF** structure is flexible. It must have one **IF (...) THEN** statement and one **END IF** statement. In between, it can have any number of **ELSE IF (...) THEN** clauses, and may also have one **ELSE** clause. With this combination of features, it is possible to implement any desired branching structure.

In addition, block **IF** structures may be **nested.** Two block **IF** structures are said to be nested if one of them lies entirely within a single code block of the other one. The following two **IF** structures are properly nested.

```
IF (X .GT. 0.) THEN
   ...
   ...
   IF (Y .LT. 0.) THEN
      ...
      ...
   END IF
   ...
END IF
```

It is sometimes possible to implement an algorithm using either **ELSE IF ( ) THEN** clauses or nested **IF** statements. In that case, a programmer may choose whichever style he or she prefers.

EXAMPLE 3-3 Suppose that we are writing a program which reads in a numerical grade and assigns a letter grade to it according to the following table:

```
95 < GRADE ≤ 100        A
86 < GRADE ≤  95        B
76 < GRADE ≤  86        C
66 < GRADE ≤  76        D
 0 < GRADE ≤  66        F
```

Write an **IF** structure that will assign the grades as described above using (*a*) **ELSE IF** clauses and (*b*) nested **IF** structures.

SOLUTION (*a*) One possible structure using **ELSE IF** clauses is

```
IF ( (GRADE .GT. 95.0) .AND. (GRADE .LE. 100.0) ) THEN
   WRITE (*,*) ' The grade is A.'
ELSE IF (GRADE .GT. 86.0) ) THEN
   WRITE (*,*) ' The grade is B.'
ELSE IF (GRADE .GT. 76.0) ) THEN
   WRITE (*,*) ' The grade is C.'
ELSE IF (GRADE .GT. 66.0) ) THEN
   WRITE (*,*) ' The grade is D.'
ELSE
   WRITE (*,*) ' The grade is F.'
END IF
```

(*b*) One possible structure using nested **IF** structures is

```
IF ( (GRADE .GT. 95.0) .AND. (GRADE .LE. 100.0) ) THEN
   WRITE (*,*) ' The grade is A.'
ELSE
   IF (GRADE .GT. 86.0) THEN
      WRITE (*,*) ' The grade is B.'
   ELSE
      IF (GRADE .GT. 76.0) THEN
         WRITE (*,*) ' The grade is C.'
      ELSE
         IF (GRADE .GT. 66.0) THEN
            WRITE (*,*) ' The grade is D.'
         ELSE
            WRITE (*,*) ' The grade is F.'
         END IF
      END IF
   END IF
END IF
```

It should be clear from the above example that if there are a lot of mutually exclusive options, a single **IF** structure with **ELSE IF** clauses will be simpler than a nested **IF** structure.

■
GOOD PROGRAMMING PRACTICE

For branches in which there are many mutually exclusive options, use a single **IF** structure with **ELSE IF** clauses in preference to nested **IF** structures.

3.3.6 The Logical IF Statement

There is an alternative form of the logical **IF** statement described above. This alternative form is

```
IF (logical expression) Statement
```

where Statement is any executable FORTRAN statement. If the logical expression is TRUE, the program executes the statement on the same line with it. If the logical expression is FALSE, then the program skips to the next executable statement in the program.

This form of the logical **IF** is equivalent to a logical block **IF** structure with only one statement in the **IF** block, and with no **ELSE** clause. It is a holdover from an earlier, unstructured version of the FORTRAN language—FORTRAN 66. There is no need to use this statement in the FORTRAN 77 language.

QUIZ 3-1

This quiz provides a quick check to see if you have understood the concepts introduced in Section 3.3. If you have trouble with the quiz, reread the section, ask your instructor, or discuss the material with a fellow student. The answers to this quiz are found in the back of the book.

Write FORTRAN statements that perform the functions described below.

1. If X is greater than or equal to zero, then assign the square root of X to variable SQRTX and print out the result. Otherwise, print out an error message about the argument of the square root function, and set SQRTX to zero.
2. A value FUN is calculated as NUM / DEN. If the absolute value of DEN is less than 1.0E-10, write "Divide by 0 error." Otherwise, calculate and print out FUN.
3. The cost per mile for a rented vehicle is $0.50 for the first 100 miles, $0.30 for the next 200 miles, and $0.20 for all miles in excess of 300 miles. Write FORTRAN statements which determine the total cost and the average cost per mile for a given number of miles (stored in variable DIST).

Examine the following FORTRAN statements. Are they correct or incorrect? If they are correct, what is output by them? If they are incorrect, what is wrong with them?

4.
```
IF ( VOLTS .GT. 125. ) THEN
   WRITE (*,*) 'WARNING: High voltage on line. '
IF ( VOLTS .LT. 105. ) THEN
   WRITE (*,*) 'WARNING: Low voltage on line. '
ELSE
   WRITE (*,*) 'Line voltage is within tolerances. '
END IF
```

5.
```
PROGRAM TEST
LOGICAL WARN
REAL DIST, LIMIT
WARN = .TRUE.
PARAMETER ( LIMIT = 100. )
DIST0 = 55. + 10.
IF ( DIST .GT. LIMIT .OR. WARN ) THEN
   WRITE (*,*) 'Warning: Distance exceeds limit.'
ELSE
   WRITE (*,*) 'Distance = ', DIST
END IF
```

6.
```
LOGICAL LTEST
REAL A, B, C
DATA A, B, C / 3.141593, -10., 3.1 /
LTEST = A .GT. 0.
LTEST = B .LT. 1. .OR. LTEST
LTEST = C .GT. SQRT(ABS(A)+ABS(B)) .AND. LTEST
IF ( LTEST ) THEN
   WRITE (*,*) 'Tests passed...'
ELSE
   WRITE (*,*) 'Tests failed...'
END IF
```

7.
```
LOGICAL LTEST
REAL A, B
DATA A, B / 3.141593, -10. /, LTEST / .TRUE. /
IF (A .GT. 0. .OR. B .LT. 1. .AND. LTEST .LT. 0 ) THEN
   WRITE (*,*) 'Tests passed...'
ELSE
   WRITE (*,*) 'Tests failed...'
END IF
```

8.
```
IF ( TEMP .GT. 37. ) THEN
   WRITE (*,*) 'Human body temperature exceeded. '
ELSE IF ( TEMP .GT. 100. ) THEN
   WRITE (*,*) 'Boiling point of water exceeded. '
END IF
```

3.4 Control Structures: Loops

Loops are FORTRAN structures that permit us to execute a sequence of statements more than once. There are two basic forms of loop structures: **while loops** and **iterative loops** (or **counting loops**). The major difference between these two types of loops is in how the repetition is controlled. The code in iterative loops is repeated a specified number of times, and the number of repetitions is known before the loops start. By contrast, the code in a while loop is repeated indefinitely as long as some user-specified condition is satisfied.

3.4.1 Iteration: The While Loop

A *while loop* is a sequence of statements that are repeated indefinitely as long as some condition is satisfied. Although there is no standard while loop in FORTRAN

77,[1] it is easy to construct one from statement types that are included in the language. One possible while structure has the form

```
k   IF (logical expression) THEN
        Statement 1  ⎫
        Statement 2  ⎪
        Statement 3  ⎬  Code block
        ...          ⎪
        Statement n  ⎭
        GO TO k
    END IF
```

Here, k is a statement label appearing in columns 1–5 on the line containing the **IF** statement. If the logical expression is TRUE, statements 1 through n are executed, and then control returns to the **IF** statement. If the logical expression is still TRUE, the statements are executed again. This process will be repeated over and over again until the logical expression becomes FALSE. When the logical expression becomes FALSE, the program executes the first statement after the **END IF.**

Note that if the logical expression is FALSE the first time we reach the while loop, then statements 1 through n will never be executed at all!

The pseudocode corresponding to a while loop is

```
WHILE logical expr
    Statement 1
    Statement 2
    Statement 3
    ...
    Statement n
End of WHILE
```

and the flowchart for this structure is shown in Figure 3-12.

The **GO TO k** statement appearing in this structure is called an **unconditional branch.** After it is executed, the next statement to be executed is always the one with statement label k.

We now show an example from statistical analysis which is implemented using a while loop.

■
EXAMPLE 3-4 *Statistical Analysis*   It is common in science and engineering to work with large sets of numbers, each of which is a measurement of some particular property that we are interested in. A simple example would be the grades on the first test in this course. Each grade is a measurement of how much a particular student has learned in the course to date.

Much of the time, we are not interested in looking closely at every single measurement that we make. Instead, we want to summarize the results of a set of measurements with a few numbers that tell us a lot about the overall data set. Two such numbers are the *average* (or *mean*) and the *standard deviation* of the set of measurements. The average or mean of a set of numbers is defined as

---

[1]However, a while loop is a common extension to FORTRAN 77. See below for the discussion of the **DO WHILE** structure.

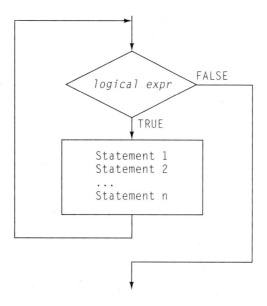

FIGURE 3-12   The flowchart representation of a while loop.

$$\bar{x} = \frac{1}{N} \sum_{i=1}^{N} x_i \qquad \text{(3-3)}$$

where x_i is sample i out of N samples. The standard deviation of a set of numbers is defined as

$$s = \sqrt{\frac{N \sum_{i=1}^{N} x_i^2 - \left(\sum_{i=1}^{N} x_i \right)^2}{N(N-1)}} \qquad \text{(3-4)}$$

Standard deviation is a measure of the amount of scatter on the measurements; the greater the standard deviation, the more scattered the points in the data set are.

Implement an algorithm that reads in a set of measurements and calculates the mean and the standard deviation of the input data set.

SOLUTION   This program must be able to read in an arbitrary number of measurements, and then calculate the mean and standard deviation of those measurements. We will use a while loop to accumulate the input measurements before performing the calculations.

When all of the measurements have been read, we must have some way of telling the program that there is no more data to enter. For now, we will assume that all the input measurements are either positive or zero, and we will use a negative input value as a *flag* to indicate that there is no more data to read. If a negative value is entered, then the program will stop reading input values and will calculate the mean and standard deviation of the data set.

1. State the problem.

Since we assume that the input numbers must be positive or zero, a proper statement of this problem would be: *Calculate the average and the standard deviation of a set of measurements, assuming that all of the measurements are either positive or zero, and assuming that we do not know in advance how many measurements are included in the data set.*

2. Define the inputs and outputs.

The inputs required by this program are an unknown number of positive or zero real (floating-point) numbers. The outputs from this program are a printout of the mean and the standard deviation of the input data set. In addition, we will print out the number of data points input to the program, since this is a useful check that the input data was read correctly.

3. Describe the algorithm.

This program can be broken down into three major steps:

```
Accumulate the input data
Calculate the mean and standard deviation
Write out the mean, standard deviation, and number of points
```

The first major step of the program is to accumulate the input data. To do this, we have to prompt the user to enter the desired numbers. When the numbers are entered, we have to keep track of the number of values entered, plus the sum and the sum of the squares of those values. The pseudocode for these steps is:

```
Initialize N, SUMX, and SUMX2 to 0
Prompt user for first number
Read in first X
WHILE X >= 0.
   N ← N + 1
   SUMX ← SUMX + X
   SUMX2 ← SUMX2 + X**2
   Prompt user for next number
   Read in next X
End of WHILE
```

Note that we have to read the first value before the loop starts so that the while loop can have a value to test the first time.

Next, we must calculate the mean and standard deviation. The pseudocode for this step is just the FORTRAN versions of Equations (3-3) and (3-4).

```
XBAR ← SUMX / REAL(N)
S ← SQRT( (REAL(N) * SUMX2 - SUMX**2) / (REAL(N) * REAL(N-1)) )
```

Finally, we must write out the results.

```
Write out the mean value XBAR
Write out the standard deviation S
Write out the number of input data points N
```

The flowchart for this program is shown in Figure 3-13.

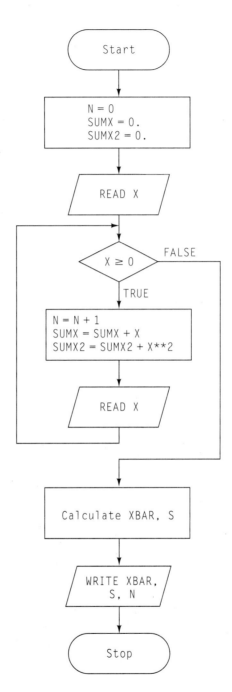

FIGURE 3-13 Flowchart for the statistical analysis program of Example 3-4.

4. Turn the algorithm into FORTRAN statements.

The final FORTRAN program is shown in Figure 3-14.

```
      PROGRAM STAT1
C
C  Purpose:
C     To calculate mean and the standard deviation of an input
C     data set containing an arbitrary number of input values.
C
C  Record of revisions:
C      Date       Programmer         Description of change
C      ====       ==========         =====================
C     12/29/90  S. J. Chapman        Original code
C
C  List of variables:
C      N      -- The number of input samples.
C      S      -- The standard deviation of the input samples.
C      SUMX   -- The sum of the input values.
C      SUMX2  -- The sum of the squares of the input values.
C      X      -- An input data value.
C      XBAR   -- The average of the input samples.
C
      IMPLICIT NONE
C
C     Declare the variables used in this program.
C
      INTEGER N
      REAL    X, SUMX, SUMX2
      REAL    XBAR, S
C
C     Initialize the counter and sums to zero.
C
      N     = 0
      SUMX  = 0.
      SUMX2 = 0.
      X     = 0.
C
C     Get first number.
C
      WRITE (*,*) 'Enter first number: '
      READ  (*,*) X
      WRITE (*,*) 'The number is ', X
C
C     Loop to read input values.
C
100   IF ( X .GE. 0. ) THEN
C
C        Accumulate sums.
C
         N     = N + 1
         SUMX  = SUMX + X
         SUMX2 = SUMX2 + X**2
C
C        Get next number, and echo it back to the user.
C
         WRITE (*,*) 'Enter next number: '
         READ  (*,*) X
         WRITE (*,*) 'The number is ', X
C
         GO TO 100
      END IF
C
C     Calculate the mean and standard deviation
C
```

```
      XBAR = SUMX / REAL(N)
      S    = SQRT( (REAL(N) * SUMX2 - SUMX**2) / (REAL(N) * REAL(N-1)) )
C
C     Tell user.
C
      WRITE (*,*) ' The mean of this data set is:', XBAR
      WRITE (*,*) ' The standard deviation is:   ', S
      WRITE (*,*) ' The number of data points is:', N
C
C     Finish up.
C
      END
```

FIGURE 3-14   The statistical analysis program of Example 3-4.

5. Test the program.

To test this program, we will calculate the answers by hand for a simple data set, and then compare the answers to the results of the program. If we used three input values: 3, 4, and 5, then the mean and standard deviation would be

$$\bar{x} = \frac{1}{N} \sum_{i=1}^{N} x_i = \frac{1}{3} 12 = 4$$

$$s = \sqrt{\frac{N \sum_{i=1}^{N} x_i^2 - \left(\sum_{i=1}^{N} x_i \right)^2}{N(N-1)}} = 1$$

When the above values are fed into the program, the results are

```
C:\BOOK\FORT>STAT1
Enter first number:
3.
The number is         3.000000
Enter next number:
4.
The number is         4.000000
Enter next number:
5.
The number is         5.000000
Enter next number:
-1.
The number is        -1.000000
 The mean of this data set is:                4.000000
 The standard deviation is:                   1.000000
 The number of data points is:               3
```

The program gives the correct answers for our test data set.   ●

In the example above, we failed to follow the design process completely. This failure has left the program with a fatal flaw! Did you spot it?

We have failed because *we did not completely test the program for all possible types of inputs.* Look at the example once again. If we enter either no numbers or only one number, then we will be dividing by zero in the above equations! The division-by-zero error will cause the program to abort. We need to modify the program to detect this problem, inform the user of it, and stop gracefully.

A modified version of the program called STAT2 is shown in Figure 3-15. Here, we check to see if there are enough input values before performing the calculations. If not, the program will print out an intelligent error message and quit. Test the modified program for yourself.

```
      PROGRAM STAT2
C
C  Purpose:
C    To calculate mean and the standard deviation of an input
C    data set containing an arbitrary number of input values.
C
C  Record of revisions:
C       Date      Programmer          Description of change
C       ====      ==========          =====================
C 0.  12/29/90   S. J. Chapman       Original code
C 1.  12/31/90   S. J. Chapman       Correct divide-by-0 error if
C                                    0 or 1 input values given.
C
C  List of variables:
C     N       -- The number of input samples.
C     S       -- The standard deviation of the input samples.
C     SUMX    -- The sum of the input values.
C     SUMX2   -- The sum of the squares of the input values.
C     X       -- An input data value.
C     XBAR    -- The average of the input samples.
C
      IMPLICIT NONE
C
C    Declare the variables used in this program.
C
      INTEGER N
      REAL    X, SUMX, SUMX2
      REAL    XBAR, S
C
C    Initialize the sums to zero.
C
      N     = 0
      SUMX  = 0.
      SUMX2 = 0.
      X     = 0.
C
C    Get first number, and echo it back to the user.
C
      WRITE (*,*) 'Enter first number: '
      READ  (*,*) X
      WRITE (*,*) 'The number is ', X
C
C    Loop to read input values.
C
  100 IF ( X .GE. 0. ) THEN
C
C         Accumulate sums.
C
          N     = N + 1
          SUMX  = SUMX + X
          SUMX2 = SUMX2 + X**2
C
```

```
C       Get next number.
C
        WRITE (*,*) 'Enter next number: '
        READ  (*,*) X
        WRITE (*,*) 'The number is ', X
C
        GO TO 100
      END IF
C
C Check to see if we have enough input data.
C
      IF ( N .LT. 2 ) THEN
C
C       Insufficient data.
C
        WRITE (*,*) ' At least 2 values must be entered.'
C
      ELSE
C
C       Calculate the mean and standard deviation
C
        XBAR = SUMX / REAL(N)
        S    = SQRT( (REAL(N) * SUMX2 - SUMX**2)
     *       / (REAL(N) * REAL(N-1)) )
C
C       Tell user.
C
        WRITE (*,*) ' The mean of this data set is:', XBAR
        WRITE (*,*) ' The standard deviation is:   ', S
        WRITE (*,*) ' The number of data points is:', N
C
      END IF
C
C Finish up.
C
      END
```

FIGURE 3-15   A modified statistical analysis program that avoids the divide-by-zero problems inherent in program STAT.

> ***FORTRAN 90 Extension (common in FORTRAN 77)***
> There is no while structure in standard FORTRAN 77. However, most modern compilers include a while structure as an extension to standard FORTRAN 77. Furthermore, this structure is a part of FORTRAN 90. The **DO WHILE** structure has the form
>
> ```
>       DO WHILE (logical expression)
>          Statement 1 ⎤
>          Statement 2 ⎟
>          Statement 3 ⎬ Code block
>          ...          ⎟
>          Statement n ⎦
>       END DO
> ```

If the logical expression is TRUE, statements 1 through n will be executed, and then control will return to the **DO WHILE** statement. If the logical expression is still TRUE, the statements will be executed again. This process will be repeated over and over again until the logical expression becomes FALSE. When control returns to the **DO WHILE** statement and the logical expression is FALSE, the program will execute the first statement after the **END DO**.

If your compiler supports the **DO WHILE** structure, you may use it in your programs with confidence that your programs will still run under FORTRAN 90. However, you may not be able to move your program to another computer having a FORTRAN 77 compiler. If your code must be portable between computers, do *not* use this structure.

The following program fragment shows how to implement the statistics program input loop using a **DO WHILE** structure.

```
C
C     Loop to read input values.
C
      DO WHILE ( X .GE. 0. )
C
C        Accumulate sums.
C
         N     = N + 1
         SUMX  = SUMX + X
         SUMX2 = SUMX2 + X**2
C
C        Get next number.
C
         WRITE (*,*) 'Enter next number: '
         READ  (*,*) X
         WRITE (*,*) 'The number is ', X
C
      END DO
```

3.4.2 Iteration: The DO loop

In the FORTRAN language, an iterative loop structure is called a **DO loop**, because the first statement of the loop begins with the word **DO**. The **DO** loop repeats the statements within the loop a fixed number of times. The **DO** loop structure has the form

```
      DO k INDEX = ISTART, IEND, INCR
          Statement 1 ⎤
          Statement 2 ⎥
          Statement 3 ⎬ Body
          ...          ⎥
          Statement n ⎦
    k CONTINUE
```

The constant k is the statement number of the last statement in the loop, and INDEX is a variable used as the loop counter (also known as the **loop index**). The quantities ISTART, IEND, and INCR are the *parameters* of the **DO** loop; they control the values of the variable INDEX during execution. The parameter INCR is optional; if it is missing, it is assumed to be 1.

The **CONTINUE** statement with label k marks the end of the **DO** loop. The **CONTINUE** statement is a FORTRAN statement which does nothing. It simply serves as a placeholder to mark the end of the **DO** loop. Note that the label k which marks the end of the **DO** loop is attached to the **CONTINUE** statement.

The statements between the **DO** statement and the **CONTINUE** statement are known as the *body* of the **DO** loop. They are executed repeatedly during each pass of the **DO** loop.

The **DO** loop structure functions as follows:

1. Each of the three **DO** loop parameters ISTART, IEND, and INCR may be a constant, a variable, or an expression. If they are variables or expressions, then their values are calculated before the start of the **DO** loop, and the resulting values are used to control the loop.
2. At the beginning of the execution of the **DO** loop, the program assigns the value ISTART to control variable INDEX. If INDEX*INCR $\leq$ IEND*INCR, the program executes the statements within the body of the loop.
3. After the statements in the body of the loop have been executed, the control variable is recalculated as

    ```
    INDEX = INDEX + INCR
    ```

    If INDEX*INCR is still $\leq$ IEND*INCR, the program executes the statements within the body again.
4. Step 2 is repeated over and over as long as INDEX*INCR $\leq$ IEND*INCR. When this condition is no longer true, execution skips to the first statement following the end of the **DO** loop.

Let's look at a number of specific examples to make the operation of the **DO** loop clearer. First, consider the following example:

```
    DO 100 I = 1, 10
        Statement 1
        Statement 2
        ...
        Statement n
100 CONTINUE
```

In this case, statements 1 through n are executed 10 times. The index variable I will be 1 on the first time, 2 on the second time, and so on. The index variable will be 10 on the last pass through the statements. After the tenth pass, the next statement following the **CONTINUE** statement will be executed.

Second, consider the following example:

```
      DO 100 I = 1, 10, 2
         Statement 1
         Statement 2
         ...
         Statement n
100 CONTINUE
```

In this case, statements 1–n are executed five times. The index variable I will be 1 on the first time, 3 on the second time, and so on. The index variable will be 9 on the fifth and last pass through the statements. When control is returned to the **DO** statement after the fifth pass, the index variable I will be increased to 11. Since $11 \times 2 > 10 \times 2$, control will transfer to the first statement after the **CONTINUE** statement.

Third, consider the following example:

```
      DO 100 I = 1, 10, -1
         Statement 1
         Statement 2
         ...
         Statement n
100 CONTINUE
```

Here, *statements 1 through n will never be executed,* since INDEX*INCR > IEND*INCR on the first time that the **DO** statement is reached. Instead, control will transfer to the first statement after the **CONTINUE** statement.
Finally, consider the example:

```
      DO 100 I = 3, -3, -2
         Statement 1
         Statement 2
         ...
         Statement n
100 CONTINUE
```

In this case, statements 1–n will be executed four times. The index variable I is 3 on the first time, 1 on the second time, −1 on the third time, and −3 on the fourth time. When control is returned to the **DO** statement after the fourth pass, the index variable I is decreased to −5. Since $-5 \times -2 > -3 \times -2$, control is transferred to the first statement after the **CONTINUE** statement.
The pseudocode corresponding to a **DO** loop is

```
DO for INDEX = ISTART to IEND by INCR
   Statement 1
   Statement 2
   Statement 3
   ...
   Statement n
End of DO
```

and the flowchart for this structure is shown in Figure 3-16.

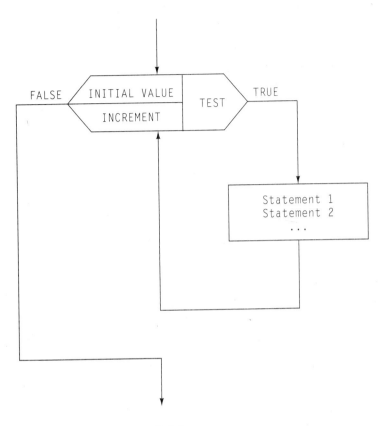

FIGURE 3-16 Flowchart for a **DO** loop structure.

EXAMPLE 3-5 *The Factorial Function*   To illustrate the operation of a **DO** loop, we use a **DO** loop to calculate the factorial function. The factorial function is defined as

$$N! = \begin{cases} 1 & N = 0 \\ N * (N-1) * (N-2) * \ldots * 3 * 2 * 1 & N > 0 \end{cases}$$

The FORTRAN code to calculate N factorial for positive value of N is:

```
      NFAC = 1
      DO 10 I = 1, N
         NFAC = NFAC * I
   10 CONTINUE
```

Suppose that we wish to calculate the value of 5!. If N is 5, the **DO** loop parameters are ISTART = 1, IEND = 5, and INCR = 1. This loop is executed 5 times, with the variable I taking on values of 1, 2, 3, 4, and 5 in the successive loops. The resulting value of NFAC is $1 \times 2 \times 3 \times 4 \times 5 = 120$. ●

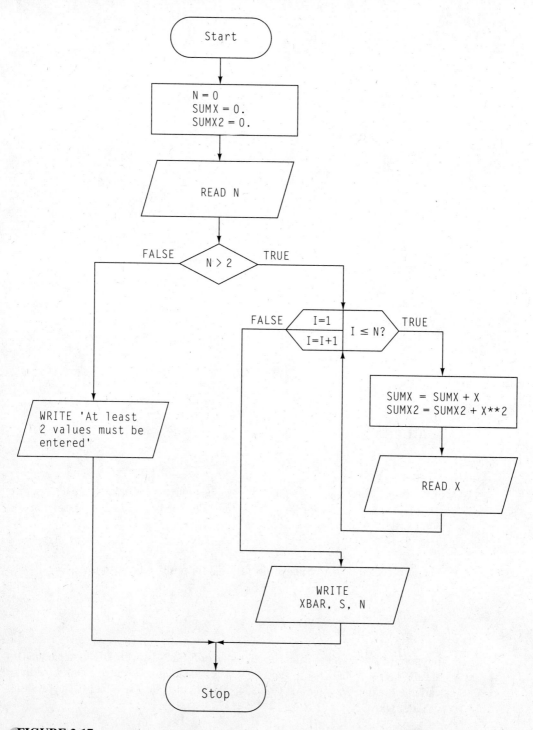

FIGURE 3-17 Flowchart for modified statistical analysis program using a **DO** loop.

EXAMPLE 3-6 *Statistical Analysis* Implement an algorithm that reads in a set of measurements and calculates the mean and the standard deviation of the input data set, when any value in the data set can be positive, negative, or zero.

SOLUTION This program must be able to read in an arbitrary number of measurements, and then calculate the mean and standard deviation of those measurements. Each measurement can be positive, negative, or zero.

Since we cannot use a data value as a flag this time, we will ask the user for the number of input values, and then use a **DO** loop to read in those values. A flowchart for this program is shown in Figure 3-17. Note that the while loop has been replaced by a **DO** loop. The modified program that permits the use of any input value is shown in Figure 3-18. Verify its operation for yourself by finding the mean and standard deviation of the following five input values: 3., −1., 0., 1., and −2.

```
      PROGRAM STAT3
C
C Purpose:
C   To calculate mean and the standard deviation of an input
C   data set, where each input value can be positive, negative,
C   or zero.
C
C Record of revisions:
C     Date        Programmer          Description of change
C     ====        ==========          =====================
C   01/02/91    S. J. Chapman        Original code
C
C List of variables:
C   N       -- The number of input samples.
C   S       -- The standard deviation of the input samples.
C   SUMX    -- The sum of the input values.
C   SUMX2   -- The sum of the squares of the input values.
C   X       -- An input data value.
C   XBAR    -- The average of the input samples.
C
      IMPLICIT NONE
C
C Declare the variables used in this program.
C
      INTEGER I, N
      REAL    X, SUMX, SUMX2
      REAL    XBAR, S
C
C Initialize the counter and sums to zero.
C
      SUMX  = 0.
      SUMX2 = 0.
      X     = 0.
C
C Get the number of points to input.
C
      WRITE (*,*) 'Enter number of points: '
      READ  (*,*) N
C
C Check to see if we have enough input data.
C
```

```
      IF ( N .LT. 2 ) THEN
C
C         Insufficient data.
C
          WRITE (*,*) ' At least 2 values must be entered.'
C
      ELSE
C
C         Loop to read input values.
C
          DO 100 I = 1, N
C
C            Get next number.
C
             WRITE (*,*) 'Enter next number: '
             READ  (*,*) X
             WRITE (*,*) 'The number is ', X
C
C            Accumulate sums.
C
             SUMX  = SUMX + X
             SUMX2 = SUMX2 + X**2
C
  100     CONTINUE
C
C         Calculate the mean and standard deviation
C
          XBAR = SUMX / REAL(N)
          S    = SQRT( (REAL(N) * SUMX2 - SUMX**2)
     *           / (REAL(N) * REAL(N-1)) )
C
C         Tell user.
C
          WRITE (*,*) ' The mean of this data set is:', XBAR
          WRITE (*,*) ' The standard deviation is: ', S
          WRITE (*,*) ' The number of data points is:', N
C
      END IF
C
C     Finish up.
C
      END
```

FIGURE 3-18 Modified statistical analysis program that works with both positive and input values. ●

Details of Operation

Now that we have seen examples of a **DO** loop in operation, we will examine some of the important details required to use **DO** loops properly.

1. It is not necessary to indent the body of the **DO** loop as we have shown above. The FORTRAN compiler recognizes the loop even if every statement in it starts in column 7. However, the code is much more readable if the body of the **DO** loop is indented, so you should always indent the bodies of your **DO** loops.

■   **GOOD PROGRAMMING PRACTICE**

Always indent the body of a **DO** loop by two or more spaces to improve the readability of the code.

2. The index variable of a **DO** loop *should not be modified anywhere within the* **DO** *loop*. Since the index variable is used to control the repetitions in the **DO** loop, changing it could produce unexpected results. In the worst case, modifying the index variable could produce an *infinite loop* that never completes. Consider the following example.

```
      PROGRAM BAD1
      INTEGER I
      DO 10 I = 1, 4
         I = 2
   10 CONTINUE
      END
```

If I is reset to 2 every time through the loop, the loop will never end, because the index variable can never be greater than 4! This loop will run forever unless the program containing it is killed.

   Most of the better FORTRAN compilers recognize this problem, and generate a compile-time error if a program attempts to modify an index variable within a loop. For example, if we compile program BAD1 with the Microsoft FORTRAN compiler, the following error is produced.

```
C:\BOOK\FORT>fl bad1.for
Microsoft (R) FORTRAN Optimizing Compiler Version 5.10
Copyright (c) Microsoft Corp 1982-1991. All rights reserved.

bad1.for
bad1.for(4) : error F2516: I : assignment using active DO variable illegal
```

PROGRAMMING PITFALLS

Never attempt to modify the value of a **DO** loop index variable while inside the loop.

3. The number of iterations to be performed by a **DO** loop is calculated using the following equation:

$$ITER = \frac{IEND - ISTART + INCR}{INCR} \qquad (3\text{-}5)$$

Many compilers permit the values of ISTART, IEND, and INCR to be modified within a **DO** loop. They should never be modified within the loop, since changing IEND and INCR can inadvertently change the number of iterations performed by the loop.

PROGRAMMING PITFALLS

Never attempt to modify the control values of a **DO** loop (ISTART, IEND, INCR) while inside the loop.

---

4. If the number of iterations calculated from Equation (3-5) is less than or equal to zero, the statements within the **DO** loop are never executed at all. For example, the statements in the following **DO** loop will never be executed:

    ```
        DO 10 I = 3, 2
          . . .
     10  CONTINUE
    ```

    since

    $$ITER = \frac{IEND - ISTART + INCR}{INCR} = \frac{2 - 3 + 1}{1} = 0$$

5. It is possible to design **DO** loops that count down as well as up. The following **DO** loop executes three times with I being 3, 2, and 1 in the successive loops.

    ```
        DO 10 I = 3, 1, -1
          . . .
     10  CONTINUE
    ```

6. The index variable and control parameters of a **DO** loop may be either integer or real quantities. However, *real index variables should never be used*. To understand why we should not use real index variables, consider the following example. Suppose that we need a loop that runs from 0 to 12 in steps of 2/3. The FORTRAN code for this loop is:

    ```
        REAL X
        DO 100 X = 0., 12., 2./3.
          . . .
          . . .
          . . .
    100    CONTINUE
    ```

There should be 19 iterations of this loop, with X = 0., 0.66666. . . , 1.33333. . . , etc. up to 12. Unfortunately, we can't be sure that there really will be 19 iterations. On some computers, there will be 19 iterations, while on others there will be only 18! This happens because of different roundoff errors on different computers. The value of X is incremented by 2./3. on each iteration, and X is compared to 12. to determine when to stop the loop. On some computers, the roundoff from the successive floating-point additions results in a number slightly greater than 12., while on other computers the roundoff results in a number slightly less than 12. Therefore, on some computers the loop will execute one more time than on other computers.

It is unacceptable to have identical programs behave differently on different computers. The following **DO** loop is much better, since integer variables do not suffer from roundoff problems. It will perform the same function, and yet will behave exactly the same way on all computers.

```
    INTEGER I
    REAL    X
    DO 100 I = 0, 18
       X = 2./3. * REAL(I)
       ...
       ...
       ...
100 CONTINUE
```

■ **GOOD PROGRAMMING PRACTICE**

DO loop index variables should always be of type **INTEGER** to avoid problems caused by roundoff errors in real variables.

7. It is not necessary to end a **DO** loop with a **CONTINUE** statement. The statement label marking the end of the **DO** loop may be attached to many different types of executable statements. For example, the following **DO** loop is legal:

```
    DO 100 I = 0, 18
       J = I ** 2
100    WRITE (*,*) I, '**2 = ', J
```

However, it is illegal to terminate a **DO** loop with certain statements. These illegal statements include **IF, ELSE, END IF,** or another **DO** statement, as well as others that we haven't met yet.

Even though it is legal to terminate a **DO** loop on certain executable statements, **DO** *loops should always be terminated with* **CONTINUE** *statements*. This practice helps prevent errors due to confusion over which statements are legal and which ones are illegal at the end of a **DO** loop, and it also makes the **DO** loop more readable by providing a "border" on either side of the body of the **DO** loop.

■ **GOOD PROGRAMMING PRACTICE**

Always terminate **DO** loops with a **CONTINUE** statement.

8. It is possible to branch out of a **DO** loop at any time while the loop is executing. If program execution does branch out of a **DO** loop before it would otherwise finish, the loop index variable retains the value that it had when the branch occurs. Consider the following example.

```
      INTEGER I
      DO 100 I = 1, 5
         ...
         ...
      IF (I .GE. 3) GO TO 200
         ...
100 CONTINUE
200 CONTINUE
      WRITE (*,*) I
```

Execution will branch out of the **DO** loop and go to statement 200 on the third pass through the loop. When execution gets to statement 200, variable I will contain a value of 3.

9. If a **DO** loop completes normally, *the value of the index variable is undefined when the loop is completed.* In the example shown below, the value written out by the **WRITE** statement is not defined in the FORTRAN 77 standard.

```
      INTEGER I
      DO 100 I = 1, 5
         ...
         ...
         ...
100 CONTINUE
      WRITE (*,*) I
```

On most computers, after the loop has completed, the index variable I will contain the first value of the index variable to fail the INDEX*INCR ≤ IEND*INCR test. In the above code, it would usually contain a 6 after the loop is finished. However, don't count on it! Since the value is officially undefined in the FORTRAN 77 standard, some compilers may produce a different result. If your code depends on the value of the index variable after the loop is completed, you may get different results as the program is moved from computer to computer.

GOOD PROGRAMMING PRACTICE

Never depend on an index variable to retain a specific value after a **DO** loop completes normally.

10. It is illegal for program execution to branch into the body of a **DO** loop. The following code will generate a compile-time error on a FORTRAN compiler.

```
      INTEGER I
      DO 100 I = 1, 5
         ...
200      ...
         ...
100 CONTINUE
      ...
      GO TO 200
```

3.4.3 Nesting DO loops and Block IF Structures

It is possible for one **DO** loop to be completely inside another one. If one loop is completely inside another one, the two **DO** loops are called *nested* **DO** loops. The following example shows two nested **DO** loops used to calculate and write out the product of two integers.

```
      DO 200 I = 1, 3
         DO 100 J = 1, 3
            MULT = I * J
            WRITE (*,*) I, ' * ', J, ' = ', MULT
100      CONTINUE
200 CONTINUE
```

In this example, the outer **DO** loop assigns a value of 1 to index variable I, and then the inner **DO** loop is executed. The inner **DO** loop is executed three times with index variable J having values 1, 2, and 3. When the entire inner **DO** loop has been completed, the outer **DO** loop assigns a value of 2 to index variable I, and the inner **DO** loop is executed again. This process repeats until the outer **DO** loop has executed three times, and the resulting output is

```
1 *  1 =   1
1 *  2 =   2
1 *  3 =   3
2 *  1 =   2
2 *  2 =   4
2 *  3 =   6
3 *  1 =   3
3 *  2 =   6
3 *  3 =   9
```

Note that the inner **DO** loop executes completely before the index variable of the outer **DO** loop is incremented.

If **DO** *loops are nested, they must have independent index variables.* Remember that it is not possible to change an index variable within the body of a **DO** loop. Therefore, it is not possible to use the same index variable for two nested **DO** loops, since the inner loop would be attempting to change the index variable of the outer loop within the body of the outer loop.

Also, *if two loops are to be nested, one of them must lie completely within the other one*. The following **DO** loops are incorrectly nested, and a compile-time error will be generated for this code.

```
      DO 200 I = 1, 3
         . . .
         . . .
      DO 100 J = 1, 3
         . . .
         . . .
  200 CONTINUE
         . . .
         . . .
  100    CONTINUE
```

It is also possible to nest **DO** loops within block **IF** structures or block **IF** structures within **DO** loops. If a **DO** loop is nested within a block **IF** structure, the **DO** loop must lie entirely within a single code block of the **IF** structure. For example, the following statements are illegal since the **DO** loop stretches between the **IF** and the **ELSE** code blocks of the **IF** structure.

```
      IF ( A .LT. B ) THEN
         . . .
         . . .
      DO 200 I = 1, 3
         . . .
         . . .
      ELSE
         . . .
         . . .
  200    CONTINUE
         . . .
      END IF
```

By contrast, the following statements are legal, since the **DO** loop lies entirely within a single code block of the **IF** structure.

```
      IF ( A .LT. B ) THEN
         . . .
         . . .
      DO 200 I = 1, 3
         . . .
         . . .
  200    CONTINUE
         . . .
      ELSE
         . . .
      END IF
```

EXAMPLE 3-7 *Physics—The Flight of a Ball*   If we assume negligible air friction and ignore the curvature of the Earth, a ball that is thrown into the air from any point on the Earth's surface will follow a parabolic flight path (see Figure 3-19(a)). The height of the ball at any time *t* after it is thrown is given by Equation (3-6):

$$y(t) = y_o + v_{yo}t + \frac{1}{2}gt^2 \tag{3-6}$$

where y_o is the initial height of the object above the ground, v_{yo} is the initial vertical velocity of the object, and *g* is the acceleration due to the earth's gravity. The horizontal distance (range) traveled by the ball as a function of time after it is thrown is given by Equation (3-7):

$$x(t) = x_o + v_{xo}t \tag{3-7}$$

· where x_o is the initial horizontal position of the ball on the ground, and v_{xo} is the initial horizontal velocity of the ball.

If the ball is thrown with some initial velocity v_o at an angle of $\theta°$ with respect to the earth's surface, then the initial horizontal and vertical components of velocity are

$$v_{xo} = v_o \cos \theta \tag{3-8}$$
$$v_{yo} = v_o \sin \theta \tag{3-9}$$

Assume that the ball is initially thrown from position $(x_o, y_o) = (0, 0)$ with an initial velocity *v* of 20 m/sec at an initial angle of $\theta°$. Write a program that will determine the horizontal distance traveled by the ball from the time it was thrown until it touches the ground again. The program should do this for all angles θ from 0 to 90

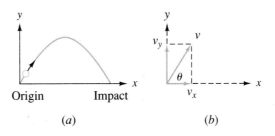

(a)   (b)

FIGURE 3-19   (*a*) When a ball is thrown upward, it follows a parabolic trajectory. (*b*) The horizontal and vertical components of a velocity vector *v* at an angle θ with respect to the horizontal.

degrees in 1-degree steps. Determine the angle θ that maximizes the range of the ball.

SOLUTION   To solve this problem, we must determine an equation for the range of the thrown ball. We can do this by first finding the time that the ball remains in the air, and then finding the horizontal distance that the ball can travel during that time.

The time that the ball remains in the air after it is thrown may be calculated from Equation (3-6). The ball touches the ground at the time t for which $y(t) = 0$. Remembering that the ball starts from ground level ($y(0) = 0$), and solving for t, we get

$$y(t) = y_o + v_{yo} t + \frac{1}{2} g t^2 \qquad (3\text{-}6)$$

$$0 = 0 + v_{yo} t + \frac{1}{2} g t^2$$

$$0 = \left(v_{yo} + \frac{1}{2} gt \right) t$$

so the ball will be at ground level at time $t_1 = 0$ (when we threw it), and at time

$$t_2 = - \frac{2v_{yo}}{g}$$

The horizontal distance that the ball travels in time t_2 is found using Equation (3-7):

$$\text{range} = x(t_2) = x_o + v_{xo} t_2 \qquad \cdot (3\text{-}7)$$

$$\text{range} = 0 + v_{xo} \left(- \frac{2v_{yo}}{g} \right)$$

$$\text{range} = - \frac{2v_{xo}v_{yo}}{g}$$

We can substitute Equations (3-8) and (3-9) for v_{xo} and v_{yo} to get an equation expressed in terms of the initial velocity v and initial angle θ:

$$\text{range} = - \frac{2(v_o \cos \theta)(v_o \sin \theta)}{g}$$

$$\text{range} = - \frac{2v_o^2}{g} \cos \theta \sin \theta \qquad \textbf{(3-10)}$$

From the problem statement, we know that the initial velocity v_o is 20 m/sec, and that the ball is thrown at all angles from 0 to 90° in 1° steps. Finally, any elementary physics textbook tells us that the acceleration due to the earth's gravity is -9.8 m/sec^2.

Now let's apply our design technique to this problem.

1. State the problem.

A proper statement of this problem would be: *Calculate the range that a ball would travel when it is thrown with an initial velocity of v_o at an initial angle θ. Calculate this range for a v_o of 20 m/sec and all angles between 0 and 90°, in 1° increments. Determine the angle θ that will result in the maximum range for the ball. Assume that there is no air friction.*

2. Define the inputs and outputs.

As the problem is defined above, no inputs are required. We know from the problem statement what v_o and θ will be, so there is no need to read them in. The outputs from this program will be a table showing the range of the ball for each angle θ, and the angle θ for which the range is maximum.

3. Describe the algorithm.

This program can be broken down into the following major steps

```
DO for THETA = 0 to 90 degrees
   Calculate the range of the ball for each angle THETA
   Determine if this THETA yields the maximum range so far
   Write out the range as a function of THETA
END of DO
WRITE out the THETA yielding maximum range
```

A **DO** loop is appropriate for this algorithm, since we are calculating the range of the ball for a specified number of angles. We calculate the range for each value of θ, and compare each range with the maximum range found so far to determine which angle yields the maximum range. Note that the trigonometric functions work in radians, so the angles in degrees must be converted to radians before the range is calculated. The detailed pseudocode for this algorithm is

```
Initialize MAXRNG and MAXDEG to 0
Initialize V0 to 20 meters/second
DO for THETA = 0 to 90 degrees
   RADIAN ← THETA * DEG2RD               Convert degrees to radians
   RANGE ← (-2. * V0**2 / GRAVTY ) * SIN(RADIAN) * COS(RADIAN)
   Write out THETA and RANGE
   IF RANGE > MAXRNG then
        MAXRNG ← RANGE
        MAXDEG ← THETA
   END of IF
END of DO
Write out MAXDEG, MAXRNG
```

The flowchart for this program is shown in Figure 3-20.

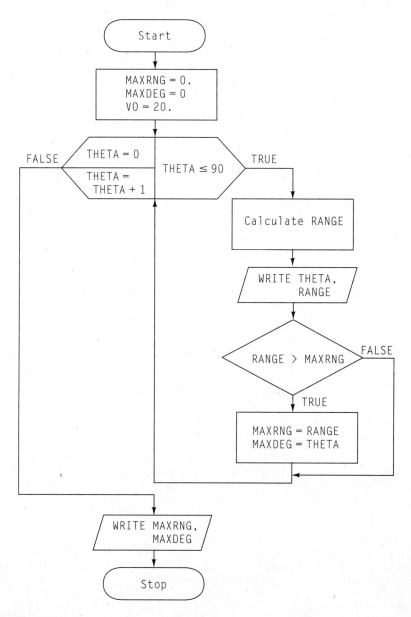

FIGURE 3-20 Flowchart for a program to determine the angle θ at which a ball thrown with an initial velocity v_o of 20 m/s will travel the farthest.

4. Turn the algorithm into FORTRAN statements.

The final FORTRAN program is shown in Figure 3-21.

```
      PROGRAM BALL
C
C Purpose:
C   To calculate distance traveled by a ball thrown at a specified
C   angle THETA and at a specified velocity VO from a point on the
C   surface of the earth, ignoring the effects of air friction and
C   the earth's curvature.
C
C Record of revisions:
C       Date      Programmer       Description of change
C       ====      ==========       =====================
C     02/02/92  S. J. Chapman      Original code
C
C List of variables:
C   DEG2RD -- Conversion factor: degrees to radians (constant)
C   GRAVTY -- The acceleration due to the earth's gravity (m/s).
C   MAXDEG -- The angle at which the max range occurs (in degrees)
C   MAXRNG -- The maximum range for the ball at velocity VO (meters).
C   RANGE  -- The range of the ball at a particular angle (meters).
C   RADIAN -- The angle at which the ball was thrown (in radians).
C   THETA  -- The angle at which the ball was thrown (in degrees).
C   VO     -- The velocity of the ball (in m/s)
C
      IMPLICIT NONE
C
C   Declare the variables used in this program.
C
      INTEGER THETA, MAXDEG
      REAL    DEG2RD, GRAVTY, RADIAN
      REAL    VO, RANGE, MAXRNG
C
C   Parameters.
C
      PARAMETER ( DEG2RD = 0.01745329 )
C
C   Data.
C
      DATA GRAVTY / -9.80 /
C
C   Initialize MAXRNG, MAXDEG, and VO.
C
      MAXRNG = 0.
      MAXDEG = 0
      VO     = 20.
C
C   Loop over all specified angles.
C
      DO 100 THETA = 0, 90
C
C       Get angle in radians.
C
```

```
      RADIAN = REAL(THETA) * DEG2RD
C
C     Calculate range in meters.
C
      RANGE = (-2. * V0**2 / GRAVTY) * SIN(RADIAN) * COS(RADIAN)
C
C     Write out the range for this angle.
C
      WRITE (*,*) 'THETA = ', THETA, ' degrees; Range = ', RANGE,
     *            ' meters'
C
C     Compare the range to the previous maximum range. If this
C     range is larger, save it and the angle at which it occurred.
C
      IF ( RANGE .GT. MAXRNG ) THEN
         MAXRNG = RANGE
         MAXDEG = THETA
      END IF
C
  100 CONTINUE
C
C     Skip a line, and then write out the maximum range and the angle
C     at which it occurred.
C
      WRITE (*,*) ' '
      WRITE (*,*) 'Max range = ', MAXRNG, ' at ', MAXDEG, ' degrees'
C
C     Finish up.
C
      END
```

FIGURE 3-21   Program BALL from Example 3-7.

The degrees-to-radians conversion factor is always a constant, so in the program it is given a name with a **PARAMETER** statement, and all references to the constant within the program use that name. On the other hand, the acceleration due to gravity is *not* a constant. At sea level, it is about 9.8 m/sec^2, directed downward. At higher altitudes, the acceleration due to gravity will be lower. Since GRAVTY may vary somewhat, it was made a variable instead of a constant. The variable is initialized to the acceleration at sea level using a **DATA** statement. With this structure, the program can easily be modified to explore the effects of different accelerations on the maximum range of the ball.

5.   Test the program.

To test this program, we calculate the answers by hand for a few of the angles, and compare the results with the output of the program.

$$\theta = 0°: \qquad \text{range} = -\frac{2(20^2)}{-9.8} \cos 0 \sin 0 = 0$$

$$\theta = 5°: \qquad \text{range} = -\frac{2(20^2)}{-9.8} \cos\left(\frac{5\pi}{180}\right) \sin\left(\frac{5\pi}{180}\right) = 7.087680$$

$$\theta = 40°: \qquad \text{range} = -\frac{2(20^2)}{-9.8} \cos\left(\frac{40\pi}{180}\right) \sin\left(\frac{40\pi}{180}\right) = 40.19623$$

$$\theta = 45°: \qquad \text{range} = -\frac{2(20^2)}{-9.8} \cos\left(\frac{45\pi}{180}\right) \sin\left(\frac{45\pi}{180}\right) = 40.81633$$

When program BALL is executed, a 90-line table of angles and ranges is produced. To save space, only a portion of the table is reproduced below.

```
C:\BOOK\FORT>BALL
THETA =              0 degrees; Range =         0.000000E+00 meters
THETA =              1 degrees; Range =             1.424469 meters
THETA =              2 degrees; Range =             2.847203 meters
THETA =              3 degrees; Range =             4.266467 meters
THETA =              4 degrees; Range =             5.680534 meters
THETA =              5 degrees; Range =             7.087680 meters
    . . .
    . . .
    . . .
THETA =             40 degrees; Range =            40.196230 meters
THETA =             41 degrees; Range =            40.419100 meters
THETA =             42 degrees; Range =            40.592730 meters
THETA =             43 degrees; Range =            40.716900 meters
THETA =             44 degrees; Range =            40.791460 meters
THETA =             45 degrees; Range =            40.816330 meters
THETA =             46 degrees; Range =            40.791460 meters
THETA =             47 degrees; Range =            40.716900 meters
THETA =             48 degrees; Range =            40.592730 meters
THETA =             49 degrees; Range =            40.419110 meters
THETA =             50 degrees; Range =            40.196240 meters
    . . .
    . . .
    . . .
THETA =             85 degrees; Range =             7.087695 meters
THETA =             86 degrees; Range =             5.680547 meters
THETA =             87 degrees; Range =             4.266479 meters
THETA =             88 degrees; Range =             2.847212 meters
THETA =             89 degrees; Range =             1.424487 meters
THETA =             90 degrees; Range =         1.589446E-05 meters

Max range =         40.816330 at             45 degrees
```

The program output matches our hand calculation for the angles calculated above. Note that the maximum range occurred at an angle of 45°. ●

QUIZ 3-2

This quiz provides a quick check to see if you have understood the concepts introduced in Section 3.4. If you have trouble with the quiz, reread the section, ask your instructor, or discuss the material with a fellow student. The answers to this quiz are found at the back of the book.

*Examine the following **DO** loops and determine how many times each loop will be executed. Assume that all of the index variables shown are of type integer.*

1. `DO 100 INDEX = 7, 10`
2. `DO 100 J = 7, 10, -1`
3. `DO 100 INDEX = 1, 10, 10`
4. `DO 100 ICOUNT = -2, 10, 2`
5. `DO 100 TIME = -2, -10, -1`
6. `DO 100 I = -10, -7, -3`

*Examine the following **DO** loops and determine the value in **IRES** at the end of each of the loops. Assume that all index variables are integers.*

7.
```
      IRES = 0
      DO 100 INDEX = 1, 10
         IRES = IRES + 1
  100 CONTINUE
```

8.
```
      IRES = 0
      DO 100 INDEX = 1, 10
         IRES = IRES + INDEX
  100 CONTINUE
```

9.
```
      IRES = 0
      DO 100 INDEX = -3, 3
         IRES = IRES + INDEX
  100 CONTINUE
```

10.
```
      IRES = 0
      DO 110 INDEX1 = 1, 10
         DO 100 INDEX2 = 1, 10
            IRES = IRES + 1
  100    CONTINUE
  110 CONTINUE
```

11.
```
      IRES = 0
      DO 110 INDEX1 = 1, 10
         DO 100 INDEX2 = INDEX1, 10
            IRES = IRES + 1
  100    CONTINUE
  110 CONTINUE
```

Examine the following FORTRAN statements and tell whether or not they are valid. If they are invalid, indicate the reason why they are invalid.

12.
```
      DO 120 I = 1, 10
         DO 110 J = 1, 10
            DO 100 I = I, J
                 . . .
  100          CONTINUE
  110    CONTINUE
  120 CONTINUE
```

```
13.      DO 120 I = 1, 10
            DO 110 J = I, 10
               DO 100 K = I, J
                  . . .
100            CONTINUE
110         CONTINUE
120 CONTINUE
14.      DO 120 I = 1, 10
            . . .
            . . .
            DO 110 J = 1, 10
               . . .
               . . .
120         CONTINUE
110 CONTINUE
15.      IF ( ITER .LE. MAX ) THEN
            DO 110 J = ITER, MAX
               . . .
               . . .
110         CONTINUE
         ELSE
            DO 110 J = ITER, MAX, -1
               . . .
               . . .
110         CONTINUE
         END IF
```

3.5   MORE ON DEBUGGING FORTRAN PROGRAMS

It is much easier to make a mistake when writing a program containing branches and loops than it is when writing simple sequential programs. Even after going through the full design process, a program of any size is almost guaranteed not to be completely correct the first time it is used. Suppose that we have built the program and tested it, only to find that the output values are in error. How do we go about finding the bugs and fixing them?

The best approach to locating the error is to insert WRITE statements into the code to print out important variables at key points in the program. When the program is run, the **WRITE** statements print out the values of the important variables. These values can be compared to the ones you expect, and the places where the actual and expected values differ will serve as a clue to help you locate the problem. For example, to verify the operation of a **DO** loop, the following **WRITE** statements could be added to the program.

```
WRITE (*,*) ' At DO 100 loop: IST, IEN, INC = ', IST, IEN, INC
DO 100 I = IST, IEN, INC
   WRITE (*,*) 'In DO 100 loop: I = ', I
   . . .
   . . .
   . . .
100 CONTINUE
   WRITE (*,*) ' DO 100 loop completed'
```

When the program is executed, its output listing will contain detailed information about the variables controlling the **DO** loop and just how many times the loop was executed. Similar **WRITE** statements could be used to debug the operation of a block **IF** structure:

```
WRITE (*,*) ' At IF #1: VAR1 = ', VAR1
IF ( SQRT(VAR1) .GT. 1. ) THEN
   WRITE (*,*) ' At IF #1: SQRT(VAR1) .GT. 1. '
   ...
   ...
ELSE IF ( SQRT(VAR1) .LT. 1. ) THEN
   WRITE (*,*) ' At IF #1: SQRT(VAR1) .LT. 1. '
   ...
   ...
ELSE
   WRITE (*,*) ' At IF #1: SQRT(VAR1) .EQ. 1. '
   ...
   ...
END IF
```

Once you have located the portion of the code in which the error occurs, you can take a look at the specific statements in that area to locate the problem. A list of some common errors is given below. Be sure to check for them in your code.

1. *If the problem is in an* **IF** *structure, check to see if you used the proper relational operator in your logical expressions.* Did you use **.GT.** when you really intended **.GE.**, etc.? Logical errors of this sort can be very hard to spot, since the compiler will not give an error message for them. Be especially careful when you encounter logical expressions that are very complex, since they are hard to understand, and very easy to mess up. You should use extra parentheses to make them easier to understand. If the logical expressions are really large, consider breaking them down into simpler expressions which are easier to follow. This can be done by making use of intermediate logical variables. For example, the structure

```
IF ( (SIN(X) .GT. 0.5) .AND. (I .LT. 5 ) .AND.
*     (DEPTH .GE. 1000. ) ) THEN
   ...
   ...
   ...
END IF
```

could be replaced by

```
LOGICAL TEST

TEST = SIN(X) .GT. 0.5
TEST = TEST .AND. (I .LT. 5)
TEST = TEST .AND. (DEPTH .GE. 1000.)
IF ( TEST ) THEN
   ...
   ...
   ...
END IF
```

2. *Another common problem with* **IF** *statements occurs when real variables are tested for equality.* Because of small roundoff errors during floating-point arithmetic operations, two numbers which theoretically should be equal will differ by a tiny amount, and the test for equality will fail. When working with real variables, it is often a good idea to replace a test for equality with a test for *near equality.* For example, instead of testing to see if $X = 10.$, you should test to see if $|X - 10.| < 0.0001$. Any value of X between 9.9999 and 10.0001 will satisfy the latter test, so roundoff error will not cause problems. In FORTRAN statements,

```
IF ( X .EQ. 10. ) THEN
```

would be replaced by

```
IF ( ABS(X - 10.) .LE. 0.0001 ) THEN
```

3. *Most errors in* **DO** *loops involve mistakes with the loop parameters.* If you add **WRITE** statements to the **DO** loop as described earlier, the problem should be fairly clear. Did the **DO** loop start with the correct value? Did it end with the correct value? Did it increment at the proper step? If not, check the parameters of the **DO** loop closely. You will probably spot an error in the control parameters.

4. *Errors in* **DO** *loops may also be caused by inadvertently modifying the* **DO** *loop index variable.* Explicit attempts to modify the index variable within a loop will be easy to see, and they will often produce a compiler error. However, the **DO** loop index may be modified indirectly within a subprogram (as we will show in Chapter 5), and the compiler will not be able to detect the problem. In this case, the **DO** loop will function incorrectly, since the **DO** loop variable will not increment properly. This problem can be detected by examining the value of the index variable in every iteration of the loop.

5. Errors in while loops are usually related to errors in the logical expression used to control their function. These errors may be detected by examining the **IF** statement of the while loop as described above.

3.6 SUMMARY

In Chapter 3 we have presented the basic types of FORTRAN branches and loops. The principal type of branch is the block **IF—ELSE IF—ELSE—END IF** structure. This structure is flexible. It can have as many **ELSE IF** clauses as needed to construct any desired test. Furthermore, block **IF** structures can be nested to produce more complex tests.

There are two basic types of loops in FORTRAN, the while loop and the **DO** (iterative or counting) loop. There is no actual while statement in standard FORTRAN 77, but one can be created using a block **IF** structure and a **GO TO** statement.[2] The while loop is used to repeat a section of code in cases where we do not know in advance how many times the loop must be repeated. The **DO** loop is used to repeat a section of code in cases where we know in advance how many times the loop should be repeated.

3.6.1 Summary of Good Programming Practice

The following guidelines should be adhered to when programming with branch or loop structures. If you follow them consistently, your code will contain fewer bugs, will be easier to debug, and will be more understandable to others who may need to work with it in the future.

1. Always indent code blocks in block **IF, DO,** and while structures to make them more readable.
2. Be cautious about testing for equality with real variables in an **IF** structure, since roundoff errors may cause two variables that should be equal to fail a test for equality. Instead, test to see if the variables are nearly equal within the roundoff error to be expected on the computer you are working with.
3. Use a while loop to repeat sections of code when you don't know in advance how often the loop will be executed.
4. Use a **DO** loop to repeat sections of code when you know in advance how often the loop will be executed.
5. Always use integer index variables and parameters in **DO** loops to avoid unexpected behavior caused by roundoff effects in calculations with real numbers.
6. Never attempt to modify the values of **DO** loop index or control variables while inside the loop.
7. Always terminate **DO** loops with a **CONTINUE** statement.

CHAPTER 3 KEY WORDS

Algorithm	Iterative loops
Alpha release	Loops
Beta release	Nested loops
Block **IF** structure	Pseudocode
Branches	Structured program
DO loop (iterative or counting loop)	Structures
Flowchart	Top-down design
IF-ELSE structure	Unconditional branch
IF-ELSE IF structure	While loop
Index	

---

[2]The **DO WHILE** structure is an extension to FORTRAN 77 that is a part of the FORTRAN 90 standard.

CHAPTER 3 SUMMARY OF FORTRAN STATEMENTS AND STRUCTURES

The following summary describes the FORTRAN statements and structures introduced in this chapter.

CONTINUE Statement:

```
k CONTINUE
```

Example:
```
100 CONTINUE
```

Description: The **CONTINUE** statement is a placeholder statement that does nothing. It is most commonly used as the termination statement for a **DO** loop.

DO Loop Structure:

```
DO k index = istart, iend, incr
    ...
k CONTINUE
```

Example:
```
DO 100 INDEX = 1, LSTVAL, 3
    ...
    ...
    ...
100 CONTINUE
```

Description: The **DO** loop is used to repeat a block of code a known number of times. During the first iteration of the **DO** loop, the variable *index* is set to the value *istart*. "The variable" is in roman type. *index* is incremented by *incr* in each successive loop until its value exceeds *iend,* at which time the loop terminates.

The loop variable *index* is incremented and tested *before* each loop, so the **DO** loop code is never executed at all if *istart*incr* > *iend*incr.*

DO WHILE Structure:

```
DO WHILE ( logical expression )
    ...
END DO
```

Example:
```
DO WHILE ( X .GE. 0. )
    ...
    ...
    ...
END DO
```

Description: The **DO WHILE** structure is used to repeat a block of code for as long as a specified *logical expression* is TRUE. It differs from a **DO** loop in that we do not know in advance how many times the loop will be repeated.

At the beginning of each pass through the loop, the *logical expression* is evaluated. If it is TRUE, the code in the loop is executed. If it is FALSE, execution skips to the next statement following the end of the loop.

The **DO WHILE** statement is an extension to FORTRAN 77 which is a part of the FORTRAN 90 standard.

GO TO Statement:

```
   GO TO k
```

Example:

```
   GO TO 100
      . . .
      . . .
100 CONTINUE
      . . .
```

Description: The **GO TO** statement causes execution to skip to the statement associated with the specified statement label.

This statement should be used with caution, since excessive use can make your code hard to read and debug. The primary use for the **GO TO** statement is in building while loop structures.

Logical Block IF Structure:

```
IF ( logical expression 1 ) THEN
    Block 1
ELSE IF ( logical expression 2 ) THEN
    Block 2
ELSE
    Block 3
END IF
```

Description: The **Logical Block IF** structure permits the execution of a code block based on the results of one or more logical expressions. If *logical expression 1* is TRUE, the first code block is executed, and then control jumps to the first statement after the end of the structure. If *logical expression 1* is FALSE, then *logical expression 2* is checked. If *logical expression 2* is TRUE, the second code block is executed, and then control jumps to the first statement after the end of the structure. If both logical expressions are FALSE, the third code block is executed, and then control jumps to the first statement after the end of the structure.

There must be one and only one **IF ( ) THEN** statement in a logical block **IF** structure. There may be any number of **ELSE IF** clauses (0 or more), and there may be at most one **ELSE** clause in the structure.

Logical IF Statement:

```
IF ( logical expression ) statement
```

Description: The Logical **IF** statement is a special case of the logical block **IF** structure. If *logical expression* is TRUE, then *statement* on the same line with the **IF** is executed, and then execution continues at the next line after the **IF** statement. If the expression is FALSE, then *statement* is skipped, and execution continues at the next line after the **IF** statement.

This statement is a holdover from FORTRAN 66. It may be used instead of the logical block **IF** structure if only one statement needs to be executed as a result of the logical condition.

WHILE Loop Structure:

```
k IF ( logical expression ) THEN
     ...
     ...
     ...
     GO TO k
  END IF
```

Example:

```
100 IF ( X .GE. 0. ) THEN
       ...
       ...
       ...
       GO TO 100
    END IF
```

Description: The while loop is used to repeat a block of code for as long as a specified *logical expression* is TRUE. It differs from a **DO** loop in that we do not know in advance how many times the loop will be repeated. When the first statement of the loop is executed with *logical expression* FALSE, execution skips to the next statement following the end of the loop.

CHAPTER 3 EXERCISES

1. The tangent function is defined as $\tan\theta = \sin\theta/\cos\theta$. This expression can be evaluated to solve for the tangent as long as the magnitude of $\cos\theta$ is not too near to 0. (If $\cos\theta$ is 0, evaluating the equation for $\tan\theta$ will produce a divide-by-zero error.) Assume that θ is given in degrees, and write FORTRAN statements to evaluate $\tan\theta$ as long as the magnitude of $\cos\theta$ is greater than or equal to 10^{-20}. If the magnitude of $\cos\theta$ is less than 10^{-20}, write out an error message instead.

2. Write the FORTRAN statements required to calculate $y(t)$ from the equation

$$y(t) = \begin{cases} -3t^2 + 5 & t \geq 0 \\ 3t^2 + 5 & t < 0 \end{cases}$$

for values of t between -9 and 9 in steps of 3.

3. Write the FORTRAN statements required to calculate and print out the squares of all the even integers between 0 and 50.

4. Write a FORTRAN program to evaluate the equation $y(x) = x^2 - 3x + 2$ for all values of x between -1 and 3, in steps of 0.1.

5. Write a FORTRAN program to calculate the factorial function, as defined in Example 3-5. Be sure to handle the special cases of 0! and of illegal input values.

6. The following FORTRAN statements are intended to alert a user to dangerously high oral thermometer readings (values are in degrees Fahrenheit). Are they correct or incorrect? If they are incorrect, explain why and correct them.

```
IF ( TEMP .LT. 97.5 ) THEN
   WRITE (*,*) 'Temperature below normal'
ELSE IF ( TEMP .GT. 97.5 ) THEN
   WRITE (*,*) 'Temperature normal'
ELSE IF ( TEMP .GT. 99.5 ) THEN
   WRITE (*,*) 'Temperature slightly high'
ELSE IF ( TEMP .GT. 103.0 ) THEN
   WRITE (*,*) 'Temperature dangerously high'
END IF
```

7. The cost of sending a package by an express delivery service is $10.00 for the first 2 lb, and $3.75 for each pound or fraction thereof over 2 lb. If the package weighs more than 70 lb, a $10.00 excess weight surcharge is added to the cost. No package over 100 lb will be accepted. Write a program that accepts the weight of a package in pounds and computes the cost of mailing the package. Be sure to handle the case of overweight packages.

8. Modify program STAT2 to use the **DO WHILE** structure instead of the FORTRAN 77 while structure currently in the program.

9. The following FORTRAN statements calculate the square root of the products of all numbers between 1 and 10, taken in any combination. Assume that I and J are integers, and RESULT is real. Is this code correct or incorrect? If it is incorrect, explain why and correct it.

```
      DO 1000 I = 1, 10
         DO 1010 J = 1, 10
            RESULT = SQRT ( REAL (I*J) )
            WRITE (*,*) 'SQRT(', I, '*', J, ') = ', RESULT
1000     CONTINUE
1010 CONTINUE
```

10. The inverse sine function ASIN(X) is only defined for the range $-1.0 \le X \le 1.0$. If X is outside this range, an error will occur when the function is evaluated. The following FORTRAN statements calculate the inverse sine of a number if it is in the proper range, and print an error message if it is not. Assume that X and INVSIN are real. Is this code correct or incorrect? If it is incorrect, explain why and correct it.

```
IF ( ABS(X) .LE. 1. ) THEN
    INVSIN = ASIN(X)
ELSE
    WRITE (*,*) X, ' is out of range!'
END IF
```

11. In Example 3-2, we wrote a program to evaluate the function $f(x, y)$ for any two user-specified values x and y, where the function $f(x, y)$ was defined as follows.

$$f(x, y) = \begin{cases} x + y & x \ge 0 \quad \text{and} \quad y \ge 0 \\ x + y^2 & x \ge 0 \quad \text{and} \quad y < 0 \\ x^2 + y & x < 0 \quad \text{and} \quad y \ge 0 \\ x^2 + y^2 & x < 0 \quad \text{and} \quad y < 0 \end{cases}$$

The problem was solved by using a single logical **IF** structure with four code blocks to calculate $f(x, y)$ for all possible combinations of x and y. Rewrite program FUNXY to use nested **IF** structures, where the outer structure evaluates the value of x and the inner structures evaluate the value of y.

12. What is the output of the following FORTRAN program for the input data sets specified below? Why? (Determine the answer in each case by following the logic of the program branches. If desired, you may check your work by actually running the program.)

```
PROGRAM ONE
LOGICAL L1, L2, L3, L4
WRITE (*,*) 'Enter L1 and L2:'
READ (*,*) L1, L2
L3 = L1 .OR. L2
L4 = L1 .AND. L2
IF ( L3 .AND. .NOT. L4 ) THEN
    WRITE (*,*) 'Both conditions are true...'
ELSE
    IF ( L3 ) THEN
        WRITE (*,*) 'Condition 1 is true...'
    END IF
    IF ( .NOT. L4 ) THEN
        WRITE (*,*) 'Condition 2 is true...'
    END IF
END IF
END
```

(*a*) Input data set 1:   T   F
(*b*) Input data set 2:   F   F
(*c*) Input data set 3:   T   T
(*d*) Input data set 4:   F   T

13. Examine the following **DO** statements and determine how many times each loop will be executed. (Assume that all loop index variables are integers.)

(*a*) `DO 32767 IRANGE = -32768, 32767`
(*b*) `DO 200 J = 100, 1, -10`
(*c*) `DO 1 KOUNT = 2, 3, 4`
(*d*) `DO 100 INDEX = -4, -7`
(*e*) `DO 101 I = -10, 10, 10`

14. How many times will the following while loop be executed? How do you know?

```
        PROGRAM AVE
        REAL VALUE
        INTEGER ICOUNT
        WRITE (*,*) 'Enter first value:'
        READ (*,*) VALUE
     1  IF ( VALUE .GE. 0. ) THEN
            SUM = SUM + VALUE
            ICOUNT = ICOUNT + 1
            WRITE (*,*) 'Enter next value:'
            READ (*,*) VALUE
            GO TO 1
        END IF
        WRITE (*,*) 'Average = ', SUM / REAL(ICOUNT)
        END
```

15. Examine the following **DO** loops and determine the value of IRES at the end of each of the loops. Assume that all variables are integers.

(*a*)
```
        IRES = 0
        DO 100 INDEX = -10, 10
            IRES = IRES + 1
    100 CONTINUE
```
(*b*)
```
        IRES = 0
        DO 100 INDEX1 = 1, 100, 5
            DO 90 INDEX2 = INDEX1, 10, 5
                IRES = IRES + INDEX2
     90     CONTINUE
    100 CONTINUE
```
(*c*)
```
        IRES = 0
        DO 100 INDEX = -10, 10
            IRES = IRES + INDEX
    100 CONTINUE
```

16. Modify program BALL from Example 3-7 to read in the acceleration due to gravity at a particular location, and to calculate the maximum range of the ball

for that acceleration. After modifying the program, run it with accelerations of -9.8, -9.7, and -9.6 m/sec^2. What effect does the reduction in gravitational attraction have on the range of the ball? What effect does the reduction in gravitational attraction have on the best angle θ at which to throw the ball?

17. Modify program BALL from Example 3-7 to read in the initial velocity with which the ball is thrown. After modifying the program, run it with initial velocities of 10, 20, and 30 m/sec. What effect does changing the initial velocity v_o have on the range of the ball? What effect does it have on the best angle θ at which to throw the ball?

18. Write a FORTRAN program to evaluate the function

$$y(x) = \ln \frac{1}{1-x}$$

for any user-specified value of x, where ln is the natural logarithm (logarithm to the base e). Write the program with a while loop, so that the program repeats the calculation for each legal value of x entered into the program. When an illegal value of x is entered, terminate the program.

19. The current flowing through the semiconductor diode shown in Figure 3-22 is given by the equation

$$i_D = I_O \left(e^{\frac{q v_D}{kT}} - 1 \right) \tag{3-11}$$

where

i_D = the voltage across the diode, in volts
v_D = the current flow through the diode, in amps
I_O = the leakage current of the diode, in amps
q = the charge on an electron, 1.602×10^{-19}
k = Boltzmann's constant, 1.38×10^{-23} J/K
T = temperature, in kelvins (K)

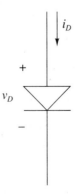

FIGURE 3-22 A semiconductor diode.

The leakage current I_O of the diode is 2.0 μA. Write a computer program to calculate the current flowing through this diode for all voltages from -1.0 to $+0.8$ V, in 0.1 steps. Repeat this process for the following temperatures: 75 and 100°F, and 125°F. Use the program of Example 2-4 to convert the temperatures from °F to kelvins (Figure 3-22).

20. Engineers often measure the ratio of two power measurements in *decibels,* or dB. The equation for the ratio of two power measurements in decibels is

$$dB = 10 \log_{10} \frac{P_2}{P_1} \tag{3-12}$$

where P_2 is the power level being measured, and P_1 is some reference power level. Assume that the reference power level P_1 is 1 W, and write a program that calculates the decibel level corresponding to power levels between 1 and 20 W, in 0.5-W steps.

21. Trigonometric functions are usually calculated on computers by using a *truncated infinite series*. An *infinite series* is an infinite set of terms that together add up to the value of a particular function or expression. For example, one infinite series used to evaluate the sine of a number is

$$\sin x = x - \frac{x^3}{3!} + \frac{x^5}{5!} - \frac{x^7}{7!} + \frac{x^9}{9!} + \ldots \tag{3-13a}$$

or

$$\sin x = \sum_{n=1}^{\infty} (-1)^{n-1} \frac{x^{2n-1}}{(2n-1)!} \tag{3-13b}$$

where x is in units of radians.

Since a computer does not have enough time to add an infinite number of terms for every sine that is calculated, the infinite series is *truncated* after a finite number of terms. The number of terms that should be kept in the series is just enough to calculate the function to the precision of the floating-point numbers on the computer on which the function is being evaluated. The truncated infinite series for $\sin x$ is

$$\sin x = \sum_{n=1}^{N} (-1)^{n-1} \frac{x^{2n-1}}{(2n-1)!} \tag{3-14}$$

where N is the number of terms to retain in the series.

Write a FORTRAN program that reads in a value for x in degrees, and then calculates the sine of x using the sine intrinsic function. Next, calculate the sine of x using Equation 3-14, with $N = 1, 2, 3, \ldots, 10$. Compare the true value of sin x with the values calculated using the truncated infinite series. How many terms are required to calculate sin x to the full accuracy of the machine?

22. The *geometric mean* of a set of numbers x_1 through x_n is defined as the nth root of the product of the numbers:

$$\text{geometric mean} = \sqrt[n]{x_1 \, x_2 \, x_3 \ldots x_n}$$

Write a FORTRAN program that will accept an arbitrary number of positive input values and calculate both the arithmetic mean (*i.e.*, the average) and the geometric mean of the numbers. Use a while loop to get the input values, and to terminate the inputs a user enters a negative number. Test your program by calculating the average and geometric mean of the four numbers 10, 5, 2, and 5.

23. The *root-mean-square* (rms) *average* is another way of calculating a mean for a set of numbers. The rms average of a series of numbers is the square root of the arithmetic mean of the squares of the numbers:

$$\text{rms average} = \sqrt{\frac{1}{N} \sum_{i=1}^{N} x_i^2} \qquad \text{(3-15)}$$

Write a FORTRAN program that accepts an arbitrary number of positive input values and calculate the rms average of the numbers. Prompt the user for the number of values to be entered, and use a **DO** loop to read in the numbers. Test your program by calculating the rms average of the four numbers 10, 5, 2, and 5.

24. The *harmonic mean* is yet another way of calculating a mean for a set of numbers. The harmonic mean of a set of numbers is given by the equation

$$\text{harmonic mean} = \frac{N}{\dfrac{1}{x_1} + \dfrac{1}{x_2} + \cdots + \dfrac{1}{x_N}} \qquad \text{(3-16)}$$

Write a FORTRAN program that will read in an arbitrary number of positive input values and calculate the harmonic mean of the numbers. Use any method that you desire to read in the input values. Test your program by calculating the harmonic mean of the four numbers 10, 5, 2, and 5.

25. Write a single FORTRAN program that calculates the arithmetic mean (average), rms average, geometric mean, and harmonic mean for a set of numbers. Use any method that you desire to read in the input values. Compare these values for each of the following sets of numbers:

(*a*) 4, 4, 4, 4, 4, 4, 4   (*c*) 4, 1, 4, 7, 4, 1, 7

(*b*) 4, 3, 4, 5, 4, 3, 5   (*d*) 1, 2, 3, 4, 5, 6, 7

26. When a ray of light passes from a region with an index of refraction n_1 into a region with a different index of refraction n_2, the light ray is bent (see Figure 3-23). The angle at which the light is bent is given by *Snell's law:*

$$n_1 \sin \theta_1 = n_2 \sin \theta_2 \qquad\qquad\qquad \textbf{(3-17)}$$

where θ_1 is the angle of incidence of the light in the first region, and θ_2 is the angle of incidence of the light in the second region. Using Snell's law, it is possible to predict the angle of incidence of a light ray in region 2 if the angle of incidence θ_1 in region 1 and the indices of refraction n_1 and n_2 are known. The equation to perform this calculation is

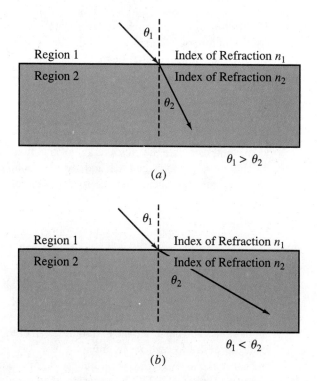

FIGURE 3-23   A ray of light bends as it passes from one medium into another one. (*a*) If the ray of light passes from a region with a low index of refraction into a region with a higher index of refraction, the ray of light bends more toward the vertical. (*b*) If the ray of light passes from a region with a high index of refraction into a region with a lower index of refraction, the ray of light bends away from the vertical.

$$\theta_2 = \sin^{-1}\left(\frac{n_1}{n_2} \sin \theta_1\right)$$ (3-18)

Write a FORTRAN program to calculate the angle of incidence in degrees of a light ray in region 2 given the angle of incidence θ_1 in region 1 and the indices of refraction n_1 and n_2. (*Note*: If $n_1 > n_2$, then for some angles θ_1, Equation 3-18 has no real solution because the absolute value of the quantity $(n_1/n_2 \sin \theta_1)$ is greater than 1.0. When this occurs, all light is reflected back into region 1, and no light passes into region 2 at all. Your program must be able to recognize and properly handle this condition.)

Basic I/O Concepts

In the previous chapters, we have read values into and written them out of our FORTRAN programs using list-directed **READ** and **WRITE** statements. List-directed input/output (I/O) statements are said to be in **free format**. Free format is specified by the second asterisk in the **READ (*,*)** and **WRITE (*,*)** statements. As we saw in the previous chapters, the results of writing out data in free format are not always pretty. There are often a large number of extra spaces in the output. In this chapter, we will learn how to write out data using *formats* which specify the exact way in which the numbers should be printed out.

Formats may be used either when writing data out or when reading it in. Since they are most useful during output, we will examine formatted **WRITE** statements first, and postpone formatted **READ** statements until a later section in the chapter.

The second major topic introduced in this chapter is disk file processing. We will learn the basics of how to read from and write to disk files. Advanced disk file processing will be postponed to Chapter 8, which deals with advanced I/O concepts.

4.1 THE **FORMAT** STATEMENT AND FORMATTED **WRITE** STATEMENTS

We normally use a **FORMAT** statement to specify the exact manner in which variables are to be printed out of a program. In general, a **FORMAT** statement can specify both the horizontal and the vertical position of the variables on the paper, and also the number of significant digits to be printed out. A typical formatted **WRITE** statement is shown below:

```
     WRITE (*,100) I, RESULT
 100 FORMAT (' The result for iteration ', I3,' is ', F7.3)
```

The number 100 which appears within the parentheses in the **WRITE** statement is the statement label associated with the **FORMAT** statement which describes how the values contained in I and RESULT are to be printed out. **I3** and **F7.3** are the **format descriptors** associated with variables I and RESULT, respectively. In this case, the **FORMAT** statement specifies that the program should first write out the phrase 'The result for iteration ', followed by the value of variable I. The format descriptor **I3** specifies that a space three characters wide should be used to print out the value of variable I. The value of I is followed by the phrase ' is ' and then the value of the variable RESULT. The format descriptor **F7.3** specifies that a space seven characters wide should be used to print out the value of variable RESULT, and that it should be printed with three digits to the right of the decimal point. The resulting output line is shown below, compared to the same line printed with free format.

```
The result for iteration  21 is   3.142                    Formatted
The result for iteration        21 is       3.141590   Free format
```

Notice that we are able to eliminate both extra spaces and undesired decimal places by using format statements. Note also that the value in variable RESULT was rounded before it was printed out in **F7.3** format. (Only the value printed out has been rounded; the contents of variable RESULT are unchanged.) Formatted I/O permits us to create neat output listings from our programs.

In the above example, each format descriptor was separated from its neighbors by commas. With a few exceptions, *multiple format descriptors in a single* FOR-MAT *statement must be separated by commas.*

4.2   OUTPUT DEVICES

To understand the structure of a **FORMAT** statement, we must know something about the **output devices** on which our data will be displayed. When we run a FORTRAN program, we see the output of the program displayed on an output device. There are many types of output devices that are used with computers. Some output devices produce permanent paper copies of the data, while others just display it temporarily for us to see. Common output devices include line printers, laser printers, and terminals.

The most common way to get a paper copy of the output of a program is on a **line printer.** A line printer is a type of printer that originally got its name from the fact that it prints output data a line at a time. Since it was the first common computer output device, FORTRAN output specifications were designed with it in mind. Other more modern output devices are generally built to be compatible with the line printer, so that the same output statement can be used for any of the devices.

A line printer prints on computer paper that is divided into pages on a continuous roll. There are perforations between the pages so that it is easy to separate them. The most common size of computer paper in the United States is 11 in. high by 14 7/8 in. wide. Each page is divided into a number of lines, and each line is divided into 132 columns, with one character per column. Since most line printers print ei-

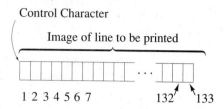

Control Character

Image of line to be printed

1 2 3 4 5 6 7   132   133

FIGURE 4-1 The output buffer is usually 133 characters long. The first
character is the control character, and the next 132 characters are
an image of what is to be printed on the line.

ther 6 lines per inch or 8 lines per inch, the printers can print either 60 or 72 lines per
page (note that this assumes a 0.5 in. margin at the top and the bottom of each page;
if the margin is made larger, fewer lines can be printed). The **FORMAT** statement
specifies where a line is to be printed on a page (vertical position), and also where
each variable is to be printed within the line (horizontal position).

The computer builds up a complete image of each line in memory before sending it to an output device. The computer memory containing the image of the line is
called the **output buffer.** The output buffer for a line printer is usually 133 characters wide. The first character in the buffer is known as the **control character;** it
specifies the vertical spacing for the line. The remaining 132 characters in the buffer
contain the data to be printed on that line (Figure 4-1).

The control character is not printed on the page by the line printer. Instead, it
provides vertical positioning control information to the printer. Table 4-1 shows the
vertical spacing resulting from different control characters.

TABLE 4-1   FORTRAN Control Characters

Control Character	*Action*
1	Skip to new page
Blank	Single spacing
0	Double spacing
+	No spacing (print over previous line)

A '1' character causes the printer to skip the remainder of the current page and print
the current line at the top of the next page. A blank character causes the printer to
print the current line right below the previous one, while a '0' character causes the
printer to skip a line before the current line is printed. A '+' character specifies no
spacing; in this case, the new line will overwrite the previous line. If any other char-

acter is used as the control character, the results are uncertain.[1] On most computers, the result will be single spacing, but don't count on that always being true!

For list-directed output **[WRITE (*,*)]**, a blank control character is automatically inserted at the beginning of each output buffer. Therefore, list-directed output is always printed in single-spaced lines.

The following **FORMAT** statements illustrate the use of the control character. They print a heading at the top of a new page, skip one line, and then print column headings for Table 4-1 below it.

```
      WRITE (*,100)
100 FORMAT ('1', 'This heading is at the top of a new page.')
      WRITE (*,110)
110 FORMAT ('0','  Control Character      Action ')
      WRITE (*,120)
120 FORMAT (' ','  ==================      ====== ')
```

The results of executing these FORTRAN statements are:

```
This heading is at the top of a new page.

Control Character      Action
==================      ======
```

where the lines represent the top and left edges of the paper.

You must be careful to avoid unpleasant surprises when writing output format statements. For example, the following statements behave in an unpredictable fashion.

```
      WRITE (*,100) N
100 FORMAT (I3)
```

The format descriptor **I3** specifies that we want to print the value of variable N in the first three characters of the output buffer. If the value of N is 25, the three positions are filled with b25 (where b denotes a blank). Because the first character is interpreted as a control character, the printer spaces down one line and prints out 25 in the first two columns of the new line. On the other hand, if N is 125, then the first three characters of the output buffer are filled with 125. Because the first character is interpreted as a control character, the printer *skips to a new page* and prints out 25 in the first two columns of the new line. This is certainly not what we intended!

---

[1] The FORTRAN 77 standard specifies that any other character should be treated as a blank, producing single-spaced output. However, some compilers assign special meanings to certain characters as an extension to the FORTRAN 77 standard. For example, some compilers define the '-' character to produce triple spacing. If you have such a character in the control character position, you might get single spacing on some computers, and triple spacing on others! It is safest to use *only* the control characters defined in the FORTRAN 77 standard.

You should be very careful not to write any format descriptors that include column 1, since they can produce erratic printing behavior and fail to display the correct results.

PROGRAMMING PITFALLS

Never write a format descriptor which includes column 1 of the output line. Erratic paging behavior and incorrectly displayed values may result if you do so.

To help avoid this error, it is a good idea to write out each control character separately in the **FORMAT** statement. For example, the following two **FORMAT** statements are equivalent:

```
100 FORMAT ('1','COUNT = ', I3)
100 FORMAT ('1COUNT = ', I3)
```

Each of these statements produces the same output buffer, containing a 1 in the control character position. However, the control character is more obvious in the first statement than it is in the second one.

■ **GOOD PROGRAMMING PRACTICE**

Write FORTRAN control characters separately from any other text in a FORMAT statement. This action highlights the control characters, making them more obvious.

4.3   FORMAT DESCRIPTORS

There are many different format descriptors. They fall into four basic categories:

1. Format descriptors which describe the *vertical position* of a line of text. (The control character mentioned previously is an example of this type of format descriptor.)
2. Format descriptors which describe the *horizontal position* of data in a line of text.
3. Format descriptors which describe the output format of a particular integer, real, logical, or character variable.
4. Format descriptors which control the repeated use of portions of a **FORMAT** statement.

We will deal with some common examples of format descriptors in this chapter. Other less common format descriptors will be postponed to a later chapter.

Five types of format descriptors are used to describe the types of variables we have studied so far. They are **I** for integer values, **F** and **E** for real (or floating-point) values, **L** for logical values, and **A** for character values.

4.3.1   Integer Output—the I Descriptor

The descriptor used to describe the display format of integer data is the **I** descriptor. It has the general form

$$rIw \quad \text{or} \quad rIw.m$$

where

I   indicates integer data

w   is the number of characters to use to display the integer data. This parameter is known as the **field width** of the descriptor.

r   is the **repetition indicator.** It indicates the number of times this descriptor will be used. For example, the format descriptor **3I5** means that there will be three consecutive integer variables output in **I5** format. The descriptor **3I5** is completely equivalent to the three descriptors **I5, I5, I5**. This field is optional; if it is absent, the format descriptor is used only once.

m   is the minimum number of digits to use when displaying the integer value. If the number does not have *m* digits, then leading zeros will be added to bring the display up to *m* digits. This field is optional.

Integer values are *right-justified* in their fields. This means that integers are printed out so that the last digit of the integer occupies the rightmost column of the field. If an integer is too large to fit into the field in which it is to be printed, then the field is filled with asterisks. For example, if the values of the integer variables INDEX, JUNK, and NUMBER are

```
INDEX  = -12
JUNK   = 4
NUMBER = -12345
```

then the following statements:

```
      WRITE (*,200) INDEX, INDEX+12, JUNK, NUMBER
      WRITE (*,210) INDEX, INDEX+12, JUNK, NUMBER
      WRITE (*,220) INDEX, INDEX+12, JUNK, NUMBER
200 FORMAT (' ', 2I5,   I6, I10 )
210 FORMAT (' ', 2I5.0, I6, I10.8 )
220 FORMAT (' ', 2I5.3, I6, I5 )
```

produce the output

```
       5    10   15   20   25   30
   ----|----|----|----|----|----|
    -12    0    4    -12345
    -12         4 -00012345
   -012  000    4*****
   ----|----|----|----|----|----|
       5    10   15   20   25   30
```

4.3.2 Real Output—the F Descriptor

One format descriptor used to describe the display format of real data is the **F** descriptor. It has the form

rF*w.d*

where

F   indicates real (floating-point) data presented in standard notation without
     an exponent
w   is the field width in which the data is to be displayed
d   is the number of digits to the right of the decimal point
r   is the repetition indicator. It indicates the number of times this descriptor
     will be used. This value is optional; if it is absent, the format descriptor is
     used only once.

Real values are printed *right-justified* within their fields. If necessary, the number will be rounded off before it is displayed. For example, suppose that the variable PI contains the value 3.141592. If this variable is displayed using the **F7.3** format descriptor, the displayed value is ⱕⱕ3.142. On the other hand, if the displayed number includes more significant digits than the internal representation of the number, extra zeros will be appended to the right of the decimal point. If the variable PI is displayed with an **F10.8** format descriptor, the resulting value is 3.14159200.

If a real number is too large to fit into the field in which it is to be printed, the field is filled with asterisks.

For example, if the variables A, B, and C are

```
A = -12.3
B = .123
C = 123.456
```

then the statements

```
      WRITE (*,200) A, B, C
      WRITE (*,210) A, B, C
200 FORMAT (' ', 2F6.3, F8.3 )
210 FORMAT (' ', 3F10.2 )
```

will produce the output

```
     5    10   15   20   25   30
----|----|----|----|----|----|
****** 0.123 123.456
   -12.30      0.12    123.46
----|----|----|----|----|----|
     5    10   15   20   25   30
```

4.3.3 Real Output—the E Descriptor

Real data can also be printed in **scientific notation** using the **E** descriptor. Scientific notation is a popular way for scientists and engineers to display very large or very small numbers. It consists of expressing a number as a normalized value between 1 and 10 multiplied by 10 raised to a power.

To understand the convenience of scientific notation, let's consider the following two examples from chemistry and physics. *Avogadro's number* is the number of atoms in a mole of a substance. It can be written out as 602,000,000,000,000,000,000,000 or it can be expressed in scientific notation as 6.02×10^{23}. On the other hand, the charge on an electron is 0.0000000000000000001602 coulombs. This number can be expressed in scientific notation as 1.602×10^{-19}. Scientific notation is clearly a much more convenient way to write these numbers!

The E format descriptor has the form

rEw.d

where

   E   indicates real (floating-point) data presented in scientific notation (with an exponent)

   w   is the field width in which the data is to be displayed

   d   is the number of digits to the right of the decimal point

   r   is the **repetition indicator.** It indicates the number of times this descriptor is used. This value is optional; if it is absent, the format descriptor is used only once.

Unlike normal scientific notation, the real values displayed with the **E** descriptor are normalized to a range between 0.1 and 1.0. That is, they are displayed as a number between 0.1 and 1.0 multiplied by a power of 10. For example, the standard scientific notation for the number 4096.0 would be 4.096×10^{3}, while the computer output with the **E** descriptor would be 0.4096×10^{4}. Since it is not easy to represent exponents on a line printer, the computer output would appear on the printer as 0.4096E+04.

If a real number is too large to fit into the field in which it is to be printed, then the field is filled with asterisks. You should be especially careful with field sizes when working with the **E** format descriptor, since many items must be considered when sizing the output field. For example, suppose that we want to print out a variable in the **E** format with four significant digits of accuracy. Then a field width of **11** characters is required, as shown below: 1 for the sign of the mantissa, 2 for the zero and decimal point, 4 for the actual mantissa, 1 for the **E**, 1 for the sign of the exponent, and 2 for the exponent itself.

   ± 0.ddddE ± ee

In general, the width of an **E** format descriptor field must satisfy the expression

$$w \geq d + 7 \tag{4-1}$$

or the field may be filled with asterisks.[2]

---

[2] If the number to be displayed in the field is positive, then the field width *w* need only be 6 characters larger than *d*. If the number is negative, an extra character is needed for the minus sign. Hence, in general *w* must be $\geq d + 7$. Also, note that some compilers suppress the leading zero, so that one less column is required.

For example, if the variables A, B, and C are given by

```
A = 1.2346E6
B = 0.001
C = -77.7E10
```

then the statements

```
      WRITE (*,200) A, B, C
200 FORMAT (' ', 2E14.4, E12.6 )
```

produce the output

```
    5    10   15   20   25   30   35   40
----|----|----|----|----|----|----|----|
    0.1235E+07    0.1000E-02***********
----|----|----|----|----|----|----|----|
    5    10   15   20   25   30   35   40
```

Notice that the third field is all asterisks, since the format descriptor does not satisfy Equation (4-1).

4.3.4 Scale Factors—the P Descriptor

As we mentioned above, the output of the **E** format descriptor doesn't exactly match conventional scientific notation. Conventional scientific notation expresses a number as a value between 1.0 and 10.0 times a power of 10, while the **E** format expresses the number as a value between 0.1 and 1.0 times a power of 10.

We can make the computer output match conventional scientific notation by adding a special format descriptor called a **scale factor** to the format statement. A scale factor has the form

nP

where

P   is the scale factor
n is the number of places by which to shift the decimal point

The **P** scale factor may precede either **E** or **F** format descriptors. The general form of the descriptors with a scale factor are

nPrF$w.d$ and nPrE$w.d$

With the **F** format descriptor, the **P** scale factor causes the displayed number to be multiplied by 10^n. With the **E** format descriptor, the **P** scale factor causes the fractional part of the displayed number to be multiplied by 10^n, and the exponent to be decreased by n.

Once a scale factor has been specified on any **E** or **F** format descriptor, the same scale factor is applied to all subsequent **E** and **F** format descriptors within the same **FORMAT** statement. If you do not want the scale factor to be applied to some later numbers in the same **FORMAT** statement, you should explicitly cancel it by using the **0P** option before the format descriptors for those numbers.

To illustrate the use of scale factors, suppose that integer variable I and real variables A, B, and C are defined as follows:

```
I = 100
A = 1.2346E6
B = 0.001
C = -1024.
```

then the statements

```
        WRITE (*,200) I, A, B, C, I
        WRITE (*,210) I, A, B, C, I
        WRITE (*,220) I, A, B, C, I
200 FORMAT (' ', I5, 2E15.4, F15.2, I5)
210 FORMAT (' ', I5, 1P2E15.4, F15.2, I5)
220 FORMAT (' ', I5, -1P2E15.4, 0PF15.2, I5)
```

will produce the output

```
     5   10   15   20   25   30   35   40   45   50   55   60
 ----|----|----|----|----|----|----|----|----|----|----|----|
     100     0.1235E+07     0.1000E-02          -1024.00   100
     100     1.2346E+06     1.0000E-03         -10240.00   100
     100     0.0123E+08     0.0100E-01          -1024.00   100
 ----|----|----|----|----|----|----|----|----|----|----|----|
     5   10   15   20   25   30   35   40   45   50   55   60
```

Notice that the **P** scale factor can shift the decimal point in either direction, depending on the sign of *n*. Notice also that *the* **P** *scale factor has affected all* **E** *and* **F** *format descriptors after it in the same* **FORMAT** *statement,* unless canceled by a **0P** scale factor. Finally, note that the **I** format descriptor was not affected by the presence of the scale factor at all.

It is a good idea to use the **1P** scale factor with **E** format data, since the user will be presented with output values in the familiar scientific notation format. However, it is a very bad idea to use a scale factor with **F** format data, since the number displayed will not be the true value inside the program, and a program user could be confused by the printed output value. Therefore, you should be careful to cancel any scale factors in effect before printing out data in the **F** format.

■   **GOOD PROGRAMMING PRACTICE**

When displaying very large or very small numbers, use the **1P** scale factor with the **E** format descriptor to cause them to be displayed in conventional scientific notation. This display will help a reader to quickly understand the output numbers.

PROGRAMMING PITFALLS

Never use a scale factor with the **F** format descriptor, since the number printed out is not the number actually in memory within the computer. This can lead to confusion on the part of both program users and other programmers trying to maintain your software. Cancel any scale factors in effect before displaying real data with the **F** descriptor.

4.3.5 Logical Output—the L Descriptor

The descriptor used to display logical data has the form

> rLw

where

L	indicates logical data
w	is the field width in which the data is to be displayed
r	is the repetition indicator. It indicates the number of times this descriptor is used. This value is optional; if it is absent, the format descriptor is used only once.

The value of a logical variable can only be TRUE or FALSE. The output of logical variable is either a T or an F, right-justified in the output field.

For example, if the logical variables OUTPUT and DEBUG are given by

```
OUTPUT = .TRUE.
DEBUG  = .FALSE.
```

then the statements

```
      WRITE (*,200) OUTPUT, DEBUG
200 FORMAT (' ', 2L5 )
```

produce the output

```
    5    10    15    20    25    30    35    40
----|----|----|----|----|----|----|----|
    T     F
----|----|----|----|----|----|----|----|
    5    10    15    20    25    30    35    40
```

4.3.6 Character Output—the A Descriptor

Character data is displayed using the **A** format descriptor.

> rA   or rAw

where

A   indicates character data

w   is the field width in which the data is to be displayed. This value is optional; if it is absent, the number of characters displayed is equal to the length of the character data being displayed.

r   is the repetition indicator. This value is optional; if it is absent, the format descriptor is used only once.

The *r*A descriptor displays character data in a field whose width is the same as the number of characters being displayed, while the *r*A*w* descriptor displays character data in a field of fixed width *w*. If the width *w* of the field is longer than the length of the character variable, the variable is printed out *right-justified* in the field. If the width of the field is shorter than the length of the character variable, only the first *w* characters of the variable are printed out in the field.

For example, if the character variable STRING is defined as

```
CHARACTER*17 STRING
STRING = 'This is a string.'
```

then the statements

```
      WRITE (*,10) STRING
      WRITE (*,11) STRING
      WRITE (*,12) STRING
10 FORMAT (' ', A)
11 FORMAT (' ', A20)
12 FORMAT (' ', A6)
```

will produce the output

```
      5    10   15   20   25   30   35   40
   ----|----|----|----|----|----|----|----|
This is a string.
    This is a string.
This i
   ----|----|----|----|----|----|----|----|
      5    10   15   20   25   30   35   40
```

4.3.7 Horizontal Positioning—the X and T Descriptors

Two format descriptors are available to control the spacing of data in the output buffer, and therefore on the final output line. They are the **X** descriptor, which inserts spaces into the buffer, and the **T** descriptor, which "tabs" over to a specific column in the buffer. The **X** descriptor has the form

*n*X

where

X   indicates that we are inserting blanks

n   is the number of blanks to insert

It is used to *add one or more blanks* between two values on the output line. The **T** descriptor has the form

    T*c*

where

    T   indicates the "tab" descriptor
    c   is the column number in the output buffer at which to begin the next for-
            mat descriptor

It is used to *jump directly to a specific column* in the output buffer. The **T** descriptor works much like a "tab" character on a typewriter, except that it is possible to jump to any position in the output line, even if we are already past that position in the **FORMAT** statement.

For example, suppose that the character variables FIRST, MI, LAST, and CLASS, and the integer variable GRADE are defined as follows:

```
CHARACTER*10 FIRST
CHARACTER*1  MI
CHARACTER*16 LAST
CHARACTER*9  CLASS
INTEGER      GRADE
```

and that they contain the values shown below.

```
FIRST = 'JAMES'
MI    = 'R'
LAST  = 'JOHNSON'
CLASS = 'COSC 2301'
GRADE = 92
```

Then the statements

```
     WRITE (*,100) FIRST, MI, LAST, GRADE, CLASS
100 FORMAT (1X, A10, 1X, A1, 1X, A10, 4X, I3, T51, A9)
```

produce the output

```
      5   10   15   20   25   30   35   40   45   50   55   60
----|----|----|----|----|----|----|----|----|----|----|----|
JAMES       R JOHNSON            92                 COSC 2301
----|----|----|----|----|----|----|----|----|----|----|----|
      5   10   15   20   25   30   35   40   45   50   55   60
```

The first **1X** descriptor produces a blank control character, so this output line is printed on the next line of the printer. The first name begins in column 1, the middle initial begins in column 12, the last name begins in column 14, the grade begins in column 28, and course name begins in column 50. (The course name begins in column 51 of the buffer, but it is printed in column 50, since the first character in the output buffer is the control character.) This same output structure could have been created with the following statements.

```
      WRITE (*,100) FIRST, MI, LAST, CLASS, GRADE
100 FORMAT (1X, A10, T13, A1, T15, A10, T51, A9, T29, I3)
```

Note that the middle initial begins in column 13 of the output buffer. This causes it to be printed in column 12 of the output line, since the first character in the output buffer is the control character. In this example, we are actually jumping backward in the output line when we print out the grade.

Since you may freely move anywhere in the output buffer with the **T** descriptor, it is possible to accidentally overwrite portions of your output data before the line is printed out. For example, if we change the tab descriptor for CLASS from **T51** to **T17**

```
      WRITE (*,100) FIRST, MI, LAST, CLASS, GRADE
100 FORMAT (1X, A10, T13, A1, T15, A10, T17, A9, T29, I3)
```

the program will produce the following output:

```
     5    10    15    20    25    30    35    40    45    50    55    60
- - - -|- - - -|- - - -|- - - -|- - - -|- - - -|- - - -|- - - -|- - - -|- - - -|- - - -|- - - -|
JAMES        R JOCOSC 2301    92
- - - -|- - - -|- - - -|- - - -|- - - -|- - - -|- - - -|- - - -|- - - -|- - - -|- - - -|- - - -|
     5    10    15    20    25    30    35    40    45    50    55    60
```

PROGRAMMING PITFALLS

When using the **T** descriptor, be careful to make certain that your fields do not overlap.

4.3.8   Repeating Groups of Format Descriptors

We have seen that many individual format descriptors can be repeated by preceding them with a repetition indicator. For example, the format descriptor **2I10** is the same as the pair of descriptors **I10, I10.**

It is also possible to repeat *whole groups* of format descriptors by enclosing the whole group within parentheses and placing a repetition count in front of the parentheses. For example, the following two **FORMAT** statements are equivalent:

```
320 FORMAT ( 1X, I6, I6, F10.2, F10.2, I6, F10.2, F10.2 )
320 FORMAT ( 1X, I6, 2(I6, 2F10.2) )
```

Groups of format descriptors may be *nested* if desired. For example, the following two **FORMAT** statements are equivalent:

```
330 FORMAT ( 1X, I6, F10.2, A, F10.2, A, I6, F10.2, A, F10.2, A )
330 FORMAT ( 1X, 2(I6, 2(F10.2,A)) )
```

However, don't go overboard with nesting. The more complicated you make your **FORMAT** statements, the harder it is for you or someone else to understand and debug them.

4.3.9 Changing Output Lines—the Slash (/) Descriptor

The slash (/) descriptor causes the current output buffer to be sent to the printer, and a new output buffer to be started. With slash descriptors, a single **WRITE** statement can display output values on more than one line. Although there are other ways to advance to a new line with format descriptors, the slash descriptor is special in that it lets the data on different lines be output in *different* formats. Several slashes can be used together to skip several lines. The slash is one of the special descriptors that does not have to be separated from other descriptors by commas. However, you may use commas if you wish.

For example, suppose that we need to print out the results of an experiment in which we have measured the amplitude and phase of a signal at a certain time and depth. Assume that the integer variable INDEX is 10 and the real variables TIME, DEPTH, AMP, and PHASE are 300., 1250., 850.65, and 30., respectively. Then the statements

```
      WRITE (*,100) INDEX, TIME, DEPTH, AMP, PHASE
  100 FORMAT ('1',T20,'Results for Test Number ',I3,///,
     *   1X,'Time       = ',F7.0/,1X,'Depth      = ',F7.1,' feet',/,
     *   1X,'Amplitude = ', F8.2/,
     *   1X,'Phase      = ',F7.1)
```

generate seven separate output buffers. The first buffer contains a '**1**' as the control character, so it skips to a new page, and puts a title on the page. The next two output buffers are empty, so two blank lines are printed. The final four output buffers have a blank control character, so the four values for **TIME, DEPTH, AMP,** and **PHASE** are printed on successive lines. The resulting output is

```
                      Results for Test Number 10


Time       =    300.
Depth      = 1250.0 feet
Amplitude =   850.65
Phase      =    30.2
```

Notice the **1X** descriptors after each slash. These descriptors place a blank in the control character of each output buffer, to ensure that the output advances by one line between buffers. Also, note that some slashes were separated from adjacent descriptors by commas and some were not. The output behavior is the same in either case.

4.3.10 How Format Statements Are Used

Most FORTRAN compilers verify the syntax of **FORMAT** statements at compilation time, but do not otherwise process them. Instead, they are saved unchanged as a character string within the compiled program. When the program is executed, the characters in the **FORMAT** statement are used as a template to guide the operation of the formatted **WRITE.**

At execution time, the list of output variables associated with the **WRITE** statement is processed together with the format of the statement. The program begins at the left end of the variable list and the left end of the **FORMAT** statement, and scans from left to right, associating the first variable in the output list with the first format descriptor in the format statement, etc. The variables in the output list must be of the same type and in the same order as the format descriptors in the format statement, or a run-time error will occur. For example, the program in Figure 4-2 will compile and link correctly, since all the statements in it are legal FORTRAN statements, and the program doesn't check for correspondence between the format descriptors and the data types until it runs. However, it will abort at run-time, when the check shows a real format descriptor corresponding to an integer variable.

```
C:\BOOK\FORT>fl fig4-2.for
Microsoft (R) FORTRAN Optimizing Compiler Version 5.10.0017
Copyright (c) Microsoft Corp 1982-1991. All rights reserved.

fig4-2.for
                                                PAGE  1
                                                05-23-91
                                                20:37:05

Line#  Source Line    Microsoft FORTRAN Optimizing Compiler Version 5.00.03

    1        PROGRAM FORMAT
    2        IMPLICIT NONE
    3        INTEGER I, J
    4        I = 10
    5        J = 20
    6        WRITE (*,100) I, J
    7    100 FORMAT ( I10, F10.0 )
    8        END


main  Local Symbols

Name                        Class   Type        Size  Offset

I . . . . . . . . . . . . . local   INTEGER*4      4  0002
J . . . . . . . . . . . . . local   INTEGER*4      4  0006


Global Symbols

Name                        Class   Type        Size  Offset

main. . . . . . . . . . . . FSUBRT  ***         ***   0000
```

```
Code size = 009c (156)
Data size = 0015 (21)
Bss size  = 000a (10)

No errors detected

Microsoft (R) Segmented-Executable Linker  Version 5.15
Copyright (C) Microsoft Corp 1984-1991.  All rights reserved.

Object Modules [.OBJ]: fig4-2.OBJ
Run File [fig4-2.exe]: fig4-2.EXE
List File [NUL.MAP]: NUL
Libraries [.LIB]:
Definitions File [NUL.DEF]: ;

C:\BOOK\FORT>fig4-2

fig4-2.for(6) : run-time error F6207: WRITE(CON)
- I edit descriptor expected for INTEGER
```

FIGURE 4-2   A FORTRAN program showing a run-time error resulting from a data/format descriptor mismatch.

PROGRAMMING PITFALLS

Make sure that there is a one-to-one correspondence between the types of the data in a **WRITE** statement and the types of the format descriptors in the associated **FORMAT** statement, or your program will fail at execution time.

As the program moves from left to right through the variable list of a **WRITE** statement, it also scans from left to right through the associated **FORMAT** statement. However, the order in which the contents of a **FORMAT** statement are used may be modified by the inclusion of repetition counters and parentheses. **FORMAT** statements are scanned according to the following rules:

1. **FORMAT** *statements are scanned in order from left to right.* The first variable format descriptor in the **FORMAT** statement is associated with the first value in the output list of the **WRITE** statement, and so forth. The type of each format descriptor must match the type of the data being output. In the example shown below, descriptor **I5** is associated with variable I, **I10** with variable J, **I15** with variable K, and **F10.2** with variable A.

   ```
       WRITE (*,10) I, J, K, A
    10 FORMAT (1X, I5, I10, I15, F10.2)
   ```

2. *If a format descriptor has a repetition count associated with it, the descriptor will be used the number of times specified in the repetition count before the next descriptor will be used.* In the example shown below, descriptor **I5** is asso-

ciated with variable I, and again with variable J. After it has been used twice, **I10** is associated with variable K, and **F10.2** with variable A.

```
    WRITE (*,20) I, J, K, A
20 FORMAT (1X, 2I5, I10, F10.2)
```

3. *If a group of format descriptors included within parentheses has a repetition count associated with it, the entire group will be used the number of times specified in the repetition count before the next descriptor will be used.* Each descriptor within the group is used in order from left to right during each repetition. In the example shown below, descriptor **F10.2** is associated with variable A. Next, the group in parentheses is used twice, so **I5** is associated with I, **E14.6** is associated with B, **I5** is associated with J, and **E14.6** is associated with C. Finally, **F10.2** is associated with D.

```
    WRITE (*,30) A, I, B, J, C, D
30 FORMAT (1X, F10.2, 2(I5, E14.6), F10.2)
```

4. If the **WRITE** statement runs out of variables before the end of the **FORMAT** statement, *the use of the **FORMAT** statement stops at the first format descriptor without a corresponding variable, or at the end of the **FORMAT** statement, whichever comes first.* For example, the statements

```
    M = 1
    WRITE (*,40) M
40 FORMAT (1X, 'M = ', I3, 'N = ', I4, 'O = ', F7.2)
```

produce the output

```
    5    10   15   20   25   30
----|----|----|----|----|----|
M =    1 N =
----|----|----|----|----|----|
    5    10   15   20   25   30
```

since the use of the **FORMAT** statement stops at **I4,** which is the first unmatched format descriptor. Similarly, the statements

```
    VOLTAGE = 13800.
    WRITE (*,50) VOLTAGE / 1000.
50 FORMAT (1X, 'VOLTAGE = ', F8.1, ' kV')
```

produce the output

```
    5    10   15   20   25   30
----|----|----|----|----|----|
VOLTAGE =      13.8 kV
----|----|----|----|----|----|
    5    10   15   20   25   30
```

since there are no unmatched descriptors, and the use of the **FORMAT** statement stops at the end of the statement.

5. If the scan reaches the end of the **FORMAT** statement before the **WRITE** statement runs out of values, the program sends the current output buffer to the printer, and starts over *at the rightmost open parenthesis in the* **FORMAT** *statement that is not preceded by a repetition count.* For example, the statements

```
      J = 1
      K = 1
      L = 3
      M = 4
      N = 5
      WRITE (*,60) J, K, L, M, N
   60 FORMAT (1X,'VALUE = ', I3)
```

produce the output

```
     5    10   15   20   25   30
 ----|----|----|----|----|----|
 VALUE =   1
 VALUE =   2
 VALUE =   3
 VALUE =   4
 VALUE =   5
 ----|----|----|----|----|----|
     5    10   15   20   25   30
```

When the program reaches the end of the **FORMAT** statement after it prints J with the **I3** descriptor, it sends that output buffer to the printer and goes back to the rightmost open parenthesis not preceded by a repetition count. In this case, the rightmost open parenthesis without a repetition count is the opening parenthesis of the statement, so the entire statement is used again to print K, L, M, and N. By contrast, the statements

```
      J = 1
      K = 2
      L = 3
      M = 4
      N = 5
      WRITE (*,60) J, K, L, M, N
   60 FORMAT (1X,'VALUE = ',/, (1X,'New Line',2(3X,I5)))
```

produce the output

```
     5    10   15   20   25   30
 ----|----|----|----|----|----|
 VALUE =
 New Line      1      2
 New Line      3      4
 New Line      5
 ----|----|----|----|----|----|
     5    10   15   20   25   30
```

In this case, the entire **FORMAT** statement is used to print values J and K. Since the rightmost open parenthesis not preceded by a repetition count is the one just before "**1X,'New Line'**", that part of the statement is used again to print L, M, and N. Note that the open parenthesis associated with (3X,I5) was ignored because it had a repetition count associated with it.

We discuss additional formatting features later on in Chapter 8, which deals with advanced I/O features.

EXAMPLE   4-1   *Generating a Table of Information*   A good way to illustrate the use of formatted **WRITE** statements is to generate and print out a table of data. The example program shown generates the square roots, squares, and cubes of all integers between 1 and 10, and presents the data in a table with appropriate headings.

```
      PROGRAM TABLE
C
C Purpose:
C   To illustrate the use of formatted WRITE statements.  This
C   program generates a table containing the square roots, squares,
C   and cubes of all integers between 1 and 10.  The table includes
C   a title and column headings.
C
C Record of revisions:
C     Date       Programmer            Description of change
C     ====       ==========            =====================
C   05/12/91  S. J. Chapman            Original code
C
C List of variables:
C   CUBE    -- The cube of I
C   I       -- Index variable
C   SQUARE  -- The square of I
C   SQOOT   -- The square root of I
C
      IMPLICIT NONE
C
C   Declare the variables used in this program.
C
      INTEGER    CUBE, I, SQUARE
      REAL       SQROOT
C
C   Print the title of the table on a new page.
C
      WRITE (*,100)
  100 FORMAT ('1', T3, 'Table of Square Roots, Squares, and Cubes')
C
C   Print the column headings.
C
```

```
       WRITE (*,110)
  110 FORMAT ('0',T4,'Number',T13,'Square Root',T29,'Square',T39,'Cube')
       WRITE (*,120)
  120 FORMAT (1X,T4,'======',T13,'============',T29,'======',T39,'===='/)
C
C    Generate the required values, and print them out.
C
       DO 10 I = 1, 10
C
          SQROOT = SQRT ( REAL(I) )
          SQUARE = I**2
          CUBE   = I**3
C
          WRITE (*,130) I, SQROOT, SQUARE, CUBE
  130     FORMAT (T4, I4, T13, F10.6, T27, I6, T37, I6)
C
   10 CONTINUE
       END
```

This program uses the tab format descriptor to set up neat columns of data for the table. When this program is compiled and executed on a PC, the result is

```
C:\BOOK\FORT>table

Table of Square Roots, Squares, and Cubes

   Number     Square Root      Square   Cube
   ======     ============     ======   ====

      1        1.000000          1        1
      2        1.414214          4        8
      3        1.732051          9       27
      4        2.000000         16       64
      5        2.236068         25      125
      6        2.449490         36      216
      7        2.645751         49      343
      8        2.828427         64      512
      9        3.000000         81      729
     10        3.162278        100     1000  ●
```

EXAMPLE 4-2 *Charge on a Capacitor*   A *capacitor* is an electrical device that stores electric charge. It essentially consists of two flat plates with an insulating material (the *dielectric*) between them (see Figure 4-3). The capacitance of a capacitor is defined as

$$C = \frac{Q}{V} \qquad\qquad\qquad \text{(4-2)}$$

where Q is the amount of charge stored in a capacitor in units of coulombs (C) and V is the voltage between the two plates of the capacitor in volts. The units of capacitance are farads (F), with 1 F = 1 C/V. When a charge is present on the plates of the

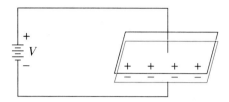

FIGURE 4-3   A capacitor consists of two metal plates separated by an insulating material.

capacitor, there is an electric field between the two plates. The energy stored in this electric field is given by the equation

$$E = \frac{1}{2}CV^2$$
                                                                        (4-3)

where E is the energy in joules. Write a program that will perform one of the following calculations:

1. For a known capacitance and voltage, calculate the charge on the plates, the number of electrons on the plates, and the energy stored in the electric field.
2. For a known charge and voltage, calculate the capacitance of the capacitor, the number of electrons on the plates, and the energy stored in the electric field.

SOLUTION   This program must be able to ask the user which calculation he or she wishes to perform, read in the appropriate values for that calculation, and write out the results in a reasonable format. Note that this problem will require us to work with very small and very large numbers, so we will have to pay special attention to the **FORMAT** statements in the program. For example, capacitors are typically rated in microfarads (μF or 10^{-6} F) or picofarads (pF or 10^{-12} F), and there are 6.241461×10^{18} electrons per coulomb of charge.

1. State the problem.
The problem may be succinctly stated as follows:

   (*a*) For a known capacitance and voltage, calculate the charge on the plates of a capacitor, the number of electrons stored on the plates, and the energy stored in the electric field between the plates.
   (*b*) For a known charge and voltage, calculate the capacitance of the capacitor, the number of electrons stored on the plates of the capacitor, and the energy stored in the electric field between the plates.

2. Define the inputs and outputs.
There are two possible sets of input values to this program:

   (*a*) Capacitance in farads and voltage in volts, or
   (*b*) Charge in coulombs and voltage in volts

The outputs from the program in either mode will be the capacitance of the capacitor, the voltage across the capacitor, the charge on the plates of the capacitor, and the number of electrons on the plates of the capacitor. The output must be printed out in a reasonable and understandable format.

3. Describe the algorithm.

This program can be broken down into four major steps:

```
Decide which calculation is required
Get the input data for that calculation
Calculate the unknown quantities
Write out the capacitance, voltage, charge and number of elec-
    trons
```

The first major step of the program is to decide which calculation is required. There are two types of calculations: type 1 requires capacitance and voltage, while type 2 requires charge and voltage. We must prompt the user for the type of input data, read the answer, and then read in the appropriate data. The pseudocode for these steps is:

```
Prompt user for the type of calculation ITYPE
Read ITYPE
WHILE ITYPE <> 1 and ITYPE <> 2
    Tell user of invalid value
    Read ITYPE
End of WHILE

IF ITYPE = 1 THEN
    Prompt the user for the capacitance C in farads
    Read capacitance C
    Prompt the user for the voltage V in volts
    Read voltage V
ELSE IF ITYPE = 2 THEN
    Prompt the user for the charge CHARGE in coulombs
    Read charge CHARGE
    Prompt the user for the voltage V in volts
    Read voltage V
END IF
```

Note that we have to read the first ITYPE value before the loop starts so that the **WHILE** loop can have a value to test the first time.

Next, we must calculate unknown values. For type 1 calculations, the unknown values are charge, the number of electrons, and the energy in the electric field, while for type 2 calculations, the unknown values are capacitance, the number of electrons, and the energy in the electric field. The pseudocode for this step is shown below.

```
IF ITYPE = 1 THEN
    CHARGE ← C * V
ELSE
    C ← CHARGE / V
END IF
ELECTR ← CHARGE * ELEPCH
ENERGY ← 0.5 * C * V**2
```

where ELEPCH is the number of electrons per coulomb of charge (6.241461×10^{18}). Finally, we must write out the results in a useful format.

```
Write out CAP, CHARGE, V, ELECTR, ENERGY
```

The flowchart for this program is shown in Figure 4-4.

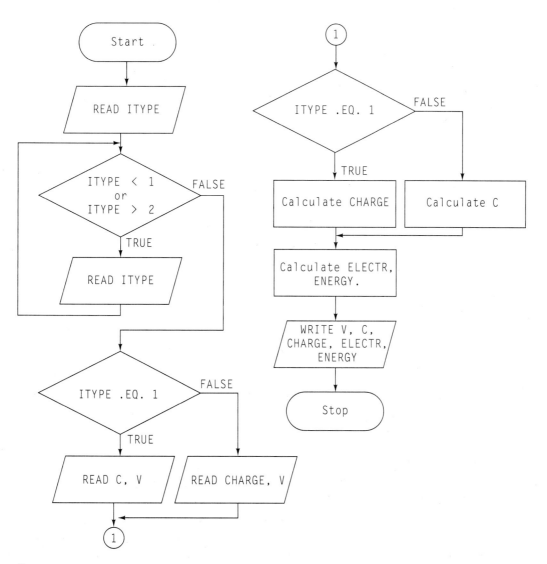

FIGURE 4-4 Flowchart for the program to calculate information about a capacitor.

4. Turn the algorithm into FORTRAN statements.

The final FORTRAN program is shown in Figure 4-5.

```
      PROGRAM CAP
C
C  Purpose:
C     To calculate the behavior of a capacitor as follows:
C     1.  If capacitance and voltage are known, calculate
C         charge, number of electrons, and energy stored.
C     2.  If charge and voltage are known, calculate capa-
C         citance, number of electrons, and energy stored.
C
C  Record of revisions:
C     Date           Programmer          Description of change
C     ====           ==========          =====================
C  05/05/91       S. J. Chapman          Original code
C
C  List of variables:
C     C       The capacitance of the capacitor, in farads.
C     CHARGE -- The charge on the capacitor, in coulombs.
C     ELECTR -- The number of electrons on the plates of the capacitor
C     ELEPCH -- The number of electrons per coulomb of charge
C     ENERGY -- The energy stored in the electric field
C     ITYPE  -- The type of input data available for the calculation:
C               1:  C and V
C               2:  CHARGE and V
C     V      -- The voltage on the capacitor
C
      IMPLICIT NONE
C
C  Declare the variables used in this program.
C
      INTEGER ITYPE
      REAL    C,   CHARGE, ELECTR
      REAL    ELEPCH, ENERGY, V
C
C  Number of electrons per coulomb
C
      DATA ELEPCH / 6.241461E18 /
C
C  Prompt user and get type of input data available.
C
      WRITE (*, 100)
 100  FORMAT (' This program calculates information about a '
     *        'capacitor.',/, ' Please specify the type of information',
     *        ' available from the following list:',/,
     *        ' 1 - capacitance and voltage ',/,
     *        ' 2 - charge and voltage ',//,
     *        ' Select options 1 or 2:')
      READ (*,*) ITYPE
C
C     See if the user gave us a valid choice.
C
 10   IF ( (ITYPE .LT. 1) .OR. (ITYPE .GT. 2) ) THEN
C
C         Invalid response—tell user.
C
          WRITE (*,110) ITYPE
 110      FORMAT (' Invalid response: ', I6, '.  Please enter 1 or 2:')
C
```

```
C          Get type of input data.
C
           READ (*,*) ITYPE
           GO TO 10
       END IF
C
C      Get additional data based upon ITYPE.
C
       IF ( ITYPE .EQ. 1 ) THEN
C
C          Get capacitance.
C
           WRITE (*,120)
 120       FORMAT (' Enter capacitance in farads: ' )
           READ (*,*) C
C
C          Get voltage.
C
           WRITE (*,130)
 130       FORMAT (' Enter voltage in volts: ' )
           READ (*,*) V
C
       ELSE
C
C          Get charge.
C
           WRITE (*,140)
 140       FORMAT (' Enter charge in coulombs: ' )
           READ (*,*) CHARGE
C
C          Get voltage.
C
           WRITE (*,130)
           READ (*,*) V
C
       END IF
C
C      Calculate the unknown quantities.
C
       IF ( ITYPE .EQ. 1 ) THEN
          CHARGE = C * V
       ELSE
          C = CHARGE / V
       END IF
       ELECTR = CHARGE * ELEPCH
       ENERGY = 0.5 * C * V**2
C
C      Write out answers.
C
       WRITE (*,150) V, C, CHARGE, ELECTR, ENERGY
 150   FORMAT (' For this capacitor: ',/,
      *         ' Voltage             = ', F10.2, ' V',/,
      *         ' Capacitance         = ', 1PE10.3, ' F',/,
      *         ' Total charge        = ', E10.3, ' C',/,
      *         ' Number of electrons = ', E10.3,/,
      *         ' Total energy        = ', 0PF10.4, ' joules' )
C
       END
```

FIGURE 4-5   The program of Example 4-2.

5. Test the program.

To test this program, we will calculate the answers by hand for a simple data set, and then compare the answers to the results of the program. If we use a voltage of 100 V and a capacitance of 100 μF, the resulting charge on the plates of the capacitor is 0.01 C, there are 6.241×10^{16} electrons on the capacitor, and the energy stored is 0.5 J.

Running these values through the program using both options 1 and 2 yields the following results:

```
C:\BOOK\FORT>CAP
This program calculates information about a capacitor.
Please specify the type of information available from the following list:
   1 - capacitance and voltage
   2 - charge and voltage

Select options 1 or 2:
1
Enter capacitance in farads:
100.E-6
Enter voltage in volts:
100.
For this capacitor:
   Voltage             =     100.00 V
   Capacitance         =  1.000E-04 F
   Total charge        =  1.000E-02 C
   Number of electrons =  6.241E+16
   Total energy        =     .5000 joules

C:\BOOK\FORT>CAP
This program calculates information about a capacitor.
Please specify the type of information available from the following list:
   1 - capacitance and voltage
   2 - charge and voltage

Select options 1 or 2:
2
Enter charge in coulombs:
0.01
Enter voltage in volts:
100.
For this capacitor:
   Voltage             =     100.00 V
   Capacitance         =  1.000E-04 F
   Total charge        =  1.000E-02 C
   Number of electrons =  6.241E+16
   Total energy        =     .5000 joules
```

The program gives the correct answers for our test data set. ●

QUIZ 4-1

*This quiz provides a quick check to see if you have understood the concepts introduced in Sections 4.1 through 4.3. If you have trouble with the quiz, reread the sections, ask your instructor, or discuss the material with a fellow student. The answers to this quiz are found in the back of the book. Unless otherwise stated, assume that variables beginning with the letters **I-N** are integers, and all other variables are reals.*

Write FORTRAN statements that perform the operations described below.

1. Skip to a new page and print the title 'THIS IS A TEST!' starting in column 25.
2. Skip a line, then display the values of I, J, and DATA1 in fields 10 characters wide. Allow two decimal points for the real variable(s).
3. Beginning in column 12, write out the string 'The result is' followed by the value of RESULT expressed to five significant digits in correct scientific notation.

Assume that real variables A, B, and C are initialized with -0.0001, 6.02×10^{23}, and 3.141593, respectively, and that integer variables I, J, and K are initialized with 32767, 24, and -1010101 respectively. What will be printed out by each of the following sets of statements?

```
4.      WRITE (*,10) A, B, C
    10 FORMAT (1X,3F10.4)
5.      WRITE (*,20) A, B, C
    20 FORMAT (1X,F10.3, 2X, E10.3, 2X, F10.5)
6.      WRITE (*,30) A, B, C
    30 FORMAT (1X,F6.4, 2X, E7.2, 2X, F6.3)
7.      WRITE (*,40) A, B, C
    40 FORMAT (1X,1PE10.4, E11.4, F10.4)
8.      WRITE (*,50) I, J, K
    50 FORMAT (I5)
9.      WRITE (*,60) I, J, K
    60 FORMAT (1X,I8, 2X, I8.8, 2X, I8)
```

Assume that STR1 is a 10-character variable initialized with the string 'ABCDEFGHIJ', and that STR2 is a five-character variable initialized with the string '12345'. What will be printed out by each of the following sets of statements?

```
10.     WRITE (*,70) STR1, STR2
    70 FORMAT (1X,2A10)
11.     WRITE (*,80) STR1, STR2
    80 FORMAT (T21,A10,T24,A5)
12.     WRITE (*,90) STR1, STR2
    90 FORMAT (1X,2A)
13.     WRITE (*,90) STR1, STR2
    90 FORMAT (1X,A5,2X,A5)
```

Examine the following FORTRAN statements. Are they correct or incorrect? If they are incorrect, why are they incorrect?

14.
```
      WRITE (*,100) ISTART, ISTOP, STEP
  100 FORMAT (2I6,F10.4)
```
15.
```
      WRITE (*,220) 'Output = ',OUTPUT, 'Error = ', ERROR
  220 FORMAT ( 1X, A, 1PE10.3, A, F10.4 )
```
16.
```
      WRITE (*,10) I, J, K, L, M, N
   10 FORMAT ( 1X, 3(I6,3X) )
```
17.
```
      LOGICAL TEST
      CHARACTER*6 NAME
      INTEGER IERROR
      WRITE (*,200) NAME, TEST, IERROR
  200 FORMAT (1X,'Test name: ',A,/,' Completion status : ',
     * I6, ' Test results: ', L6 )
```

What output is generated by each of the following programs? Describe the output from each of these programs, including both the horizontal and vertical position of each output item.

18.
```
      INTEGER INDEX1, INDEX2
      REAL X1, Y1, X2, Y2
      DATA INDEX1, INDEX2 / 1, 2 /
      DATA X1, Y1, X2, Y2 / 1.2, 2.4, 2.4, 4.8 /
      WRITE (*,120) INDEX1, X1, Y1, INDEX2, X2, Y2
  120 FORMAT ('1',T11,'Output Data',/,
     *         ' ',T11,'============',//,
     *         (' ','POINT(',I2,') = ',2F14.6))
```
19.
```
      WRITE (*,210)
  210 FORMAT ('1',8('**********'),/,
     *        ' ','*',T81,'*',/,
     *        ' ','*',T81,'*',T31,'This is a title box!',/,
     *        ' ','*',T81,'*',/,
     *        ' ',8('**********'))
```
20.
```
      INTEGER I, J
      REAL X, Y
      DATA I, J, X, Y / -17, 0, 0.1001E9, 100. /
      WRITE (*,100) I, X, Y, J
  100 FORMAT (I6,1PE10.4,F10.4,I6)
```
21.
```
      PROGRAM OUT1
      CHARACTER*16 LAST, FIRST, MI*1
      CHARACTER*1 GRADE
      REAL AVE
      LAST  = 'DOE'
      FIRST = 'JOHN'
      MI    = 'Q'
      GRADE = 'B'
      AVE   = 88.0
      WRITE (*,100)
  100 FORMAT ('1',T21,'Grade List')
      WRITE (*,110) LAST, FIRST, MI, AVE, GRADE
  110 FORMAT (//'0',A16,2X,A16,2X,A,T41,F6.1,T50,A1)
      WRITE (*,120)
  120 FORMAT (///,21X,'End of Grade List')
      STOP
      END
```

22.
```
      PROGRAM OUT2
      REAL PI, SQRT2, ONEAU
      INTEGER I, J
      DATA PI, SQRT2 / 3.141592, 1.4142156 /
      DATA ONEAU / 93000000. /
      DATA I, J / -32767, 12 /
      WRITE (*,1000)
 1000 FORMAT (///' This is a test!',/'1This too!'//)
      WRITE (*,1010) I, PI, SQRT2, ONEAU, J
 1010 FORMAT ('0',I3,17X,F5.3,10X,F5.3,10X,F5.3,10X,I3)
      WRITE (*,1020) I, PI, SQRT2, ONEAU, J
 1020 FORMAT ('0',I10,T21,1PE10.3,5X,F10.3,5X,E10.3,5X,I8)
      WRITE (*,1030) I, PI, SQRT2, ONEAU
 1030 FORMAT (' ',I1,' ',T21,E10.3,T36,F10.3,T51,F10.1,I8.6)
      END
```

4.4 FORMATTED **READ** STATEMENTS

An *input device* is a piece of equipment that can enter data into a computer. The most common input device on a modern computer is a keyboard. As data is entered into the input device, it is stored in an **input buffer** in the computer's memory. Once an entire line has been typed into the input buffer, the user hits the RETURN (or ENTER) key on the keyboard, and the input buffer is made available for processing by the computer.

A **READ** statement reads one or more data values from the input buffer associated with an input device. The particular input device to read from is specified by the logical unit number in the **READ** statement. It is possible to use a **formatted READ statement** to specify the exact manner in which the contents of an input buffer are to be interpreted.

In general, a **FORMAT** statement specifies which columns of the input buffer are to be associated with a particular variable and how those columns are to be interpreted. A typical formatted **READ** statement is

```
      READ (*,100) INCR
  100 FORMAT (6X,I6)
```

This statement specifies that the first six columns of the input buffer are to be skipped, and then the contents of columns 7–12 are to be interpreted as an integer, with the resulting value stored in variable INCR.

FORMAT statements associated with **READ**s use many of the same format descriptors as **FORMAT** statements associated with **WRITE**s. However, the interpretation of those descriptors is different. The meanings of the format descriptors commonly found with **READ**s are described below.

4.4.1   Integer Input—the I Descriptor

The descriptor used to read integer data is the **I** descriptor. It has the general form

rIw

where

I   indicates integer data

w is the width of the field from which the data is read

r is the **repetition indicator.** It indicates the number of times this descriptor is used. This field is optional; if it is absent, the format descriptor is used only once.

According to the FORTRAN 77 standard, an integer value may be placed anywhere within its field, and it will be read and interpreted correctly. For example, consider the following statements

```
      READ (*,100) I
      READ (*,100) J
      READ (*,100) K
100 FORMAT (I4)
```

If the input data for these statements is

```
      5    10
- - - -|- - - -|
   12
  12
 12
- - - -|- - - -|
  5    10
```

then after the reads occur, I, J, and K all contain the value 12. Unfortunately, *not all compilers follow the FORTRAN 77 standard in this respect.* All earlier versions of FORTRAN assumed that any blank characters within an input field were really zeros. If a value did not end in the rightmost column of its field, then the blanks to the right of it were interpreted as zeros. For those compilers, the statements

```
      READ (*,100) I
      READ (*,100) J
      READ (*,100) K
100 FORMAT (I4)
```

and the input values

```
      5    10
- - - -|- - - -|
   12
  12
 12
- - - -|- - - -|
  5    10
```

would leave I with the value 12, J with the value 120, and K with the value 1200! Some FORTRAN 77 compilers interpret blanks as zeros by default in this manner so that they are backward-compatible with earlier versions of FORTRAN.

As we will see in Chapter 8, FORTRAN 77 includes a standard mechanism to control the way blanks are interpreted in a formatted **READ** statement (the **BN** and **BZ** format descriptors). If this mechanism is used, it is possible to write programs that interpret input numbers in a consistent fashion on any computers, and so are more portable between computers.

It is also possible to guarantee that your input data will be interpreted correctly on any computer, regardless of its default treatment of blanks. If each input data item is right-justified within its field, then it will be interpreted the same way on all FORTRAN compilers. It is a good idea to always right-justify any integer input data, so that it will be processed correctly on any computer.

■ **GOOD PROGRAMMING PRACTICE**

Always right-justify any integer input values within their fields.

4.4.2 Real Input—the F Descriptor

The format descriptor used to describe the input format of real data is the **F** descriptor. It has the form

  $rFw.d$

where

F	indicates real (floating-point) data
w	is the width of the field from which the data is read
d	is the number of digits to the right of the decimal point
r	is the repetition indicator. It indicates the number of times this descriptor will be used. This value is optional; if it is absent, the format descriptor is used only once.

The interpretation of real data in a formatted **READ** statement is rather complicated. The input value in an **F** input field may consist of a real number with a decimal point, a real number in exponential notation, or a number without a decimal point. *If a real number with a decimal point or a real number in exponential notation is present in the field, then the number is always interpreted correctly regardless of its position in the input field.* For example, consider the following statements:

```
     READ (*,100) A
     READ (*,100) B
     READ (*,100) C
     READ (*,100) D
 100 FORMAT (F10.4)
```

Assume that the input data for these statements is

```
     5    10
---- | ---- |
   1.5
          1.5
  0.15E+01
    15.0E-01
---- | ---- |
   5    10
```

After the statements are executed, all four variables will contain the number 1.5.

If a number without a decimal point appears in the field, then a decimal point is assumed to be in the position specified by the *d* term of the format descriptor. For example, if the format descriptor is **F10.4**, then the four rightmost digits of the number are assumed to be the fractional part of the input value, and the remaining digits are assumed to be the integer part of the input value. Consider the following FOR-TRAN statements:

```
     READ (*,100) A
     READ (*,100) B
     READ (*,100) C
     READ (*,100) D
 100 FORMAT (F10.4)
```

Assume that the input data for these statements is

```
      5    10
 ---- | ---- |
           15
         150
      150
   15000
 ---- | ---- |
    5    10
```

and that the compiler conforms to the FORTRAN 77 standard that blank characters are ignored. Then after these statements are executed, A will contain 0.0015, B will contain 0.0150, C will contain 0.0150, and D will contain 1.5000. (On a compiler that interprets blanks as zeros, the four values would have been 0.0015, 0.0150, 1.500, and 1500.) As you can see, the use of values without decimal points in a real input field is very confusing. It is a relic from an earlier version of FORTRAN that should never be used in your programs.

■ **GOOD PROGRAMMING PRACTICE**

Always include a decimal point in any real values used with a formatted **READ** statement.

The **E** descriptor may be used in the same manner as the **F** descriptor, if desired.

4.4.3   Logical Input—the L Descriptor

The descriptor used to read logical data has the form

     *r*L*w*

where

    L   indicates logical data
    w   is the width of the field from which the data is read
    r   is the repetition indicator. It indicates the number of times this descriptor
          will be used. This value is optional; if it is absent, the format descriptor is
          used only once.

The value of a logical variable can only be TRUE or FALSE. The input to a logical variable is either a T or an F, appearing as the first nonblank character in the input field.

For example, consider the following statements:

```
      READ (*,100) TEST1
      READ (*,100) TEST2
      READ (*,100) TEST3
      READ (*,100) TEST4
  100 FORMAT (L10)
```

Assume that the input data for these statements is

```
 0    5    10
 |----|----|
      T
          TRUE
          FALSE
       J2
 |----|----|
 0    5    10
```

After the statements are executed, the values of TEST1 and TEST2 are TRUE, and the value of TEST3 is FALSE. The fourth statement will produce a run-time error, since the first nonblank character is neither T nor F. The logical input format descriptor is rarely used.

4.4.4   Character Input—the A Descriptor

Character data is read using the **A** format descriptor.

    *r*A   or   *r*A*w*

where

    A   indicates character data

    w   is the width of the field from which the data is read. This value is optional. If it is absent, the width of the field will be equal to the length of the character variable being read

    r   is the repetition indicator. This value is optional; if it is absent, the format descriptor is used only once.

The *r*A descriptor reads character data in a field whose width is the same as the length of the character variable being read, while the *r*A*w* descriptor reads character data in a field of fixed width *w*. If the width *w* of the field is larger than the length of the character variable, the data from the *rightmost* portion of the field is loaded into the character variable. If the width of the field is smaller than the length of the character variable, the characters in the field will be stored in the leftmost characters of the variable, and the remainder of the variable will be padded with blanks.

For example, consider the following statements:

```
CHARACTER STR1*10, STR2*10, STR3*5, STR4*15, STR5*15
READ (*,100) STR1
READ (*,110) STR2
READ (*,110) STR3
READ (*,110) STR4
READ (*,100) STR5
100 FORMAT (A)
110 FORMAT (A10)
```

Assume that the input data for these statements is

```
    5    10   15
----|----|----|
ABCDEFGHIJKLMNO
ABCDEFGHIJKLMNO
ABCDEFGHIJKLMNO
ABCDEFGHIJKLMNO
ABCDEFGHIJKLMNO
----|----|----|
    5    10   15
```

After the statements are executed, variable STR1 will contain 'ABCDEFGHIJ', since STR1 is 10 characters long, and the A descriptor will read as many characters as the length of variable. Variable STR2 will contain 'ABCDEFGHIJ', since STR2 is 10 characters long, and the A10 descriptor will read 10 characters. Variable STR3 is only 5 characters long, and the A10 descriptor is 10 characters long, so STR3 will contain the 5 rightmost of the 10 characters in the field: 'FGHIJ'. Finally STR4 will contain 'ABCDEFGHIJ♭♭♭♭♭', since STR2 is 15 characters long, and the A10 descriptor will only read 10 characters. Finally STR5 contains 'ABCDEFGHIJKLMNO', since STR5 is 15 characters long, and the A descriptor will read as many characters as the length of variable.

When character values are read in free format, the values must be enclosed in single quotes. By contrast, when character values are read with formatted **READ** statements, they should *not* be enclosed in single quotes. The statements shown below read two character variables, one with a formatted **READ** and one with a free-format **READ.**

```
      CHARACTER STR1*6, STR2*6
      READ (*,100) STR1
      READ (*,*) STR2
100 FORMAT (A)
```

If the input data for these statements is

```
      5    10    15
 ----|----|----|
 ABCDEF
 'ABCDEF'
 ----|----|----|
      5    10    15
```

then the values stored in STR1 and STR2 will be identical. Since it is more convenient for users to enter character strings without enclosing them in single quotes, it is a good idea to always read any character data into your program with formatted **READ** statements.

■   **GOOD PROGRAMMING PRACTICE**

Use formatted **READ** statements (instead of free-format **READ**s) to read character values into your program. By doing so, a user will not have to enclose the input values between single quotes.

4.4.5   Horizontal Positioning—the X and T Descriptors

The **X** and **T** format descriptors may be used when reading formatted input data. The chief use of the **X** descriptor is to skip over fields in the input data that we do not wish to read. The **T** descriptor may be used for the same purpose, but it may also be used to read the same data twice in two different formats. For example, the following code reads the values in characters 1–6 of the input buffer twice—once as an integer, and once as a character string.

```
      CHARACTER*6 STRING
      INTEGER INPUT
      READ (*,100) INPUT, STRING
100 FORMAT (I6,T1,A6)
```

4.4.6 Vertical Positioning—the Slash (/) Descriptor

The slash (/) format descriptor causes a formatted **READ** statement to discard the current input buffer, get another one from the input device, and start processing from the beginning of the new input buffer. For example, the following formatted **READ** statement reads the values of variables A and B from the first input line, skips down two lines, and reads the values of variables C and D from the third input line.

```
      REAL A, B, C, D
      READ (*,300) A, B, C, D
  300 FORMAT (2F10.2,//,2F10.2)
```

If the input data for these statements is

```
    5    10   15   20   25   30
----|----|----|----|----|----|
        1.0        2.0        3.0
        4.0        5.0        6.0
        7.0        8.0        9.0
----|----|----|----|----|----|
    5    10   15   20   25   30
```

then the contents of variables A, B, C, and D will be 1.0, 2.0, 7.0, and 8.0, respectively.

4.4.7 How FORMAT Statements Are Used During READs

Most FORTRAN compilers verify the syntax of **FORMAT** statements at compilation time, but do not otherwise process them. Instead, they are saved unchanged as a character string within the compiled program. When the program is executed, the characters in the **FORMAT** statement are used as a template to guide the operation of the formatted **READ.**

At execution time, the list of input variables associated with the **READ** statement is processed together with the format of the statement. The program begins at the left end of the variable list and the left end of the **FORMAT** statement, and scans from left to right, associating the first variable in the input list with the first format descriptor in the format statement, etc. The variables in the input list must be of the same type and in the same order as the format descriptors in the format statement, or a run-time error will occur.

As the program moves from left to right through the variable list of a **READ** statement, it also scans from left to right through the associated **FORMAT** statement. The rules for scanning a **FORMAT** statement are essentially the same for **READs** as they are for **WRITEs**. **FORMAT** statements are scanned according to the following rules:

1. **FORMAT** statements are scanned in order from left to right. The first format descriptor in the **FORMAT** statement is associated with the first value in the input list of the **READ** statement, and so forth. The type of each format descriptor must match the type of the data being input.

2. If a format descriptor has a repetition count associated with it, the descriptor will be used the number of times specified in the repetition count before the next descriptor will be used.

3. If a group of format descriptors has a repetition count associated with it, the entire group will be used the number of times specified in the repetition count before the next descriptor will be used. Each descriptor within the group will be used in order from left to right during each repetition.

4. If the **READ** statement runs out of variables before the end of the **FORMAT** statement, the use of the **FORMAT** statement stops after the last variable has been read. The next **READ** statement will start with a new input buffer, and all of the other data in the original input buffer will be lost. For example, consider the following statements:

```
    READ (*,30) I, J
    READ (*,30) K, L, M
 40 FORMAT (5I5)
```

and the following input data:

```
     5    10    15    20    25    30
----|----|----|----|----|----|----|
     1     2     3     4     5
     6     7     8     9    10
----|----|----|----|----|----|----|
     5    10    15    20    25    30
```

After the first statement is executed, the values of I and J will be 1 and 2 respectively. The first **READ** ends at that point, so that input buffer is thrown away without ever using the remainder of the buffer. The next **READ** uses the second input buffer, so the values of K, L, and M will be 6, 7, and 8.

5. If the scan reaches the end of the **FORMAT** statement before the **READ** statement runs out of values, the program discards the remainder of the output buffer. It gets a new output buffer, and starts over *at the rightmost open parenthesis in the **FORMAT** statement that is not preceded by a repetition count.* For example, the statements

```
    READ (*,40) I, J, K, L, M
 40 FORMAT (I5,(T6,2I5))
```

and the input data

```
     5    10    15    20    25    30
----|----|----|----|----|----|----|
     1     2     3     4     5
     6     7     8     9    10
----|----|----|----|----|----|----|
     5    10    15    20    25    30
```

When the **READ** statement is executed, variables I, J, and K will be read from the first input buffer. They will contain 1, 2, and 3 respectively. The **FORMAT** statement ends at that point, so the first input buffer is discarded, and the next one is used. The **FORMAT** statement starts over at the rightmost open parenthesis not preceded by a repetition count, so variables L and M contain 7 and 8, respectively.

QUIZ 4-2

*This quiz provides a quick check to see if you have understood the concepts introduced in Section 4.4. If you have trouble with the quiz, reread the section, ask your instructor, or discuss the material with a fellow student. The answers to this quiz are found in the back of the book. Unless otherwise stated, assume that variables beginning with the letters **I-N** are integers, and all other variables are reals.*

Write FORTRAN statements that perform the functions described below.

1. Read the values of a real variable AMP from columns 10–20, an integer variable COUNT from columns 30–35, and a character variable IDENT from columns 60–72 of the current input buffer.
2. Read a 25-character variable called TITLE from columns 10–34 of the first input line, and then read 5 integer variables I1 through I5 from columns 5–12 on each of the next five lines.
3. Read columns 11–20 from the current input line into a character variable STRING, skip two lines, and read columns 11–20 into an integer variable NUMBER. Do this with a single formatted **READ** statement.

What will be stored in each of the following variables? Assume that blanks within a field are treated as nulls.

4.
```
      READ (*,10) A, B, C
   10 FORMAT (3F10.4)
```

With the input data
```
    5    10   15   20   25   30   35   40   45   50
----|----|----|----|----|----|----|----|----|----|
    1.65E-10   17.     -11.7
----|----|----|----|----|----|----|----|----|----|
    5    10   15   20   25   30   35   40   45   50
```

5.
```
      READ (*,20) A, B, C
   20 FORMAT (E10.2,F10.2,/,20X,F10.2)
```

With the input data
```
    5    10   15   20   25   30   35   40   45   50
----|----|----|----|----|----|----|----|----|----|
   -3.1415932.7182818210.1E10
        -11.        -5.       37.5532
----|----|----|----|----|----|----|----|----|----|
    5    10   15   20   25   30   35   40   45   50
```

6.
```
     READ (*,30) A, B, C
  30 FORMAT (3F10.3)
```

With the input data

```
      5    10   15   20   25   30   35   40   45   50
  ----|----|----|----|----|----|----|----|----|----|
      1024         1024  1024
  ----|----|----|----|----|----|----|----|----|----|
      5    10   15   20   25   30   35   40   45   50
```

7.
```
     READ (*,40) I, J, K
  40 FORMAT (3I5)
```

With the input data

```
      5    10   15   20   25   30   35   40   45   50
  ----|----|----|----|----|----|----|----|----|----|
   -35    67053687
  ----|----|----|----|----|----|----|----|----|----|
      5    10   15   20   25   30   35   40   45   50
```

8. If the blanks within a field were treated as zeros, how would the values stored in the variables change in Problems 4 through 7?

9.
```
     CHARACTER STR1*5 STR2*10, STR3*15, STR4*10
     READ (*,50) STR1, STR2, STR3, STR4
  50 FORMAT (4A10)
```

With the input data

```
      5    10   15   20   25   30   35   40   45   50
  ----|----|----|----|----|----|----|----|----|----|
  ABCDEFGHIJLKMNOPQRSTUVWXYZ0123    _TEST_1
  ----|----|----|----|----|----|----|----|----|----|
      5    10   15   20   25   30   35   40   45   50
```

Examine the following FORTRAN statements. Are they correct or incorrect? If they are incorrect, why are they incorrect? If they are correct, what do they do?

10.
```
     READ (*,100) NVALS, TIME1, TIME2
 100 FORMAT (10X,I10,F10.2,F10.4)
```

11.
```
     READ (*,220) JUNK, SCRATCH
 220 FORMAT ( T60,I15,/,E15.3)
```

12.
```
     READ (*,220) ICNT, RANGE, AZ, EL
 220 FORMAT ( I6, 4X, F20.2)
```

What values will be read into each of the variables in the following programs, given the associated input data sets? If any of the input values produces an error, explain the nature of the error.

13.
```
     INTEGER INDEX1, INDEX2
     REAL X1, Y1, X2, Y2
     CHARACTER*20 TITLE
     READ (*,12) TITLE, INDEX1, X1, Y1, INDEX2, X2, Y2
  12 FORMAT (A,/,(I10,T20,F13.6,T35,F13.6))
```

With the input data

```
      5    10   15   20   25   30   35   40   45   50
----|----|----|----|----|----|----|----|----|----|
Measurement Summary
              1              -230.3              121221
              2                         87.65    -11.352
              3                    65.                62.2
----|----|----|----|----|----|----|----|----|----|
      5    10   15   20   25   30   35   40   45   50
```

14.
```
      LOGICAL VALID
      REAL X1, Y1, X2, Y2
      CHARACTER*10 TITLE
      READ (*,400) X1, X2, X3, X4, A, B
  400 FORMAT (10X,F14.0,T11,F14.4,T11,F14.6,T15,F14.4)
      READ (*,500) TITLE, VALID, A, B
  500 FORMAT (/,10X,A10,5X,L5,F10.0,E10.2)
```

With the input data

```
      5    10   15   20   25   30   35   40   45   50
----|----|----|----|----|----|----|----|----|----|
              31415926536              3.1415926536
          PRELIM          FALSE   -10.        -17.E2
          TEST DATA              -12.6E-1  16.2
----|----|----|----|----|----|----|----|----|----|
      5    10   15   20   25   30   35   40   45   50
```

4.5   AN INTRODUCTION TO FILES AND FILE PROCESSING

The programs that we have written up to now have involved relatively small amounts of input and output data. We have typed in the input data from the keyboard each time that a program has been run, and the output data has gone directly to a terminal or printer. This is acceptable for small data sets, but it rapidly becomes prohibitive when we are working with large volumes of data. Imagine having to type in 100,000 input values each time a program is run! Such a process would be both time-consuming and prone to typing errors. We need a convenient way to read in and write out large data sets, and to be able to use them repeatedly without retyping.

Fortunately, computers have a standard structure for holding data that we will be able to use in our programs. This structure is called a **file.** A file consists of many lines of data which are related to each other, and which can be accessed as a unit. Each line of information in a file is called a **record.** FORTRAN can read information from a file or write information to a file one record at a time.

The files on a computer can be stored on various types of devices, which are collectively know as **secondary storage devices.** (The computer's memory is its primary storage device.) Secondary storage devices are slower than the computer's main memory, but they still allow relatively quick access to the data. Common secondary storage devices include hard disk drives, floppy disk drives, and magnetic tapes.

In the early days of computers, magnetic tapes were the most common type of secondary storage device. Computer magnetic tapes store data in a manner similar to the audio cassette tapes that we use to play music. Like them, computer magnetic tapes must be read (or "played") in order from the beginning of the tape to the end of it. When we read data in consecutive order one record after another in this manner, we are using **sequential access.** Other devices such as hard disks have the ability to jump from one record to another anywhere within a file. When we jump freely from one record to another following no specific order, we are using **direct access.** For historical reasons, sequential access is the default access technique in FORTRAN, even if we are working with devices capable of direct access.

To use files within a FORTRAN program, we will need some way to select the file that we want and to read from or write to it. Fortunately, FORTRAN has a wonderfully flexible method to read from and write to files, whether they are on disk, magnetic tape, or some other device attached to the computer. This mechanism is known as the **logical unit** (LU). The logical unit corresponds to the *first* asterisk in the **READ (*,*)** and **WRITE (*,*)** statements. If that asterisk is replaced by a logical unit number, then the *corresponding read or write will be to the device assigned to that unit* instead of to the standard input or output device. Note that the statements to read from or write to any file or device attached to the computer are exactly the same except for the logical unit number in the first position, so we already know most of what we need to know to use file I/O.

A LU number must be of type INTEGER. The range of integers which may be legally assigned as logical units varies from system to system, but typically at least the numbers between 1 and 99 are legal LUs. On some systems, any integer may be a LU. You must check with your instructor or the FORTRAN manuals for your system to find out which integers are legal LUs on that system.

Logical unit numbers are assigned to disk files or devices using the **OPEN** statement, and detached from them using the **CLOSE** statement. Once a file is attached to an LU using the **OPEN** statement, we can read and write in exactly the same manner that we have already learned. When we are through with the file, the **CLOSE** statement closes the file and releases the LU to be assigned to some other file.

Certain LU numbers are predefined to be connected to certain input or output devices, so that we don't need an **OPEN** statement to use these devices. These predefined LUs vary from computer system to computer system. Typically, LU 5 is predefined to be the *standard input device* for your program (i.e., the keyboard if you are running at a terminal, or the input batch file if you are running in batch mode). Similarly, LU 6 is usually predefined to be the *standard output device* for your program (the screen if you are running at a terminal, or the line printer if you are running in batch mode). These assignments date back to the early days of FORTRAN on IBM computers, so they have been copied by most other manufacturers in their FORTRAN compilers. However, you cannot count on these associations always being true on every computer. If you need to read from and write to the standard devices, always use the asterisk instead of the standard LU number for that device. The asterisk is guaranteed to work correctly on any computer system.

■ **GOOD PROGRAMMING PRACTICE**

Always use asterisks instead of LU numbers when referring to the standard input or standard output devices. The standard LU numbers vary from machine to machine, but the asterisk works correctly on all computers.

If we want to access any files or devices other than the predefined standard devices, we must first use an **OPEN** statement to associate the file or device with a specific LU number. Once the association has been established, we can use ordinary FORTRAN **READ**s and **WRITE**s with that LU to work with the data in the file.[3]

4.5.1 The OPEN Statement

The **OPEN** statement associates a file with a given LU number. Its form is

```
OPEN (open list)
```

where *open list* contains a series of clauses specifying the LU number, the file name, and information about how to access the file. The clauses in the list are separated by commas. The full details of the **OPEN** statement will be postponed until Chapter 8. For now, we will introduce only the four most important items from the list. They are

1. A **UNIT**= clause indicating the logical unit number to associate with this file. This clause has the form,

```
UNIT= integer expression
```

where *integer expression* can be a non-negative integer constant, variable, or expression.

2. A **FILE**= clause specifying the file name of the file to be opened. This clause has the form

```
FILE= character expression
```

where *character expression* is a character constant, variable, or expression containing the file name to be opened.

3. A **STATUS**= clause specifying the status of the file to be opened. This clause has the form

```
STATUS= character expression
```

where *character expression* is one of the following: 'OLD', 'NEW', 'UNKNOWN', or 'SCRATCH'.

---

[3]Some FORTRAN compilers attach default files to logical units that have not been opened. For example, in VAX FORTRAN, a write to an unopened LU 26 automatically goes into a file called FOR026.DAT. You should never use this feature, since it is non-standard and varies from computer to computer. Your programs will be much more portable if you always use an **OPEN** statement before writing to a file.

4. An **IOSTAT**= clause specifying the name of an integer variable in which the status of the open operation can be returned. This clause has the form

```
IOSTAT= integer variable
```

where *integer variable* is an integer variable. If the **OPEN** statement is successful, a 0 will be returned in the integer variable. If it is not successful, a positive number corresponding to a system error message will be returned in the variable. The system error messages vary from computer to computer, but a zero always means success.

The above clauses may appear in any order in the **OPEN** statement. Some examples of correct **OPEN** statements are shown below.

Case 1: Opening a File for Input

The statement below opens a file named EXAMPLE.DAT and attaches it to LU 8.

```
INTEGER IERROR
OPEN (UNIT=8, FILE='EXAMPLE.DAT', STATUS='OLD', IOSTAT=IERROR)
```

The **STATUS**=**'OLD'** clause specifies that the file already exists; if it does not exist, then the **OPEN** statement will return an error code in variable IERROR. This is the proper form of the open statement for an *input file*. If we are opening a file to read input data from, then the file had better be present with data in it! If it is not there, something is obviously wrong. By checking the returned value in IERROR, we can tell that there is a problem and take appropriate action.

Case 2: Opening a File for Output

The statements below open a file named OUTDAT and attach it to LU 25.

```
INTEGER    LU, IERROR
CHARACTER*6 FILENM
LU     = 25
FILENM = 'OUTDAT'
OPEN (UNIT=LU, FILE=FILENM, STATUS='NEW', ISTAT=IERROR)
```

or

```
OPEN (UNIT=LU, FILE=FILENM, STATUS='UNKNOWN', ISTAT=IERROR)
```

The **STATUS**=**'NEW'** clause specifies that the file is a new file; if it already exists, then the **OPEN** statement will return an error code in variable IERROR. This is the proper form of the **OPEN** statement for an *output file* if we want to make sure that we don't overwrite the data in a file that already exists.

The **STATUS**=**'UNKNOWN'** clause specifies that the file should be opened whether it exists or not. If the file already exists, the program will open it. If it does not exist, the program will create a new file by that name and open it. This is the proper form of the **OPEN** statement for an output file if we want to open the file whether or not a previous file exists with the same name.

Case 3: Opening a Scratch File

The statement below opens a *scratch file* and attaches it to LU 12.

```
OPEN (UNIT=12, STATUS='SCRATCH', ISTAT=IERROR)
```

A scratch file is a temporary file which is created by the program, and which will be deleted automatically when the file is closed or when the program terminates. This type of file may be used for saving intermediate results while a program is running, but it may not be used to save anything that we want to keep after the program finishes. Notice that no file name is specified in the **OPEN** statement. In fact, it is an error to specify a file name with a scratch file.

■ **GOOD PROGRAMMING PRACTICE**

Always be careful to specify the proper status in **OPEN** statements, depending on whether you are reading from or writing to a file. This practice helps prevent errors such as accidentally overwriting data files that you want to keep.

4.5.2   The CLOSE Statement

The **CLOSE** statement closes a file and releases the LU number associated with it. Its form is

```
CLOSE (close list)
```

where *close list* must contain a clause specifying the LU number, and may specify other options that will be discussed with the advanced I/O material in Chapter 8. If no **CLOSE** statement is included in the program for a given file, that file will be closed automatically when the program terminates.

After a nonscratch file is closed, it may be reopened at any time using a new **OPEN** statement. When it is reopened, it may be associated with the same LU or with a different LU. After the file is closed, the LU that was associated with it is free to be reassigned to any other file in a new **OPEN** statement.

4.5.3   READs and WRITEs to Disk Files

Once a file has been connected to a logical unit via the **OPEN** statement, it is possible to read from or write to the file using the same **READ** and **WRITE** statements that we have been using. For example, the statements

```
OPEN (UNIT=8, FILE='INPUT.DAT',STATUS='OLD',IOSTAT=IERROR)
READ (8,*) X, Y, Z
```

read the values of variables X, Y, and Z in free format from the file INPUT.DAT, and the statements

```
     OPEN(UNIT=9,FILE='OUTPUT.DAT',STATUS='UNKNOWN',IOSTAT=IERROR)
     WRITE (9,100) X, Y, Z
100 FORMAT (' X = ', F10.2, ' Y = ', F10.2, ' Z = ', F10.2 )
```

write the values of variables X, Y, and Z to the file OUTPUT.DAT in the specified format.

4.5.4 The IOSTAT= Clause in the READ Statement

The **IOSTAT=** clause is an important additional feature that may be added to the **READ** statement when working with disk files. The form of this clause is

```
IOSTAT= integer variable
```

where *integer variable* is an integer variable. If the **READ** statement is successful, a 0 is returned in the integer variable. If it is not successful due to a file error, a positive number corresponding to a system error message is returned in the variable. If it is not successful because the end of the input data file has been reached, a negative number is returned in the variable.[4]

If no **IOSTAT=** clause is present in a **READ** statement, *any attempt to read a line beyond the end of a file will abort the program.* This behavior is unacceptable in a well-designed program. We often want to read all of the data from a file until the end is reached, and then perform some sort of processing on that data. This is where the **IOSTAT=** clause comes in: if an **IOSTAT=** clause is present, the program will not abort on an attempt to read a line beyond the end of a file. Instead, the **READ** will complete with the **IOSTAT** variable set to a negative number. We can then test the value of the variable, and process the data accordingly.[5]

■
GOOD PROGRAMMING PRACTICE

Always include the **IOSTAT=** clause when reading from a disk file. This clause provides a graceful way to detect end-of-data conditions on the input files.

■
EXAMPLE 4-3 *Reading Data from a File* It is common to read a large data set into a program from a file, and then to process the data in some fashion. Often, the program has no way of knowing in advance just how much data is present in the file. In that case, the program needs to read the data in a while loop until the end of the

---

[4]There is an alternate method of detecting file read errors and end-of-file conditions using **ERR=** and **END=** clauses. These clauses of the **READ** statement will be described in Chapter 8. The **IOSTAT=** clause lends itself better to structured programming than the other clauses do, so they are being postponed to the later chapter.

[5]The **END=** clause also prevents the **READ** from aborting, as we will see in Chapter 8.

data set is reached, and then must detect that there is no more data to read. Once it has read in all of the data, the program can process it in whatever manner is required.

Let's illustrate this process by writing a program that can read in an unknown number of real values from a disk file, and detect the end of the data in the disk file.

SOLUTION   This program must open the input disk file, and then read the values in from it using the **IOSTAT**= clause to detect problems. If the **IOSTAT** variable contains a negative number after a **READ,** then the end of the file has been reached. If the **IOSTAT** variable contains 0 after a **READ,** then everything was OK. In this example, the program should stop if a **READ** error occurs.

1.   State the problem.
The problem may be succinctly stated as follows: Write a program that can read an unknown number of real values from a user-specified input data file, detecting the end of the data file as it occurs.

2.   Define the inputs and outputs.
The inputs to this program consist of:

(*a*) The name of the file to be opened.
(*b*) The data contained in that file.

The outputs from the program are the input values in the data file. At the end of the file, an informative message is written out telling how many valid input values were found.

3.   Describe the algorithm.
This pseudocode for this program is

```
Initialize NVALS to 0
*
*   Get and open file to read
*
Prompt user for file name
Get the name of the input file
OPEN the input file
Check for errors on OPEN
*
*   Read input data
*
If no OPEN error THEN
    READ first value
    WHILE ISTAT = 0
        NVALS ← NVALS + 1
        WRITE valid data to screen
        READ next value
    END of WHILE
*
*   Check to see if the WHILE terminated due to end of file
*   or READ error
*
```

```
    IF ISTAT > 0
        WRITE 'READ error occurred on line', NVALS
    ELSE
        WRITE number of valid input values NVALS
    END of IF ( ISTAT > 0 )
END of IF ( no OPEN error )
END
```

A flowchart for the program is shown in Figure 4-6.

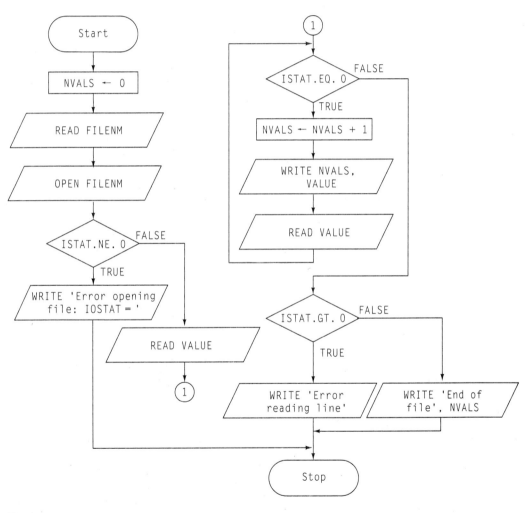

FIGURE 4-6 Flowchart for a program to read an unknown number of values from an input data file.

4. Turn the algorithm into FORTRAN statements.

The final FORTRAN program is shown in Figure 4-7.

```
      PROGRAM READ
C
C  Purpose:
C    To illustrate how to read an unknown number of values from
C    an input data file, detecting both any formatting errors and
C    the end of file.
C
C  Record of revisions:
C      Date        Programmer        Description of change
C      ====        ==========        =====================
C    08/29/92   S. J. Chapman        Original code
C
C  List of variables:
C    FILENM -- The name of the input file to open
C    ISTAT  -- I/O Status Variable
C    NVALS  -- Number of values read in
C    VALUE  -- The real value read in
C
      IMPLICIT NONE
C
C    Declare the variables used in this program.
C
      CHARACTER*20 FILENM
      INTEGER    NVALS, ISTAT
      REAL       VALUE
C
C    Initialize variables.
C
      NVALS = 0
C
C    Get the file name, and echo it back to the user.
C
      WRITE (*,*) 'Please enter input file name: '
      READ  (*,*) FILENM
      WRITE (*,1000) FILENM
 1000 FORMAT (' ','The input file name is: ', A)
C
C    Open the file, and check for errors on open.
C
      OPEN (UNIT=3, FILE=FILENM, STATUS='OLD', IOSTAT=ISTAT )
      IF ( ISTAT .NE. 0 ) THEN
         WRITE (*,1010) ISTAT
 1010    FORMAT (' ','Error opening file: IOSTAT = ', I6 )
      ELSE
C
C        OPEN was ok. Read first value.
C
         READ (3,*,IOSTAT=ISTAT) VALUE
C
C        Begin WHILE loop.
C
   10    IF ( ISTAT .EQ. 0 ) THEN
C
C           READ was ok. Echo value to screen.
C
```

```
                  NVALS = NVALS + 1
                  WRITE (*,1020) NVALS, VALUE
     1020          FORMAT (' ','Line ', I6, ': VALUE = ',F10.4 )
C
C                 READ next value.
C
                  READ (3,*,IOSTAT=ISTAT) VALUE
C
                  GO TO 10
              END IF
C
C             The WHILE loop has terminated. Was it because of a READ error
C             or because of the end of the input file?
C
              IF ( ISTAT .GT. 0 ) THEN
C
C                 An error occurred.
C
                  WRITE (*,1030) NVALS+1
     1030          FORMAT ('0','An error occurred reading line ', I6)
          ELSE
C
C             End of data reached.
C
                  WRITE (*,1040) NVALS
     1040          FORMAT ('0','End of file reached. There were ', I6,
          *              ' values in the file.')
              END IF
          END IF
C
C     Close file.
C
          CLOSE ( UNIT=8 )
C
          END
```

FIGURE 4-7 The program of Example 4-3.

Note that the input file is opened with **STATUS='OLD',** since we are reading from the file, and the input data must already exist before the program is executed.

5. Test the program.

To test this program, we will create two input files, one with valid data, and one with an input data error. We run the program with both input files, and verify that it both works correctly for valid data and can properly handle input errors. Also, we run the program with an invalid file name to show that it can properly handle missing input files.

The valid input file is called READ1.DAT. It contains the following lines:

```
-17.0
30.001
1.0
12000.
-0.012
```

The invalid input file is called READ2.DAT. It contains the following lines:

```
-17.0
30.001
ABCDEF
12000.
-0.012
```

Running these files through the program yields the following results:

```
C:\BOOK\FORT>READ
Please enter input file name:
'READ1.DAT'
The input file name is: READ1.DAT
Line      1: VALUE =    -17.0000
Line      2: VALUE =     30.0010
Line      3: VALUE =      1.0000
Line      4: VALUE = 12000.0000
Line      5: VALUE =      -.0120

End of file reached.  There were       5 values in the file.

C:\BOOK\FORT>READ
Please enter input file name:
'READ2.DAT'
The input file name is: READ2.DAT
Line      1: VALUE =    -17.0000
Line      2: VALUE =     30.0010

An error occurred reading line       3
```

Finally, let's test the program with an invalid input file name.

```
C:\BOOK\FORT>READ
Please enter input file name:
'JUNK.DAT'
The input file name is: JUNK.DAT
Error opening file: IOSTAT =   6416
```

The number of the **IOSTAT** error reported by this program will vary from compiler to compiler, but it will always be positive. You must consult a listing of the run-time error codes for your particular compiler to find the exact meaning of the error code that your computer reports. For Microsoft FORTRAN, run-time error 6416 means "File not found."

This program correctly read all of the values in the input file, and detected the end of the data set when it occurred. ●

4.5.5   File Positioning

As we stated previously, ordinary FORTRAN files are sequential—they are read in order from the first record in the file to the last record in the file. However, we sometimes need to read a piece of data more than once, or to process a whole file more than once during a program. How can we skip around within a sequential file?

FORTRAN provides two statements to help us move around within a sequential file. They are the **BACKSPACE** statement, which moves back one record each time it is called, and the **REWIND** statement, which restarts the file at its beginning. The form of these statements are

```
BACKSPACE (lu)
```

and

```
REWIND (lu)
```

where **lu** is the logical unit number associated with the file that we want to work with.[6]

EXAMPLE   4-4   *Using File Positioning Commands*   We now illustrate the use of scratch files and file positioning commands in a simple example problem. We will write a program that accepts a series of non-negative real values and stores them in a scratch file. After the data is input, the program should ask the user what data record he or she is interested in, and then recover and display that value from the disk file.

SOLUTION   Since the program is expected to read only positive or zero values, we can use a negative value as a flag to terminate the input to the program. A FORTRAN program that does this is shown in Figure 4-8. This program opens a scratch file, and then reads input values from the user. If a value is non-negative, is it written to the scratch file. When a negative value is encountered, the program asks the user for the record to display. It checks to see if a valid record number was entered. If the record number is valid, it rewinds the file and reads forward to that record number. Finally, it displays the contents of that record to the user.

```
      PROGRAM SCRTCH
C
C  Purpose:
C    To illustrate the use of a scratch file and positioning
C    commands as follows:
C    1. Read in an arbitrary number of positive or zero
C       values, saving them in a scratch file. Stop
C       reading when a negative value is encountered.
C    2. Ask the user for a record number to display.
```

---

[6]Alternate forms of these statements are described in Chapter 8.

```
C     3. Rewind the file, get that value, and display it.
C
C  Record of revisions:
C     Date        Programmer        Description of change
C     ====        ==========        =====================
C   03/12/91  S. J. Chapman      Original code
C
C  List of variables:
C     DATA   -- The data stored in a disk record
C     ICOUNT -- The number of input data records
C     IREC   -- The record number to recover and display
C     J      -- Do loop index
C     LU     -- The logical unit of the scratch file
C
      IMPLICIT NONE
C
C     Declare the variables used in this program.
C
      INTEGER ICOUNT, IREC, J, LU
      REAL    DATA
C
C     Use LU 8 for the scratch file
C
      PARAMETER ( LU = 8 )
C
C     Open the scratch file
C
      OPEN (UNIT=LU, STATUS='SCRATCH' )
C
C     Prompt user and get input data.
C
      WRITE (*, 100)
  100 FORMAT (1X,'Enter positive or zero input values. ',/,
     *        1X,'A negative value terminates input.' )
C
C     Get the first value.
C
      ICOUNT = 1
      WRITE (*, 110) ICOUNT
  110 FORMAT (1X,'Enter sample ',I4,':' )
      READ (*,*) DATA
C
C     Begin WHILE loop.
C     See if the user gave us a valid choice.
C
   10 IF ( DATA .GE. 0. ) THEN
C
C        Put value in the file.
C
         WRITE (LU,120) DATA
  120    FORMAT ( 1X, 1PE16.6 )
C
C        Prompt user and get more data.
C
         ICOUNT = ICOUNT + 1
         WRITE (*, 110) ICOUNT
         READ (*,*) DATA
C
```

```
          GO TO 10
      END IF
C
C     End of WHILE loop.
C
C     When we get here, we have had a negative input value.
C     Decrease the counter by 1 since the last value was
C     not valid.
C
      ICOUNT = ICOUNT - 1
C
C     Ask which record to see.
C
      WRITE (*,140) ICOUNT
  140 FORMAT (1X,'Which record do you want to see (1 to ',
     *        I4, '): ')
      READ (*,*) IREC
C
C     Do we have a legal record number?  If so, get the
C     record. If not, tell the user and stop.
C
      IF ( (IREC .GE. 1) .AND. (IREC .LE. ICOUNT) ) THEN
C
C         This is a legal record. Rewind the scratch file.
C
          REWIND (LU)
C
C         Read forward to the desired record.
C
          DO 20 J = 1, IREC
             READ (LU,*) DATA
   20     CONTINUE
C
C         Tell user.
C
          WRITE (*,150) IREC, DATA
  150     FORMAT (1X,'The value of record ', I4, ' is ', 1PE14.5 )
C
      ELSE
C
C         We have an illegal record number. Tell user.
C
          WRITE (*,160) IREC
  160     FORMAT (1X,'Illegal record number entered: ', I8)
      END IF
C
      END
```

FIGURE 4-8   Sample program illustrating the use of file positioning commands.

Now let us test the program with valid data:

```
C:\BOOK\FORT>SCRTCH
Enter positive or zero input values.
A negative input value terminates input.
Enter sample    1:
234.
```

```
Enter sample     2:
12.34
Enter sample     3:
0.
Enter sample     4:
16.
Enter sample     5:
11.235
Enter sample     6:
2.
Enter sample     7:
-1
Which record do you want to see (1 to     6):
5
The value of record 5 is        1.12350E+01
```

Finally, let us test the program with an invalid record number to see that the error condition is handled properly.

```
C:\BOOK\FORT>SCRTCH
Enter positive or zero input values.
A negative input value terminates input.
Enter sample     1:
234.
Enter sample     2:
12.34
Enter sample     3:
0.
Enter sample     4:
16.
Enter sample     5:
11.235
Enter sample     6:
2.
Enter sample     7:
-1
Which record do you want to see (1 to     6):
7
Illegal record number entered:        7
```

The program appears to be functioning correctly. ●

EXAMPLE 4-5 *Least-Squares Fit to a Straight Line*   The velocity of a falling object in the presence of a constant gravitational field is given by the equation

$$v(t) = at + v_0$$

(4-4)

where

$v(t)$ is the velocity at any time t
a is the acceleration due to gravity
v_0 is the velocity at time 0.

This equation is derived from elementary physics—it is known to every freshman physics student. If we plot velocity versus time for the falling object, our (v, t) measurement points should fall along a straight line. However, the same freshman physics student also knows that if we go out into the laboratory and attempt to *measure* the velocity versus time of an object, our measurements will *not* fall along a straight line. They may come close, but they will never line up perfectly. Why not? Because we can never make perfect measurements. There is always some *noise* included in the measurements which distorts them.

There are many cases in science and engineering where there are noisy sets of data such as this, and we wish to estimate the straight line which "best fits" the data. This problem is called the **linear regression** problem. Given a noisy set of measurements (x, y) that appear to fall along a straight line, how can we find the equation of the line

$$y = mx + b \tag{4-5}$$

which "best fits" the measurements? If we can determine the **regression coefficients** m and b, then we can use this equation to predict the value of y at any given x by evaluating Equation (4-5) for that value of x.

A standard method for finding the regression coefficients m and b is the **method of least squares.** This method is named "least squares" because it produces the line $y = mx + b$ for which the sum of the squares of the differences between the observed y values and the predicted y values is as small as possible. The slope of the least squares line is given by

$$m = \frac{(\Sigma xy) - (\Sigma x)\bar{y}}{(\Sigma x^2) - (\Sigma x)\bar{x}} \tag{4-6}$$

and the intercept of the least-squares line is given by

$$b = \bar{y} - m\bar{x} \tag{4-7}$$

where:

Σx is the sum of the x values
Σx^2 is the sum of the squares of the x values
Σxy is the sum of the products of the corresponding x and y values
$\bar{x}$ is the mean (average) of the x values
$\bar{y}$ is the mean (average) of the y values

Write a program which will calculate the least-squares slope m and y-axis intercept b for a given set of measured data points (x, y) which are to be found in an input data file.

SOLUTION

1. State the problem.

Calculate the slope m and intercept b of a least-squares line that best fits an input data set consisting of an arbitrary number of (x, y) pairs. The input (x, y) data resides in a user-specified input file.

2. Define the inputs and outputs.

The inputs required by this program are pairs of points (x, y), where x and y are real quantities. Each pair of points is located on a separate line in the input disk file. The number of points in the disk file is not known in advance.

The outputs from this program are the slope and intercept of the least-squares fitted line, plus the number of points going into the fit.

3. Describe the algorithm.

This program can be broken down into four major steps:

```
Get the name of the input file and open it
Accumulate the input statistics
Calculate the slope and intercept
Write out the slope and intercept
```

The first major step of the program is to get the name of the input file and to open the file. To do this, we will have to prompt the user to enter the name of the input file. After the file is opened, we must check to see that the open was successful. Next we must read the file and keep track of the number of values entered, plus the sums Σx, Σy, Σx^2, Σxy. The pseudocode for these steps is

```
Initialize N, SUMX, SUMX2, SUMY, and SUMXY to 0
Prompt user for input file name
Open file FILENM
Check for error on OPEN
READ x, y from file FILENM
WHILE not end of file
    N ← N + 1
    SUMX ← SUMX + X
    SUMY ← SUMY + Y
    SUMX2 ← SUMX2 + X**2
    SUMXY ← SUMXY + X*Y
    READ x, y from file FILENM
End of WHILE
```

Note that we have to read the first value before the loop starts so that the while loop can have a value to test the first time in.

Next we must calculate the slope and intercept of the least-squares line. The pseudocode for this step is just the FORTRAN versions of Equations (4-6) and (4-7).

```
            XBAR ← SUMX / REAL(N)
            YBAR ← SUMY / REAL(N)
            SLOPE ← (SUMXY - SUMX * YBAR) / ( SUMX2 - SUMX * XBAR)
            YINT ← YBAR - SLOPE * XBAR
```

Finally we must write out the results.

```
            Write out slope SLOPE and intercept YINT.
```

4. Turn the algorithm into FORTRAN statements.
The final FORTRAN program is shown in Figure 4-9.

```
      PROGRAM LSQFIT
C
C Purpose:
C    To perform a least-squares fit of an input data set
C    to a straight line, and print out the resulting slope
C    and intercept values. The input data for this fit
C    comes from a user-specified input data file.
C
C Record of revisions:
C     Date      Programmer         Description of change
C     ====      ==========         =====================
C   03/14/91  S. J. Chapman        Original code
C
C List of variables:
C    FILENM -- The input file name (<= 24 characters)
C    IERROR -- The status flag returned by the I/O statements
C    LU     -- The logical unit number to use for file I/O
C    N      -- The number of input data pairs (x,y)
C    SLOPE  -- The slope of the line
C    SUMX   -- The sum of all input X values
C    SUMX2  -- The sum of all input X values squared
C    SUMXY  -- The sum of all X*Y values
C    SUMY   -- The sum of all input Y values
C    X      -- An input X value
C    XBAR   -- The average X value
C    Y      -- An input Y value
C    YBAR   -- The average Y value
C    YINT   -- The Y-axis intercept of the line
C
      IMPLICIT NONE
C
C Declare the variables used in this program.
C
      CHARACTER*24 FILENM
      INTEGER N, IERROR, LU
      REAL    SUMX, SUMY, SUMX2, SUMXY
      REAL    X, Y, XBAR, YBAR, SLOPE, YINT
C
C Use LU 12 for the input file
C
      PARAMETER ( LU = 12 )
C
C Initialize variables to zero.
C
      N    = 0
      SUMX = 0.
```

```
        SUMY  = 0.
        SUMX2 = 0.
        SUMXY = 0.
C
C     Prompt user and get the name of the input file.
C
        WRITE (*,1000)
 1000 FORMAT (1X,'This program performs a least-squares fit of an ',/,
      *        1X,'input data set to a straight line. Enter the name',/,
      *        1X,'of the file containing the input (x,y) pairs:' )
        READ (*,1010) FILENM
 1010 FORMAT (A)
C
C     Open the input file
C
        OPEN (UNIT=LU, FILE=FILENM, STATUS='OLD', IOSTAT=IERROR )
C
C     Check to see if the OPEN failed.
C
        IF ( IERROR .GT. 0 ) THEN
           WRITE (*,1020) FILENM
 1020      FORMAT (1X,'ERROR: File ',A,' does not exist!')
           STOP
        END IF
C
C     Read the first (x,y) pair from the input file.
C
        READ (LU,*,IOSTAT=IERROR) X, Y
C
C     Beginning of WHILE loop to process (x,y) pairs.
C
   10 IF ( IERROR .EQ. 0 ) THEN
C
C        Sum the statistics.
C
           N     = N + 1
           SUMX  = SUMX + X
           SUMY  = SUMY + Y
           SUMX2 = SUMX2 + X**2
           SUMXY = SUMXY + X * Y
C
C        Get the next data point.
C
           READ (LU,*,IOSTAT=IERROR) X, Y
C
C        End of WHILE loop
C
           GO TO 10
        END IF
C
C     Now calculate the slope and intercept.
C
        XBAR  = SUMX / REAL(N)
        YBAR  = SUMY / REAL(N)
        SLOPE = (SUMXY - SUMX * YBAR) / ( SUMX2 - SUMX * XBAR)
        YINT  = YBAR - SLOPE * XBAR
C
C     Tell user.
C
```

```
        WRITE (*, 1030 ) SLOPE, YINT, N
  1030 FORMAT ('0','Regression coefficients for the least-squares line:',
      *          /,1X,'  Slope (m)     = ', F12.3,
      *          /,1X,'  Intercept (b) = ', F12.3,
      *          /,1X,'  No of points  = ', I12 )
C
C     Close input file, and quit.
C
        CLOSE (LU)
        END
```

FIGURE 4-9   The least-squares fit program of Example 4-5.

5. Test the program.

To test this program, we will try a simple data set. For example, if every point in the input data set actually falls along a line, then the resulting slope and intercept should be exactly the slope and intercept of that line. Thus the data set

```
    1.1, 1.1
    2.2, 2.2
    3.3, 3.3
    7.7, 7.7
```

should produce a slope of 1.0 and an intercept of 0.0. If we place these values in a file called INPUT, and run the program, the results are

```
C:\BOOK\FORT>LSQFIT
This program performs a least-squares fit of an
input data set to a straight line. Enter the name
of the file containing the input (x,y) pairs:
INPUT
Regression coefficients for the least-squares line:
  Slope (m)     =        1.000
  Intercept (b) =         .000
  No of points  =           4
```

Now let's add some noise to the measurements. The data set becomes

```
    1.125, 1.089
    2.172, 2.201
    3.304, 3.312
    7.688, 7.691
```

If these values are placed in a file called INPUT1, and the program is run on that file, the results are

```
C:\BOOK\FORT>LSQFIT
This program performs a least-squares fit of an
input data set to a straight line. Enter the name
of the file containing the input (x,y) pairs:
INPUT1
Regression coefficients for the least-squares line:
  Slope (m)     =        1.002
  Intercept (b) =        -.007
  No of points  =           4
```

If we calculate the answer by hand, it is easy to show that the program gives the correct answers for our two test data sets.   ●

Quiz 4-3

This quiz provides a quick check to see if you have understood the concepts introduced in Section 4.5. If you have trouble with the quiz, reread the section, ask your instructor, or discuss the material with a fellow student. The answers to this quiz are found in the back of the book.

Write FORTRAN statements that perform the functions described below. Unless otherwise stated, assume that variables beginning with the letters I-N are integers, and all other variables are reals.

1. Open an existing file named IN052691 on LU 25 for input, and check the status to see if the **OPEN** was successful.
2. Open a new output file, making sure that you do not overwrite any existing file by the same name. The name of the output file is stored in character variable OUTNAM.
3. Close the file attached to LU 24.
4. Read variables FIRST and LAST from LU 8 in free format, checking for end of data during the **READ.**
5. Backspace eight lines in the file attached to LU 13.

Examine the following FORTRAN statements. Are they correct or incorrect? If they are incorrect, why are they incorrect?

```
6.  OPEN (UNIT=35, FILE='DATA1', STATUS='UNKNOWN',IOSTAT=IERROR)
    READ (35,*) N, DATA1, DATA2
7.  OPEN (UNIT=11, FILE='DATA1', STATUS='SCRATCH',IOSTAT=IERROR)
8.  OPEN (UNIT=X, FILE='JUNK', STATUS='NEW',IOSTAT=IERROR)
9.  OPEN (UNIT=9, FILE='TEMP.DAT', STATUS='OLD',IOSTAT=IERROR)
    READ (9,*) X, Y
10. OPEN (UNIT=9, FILE='TEMP.DAT', STATUS='OLD',IOSTAT=IERROR)
    . . .
    A = 8
    CLOSE (A)
```

4.6   SUMMARY

In Chapter 4, we presented a basic introduction to formatted **WRITE** statements, and to the use of disk files for input and output of data.

In a formatted **WRITE** statement, the second asterisk of the unformatted **WRITE** statement (**WRITE (*,*)**) is replaced by a **FORMAT** statement number. The **FORMAT** statement describes how the output data is to be displayed. It is composed of format descriptors which describe the vertical and horizontal position of the data on a page, as well as the display format for integer, real, logical and character data types.

The format descriptors discussed in this chapter are summarized in Table 4-2.

TABLE 4-2 FORTRAN 77 Format Descriptors Discussed in Chapter 4

FORMAT Descriptors		*Usage*
A	**A**w	Character data
E$w.d$		Real data in exponential notation
F$w.d$		Real data in decimal notation
Iw	**I**$w.m$	Integer data
Lw		Logical data
k**P**		Scale factor for display of real data
Tc		TAB: move to column c of current line
n**X**		Horizontal spacing: skip n spaces
/		Vertical spacing: move down one line

where

c	is the column number
d	is the number of digits to right of decimal place
k	is the scale factor (number of places to shift decimal point)
m	is the minimum number of digits to be displayed
w	is the field width in characters

Formatted **READ** statements use a **FORMAT** statement to describe how the input data is to be interpreted. All of the above format descriptors are also legal in formatted **READ** statements.

A disk file is opened using the **OPEN** statement, read and written using **READ** and **WRITE** statements, and closed using the **CLOSE** statement. The **OPEN** statement associates a file with an LU number, and that LU number is used by the **READ** statements and **WRITE** statements in the program to access the file. When the file is closed, the association is broken.

It is possible to move around within a sequential disk file using the **BACKSPACE** and **REWIND** statements. The **BACKSPACE** statement moves the current position in the file backward by one record whenever it is executed, and the **REWIND** statement moves the current position back to the first record in the file.

4.6.1 Summary of Good Programming Practice

The following guidelines should be adhered to when programming with formatted output statements or with disk I/O. By following them consistently, your code will contain fewer bugs, will be easier to debug, and will be more understandable to others who may need to work with it in the future.

1. The first column of any output line is reserved for a control character. Never put anything in the first column except for the control character. Be especially careful not to write a format descriptor that includes column 1, since the pro-

gram could behave erratically depending on the value of the data being written out. To highlight the presence of the control character, write it out separately from any other text in a **FORMAT** statement.

2. Always be careful to match the type of data in a **WRITE** statement to the type of descriptors in the **FORMAT** statement. Integers should be associated with **I** format descriptors, reals with **E** or **F** format descriptors, logicals with **L** descriptors, and characters with **A** descriptors. A mismatch between data types and format descriptor types will result in an error at execution time.

3. Use a **1P** scale factor when displaying data in **E** format to make the output data appear to be in conventional scientific notation. This display helps a reader to quickly understand the output numbers.

4. Use formatted **READ** statements (instead of free-format **READ**s) to read character values into your program. By doing so, a user will not have to enclose the input values between single quotes.

5. Use an asterisk instead of an LU number when reading from the standard input device or writing to the standard output device. This makes your code more portable, since the asterisk is the same on all systems, while the actual LU numbers assigned to standard input and standard output devices may vary from system to system.

6. Always open input files with **STATUS='OLD'.** By definition, an input file must already exist if we are to read data from it. If the file does not exist, this is an error, and the **STATUS='OLD'** will catch that error.

7. Open output files with **STATUS='NEW'** or **STATUS='UNKNOWN'**, depending on whether or not you want to preserve the existing contents of the output file. If the file is opened with **STATUS='NEW',** it should be impossible to overwrite an existing file, so the program cannot accidentally destroy data. If we don't care about the existing data in the output file, open the file with **STATUS='UNKNOWN',** and the file will be overwritten if it exists. Open scratch files with **STATUS='SCRATCH',** so that they will be automatically deleted on closing.

8. Always include the **IOSTAT=** clause when reading from disk files to detect an end-of-file or error condition.

CHAPTER 4 KEY WORDS

Control character	Method of least squares
Direct access	Output buffer
Field width	Output device
File	Record
Formatted output	Regression coefficients
Free format	Repetition indicator
Input buffer	Scale factor
Input device	Scientific notation
Linear regression	Secondary storage device
Logical unit	Sequential access

CHAPTER 4 SUMMARY OF FORTRAN STATEMENTS AND STRUCTURES

The following summary describes the FORTRAN statements and structures introduced in this chapter.

Formatted READ Statement:

```
READ (lu,label) output list
```

Example:

```
      READ (1,100) TIME, SPEED
100 FORMAT ( F10.4, F18.4 )
```

Description: The formatted **READ** statement reads data from an input buffer according to the formats specified in the **FORMAT** statement with statement label *label*.

Formatted WRITE Statement:

```
WRITE (lu,label) output list
```

Example:

```
      WRITE (*,100) I, J, SLOPE
100 FORMAT ( 1X, 2I10, F10.2 )
```

Description: The formatted **WRITE** statement outputs the data in the output list according to the formats specified in the **FORMAT** statement with statement label *label*.

FORMAT Statement:

```
label FORMAT (format descriptor, ... )
```

Example:

```
100 FORMAT (' This is a test: ', I6 )
```

Description: The **FORMAT** statement describes the position and format of the data being written out.

OPEN Statement:

```
OPEN (open list)
```

Example:

```
OPEN (UNIT=8, FILE='X', STATUS='OLD', IOSTAT=IER)
```

Description: The **OPEN** statement associates a file with an LU number, so that it can be accessed by **READ** or **WRITE** statements.

CLOSE Statement:

```
CLOSE (close list)
```

Example:

```
CLOSE (8)
```

Description: The **CLOSE** statement closes the file associated with an LU number.

BACKSPACE Statement:

```
BACKSPACE (lu)
```

Example:

```
BACKSPACE (8)
```

Description: The **BACKSPACE** statement moves the current position of a file back by one record.

REWIND Statement:

```
REWIND (lu)
```

Example:

```
REWIND (8)
```

Description: The **REWIND** statement moves the current position of a file back to the beginning.

■ CHAPTER 4 EXERCISES

1. What is the purpose of a **FORMAT** statement?
2. What is the effect of each of the following characters when it appears in the control character of the FORTRAN output buffer?
    (a)   '1'
    (b)   ' '
    (c)   '0'
    (d)   '+'
    (e)   '2'
3. What is printed out by the following FORTRAN statements?
    (a)
```
      INTEGER I
      I = -123456
      WRITE (*,100) I
100   FORMAT ('1','I = ', I6)
```
    (b)
```
      INTEGER I
      I = 16
      WRITE (*,200) I
200   FORMAT ('1','I = ', I6.5)
```
    (c)
```
      REAL A, B, SUM, DIFF
      A    = 1.0020E6
      B    = 1.0001E6
      SUM  = A + B
      DIFF = A - B
      WRITE (*,101) A, B, SUM, DIFF
101   FORMAT (1X,'A = ',1PE14.6,' B = ',E14.6,' SUM = ',E14.6,
     *            ' DIFF = ', F14.6)
```
    (d)
```
      INTEGER I1, I2
      I1 = 10
      I2 = 4**2
      WRITE (*,400) I1 .GT. I2
400   FORMAT (' ','RESULT = ', L6)
```

4. What is printed out by the following FORTRAN statements?

(*a*)
```
        REAL A, B, C
        DATA A, B, C / 1.602E-19, 57.2957795, -1. /
        WRITE (*,100) A, B, C
   100 FORMAT (' ',1PE14.7,2(1X,E13.7))
        WRITE (*,110) A, B, C
   110 FORMAT (' ',1PE14.7,1X,E13.7,1X,F13.7)
```

(*b*)
```
        INTEGER I, J, K
        DATA I, J, K / 1234567, -1234567, -5 /
        WRITE (*,100) I, J, K
   100 FORMAT ('0',I8.8,2X,I8,2X,I3)
```

5. For the FORTRAN statements and input data given below, state what the values of each variable will be when the **READ** statement has been completed.

Statements:

```
    CHARACTER A*5, B*10, C*15
    READ (*,10) A, B, C
 10 FORMAT ( 3A10 )
```

Input Data:

```
     5    10   15   20   25   30   35   40   45   50
 ----|----|----|----|----|----|----|----|----|----|
 This is a test of reading characters.
 ----|----|----|----|----|----|----|----|----|----|
     5    10   15   20   25   30   35   40   45   50
```

6. For the FORTRAN statements and input data given below, state what the values of each variable will be when the **READ** statement has been completed.

(*a*) *Statements:*

```
    INTEGER ITEM1, ITEM2, ITEM3, ITEM4, ITEM5
    INTEGER ITEM6, ITEM7, ITEM8, ITEM9, ITEM10
    READ (*,*) ITEM1, ITEM2, ITEM3, ITEM4, ITEM5, ITEM6
    READ (*,*) ITEM7, ITEM8, ITEM9, ITEM10
```

Input Data:

```
     5    10   15   20   25   30   35   40   45   50
 ----|----|----|----|----|----|----|----|----|----|
        -300      -250      -210      -160      -135
        -105       -70       -55       -28       -11
          17        55       102       165       225
 ----|----|----|----|----|----|----|----|----|----|
     5    10   15   20   25   30   35   40   45   50
```

(*b*) *Statements:*

```
    INTEGER ITEM1, ITEM2, ITEM3, ITEM4, ITEM5
    INTEGER ITEM6, ITEM7, ITEM8, ITEM9, ITEM10
    READ (*,8) ITEM1, ITEM2, ITEM3, ITEM4, ITEM5, ITEM6
    READ (*,8) ITEM7, ITEM8, ITEM9, ITEM10
  8 FORMAT (4I10)
```

Input Data:

```
     5    10   15   20   25   30   35   40   45   50
----|----|----|----|----|----|----|----|----|----|
      -300        -250       -210       -160      -135
      -105         -70        -55        -28       -11
        17          55        102        165       225
----|----|----|----|----|----|----|----|----|----|
     5    10   15   20   25   30   35   40   45   50
```

(**c**)   *Statements:*

```
      CHARACTER LAST*16, FIRST*16, MI*1, SEX*1, SKILL*20
      INTEGER AGE
      READ (*,100) LAST, FIRST, MI, SEX, AGE, SKILL
  100 FORMAT (A16,T20,A16,T40,A1,///,A1,T16,I3,1X,A20)
```

Input Data:

```
     5    10   15   20   25   30   35   40   45   50
----|----|----|----|----|----|----|----|----|----|
JOHNSON             JAMES                R
Rt. 4 Box 206
Anytown, TX 99999
M               45 ELECTRICAL ENGR
----|----|----|----|----|----|----|----|----|----|
     5    10   15   20   25   30   35   40   45   50
```

(**d**)   *Statements:*

```
      CHARACTER*20 STR1, STR2
      LOGICAL MYTEST
      REAL X, Y
      READ (*,*) STR1
      READ (*,100) STR2
  100 FORMAT (A20)
      MYTEST = STR1 .EQ. STR2
      IF ( MYTEST ) THEN
          READ (*,110) X, Y
  110     FORMAT (F20.2)
      ELSE
          READ (*,120) X, Y
  120     FORMAT (F18.4)
      END IF
```

Input Data:

```
     5    10   15   20   25   30   35   40   45   50
----|----|----|----|----|----|----|----|----|----|
'TEST1'
'TEST1'
            -37.1615
            12345678
----|----|----|----|----|----|----|----|----|----|
     5    10   15   20   25   30   35   40   45   50
```

(e) *Statements:*

```
CHARACTER*15 STRING
LOGICAL TEST
INTEGER INT1
REAL REAL1, REAL2
READ (*,400) TEST, STRING, REAL1, INT1, REAL2
400 FORMAT (L10,T1,A10,T11,F10.3,T13,I4,F10.2)
```

Input Data:

```
     5    10   15   20   25   30   35   40   45   50
----|----|----|----|----|----|----|----|----|----|
     FIRST    3375.62
----|----|----|----|----|----|----|----|----|----|
     5    10   15   20   25   30   35   40   45   50
```

7. Write a FORTRAN program to generate a table of the base-10 logarithms between 1 and 10 in steps of 0.1. The table should start in a new page, and should include a title describing the table and row and column headings. This table should be organized as shown.

	X.0	X.1	X.2	X.3	X.4	X.5	X.6	X.7	X.8	X.9
1.0	0.000	0.041	0.079	0.114	...					
2.0	0.301	0.322	0.342	0.362	...					
3.0	...									
4.0	...									
5.0	...									
6.0	...									
7.0	...									
8.0	...									
9.0	...									
10.0	...									

8. Example 4-3 illustrates the technique of reading an arbitrary amount of real data from an input data file. Modify that program to read in the data from an input data file and to calculate the mean and standard deviation of the samples in the file.

9. A real number LENGTH is to be displayed in **Fw.d** format with four digits to the right of the decimal point ($d = 4$). If the number is known to lie within the range $-10000. \le$ LENGTH $\le 10000.$, what is the minimum field width w that will always be able to display the value of LENGTH?

10. In what columns will the following characters be printed?

```
    WRITE (*,1700) 'Garbage!'
1700 FORMAT (T30,A)
```

11. Write FORTRAN statements to perform the functions described below. Assume that variables beginning with I-N are integers, and all other variables are reals.

(*a*)   Skip to a new page and print the title 'INPUT DATA' starting in column 40.

(*b*)   Skip a line, and then display the data point number IPOINT in columns 6–10, and the data point value DATA in columns 15–26. Display the data in scientific notation with seven significant digits.

12.   What is the major advantage of the scaling factor (**P**) descriptor? What is its major disadvantage?

13.   What is the minimum field width necessary to display any real data value in **E** format with 6 significant bits of accuracy? What is the minimum field width necessary to display the data with six significant bits of accuracy if the **1P** scale factor is used with the **E** format?

14.   Examine the following FORTRAN statements. Are they correct or incorrect? If they are incorrect, why are they incorrect? (Unless otherwise indicated, assume that variables beginning with I-N are integers, and all other variables are reals.)

(*a*)
```
      INTEGER COUNT
      LOGICAL STATUS
      REAL FREQ, PERIOD
      ...
      WRITE (*, 1001) 'FREQ, PERIOD = ', FREQ, PERIOD, COUNT,
     *    STATUS
 1001 FORMAT (1X,A10,F15.5,L10,I10)
```
(*b*)
```
      WRITE (*,100) X .LT. Y
  100 FORMAT (1X,'X < Y?', I6)
```
(*c*)
```
      WRITE (*,200) X1, X2, X3, Y1, Y2, Y3
  200 FORMAT ('1','OUTPUT:'//,2(3F14.6))
```

15.   Write a FORTRAN program that reads in a time in seconds since the start of the day (this value will be somewhere between 0. and 86400.), and writes out the time in the form HH:MM:SS using the 24-hour clock convention. Use the **Iw.m** format descriptor to ensure that leading zeros are preserved in the MM and SS fields. Also, be sure to check the input number of seconds for validity, and write an appropriate error message if an invalid number is entered.

16.   Modify the program of the previous problem to write out the time in 12-hour clock format, with AM or PM (as appropriate) appended to the time.

17.   What is the proper STATUS to use when opening a file to read input data from? What is the proper STATUS to use when opening a file to write output data to? What is the proper STATUS to use when opening a temporary storage file?

18.   Is a **CLOSE** statement always required in a FORTRAN program that uses disk files? Why or why not?

19.   Write FORTRAN statements to perform the functions described below. Assume that file INPUT.DAT contains a series of real values organized with one value per record.

(*a*)   Open an existing file named INPUT.DAT on LU 98 for input, and a new file named NEWOUT.DAT on LU 99 for output.

(*b*)   Read data values from file INPUT.DAT until the end-of-file is reached. Write all positive data values to the output file.

(*c*)   Close the input and output data files.

20.   Write a program that reads an arbitrary number of real values from a user-specified input data file, rounds the values to the nearest integer, and writes the integers to a user-specified output file. Open the input and output files with the appropriate status, and be sure to handle end-of-file and error conditions properly.

21.   Write a program that opens a scratch file and writes the integers 1–10 in the first 10 records. Next, move back six records in the file, and read the value stored in that record. Save that value in variable X. Next, move back three records in the file, and read the value stored in that record. Save that value in variable Y. Multiply the two values X and Y together. What is their product?

22.   Write FORTRAN statements to perform the functions described below. Assume that file STATS.DAT contains a series of real values organized with one value per record.

(*a*)   Open an existing file named STATS.DAT on logical unit 7 for input.

(*b*)   Read the fifth line in the input data file, and store the value in variable X5.

(*c*)   Next, backspace in the input data file to read the third line, and store the value in variable Y3.

(*d*)   Finally, rewind the file and read the first line in the file. Store the value in Z1.

Assume that file STATS.DAT contains the following 10 items organized one per record: 1.25, 88.0, 95.0, 100.0, 35.5, −89.3, 78.9, 100.02, 47.2, 16.5. What will be stored in variables X5, Y3, and Z1?

23.   Examine the following FORTRAN statements. Are they correct or incorrect? If they are incorrect, why are they incorrect? (Unless otherwise indicated, assume that variables beginning with I-N are integers, and all other variables are reals.)

(*a*)
```
OPEN (UNIT=1, FILE='INFO.DAT', STATUS='NEW', IOSTAT=IERROR)
READ (1,*) I, J, K
```

(*b*)
```
OPEN (UNIT=17,FILE='TEMP.DAT',STATUS='SCRATCH',IOSTAT=IERROR)
```

(*c*)
```
LU = 8
OPEN (UNIT=LU, FILE='INFO.DAT', STATUS='OLD', IOSTAT=IERROR)
READ (8,*) LU
CLOSE (UNIT=LU)
```

(*d*)
```
OPEN (UNIT=9, FILE='OUTPUT.DAT', STATUS='NEW', IOSTAT=IERROR)
WRITE (9,*) MYDAT1, MYDAT2
WRITE (9,*) MYDAT3, MYDAT4
CLOSE (UNIT=9)
```

24.   Write a program to generate a table containing the sine and cosine of θ for θ between 0 and 90°, in 1° increments. The program should properly label each of the columns in the table.

25. Suppose that you have a sum of money P in an interest-bearing account at a local bank (P stands for *present value*). If the bank pays you interest on the money at a rate of i percent per year and compounds the interest monthly, the amount of money that you will have in the bank after n months is given by the equation

$$F = P\left(1 + \frac{i}{1200}\right)^n$$

where F is the future value of the account and $i/12$ is the monthly percentage interest rate (the extra factor of 100 in the denominator converts the interest rate from percentages to fractional amounts). Write a FORTRAN program that will read an initial amount of money P and an annual interest rate i, and will calculate and print out a table showing the future value of the account every month for the next five years. Be sure to label the columns of your table properly.

26. Write a program to read a set of integers from an input data file, and locate the largest and smallest values within the data file. Print out the largest and smallest values, together with the lines on which they were found. Assume that you do not know the number of values in the file before the file is read.

27. In Problem 25 in Chapter 3, we wrote a FORTRAN program that calculated the arithmetic mean (average), root-mean-square (rms) average, geometric mean, and harmonic mean for a set of numbers. Modify that program to read an arbitrary number of values from an input data file, and calculate the means of those numbers. To test the program, place the following values into an input data file and run the program on that file: 1.0, 2.0, 5.0, 4.0, 3.0, 2.1, 4.7, 3.0.

28. There is a logical error in program LSQFIT from Example 4-5. The error can cause the program to abort with a divide-by-zero error. It slipped through the example because we did not test the program exhaustively for all possible inputs. Find the error, and rewrite the program to eliminate it.

29. The method of least squares is used to fit a straight line to a noisy input data set consisting of pairs of values (x, y). As we saw in Example 4-5, the best fit to the equation

$$y = mx + b \qquad \text{(4-5)}$$

is given by

$$m = \frac{(\Sigma xy) - (\Sigma x)\bar{y}}{(\Sigma x^2) - (\Sigma x)\bar{x}} \qquad \text{(4-6)}$$

and

$$b = \bar{y} - m\bar{x} \qquad \text{(4-7)}$$

where

Σx	is the sum of the x values
Σx^2	is the sum of the squares of the x values
Σxy	is the sum of the products of the corresponding x and y values
$\bar{x}$	is the mean (average) of the x values
$\bar{y}$	is the mean (average) of the y values

Figure 4-10 shows two data sets and the least-squares fits associated with each one. As you can see, the low-noise data fits the least-squares line much better than the noisy data does. It would be useful to have some quantitative way to describe how well the data fits the least-squares line given by Equations (4-5) through (4-7).

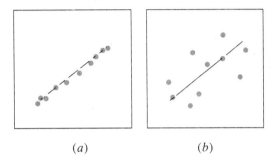

(a)   (b)

FIGURE 4-10   Two different least-squares fits: (a) with good, low-noise data; (b) with very noisy data.

There is a standard statistical measure of the "goodness of fit" of a data set to a least-squares line. It is called a *correlation coefficient*. The correlation coefficient is equal to 1.0 when there is a perfect positive linear relationship between data x and y, and it is equal to -1.0 when there is a perfect negative linear relationship between data x and y. The correlation coefficient is 0.0 when there is no linear relationship between x and y at all. The correlation coefficient is given by the equation

$$r = \frac{n(\Sigma xy) - (\Sigma x)(\Sigma y)}{\sqrt{[(n\Sigma x^2) - (\Sigma x)^2][(n\Sigma y^2) - (\Sigma y)^2]}}$$

where r is the correlation coefficient and n is the number of data points included in the fit.

Write a program to read an arbitrary number of (x, y) data pairs from an input data file, and to calculate and print out both the least-squares fit to the data and the correlation coefficient for the fit. If the correlation coefficient is small ($|r| < 0.2$), write out a warning message to the user.

5

Arrays

An **array** is a group of variables, all of the same type, that are referred to by a single name. The variables in the group occupy consecutive locations in the computer's memory (see Figure 5-1). An individual variable within the array is called an **array element;** it is identified by the name of the array together with a **subscript** pointing to the particular variable within the array. For example, the first variable shown in Figure 5-1 is referred to as A(1), and the fifth variable shown in the figure is referred

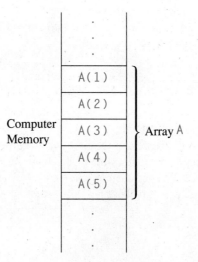

FIGURE 5-1   The elements of an array occupy successive locations in a computer's memory.

to as A(5). The subscript of an array is of type **INTEGER.** Either constants or variables may be used for array subscripts.

As we will see, arrays can be extremely powerful tools. They permit us to apply the same algorithm over and over again to many different data items with a simple **DO** loop. For example, suppose that we need to take the square root of 100 different real numbers. If the numbers are stored as elements of an array A consisting of 100 real values, then the code

```
      DO 10 I = 1, 100
         A(I) = SQRT(A(I))
  10 CONTINUE
```

will take the square root of each real number, and store it back into the memory location that it came from. If we wanted to take the square root of 100 real numbers without using arrays, we would have to write out

```
  A1   = SQRT(A1)
  A2   = SQRT(A2)
  A3   = SQRT(A3)
  A4   = SQRT(A4)
       . . .
  A100 = SQRT(A100)
```

on 100 separate lines! Arrays are obviously a *much* cleaner way to handle repeated similar operations.

5.1 DECLARING ARRAYS

Before an array can be used, its *type* and *size* must be **declared** to the compiler, so that the compiler will know what sort of data is to be stored in the array, and how much memory is required to hold it. An array may be of any type: real, integer, logical, or character. The type and size of an array are declared using a type declaration statement.[1] For example, a real array TRASH containing 16 elements could be declared as follows:

```
  REAL TRASH(16)
```

The elements in array TRASH would be addressed as TRASH(1), TRASH(2), etc., up to TRASH(16). Similarly, an array of fifty 20-character-long variables could be declared as follows:

```
  CHARACTER*20 LASTNM(50)
```

Each of the elements in array LASTNM would be a **CHARACTER*20** variable, and the elements would be addressed as LASTNM(1), LASTNM(2), etc.

---

[1]There is an alternate way to declare array sizes using a **DIMENSION** statement. The **DIMENSION** statement is described in Chapter 12.

5.2   USING ARRAYS

This section contains some of the practical details involved in using arrays in FOR-TRAN programs.

5.2.1   Array Elements Are Just Ordinary Variables

Each element of an array is a variable just like any other variable, and *an array element may be used in any place where an ordinary variable of the same type may be used.* Array elements may be included in arithmetic and logical expressions, and the results of an expression may be assigned to an array element. Assume that arrays I, L, TEMP, and STRING are declared as:

```
INTEGER I(10)
LOGICAL L(2)
REAL    TEMP(3)
CHARACTER*10 STRING(5)
```

Then the following FORTRAN 77 statements are perfectly valid:

```
I(1) = 1
L(2) = .TRUE.
TEMP(3) = REAL(I(1)) / 4.
STRING(3) = 'Your name:'
WRITE (*,*) ' I(1) = ', I(1)
WRITE (*,*) STRING(3)
```

Note that although array elements can be used freely like any other variables in FORTRAN 77 statements, arrays themselves *may not* be used like variables in FOR-TRAN 77 statements. For example, assume that arrays I and TEMP are declared as above. Then each of the following statements are illegal, and will produce a compile-time error:

```
I = 1
TEMP = REAL(I)
RESULT = SIN(TEMP)
```

The only exceptions to this general rule occur in certain I/O statements, which are covered later in this chapter, and in subprograms, which are covered in Chapter 6.

PROGRAMMING PITFALLS

Be careful not to confuse arrays with array elements in your code. Array elements may be freely used anywhere a FORTRAN variable is required, but entire arrays are restricted to certain special uses which will be described later.

5.2.2   Initialization of Array Elements

Just as with ordinary variables, the values in an array must be *initialized* before use. If an array is not initialized, the contents of the array elements are undefined. In the following FORTRAN 77 statements, array J is an example of an **uninitialized array.**

```
INTEGER J(10)
WRITE (*,*) ' J(1) = ', J(1)
```

The array J has been declared by the INTEGER J(10) statement, but no values have been placed into it yet. The values of the elements in an uninitialized array are not defined by the FORTRAN 77 standard. Some compilers automatically set uninitialized array elements to zero, and some set them to different arbitrary patterns. Other compilers leave in memory whatever values previously existed in the computer's memory at the location of the array elements. Some compilers even produce a run-time error if an array element is used without first being initialized.

Because of these differences, a program that works perfectly well on one computer may fail when it is moved to another one. To ensure that a program performs consistently from computer to computer, *the elements in an array should always be initialized before they are used.*

■ **GOOD PROGRAMMING PRACTICE**

Always initialize the elements in an array before they are used.

The elements in an array may be initialized by one of three techniques:

---

1. Initial values may be assigned to the array using assignment statements in a **DO** loop.
2. Initial values may be loaded into the array at compilation time using **DATA** statements.
3. Initial values may be read into the array using FORTRAN 77 **READ** statements.

Initializing Arrays with DO Loops

Initial values may be assigned to the array during program execution by using assignment statements in a **DO** loop. For example, the following code initializes all of the elements of array ARRAY1 to 0.0:

```
REAL ARRAY1(100)
DO 10 I = 1, 100
   ARRAY1(I) = 0.0
10 CONTINUE
```

The simple program shown in Figure 5-2 calculates the squares of the numbers in array NUMBER, and then prints out the numbers and their squares. Note that the values in array NUMBER are initialized with a **DO** loop.

```
      PROGRAM SQR1
C
      IMPLICIT NONE
C
      INTEGER I, NUMBER(10), SQUARE(10)
C
C     Initialize array NUMBER.
C
      DO 10 I = 1, 10
         NUMBER(I) = I
   10 CONTINUE
C
C     Calculate the squares of the numbers.
C
      DO 20 I = 1, 10
         SQUARE(I) = NUMBER(I)**2
   20 CONTINUE
C
C     Write out each number and its square.
C
      DO 30 I = 1, 10
         WRITE (*,100) NUMBER(I), SQUARE(I)
  100    FORMAT (1X,'NUMBER = ',I6,'  SQUARE = ',I6)
   30 CONTINUE
C
      END
```

FIGURE 5-2   A program to calculate the squares of the integers from 1 to 10, using a **DO** loop to initialize the values in array NUMBER.

Initializing Arrays with DATA Statements

Initial values may be loaded into the array at compilation time using **DATA** statements. Either individual array elements or entire arrays may be initialized with **DATA** statements. To initialize an array element with a **DATA** statement, we name the array element and then declare its initial value between slashes. For example, the following statement initializes element 2 of ARRAY1 to 10.

```
      REAL ARRAY1(100)
      DATA ARRAY1(2) / 10. /
```

To initialize the values of an entire array with a **DATA** statement, we name the array and then declare the initial values of all of its elements between slashes. For example, the following statement initializes each of the values of array ARRAY1.

```
      REAL ARRAY1(100)
      DATA ARRAY1 / 1., 2., 98*100. /
```

This statement initializes array element ARRAY1(1) to 1., array element ARRAY1(2) to 2., and array elements ARRAY1(3) through ARRAY1(100) to 100.

If the **DATA** statement used to initialize an array contains either fewer data values or more data values than there are elements in the array, the behavior of the **DATA** statement will be unpredictable. On some compilers, a mismatch in the number of values will produce a compile-time error. On others, the data values are used to initialize as many array elements as possible, and then any excess array elements or data values will be ignored. For example, the following code will produce a compilation error on some compilers. On others, the first three elements of ARRAY1 are initialized to 1., 2., and 3., respectively, while all of the other elements of the array remain uninitialized.

```
REAL ARRAY1(100)
DATA ARRAY1 / 1., 2., 3. /
```

Since we would like for our programs to be as portable as possible between computers, it is a good idea to always make the number of array elements and the number of data values match in any **DATA** statement.

■ **GOOD PROGRAMMING PRACTICE**

Always make the number of array elements equal to the number of data values in a **DATA** statement.

The program in Figure 5-3 illustrates the use of **DATA** statements to initialize the values in an array. It calculates the square roots of the numbers in array VALUE, and then prints out the numbers and their square roots. Note that the elements of array SQRT1 are initialized by assignment statements as a part of the calculation.

```
      PROGRAM SQRT1
C
      IMPLICIT NONE
C
      INTEGER I
      REAL VALUE(10), SQRT1(10)
C
C     Initialize array VALUE.
C
      DATA VALUE / 1., 2., 3., 4., 5., 6., 7., 8., 9., 10. /
C
C     Calculate the square roots of the numbers.
C
      DO 20 I = 1, 10
         SQRT1(I) = SQRT (VALUE(I))
   20 CONTINUE
C
C     Write out each number and its square root.
C
      DO 30 I = 1, 10
```

```
           WRITE (*,100) VALUE(I), SQRT1(I)
   100     FORMAT (1X,'VALUE = ',F10.4,'  SQUARE ROOT = ',F10.4)
    30 CONTINUE
C
       END
```

FIGURE 5-3 A program to calculate the square roots of the integers from 1 to 10, using a
DATA statement to initialize the values in array VALUE.

Initializing Arrays with FORTRAN READ Statements

Arrays may also be initialized with FORTRAN **READ** statements. The use of arrays
in I/O statements is described in detail in Section 5.3.

5.2.3 Changing the Declared Subscript Range of an Array

The elements of an *N*-element array are normally addressed using the subscripts 1,
2, . . . , *N*. Thus the elements of array A declared with the statement

```
    REAL A(5)
```

would be addressed as A(1), A(2), A(3), A(4), and A(5). In some problems, however, it is more convenient to address the array elements with other subscripts. For
example, the possible grades on an exam range from 0 to 100. If we wished to accumulate statistics on the number of people scoring any given grade, it would be convenient to have a 101-element array whose subscripts ranged from 0 to 100 instead
of 1 to 101. If the subscripts ranged from 0 to 100, each student's exam grade could
be used directly as an index into the array.

For those problems, FORTRAN 77 provides a mechanism for specifying the
range of numbers which will be used to address the elements of an array. To specify
the subscript range, we include the starting and ending subscript numbers in the declaration statement, with the two numbers separated by a colon. For example, the following three arrays all consist of five elements:

```
    REAL A(5)
    REAL B(-2:2)
    REAL C(5:9)
```

Array A is addressed with subscripts 1 through 5, array B is addressed with subscripts −2 through 2, and array C is addressed with subscripts 5 through 9.

The simple program SQR2 shown in Figure 5-4 calculates the squares of the
numbers in array NUMBER, and then prints out the numbers and their squares. The
arrays in this example contain 11 elements, addressed by the subscripts −5, −4, . . .
0, . . . , 4, 5.

```
PROGRAM SQR2
C
    IMPLICIT NONE
C
    INTEGER I, NUMBER(-5:5), SQUARE(-5:5)
```

```
C
C      Initialize array NUMBER.
C
       DO 10 I = -5, 5
          NUMBER(I) = I
    10 CONTINUE
C
C      Calculate the squares of the numbers, and write out
C      the result.
C
       DO 20 I = -5, 5
          SQUARE(I) = NUMBER(I)**2
          WRITE (*,100) I, NUMBER(I), SQUARE(I)
   100    FORMAT (1X,'I = ',I6,'  NUMBER = ',I6,'  SQUARE = ',I6)
    20 CONTINUE
C
       END
```

FIGURE 5-4   A program to calculate the squares of the integers from -5 to 5, using array elements addressed by subscripts -5 through 5.

When program SQR2 is executed, the results are

```
C:\BOOK\FORT>sqr2
I =  -5  NUMBER =  -5  SQUARE =  25
I =  -4  NUMBER =  -4  SQUARE =  16
I =  -3  NUMBER =  -3  SQUARE =   9
I =  -2  NUMBER =  -2  SQUARE =   4
I =  -1  NUMBER =  -1  SQUARE =   1
I =   0  NUMBER =   0  SQUARE =   0
I =   1  NUMBER =   1  SQUARE =   1
I =   2  NUMBER =   2  SQUARE =   4
I =   3  NUMBER =   3  SQUARE =   9
I =   4  NUMBER =   4  SQUARE =  16
I =   5  NUMBER =   5  SQUARE =  25
```

5.2.4   Out-of-Bounds Array Subscripts

Each element of an array is addressed using an integer subscript. The range of integers that correspond to elements in the array depends on the size of the array as declared in a program. For a real array declared as

```
REAL A(5)
```

the integer subscripts 1, 2, 3, 4, and 5 would correspond to elements in the array. *Any other integers* (less than 1 or greater than 5) *could not be used as subscripts, since they do not correspond to allocated memory locations.* Such integers subscripts are said to be **out of bounds** for the array. But what would happen if we make a mistake and try to access the out of bounds element A(6) in a program?

The answer to this question is complicated, since it varies from computer to computer. On some computers, a running FORTRAN 77 program checks *every subscript* used to reference an array to see if it is in bounds. If an out-of-bounds subscript is detected, the program issues an informative error message and stops. Unfortunately, such **bounds checking** requires a lot of computer time, and the program will run very slowly. To make programs run faster, most FORTRAN compilers make bounds checking optional. If it is turned on, programs run slower, but they are protected from out-of-bounds references. If it is turned off, programs run much faster, but out-of-bounds references are not checked. If your FORTRAN compiler has a bounds checking option, you should always turn it on during debugging to help detect programming errors. Once the program has been debugged, bounds checking can be turned off if necessary to increase the execution speed of the final program.

■ GOOD PROGRAMMING PRACTICE

Always turn on the bounds-checking option on your FORTRAN compiler during program development and debugging to help you catch programming errors producing out-of-bounds references. The bounds-checking option may be turned off if necessary for greater speed in the final program.

What happens in a program if an out-of-bounds reference occurs and the bounds checking option is not turned on? Sometimes the program aborts. Much of the time, though, the computer will simply go to the location in memory *at which the referenced array element would have been if it had been allocated,* and use that memory location. For example, the array A declared above has five elements in it. If A(6) were used in a program, the computer would access the first word beyond the end of array A. Since that word will be allocated for a totally different purpose, the program can fail in subtle and bizarre ways which can be almost impossible to track down. Be careful with your array subscripts, and always use the bounds checker when you are debugging!

The program shown in Figure 5-5 illustrates the behavior of a FORTRAN program containing incorrect array references with and without bounds checking turned on. This simple program declares a five-element real array A and a real variable B. The array A is initialized with the values 1, 2, 3, 4, and 5, and B is initialized with the value 6 (see Figure 5-6). It uses a **DO** loop to write out the values in the array elements 1 through 6 (note that array element A(6) is out of bounds).

```
      PROGRAM ARRAY1
C
C  Purpose:
C    To illustrate the effect of accessing an out-of-bounds
C    array element.
C
C  Record of revisions:
C      Date       Programmer        Description of change
C      ====       ==========        =====================
C    04/10/91  S. J. Chapman        Original code
C
C  List of variables:
```

```
C      A      -- Name of a 5-element real array
C      B      -- Real variable allocated after the end of the array
C
       IMPLICIT NONE
C
C      Declare the and initialize the variables used in this program.
C
       REAL A(5), B
       DATA A / 1., 2., 3., 4., 5. /
       DATA B / 6. /
C
C      Write out the values of array A
C
       DO 10 I = 1, 6
          WRITE (*,100) I, A(I)
  100     FORMAT ( 1X,'A(', I1, ') = ', F6.2 )
   10 CONTINUE
C
C      Write out the value of variable B
C
       WRITE (*,110) B
  110 FORMAT ( 1X,'B = ', F6.2 )
C
       END
```

FIGURE 5-5   A simple program to illustrate the effect of out-of-bounds array references with and without bounds checking turned on.

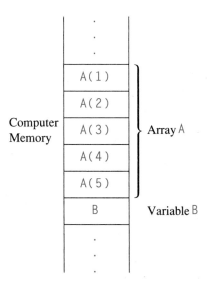

FIGURE 5-6   A computer memory showing a five-element array A followed by a variable B. If bounds checking is turned off, some computers may not recognize the end of array A, and may treat B as A(6).

If this program is compiled with the MICROSOFT FORTRAN compiler on a PC-compatible computer with bounds checking turned on, the result is

```
C:\BOOK\FORT>array1
A(1) =    1.00
A(2) =    2.00
A(3) =    3.00
A(4) =    4.00
A(5) =    5.00
array1.for(12) : run-time error F6096: $DEBUG
- array subscript expression out of range
```

The program checked each array reference, and aborted when an out-of-bounds expression was encountered. Note that the error message tells us what is wrong, and even the line number at which it occurred. If bounds checking is turned off, the result is

```
C:\BOOK\FORT>array1
A(1) =    1.00
A(2) =    2.00
A(3) =    3.00
A(4) =    4.00
A(5) =    5.00
A(6) =    6.00
B    =    6.00
```

Since variable B was allocated immediately after array A in the computer's memory, the value stored in B was displayed when the program wrote out array element A(6).

5.2.5   The PARAMETER Statement

In many FORTRAN programs, arrays are used to store large amounts of information. The amount of information that a program can process depends on the size of the arrays included in it. If the arrays are made relatively small, the program will be small and will not require much memory to run, but it will only be able to handle a small amount of data. On the other hand, if the arrays are made large, the program will be able to handle a lot of information, but it will require a lot of memory to run. The array sizes in such a program are frequently changed to make the program run better for different problems or on different computers.

It is good practice to always declare the array sizes using **PARAMETER** statements. As we mentioned in Chapter 2, a parameter is essentially a named constant that may be used in place of an ordinary constant anywhere in a FORTRAN program. Parameters make it easy to resize the arrays in a FORTRAN program. In the following code, the sizes of all arrays can be changed by simply changing the single parameter ISIZE.

```
      INTEGER ISIZE
      PARAMETER ( ISIZE = 1000 )
C
      REAL ARRAY1(ISIZE)
      REAL ARRAY2(ISIZE)
      REAL ARRAY3(2*ISIZE)
```

This may seem like a small point, but it is *very* important to the proper maintenance of large FORTRAN programs. If all related array sizes in a program are declared using parameters, and if those same parameters are used in any size tests that may be in the program, then it will be much simpler to modify the program later. Imagine what it would be like if you had to locate and change every reference to array sizes within a 50,000-line program! The process could take you weeks to complete and debug. By contrast, the size of a well-designed program could be modified in five minutes by changing only one statement in the code.

GOOD PROGRAMMING PRACTICE

Always declare the sizes of arrays in a FORTRAN program using **PARAMETER** statements to make them easy to change.

EXAMPLE 5-1 *Finding the Largest and Smallest Values in a Data Set* To illustrate the use of arrays, we write a simple program that reads in data values supplied by a user, and finds the largest and smallest numbers in the data set. The program then writes out the values, with the word LARGEST printed by the largest value and the word SMALLEST printed by the smallest value in the data set.

SOLUTION This program must be able to ask the user for the number of values to be input, and then must read the input values into an array. Once the values are all read in, it must go through the data to find the largest and smallest values in the data set. Finally, it must print out the input values, with the appropriate annotations beside the largest and smallest values in the data set.

1. State the problem.
We have not yet specified the type of data we will be processing. If we are processing integer data, then the problem that we are solving may be stated as follows:

> Develop a program to read a user-specified number of integer values from the standard input device, locate the largest and smallest values in the data set, and write out all of the values with the words 'LARGEST' and 'SMALLEST' printed by the largest and smallest values in the data set.

2. Define the inputs and outputs.

There are two types of inputs to this program:

> (*a*) An integer containing the number of integer values to read. This value will come from the standard input device.
>
> (*b*) The integer values in the data set. These values will also come from the standard input device.

The outputs from this program are the values in the data set, with the word 'LARGEST' printed by the largest value, and the word 'SMALLEST' printed by the smallest value.

3. Describe the algorithm.

The program can be broken down into four major steps

```
Get the number of values to read in
Read the input values into an array
Find the largest and smallest values in the array
Write out the data with the words 'LARGEST' and 'SMALLEST' at
    the appropriate places
```

The first two major steps of the program are to get the number of values to read in and to read the values into an input array. We must prompt the user for the number of values to read in. If that number is less than or equal to the size of the input array, we should read in the data values. Otherwise we should warn the user and quit. The detailed pseudocode for these steps is

```
Prompt user for the number of input values NVAL
Read in NVALS
IF NVAL <= MAXSIZ then
    DO for J = 1 to NVALS
        Read in input values
    End of DO
    ...
    ...(Further processing here)
    ...
ELSE
    Tell user that there are too many values for array to hold
End of IF
END
```

Next we have to locate the largest and smallest values in the data set. We will use variables ILARGE and ISMALL to hold pointers to the array elements having the largest and smallest values. The pseudocode to find the largest and smallest values is

```
*
* Find largest value
*
    TEMP ← INPUT(1)
    ILARGE ← 1
    DO for J = 2 to NVALS
```

```
            IF INPUT(J) > TEMP then
                TEMP ← INPUT(J)
                ILARGE ← J
            End of IF
         End of DO
   *
   *   Find smallest value
   *
         TEMP ← INPUT(1)
         ISMALL ← 1
         DO for J = 2 to NVALS-1
            IF INPUT(J) > TEMP then
                TEMP ← INPUT(J)
                ISMALL ← J
            End of IF
         End of DO
```

The final step is writing out the values with the largest and smallest numbers labeled

```
         DO for J = 1 to NVALS
            IF ISMALL = J then
                Write INPUT(J) and 'SMALLEST'
            ELSE IF ILARGE = J then
                Write INPUT(J) and 'LARGEST'
            ELSE
                Write INPUT(J)
         End of DO
```

4. Turn the algorithm into FORTRAN statements.
The resulting FORTRAN program is shown in Figure 5-7.

```
      PROGRAM EXTRME
C
C  Purpose:
C    To find the largest and smallest values in a data set,
C    and to print out the data set with the largest and smallest
C    values labeled.
C
C  Record of revisions:
C      Date      Programmer         Description of change
C      ====      ==========         =====================
C    07/19/93  S. J. Chapman       Original code
C
C  List of parameters:
C     MAXSIZ — Maximum size of input data set.
C
C  List of variables:
C     INPUT  -- Array of input values.
C     ILARGE -- Pointer to largest value in data set
C     ISMALL -- Pointer to smallest value in data set
C     J      -- DO loop index
C     NVALS  -- number of values in input data set (<= MAXSIZ)
C     TEMP   -- Temporary variable used when looking for big/small values.
C
      IMPLICIT NONE
C
```

```
      INTEGER MAXSIZ
      PARAMETER ( MAXSIZ = 10 )
C
C     Declare variables.
C
      INTEGER INPUT(MAXSIZ), ILARGE, ISMALL, J, TEMP, NVALS
C
C     Get number of values in data set
C
      WRITE (*,*) 'Enter number of values in data set:'
      READ (*,*) NVALS
C
C     Is the number <= MAXSIZ?
C
      IF ( NVALS .LE. MAXSIZ ) THEN
C
C         Yes!  Get values.
C
          DO 10 J = 1, NVALS
              WRITE (*,100) 'Enter value ', J
  100         FORMAT (' ',A,I3,':')
              READ (*,*) INPUT(J)
   10     CONTINUE
C
C         Find the largest value.
C
          TEMP = INPUT(1)
          ILARGE = 1
          DO 20 J = 2, NVALS
              IF ( INPUT(J) .GT. TEMP ) THEN
                  TEMP = INPUT(J)
                  ILARGE = J
              END IF
   20     CONTINUE
C
C         Find the smallest value.
C
          TEMP = INPUT(1)
          ISMALL = 1
          DO 30 J = 2, NVALS
              IF ( INPUT(J) .LT. TEMP ) THEN
                  TEMP = INPUT(J)
                  ISMALL = J
              END IF
   30     CONTINUE
C
C         Write out list.
C
          WRITE (*,110)
  110     FORMAT ('0','The values are:')
          DO 40 J = 1, NVALS
              IF ( J .EQ. ILARGE ) THEN
                  WRITE (*,120) INPUT(J), 'LARGEST'
  120             FORMAT (' ',I6,2X,A)
              ELSE IF ( J .EQ. ISMALL ) THEN
                  WRITE (*,120) INPUT(J), 'SMALLEST'
              ELSE
                  WRITE (*,120) INPUT(J)
              END IF
```

```
    40    CONTINUE
C
      ELSE
C
C         NVALS > MAXSIZ.  Tell user and quit.
C
          WRITE (*,130) NVALS, MAXSIZ
   130    FORMAT (1X,'Too many input values: ', I6, '>', I6)
C
      END IF
C
      END
```

FIGURE 5-7 A program to read in a data set from the standard input, find the largest and smallest values, and print the values with the largest and smallest values labeled.

5. Test the program.

To test this program, we use two data sets, one with 6 values and one with 12 values. Running this program with six values yields the following result:

```
C:\BOOK\FORT>extrme
Enter number of values in data set:
6
Enter value 1:
-6
Enter value 2:
5
Enter value 3:
-11
Enter value 4:
16
Enter value 5:
9
Enter value 6:
0

The values are:
     -6
      5
    -11   SMALLEST
     16   LARGEST
      9
      0
```

The program correctly labeled the largest and smallest values in the data set. Running this program with 12 values yields the following result:

```
C:\BOOK\FORT>extrme
Enter number of values in data set:
12
Too many input values:      12 >    10
```

The program recognized that there were too many input values, and quit. Thus, the program gives the correct answers for both of our test data sets. ●

5.3   INPUT AND OUTPUT

It is possible to perform I/O operations on either individual array elements or entire arrays. Both types of I/O operations are described in this section.

5.3.1   Input and Output of Array Elements

We previously stated that an *array element* is a variable just like any other variable, and that an array element may be used in any place where an ordinary variable of the same type may be used. Therefore, **READ** and **WRITE** statements containing array elements are just like **READ** and **WRITE** statements for any other variables.

To write out specific elements from an array, we just name them in the argument list of the **WRITE** statement. For example, the following code writes out the first five elements of the real array A.

```
    WRITE (*,100) A(1), A(2), A(3), A(4), A(5)
100 FORMAT (1X,'A = ', 5F10.2 )
```

5.3.2   The Implied DO Loop

FORTRAN 77 includes a shorthand way to write such an argument list: the **implied DO loop.** An implied **DO** loop permits an argument list to be written many times as a function of an index variable. Every argument in the argument list is written once for each value of the index variable in the implied **DO** loop. With an implied **DO** loop, the above statement becomes

```
    WRITE (*,100) ( A(I), I = 1, 5 )
100 FORMAT (1X,'A = ', 5F10.2 )
```

The argument list in this case contains only one item: A(I). This list is repeated once for each value of the index variable I. Since I takes on the values from 1 to 5, the array elements A(1), A(2), A(3), A(4), and A(5) will be written out.

The general form of a **WRITE** or **READ** statement with an implied **DO** loop is

```
    WRITE (lu,format) (arg1, arg2, ... , index = istart, iend, incr)
    READ  (lu,format) (arg1, arg2, ... , index = istart, iend, incr)
```

where *arg1, arg2,* etc., are the values to be written out or read in. Each argument in an output list may be a constant, a variable, an expression, or an array element; each argument in an input list must be a variable. The variable *index* is the **DO** loop index, and *istart, iend,* and *incr* are, respectively, the starting value, ending value, and increment of the loop index variable. The index and all of the loop control parameters should be of type **INTEGER**.

For a **WRITE** statement containing an implied **DO** loop, each argument in the argument list is written out once each time the loop is executed. Therefore, a statement like

```
        WRITE (*,1000) (I, 2*I, 3*I, I = 1, 3)
   1000 FORMAT (1X,9I6)
```

will write out nine values on a single line:

```
    1     2     3     2     4     6     3     6     9
```

Now let's look at a slightly more complicated example of using arrays with an implied **DO** loop. Figure 5-8 shows a program that calculates the square root and cube root of a set of numbers, and prints out a table of square and cube roots. The program computes square roots and cube roots for all numbers between 1 and MAXSIZ, where MAXSIZ is a parameter. What does the output of this program look like?

```
      PROGRAM ROOT23
C
C  Purpose:
C    To calculate a table of numbers, square roots, and cube roots
C    using an implied DO loop to output the table.
C
C  Record of revisions:
C      Date      Programmer        Description of change
C      ====      ==========        =====================
C    07/21/93  S. J. Chapman       Original code
C
C  List of parameters:
C     MAXSIZ -- Maximum number of values to process.
C
C  List of variables:
C     VALUE  -- Array of numbers.
C     SQRT1  -- Array of square roots.
C     CUBERT -- Array of cube roots.
C     J      -- DO loop index
C
      IMPLICIT NONE
C
      INTEGER MAXSIZ
      PARAMETER ( MAXSIZ = 10 )
C
      INTEGER J
      REAL VALUE(MAXSIZ), SQRT1(MAXSIZ), CUBERT(MAXSIZ)
C
C     Calculate the square roots & cube roots of the numbers.
C
      DO 10 J = 1, MAXSIZ
         VALUE(J)  = REAL(J)
         SQRT1(J)  = SQRT (VALUE(J))
         CUBERT(J) = VALUE(J)**(1./3.)
   10 CONTINUE
C
C     Write out each number, its square root, and its cube root.
C
```

```
      WRITE (*,100)
  100 FORMAT ('0',20X,'Table of Square and Cube Roots',/,
     *          4X,'  Number Square Root  Cube Root',
     *          3X,'  Number Square Root  Cube Root',/,
     *          4X,'  ====== ============  =========',
     *          3X,'  ====== ============   =========')
      WRITE (*,110) (VALUE(J), SQRT1(J), CUBERT(J), J = 1, MAXSIZ)
  110 FORMAT (2(4X,F6.0,9X,F6.4,6X,F6.4))
C
      END
```

FIGURE 5-8   A program that computes the square and cube roots of a set of numbers, and writes them out using an implied **DO** loop.

The implied **DO** loop in this example is executed 10 times, with J taking on every value between 1 and 10 (the loop increment is defaulted to 1 here). During each iteration of the loop, the entire argument list will be written out. Therefore, this **WRITE** statement writes out 30 values, six per line. The resulting output is

```
               Table of Square and Cube Roots
      Number  Square Root  Cube Root   Number  Square Root  Cube Root
      ======  ===========  =========   ======  ===========  =========
        1.      1.0000       1.0000      2.      1.4142       1.2599
        3.      1.7321       1.4422      4.      2.0000       1.5874
        5.      2.2361       1.7100      6.      2.4495       1.8171
        7.      2.6458       1.9129      8.      2.8284       2.0000
        9.      3.0000       2.0801     10.      3.1623       2.1544
```

Nested Implied DO Loops

Like ordinary **DO** loops, implied **DO** loops may be *nested*. If they are nested, the inner loop executes completely for each step in the outer loop. As a simple example, consider the following statements

```
      WRITE (*,100) ((I, J, J = 1, 3), I = 1, 2)
  100 FORMAT (1X,I5,1X,I5)
```

There are two implicit **DO** loops in this **WRITE** statement. The index variable of the inner loop is J, and the index variable of the outer loop is I. When the **WRITE** statement is executed, variable J takes on values 1, 2, and 3 while I is 1, and then 1, 2, and 3 while I is 2. The output from this statement is

```
      1      1
      1      2
      1      3
      2      1
      2      2
      2      3
```

Nested implied **DO** loops are important when working with arrays having two or more dimensions, as we will see later in the chapter.

The Difference Between I/O with Standard DO Loops and I/O with Implied DO Loops

Array input and output can be performed either with a standard **DO** loop containing I/O statements or with an implied **DO** loop. However, *there are subtle differences between the two types of loops*. To better understand those differences, let's compare the same output statement written with both types of loops. We will assume that integer array ARR is initialized as follows

```
INTEGER ARR(5)
DATA ARR / 1, 2, 3, 4, 5 /
```

and compare output using a regular **DO** loop with output using an implied **DO** loop. An output statement using an ordinary **DO** loop is shown below:

```
      DO 10 I = 1, 5
         WRITE (*,1000) ARR(I), 2.*ARR(I), 3*ARR(I)
1000     FORMAT (1X,6I6)
   10 CONTINUE
```

In this loop, the **WRITE** statement is executed *five times*. In fact, this loop is equivalent to the following statements

```
      WRITE (*,1000) ARR(1), 2.*ARR(1), 3*ARR(1)
      WRITE (*,1000) ARR(2), 2.*ARR(2), 3*ARR(2)
      WRITE (*,1000) ARR(3), 2.*ARR(3), 3*ARR(3)
      WRITE (*,1000) ARR(4), 2.*ARR(4), 3*ARR(4)
      WRITE (*,1000) ARR(5), 2.*ARR(5), 3*ARR(5)
1000 FORMAT (1X,6I6)
```

An output statement using an implied **DO** loop is shown below:

```
      WRITE (*,1000) (ARR(I), 2.*ARR(I). 3*ARR(I), I = 1, 5)
1000 FORMAT (1X,6I6)
```

Here, there is only *one* **WRITE** statement, but the **WRITE** statement has 15 arguments. In fact, the **WRITE** statement with the implied **DO** loop is equivalent to

```
      WRITE (*,1000) ARR(1), 2.*ARR(1), 3*ARR(1),
     *               ARR(2), 2.*ARR(2), 3*ARR(2),
     *               ARR(3), 2.*ARR(3), 3*ARR(3),
     *               ARR(4), 2.*ARR(4), 3*ARR(4),
     *               ARR(5), 2.*ARR(5), 3*ARR(5)
1000 FORMAT (1X,6I6)
```

The main difference beween having many **WRITE** statements with few arguments and one **WRITE** statement with many arguments is in the behavior of the associated **FORMAT** statement. Remember that each **WRITE** statement starts at the beginning of the **FORMAT** statement. Therefore, each of the five **WRITE** statements in the standard **DO** loop starts over at the beginning of the **FORMAT** statement, and only the first three of the six **I6** descriptors will be used. The output of the standard **DO** loop is

```
1     2     3
2     4     6
3     6     9
4     8    12
5    10    15
```

On the other hand, the implied **DO** loop contains a single **WRITE** statement with 15 arguments, so the associated **FORMAT** statement will be used completely 2½ times. The output of the implied **DO** loop is

```
1     2     3     2     4     6
3     6     9     4     8    12
5    10    15
```

The same concept applies to a comparison of **READ** statements using standard **DO** loops with **READ** statements using implied **DO** loops. (See exercise 8 at the end of the chapter.)

5.3.3 Input and Output of Whole Arrays

In addition to array elements, *entire arrays* may be read in or written out with **READ** and **WRITE** statements. If an array name is mentioned *without subscripts* in a FORTRAN I/O statement, then the compiler assumes that *every element in the array is to be read in or written out*. Figure 5-9 shows a simple example of using an array in an I/O statement. The array A contains five elements, so the **WRITE** statement in this example writes out five values.

```
      PROGRAM EXMPL2
C
C Purpose:
C   To illustrate array I/O.
C
C Record of revisions:
C     Date      Programmer        Description of change
C     ====      ==========        =====================
C   04/10/91  S. J. Chapman       Original code
C
C   List of variables:
C     A       -- Name of a 5-element real array
C
      IMPLICIT NONE
C
      REAL A(5)
      DATA A / 1., 2., 3., 2., 1. /
C
      WRITE (*,100) A
  100 FORMAT ( 2X, 6F8.4 )
C
      END
```

FIGURE 5-9   An example program illustrating array I/O.

The output from this program is:

```
1.0000  2.0000  3.0000  2.0000  1.0000
```

Quiz 5-1

This quiz provides a quick check to see if you have understood the concepts introduced in Sections 5.1 through 5.3. If you have trouble with the quiz, reread the sections, ask your instructor, or discuss the material with a fellow student. The answers to this quiz are found in the back of the book.

For questions 1–3, determine the length of the array specified by each of the following declaration statements and the valid subscript range for each array.

1. `INTEGER ITEMP(15)`

2. `LOGICAL TEST(0:255)`

3. `PARAMETER ( I1 = -20 )`
`PARAMETER ( I2 = -1 )`
`REAL A(I1:I1*I2)`

Determine which of the following FORTRAN statements are valid. For each valid statement, specify what will happen in the program.

4.
```
      REAL PHASE(0:11)
      DATA PHASE / 0., 1., 2., 6*3., 2., 1., 0. /
```

5.
```
      REAL PHASE(10)
      DATA PHASE(0) / 0. /
```

6.
```
      INTEGER DATA1(256)
      DATA1 = 100
      WRITE (*,10) DATA1
  100 FORMAT (1X,10I8)
```

7.
```
      INTEGER INDEX(15:20)
      DATA INDEX / 0, 1, 2, 10, 256, -9999 /
      WRITE (*,10) INDEX
   10 FORMAT ('1',5X,INDEX = ,/,(3X,I6))
```

8.
```
      REAL ERROR(-5:0)
      ERROR(-5) = 1.12E-4
      ERROR(-4) = -0.0035
      ERROR(-3) = 0.00012
      ERROR(-2) = 0.0152
      ERROR(-1) = 0.0
      WRITE (*,500) ERROR
  500 FORMAT (T6,ERROR = ,/,(3X,I6))
```

9.
```
      INTEGER SIZE
      PARAMETER ( SIZE = 10 )
      REAL SQUARE(SIZE)
      DO 100 I = 1, SIZE
         SQUARE(I) = REAL(I)**2
  100 CONTINUE
      WRITE (*,1000) (I, SQUARE(I), I = 1, SIZE)
 1000 FORMAT ( '1',9X,'Table of Squares:',//,
     *          (10X,I4,3X,F10.2))
```

10.
```
        INTEGER NPOINT
        PARAMETER ( NPOINT = 10 )
        REAL MYDATA(NPOINT)
        DO 10 I = 1, NPOINT
           READ (*,*) MYDATA
     10 CONTINUE
```

11.
```
        INTEGER NVALUE
        PARAMETER ( NVALUE = 6 )
        INTEGER INPUT(NVALUE)
        READ (*,*) ( INPUT(I), I = 1, NVALUE )
```

What will the output of the following program be?

12.
```
        PROGRAM TEST
        INTEGER MAXSTR, I
        PARAMETER ( MAXSTR = 5 )
        CHARACTER*6 STRING(MAXSTR)
        DATA STRING / 'FRIEND', 'BBBBBB', '123456',
       *              'ABCDEF', 'BUDDY ' /
        DO 10 I = 1, MAXSTR
           WRITE (*,100) STRING(I)
    100    FORMAT (2(1X,A))
     10 CONTINUE
        WRITE (*,100) (STRING(I), I = 1, MAXSTR)
        END
```

5.4   EXAMPLE PROBLEMS

We will now show two additional example problems that illustrate the use of arrays.

EXAMPLE 5-2 *Sorting Data*   In many scientific and engineering applications, it is necessary to take a random input data set and sort it so that the numbers in the data set are either all in *ascending order* (lowest-to-highest) or all in *descending order* (highest-to-lowest). For example, suppose that you were a zoologist studying a large population of animals, and that you wanted to identify the largest 5% of the animals in the population. The most straightforward way to approach this problem would be to sort the sizes of all of the animals in the population into ascending order, and take the top 5% of the values.

Sorting data into ascending or descending order seems to be an easy job. After all, we do it all the time. It is a simple matter for us to sort the data (10, 3, 6, 4, 9) into the order (3, 4, 6, 9, 10). How do we do it? We first scan the input data list (10, 3, 6, 4, 9) to find the smallest value in the list (3), and then scan the remaining input data (10, 6, 4, 9) to find the next smallest value (4), etc. until the complete list is sorted.

In fact, sorting can be a difficult job. As the number of values to be sorted increases, the time required to perform the simple sort described above increases rapidly, since we must scan the input data set once for each value that we are sorting. For very large data sets, this technique just takes too long to be practical. Even worse, how would we sort the data if there were too many numbers to fit into the main memory of the computer? The development of efficient sorting techniques for large data sets is an active area of research, and is the subject of whole courses all by itself.

In this example, we will confine ourselves to the simplest possible algorithm to illustrate the concept of sorting. This simplest algorithm is called the **selection sort.** It is just a computer implementation of the mental math described above. The basic algorithm for the selection sort is illustrated in Figure 5-10. The steps required for this sort are

1. Scan the list of numbers to be sorted to locate the smallest value in the list. Place that value at the front of the list by swapping it with the value currently at the front of the list. If the value at the front of the list is already the smallest value, then do nothing.
2. Scan the list of numbers from position 2 to the end to locate the next smallest value in the list. Place that value in position 2 of the list by swapping it with the value currently at that position. If the value in position 2 is already the next smallest value, then do nothing.
3. Scan the list of numbers from position 3 to the end to locate the third smallest value in the list. Place that value in position 3 of the list by swapping it with the value currently at that position. If the value in position 3 is already the third smallest value, then do nothing.
4. Repeat this process until the next-to-last position in the list is reached. After the next-to-last position in the list has been processed, the sort is complete.

Note that if we are sorting N values, this sorting algorithm requires $N-1$ scans through the data to accomplish the sort.

This process is illustrated in Figure 5-10. Since there are five values in the data set to be sorted, we will make four scans through the data. During the first pass through the entire data set, the minimum value is 3, so the 3 is swapped with the 10 which was in position 1. Pass 2 searches for the minimum value in positions 2 through 5. That minimum is 4, so the 4 is swapped with the 10 in position 2. Pass 3 searches for the minimum value in positions 3 through 5. That minimum is 6, which is already in position 3, so no swapping is required. Finally, pass 4 searches for the

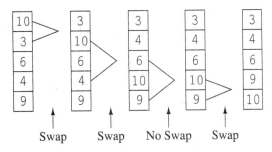

FIGURE 5-10 An example problem demonstrating the selection sort algorithm.

minimum value in positions 4 through 5. That minimum is 9, so the 9 is swapped with the 10 in position 4, and the sort is completed.

PROGRAMMING PITFALLS

The selection sort algorithm is the easiest sorting algorithm to understand, but it is computationally inefficient. *It should never be applied to sort really large data sets* (say, sets with more than 1000 elements). Over the years, computer scientists have developed much more efficient sorting algorithms. We will encounter one such algorithm (the *heapsort algorithm*) in Chapter 11.

We will now develop a program to read in a data set from a file, sort it into ascending order, and display the sorted data set.

SOLUTION This program must be able to ask the user for the name of the file to be sorted, open that file, read the input data, sort the data, and write out the sorted data. The design process for this problem is given below.

1. State the problem.
We have not yet specified the type of data we will be sorting. If we are sorting real data, the problem we are solving may be stated as follows:

> Develop a program to read an arbitrary number of real input data values from a user-supplied file, sort the data into ascending order, and write the sorted data to the standard output device.

2. Define the inputs and outputs.
There are two types of inputs to this program:

(*a*) A character string containing the file name of the input data file. This string will come from the standard input device.

(*b*) The real data values in the file.

The outputs from this program are the sorted real data values written to the standard output device.

3. Describe the algorithm.
This program can be broken down into five major steps:

```
Get the input file name
Open the input file
Read the input data into an array
Sort the data in ascending order
Write the sorted data
```

The first three major steps of the program are to get the name of the input file, to open the file, and to read in the data. We must prompt the user for the input file name, read in the name, and open the file. If the file open is successful, we must read in the data, keeping track of the number of values that we have read. Since we don't know how many data values to expect, a while loop is appropriate for the **READ**. A flowchart for these steps is shown in Figure 5-11, on page 252, and the detailed pseudocode is shown below:

```
Prompt user for the input file name FILENM
Read the file name FILENM
OPEN file FILENM
IF OPEN is successful THEN
    Read first value into TEMP
    WHILE Read successful
        NVALS ← NVALS + 1
        A(NVALS) ← TEMP
        Read next value into TEMP
    End of WHILE
    ...
    ...                              Insert sorting step here
    ...                              Insert writing step here
End of IF
```

Next we have to sort the data. We will need to find the smallest remaining value NVALS-1 times as we sort the array. We will use a pointer to locate the smallest value in the array. Once the smallest value is found, it will be swapped to the top of the list. A flowchart for these steps is shown in Figure 5-12, on page 253, and the detailed pseudocode is shown below:

```
  DO for I = 1 to NVALS-1
*
*     Find the minimum value in A(I) through A(NVALS)
*
      IPTR ← I
      DO for J = I+1 to NVALS
         IF A(J) < A(IPTR) THEN
             IPTR = J
         END of IF
      END of DO
*
*     IPTR now points to the minimum value, so swap A(IPTR) with A(I)
*     if IPTR ≠ I.
*
      IF I ≠ IPTR THEN
          TEMP ← A(I)
          A(I) ← A(IPTR)
          A(IPTR) ← TEMP
      END of IF
  END of DO
```

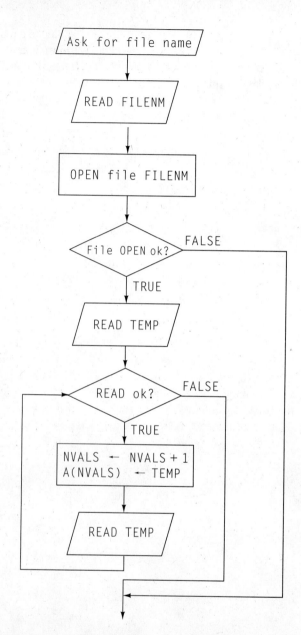

FIGURE 5-11   Flowchart for reading values to sort from an input file.

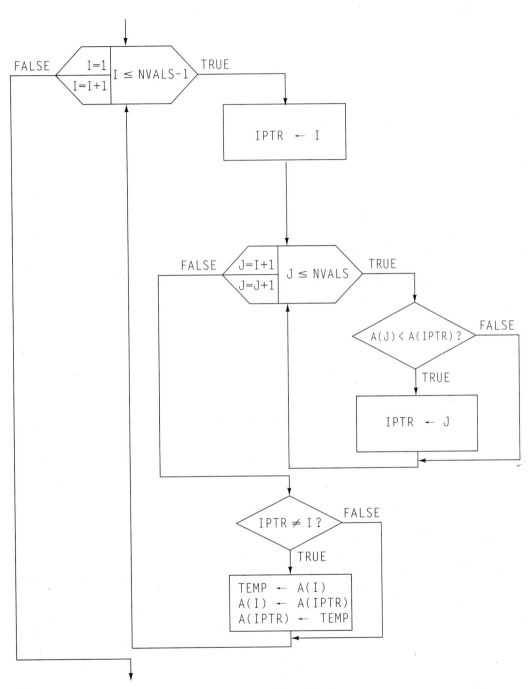

FIGURE 5-12   Flowchart for sorting values with a selection sort.

The final step is writing out the sorted values. No refinement of the pseudocode is required for that step. The final pseudocode for the entire program is

```
Prompt user for the input file name FILENM
Read the file name FILENM

OPEN file FILENM
IF OPEN is successful THEN
    NVALS ← 0
    Read first value into TEMP
    WHILE Read successful
        NVALS ← NVALS + 1
        A(NVALS) ← TEMP
        Read next value into TEMP
    End of WHILE
*
*   Sort the data
*
    DO for I = 1 to NVALS-1
*
*       Find the minimum value in A(I) through A(NVALS)
*
        IPTR ← I
        DO for J = I+1 to NVALS
            IF A(J) < A(IPTR) THEN
                IPTR = J
            END of IF
        END of DO (for J = I+1 to NVALS)
*
*       IPTR now points to the minimum value, so swap A(IPTR) with A(I)
*       if IPTR ≠ I.
*
        IF I ≠ IPTR THEN
            TEMP ← A(I)
            A(I) ← A(IPTR)
            A(IPTR) ← TEMP
        END of IF
    END of DO (for I = 1 to NVALS-1)
*
    WRITE the sorted output data to the standard output device
End of IF (OPEN is successful)
```

    4. Turn the algorithm into FORTRAN statements.
    The resulting FORTRAN program is shown in Figure 5-13.

```
      PROGRAM SORT1
C
C Purpose:
C   To read in a REAL input data set, sort it into ascending order
C   using the selection sort algorithm, and to write the sorted
C   data to the standard output device.
C
```

```
C   Record of revisions:
C        Date     Programmer        Description of change
C        ====     ==========        =====================
C      04/14/91  S. J. Chapman      Original code
C
C   List of variables:
C      A       -- REAL data array to sort.
C      FILENM  -- Name of input data file to read.
C      I       -- Index variable.
C      IPTR    -- Pointer to the smallest value found during a search.
C      ISTAT   -- I/O status variable: 0 for success
C      NVALS   -- Number of data values to sort.
C      J       -- Index variable.
C      TEMP    -- Temporary variable used to read in values, and to
C                 swap values in array A
C
      IMPLICIT NONE
C
C   Parameters
C
      INTEGER   MAXSIZ
      PARAMETER ( MAXSIZ = 10 )
C
C   Declare the variables used in this program.
C
      INTEGER    I, J, IPTR, ISTAT, NVALS
      REAL       A(MAXSIZ), TEMP
      CHARACTER*20 FILENM
C
C   Initialize variables.
C
      NVALS = 0
C
C   Get the name of the file containing the input data.
C
      WRITE (*,1000)
 1000 FORMAT (1X,'Enter the file name with the data to be sorted: ')
      READ (*,1010) FILENM
 1010 FORMAT ( A20 )
C
C   Open input data file.  Status is OLD because the input data must
C   already exist.
C
      OPEN ( UNIT=9, FILE=FILENM, STATUS='OLD', IOSTAT=ISTAT )
C
C   Was the OPEN successful?
C
      IF ( ISTAT .EQ. 0 ) THEN
C
C      The file was opened successfully, so read the data to sort
C      from it, sort the data, and write out the results.
C
         READ (9, *, IOSTAT=ISTAT) TEMP
C
C      Begin WHILE loop.  Did we read the value successfully?
C
```

```
       10     IF ( ISTAT .EQ. 0 ) THEN
C
C              Yes.   Increment pointer and store value in array A.
C
              NVALS = NVALS + 1
              A(NVALS) = TEMP
C
C              Read next value.
C
              READ (9, *, IOSTAT=ISTAT) TEMP
              GO TO 10
C
C              End of WHILE Loop
C
          END IF
C
C       Now, sort the data.
C
          DO 30 I = 1, NVALS-1
C
C              Find the minimum value in A(I) through A(NVALS)
C
              IPTR = I
              DO 20 J = I+1, NVALS
                 IF ( A(J) .LT. A(IPTR) ) THEN
                    IPTR = J
                 END IF
       20     CONTINUE
C
C
C              IPTR now points to the minimum value, so swap A(IPTR) with A(I)
C              if I <> IPTR.
C
              IF ( I .NE. IPTR ) THEN
                 TEMP  = A(I)
                 A(I)  = A(IPTR)
                 A(IPTR) = TEMP
              END IF
C
       30     CONTINUE
C
C       Now write out the sorted data.
C
          WRITE (*,1030) ' The sorted output data values are: '
     1030 FORMAT (A)
          WRITE (*,1040) ( A(I), I = 1, NVALS )
     1040 FORMAT (4X,F10.4)
C
C              END of IF OPEN successful...
C
       END IF
C
       END
```

FIGURE 5-13   A program to read in values from an input data file, and to sort them into ascending order.

5. Test the program.

To test this program, we will create an input data file and run the program with it. The data set contains a mixture of positive and negative numbers as well as at least one duplicated value to see if the program works properly under those conditions. The following data set is placed in file INPUT2:

```
13.3
12.
-3.0
 0.
 4.0
 6.6
 4.
-6.
```

Running this file's values through the program yields the following result:

```
C:\BOOK\FORT>sort1
Enter the file name containing the data to be sorted:
input2
The sorted output data values are:
    -6.0000
    -3.0000
      .0000
     4.0000
     4.0000
     6.6000
    12.0000
    13.3000
```

The program gives the correct answers for our test data set. Note that it works for both positive and negative numbers as well as for repeated numbers.   ●

To be certain that our program works properly, we must test it for every possible type of input data. This program worked properly for the test input data set, but will it work for *all* input data sets? Study the code now and see if you can spot any flaws before continuing to the next paragraph.

The program has a major flaw that must be corrected. If there are more than 10 values in the input data file, this program will attempt to store input data in memory locations A(11), A(12), etc., that have not been allocated in the program (this is an out-of-bounds or **array overflow** condition). If bounds checking is turned on, the program will abort when we try to write to A(11). If bounds checking is not turned on, the results are unpredictable and vary from computer to computer. This program must be rewritten to prevent it from attempting to write into locations beyond the end of the allocated array. This can be done by checking to see if the number of values exceeds MAXSIZ before storing each number into array A. The corrected flow-chart for reading in the data is shown in Figure 5-14, and the corrected program is shown in Figure 5-15 on pages 259–261.

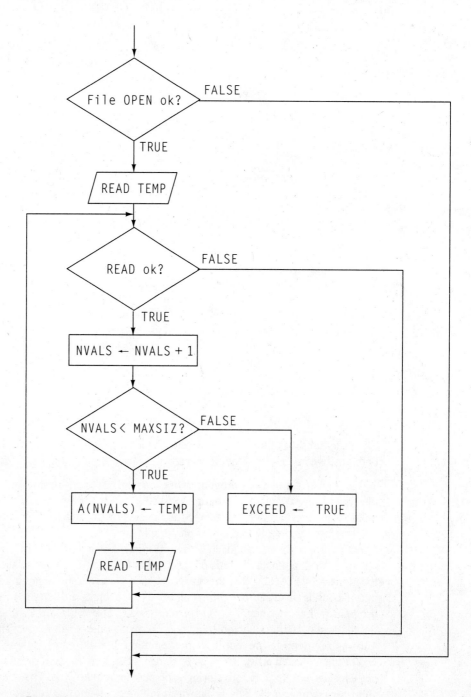

FIGURE 5-14   Corrected flowchart for reading the values to sort from an input
file without causing an array overflow.

```
      PROGRAM SORT2
C
C   Purpose:
C     To read in a REAL input data set, sort it into ascending order
C     using the selection sort algorithm, and to write the sorted
C     data to the standard output device.
C
C   Record of revisions:
C       Date      Programmer        Description of change
C       ====      ==========        =====================
C 0  04/14/91  S. J. Chapman       Original code
C 1  04/15/91  S. J. Chapman       Modified to protect against array
C                                  overflow.
C
C   List of variables:
C     A      -- REAL data array to sort.
C     EXCEED -- Logical indicating that array limits are exceeded.
C     FILENM -- Name of input data file to read.
C     I      -- Index variable.
C     IPTR   -- Pointer to the smallest value found during a search.
C     ISTAT  -- I/O status variable:  0 for success
C     NVALS  -- Number of data values to sort.
C     J      -- Index variable.
C     TEMP   -- Temporary variable used to read in values, and to
C                 swap values in array A
C
      IMPLICIT NONE
C
C     Parameters
C
      INTEGER    MAXSIZ
      PARAMETER ( MAXSIZ = 10 )
C
C     Declare the variables used in this program.
C
      INTEGER       I, J, IPTR, ISTAT, NVALS
      REAL          A(MAXSIZ), TEMP
      LOGICAL       EXCEED
      CHARACTER*20 FILENM
C
C     Initialize variables.
C
      NVALS  = 0
      EXCEED = .FALSE.
C
C     Get the name of the file containing the input data.
C
      WRITE (*,1000)
 1000 FORMAT (1X,'Enter the file name with the data to be sorted: ')
      READ (*,1010) FILENM
 1010 FORMAT ( A20 )
C
C     Open input data file.  Status is OLD because the input data must
C     already exist.
C
      OPEN ( UNIT=9, FILE=FILENM, STATUS='OLD', IOSTAT=ISTAT )
C
C     Was the OPEN successful?
C
      IF ( ISTAT .EQ. 0 ) THEN
C
```

```
C          The file was opened successfully, so read the data to sort
C          from it, sort the data, and write out the results.
C
           READ (9, *, IOSTAT=ISTAT) TEMP
C
C          Begin WHILE loop.  Did we read the value successfully?
C
   10      IF ( ISTAT .EQ. 0 ) THEN
C
C          Yes.  Increment number of values.
C
           NVALS = NVALS + 1
C
C          Is NVALS <= MAXSIZ?  If so, store the value in array A.
C          If not, set the array size exceeded flag to .TRUE.
C
           IF ( NVALS .LE. MAXSIZ ) THEN
              A(NVALS) = TEMP
           ELSE
              EXCEED = .TRUE.
           END IF
C
C          Read next value.
C
           READ (9, *, IOSTAT=ISTAT) TEMP
           GO TO 10
C
C          End of WHILE Loop
C
        END IF
C
C       Was the array size exceeded?  If so, tell user and quit.
C
        IF ( EXCEED ) THEN
           WRITE (*,1020) NVALS, MAXSIZ
 1020      FORMAT (' Maximum array size exceeded: ', I6, '>', I6 )
        ELSE
C
C          Array size not exceeded.  Sort the data.
C
           DO 30 I = 1, NVALS-1
C
C             Find the minimum value in A(I) through A(NVALS)
C
              IPTR = I
              DO 20 J = I+1, NVALS
                 IF ( A(J) .LT. A(IPTR) ) THEN
                    IPTR = J
                 END IF
   20         CONTINUE
C
C             IPTR now points to the minimum value, so swap A(IPTR) with
C             A(I) if I <> IPTR.
C
              IF ( I .NE. IPTR ) THEN
                 TEMP     = A(I)
                 A(I)     = A(IPTR)
                 A(IPTR) = TEMP
              END IF
C
```

```
      30          CONTINUE
C
C              Now write out the sorted data.
C
               WRITE (*,1030) ' The sorted output data values are: '
    1030        FORMAT (A)
               WRITE (*,1040) ( A(I), I = 1, NVALS )
    1040        FORMAT (4X,F10.4)
C
C              END of IF array size exceeded...
C
          END IF
C
C         END of IF OPEN successful...
C
      END IF
C
      END
```

FIGURE 5-15   A corrected version of the sort program that detects array overflows.

Note that in our test for array overflow conditions, we have used a logical variable EXCEED. If the next value to be read into the array would result in an array overflow, then EXCEED is set to TRUE, and the value is not stored. When all values have been read from the input file, the program checks to see if the array size would have been exceeded. If so, it writes out an error message and quits. If not, it calculates the mean, median, and standard deviation of the numbers.

This program also illustrates the proper use of parameters to allow the size of a program to be changed easily. The size of array A is set by parameter MAXSIZ, and the test for array overflow within the code also uses parameter MAXSIZ. The maximum sorting capacity of this program could be changed from 10 to 1000 by simply modifying the **PARAMETER** statement at the top of the program.

EXAMPLE 5-3   *The Median*   In Chapter 3 we examined two common statistical measures of data: averages (or means) and standard deviations. Another common statistical measure of data is the **median.** The median of a data set is the value such that half of the numbers in the data set are larger than the value and half of the numbers in the data set are smaller than the value. If there are an even number of values in the data set, then there cannot be a value exactly in the middle. In that case, the median is usually defined as the average of the two elements in the middle. The median value of a data set is often close to the average value of the data set, but not always. For example, consider the following data set:

```
          1
          2
          3
          4
        100
```

The average or mean of this data set is 22, while the median of this data set is 3!

An easy way to compute the median of a data set is to sort it into ascending order, and then to select the value in the middle of the data set as the median. If there are an even number of values in the data set, then average the two middle values to get the median.

Write a program to calculate the mean, median, and standard deviation of an input data set which is read from a user-specified file.

SOLUTION   This program must be able to read in an arbitrary number of measurements from a file, and then calculate the mean and standard deviation of those measurements.

1.   State the problem.

Calculate the average, median, and standard deviation of a set of measurements that are read from a user-specified input file, and write those values out on the standard output device.

2.   Define the inputs and outputs.

There are two types of inputs to this program:

(*a*)   A character string containing the file name of the input data file. This string will come from the standard input device.

(*b*)   The real data values in the file.

The outputs from this program are the average, median, and standard deviation of the input data set. They are written to the standard output device.

3.   Describe the algorithm.

This program can be broken down into six major steps:

```
Get the input file name
Open the input file
Read the input data into an array
Sort the data in ascending order
Calculate the average, mean, and standard deviation
Write average, median, and standard deviation
```

The detailed pseudocode for the first four steps is similar to that of the previous example:

```
Initialize variables.
Prompt user for the input file name FILENM
Read the file name FILENM
OPEN file FILENM
IF OPEN is successful THEN
   Read first value into TEMP
   WHILE Read successful
      NVALS ← NVALS + 1
      IF NVALS <= MAXSIZ then
         A(NVALS) ← TEMP
```

```
      ELSE
          EXCEED ← .TRUE.
      End of IF
      Read next value into TEMP
   End of WHILE
*
*  Notify user if array size exceeded.
*
   IF array size exceeded then
      Write out message to user
    ELSE
*     Sort the data
*
      DO for I = 1 to NVALS-1
*
*         Find the minimum value in A(I) through A(NVALS)
*
          IPTR ← I
          DO for J = I+1 to NVALS
             IF A(J) < A(IPTR) THEN
                 IPTR = J
             END of IF
          END of DO (for J = I+1 to NVALS)
*
*         IPTR now points to the minimum value, so swap A(IPTR) with
*         A(I) if IPTR <> I.
*
          IF  I ≠ IPTR THEN
              TEMP ← A(I)
              A(I) ← A(IPTR)
              A(IPTR) ← TEMP
          END of IF
      END of DO (for I = 1 to NVALS-1)
*
      (Add code here)
*
   End of IF array size exceeded...
*
End of IF open successful...
```

The fifth step is to calculate the required average, median, and standard deviation. To do this, we must first accumulate some statistics on the data ($\sum x$ and $\sum x^2$), and then apply the definitions of average, mean, and standard deviation given previously. The pseudocode for this step is

```
SUMX ← 0.
SUMX2 ← 0.
DO for I = 1 to NVALS
   SUMX ← SUMX + A(I)
   SUMX2 ← SUMX2 + A(I)**2
End of DO
```

```
IF NVALS >= 2 THEN
   XBAR ← SUMX / REAL(NVALS)
   S ← SQRT((REAL(NVALS)*SUMX2-SUMX**2)/(REAL(NVALS)*REAL(NVALS-1)))
   IF NVALS is an even number THEN
      MEDIAN ← (A(NVALS/2) + A(NVALS/2+1)) / 2.
   ELSE
      MEDIAN ← A(NVALS/2+1)
   END of IF
END of IF
```

We will decide if NVALS is an even number by using the modulo function MOD(NVALS,2). If NVALS is even, this function returns a 0; if NVALS is odd, it returns a 1. Finally, we must write out the results.

```
Write out average, median, standard deviation, and number of points
```

4. Turn the algorithm into FORTRAN statements.
The resulting FORTRAN program is shown in Figure 5-16.

```
      PROGRAM STAT4
C
C Purpose:
C    To calculate mean, median, and standard deviation of an input
C    data set.
C
C Record of revisions:
C      Date       Programmer        Description of change
C      ====       ==========        =====================
C    04/20/91  S. J. Chapman        Original code
C
C List of variables:
C    A       -- REAL data array to sort.
C    EXCEED  -- Logical indicating that array limits are exceeded.
C    FILENM  -- Name of input data file to read.
C    I       -- Index variable.
C    IPTR    -- Pointer to the smallest value found during a search.
C    ISTAT   -- I/O status variable:  0 for success
C    MEDIAN  -- The median of the input samples.
C    NVALS   -- Number of data values to sort.
C    J       -- Index variable.
C    S       -- The standard deviation of the input samples.
C    SUMX    -- The sum of the input values.
C    SUMX2   -- The sum of the squares of the input values,
C               units of reciprocal years.
C    TEMP    -- Temporary variable used to read in values, and to
C               swap values in array A
C    XBAR    -- The average of the input samples.
C
      IMPLICIT NONE
C
C    Parameters
C
      INTEGER    MAXSIZ
      PARAMETER ( MAXSIZ = 100 )
C
```

```
C      Declare the variables used in this program.
C
       INTEGER      I, J, IPTR, ISTAT, NVALS
       REAL         A(MAXSIZ), MEDIAN, S, SUMX, SUMX2, TEMP, XBAR
       LOGICAL      EXCEED
       CHARACTER*20 FILENM
C
C      Initialize variables.
C
       NVALS  = 0
       SUMX   = 0.
       SUMX2  = 0.
       EXCEED = .FALSE.
C
C      Get the name of the file containing the input data.
C
       WRITE (*,1000)
 1000  FORMAT (1X,'Enter the file name with the data to be processed: ')
       READ (*,1010) FILENM
 1010  FORMAT ( A20 )
C
C      Open input data file.  Status is OLD because the input data must
C      already exist.
C
       OPEN ( UNIT=9, FILE=FILENM, STATUS='OLD', IOSTAT=ISTAT )
C
C      Was the OPEN successful?
C
       IF ( ISTAT .EQ. 0 ) THEN
C
C         The file was opened successfully, so read the data to sort
C         from it, sort the data, and write out the results.
C
          READ (9, *, IOSTAT=ISTAT) TEMP
C
C         Begin WHILE loop.  Did we read the value successfully?
C
   10     IF ( ISTAT .EQ. 0 ) THEN
C
C            Yes.  Increment number of values.
C
             NVALS = NVALS + 1
C
C            Is NVALS <= MAXSIZ?  If so, store the value in array A.
C            If not, set the array size exceeded flag to .TRUE.
C
             IF ( NVALS .LE. MAXSIZ ) THEN
                A(NVALS) = TEMP
             ELSE
                EXCEED = .TRUE.
             END IF
C
C            Read next value.
C
             READ (9, *, IOSTAT=ISTAT) TEMP
             GO TO 10
C
C            End of WHILE Loop
C
```

```
      END IF
C
C     Was the array size exceeded?  If so, tell user and quit.
C
      IF ( EXCEED ) THEN
         WRITE (*,1020) NVALS, MAXSIZ
 1020    FORMAT (' Maximum array size exceeded: ', I6, '>', I6 )
      ELSE
C
C        Array size not exceeded.  Sort the data.
C
         DO 30 I = 1, NVALS-1
C
C           Find the minimum value in A(I) throug A(NVALS)
C
            IPTR = I
            DO 20 J = I+1, NVALS
               IF ( A(J) .LT. A(IPTR) ) THEN
                  IPTR = J
               END IF
 20         CONTINUE
C
C           IPTR now points to the minimum value, so swap A(IPTR) with
C           A(I) if I <> IPTR.
C
            IF ( I .NE. IPTR ) THEN
               TEMP   = A(I)
               A(I)   = A(IPTR)
               A(IPTR) = TEMP
            END IF
C
 30      CONTINUE
C
C        Accumulate sums.
C
         DO 40 I = 1, NVALS
            SUMX  = SUMX + A(I)
            SUMX2 = SUMX2 + A(I)**2
 40      CONTINUE
C
C        Check to see if we have enough input data.
C
         IF ( NVALS .LT. 2 ) THEN
C
C           Insufficient data.
C
            WRITE (*,*) ' At least 2 values must be entered.'
C
         ELSE
C
C           Calculate the mean, median, and standard deviation
C
            XBAR = SUMX / REAL(NVALS)
            S    = SQRT( (REAL(NVALS) * SUMX2 - SUMX**2)
     *             / (REAL(NVALS) * REAL(NVALS-1)) )
            IF ( MOD(NVALS,2) .EQ. 0 ) THEN
               MEDIAN = ( A(NVALS/2) + A(NVALS/2+1) ) / 2.
            ELSE
               MEDIAN = A(NVALS/2+1)
```

```
          END IF
C
C         Tell user.
C
          WRITE (*,*) ' The mean of this data set is:  ', XBAR
          WRITE (*,*) ' The median of this data set is:', MEDIAN
          WRITE (*,*) ' The standard deviation is:     ', S
          WRITE (*,*) ' The number of data points is:  ', NVALS
C
       END IF
C
C      END of IF array size exceeded...
C
    END IF
C
C   END of IF OPEN successful...
C
  END IF
C
  END
```

FIGURE 5-16   A program to read in values from an input data file, and to calculate their mean, median, and standard deviation.

5. Test the program.

To test this program, we will calculate the answers by hand for a simple data set, and then compare the answers to the results of the program. If we use five input values: 5, 3, 4, 1, and 9, then the mean and standard deviation would be

$$\bar{x} = \frac{1}{N} \sum_{i=1}^{N} x_i = \frac{1}{5} \, 22 = 4.4$$

$$s = \sqrt{\frac{N \sum_{i=1}^{N} x_i^2 - \left(\sum_{i=1}^{N} x_i\right)^2}{N(N-1)}} = 2.966$$

median = 4

If these values are placed in the file INPUT4 and the program is run with that file as an input, the results are

```
C:\BOOK\FORT>STAT4
Enter the file name containing the input data:
input4
 The mean of this data set is:       4.400000
 The median of this data set is:     4.000000
 The standard deviation is:          2.966479
 The number of data points is:              5
```

The program gives the correct answers for our test data set.   ●

5.5   TWO-DIMENSIONAL ARRAYS

The arrays which we have worked with so far in this chapter are **one-dimensional arrays,** or **vectors.** These arrays can be visualized as a series of values laid out in a column, with a single subscript used to select the individual array elements (Figure 5-17(*a*)). Such arrays are useful to describe data that is a function of one independent variable, such as a series of temperature measurements made at fixed intervals of time.

Some types of data are functions of more than one independent variable. For example, we might measure the power output of each of four different electrical generators at six different times. In this case, our 24 measurements could logically be grouped into four different columns of 6 measurements each, with a separate column for each generator. FORTRAN has a structure especially designed to hold this sort of data—a **two-dimensional array,** or **matrix** (Figure 5-17(*b*)).

Two-dimensional arrays are functions of two subscripts, and a particular element in the array is selected by simultaneously choosing values for both of them. Figure 5-18(*b*) shows the array consisting of six different power measurements for each of four different generators. In this example, each row specifies a measurement time, and each column specifies a generator number. The array element containing the power supplied by generator 3 at time 4 would be POWER(4,3); its value is 41.1 MW.

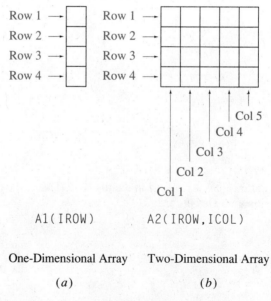

A1(IROW)   A2(IROW,ICOL)

One-Dimensional Array   Two-Dimensional Array

(*a*)   (*b*)

FIGURE 5-17   One- and two-dimensional arrays.

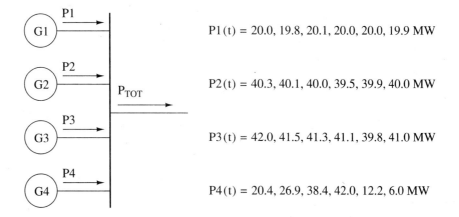

$P1(t) = 20.0, 19.8, 20.1, 20.0, 20.0, 19.9$ MW

$P2(t) = 40.3, 40.1, 40.0, 39.5, 39.9, 40.0$ MW

$P3(t) = 42.0, 41.5, 41.3, 41.1, 39.8, 41.0$ MW

$P4(t) = 20.4, 26.9, 38.4, 42.0, 12.2, 6.0$ MW

(*a*) Power measurements from four different generators at six different times.

	G1	G2	G3	G4
Time 1	20.0	40.3	42.0	20.4
Time 2	19.8	40.1	41.5	26.9
Time 3	20.1	40.0	41.3	38.4
Time 4	20.0	39.5	41.1	42.0
Time 5	20.0	39.9	39.8	12.2
Time 6	19.9	40.0	41.0	6.0

(*b*) Two-dimensional matrix of power measurements.

FIGURE 5-18   A power generating station consisting of four different generators. The power output of each generator is measured at six different times. (*a*) Power measurements from four generators at six different times. (*b*) Two-dimensional matrix of power measurements.

5.5.1 Declaring Two-Dimensional Arrays

Like one-dimensional arrays, the type and size of a two-dimensional array must be declared to the compiler using a type statement. Some example array declarations are shown below:

1. `REAL SUM(3,6)`
   This type statement declares a **REAL** array consisting of three rows and six columns, for a total of 18 elements. The legal values of the first subscript are

1–3, and the legal values of the second subscript are 1–6. Any other subscript values are out of bounds.

2. `INTEGER HIST(0:100,0:20)`

   This type statement declares an **INTEGER** array consisting of 101 rows and 21 columns, for a total of 2121 elements. The legal values of the first subscript are 0–100, and the legal values of the second subscript are 0–20. Any other subscript values are out of bounds.

3. `CHARACTER*6 COUNTS(-3:3,10)`

   This type statement declares an array consisting of 7 rows and 10 columns, for a total of 70 elements. Its type is **CHARACTER,** with each array element capable of holding six characters. The legal values of the first subscript are −3 to 3, and the legal values of the second subscript are 1 to 10. Any other subscript values are out of bounds.

5.5.2 Two-Dimensional Array Storage

We have already learned that a one-dimensional array of length N occupies N successive locations in the computer's memory. Similarly, a two-dimensional array of size M by N occupies M × N successive locations in the computer's memory. How are the two dimensions of the array allocated in the computer's memory? FORTRAN always allocates arrays in **column order.** That is, FORTRAN allocates the first column in memory, then the second one, then the third one, etc. until all columns have been allocated. Figure 5-19 illustrates this memory allocation scheme

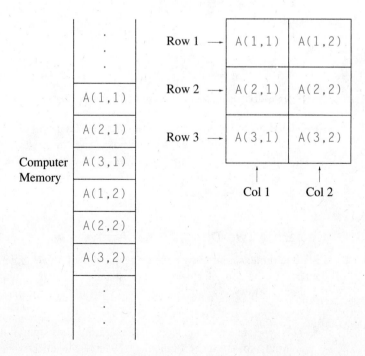

FIGURE 5-19   Memory allocation for a 3 × 2 two-dimensional array A.

for a 3 × 2 array A. As we can see from the picture, the array element A(2,2) is really the fifth location reserved in memory. The order of memory allocation will become important when we discuss **DATA** statements and I/O statements later in this section.

5.5.3 Initializing Two-Dimensional Arrays

Like one-dimensional arrays, two-dimensional arrays may be initialized with **DO** loops, **DATA** statements, or FORTRAN **READ** statements.

Initializing Two-Dimensional Arrays with DO Loops

Initial values may be assigned to the array during program execution by using assignment statements in a nested **DO** loop. For example, suppose we have an **INTEGER** array ISTAT(4,3) that we wish to initialize with the values shown in Figure 5-20.

1	2	3
1	2	3
1	2	3
1	2	3

ISTAT(4,3)

FIGURE 5-20   Initial values for **INTEGER** array ISTAT.

This array could be initialized at run-time with **DO** loops as follows:

```
       INTEGER ISTAT(4,3)
       DO 20 I = 1, 4
          DO 10 J = 1, 3
             ISTAT(I,J) = J
10        CONTINUE
20 CONTINUE
```

Initializing Two-Dimensional Arrays with DATA Statements

Initial values may also be loaded into the array at compilation time using **DATA** statements. When a **DATA** statement is used to initialize a two-dimensional array, the data values are loaded into the array in the order in which memory is allocated by the FORTRAN compiler. *Since arrays are allocated in column order, the values listed in the* **DATA** *statement must be in column order.* That is, all of the elements in column 1 must be listed in the data statement first, and then all of the elements in column 2, etc. Array ISTAT contains four rows and three columns, so to initialize the array with a data statement the four values of column 1 must be listed first, then the four values for column 2, and finally the four values for column 3. Therefore, array ISTAT could be initialized with the following **DATA** statement:

```
INTEGER ISTAT(4,3)
DATA ISTAT / 4*1, 4*2, 4*3 /
```

It is interesting to note that implied **DO** loops work in **DATA** statements as well as in I/O statements, so another way to initialize this array with **DATA** statements would be to use nested implied **DO** loops

```
INTEGER ISTAT(4,3)
DATA ((ISTAT(I,J), I=1,4), J=1,3) / 4*1, 4*2, 4*3 /
```

If implied **DO** loops are used, the order in which values are initialized may be changed. For example, the following statements are equivalent to the two **DATA** statements above.

```
INTEGER ISTAT(4,3)
DATA ((ISTAT(I,J), J=1,3), I=1,4) / 1,2,3,1,2,3,1,2,3,1,2,3 /
```

PROGRAMMING PITFALLS

Implied **DO** loops only work in I/O statements and **DATA** statements. They may not be used anywhere else in a FORTRAN program.

Initializing Two-Dimensional Arrays with READ Statements

Arrays may be initialized with FORTRAN **READ** statements. If an array name appears without subscripts in the argument list of a **READ** statement, the program will attempt to read values for all of the elements in the array, and the values read in will be assigned to the array elements in the order in which they are stored in the computer's memory. Therefore, if file INITL contains the values

```
1   1   1   1   2   2   2   2   3   3   3   3
```

the following code will initialize array ISTAT to have the values shown in Figure 5-20.

```
INTEGER ISTAT(4,3)
OPEN (7, FILE='INITL', STATUS='OLD')
READ (7,*) ISTAT
```

Implied **DO** loops may be used in **READ** statements to change the order in which array elements are initialized, or to initialize only a portion of an array. For example, if file INITL1 contains the values

```
1   2   3   1   2   3   1   2   3   1   2   3
```

the following code will initialize array **ISTAT** to have the values shown in Figure 5-20.

```
INTEGER ISTAT(4,3)
OPEN (7, FILE='INITL1', STATUS='OLD')
READ (7,*) ((ISTAT(I,J), J=1,3), I=1,4)
```

The values would have been read from file INITL1 in a different order than in the previous example, but the implied **DO** loops would ensure that the proper input values went into the proper array elements.

Implied **DO** loops may be also used in **READ** statements to initialize only a portion of an array. For example, the following implied **DO** loop would initialize a portion of array ISTAT. It would initialize the first row of array ISTAT to have the values shown in Figure 5-20, while leaving the remaining two rows undefined.

```
INTEGER ISTAT(4,3)
OPEN (7, FILE='INITL1', STATUS='OLD')
READ (7,*) (ISTAT(1,J), J=1,3)
```

5.5.4 Example Problem

EXAMPLE 5-4 *Electric Power Generation*   Figure 5-18(*b*) shows a series of electrical output power measurements at six different times for four different generators at the Acme Electric Power generating station. Write a program to read these values from a disk file, and to calculate the average power supplied by each generator over the measurement period, and the total power supplied by all of the generators at each time in the measurement period.

SOLUTION

1. State the problem.

Calculate the average power supplied by each generator in the station over the measurement period, and calculate the total instantaneous power supplied by the generating station at each time within the measurement period. Write those values out on the standard output device.

2. Define the inputs and outputs.

There are two types of inputs to this program:

(*a*) A character string containing the file name of the input data file. This string will come from the standard input device.

(*b*) The 24 real data values in the file, representing the power supplied by each of the four generators at each of six different times. The data in the input file must be organized so that the six values associated with generator G1 appear first, followed by the six values associated with generator G2, etc.

The outputs from this program are the average power supplied by each generator in the station over the measurement period, and the total instantaneous power supplied by the generating station at each time within the measurement period.

3. Describe the algorithm.

This program can be broken down into six major steps:

```
Get the input file name
Open the input file
Read the input data into an array
Calculate the instantaneous output power of the station at each
    time
Calculate the average output power of each generator
Write the output values
```

The detailed pseudocode for the problem is given below:

```
Prompt user for the input file name FILENM
Read file name FILENM
OPEN file FILENM
IF OPEN is successful THEN
   Read array POWER
*
*  Calculate the instantaneous output power of the station
*
   DO for ITIME = 1 to 6
      DO for IGEN = 1 to 4
         PWRSUM(ITIME) ← POWER(ITIME,IGEN) + PWRSUM(ITIME)
      END of DO
   END of DO
*
*  Calculate the average output power of each generator
*
   DO for IGEN = 1 to 4
      DO for ITIME = 1 to 6
         PWRAVE(IGEN) ← POWER(ITIME,IGEN) + PWRAVE(IGEN)
      END of DO
      PWRAVE(IGEN) ← PWRAVE(IGEN) / 6
   END of DO
*
*  Write out the total instantaneous power at each time
*
   Write out PWRSUM for ITIME = 1 to 6
*
*  Write out the average output power of each generator
*
   Write out PWRAVE for IGEN = 1 to 4
*
End of IF
```

4. Turn the algorithm into FORTRAN statements.

The resulting **FORTRAN** program is shown in Figure 5-21.

```fortran
      PROGRAM GENRAT
C
C  Purpose:
C    To calculate total instantaneous power supplied by a generating
C    station at each instant of time, and to calculate the average
C    power supplied by each generator over the period of measurement.
C
C  Record of revisions:
C      Date       Programmer        Description of change
C      ====       ==========        =====================
C    04/22/91  S. J. Chapman       Original code
C
C  List of variables:
C    FILENM -- Name of input data file to read.
C    IGEN   -- Index variable over number of generators.
C    ISTAT  -- I/O status variable:  0 for success
C    ITIME  -- Index variable over number of time samples.
C    MAXGEN -- Maximum number of generators supported.
C    MAXTIM -- Maximum number of times supported.
C    POWER  -- Array containing power of generator IGEN at time ITIME.
C    PWRAVE -- Average power of each generator over all times.
C    PWRSUM -- Instantaneous power of station at each time.
C
      IMPLICIT NONE
C
C    Parameters
C
      INTEGER    MAXGEN
      PARAMETER ( MAXGEN = 4 )
C
      INTEGER    MAXTIM
      PARAMETER ( MAXTIM = 6 )
C
C    Declare the variables used in this program.
C
      INTEGER      ITIME, IGEN, ISTAT
      REAL         POWER(MAXTIM,MAXGEN), PWRSUM(MAXTIM), PWRAVE(MAXGEN)
      CHARACTER*20 FILENM
C
C    Initialize data.
C
      DO 6 IGEN = 1, MAXGEN
         PWRAVE(IGEN) = 0.
    6 CONTINUE
C
      DO 8 ITIME = 1, MAXTIM
         PWRSUM(ITIME) = 0.
    8 CONTINUE
C
C    Get the name of the file containing the input data.
C
      WRITE (*,1000)
 1000 FORMAT (' Enter the file name containing the input data: ')
      READ (*,1010) FILENM
```

```
 1010 FORMAT ( A20 )
C
C     Open input data file.  Status is OLD because the input data must
C     already exist.
C
      OPEN ( UNIT=9, FILE=FILENM, STATUS='OLD', IOSTAT=ISTAT )
C
C     Was the OPEN successful?
C
      IF ( ISTAT .EQ. 0 ) THEN
C
C         The file was opened successfully, so read the data to process.
C
          READ (9, *, IOSTAT=ISTAT) POWER
C
C         Calculate the instantaneous output power of the station at each
C         time.
C
          DO 20 ITIME = 1, MAXTIM
             DO 10 IGEN = 1, MAXGEN
                PWRSUM(ITIME) = POWER(ITIME,IGEN) + PWRSUM(ITIME)
   10        CONTINUE
   20     CONTINUE
C
C         Calculate the average output power of each generator over the time
C         being measured.
C
          DO 40 IGEN = 1, MAXGEN
             DO 30 ITIME = 1, MAXTIM
                PWRAVE(IGEN) = POWER(ITIME,IGEN) + PWRAVE(IGEN)
   30        CONTINUE
             PWRAVE(IGEN) = PWRAVE(IGEN) / REAL(MAXTIM)
   40     CONTINUE
C
C         Tell user.
C
          DO 50 ITIME = 1, MAXTIM
             WRITE (*,1020) ITIME, PWRSUM(ITIME)
 1020        FORMAT (' The instantaneous power at time ', I1, ' is ',
     *               F7.2, ' MW.')
   50     CONTINUE
C
          DO 60 IGEN = 1, MAXGEN
             WRITE (*,1030) IGEN, PWRAVE(IGEN)
 1030        FORMAT (' The average power of generator  ', I1, ' is ',
     *               F7.2, ' MW.')
   60     CONTINUE
C
C         END of IF OPEN successful...
C
      END IF
C
 9999 CONTINUE
      END
```

FIGURE 5-21   The program of Example 5-3.

5. Test the program.

To test this program, we will place the data from Figure 5-18(*b*) into a file called GENDAT. The contents of file GENDAT are shown below:

```
20.0    19.8    20.1    20.0    20.0    19.9
40.3    40.1    40.0    39.5    39.9    40.0
42.0    41.5    41.3    41.1    39.8    41.0
20.4    26.9    38.4    42.0    12.2     6.0
```

Note that each row of the file corresponds to a specific generator, and each column corresponds to a specific time. Next, we will calculate the answers by hand for one generator and one time, and compare the results with those from the program. At time 3, the total instantaneous power being supplied by all of the generators is

$$P_{\text{TOT}} = 20.1 \text{ MW} + 40.0 \text{ MW} + 41.3 \text{ MW} + 38.4 \text{ MW} = 139.8 \text{ MW}$$

The average power for Generator 1

$$P_{\text{G1,AVE}} = \frac{(20.1 + 19.8 + 20.1 + 20.0 + 20.0 + 19.9)}{6} = 19.97 \text{ MW}$$

The output from the program is

```
C:\BOOK\FORT>genrat
Enter the file name containing the input data:
gendat
The instantaneous power at time 1 is   122.70 MW.
The instantaneous power at time 2 is   128.30 MW.
The instantaneous power at time 3 is   139.80 MW.
The instantaneous power at time 4 is   142.60 MW.
The instantaneous power at time 5 is   111.90 MW.
The instantaneous power at time 6 is   106.90 MW.
The average power of generator  1 is    19.97 MW.
The average power of generator  2 is    39.97 MW.
The average power of generator  3 is    41.12 MW.
The average power of generator  4 is    24.32 MW.
```

so the numbers match, and the program appears to be working correctly.   ●

Note in the previous problem that the raw data array POWER was organized as a 6 × 4 matrix (6 times by 4 generators), but the input data file was organized as a 4 × 6 matrix (4 generators by 6 times)! This reversal is caused by the fact that FORTRAN stores array data in columns, but reads in data along lines. For the columns to be filled correctly in memory, the data had to be transposed in the input file! Needless to say, this can be very confusing for people having to work with the program and its input data.

It would be much better if we could eliminate this source of confusion by making organization of the data in the input file match the organization of the data within the computer. How can we do that? With implied **DO** loops! If we were to replace the statement

```
READ (9, *, IOSTAT=ISTAT) POWER
```

with the statement

```
READ (9, *, IOSTAT=ISTAT) ((POWER(ITIME,IGEN), IGEN=1,MAXGEN), ITIME=1, MAXTIM)
```

then the data along a row in the input file would go into the corresponding row of the matrix in the computer's memory. With the new **READ** statement, the input data file could be structured as follows:

```
20.0   40.3   42.0   20.4
19.8   40.1   41.5   26.9
20.1   40.0   41.3   38.4
20.0   39.5   41.1   42.0
20.0   39.9   39.8   12.2
19.9   40.0   41.0    6.0
```

and after the **READ** statement, the contents of array POWER would be

$$
\text{POWER} = \begin{bmatrix}
20.0 & 40.3 & 42.0 & 20.4 \\
19.8 & 40.1 & 41.5 & 26.9 \\
20.1 & 40.0 & 41.3 & 38.4 \\
20.0 & 39.5 & 41.1 & 42.0 \\
20.0 & 39.9 & 39.8 & 12.2 \\
19.9 & 40.0 & 41.0 & 6.0
\end{bmatrix}
$$

■   **GOOD PROGRAMMING PRACTICE**

Use **DO** loops and/or implied **DO** loops when reading or writing two-dimensional arrays in order to keep the structure of the matrix in the file the same as the structure of the matrix within the program. This correspondence makes the programs easier to understand.

5.6   MULTIDIMENSIONAL ARRAYS

FORTRAN supports more complex arrays with as many as seven different subscripts. These larger arrays are declared, initialized, and used in the same manner as the two-dimensional arrays described in the previous section.

Multidimensional arrays are allocated in memory in a manner which is an extension of the column order used for two-dimensional arrays. Memory allocation for a three-dimensional array is illustrated in Figure 5-22. Note that the first subscript

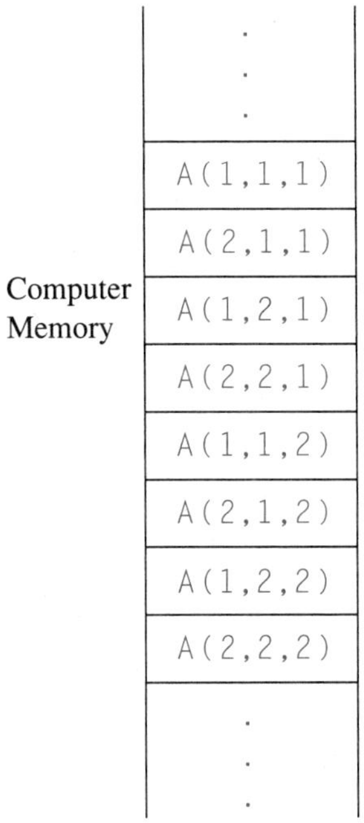

FIGURE 5-22   Memory allocation for a 2 × 2 × 2 array A.

runs through its complete range before the second subscript is incremented, and the second subscript runs through its complete range before the third subscript is incremented. This process repeats for whatever number of subscripts are declared for the array, with the first subscript always changing most rapidly, and the last subscript always changing most slowly. We must keep this allocation structure in mind if we wish to initialize or perform I/O operations with multidimensional arrays.

Quiz 5-2

This quiz provides a quick check to see if you have understood the concepts introduced in Sections 5.4 through 5.6. If you have trouble with the quiz, reread the sections, ask your instructor, or discuss the material with a fellow student. The answers to this quiz are found in the back of the book.

For questions 1–4, determine the number of elements in the array specified by the declaration statements and the valid subscript range(s) for each array.

   1.   INTEGER IRES(-10:10,0:10)
   2.   REAL DATAIN(-64:64,0:4)

3. PARAMETER (MINLU =   1)
    PARAMETER (MAXLU =   70)
    PARAMETER (MAXFIL =   3)
    CHARACTER*16 FILENM(MAXFIL,MINLU:MAXLU)
4. INTEGER IN(-3:3,-3:3,6)

Determine which of the following FORTRAN statements are valid. For each valid statement, specify what will happen in the program.

5.   REAL DIST(0:11,2)
        DATA DIST / 0.00,   0.25,   1.00,   2.25,   4.00,   6.25,
        *   9.00, 12.25, 16.00, 20.25, 25.00, 30.25,
        *   0.00,   0.25,   1.00,   2.25,   4.00,   6.25,
        *   9.00, 12.25, 16.00, 20.25, 25.00, 30.25/
6.   REAL TEMP(10,6)
        DATA (TEMP(I,1),I=1,10) / 10*33.0 /
        WRITE (*,*) TEMP
7.   LOGICAL KDELTA(10,10)
        DO 20 I = 1, 10
            DO 10 J = 1, 10
                KDELTA(I,J) = I .EQ. J
    10   CONTINUE
    20 CONTINUE
        WRITE (*,100) ((KDELTA(I,J), J=1,10), I=1,10)
    100 FORMAT ('1',5X,'Kronecker Delta Truth Table',/,
        *   ' ',5X,'===========================',//,
        *   (T15,10L1))
8.   INTEGER INDEX(0:6,12:22)
        OPEN (UNIT=2,FILE='INPUT',STATUS='OLD')
        READ (2,*) INDEX

Suppose that a file INPUT contained the following data:

11.2	16.5	31.3	3.1414	16.0
1.1	9.0	17.1	11.	15.0
10.0	11.0	12.0	13.0	14.0
15.1	16.7	18.9	21.1	24.0

What data would be read in from file INPUT in each of the following statements? What would the value of MYDATA(2,4) be in each case?

9.   REAL MYDATA(3,5)
        OPEN (UNIT=2,FILE='INPUT',STATUS='OLD')
        READ (2,*) MYDATA
10.   REAL MYDATA(3,5)
        OPEN (UNIT=2,FILE='INPUT',STATUS='OLD')
        READ (2,*) ((MYDATA(I,J), J=1,5), I=1,3)
11.   REAL MYDATA(3,5)
        OPEN (UNIT=2,FILE='INPUT',STATUS='OLD')
        DO 10 I = 1, 3
            READ (2,*) (MYDATA(I,J), J=1,5)
    10 CONTINUE

Answer the following questions.

12. What is the value DIST(6,2) in Question 5 of this quiz?

13. What is the maximum number of dimensions that an array can have in FOR-TRAN 77?

5.7   WHEN SHOULD YOU USE AN ARRAY?

We have now learned *how* to use arrays in our FORTRAN programs, but we have not yet learned *when* to use them. At this point in a typical FORTRAN course, many students are tempted to use arrays to solve problems whether they are needed or not, just because they know how to do so. How can we decide whether or not it makes sense to use an array in a particular problem?

In general, *if much or all of the input data must be in memory at the same time in order to solve a problem efficiently, then the use of arrays to hold that data is appropriate for that problem.* Otherwise, arrays are not needed. For example, let's contrast the statistics programs that we have written in Examples 3-4 and 5-3. Example 3-4 calculated the mean and standard deviation of a data set, while Example 5-3 calculated the mean, median, and standard deviation of a data set.

Recall that the equations for the mean and standard deviation of a data set are

$$\bar{x} = \frac{1}{N} \sum_{i=1}^{N} x_i \qquad (3\text{-}3)$$

and

$$s = \sqrt{\frac{N \sum_{i=1}^{N} x_i^2 - \left(\sum_{i=1}^{N} x_i \right)^2}{N(N-1)}} \qquad (3\text{-}4)$$

The sums in Equations (3-3) and (3-4) that are required to find the mean and standard deviation can easily be formed as data points are read in one by one. There is no need to wait until all of the data is read in before starting to build the sums. Therefore, a program to calculate the mean and standard deviation of a data set does not need to use arrays. You *could* use an array to hold all of the input values before calculating the mean and standard deviation, but since the array is not necessary, you should not do so. Example 3-4 works fine, and is built entirely without arrays.

On the other hand, finding the median of a data set requires that the data be sorted into ascending order. Since sorting requires all data to be in memory, a program that calculates the median must use an array to hold all of the input data before the calculations start. Therefore, Example 5-3 uses an array to hold its input data.

What's wrong with using an array within a program even if it is not needed? There are two major problems associated with using unnecessary arrays:

1. *Unnecessary arrays waste memory.* Unnecessary arrays can eat up a lot of memory, making a program larger than it needs to be. A large program requires more memory to run it, which makes the computer that it runs on more expensive. In some cases, the extra size may make it impossible to run on a particular computer at all.

2. *Unnecessary arrays restrict program capabilities.* To understand this point, let's consider an example program that calculates the mean and standard deviation of a data set. If the program is designed with a 1000-element input array, then it will only work for data sets with fewer than 1000 elements. If we encounter a data set with more than 1000 elements, the program would have to be recompiled and relinked with a larger array size. On the other hand, a program that calculates the mean and standard deviation of a data set as the values are input has no upper limit on data set size.

■
GOOD PROGRAMMING PRACTICE

Do not use arrays to solve a problem unless they are actually needed.

5.8   SUMMARY

In Chapter 5, we presented an introduction to arrays and to their use in FORTRAN programs. An array is a group of variables, all of the same type, which are referred to by a single name. The variables in the group occupy consecutive locations in the computer's memory. An individual variable within the array is called an array element. Individual array elements are addressed by means of one or more (up to seven) **INTEGER** subscripts.

An array is declared using a type statement by naming the array and specifying the maximum (and, optionally, the minimum) subscript values in parentheses following the array name. The compiler uses the declared subscript ranges to reserve space in the computer's memory to hold the array. The array elements are allocated in the computer's memory in an order such that the first subscript of the array changes most rapidly, and the last subscript of the array changes most slowly.

As with any variable, an array must be initialized before use. An array may be initialized at compile time using **DATA** statements, or at run time using **DO** loops or FORTRAN **READ**s.

Individual array elements may be used freely in a FORTRAN program just like any other variable. They may appear in assignment statements on either side of the equal sign. By contrast, an entire array (the array name without subscripts) may only be used in a few specific places (**DATA** statements, I/O statements, and some we will see in later chapters). Be careful not to confuse arrays with array elements in your code.

Arrays are especially useful for storing data values which change as a function of one or more variables (time, location, etc.). Once the data values are stored in an array, they can be easily manipulated to derive statistics or other information that may be desired.

5.8.1   Summary of Good Programming Practice

The following guidelines should be adhered to when working with arrays.

1. Before writing a program that uses arrays, you should decide whether an array is really needed to solve the problem or not. If arrays are not needed, don't use them!
2. All arrays should be declared with a type statement to explicitly specify both the type and the size of the array.
3. All array sizes should be declared using parameters. If the sizes are declared using parameters, and if those same parameters are used in any size tests within the program, then it will be very easy to modify the maximum capacity of the program at a later time.
4. All arrays should be initialized before use. The results of using an uninitialized array are unpredictable and vary from computer to computer.
5. The most common problem when programming with arrays is attempting to read from or write to locations outside the bounds of the array. To detect these problems, the bounds-checking option of your compiler should always be turned on during program testing and debugging. Because bounds checking slows down the execution of a program, the bounds-checking option may be turned off once debugging is completed.
6. Use implicit **DO** loops to read in or write out two-dimensional arrays so that each row of the array appears as a row of the input or output file. This correspondence makes it easier for a programmer to relate the data in the file to the data present within the program.

CHAPTER 5 KEY WORDS

Array	One-dimensional array
Array element	Out of bounds
Array overflow	Selection sort
Bounds checking	Sorting
Declaring arrays	Subscript
Exception handling	Two-dimensional array
Matrix	Uninitialized array
Multidimensional array	Vector

CHAPTER 5 SUMMARY OF FORTRAN STATEMENTS AND STRUCTURES

Type Declaration Statements with Arrays:

```
type array( [i1:]i2, [j1:]j2, ... ), ...
```

Example:

```
REAL A1(100), A2(-5:5)
INTEGER I(2)
CHARACTER*20 NAME(10), INITL(10)*1
```

Description: These type declaration statements declare both type and the size of an array. The example statements above are equivalent to the following statements:

```
REAL A1, A2
INTEGER I
DIMENSION A1(100), A2(-5:5), I(2)
```

Implied DO loop structure:

```
READ (lu,format) (arg1, arg2, ... , index = istart, iend, incr)
WRITE (lu,format) (arg1, arg2, ... , index = istart, iend, incr)
DATA (arg1, arg2, ... , index = istart, iend, incr) / dat1, ... /
```

Examples:

```
      WRITE (*,100) ( A(I), I = 1, 10 )
100 FORMAT (1X,10F7.2)

DATA / (A(I), I=1,5) / 1., 2*0., -17., 6. /
```

Description: The implied **DO** loop is used to repeat the values in an argument list a known number of times. The values in the argument list may be functions of the **DO** loop index variable. During the first iteration of the **DO** loop, the variable *index* is set to the value *istart*. *index* is incremented by *incr* in each successive loop until its value exceeds *iend*, at which time the loop terminates.

The loop variable *index* is incremented and tested *before* each loop, so the **DO** loop code will never be executed at all if *istart*incr* > *iend*incr*.

CHAPTER 5 EXERCISES

1. How may arrays be declared?
2. What is the difference between an array and an array element? Where may arrays be used in a FORTRAN program? Where may array elements be used?
3. Execute the following FORTRAN program on your computer with both bounds checking turned on and bounds checking turned off. What happens in each case?

```
      PROGRAM BOUNDS
      IMPLICIT NONE
      REAL TEST(20), TEST1
      INTEGER I
      DO 10 I = 1, 21
         TEST(I) = SQRT(REAL(I))
         WRITE (*,100) 'TEST(', I, ') = ', TEST(I)
100      FORMAT (1X,A,I2,A,F14.4)
   10 CONTINUE
      TEST1 = SQRT(100.)
      WRITE (*,110) 'TEST1 = ', TEST1
  110 FORMAT (1X,A,F14.4)
      END
```

4. Determine the length of the array (total number of elements) specified by each of the following declaration statements, and the valid subscript range for each array.

(*a*) `CHARACTER*80 LINE(60)`

(*b*) `CHARACTER*1 LINE(80,60)`

(*c*)
```
PARAMETER ( ISTART =  32 )
PARAMETER ( ISTOP  = 256 )
INTEGER ICHAR(ISTART:IEND)
```

(*d*)
```
PARAMETER ( NCLASS =  3 )
PARAMETER ( NSTDNT = 35 )
LOGICAL PSFAIL(NSTDNT,NCLASS)
```

(*e*) `REAL RANGE(-5:5,-5:5,-5:5,-5:5,-5:5)`

5. Determine which of the following FORTRAN program fragments are valid. For each valid statement, specify what will happen in the program. (Assume default typing for any variables that are not explicitly typed within the program fragments.)

(*a*)
```
      INTEGER ICOUNT(100), JCOUNT(100)
      ...
      DO 10 ICOUNT = 1, 100
         JCOUNT(ICOUNT) = ICOUNT + 1
   10 CONTINUE
```

(*b*)
```
      REAL B(6,4)
      ...
      DO 100 I = 1, 6
         DO 90 J = 1, 4
            TEMP   = B(I,J)
            B(I,J) = B(J,I)
            B(J,I) = TEMP
   90    CONTINUE
  100 CONTINUE
```

(*c*)
```
      REAL VALUE(10)
      DATA (VALUE(J), J=1,10,2) /  5., 4., 3., 2., 1. /
      DATA (VALUE(J), J=2,11,2) / 10., 9., 8., 7., 6. /
      WRITE (*,100) VALUE
  100 FORMAT ('1','VALUE = ',/,(F10.2))
```

(*d*)
```
      REAL ARRAY(100)
      WRITE (*,100) ARRAY
  100 FORMAT (1X,10F10.2)
```

6. Modify the program of Example 5-2 to sort an integer data set instead of a real data set.

7. What will be the output from each of the **WRITE** statements in the following program?

```
      PROGRAM TSTOUT
      INTEGER MINVAL, MAXVAL
      PARAMETER ( MINVAL = 0 )
      PARAMETER ( MAXVAL = 3 )
      INTEGER MYDAT(MINVAL:MAXVAL,MINVAL:MAXVAL)
      DATA (MYDAT(0,I),I=MINVAL,MAXVAL) /  1,  2,  3,  4 /
      DATA (MYDAT(1,I),I=MINVAL,MAXVAL) /  5,  6,  7,  8 /
      DATA (MYDAT(2,I),I=MINVAL,MAXVAL) /  9, 10, 11, 12 /
      DATA (MYDAT(3,I),I=MINVAL,MAXVAL) / 13, 14, 15, 16 /
      WRITE (*,100) MYDAT
100   FORMAT (/,(4(1X,I4)))
      WRITE (*,110) MYDAT
110   FORMAT (/,(6(1X,I4)))
      WRITE (*,120) ((MYDAT(I,J), J=MINVAL,MAXVAL),
     I=MINVAL,MAXVAL)
120   FORMAT (/,(6(1X,I4)))
      WRITE (*,130) ((MYDAT(I,J), J=MINVAL,MAXVAL),
     I=MINVAL,MAXVAL)
130   FORMAT (/,(4(1X,I4)))
      WRITE (*,140) ' '
140   FORMAT (A)
      DO 10 I = MINVAL, MAXVAL
         WRITE (*,150) (MYDAT(I,J), J=MINVAL,MAXVAL)
150      FORMAT (6(1X,I4))
10    CONTINUE
      END
```

8. An input data file INPUT1 contains the following values:

```
 27   17    10     8     6
 11   13   -11    12   -21
 -1    0     0     6    14
-16   11    21    26   -16
 04   99   -99    17     2
```

Assume that file INPUT1 has been opened on LU 8, and that array IVAL is a 4 × 4 integer array, all of whose elements have been initialized to zero. What will be the contents of array IVAL after each of the following **READ** statements has been executed?

(a)
```
      DO 10 I = 1, 4
         READ (8,*) IVAL(I,I)
10    CONTINUE
```

(b)
```
      READ (8,*) (IVAL(I,I), I=1,4)
```

(c)
```
      DO 10 I = 1, 4
         READ (8,*) (IVAL(I,J), J = 1, 4)
10    CONTINUE
```

(***d***)   `READ (8,*) ((IVAL(I,J), J = 1, 4), I=1,4)`

(***e***)
```
       DO 20 I = 1, 4
          DO 10 J = 1, 4
             READ (8,*) IVAL(I,J)
   10     CONTINUE
   20 CONTINUE
```

(***f***)   `READ (8,*) IVAL`

9. A *scalar* is a quantity that can be represented by a single number. For example, the temperature at a given location is a scalar. By contrast, a *vector* is a quantity that has both a magnitude and a direction associated with it. For example, the velocity of an automobile is a vector, since it has both a magnitude and a direction.

Vectors can be defined either by a magnitude and a direction, or by the components of the vector projected along the axes of a rectangular coordinate system. The two representations are equivalent. For two-dimensional vectors, we can convert back and forth between the representations using the following equations:

$$\mathbf{V} = V\underline{/\theta} = V_x\,\mathbf{i} + V_y\,\mathbf{j}$$
$$V_x = V\cos\theta$$
$$V_y = V\sin\theta$$
$$V = \sqrt{V_x^2 + V_y^2}$$
$$\theta = \tan^{-1}\frac{V_y}{V_x}$$

where **i** and **j** are the unit vectors in the x and y directions, respectively. The representation of the vector in terms of magnitude and angle is known as polar coordinates, and the representation of the vector in terms of components along the axes is known as rectangular coordinates (Figure 5-23).

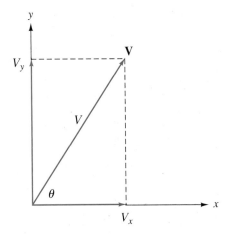

FIGURE 5-23 Representations of a vector.

Write a program that reads the polar components (magnitude and angle) of a two-dimensional vector into a one-dimensional array POLAR (POLAR(1) will contain the magnitude V and POLAR(2) will contain the angle θ in degrees). The program should then convert the vector from polar to rectangular form, storing the result in a one-dimensional array RECT. The first element of RECT should contain the x-component of the vector, and the second element should contain the y-component of the vector. After the conversion, display the contents of array RECT. Test your program by converting the following polar vectors to rectangular form:

(*a*) $5/-36.87°$
(*b*) $10/45°$
(*c*) $25/233.13°$

10. Write a program that reads the rectangular components of a two-dimensional vector into a one-dimensional array RECT (RECT(1) will contain the component V_x and RECT(2) will contain the component V_y). The program should then convert the vector from rectangular to polar form, storing the result in a one-dimensional array POLAR. The first element of POLAR should contain the magnitude of the vector, and the second element should contain the angle of the vector in degrees. After the conversion, display the contents of array POLAR. Test your program by converting the following rectangular vectors to polar form:

(*a*) $3\,i - 4\,j$
(*b*) $5\,i + 5\,j$
(*c*) $-5\,i + 12\,j$

11. Suppose that FLAGS is an 80-element logical array containing the status of 80 different alarms in the control system of an industrial plant. A flag with a TRUE status corresponds to an alarm condition (motor off line, etc.), and a flag with a FALSE status corresponds to normal operation. Write the FORTRAN statements that would check for alarms in the plant, and tell the user both that an alarm has occurred and which flag(s) triggered the alarm.

12. Assume that VALUES is a 101-element array containing a list of measurements from a scientific experiment, which has been declared by the statement

```
REAL VALUES(-50:50)
```

Write the FORTRAN statements that would count the number of positive values, negative values, and zero values in the array, and write out a message summarizing how many values of each type were found.

13. Write the FORTRAN statements that would print out every fifth value in the array VALUES described in the previous exercise. The output should take the form

```
VALUES(-50) = xxx.xxxx
VALUES(-45) = xxx.xxxx
...
VALUES( 50) = xxx.xxxx
```

14. Write a program that can read in a two-dimensional array from an input disk file, and calculate the sums of all the data in each row and each column in the array. The size of the array to read in will be specified by two numbers on the first line in the input file, and the elements in each row of the array will be found on a single line of the input file. An example of an input data file containing a 2 row $\times$ 4 column array is shown below:

```
      2          4
 -24.0     -1121.       812.1       11.1
  35.6      8.1E3       135.23     -17.3
```

Write out the results in the form

```
Sum of row  1 =
Sum of row  2 =
     ...
Sum of col  1 =
     ...
```

15. Test the program that you wrote in exercise 14 by running it on the following array:

$$\text{ARRAY} = \begin{bmatrix} 33. & -12. & 16. & 0.5 & -1.9 \\ -6. & -14. & 3.5 & 11. & 2.1 \\ 4.4 & 1.1 & -7.1 & 9.3 & -16.1 \\ 0.3 & 6.2 & -9.9 & -12. & 6.8 \end{bmatrix}$$

16. A three-dimensional vector can be represented in rectangular coordinates as

$$\mathbf{V} = V_x \mathbf{i} + V_y \mathbf{j} + V_z \mathbf{k}$$

where V_x is the component of vector $\mathbf{V}$ in the x direction, V_y is the component of vector $\mathbf{V}$ in the y direction, and V_z is the component of vector $\mathbf{V}$ in the z direction. A three-dimensional vector can be stored in a one-dimensional array containing three elements, since there are three dimensions in the coordinate system. The same idea applies to an n-dimensional vector. An n-dimensional vector can be stored in a one-dimensional array containing n elements. This is the reason why one-dimensional arrays are sometimes called vectors.

One common mathematical operation between two vectors is the *dot product*. The dot product of two vectors $\mathbf{V}_1 = V_{x1} \mathbf{i} + V_{y1} \mathbf{j} + V_{z1} \mathbf{k}$ and $\mathbf{V}_2 = V_{x2} \mathbf{i} + V_{y2} \mathbf{j} + V_{z2} \mathbf{k}$ is a scalar quantity defined by the equation

$$\mathbf{V}_1 \cdot \mathbf{V}_2 = V_{x1}V_{x2} + V_{y1}V_{y2} + V_{z1}V_{z2}$$

Write a FORTRAN program that will read two vectors $\mathbf{V}_1$ and $\mathbf{V}_2$ into two one-dimensional arrays in computer memory, and then calculate their dot product according to the equation given above. Test your program by calculating the dot product of vectors $\mathbf{V}_1 = 5\,\mathbf{i} - 3\,\mathbf{j} + 2\,\mathbf{k}$ and $\mathbf{V}_2 = 2\,\mathbf{i} + 3\,\mathbf{j} + 4\,\mathbf{k}$.

17. The dot product of two n-dimensional vectors is calculated in the same fashion as the dot product of two three-dimensional vectors. The general equation for calculating the dot product of two n-dimensional vectors A and B is

$$\mathbf{A} \cdot \mathbf{B} = \sum_{i=1}^{n} a_i b_i$$

Write a FORTRAN program that will read two n-dimensional vectors $\mathbf{V}_1$ and $\mathbf{V}_2$ into two arrays in computer memory, and then calculate their dot product according to the equation given above. Note that you will have to specify the number of dimensions in the vectors when they are read in. Test your program by calculating the dot product of vectors $\mathbf{V}_1 = [2\ -1\ 3\ 2\ 4]$ and $\mathbf{V}_2 = [-3\ -2\ 3\ 1\ -1]$.

18. If an object is being pushed by a force $\mathbf{F}$ at a velocity $\mathbf{v}$, then the power supplied to the object by the force is given by the equation

$$P = \mathbf{F} \cdot \mathbf{v}$$

where the force $\mathbf{F}$ is measured in newtons, the velocity $\mathbf{v}$ is measured in meters per second, and the power P is measured in watts. Use the FORTRAN program written in exercise 16 to calculate the power supplied by a force of $\mathbf{F} = 4\,\mathbf{i} + 3\,\mathbf{j} - 2\,\mathbf{k}$ newtons to an object moving with a velocity of $\mathbf{v} = 4\,\mathbf{i} - 2\,\mathbf{j} + 1\,\mathbf{k}$ m/sec (Figure 5-24).

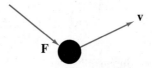

FIGURE 5-24

19. Another common mathematical operation between two vectors is the *cross product*. The cross product of two vectors $\mathbf{V}_1 = V_{x1}\,\mathbf{i} + V_{y1}\,\mathbf{j} + V_{z1}\,\mathbf{k}$ and $\mathbf{V}_2 = V_{x2}\,\mathbf{i} + V_{y2}\,\mathbf{j} + V_{z2}\,\mathbf{k}$ is a vector quantity defined by the equation

$$\mathbf{V}_1 \times \mathbf{V}_2 = (V_{y1}V_{z2} - V_{y2}V_{z1})\mathbf{i} + (V_{z1}V_{x2} - V_{z2}V_{x1})\mathbf{j} + (V_{x1}V_{y2} - V_{x2}V_{y1})\mathbf{k}$$

Write a FORTRAN program that will read two vectors $\mathbf{V}_1$ and $\mathbf{V}_2$ into arrays in computer memory, and then calculate their cross product according to the equation given above. Test your program by calculating the cross product of vectors $\mathbf{V}_1 = 5\,\mathbf{i} - 3\,\mathbf{j} + 2\,\mathbf{k}$ and $\mathbf{V}_2 = 2\,\mathbf{i} + 3\,\mathbf{j} + 4\,\mathbf{k}$.

20. The vector angular velocity ω of an object moving with a velocity $\mathbf{v}$ at a distance $\mathbf{r}$ from the origin of the coordinate system is given by the equation

$$\mathbf{v} = \mathbf{r} \times \omega$$

where $\mathbf{r}$ is the distance in meters, ω is the angular velocity in radians per second, and $\mathbf{v}$ is the velocity in meters per second. If the distance from the center of the earth to an orbiting satellite is $\mathbf{r} = 300000\,\mathbf{i} + 400000\,\mathbf{j} + 50000\,\mathbf{k}$ meters, and the angular velocity of the satellite is $\omega = -6 \times 10^{-3}\,\mathbf{i} + 2 \times 10^{-3}\,\mathbf{j} - 9 \times 10^{-4}\,\mathbf{k}$ radians per second, what is the velocity of the satellite in meters per second? Use the program written in the previous exercise to calculate the answer (Figure 5-25).

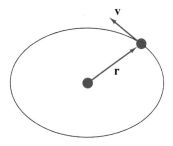

FIGURE 5-25

21. Program STAT4 in Example 5-3 will behave incorrectly if a user enters an invalid value in the input data set. For example, if the user enters the characters 1.o instead of 1.0 on a line, then the **READ** statement will return a non-zero **IOSTAT** for that line. This non-zero **IOSTAT** will be misinterpreted as the end of the data set, and only a portion of the input data will be processed. Modify the program to protect against invalid values in the input data file. If a bad value is encountered in the input data file, the program should display the line number containing the bad value, and skip it. The program should process all of the good values in the file, even those after a bad value.

22. The location of any point P in a three-dimensional space can be represented by a set of three values (x, y, z), where x is the distance along the x axis to the point, y is the distance along the y axis to the point, and z is the distance along the z axis to the point. If two points P_1 and P_2 are represented by the values (x_1, y_1, z_1) and (x_2, y_2, z_2), then the distance between the points P_1 and P_2 can be calculated from the equation

$$distance = \sqrt{(x_1 - x_2)^2 + (y_1 - y_2)^2 + (z_1 - z_2)^2}$$

Write a FORTRAN program to read in two points (x_1, y_1, z_1) and (x_2, y_2, z_2), and to calculate the distance between them. Test your program by calculating the distance between the points $(-1, 4, 6)$ and $(1, 5, -2)$.

23. As a part of a meteorological experiment, average annual temperature measurements were collected at 36 locations specified by latitude and longitude as shown in the chart below.

	90.0° W long	*90.5° W long*	*91.0° W long*	*91.5° W long*	*92.0° W long*	*92.5° W long*
30.0° N lat	68.2	72.1	72.5	74.1	74.4	74.2
30.5° N lat	69.4	71.1	71.9	73.1	73.6	73.7
31.0° N lat	68.9	70.5	70.9	71.5	72.8	73.0
31.5° N lat	68.6	69.9	70.4	70.8	71.5	72.2
32.0° N lat	68.1	69.3	69.8	70.2	70.9	71.2
32.5° N lat	68.3	68.8	69.6	70.0	70.5	70.9

Write a FORTRAN program that calculates the average annual temperature along each latitude included in the experiment, and the average annual temperature along each longitude included in the experiment. Finally, calculate the average annual temperature for all of the locations in the experiment.

24. The *size* of a matrix is specified by the number of rows and columns in the matrix. For example, an N × M matrix has N rows and M columns. Matrix addition and subtraction are only defined for two matrices of the same size. If two matrices are of the same size, then the sum of the two matrices is just the sum of the corresponding components in each matrix. For example, if matrices A and B are 2 × 2 matrices:

$$A = \begin{bmatrix} a_{11} & a_{12} \\ a_{21} & a_{22} \end{bmatrix} \text{ and } B = \begin{bmatrix} b_{11} & b_{12} \\ b_{21} & b_{22} \end{bmatrix}$$

then their sum C = A + B is

$$C = \begin{bmatrix} a_{11} + b_{11} & a_{12} + b_{12} \\ a_{21} + b_{21} & a_{22} + b_{22} \end{bmatrix}$$

Write a program that can read in two matrices of arbitrary size from two input disk files, and add them if they are of the same size. If they are of different sizes, an appropriate error message should be printed. The size of each matrix is specified by two numbers on the first line in each file, and the elements in each row of the matrix are found on a single line of the input file. An example of an input data file containing a 3 × 4 matrix is shown below:

```
      3         4
  -24.0     11.21      1.23        0.
   1.22       -6.      1.0        -6.
 1.12E+2     .0056      6.2       45.6
```

Verify your program by creating two input data files containing matrices of the same size, calculating the resulting sums with the program, and checking the answers by hand. Also, verify the proper behavior of the program if it is given two matrices that are of different sizes. (*Note:* Be sure to use the proper form of implied **DO** statements to read in and write out the data correctly.)

25. Use the program produced in exercise 25 to find the sum of the following two matrices:

$$A = \begin{bmatrix} 1.0 & -3.0 & 17.2 & 0.0 & -0.5 \\ -6.1 & 3.33 & 11.1 & 0.25 & -17.0 \\ 14.1 & 2.2 & -3.1 & 0.0 & -0.05 \\ 1.0 & -1.0 & 1.0 & 10.0 & -5.65 \end{bmatrix}$$

and

$$B = \begin{bmatrix} 13.1 & 3.0 & 0.0 & 0.05 & -1.667 \\ -1.2 & 1.667 & -11.1 & -4.5 & 5.5 \\ -9.25 & -4.05 & 5.01 & 0.0 & 6.2 \\ -1.0 & 6.0 & 1.0 & 4.0 & -2.0 \end{bmatrix}$$

26. Matrix multiplication is only defined for two matrices in which *the number of columns in the first matrix is equal to the number of rows in the second matrix.* If matrix A is an $N \times L$ matrix, and matrix B is an $L \times M$ matrix, then the product $C = A \times B$ is an $N \times M$ matrix whose elements are given by the equation

$$c_{ik} = \sum_{j=1}^{L} a_{ij} b_{jk}$$

For example, if matrices A and B are 2×2 matrices

$$A = \begin{bmatrix} 3.0 & -1.0 \\ 1.0 & 2.0 \end{bmatrix} \quad \text{and} \quad B = \begin{bmatrix} 1.0 & 4.0 \\ 2.0 & -3.0 \end{bmatrix}$$

then the elements of matrix C will be

$$c_{11} = a_{11}b_{11} + a_{12}b_{21} = (3.0)(1.0) + (-1.0)(2.0) = 1.0$$
$$c_{12} = a_{11}b_{12} + a_{12}b_{22} = (3.0)(4.0) + (-1.0)(-3.0) = 15.0$$
$$c_{21} = a_{21}b_{11} + a_{22}b_{21} = (1.0)(1.0) + (2.0)(2.0) = 5.0$$
$$c_{22} = a_{21}b_{12} + a_{22}b_{22} = (1.0)(4.0) + (2.0)(-3.0) = -2.0$$

Write a program that can read in two matrices of arbitrary size from two input disk files, and multiply them if they are of compatible sizes. If they are of incompatible sizes, an appropriate error message should be printed. The number of rows and columns in each matrix are specified by two integers on the first line in each file, and the elements in each row of the matrix are found on a single line of the input file (this is the same format as exercise 26). Verify your program by creating two input data files containing matrices of the compatible sizes, calculating the resulting values, and checking the answers by hand. Also, verify the proper behavior of the program if it is given two matrices that are of incompatible sizes. (*Note:* Be sure to use the proper form of implied **DO** statements to read in and write out the data correctly.)

27. Use the program produced in exercise 27 to multiply the following two matrices *A* and *B*:

$$C = A \times B$$

where

$$A = \begin{bmatrix} 1. & -5. & 4. & 2. \\ -6. & -4. & 2. & 2. \end{bmatrix}$$

and

$$B = \begin{bmatrix} 1. & -2. & -1. \\ 2. & 3. & 4. \\ 0. & -1. & 2. \\ 0. & -3. & 1. \end{bmatrix}$$

How many rows and how many columns are present in the resulting matrix *C*?

28. Write a FORTRAN program that scans a one-dimensional array to find both the maximum value in the array, and the index of the array element containing the maximum value. The program should be able to read an arbitrary number of values (up to 1000) from a user-specified input disk file, with one input value per line. Test the program using a file containing the following 10 input values: $-10.$, $-20.$, $0.$, $45.$, $0.$, $17.$, $32.$, $100.$, $-34.$, and $-200.$

29. A point in a two-dimensional array is said to be a *relative maximum* if it is higher than any of the eight points surrounding it. For example, the element at position (2, 2) in the array shown below is a relative maximum, since it is larger than any of the surrounding points.

$$\begin{bmatrix} 11 & 7 & -2 \\ -7 & 14 & 3 \\ 2 & -3 & 5 \end{bmatrix}$$

Write a program to read a matrix *A* from an input disk file, and to scan for all relative maxima within the matrix. The first line in the disk file should contain the number of rows and the number of columns in the matrix, and then the next lines should contain the values in the matrix, with all of the values in a given row on a single line of the input disk file. (Be sure to use the proper form of implied **DO** statements to read in the data correctly.) The program should only consider interior points within the matrix, since any point along an edge of the matrix cannot possibly be completely surrounded by points lower than itself.

Test your program by finding all of the relative maxima in the following matrix:

$$
A = \begin{bmatrix}
2. & -1. & -2. & 1. & 3. & -5. \\
-2. & 0. & -2.5 & 5. & -2. & 2. \\
-3. & -3. & -3. & 3. & 0. & 0. \\
-4.5 & -4. & -7. & 6. & 1. & -3. \\
-3.5 & -3. & -5. & 0. & 4. & 2. \\
-9. & -6. & -5. & -3. & 1. & 17.
\end{bmatrix}
$$

30. Modify the relative maximum program of the previous example to consider points on the edge of the matrix as well as points in the center. Consider a point on the edge of the matrix to be a relative maximum if and only if the magnitudes of all of the neighbor points that exist are smaller than the point itself. Test the modified program using the same matrix that the original program was tested with. How many more maxima were found using this new definition?

Subprograms and Structured Programming

In Chapter 3 we learned the importance of good program design. The basic technique that we employed is *top-down design*. In top-down design, the programmer starts with a statement of the problem to be solved and the required inputs to and outputs from the program. Next, he or she describes the algorithm to be implemented by the program in broad outline, and applies *decomposition* to break the algorithm down into logical subdivisions called subtasks. Then, the user breaks down each subtask until he or she winds up with many small pieces, each of which does a simple, clearly understandable job. Finally, the individual pieces are turned into FORTRAN code.

Although we have followed this design process in our examples, the results have been somewhat restricted, since we have had to combine the final FORTRAN code we generated for each subtask into a single large program. We have had no way to code, verify, and test each of our subtasks independently before combining them into the final program.

Fortunately, FORTRAN has a special mechanism designed to make subtasks easy to develop and debug independently before building the final program. It is possible to code each subtask as a separate **subprogram,** and each subprogram can be compiled, tested, and debugged independently of all of the other subtasks (subprograms) in the program.

There are two kinds of subprograms in FORTRAN: **function subprograms** (or functions) and **subroutines.** Function subprograms are subprograms whose result is a single number, logical value, or character string, while subroutines are subprograms whose results include more than one number, logical values, or character strings. These subprograms will be described in this chapter.

Subprograms are marvelous! Well-designed subprograms enormously reduce the effort required on a large programming project. Their benefits include:

1. **Independent testing of subtasks.** Each subtask can be coded and compiled as an independent unit. The subtask can be tested separately to ensure that it performs properly by itself before combining it into the larger task. This step is known as **unit testing.** It eliminates a major source of problems before the final program is even built.

2. **Reusable code.** In many cases, the same basic subtask is needed over and over again in many parts of a program. For example, it may be necessary to sort a list of values into ascending order many different times within a program, or even in other programs. It is possible to design, code, test, and debug a *single* subprogram to do the sorting, and then to reuse that subprogram over and over whenever sorting is required. This reusable code has two major advantages: it reduces the total programming effort required, and it simplifies debugging, since the sorting function only needs to be debugged once.

3. **Isolation from unintended side effects.** Subprograms communicate with the main programs that use them through a list of variables called an **argument list.** *The only variables in the main program which can be changed by the subprogram are those in the argument list.* This is very important, since accidental programming mistakes can only affect the variables in the module in which the mistake occurred.

Once a large program is written and released, it has to be **maintained.** Program maintenance involves fixing bugs and modifying the program to handle new and unforeseen circumstances. The programmer who modifies the program during maintenance is usually not the same one that originally wrote it. In poorly written programs, it is common for the programmer modifying the program to make a change in one region of the code, and to have that change cause unintended side effects in a totally different part of the program. This happens because variable names are reused in different portions of the program. When the programmer changes the values left behind in some of the variables, those values are accidentally picked up and used in other portions of the code.

The use of well-designed subprograms minimizes this problem by **variable hiding.** All of the variables in the subprogram except for those in the argument list are not visible to the main program, and therefore mistakes or changes in those variables cannot accidentally cause unintended side effects in the other parts of the program.

■ GOOD PROGRAMMING PRACTICE

Break large program tasks into subprograms whenever practical to achieve the important benefits of independent component testing, reusability, and isolation from undesired side effects.

We will now examine the two different types of FORTRAN 77 subprograms: subroutines and functions.

6.1   SUBROUTINES

A **subroutine** is a FORTRAN subprogram that receives its input values and returns its results through an *argument list*. The general form of a subroutine is

```
SUBROUTINE subroutine name ( argument list )
...
   (Declaration section)
...
   (Execution section)
...
   (Termination section)
RETURN
END
```

The subroutine name must follow standard FORTRAN conventions: it may be up to six characters long and contain both alphabetic characters and digits, but the first character must be alphabetic. The argument list contains a list of the variables and/or arrays which are being passed from the calling program to the subroutine. These variables are called **dummy arguments,** since the subroutine does not actually allocate any memory for them. They are just placeholders for variables in the calling program.

Note that like any FORTRAN program, a subroutine must have a declaration section, an execution section, and a termination section. When a program calls the subroutine, the execution of the calling program stops, and the execution section of the subroutine is run. When a **RETURN** or **END** statement is reached in the subroutine, the calling program starts running again at the line following the subroutine call.

Each subroutine is an independent program unit, beginning with a **SUBROUTINE** statement and terminated by an **END** statement. It is compiled separately from the main program and from any other subprograms. Because each program unit in a program is compiled separately, statement labels and variable names may be reused in different routines without causing an error.

Any program may call a subroutine, including another subroutine. However, a subroutine may not call itself (FORTRAN 77 subroutines are not *recursive*). To call a subroutine, the calling program places a **CALL** statement in its code. The format of a call statement is

```
CALL subroutine name ( argument list )
```

where the order and type of the values in the argument list must match the order and type of the dummy arguments declared in the subroutine. Each input argument in the argument list of the **CALL** statement may be a variable, constant, or expression. Each output argument in the argument list of the **CALL** statement must be a variable.

A simple example subroutine is shown in Figure 6-1. This subroutine calculates the hypotenuse of a right triangle from the lengths of the other two sides.

```
         SUBROUTINE CHYPOT ( SIDE1, SIDE2, HYPOT )
C
C  Purpose:
C    To calculate the hypotenuse of a right triangle from the two
C    other sides.
C
C  Record of revisions:
C      Date         Programmer          Description of change
C      ====         ==========          =====================
C    04/27/91    S. J. Chapman          Original code
C
C  List of calling arguments:
C     NAME    I/O   TYPE         DESCRIPTION
C     ====    ===   ====         ===========
C     SIDE1    I    REAL         Length of side 1.
C     SIDE2    I    REAL         Length of side 2.
C     HYPOT    O    REAL         Length of hypotenuse.
C
C  List of local variables:
C     TEMP    -- REAL variable to hold intermediate results.
C
      IMPLICIT NONE
C
C  Declare calling parameters.
C
      REAL    SIDE1, SIDE2, HYPOT
C
C  Declare local variables.
C
      REAL    TEMP
C
C  Execution section.
C
      TEMP  = SIDE1**2 + SIDE2**2
      HYPOT = SQRT ( TEMP )
C
C  Termination section.
C
      RETURN
      END
```

FIGURE 6-1   A simple subroutine to calculate the hypoteneuse of a right triangle.

This subroutine has three arguments in its argument list. SIDE1 and SIDE2 are placeholders for real variables containing the lengths of sides 1 and 2 of the triangle. These variables are used in the subroutine but are not changed, so their I/O type is input ("I" above). HYPOT is a placeholder for a real variable that will receive the length of the hypotenuse of the triangle. The value of HYPOT is set in the subroutine, so its I/O type is output ("O" above).

Variable TEMP is actually defined within the subroutine. It is used in the subroutine, but it is not accessible to any calling program. Variables which are used within a subroutine and which are not accessible by calling programs are called **local variables.**

To test a subroutine, it is necessary to write a main program called a **test driver program** (or just a driver). The test driver program is a main program that calls the subroutine with a sample data set, and displays the results from the subroutine. A test driver program for subroutine CHYPOT is shown in Figure 6-2:

```
      PROGRAM THYPOT
C
C  Purpose:
C     Program to test the operation of subroutine CHYPOT.
C
C  Record of revisions:
C      Date        Programmer         Description of change
C      ====        ==========         =====================
C     04/27/91   S. J. Chapman        Original code
C
C  List of variables:
C     HYP     -- Length of hypotenuse.
C     S1      -- Length of side 1.
C     S2      -- Length of side 2.
C
      IMPLICIT NONE
C
C     Declare the variables used in this program.
C
      REAL S1, S2, HYP
C
C     Get the lengths of the two sides.
C
      WRITE (*,1000)
 1000 FORMAT (' Program to test subroutine CHYPOT: ')
      WRITE (*,1010)
 1010 FORMAT (' Enter the length of side 1: ')
      READ (*,*) S1
      WRITE (*,1020)
 1020 FORMAT (' Enter the length of side 2: ')
      READ (*,*) S2
C
C     Call CHYPOT.
C
      CALL CHYPOT ( S1, S2, HYP )
C
C     Write out hypotenuse.
C
      WRITE (*,1030) HYP
 1030 FORMAT (' The length of the hypotenuse is: ', F10.4 )
C
      END
```

FIGURE 6-2   A test driver program for subroutine CHYPOT.

This program calls subroutine CHYPOT with an argument list of variables S1, S2, and HYP. Therefore, wherever the dummy argument SIDE1 appears in the subroutine, variable S1 is really used instead. Similarly, the hypotenuse is really written into variable HYP.

This example subroutine is so simple that it does not properly illustrate all of the advantages of subprograms. We will see more benefits as we start working more complex problems later on in the book.

6.1.1 Example Problem—Sorting

Let us now reexamine the sorting problem of Example 5-2 in the previous chapter, using subroutines where appropriate.

■───────

EXAMPLE 6-1 *Sorting Data* Develop a program to read in a data set from a file, sort it into ascending order, and display the sorted data set. Use subroutines where appropriate.

SOLUTION The program in Example 5-2 read an arbitrary number of real input data values from a user-supplied file, sorted the data into ascending order, and wrote the sorted data to the standard output device. The sorting process would make a good candidate for a subroutine, since only the array A and its length NVALS are in common between the sorting process and the rest of the program. The rewritten program using a sorting subroutine is shown in Figure 6-3:

```
      PROGRAM SORT3
C
C Purpose:
C   To read in a REAL input data set, sort it into ascending order
C   using the selection sort algorithm, and to write the sorted
C   data to the standard output device. This program calls subroutine
C   SORT to do the actual sorting.
C
C Record of revisions:
C     Date        Programmer          Description of change
C     ====        ==========          =====================
C   05/03/91      S. J. Chapman       Original code
C
C List of variables:
C   A       -- REAL data array to sort.
C   EXCEED  -- Logical indicating that array limits are exceeded.
C   FILENM  -- Name of input data file to read.
C   I       -- Index variable.
C   ISTAT   -- I/O status variable:  0 for success
C   NVALS   -- Number of data values to sort.
C   TEMP    -- Temporary variable used to read in values, and to
C              swap values in array A
C
      IMPLICIT NONE
C
C   Parameters
C
      INTEGER    MAXSIZ
      PARAMETER ( MAXSIZ = 10 )
C
```

```
C     Declare the variables used in this program.
C
      INTEGER      I, ISTAT, NVALS
      REAL         A(MAXSIZ), TEMP
      LOGICAL      EXCEED
      CHARACTER*20 FILENM
C
C     Get the name of the file containing the input data.
C
      WRITE (*,1000)
 1000 FORMAT (' Enter the file name containing the data to be sorted: ')
      READ (*,1010) FILENM
 1010 FORMAT ( A20 )
C
C     Open input data file.  Status is OLD because the input data must
C     already exist.
C
      OPEN ( UNIT=9, FILE=FILENM, STATUS='OLD', IOSTAT=ISTAT )
C
C     Was the OPEN successful?
C
      IF ( ISTAT .EQ. 0 ) THEN
C
C        The file was opened successfully, so read the data to sort
C        from it, sort the data, and write out the results.
C
         READ (9, *, IOSTAT=ISTAT) TEMP
C
C        Begin WHILE loop.  Did we read the value successfully?
C
   10    IF ( ISTAT .EQ. 0 ) THEN
C
C           Yes.  Increment number of values.
C
            NVALS = NVALS + 1
C
C           Is NVALS <= MAXSIZ?  If so, store the value in array A.
C           If not, set the array size exceeded flag to .TRUE.
C
            IF ( NVALS .LE. MAXSIZ ) THEN
               A(NVALS) = TEMP
            ELSE
               EXCEED = .TRUE.
            END IF
C
C           Read next value.
C
            READ (9, *, IOSTAT=ISTAT) TEMP
            GO TO 10
C
C           End of WHILE Loop
C
         END IF
C
C        Was the array size exceeded?  If so, tell user and quit.
C
         IF ( EXCEED ) THEN
```

```
            WRITE (*,1020) NVALS, MAXSIZ
 1020       FORMAT (' Maximum array size exceeded: ', I6, '>', I6 )
         ELSE
C
C           Array size not exceeded.  Sort the data.
C
            CALL SORT ( A, NVALS )
C
C           Now write out the sorted data.
C
            WRITE (*,1030) ' The sorted output data values are: '
 1030       FORMAT (A)
            WRITE (*,1040) ( A(I), I = 1, NVALS )
 1040       FORMAT (4X,F10.4)
         END IF
C
C        END of IF OPEN successful...
C
      END IF
C
      END
      SUBROUTINE SORT ( ARRAY, N )
C
C  Purpose:
C    To sort REAL array ARRAY into ascending order using a selection
C    sort.
C
C  List of calling arguments:
C    NAME    I/O    TYPE        DESCRIPTION
C    ====    ===    ====        ===========
C    ARRAY   IO     REAL ARRAY  Input:  array to be sorted.
C                               Output: sorted array.
C    N       I      INTEGER     Number of values in array ARRAY.
C
C  List of local variables:
C    I      -- Index variable.
C    IPTR   -- Pointer to the smallest value found during a search.
C    J      -- Index variable.
C    TEMP   -- Temporary variable used to swap values in array.
C
      IMPLICIT NONE
C
C     Declare calling parameters.
C
      REAL    ARRAY(*)
      INTEGER N
C
C     Declare local variables.
C
      INTEGER I, IPTR, J
      REAL    TEMP
C
      DO 20 I = 1, N-1
C
C        Find the minimum value in ARRAY(I) through ARRAY(N)
C
         IPTR = I
```

```
          DO 10 J = I+1, N
             IF ( ARRAY(J) .LT. ARRAY(IPTR) ) THEN
                IPTR = J
             END IF
   10     CONTINUE
C
C         IPTR now points to the minimum value, so swap ARRAY(IPTR) with
C         ARRAY(I) if I <> IPTR.
C
          IF ( I .NE. IPTR ) THEN
             TEMP        = ARRAY(I)
             ARRAY(I)    = ARRAY(IPTR)
             ARRAY(IPTR) = TEMP
          END IF
C
   20 CONTINUE
C
C     Termination section.
C
       RETURN
       END
```

FIGURE 6-3   Program to sort real data values into ascending order using a SORT subroutine.

This new program can be tested just as the original program was, with identical results. If the following data set is placed in file INPUT2,

```
    13.3
    12.
    -3.0
     0.
     4.0
     6.6
     4.
    -6.
```

the results of the test run are:

```
C:\BOOK\FORT>sort3
Enter the file name containing the data to be sorted:
input2
The sorted output data values are:
      -6.0000
      -3.0000
        .0000
       4.0000
       4.0000
       6.6000
      12.0000
      13.3000
```

The program gives the correct answers for our test data set, as before.   ●

Subroutine SORT performs the same function as the sorting code in the original example, but now SORT is an independent subroutine that we can reuse unchanged whenever we need to sort any array of real numbers. As we build up collections of subroutines performing common functions such as sorting, it becomes easier and easier to implement new programs.

Note in the sort subroutine that the array was declared as

```
REAL ARRAY(*)
```

The asterisk tells the FORTRAN compiler that dummy argument ARRAY is an array whose length is unknown. The dummy argument ARRAY is only a place-holder for whatever array is passed as an argument when the subroutine is called. The actual size of the array is the size of the array that passed from the calling program.

Also, note that statement label 10 was used twice, once in the main program SORT3 and once in subroutine SORT. Since the two program units are compiled independently, this does not cause an error.

6.1.2 Variable Passing in FORTRAN: The Pass-by-Reference Scheme

FORTRAN programs communicate with their subroutines using a **pass-by-reference** scheme. When a subroutine call occurs, the main program passes a pointer to the location in memory of each argument in the argument list. The subroutine looks at the memory location pointed to by the calling program to get the values of the dummy arguments it needs. This process is illustrated in Figure 6-4.

The figure shows a main program TEST calling a subroutine SUB1. There are three arguments being passed to the subroutine, a real variable A, a four-element real array B, and an integer variable NEXT. These variables occupy memory addresses 001, 002-005, and 006, respectively, in the computer. Three dummy arguments are declared in SUB1: a real variable X, a real array Y, and an integer variable I. When the main program calls SUB1, *what is passed to the subroutine are the pointers to the memory locations containing the calling arguments:* 001, 002, and 006. Whenever variable X is referred to the subroutine, the contents of memory location 001 are accessed, etc. This parameter passing scheme is called pass-by-reference, since only pointers to the values are passed to the subroutine, not the actual values themselves.

There are some possible pitfalls associated with the pass-by-reference scheme. *The programmer must ensure that the values in the calling argument list match the subroutine's calling parameters in number, type, and order.* If there is a mismatch, the FORTRAN program is not able to recognize that fact, and it misuses the parameters without informing you of the problem.[1] For example, consider the program shown in Figure 6-5.

---

[1] Some FORTRAN compilers are smart enough to check for argument mismatches if both the calling program and the subroutine are in the same file at compilation time. If they are in separate files, even these compilers cannot detect the argument mismatch.

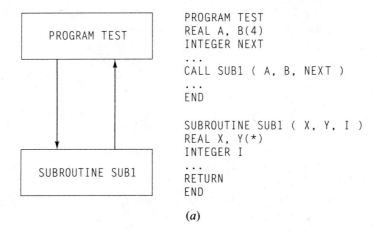

```
                                PROGRAM TEST
                                REAL A, B(4)
     ┌─────────────────────┐    INTEGER NEXT
     │                     │    ...
     │    PROGRAM TEST     │    CALL SUB1 ( A, B, NEXT )
     │                     │    ...
     └─────────────────────┘    END
         │          ▲
         │          │           SUBROUTINE SUB1 ( X, Y, I )
         │          │           REAL X, Y(*)
         ▼          │           INTEGER I
     ┌─────────────────────┐    ...
     │                     │    RETURN
     │   SUBROUTINE SUB1   │    END
     │                     │
     └─────────────────────┘
```

(a)

Memory Address	Main Program Name	Subroutine Name
001	A	X
002	B(1)	Y(1)
003	B(2)	Y(2)
004	B(3)	Y(3)
005	B(4)	Y(4)
006	NEXT	I
007		

(b)

FIGURE 6-4   The pass-by-reference memory scheme. Note that only pointers to the memory addresses of the calling arguments are passed to the subroutine.

```
       PROGRAM BADCAL
C
C  Purpose:
C     To illustrate misinterpreted calling arguments.
C
       IMPLICIT NONE
C
C     Local variables.
C
```

```
      REAL X
C
C     Set X
C
      X = 1.
C
C     Call subroutine BADARG.
C
      CALL BADARG ( X )
C
      END
      SUBROUTINE BADARG ( I )
C
      IMPLICIT NONE
C
      INTEGER I
C
      WRITE (*,*) ' I = ', I
C
      RETURN
      END
```

FIGURE 6-5   Example illustrating the effects of a type mismatch when calling a subroutine.

The argument in the call to subroutine BADARG is real, but the corresponding dummy argument is type integer. FORTRAN passes the address of the real variable X to the subroutine, which then treats it as an integer. The results are quite bad. When the program is compiled with the Microsoft FORTRAN compiler, we get

```
C:\BOOK\FORT>badcal
 I = 1065353216
```

Another serious problem can occur if a variable is placed in the calling argument list in a position at which an array is expected. The subroutine cannot tell the difference between a variable and an array, so it will treat the variable and the variables following it in memory as though they were all part of one big array! This behavior can produce a world of problems. A subroutine containing a variable named X in its calling sequence could wind up modifying another variable Y that wasn't even passed to the subroutine, just because Y happens to be allocated after X in the computer's memory. Problems like that can be *extremely* difficult to find and debug (see Figure 6-6).

```
      PROGRAM BADARR
C
C  Purpose:
C    To illustrate how a subroutine can modify variables not
C    in its argument list if variables and arrays are mismatched
C    in the argument list.
C
      IMPLICIT NONE
C
C     Local variables.
C
```

```
      REAL X, Y, Z
C
C     Initialize values
C
      X = 1.
      Y = 2.
      Z = 3.
C
C     Write out X, Y, Z before call to BADSUB.
C
      WRITE (*,100) 'Before: X = ', X, ' Y = ', Y, ' Z = ', Z
  100 Format (1X,3(A,F10.2))
C
C     Call subroutine BADSUB.
C
      Call BADSUB ( X )
C
C     Write out X, Y, Z after call to BADSUB.
C
      WRITE (*,100) 'After: X = ', X, ' Y = ', Y, ' Z = ', Z
C
      END
      SUBROUTINE BADSUB ( X )
C
      IMPLICIT NONE
C
      INTEGER I
      REAL    X(3)
C
      DO 10 I = 1, 3
         X(I) = -REAL(I)
   10 CONTINUE
C
      RETURN
      END
```

(a)

```
C:\BOOK\FORT>badarr
Before: X =        1.00 Y =        2.00 Z =        3.00
After:  X =       -1.00 Y =       -2.00 Z =       -3.00
```

(b)

FIGURE 6-6 (*a*) A sample program showing how a subroutine can modify the contents of variables not in its calling argument list if there is a mismatch between the subroutine argument list and the calling argument list. (*b*) The result of executing program BADARR.

PROGRAMMING PITFALLS

Make sure that the values in the argument list of a subroutine call match the subroutine's declared parameters in number, type, and order. Since FORTRAN cannot tell what type of value is being passed between subroutines, very bad results may occur if you do not ensure that the arguments match properly.

6.1.3 Passing Arrays to Subroutines

As we observed above, an argument is passed to a subroutine by passing a pointer to the memory location of the constant, variable, or array. If the argument happens to be an array, then the memory pointer points to the first word in the array. There is no intrinsic way for the subroutine to know just how big the array is. However, the subroutine needs to know how big the array is to ensure that it stays within the boundaries of the array. How can we supply this information to the subroutine?

There are two possible approaches to specifying the length of an array in a subroutine. One approach is to declare the length of the array with an asterisk (length unknown) and then to pass other values in the argument list to specify the processing limits. For example, the following code declares array DATA1 and then processes NVALS values in the array.

```
      SUBROUTINE SUM ( DATA, NVALS, OUTPUT )
      REAL    DATA1(*), OUTPUT
      INTEGER NVALS
C
      DO 10 I = 1, NVALS
         OUTPUT = OUTPUT + DATA1(I)
10    CONTINUE
      . . .
```

Array DATA1 had better be at least NVALS values long. If it is not, the FORTRAN code will probably abort with an error at run time. Subroutines written like this are hard to debug, since the bounds-checking option of most compilers will not work for unknown-length arrays.

The second approach is to pass the length of the array to the subroutine as an argument in the subroutine call, and to declare the array to be that length. If this is done, then the subroutine will know how long the array is, and the bounds checkers on most FORTRAN compilers will be able to report out-of-bounds memory references. For example, the following code declares array DATA1 of length N, and then processes NVALS values in the array. If an out-of-bounds reference occurs in this subroutine, it can be detected and reported.

```
      SUBROUTINE SUM ( DATA1, N, NVALS, OUTPUT )
      INTEGER N
      REAL    DATA1(N)
      INTEGER NVALS
C
      DO 10 I = 1, NVALS
         OUTPUT = OUTPUT + DATA1(I)
10    CONTINUE
      . . .
```

Note that the size of the array DATA1 was declared in a type specification statement before the array itself. Some compilers require that the variables be declared in this order, while others don't care. To make sure that the code we write is portable between computers, the type specification statement for the length of an array should always be declared before the type specification statement for the array itself.

■ **GOOD PROGRAMMING PRACTICE**

Declare the lengths of arrays passed to subroutines instead of defaulting them with an asterisk. This practice allows for easier debugging, since out-of-bounds references can be detected.

If a multidimensional array is passed to a subroutine, then sizes of all subscripts except the last one *must* be passed to the subroutine. Recall that multidimensional arrays are stored in linear memory in a computer. There is no possible way for a subroutine to translate an address like A(3,4) into a specific location in memory unless it knows how many rows are included in the array. Such an array would have to be declared as either

```
SUBROUTINE SUB1 ( M, DATA1, ... )
INTEGER M
REAL    DATA1(M,*)
...
```

or as

```
SUBROUTINE SUB1 ( M, N, DATA1, ... )
INTEGER M, N
REAL    DATA1(M,N)
...
```

The latter form of declaration is preferred, since it permits the program to detect out-of-bounds references.

■ **EXAMPLE 6-2** *Bounds Checking in Subroutines* Write a simple FORTRAN program containing a subroutine that oversteps the limits of an array in its argument list. Compile and execute the program both with bounds checking turned off and with bounds checking turned on.

SOLUTION The program in Figure 6-7 allocates a five-element array A and a scalar B. It initializes all the elements of A and B to zero, and then calls subroutine SUB1. Subroutine SUB1 modifies six elements of array A, despite the fact that A has only five elements.

```
      PROGRAM ARRAY2
C
C  Purpose:
C    To illustrate the effect of accessing an out-of-bounds
C    array element.
C
C  Record of revisions:
C      Date       Programmer          Description of change
C      ====       ==========          =====================
C    04/10/91   S. J. Chapman        Original code
C
```

```
C  List of variables:
C      A        -- Name of a 5-element real array
C      B        -- Real variable allocated after the end of the array
C
       IMPLICIT NONE
C
C      Declare and initialize the variables used in this program.
C
       REAL A(5), B
       INTEGER I
       DATA A, B / 6*0. /
C
C      Call subroutine SUB1.
C
       CALL SUB1( A, 5 )
C
C      Write out the values of array A
C
       DO 10 I = 1, 5
          WRITE (*,100) I, A(I)
  100     FORMAT ( 1X,'A(', I1, ') = ', F6.2 )
   10 CONTINUE
C
C      Write out the value of variable B
C
       WRITE (*,110) B
  110 FORMAT ( 1X,'B    = ', F6.2 )
C
       END
       SUBROUTINE SUB1 ( A, N )
C
       IMPLICIT NONE
C
       INTEGER N
       REAL A(N)
C
       INTEGER I
C
       DO 10 I = 1, 6
          A(I) = I
   10 CONTINUE
C
       RETURN
       END
```

FIGURE 6-7   A program illustrating the effect of exceeding the boundaries of an array in a subroutine.

When this program is compiled with the Microsoft FORTRAN compiler with bounds checking turned *off*, the result is

```
C:\BOOK\FORT>array2
A(1) =    1.00
A(2) =    2.00
A(3) =    3.00
A(4) =    4.00
A(5) =    5.00
B    =    6.00
```

When this program is compiled with the Microsoft FORTRAN compiler with bounds checking turned *on,* the result is

```
C:\BOOK\FORT>array2
array2.for(51) : run-time error F6096: $DEBUG
- array subscript expression out of range
```

If the length of array A in SUB1 is replaced by an asterisk (REAL A(*)), and the program is recompiled with the Microsoft FORTRAN compiler with bounds checking turned *on,* the result is

```
C:\BOOK\FORT>array2
A(1) =   1.00
A(2) =   2.00
A(3) =   3.00
A(4) =   4.00
A(5) =   5.00
B    =   6.00
```

When the asterisk is used to default the length of the array, the compiler could not detect programming errors causing out-of-bounds conditions even if bounds checking is turned on. Some compilers may behave differently, but in general bounds checkers only work on arrays passed to a subroutine if the size of the array is passed to the subroutine as an argument. ●

6.1.4   Error Handling in Subroutines

What happens if a program calls a subroutine with insufficient or invalid data for proper processing? For example, suppose that we are writing a subroutine that subtracts two input variables and takes the square root of the result. What should we do if the difference of the two variables is a negative number?

```
SUBROUTINE PROC (A, B, RES)
IMPLICIT NONE
REAL A, B, RES, TEMP
TEMP = A - B
RES = SQRT ( TEMP )
RETURN
END
```

Suppose that A is 1 and B is 2. If we just process the values in the subroutine, a run-time error will occur when we attempt to take the square root of a negative number, and the program will abort. This is clearly not an acceptable result.

An alternative version of the subroutine is shown below. In this version, we test for a negative number, and if one is present, we print out an informative error message and stop.

```
SUBROUTINE PROC (A, B, RES)
IMPLICIT NONE
REAL A, B, RES, TEMP
TEMP = A - B
IF ( TEMP .GE. 0. ) THEN
   RES = SQRT ( TEMP )
```

```
ELSE
   WRITE (*,*) 'Square root of negative value in routine PROC!'
   STOP
END IF
RETURN
END
```

While better than the previous example, this design is also bad. If TEMP is ever negative, the program will just stop without ever returning from the call to subroutine PROC. If this happens, the user will lose all of the data and processing that has occurred up to that point in the program.

A much better way to design the subroutine is to detect the possible error condition, and to report it to the calling program by setting a value into an **error flag.** The calling program can then take appropriate actions about the error. For example, it can be designed to recover from the error if possible. If not, it can at least write out an informative error message, save the partial results calculated so far, and then shut down gracefully.

In the example shown below, a zero returned in the error flag means successful completion, and a 1 means that the square-root-of-a-negative-number error occurred.

```
SUBROUTINE PROC (A, B, RES, ERROR)
IMPLICIT NONE
REAL A, B, RES, TEMP
INTEGER ERROR
TEMP = A - B
IF ( TEMP .GE. 0. ) THEN
   RES = SQRT ( TEMP )
   ERROR = 0
ELSE
   RES = 0.
   ERROR = 1
END IF
RETURN
END
```

PROGRAMMING PITFALLS

Never include **STOP** statements in any of your subroutines. If you do, you might create a working program, and release it to users, only to find that it mysteriously halts from time to time on certain unusual data sets.

■ GOOD PROGRAMMING PRACTICE

If there are possible error conditions within a subroutine, you should test for them, and set an error flag to be returned to the calling routine. The calling program should test for the error conditions after a subroutine call, and take appropriate actions.

QUIZ 6-1

This quiz provides a quick check to see if you have understood the concepts introduced in Section 6.1. If you have trouble with the quiz, reread the section, ask your instructor, or discuss the material with a fellow student. The answers to this quiz are found in the back of the book.

For questions 1–3, determine whether the subroutine calls are correct or not. If they are in error, specify what is wrong with them.

1.
```
PROGRAM TEST1
INTEGER I(15), J
REAL A(3)
...
CALL SUB1 ( I, J, A )
...
END
SUBROUTINE SUB1( X, Y, Z )
INTEGER X, Y(*)
REAL Z(*)
...
RETURN
END
```

2.
```
PROGRAM TEST2
REAL A(120), AVE, SD
INTEGER N
...
CALL AVESD ( A, N, AVE, SD )
...
END
SUBROUTINE AVESD( ARR, NVALS, AVE, SD )
REAL ARR(NVALS), NVALS, AVE, SD
...
RETURN
END
```

3.
```
PROGRAM TEST3
INTEGER IDATA(25)
REAL SUM
...
CALL SUB3 ( IDATA, SUM )
...
END
SUBROUTINE SUB3( IARRAY, SUM )
INTEGER IARRAY(*)
REAL    SUM
SUM = 0.
SO 10 I = 1, 30
   SUM = SUM + IARRAY(I)
10 CONTINUE
RETURN
END
```

6.1.5 Examples

EXAMPLE 6-3 *Statistics Subroutines* Develop a set of reusable subroutines capable of determining the statistical properties of a data set consisting of real numbers in an array. The set of subroutines should include:

1. A subroutine to determine the maximum value in a data set, and the sample number containing that value.
2. A subroutine to determine the minimum value in a data set, and the sample number containing that value.
3. A subroutine to determine the average (mean) and standard deviation of the data set.
4. A subroutine to determine the median of the data set.

SOLUTION We will be generating four different subroutines, each of which works on a common input data set consisting of an array of real numbers.

1. State the problem.
The problem is clearly stated above. We will write four different subroutines: RMAX to find the maximum value and the location of that value in a real array, RMIN to find the minimum value and the location of that value in a real array, AVESD to find the average and standard deviation of a real array, and MEDIAN to find the median of a real array.

2. Define the inputs and outputs.
The input to each subroutine is an array of values, plus the number of values in the array. The outputs are as follows:

a. The output of subroutine RMAX will be a real variable containing the maximum value in the input array, and an integer variable containing the offset in the array at which the maximum value occurred.
b. The output of subroutine RMIN will be a real variable containing the minimum value in the input array, and an integer variable containing the offset in the array at which the minimum value occurred.
c. The output of subroutine AVESD will be two real variables containing the average and standard deviation of the input array.
d. The output of subroutine MEDIAN will be a real variable containing the median value of the input array.

3. Describe the algorithm.
The pseudocode for the RMAX routine is

```
*
*    Initialize AMX to the first value in the array and IMAX to 1.
*
     AMX ← A(1)
     IMAX ← 1
*
```

```
*  Find the maximum value in A(1) through A(N)
*
   DO for I = 2 to N
      IF A(I) > AMX THEN
          AMX ← A(I)
          IMAX ← I
      END of IF
   END of DO
*
   RETURN
   END
```

The pseudocode for the RMIN routine is

```
*
*  Initialize AMN to the first value in the array and IMIN to 1.
*
   AMN ← A(1)
   IMIN ← 1
*
*  Find the minimum value in A(1) through A(N)
*
   DO for I = 2 to N
      IF A(I) < AMN THEN
          AMN ← A(I)
          IMIN ← I
      END of IF
   END of DO
*
   RETURN
   END
```

The pseudocode for the AVESD routine is similar to the code we developed in the last chapter:

```
*
*  Accumulate sums
*
   SUMX ← 0.
   SUMX2 ← 0.
   DO for I = 1 to N
      SUMX ← SUMX + A(I)
      SUMX2 ← SUMX2 + A(I)**2
   End of DO
*
*  Get AVE and SD
*
   IF N >= 2 THEN
      AVE ← SUMX / REAL(N)
      SD ← SQRT( (REAL(N)*SUMX2-SUMX**2)/(REAL(N)*REAL(N-1)))
   ELSE IF N = 1 THEN
*     Only one value, so AVE = SUMX & SD = 0.
      AVE ← SUMX
      SD ← 0.
   ELSE
```

```
   *        No values, so AVE = 0. & SD = 0.
            AVE ← 0.
            SD ← 0.
         END of IF
   *
         RETURN
         END
```

For the MEDIAN calculation, we will be able to take advantage of the SORT subroutine we have already written. (Here is an example of reusable code saving us time and effort.) The pseudocode for the MEDIAN subroutine is

```
   *
   *  Sort the data
   *
         CALL SORT ( A, N )
         IF N is an even number THEN
            MED ← (A(N/2) + A(N/2+1)) / 2.
         ELSE
            MED ← A(N/2+1)
         END of IF
   *
         RETURN
         END
```

4. Turn the algorithm into FORTRAN statements.

The resulting FORTRAN subroutines are shown in Figure 6-8.

```
      SUBROUTINE RMAX ( A, N, AMX, IMAX )
C
C  Purpose:
C    To find the maximum value in an array, and the location
C    of that value in the array.
C
C  List of calling arguments:
C    NAME    I/O  TYPE          DESCRIPTION
C    ====    ===  ====          ===========
C    A       I    REAL ARRAY    Input data.
C    N       I    INTEGER       Number of values in array A.
C    AMX     O    REAL          Maximum value in array A.
C    IMAX    O    INTEGER       Location of maximum value in array A.
C
C  List of local variables:
C    I        -- Index variable.
C
      IMPLICIT NONE
C
C    Declare calling parameters.
C
      INTEGER N
      REAL    A(N)
      REAL    AMX
      INTEGER IMAX
C
C    Declare local variables.
C
      INTEGER I
C
```

```
C      Initialize the maximum value to first value in array.
C
       AMX  = A(1)
       IMAX = 1
C
C      Find the maximum value.
C
       DO 10 I = 2, N
          IF ( A(I) .GT. AMX ) THEN
             AMX  = A(I)
             IMAX = I
          END IF
   10 CONTINUE
C
       RETURN
       END
       SUBROUTINE RMIN ( A, N, AMN, IMIN )
C
C  Purpose:
C    To find the minimum value in an array, and the location
C    of that value in the array.
C
C  List of calling arguments:
C    NAME    I/O  TYPE          DESCRIPTION
C    ====    ===  ====          ===========
C    A       I    REAL ARRAY    Input data.
C    N       I    INTEGER       Number of values in array A.
C    AMN     O    REAL          Minimum value in array A.
C    IMIN    O    INTEGER       Location of minimum value in array A.
C
C  List of local variables:
C    I        -- Index variable.
C
       IMPLICIT NONE
C
C      Declare calling parameters.
C
       INTEGER N
       REAL    A(N)
       REAL    AMN
       INTEGER IMIN
C
C      Declare local variables.
C
       INTEGER I
C
C      Initialize the minimum value to first value in array.
C
       AMN  = A(1)
       IMIN = 1
C
C      Find the minimum value.
C
       DO 10 I = 2, N
          IF ( A(I) .LT. AMN ) THEN
             AMN  = A(I)
             IMIN = I
          END IF
   10 CONTINUE
C
```

```
      RETURN
      END
      SUBROUTINE AVESD ( A, N, AVE, SD, ERROR )
C
C  Purpose:
C    To calculate the average and standard deviation of an array.
C
C  List of calling arguments:
C     NAME      I/O  TYPE          DESCRIPTION
C     ====      ===  ====          ===========
C     A          I   REAL ARRAY    Input data.
C     N          I   INTEGER       Number of values in array A.
C     AVE        O   REAL          Average of values in array A.
C     SD         O   REAL          Standard deviation of values in array A.
C     ERROR      O   INTEGER       Error flag: 0 -- No error
C                                              1 -- SD Invalid
C                                              2 -- AVE & SD invalid
C
C  List of local variables:
C     I      -- Index variable.
C     SUMX   -- The sum of the input values.
C     SUMX2  -- The sum of the squares of the input values.
C
      IMPLICIT NONE
C
C     Declare calling parameters.
C
      INTEGER N
      REAL    A(N)
      REAL    AVE
      REAL    SD
      INTEGER ERROR
C
C     Declare local variables.
C
      INTEGER I
      REAL    SUMX, SUMX2
C
C     Initialize the sums to zero.
C
      SUMX  = 0.
      SUMX2 = 0.
C
C     Accumulate sums.
C
      DO 10 I = 1, N
         SUMX  = SUMX + A(I)
         SUMX2 = SUMX2 + A(I)**2
   10 CONTINUE
C
C     Check to see if we have enough input data.
C
      IF ( N .GE. 2 ) THEN
C
C        Calculate the mean and standard deviation
C
         AVE   = SUMX / REAL(N)
         SD    = SQRT( (REAL(N) * SUMX2 - SUMX**2)
     *           / (REAL(N) * REAL(N-1)) )
         ERROR = 0
C
```

```
      ELSE IF ( N .EQ. 1 ) THEN
C
C         Set AVE to the input value, and set SD to 0.
C
          AVE   = SUMX
          SD    = 0.
          ERROR = 1
C
      ELSE
C
C         Set AVE and SD to zero.
C
          AVE   = 0.
          SD    = 0.
          ERROR = 2
      END IF
C
      RETURN
      END
      SUBROUTINE MEDIAN ( A, N, MED )
C
C  Purpose:
C    To calculate the median value of an array.
C
C  List of calling arguments:
C    NAME    I/O  TYPE        DESCRIPTION
C    ====    ===  ====        ===========
C    A       I    REAL ARRAY  Input data.
C    N       I    INTEGER     Number of values in array A.
C    MED     O    REAL        Median of values in array A.
C
C  List of local variables:
C    None
C
      IMPLICIT NONE
C
C    Declare calling parameters.
C
      INTEGER N
      REAL    A(N)
      REAL    MED
C
C    Sort the data into ascending order.
C
      CALL SORT ( A, N )
C
C    Get median.
C
      IF ( MOD(N,2) .EQ. 0 ) THEN
         MED = ( A(N/2) + A(N/2+1) ) / 2.
      ELSE
         MED = A(N/2+1)
      END IF
C
      RETURN
      END
```

FIGURE 6-8 The subroutines of Example 6-3.

5. Test the resulting FORTRAN programs.

To test these subroutines, it is necessary to write a driver program to read the input data, call the subroutines, and write out the results. This test is left as an exercise to the student (see problem 12 at the end of the chapter.) ●

EXAMPLE 6-4 *Gaussian Elimination* Many important problems in science and engineering require the solution of a system of N simultaneous linear equations in N unknowns. Some of these problems require the solution of small systems of equations, say 3×3 or 4×4. Such problems are relatively easy to solve. Other problems might require the solution of really large sets of simultaneous equations, like 1000 equations in 1000 unknowns. Those problems are *much* harder to solve, and the solution requires a variety of special iterative techniques. A whole branch of the science of numerical methods is devoted to different ways to solve systems of simultaneous linear equations.

We will now develop a subroutine to solve a system of simultaneous linear equations using the straightforward approach known as **Gaussian elimination.** The subroutine that we develop should work fine for systems of up to about 20 equations in 20 unknowns.

Gaussian elimination depends on the fact that you can multiply one equation by a constant and add it to another equation, and the new system of equations will still be equivalent to the old one. In fact, it works in exactly the same way that we solve systems of simultaneous equations by hand.

To understand the technique, consider the 3×3 system of equations shown below.

$$
\begin{array}{llll}
1.0\ X1\ +\ 1.0\ X2\ +\ 1.0\ X3\ =\ 1.0 & \\
2.0\ X1\ +\ 1.0\ X2\ +\ 1.0\ X3\ =\ 2.0 & \textbf{(6-1)} \\
1.0\ X1\ +\ 3.0\ X2\ +\ 2.0\ X3\ =\ 4.0 &
\end{array}
$$

We would like to manipulate this set of equations by multiplying one of the equations by a constant and adding it to another one until we eventually wind up with a set of equations of the form

$$
\begin{array}{llll}
1.0\ X1\ +\ 0.0\ X2\ +\ 0.0\ X3\ =\ B1 & \\
0.0\ X1\ +\ 1.0\ X2\ +\ 0.0\ X3\ =\ B2 & \textbf{(6-2)} \\
0.0\ X1\ +\ 0.0\ X2\ +\ 1.0\ X3\ =\ B3 &
\end{array}
$$

When we get to this form, the solution to the system is obvious: $X1 = B1$, $X2 = B2$, and $X3 = B3$.

To get from Equations (6-1) to Equations (6-2), we must go through three steps:

1. Eliminate all coefficients of X1 except in the first equation
2. Eliminate all coefficients of X2 except in the second equation
3. Eliminate all coefficients of X3 except in the third equation.

First, let's eliminate all coefficients of X1 except that in the first equation. If we multiply the first equation by -2 and add it to the second equation, and multiply the first equation by -1 and add it to the third equation, the results are

```
1.0 X1 + 1.0 X2 + 1.0 X3 = 1.0
0.0 X1 - 1.0 X2 - 1.0 X3 = 0.0          (6-3)
0.0 X1 + 2.0 X2 + 1.0 X3 = 3.0
```

Next, let's eliminate all coefficients of X2 except in the second equation. If we add the second equation as it is to the first equation, and multiply the second equation by 2 and add it to the third equation, the results are

```
1.0 X1 + 0.0 X2 + 0.0 X3 = 1.0
0.0 X1 - 1.0 X2 - 1.0 X3 = 0.0          (6-4)
0.0 X1 + 0.0 X2 - 1.0 X3 = 3.0
```

Finally, let's eliminate all coefficients of X3 except in the third equation. In this case, there is no coefficient of X3 in the first equation, so we don't have to do anything there. If we multiply the third equation by -1 and add it to the second equation, the results are

```
1.0 X1 + 0.0 X2 + 0.0 X3 = 1.0
0.0 X1 - 1.0 X2 + 0.0 X3 = -3.0         (6-5)
0.0 X1 + 0.0 X2 - 1.0 X3 = 3.0
```

The last step is almost trivial. If we divide equation 1 by the coefficient of X1, equation 2 by the coefficient of X2, and equation 3 by the coefficient of X3, then the solution to the equations appears on the right-hand side of the equations.

```
1.0 X1 + 0.0 X2 + 0.0 X3 = 1.0
0.0 X1 + 1.0 X2 + 0.0 X3 = 3.0          (6-6)
0.0 X1 + 0.0 X2 + 1.0 X3 = -3.0
```

The final answer is X1 = 1, X2 = 3, and X3 = -3!

Sometimes the technique shown above does not produce a solution. This happens when the set of equations being solved are not all *independent*. For example, consider the following 2×2 system of simultaneous equations:

```
2.0 X1 + 3.0 X2 = 4.0
4.0 X1 + 6.0 X2 = 8.0                    (6-7)
```

If equation 1 is multiplied by -2 and added to equation 1, we get

```
2.0 X1 + 3.0 X2 = 4.0
0.0 X1 + 0.0 X2 = 0.0                    (6-8)
```

There is no way to solve this system for a unique solution, since there are infinitely many values of X1 and X2 that satisfy Equations (6-8). These conditions can be recognized by the fact that the coefficient of X2 in the second equation is 0. The solution to this system of equations is said to be nonunique. Our computer program will have to test for problems like this, and report them as an error code.

We will now write a subroutine to solve a system of N simultaneous equations in N unknowns. The computer program works in the manner shown above, except that at each step in the process we reorder the equations. In the first step, we reorder the N equations such that the first equation is the one with the largest coefficient (absolute value) of the first variable. In the second step, we reorder equations 2 through N such that the second equation is the one with the largest coefficient (absolute value) of the second variable. This process is repeated for each step in the solution. Reordering the equations is important, because it reduces roundoff errors in large systems of equations, and also avoids divide-by-zero errors. (This reordering of equations is called the *maximum pivot* technique in the literature of numerical methods.)

1.   State the problem
Write a subroutine to solve a system of N simultaneous equations in N unknowns using Gaussian elimination and the maximum pivot technique to avoid roundoff errors. The subroutine must be able to detect singular sets of equations, and set an error flag if they occur.

2.   Define the inputs and outputs
The input to the subroutine consists of an $N \times N$ matrix A with the coefficients of the variables in the simultaneous equations, and a vector B with the contents of the right-hand sides of the equations. The outputs from the subroutine are the solutions to the set of equations (in vector B), and an error flag. Note that the matrix of coefficients A is destroyed during the solution process.

3.   Describe the algorithm
The pseudocode for this subroutine is

```
DO for IROW = 1 to N
*
*       Find peak pivot for column IROW in rows I to N
*
        IPEAK ← IROW
        DO for JROW ← IROW to N
           IF |A(JROW,IROW)| > |A(IPEAK,IROW)| then
              IPEAK ← JROW
           END of IF
        END of DO
*
*       Check for singular equations
*
        IF |A(IPEAK,IROW)| < EPSLON THEN
           Equations are singular; set error code & exit
        END of IF
*
*       Otherwise, if IPEAK <> IROW, swap equations IROW & IPEAK
*
        IF IPEAK <> IROW
           DO for KCOL = 1 to N
              TEMP ← A(IPEAK,KCOL)
              A(IPEAK,KCOL) ← A(IROW,KCOL)
              A(IROW,KCOL) ← TEMP
```

```
                         END of DO
                         TEMP ← B(IPEAK)
                         B(IPEAK) ← B(IROW)
                         B(IROW) ← TEMP
                      END of IF
  *
  *       Multiply equation IROW by -A(JROW,IROW)/A(IROW,IROW), and
  *       add it to Eqn JROW
  *
          DO for JROW = 1 to N except for IROW
             FACTOR ← -A(JROW,IROW)/A(IROW,IROW)
             DO for KCOL = 1 to N
                A(JROW,KCOL) ← A(IROW,KCOL) * FACTOR + A(JROW,KCOL)
             END of DO
             B(JROW) ← B(IROW) * FACTOR + B(JROW)
          END of DO
       END of DO
  *
  *    End of main loop over all equations.  All off-diagonal
  *    terms are now zero.  To get the final answer, we must
  *    divide each equation by the coefficient of its on-diagonal
  *    term.  End of main loop over all equations
  *
       DO for IROW = 1 to N
          B(IROW) ← B(IROW) / A (IROW,IROW)
          A(IROW,IROW) ← 1.
       END of DO
  *
       RETURN
       END
```

4. Turn the algorithm into FORTRAN statements.

The resulting FORTRAN subroutine is shown in Figure 6-9.

Note that the sizes of arrays A and B are passed explicitly to the subroutine as A(NDIM,NDIM) and B(NDIM). It is absolutely essential that at least the number of rows in matrix A be passed. The subroutine is unable to locate a value like A(2,2) unless it knows how many rows were declared in matrix A by the calling program. The second dimension of A and the single dimension of B could have been defaulted with an asterisk: A(NDIM,*) and B(*). However, it is better to pass the dimensions explicitly, so that we can use the compiler's bounds checker while we are debugging the subroutine.

```
      SUBROUTINE SIMUL ( A, B, NDIM, N, ERROR )
C
C  Purpose:
C    Subroutine to solve a set of N linear equations in N
C    unknowns using Gaussian elimination and the maximum
C    pivot technique.
C
C  Record of revisions:
C     Date        Programmer          Description of change
C     ====        ==========          =====================
C    06/11/91    S. J. Chapman        Original code
C
```

```
C   List of calling arguments:
C     NAME    I/O  TYPE      DIM     DESCRIPTION
C     ====    ===  ====      ===     ===========
C     A       I    REAL ARR NDIMxNDIM Array of coefficients (N x N).
C                                    This array is of size NDIM x
C                                    NDIM, but only N x N of the
C                                    coefficients are being used.
C                                    The declared dimension NDIM
C                                    must be passed to the sub, or
C                                    it won't be able to interpret
C                                    subscripts correctly.  (This
C                                    array is destroyed during
C                                    processing.)
C     B       IO   REAL ARR   NDIM    Input: Right-hand side of eqns.
C                                    Output: Solution vector.
C     N       I    INTEGER           Number of equations to solve.
C     ERROR   O    INTEGER           Error flag:
C                                    0 -- No error
C                                    1 -- Singular equations
C
C   List of local parameters:
C     EPSLON -- A "small" number for comparison when determining that
C               a matrix is singular.
C
C   List of local variables:
C     FACTOR -- Factor to multiply eqn IROW by before adding to
C               eqn JROW
C     IROW   -- Number of equation currently being processed
C     IPEAK  -- Pointer to equation containing maximum pivot value
C     JROW   -- Number of equation compared to current equation
C     KCOL   -- Index over all columns of equation
C     TEMP   -- Scratch real variable
C
      IMPLICIT NONE
C
C   Calling arguments.
C
      INTEGER NDIM, N, ERROR
      REAL    A(NDIM,NDIM), B(NDIM)
C
C   Parameters.
C
      REAL       EPSLON
      PARAMETER ( EPSLON = 1.0E-6 )
C
C   Local variables.
C
      INTEGER IROW, JROW, KCOL, IPEAK
      REAL    FACTOR, TEMP
C
C   Process N times to get all equations...
C
      DO 50 IROW = 1, N
C
C      Find peak pivot for column IROW in rows I to N
C
         IPEAK = IROW
         DO 10 JROW = IROW+1, N
```

```
            IF (ABS(A(JROW,IROW)) .GT. ABS(A(IPEAK,IROW))) THEN
               IPEAK = JROW
            END IF
   10    CONTINUE
C
C        Check for singular equations.
C
         IF ( ABS(A(IPEAK,IROW)) .LT. EPSLON ) THEN
            ERROR = 1
            RETURN
         END IF
C
C        Otherwise, if IPEAK <> IROW, swap equations IROW & IPEAK
C
         IF ( IPEAK .NE. IROW ) THEN
            DO 20 KCOL = 1, N
               TEMP            = A(IPEAK,KCOL)
               A(IPEAK,KCOL) = A(IROW,KCOL)
               A(IROW,KCOL)  = TEMP
   20       CONTINUE
            TEMP     = B(IPEAK)
            B(IPEAK) = B(IROW)
            B(IROW)  = TEMP
         END IF
C
C        Multiply equation IROW by -A(JROW,IROW)/A(IROW,IROW), and
C        add it to Eqn JROW (for all eqns except IROW itself).
C
         DO 40 JROW = 1, N
            IF ( JROW .NE. IROW ) THEN
               FACTOR = -A(JROW,IROW)/A(IROW,IROW)
               DO 30 KCOL = 1, N
                  A(JROW,KCOL) = A(IROW,KCOL)*FACTOR + A(JROW,KCOL)
   30          CONTINUE
               B(JROW) = B(IROW)*FACTOR + B(JROW)
            END IF
   40    CONTINUE
   50 CONTINUE
C
C     End of main loop over all equations.  All off-diagonal
C     terms are now zero.  To get the final answer, we must
C     divide each equation by the coefficient of its on-diagonal
C     term.
C
      DO 60 IROW = 1, N
         B(IROW)       = B(IROW) / A (IROW,IROW)
         A(IROW,IROW) = 1.
   60 CONTINUE
C
C     Set error flag to 0 and return.
C
      ERROR = 0
      RETURN
      END
```

FIGURE 6-9   Subroutine SIMUL.

5. Test the resulting FORTRAN programs.

To test this subroutine, it is necessary to write a driver program. The driver program opens an input data file to read the equations to be solved. The first line of the file contains the number of equations N in the system, and each of the next N lines contains the coefficients of one of the equations. To show that the simultaneous equation subroutine is working correctly, we display the contents of arrays A and B both before and after the call to SIMUL.

The test driver program for subroutine SIMUL is shown in Figure 6-10.

```
      PROGRAM TSIMUL
C
C Purpose:
C   To test subroutine SIMUL, which solves a set of N linear
C   equations in N unknowns.
C
C Record of revisions:
C     Date        Programmer          Description of change
C     ====        ==========          =====================
C   06/11/91    S. J. Chapman        Original code
C
      IMPLICIT NONE
C
      INTEGER    MAXSIZ
      PARAMETER ( MAXSIZ = 10 )
C
      INTEGER   I, J, N, ISTAT, ERROR
      REAL      A(MAXSIZ,MAXSIZ), B(MAXSIZ)
      CHARACTER FILENM*20
C
C   Get the name of the disk file containing the equations.
C
      WRITE (*,1000)
 1000 FORMAT (' Enter the file name containing the eqns: ')
      READ (*,1010) FILENM
 1010 FORMAT ( A20 )
C
C   Open input data file.  Status is OLD because the input data must
C   already exist.
C
      OPEN ( UNIT=1, FILE=FILENM, STATUS='OLD', IOSTAT=ISTAT )
C
C   Was the OPEN successful?
C
      IF ( ISTAT .EQ. 0 ) THEN
C
C       The file was opened successfully, so read the number of
C       equations in the system.
C
        READ (1,*) N
C
C       If the number of equations is <= MAXSIZ, read them in
C       and process them.
C
        IF ( N .LE. MAXSIZ ) THEN
          DO 10 I = 1, N
            READ (1,*) (A(I,J), J=1,N), B(I)
```

```
      10        CONTINUE
C
C             Display coefficients.
C
                WRITE (*,1020)
    1020        FORMAT (/,1X,'Coefficients before call:')
                DO 20 I = 1, N
                   WRITE (*,1030) (A(I,J), J=1,N), B(I)
    1030           FORMAT (1X,7F11.4)
      20        CONTINUE
C
C             Solve equations.
C
                CALL SIMUL (A, B, MAXSIZ, N, ERROR )
C
C             Check for error.
C
                IF ( ERROR .NE. 0 ) THEN
                   WRITE (*,1040)
    1040           FORMAT (/1X,'Zero pivot encountered!',
         *              //1X,'There is no unique solution to this system.')
                      ELSE
C
C             No errors. Display coefficients.
C
                   WRITE (*,1050)
    1050           FORMAT (/,1X,'Coefficients after call:')
                   DO 30 I = 1, N
                      WRITE (*,1030) (A(I,J), J=1,N), B(I)
      30           CONTINUE
C
C             Write final answer.
C
                   WRITE (*,1060)
    1060           FORMAT (/,1X,'The solutions are:')
                   DO 40 I = 1, N
                   WRITE (*,1070) I, B(I)
    1070           FORMAT (3X,'X(',I2,') = ',F16.6)
      40           CONTINUE
                END IF
C
            END IF
         END IF
         END
```

FIGURE 6-10   Test driver routine for subroutine SIMUL.

To test the subroutine, we need to call it with two different data sets. One of them should have a unique solution, and the other one should be singular. We will test the system with two sets of equations. The original equations that we solved by hand are placed in file INPUTS1

$$1.0 \ X1 + 1.0 \ X2 + 1.0 \ X3 = 1.0$$
$$2.0 \ X1 + 1.0 \ X2 + 1.0 \ X3 = 2.0 \qquad (6\text{-}1)$$
$$1.0 \ X1 + 3.0 \ X2 + 2.0 \ X3 = 4.0$$

and the following set of equations are placed in file INPUTS2.

```
1.0 X1 + 1.0 X2 + 1.0 X3 = 1.0
2.0 X1 + 6.0 X2 + 4.0 X3 = 8.0
1.0 X1 + 3.0 X2 + 2.0 X3 = 4.0
```

The second equation of this set is a multiple of the third equation, so the second set of equations is singular. When we run program TSIMUL with these data sets, the results are

```
C:\BOOK\FORT>tsimul
Enter the file name containing the eqns:
inputs1

Coefficients before call:
      1.0000      1.0000      1.0000      1.0000
      2.0000      1.0000      1.0000      2.0000
      1.0000      3.0000      2.0000      4.0000

Coefficients after call:
      1.0000       .0000       .0000      1.0000
       .0000      1.0000       .0000      3.0000
       .0000       .0000      1.0000     -3.0000

The solutions are:
  X( 1) =          1.000000
  X( 2) =          3.000000
  X( 3) =         -3.000000

C:\BOOK\FORT>tsimul
Enter the file name containing the eqns:
inputs2

Coefficients before call:
      1.0000      1.0000      1.0000      1.0000
      2.0000      6.0000      4.0000      8.0000
      1.0000      3.0000      2.0000      4.0000

Zero pivot encountered!

There is no unique solution to this system.
```

The subroutine appears to be working correctly for both unique and singular sets of simultaneous equations. ●

6.2   THE **SAVE** STATEMENT

According to the FORTRAN 77 standard, the values of all the local variables in a subroutine or function become *undefined* whenever we exit the subprogram. The next time that the subprogram is called, the values of the local variables in the subprogram may or may not be the same as they were the last time we left it, depending on the particular compiler being used. If we write a subprogram that depends on having its local variables undisturbed between calls, the subprogram will work fine on some computers and fail miserably on other ones!

FORTRAN provides a mechanism to guarantee that local variables are saved unchanged between calls to a subprogram. This is the **SAVE** statement. The **SAVE** statement is a nonexecutable statement that goes into the declaration portion of the subprogram along with the type declaration statements. Any local variables listed in the **SAVE** statement are saved unchanged between calls to the subprogram. If no variables are listed in the **SAVE** statement, then *all* of the local variables are saved unchanged.

The format of the **SAVE** statement is

```
SAVE var1, var2, ...
```

or simply

```
SAVE
```

■ GOOD PROGRAMMING PRACTICE

If a subroutine requires that the value of a local variable not change between successive calls to the subroutine, include the variable in a **SAVE** statement. If you do not do so, the subroutine will work correctly on some compilers but will fail on other ones.

EXAMPLE 6-5 *Running Averages* It is sometimes desirable to keep running statistics on a data set as the values are being entered. The subroutine RUNAVE shown in Figure 6-11 accumulates running averages and standard deviations for use in problems where we would like to keep statistics on data as it is coming in to the program. As each new data value is added, the running averages and standard deviations of all data up to that point are updated. The running sums used to derive the statistics are reset when the logical argument RESET is TRUE. Note that the sums N, SUMX, and SUMX2 are being accumulated in local variables in this subroutine. To ensure that they remain unchanged between subroutine calls, *those local variables must appear in a* **SAVE** *statement.*

```
      SUBROUTINE RUNAVE ( X, AVE, SD, RESET )
C
C  Purpose:
C    To calculate the running sums N, SUMX, and SUMX**2 as data
C    values X are received.  If RESET is .TRUE., clear sums and
C    exit.
C
C
C  List of calling arguments:
C    NAME    I/O  TYPE        DESCRIPTION
C    ====    ===  ====        ============
C    X        I   REAL        Input data value.
C    AVE      O   REAL        Running average.
```

```
C      SD       O    REAL         Running standard deviation.
C      RESET    I    LOGICAL       Reset flag: clear sums if .TRUE.
C
C  List of local variables:
C     N        -- Number of input values
C     SUMX     -- Sum of input values
C     SUMX2    -- Sum of input values squared
C
       IMPLICIT NONE
C
C      Declare calling parameters.
C
       REAL     X
       REAL     AVE
       REAL     SD
       LOGICAL RESET
C
C      Declare local variables.
C
       INTEGER N
       REAL     SUMX, SUMX2
       SAVE     N, SUMX, SUMX2
C
C      If the RESET flag is set, clear the running sums at this time.
C
       IF ( RESET ) THEN
          N     = 0
          SUMX  = 0.
          SUMX2 = 0.
       ELSE
C
C         Accumulate sums.
C
          N     = N + 1
          SUMX  = SUMX + X
          SUMX2 = SUMX2 + X**2
C
C         Calculate running statistics.
C
          AVE = SUMX / REAL(N)

          IF ( N .GE. 2 ) THEN
             SD    = SQRT( (REAL(N) * SUMX2 - SUMX**2)
     *             / (REAL(N) * REAL(N-1)) )
          ELSE
             SD = 0.
          END IF
       END IF
C
       RETURN
       END
```

FIGURE 6-11   A subroutine to calculate the running mean and standard deviation of an input data set.

A test driver for this subroutine is shown in Figure 6-12.

```
      PROGRAM TRUNAV
C
C  Purpose:
C     To test to functions of running average subroutine RUNAVE.
C
C  List of variables:
C     AVE    -- Average of array A.
C     FILENM -- Name of input data file to read.
C     ISTAT  -- I/O status variable:  0 for success
C     SD     -- Standard deviation of array A.
C     X      -- Input data value.
C
      IMPLICIT NONE
C
C     Declare the variables used in this program.
C
      INTEGER      ISTAT
      REAL         AVE, SD, X
      CHARACTER*20 FILENM
C
C     Clear the running sums.
C
      CALL RUNAVE ( 0., AVE, SD, .TRUE. )
C
C     Get the name of the file containing the input data.
C
      WRITE (*,1000)
 1000 FORMAT (' Enter the file name containing the data: ')
      READ (*,1010) FILENM
 1010 FORMAT ( A20 )
C
C     Open input data file.  Status is OLD because the input data must
C     already exist.
C
      OPEN ( UNIT=21, FILE=FILENM, STATUS='OLD', IOSTAT=ISTAT )
C
C     Was the OPEN successful?
C
      IF ( ISTAT .EQ. 0 ) THEN
C
C        The file was opened successfully, so read the data to calculate
C        running averages for.
C
         READ (21, *, IOSTAT=ISTAT) X
C
C        Begin WHILE loop.  Did we read the value successfully?
C
   10    IF ( ISTAT .EQ. 0 ) THEN
C
C           Get running averages.
C
            CALL RUNAVE ( X, AVE, SD, .FALSE. )
C
C           Now write out the running statistics.
C
            WRITE (*,1030) ' VALUE = ', X, '  AVE = ', AVE,
     *                     ' SD = ', SD
```

```
 1030          FORMAT (1X,3(A,F10.4))
C
C              Read next value.
C
               READ (21, *, IOSTAT=ISTAT) X
               GO TO 10
C
C              End of WHILE Loop
C
          END IF
       END IF
C
 9999 CONTINUE
       END
```

FIGURE 6-12   A test driver program to test subroutine RUNAVE.

To test the results of this subroutine, we calculate running statistics by hand for a set of five numbers, and compare the hand calculations to the results from the computer program. Recall that the average and standard deviation are defined as

$$\bar{x} = \frac{1}{N}\sum_{i=1}^{N} x_i \qquad (3\text{-}3)$$

and

$$s = \sqrt{\frac{N\sum_{i=1}^{N} x_i^2 - \left(\sum_{i=1}^{N} x_i\right)^2}{N(N-1)}} \qquad (3\text{-}4)$$

where x_i is sample i of N samples. If the five values are

3.,   2.,   3.,   4.,   2.8

then the running statistics calculated by hand would be

Value	N	SUMX	SUMX2	AVE	SD
3.0	1	3.0	9.0	3.00	0.000
2.0	2	5.0	13.0	2.50	0.707
3.0	3	8.0	22.0	2.67	0.577
4.0	4	12.0	38.0	3.00	0.816
2.8	5	14.8	45.84	2.96	0.713

The output of the test program for the same data set is

```
C:\BOOK\FORT>trunav
Enter the file name containing the data:
input6
  VALUE =      3.0000  AVE =      3.0000  SD =       .0000
  VALUE =      2.0000  AVE =      2.5000  SD =       .7071
  VALUE =      3.0000  AVE =      2.6667  SD =       .5774
  VALUE =      4.0000  AVE =      3.0000  SD =       .8165
  VALUE =      2.8000  AVE =      2.9600  SD =       .7127
```

so the results check. ●

6.3   COMMON BLOCKS

We have seen that programs exchange data with the subroutines they call through an argument list. Each item in the argument list of the program's **CALL** statement must be matched by a dummy argument in the argument list of the subroutine being called. A pointer to the memory location of each argument is passed from the calling program to the subroutine for use in accessing the arguments.

In addition to the argument list, FORTRAN programs, subroutines, and functions can also exchange data through **COMMON** blocks. A **COMMON** block is a declaration of a region of computer memory that is accessible to every routine containing the common block. The structure of a **COMMON** block is

```
COMMON / name / var1, var2, var3, ...
```

where *name* is the name of the **COMMON** block, and *var1, var2,* etc. are variables or arrays allocated in successive memory locations starting at the beginning of the block. A **COMMON** block can contain any mixture of real and integer variables and arrays, or it can contain character data, but numeric and character data may not be mixed in a single **COMMON** block.[2]

A routine can have as many **COMMON** blocks as the programmer wants to declare, so it is simple to declare separate **COMMON**s for numeric and **CHARACTER** data. Each separate **COMMON** block must have a unique name.

When an array appears in a **COMMON** block, the size of the array may be declared in either the **COMMON** block or the type declaration statement, but *not* in both places. The following pairs of statements are legal and completely equivalent:

```
REAL A(10)
COMMON / DATA1 / A

REAL A
COMMON / DATA1 / A(10)
```

---

[2] Many FORTRAN 77 compilers ignore the standard, and permit numeric and character data to be mixed in a single **COMMON** block. Do not use this feature, it will make your programs less portable.

while the following statements are illegal and will produce an error at compilation time:

```
REAL A(10)
COMMON / DATA1 / A(10)
```

COMMON blocks permit routines to share data by sharing a common region of memory. The FORTRAN compiler allocates all **COMMON** blocks with the same name in any routine to the same region of memory, so any data stored there by one routine may be read and used by any of the other ones. The **COMMON** blocks with a given name do not all have to be the same length in every routine, since the FORTRAN compiler and linker are smart enough to allocate enough memory to hold the largest block declared in any of the routines.

A sample pair of routines with **COMMON** blocks are shown in Figure 6-13.

```
PROGRAM MAIN
REAL A, B, C(5)
INTEGER I
COMMON / COM1 / A, B, C, I
...
CALL SUB1
END
SUBROUTINE SUB1
REAL X, Y(5)
INTEGER I, J
COMMON / COM1 / X, Y, I, J
...
RETURN
END
```

FIGURE 6-13   A main program and subroutine sharing data through a **COMMON** block.

Variables and arrays are allocated in a **COMMON** block in the order in which they are declared in the **COMMON** statement. In the main program, variable A occupies the first word in the block, variable B occupies the second word, etc. In the subroutine, variable X occupies the first word in the block, and array element Y(1) occupies the second word, etc. Therefore, *variable* A *in the main program is really the same as variable* X *in the subroutine*. They are two different ways to refer to the identical memory location (Figure 6-14).

COMMON blocks are convenient ways to share large volumes of data between routines. However, they must be used carefully to avoid problems. Two common mistakes appear in Figures 6-13 and 6-14. Note that the five-element array C in the main program and the corresponding five-element array Y in the subroutine are misaligned because there is one fewer word declared before the arrays in the subroutine than in the main program. Therefore, C(1) in the main program is the same variable as Y(2) in the subroutine. If arrays C and Y are supposed to be the same, then this misalignment will cause severe problems. Note also that REAL array element C(5) in the main program is identical to **INTEGER** variable I in the subroutine. It is ex-

Memory Allocation in COMMON /DATA1/

Memory Address	Program MAIN	Subroutine SUB1
0000	A	X
0001	B	Y(1)
0002	C(1)	Y(2)
0003	C(2)	Y(3)
0004	C(3)	Y(4)
0005	C(4)	Y(5)
0006	C(5)	I
0007	I	J

FIGURE 6-14   Memory allocation in **COMMON** block /DATA1/, showing the misalignment between arrays C and Y.

tremely unlikely that the variable stored in C(5) will be usable as an integer in subroutine SUB1. This type mismatch must also be prevented.

To properly use a **COMMON** block, we must ensure that variables the in the block appear *in the same order* and have *the same type and size* in every routine containing the block. In addition, it is good programming practice to keep the *same names* for each of the variables in every routine containing the block. The program is much more understandable if the same names apply to the same variables in all routines.

■ **GOOD PROGRAMMING PRACTICE**

You may use **COMMON** blocks to pass large amounts of data between routines within a program. If you do so, you should always declare the **COMMON** blocks identically in every routine containing them, so that the variables always have the same name and type in each routine.

The principal disadvantage of using a **COMMON** block to pass data to a subroutine is that the data passed to the subroutine is always the data in the **COMMON** block, and the subroutine can only process that data. If the data is passed through calling arguments instead, the subroutine can be used to perform the same calculations on different data sets by calling the subroutine many times with different calling arguments. Because of this difference, small subroutines which are used over and over in a program always exchange data via calling arguments, while single-use subroutines sharing large volumes of data often exchange data via **COMMON** blocks.

6.4 INITIALIZING DATA IN **COMMON** BLOCKS: THE **BLOCK DATA** SUBPROGRAM

The **DATA** statement was introduced in Chapter 2. It is used to initialize the values associated with a variable in a main program or subprogram. An example of a **DATA** statement is

```
PROGRAM TEST
INTEGER IVAL1, IVAL2
DATA IVAL1, IVAL2 /1, 2/
...
END
```

Here, the variable IVAL1 is initialized to the value 1 and the variable IVAL2 is initialized to the value 2.

There are three types of variables in FORTRAN programs and subprograms: *local variables, common variables,* and *dummy arguments.* Local variables are those variables defined only within a single program or subprogram. (However, they may be used as calling arguments in subroutine or function calls.) Common variables are those variables that are shared between subprograms in common blocks. Dummy arguments are those variables in a subroutine that correspond to arguments passed in the **CALL** statement. Of these three types, *a **DATA** statement can only initialize the local variables in a program.*

Dummy subroutine arguments may not be initialized with a **DATA** statement. Remember that subroutine arguments are merely placeholders for the variables that will be passed to the subroutine at execution time by the calling program. Since subroutine arguments are not real variables, it is understandable that they cannot be initialized with a **DATA** statement.

The argument about initializing variables in **COMMON** blocks is a little more subtle. Consider the following example program.

```
PROGRAM TEST
CALL SUB1
CALL SUB2
END
SUBROUTINE SUB1
```

```
INTEGER IVAL1, IVAL2
COMMON / MYDATA / IVAL1, IVAL2
DATA IVAL1, IVAL2 /1, 2/
...
END
SUBROUTINE SUB2
INTEGER IVAL1, IVAL2
COMMON / MYDATA / IVAL1, IVAL2
DATA IVAL1, IVAL2 /3, 4/
...
END
```

In this example, **COMMON** block /MYDATA/ is exchanged between subroutines SUB1 and SUB2. Subroutine SUB1 attempts to initialize IVAL1 and IVAL2 to 1 and 2, respectively, while subroutine SUB2 attempts to initialize IVAL1 and IVAL2 to 3 and 4, respectively. And yet, they are the same two variables! How could the FORTRAN compiler possibly make sense of this situation? The simple answer is that it can't.

To guarantee that there is only one set of initial values for the variables in a **COMMON** block, the FORTRAN language prohibits the use of **DATA** statements with common variables in any FORTRAN program, subroutine, or function. Instead, it includes a special type of subprogram *whose only function is to initialize the variables in a* **COMMON** *block*: the **BLOCK DATA subprogram.** Since there is one and only one place where COMMON variables may be initialized, there is no ambiguity about what values to assign to them.

A **BLOCK DATA** subprogram begins with a **BLOCK DATA** statement, and may contain any number of type definition statements, **COMMON** statements, and **DATA** statements. *It must not contain any executable statements.* An example **BLOCK DATA** subprogram is shown below.

```
BLOCK DATA INITL
INTEGER IVAL1, IVAL2
COMMON / MYDATA / IVAL1, IVAL2
DATA IVAL1, IVAL2 /1, 2/
END
```

The name of this **BLOCK DATA** subprogram is INITL. (**BLOCK DATA** subprogram names are optional: This subprogram would have worked equally well with no name.) The subprogram initializes the variables IVAL1 and IVAL2 in **COMMON** block /MYDATA/ to 1 and 2, respectively.

■ GOOD PROGRAMMING PRACTICE

Use **BLOCK DATA** subprograms to initialize variables in **COMMON** blocks.

EXAMPLE 6-6 *Random Number Generator*   It is always impossible to make perfect measurements in the real world. No matter how we try, there will always be some *measurement noise* associated with each measurement. This fact is an important consideration in the design of control systems to control the operation of such real-world devices as airplanes, refineries, etc. A good engineering design must take these measurement errors into account when a control system is being designed, so that the noise on the measurements will not lead to unstable behavior (no plane crashes or refinery explosions!).

Most engineering designs are tested by running *simulations* of the operation of the system before it is ever built. These simulations consist of creating mathematical models of the behavior of the system, and feeding the models a realistic string of input data. If the models respond correctly to the simulated input data, we can have reasonable confidence that the real-world system will respond correctly to the real-world input data.

The simulated input data supplied to these models must be corrupted by a simulated measurement noise, which is just a string of random numbers added to the theoretical input data. The simulated noise is usually produced by a *random number generator*.

A random number generator is a subroutine that will return a different and apparently random number each time it is called. Since the numbers are in fact generated by a deterministic algorithm, they only appear to be random.[3] However, if the algorithm used to generate them is complex enough, the numbers will be random enough to use in the simulation.

One simple random number generator algorithm is shown below.[4] It relies on the unpredictability of the modulo function when applied to large numbers. Consider the following equation:

$$n_{i+1} = \text{MOD} (2041 \, n_i + 25673, 121500) \tag{6-9}$$

Assume that n_i is a nonnegative integer. Then because of the modulo function, n_{i+1} will be a number between 0 and 121499. Next, n_{i+1} can be fed into the equation to produce a number n_{i+2} that is also between 0 and 121499. This process can be repeated forever to produce a series of numbers in the range [0,121499]. If we didn't know the numbers 2041, 25673, and 121500 in advance, it would be impossible to guess the order in which the values of n would be produced. Furthermore, it turns out that there is an equal probability that any given number will appear in the sequence. Because of these properties, Equation (6-9) can serve as the basis for a uniform random number generator.

---

[3] For this reason, some people refer to the subroutines as *pseudorandom number generators*.

[4] This algorithm is adapted from the discussion found in Chapter 7 of *Numerical Recipes: The Art of Scientific Programming*, by Press, Flannery, Teukolsky, and Vetterling, Cambridge University Press, 1986.

We will now use Equation (6-9) to design a random number generator whose output is a real number in the range [0.0, 1.0).[5]

SOLUTION   We write a subroutine that generates one random number in the range $0 \le ran < 1.0$ each time that it is called. The random number is based on the equation

$$ran_i = \frac{n_i}{121500} \tag{6-10}$$

where n_i is a number in the range 0–121499 produced by Equation (6-9).

The particular sequence produced by Equations (6-9) and (6-10) will depend on the initial value of n_0 (called the *seed)* of the sequence. We must provide a way for the user to specify n_0 so that the sequence may be varied from run to run.

1.   State the problem.

Write a subroutine RAN0 that generates and returns a single number RAN in the range $0 \le RAN < 1.0$, based on the sequence specified by Equations (6-9) and (6-10). The initial value of the seed n_0 is specified by a call to a subroutine called SEED.

2.   Define the inputs and outputs.

There are two subroutines in this problem: SEED and RAN0. The input to subroutine SEED is an integer to serve as the starting point of the sequence. There is no output from this subroutine. There is no input to subroutine RAN0, and the output from the subroutine is a single real value in the range [0.0, 1.0).

3.   Describe the algorithm

The pseudocode for subroutine RAN0 is simple:

```
SUBROUTINE RAN0 ( RAN )
N ← MOD (2041 * N + 25673, 121500 )
RAN ← REAL(N) / 121500.
RETURN
END
```

where the value of N is saved between calls to the subroutine. The pseudocode for subroutine SEED is also trivial:

```
SUBROUTINE SEED ( ISEED )
N ← ABS ( ISEED )
RETURN
END
```

The absolute value function is used so that the user can enter any integer as the starting point. The user will not have to know in advance that only positive integers are legal seeds.

The variable N is placed in a **COMMON** block so that it may be accessed by both subroutines. In addition, we will use a **BLOCK DATA** subprogram to initialize

---

[5] The notation [0.0,1.0) implies that the range of the random numbers is between 0.0 and 1.0, including the number 0.0, but excluding the number 1.0.

N to a reasonable value so that we get good results even if subroutine SEED is not called to set the seed before the first call to RAN0.

4. Turn the algorithm into FORTRAN statements.

The resulting FORTRAN subroutines are shown in Figure 6-15.

```
      SUBROUTINE RAN0 ( RAN )
C
C  Purpose:
C    Subroutine to generate a pseudorandom number with a uniform
C    distribution in the range 0. <= RAN < 1.0.
C
C  Record of revisions:
C      Date        Programmer          Description of change
C      ====        ==========          =====================
C    06/20/91    S. J. Chapman         Original code
C
C  List of calling arguments:
C    NAME    I/O  TYPE         DESCRIPTION
C    ====    ===  ====         ===========
C    RAN      O   REAL         Random number.
C
C  List of variables in COMMON /RAN001/:
C    N         -- The current value in the pseudorandom sequence
C
C  List of local variables:
C    None
C
      IMPLICIT NONE
C
C    Calling arguments.
C
      REAL    RAN
C
C    Include common /RAN001/.
C
      INTEGER N
      COMMON /RAN001/ N
C
C    Calculate next number in sequence.
C
      N = MOD (2041 * N + 25673, 121500 )
C
C    Calculate RAN.
C
      RAN = REAL(N) / 121500.
C
      RETURN
      END
      SUBROUTINE SEED ( ISEED )
C
C  Purpose:
C    Subroutine to set the seed for random number generator RAN0.
C
C  Record of revisions:
C      Date        Programmer          Description of change
C      ====        ==========          =====================
C    06/20/91    S. J. Chapman         Original code
C
```

```
C   List of calling arguments:
C      NAME     I/O  TYPE          DESCRIPTION
C      ====     ===  ====          ============
C      ISEED    I    INTEGER       Seed.
C
C   List of variables in COMMON /RAN001/:
C      N        -- The current value in the pseudorandom sequence
C
C   List of local variables:
C      None
C
       IMPLICIT NONE
C
C      Calling arguments.
C
       INTEGER ISEED
C
C      Include common /RAN001/.
C
       INTEGER N
       COMMON /RAN001/ N
C
C      Set seed.
C
       N = ABS ( ISEED )
C
       RETURN
       END
       BLOCK DATA
C
C   Purpose:
C     To initialize N to a default value.
C
C   Record of revisions:
C      Date          Programmer          Description of change
C      ====          ==========          =====================
C      06/20/91      S. J. Chapman       Original code
C
C   List of variables in COMMON /RAN001/:
C      N        -- The current value in the pseudorandom sequence
C
       IMPLICIT NONE
C
C      Include common /RAN001/.
C
       INTEGER N
       COMMON /RAN001/ N
C
C      Data.
C
       DATA N / 1021 /
C
       END
```

FIGURE 6-15 Subroutines to generate a random number sequence, and to set the seed of the sequence.

5. Test the resulting FORTRAN programs.

If the numbers generated by these routines are truly uniformly distributed random numbers in the range $0 \leq RAN < 1.0$, then the average of many numbers should be close to 0.5. To test the results, we write a test program that prints out the first 10 values produced by RAN0 to see if they are indeed in the range $0 \leq RAN < 1.0$. Then, the program will average five consecutive 100-sample intervals to see how close the averages come to 0.5. The test code to call subroutines SEED and RAN0 is shown in Figure 6-16:

```
      PROGRAM TRANO
C
C  Purpose:
C    Subroutine test the random number generator RANO.
C
C  Record of revisions:
C      Date        Programmer        Description of change
C      ====        ==========        =====================
C    06/20/91    S. J. Chapman       Original code
C
C  List of local variables:
C     AVE    -- Average of random numbers
C     I      -- DO Loop index
C     ISEED  -- Seed for random number
C     ISEQ   -- DO Loop index
C     RAN    -- A random number
C     SUM    -- Sum of random numbers
C
      IMPLICIT NONE
C
C  Local variables.
C
      INTEGER I, ISEED, ISEQ
      REAL    AVE, RAN, SUM
C
C  Get seed.
C
      WRITE (*,*) 'Enter seed:'
      READ (*,*) ISEED
C
C  Set seed.
C
      CALL SEED ( ISEED )
C
C  Print out 10 random numbers.
C
      WRITE (*,*) '10 random numbers:'
      DO 10 I = 1, 10
         CALL RANO ( RAN )
         WRITE (*,1000) RAN
 1000    FORMAT (3X,F16.6)
   10 CONTINUE
C
C  Average 5 consecutive 100-value sequences.
C
```

```
      WRITE (*,*) 'Averages of 5 consecutive 100-sample sequences:'
      DO 30 ISEQ = 1, 5
         SUM = 0.
         DO 20 I = 1, 100
            CALL RANO ( RAN )
            SUM = SUM + RAN
  20     CONTINUE
         AVE = SUM / 100.
         WRITE (*,1000) AVE
  30 CONTINUE
C
      END
```

FIGURE 6-16   Test driver program for subroutines SEED and RAN0.

The results of compiling and running the test program are shown below:

```
C:\BOOK\FORT>tran0
Enter seed:
12
10 random numbers:
            .412881
            .900724
            .589556
            .494189
            .851663
            .454568
            .984387
            .344823
            .995136
            .283473
Averages of 5 consecutive 100-sample sequences:
            .545502
            .509741
            .482004
            .539329
            .514309
```

The numbers do appear to be between 0 and 1, and the averages of long sets of these numbers are nearly 0.5, so these subroutines appear to be functioning correctly. You should try them again using different seeds to see if they behave consistently for all starting seeds. ●

QUIZ 6-2

This quiz provides a quick check to see if you have understood the concepts introduced in Section 6.2 through 6.4. If you have trouble with the quiz, reread the sections, ask your instructor, or discuss the material with a fellow student. The answers to this quiz are found in the back of the book.

1. When should a **SAVE** statement be used in a program or subprogram? Why should it be used?
2. What is the major disadvantage of a **COMMON** block relative to an argument list when they are being used to pass data to a subroutine?

For questions 3–5, determine whether there are any errors in these programs. If possible, tell what the output from each program will be.

3.
```
      PROGRAM TEST1
      IMPLICIT NONE
      INTEGER I(10), J
      DO 10 J = 1, 10
         CALL SUB1 ( I(J) )
         WRITE (*,*) ' I = ', I(J)
   10 CONTINUE
      END
      SUBROUTINE SUB1 ( IVAL )
      IMPLICIT NONE
      INTEGER IVAL, ISUM
      ISUM = ISUM + 1
      IVAL = ISUM
      RETURN
      END
```

4.
```
      PROGRAM TEST2
      IMPLICIT NONE
      REAL A(10), B
      INTEGER I
      COMMON / DATA2 / A, B
      DO 10 I = 1, 10
         A(I) = REAL(I)
   10 CONTINUE
      B = 37.
      CALL SUB2
      END
      SUBROUTINE SUB2
      IMPLICIT NONE
      REAL X(10), W
      COMMON / DATA2 / W, X
      WRITE (*,*) ' X(5) = ' , X(5)
      RETURN
      END
```

5.
```
      BLOCK DATA MYDATA
      IMPLICIT NONE
      INTEGER I
      REAL A(10), B, C, D
      COMMON / DATA3 / A(10), B, C
      DATA B, C / -123.0, 17. /
      DO 10 I = 1, 10
         A(I) = REAL(I)
   10 CONTINUE
      END
```

6.5   FORTRAN FUNCTIONS

A FORTRAN **function** is a subprogram whose result is a single number, logical value, or character string. The result of a function is a single value that can be combined with variables and constants to form FORTRAN expressions. These expressions may appear on the right side of an assignment statement in the calling program. There are two different types of FORTRAN functions: **intrinsic functions** and **user-defined functions** (or function subprograms). Intrinsic functions are those functions built into the FORTRAN language, such as SIN(X), LOG(X), etc. These functions were described in Chapter 2.

User-defined functions are functions defined by individual programmers to meet a specific need not addressed by the standard intrinsic functions. They are used just like intrinsic functions in expressions.

The general form of a user-defined FORTRAN function is:

```
FUNCTION name ( argument list )
...
   (Declaration section must declare type of name)
...
   (Execution section)
...
name =
   (Termination section)
RETURN
END
```

The name of the function must appear on the left side of a least one assignment statement in the function. The value assigned to *name* when the function returns to the calling routine will be the value of the function. Note that the argument list may be blank if the function can perform all of its calculations with no input arguments. The parentheses around the argument list are required even if the list is blank.

Since a function returns a value, it is necessary to assign a *type* to the function. If **IMPLICIT NONE** is used, *the type of the function must be declared both in the function subprogram and in the calling programs.* If **IMPLICIT NONE** is not used, the default type of the function will follow the standard rules of FORTRAN unless they are overridden by a type declaration statement. The type declaration of a user-defined FORTRAN function can take one of two equivalent forms:

```
INTEGER FUNCTION MYFUNC ( I, J )
```

or

```
FUNCTION MYFUNC ( I, J )
INTEGER MYFUNC
```

An example of a user-defined function is shown in Figure 6-17. Function QUADF evaluates a quadratic expression with user-specified coefficients at a user-specified position.

```
         FUNCTION QUADF ( X, A, B, C )
C
C  Purpose:
C     To evaluate a quadratic polynomial of the form
C        QUADF = A * X**2 + B * X + C
C     for a given A, B, C, and X.
C
C  Record of revisions:
C       Date         Programmer          Description of change
C       ====         ==========          =====================
C     06/20/91     S. J. Chapman         Original code
C
C  List of calling arguments:
C     NAME    I/O  TYPE       DESCRIPTION
C     ====    ===  ====       ===========
C     X        I   REAL       Value for which to evaluate equation
C     A        I   REAL       Coefficient of X**2 term
C     B        I   REAL       Coefficient of X term
C     C        I   REAL       Coefficient of constant term
C     QUADF    O   REAL       Output value.
C
C  List of local variables:
C     None
C
       IMPLICIT NONE
C
C     Declare calling arguments.
C
       REAL X, A, B, C, QUADF
C
C     Evaluate expression.
C
       QUADF = A * X**2 + B * X + C
C
C     Termination section.
C
       RETURN
       END
```

FIGURE 6-17   A function to evaluate a quadratic polynomial of the form
$$f(x) = ax^2 + bx + c.$$

This function produces a result of type real. A simple test program using the function is shown in Figure 6-18.

```
         PROGRAM TQUADF
C
C  Purpose:
C     Program to test function QUADF.
C
       IMPLICIT NONE
C
       REAL A, B, C, QUADF, X
C
C     Get input data.
C
```

```
      WRITE (*,*) ' Enter quadratic coefficients A, B, and C: '
      READ  (*,*) A, B, C
      WRITE (*,*) ' Enter location at which to evaluate equation: '
      READ  (*,*) X
C
C     Write out result.
C
      WRITE (*,100) ' QUADF(', X, ') = ', QUADF(X,A,B,C)
  100 FORMAT ( A, F10.4, A, F12.4 )
C
      END
```

FIGURE 6-18   A test driver program for function QUADF.

Notice that function QUADF is declared as type real both in the function itself and in the test program. In this example, function QUADF was used in the argument list of a **WRITE** statement. It could also have been used in assignment statements or wherever a FORTRAN expression is permissible. It could *not* be used be used on the left side of an assignment statement.

■ **GOOD PROGRAMMING PRACTICE**

Be sure to declare the type of any user-defined functions both in the function itself and in any routines that call the function.

6.5.1   Unintended Side Effects: The Pass-by-Reference Scheme

Input variables are passed to a user-defined function through its argument list. The data in the argument list is communicated to the function using the same pass-by-reference scheme that is used with subroutines. The function receives pointers to the memory locations containing the arguments, and it is just as free to modify the memory in those locations as a subroutine would be. Therefore, *it is possible for a user-defined* FORTRAN *function to modify its own input arguments*. If any of the function's dummy arguments appear on the left side of an assignment statement within the function, then the values of the input variables corresponding to those arguments will be changed.

By definition, a function should produce a single output value using one or more input values. The function should never modify its own input arguments. If the programmer needs to produce more than one output value from a subprogram, then the subprogram should be written as a subroutine and not as a function.

■ **GOOD PROGRAMMING PRACTICE**

A well-designed FORTRAN function should produce a single output value from one or more input values. It should never modify its own input arguments.

6.5.2 COMMON Blocks in User-Defined Functions

A user-defined function may also communicate with a main program via **COMMON** blocks. The **COMMON** blocks work in just the same way in user-defined functions as they do in subroutines. However, they are relatively rare, since a function is usually designed to work with many different sets of input data, and the argument list is an easy way to provide different sets of input data to a function.

QUIZ 6-3

This quiz provides a quick check to see if you have understood the concepts introduced in Section 6.5. If you have trouble with the quiz, reread the section, ask your instructor, or discuss the material with a fellow student. The answers to this quiz are found in the back of the book.

Write a user-defined function to perform the following calculations:

1. $f(x) = x^2 - 1$
2. $f(x) = \dfrac{x - 1}{x + 1}$
3. The hyperbolic tangent function $\tanh(x) = \dfrac{e^x - e^{-x}}{e^x + e^{-x}}$
4. The factorial function $n! = (n)(n - 1)(n - 2)\ldots(2)(1)$
5. Write a logical function that has two input arguments, x and y. The function should return a TRUE value if $x^2 + y^2 > 1.0$, and a FALSE value otherwise.

For questions 6 and 7, determine whether there are any errors in these functions. If so, show how to correct them.

6.
```
      FUNCTION AVE ( X, N )
      IMPLICIT NONE
      INTEGER N, J
      REAL X(N), SUM
C
      DO 10 J = 1, N
         SUM = SUM + X(J)
10    CONTINUE
      AVE = SUM / N
      RETURN
      END
```

7.
```
      LOGICAL FUNCTION BADVAL ( X, Y )
      IMPLICIT NONE
      REAL X, Y
      BADVAL = X .GT. Y
      RETURN
      END
```

EXAMPLE 6-7   *The sinc function*   The sinc function is defined by the equation

$$\text{sinc}(x) = \frac{\sin(x)}{x} \tag{6-11}$$

This function occurs in many different types of engineering analysis problems. For example, the sinc function describes the frequency spectrum of a rectangular time pulse. A plot of the function sinc(x) versus x is shown in Figure 6-19.

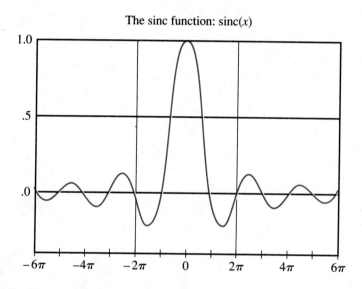

The sinc function: sinc(x)

FIGURE 6-19   Plot of sinc(x) versus x.

Write a user-defined FORTRAN function to calculate the sinc function.

SOLUTION   The sinc function looks easy to implement, but there is a calculation problem when $x = 0$. The value of sinc(0) = 1, since

$$\text{sinc}(0) = \lim_{x \to 0}\left(\frac{\sin(x)}{x}\right) = 1$$

Unfortunately, a computer program would blow up on the division by 0. We must include a logical **IF** structure in the function to handle the special case where x is nearly 0.

1. State the problem.

Write a FORTRAN function that calculates sinc(x).

2. Define the inputs and outputs.

The input to the function is the real argument x. The function is of type real, and its output is the value of sinc(x).

3. Describe the algorithm.

The pseudocode for this function is

```
IF |X| > EPSLON THEN
    SINC ← SIN(X) / X
ELSE
    SINC ← 1.
END IF

RETURN
END
```

where EPSLON is chosen to ensure that the division does not cause divide-by-zero errors. For most computers, a good choice for EPSLON might be 1.0E-30.

4. Turn the algorithm into FORTRAN statements.

The resulting FORTRAN subroutines are shown in Figure 6-20.

```
      FUNCTION SINC ( X )
C
C  Purpose:
C    To calculate the sinc function
C       SINC(X) = SIN(X) / X
C
C  Record of revisions:
C     Date        Programmer         Description of change
C     ====        ==========         =====================
C    06/22/91    S. J. Chapman       Original code
C
C  List of calling arguments:
C     NAME    I/O  TYPE         DESCRIPTION
C     ====    ===  ====         ===========
C     X        I   REAL         Value for which to evaluate equation
C     SINC     O   REAL         Output value SINC(X).
C
C  List of local parameters:
C     EPSLON -- the smallest value of X for which to calculate SIN(X)/X
C
C  List of local variables:
C     None
C
      IMPLICIT NONE
C
C     Parameters.
C
      REAL         EPSLON
      PARAMETER ( EPSLON = 1.0E-30 )
C
```

```
C      Declare calling arguments.
C
       REAL X, SINC
C
C      Check to see of ABS(X) > EPSLON.
C
       IF ( ABS(X) .GT. EPSLON ) THEN
          SINC = SIN(X) / X
       ELSE
          SINC = 1.
       END IF
C
       RETURN
       END
```

FIGURE 6-20   The FORTRAN function SINC(X).

5. Test the resulting FORTRAN program.

To test this function, it is necessary to write a driver program to read an input value, call the function, and write out the results. We will calculate several values of sinc(x) on a hand calculator and compare them with the results of the test program. Note that we must verify the function of the program for input values both greater than and less than EPSLON.

A test driver program is shown in Figure 6-21:

```
       PROGRAM TSINC
C
C  Purpose:
C    To test the sinc function SINC(X)
C
       IMPLICIT NONE
C
C      Declare the SINC function.
C
       REAL SINC
C
C      Declare local variables.
C
       REAL X
C
C      Get X.
C
       WRITE (*,*) ' Enter X: '
       READ (*,*) X
C
C      Write answer.
C
       WRITE (*,100) ' SINC(X) = ', SINC(X)
   100 FORMAT (A,F8.5)
C
       END
```

FIGURE 6-21   A test driver program for the function SINC(X).

Hand calculations yield the following values for sinc(x):

x	sinc(x)
0	1.00000
10^{-29}	1.00000
$\dfrac{\pi}{2}$	0.63662
π	0.00000

The results from the test program for these input values are:

```
C:\BOOK\FORT>tsinc
Enter X:
0
SINC(X) = 1.0000

C:\BOOK\FORT>tsinc
Enter X:
1.E-29
SINC(X) = 1.0000

C:\BOOK\FORT>tsinc
Enter X:
1.570796
SINC(X) = 0.63662

C:\BOOK\FORT>tsinc
Enter X:
3.141593
SINC(X) = 0.0000
```

The function appears to be working correctly. ●

6.6 PASSING SUBPROGRAM NAMES AS ARGUMENTS TO OTHER SUBPROGRAMS

We have shown that when a subroutine or function is called, the calling argument list is passed to the subprogram as a series of *pointers* to specific locations in memory, and that how the memory at each location is interpreted depends upon the type and size of the formal arguments declared in the subprogram.

This mechanism can be extended to permit us to pass a pointer to a *user-defined subprogram* as a calling argument to another subprogram. Both FORTRAN functions and subroutines can be passed as calling arguments. For simplicity, we will first discuss passing user-defined functions to subprograms, and afterward discuss passing subroutines to subprograms.

6.6.1   Passing User-Defined Function Names as Arguments

If a user-defined function name is included as a calling argument, then a *pointer to that function* is passed to the subprogram being called. If the corresponding formal argument in the subprogram is used as a function, then when the subprogram is executed, the function in the calling argument list will be used in place of the dummy function in the subprogram. Consider the following example:

```
PROGRAM TEST
REAL MYFUN1, MYFUN2, X, Y, OUTPUT
...
CALL EVAL ( MYFUN1, X, Y, OUTPUT )
CALL EVAL ( MYFUN2, X, Y, OUTPUT )
...
END
SUBROUTINE EVAL ( FUNC, A, B, RESULT )
REAL FUNC, A, B, RESULT
RESULT = B * FUNC(A)
RETURN
END
```

Assume that MYFUN1 and MYFUN2 are two user-supplied functions. Then a pointer to function MYFUN1 is passed to subroutine EVAL on the first occasion that it is called, and function MYFUN1 is used in place of the formal argument FUNC in the subroutine. A pointer to function MYFUN2 is passed to subroutine EVAL the second time that it is called, and function MYFUN2 is used in place of the formal argument FUNC in the subroutine.

User-supplied functions may only be passed to a calling subroutine if they are declared in an **EXTERNAL** statement in the calling program. The **EXTERNAL** statement is a specification statement of the form

```
EXTERNAL name1, name2, ...
```

It states that *name1*, *name2*, etc. are names of subprograms that are defined outside of the current routine. The **EXTERNAL** statement must appear in the declaration section of a routine, before the first executable statement.

Why is an **EXTERNAL** statement required? Without it, a calling program could not tell whether a particular calling argument is a variable or a function! Look again at the above example. Note that MYFUN1 and MYFUN2 were declared as type real. How can the compiler possibly tell that they are real functions instead of real variables? The answer is that it can't. Only by including the **EXTERNAL** statement do we tell the compiler that MYFUN1 and MYFUN2 are functions instead of variables. The correct form of the calling program is shown below.

```
PROGRAM TEST
REAL MYFUN1, MYFUN2, X, Y, OUTPUT
EXTERNAL MYFUN1, MYFUN2
...
CALL EVAL ( MYFUN1, X, Y, OUTPUT )
CALL EVAL ( MYFUN2, X, Y, OUTPUT )
...
END
```

■
EXAMPLE 6-8 *Passing User-Defined Functions to Subprograms in an Argument List* The function AVEVAL in the example program shown in Figure 6-22 determines the average amplitude of a function between user-specified limits FSTVAL and LSTVAL by sampling the function at N evenly spaced points, and calculating the overall average amplitude between those points. The function to be evaluated is passed to function AVEVAL as a calling line argument.

```
      REAL FUNCTION AVEVAL ( FUNC, FSTVAL, LSTVAL, N )
C
C  Purpose:
C    To calculate the average value of function FUNC over the range
C    [FSTVAL, LSTVAL] by taking N evenly spaced samples over the
C    range, and averaging the results.  Function FUNC is passed to
C    this routine via a command-line argument.
C
C  Record of revisions:
C      Date        Programmer          Description of change
C      ====        ==========          =====================
C    07/31/91    S. J. Chapman         Original code
C
C  List of calling arguments:
C    NAME      I/O  TYPE          DESCRIPTION
C    ====      ===  ====          ===========
C    FUNC      I    REAL FUNC     Function to be evaluated.
C    FSTVAL    I    REAL          First value in range to be averaged.
C    LSTVAL    I    REAL          Last value in range to be averaged.
C    N         I    INTEGER       Number of evenly-spaced samples to average.
C    AVEVAL    O    REAL          Resulting average output value.
C
C  List of local variables:
C    DELTA  -- Step size between samples
C    I      -- Index variable
C    SUM    -- Sum of values to average
C
      IMPLICIT NONE
C
C  Declare calling arguments.
C
      REAL    FUNC, FSTVAL, LSTVAL
      INTEGER N
C
C  Declare local variables.
C
      REAL    DELTA, SUM
      INTEGER I
C
C  Get step size.
C
      DELTA = ( LSTVAL - FSTVAL ) / REAL (N-1)
C
C  Accumulate sum.
C
```

```
      SUM = 0.
      DO 10 I = 1, N
         SUM = SUM + FUNC ( REAL(I-1) * DELTA )
   10 CONTINUE
C
C     Get average.
C
      AVEVAL = SUM / REAL(N)
C
      RETURN
      END
```

FIGURE 6-22   Function AVEVAL calculates the average amplitude of a function between two points FSTVAL and LSTVAL. The function whose average amplitude is to be determined is passed to function AVEVAL as a calling argument.

We must write a test driver program in order to test function AVEVAL. Such a test driver program is shown in Figure 6-23. In that program, function AVEVAL is called with the user-defined function MYFUNC as a calling argument. Note that function MYFUNC is declared as **EXTERNAL** in the test driver program TAVEVL. The function MYFUNC is averaged over 101 samples in the interval [0, 1], and the results are printed out.

```
      PROGRAM TAVEVL
C
C  Purpose:
C    To test the AVEVAL function by calling it with a user-defined
C    function MYFUNC.
C
C  Record of revisions:
C      Date        Programmer          Description of change
C      ====        ==========          =====================
C    07/31/91    S. J. Chapman         Original code
C
      IMPLICIT NONE
C
C     Declare functions.
C
      REAL      MYFUNC, AVEVAL
      EXTERNAL MYFUNC
C
C     Declare local variables.
C
      REAL      AVE
C
C     Call function with FUNC=MYFUN.
C
      AVE = AVEVAL ( MYFUNC, 0., 1., 101 )
      WRITE (*,1000) 'MYFUNC', AVE
 1000 FORMAT (1X,'The average value of ',A,' between 0. and 1. is ',
     *           F16.6,'.')
C
      STOP
      END
```

```
REAL FUNCTION MYFUNC ( X )
IMPLICIT NONE
REAL X
MYFUNC = 3. * X
RETURN
END
```

FIGURE 6-23   Test driver program for function AVEVAL, illustrating how to pass a user-defined function as a calling argument.

When program TAVEVL is executed, the results are

```
C:\BOOK\FORT>tavevl
The average value of MYFUNC between 0. and 1. is      1.500000.
```

Since for this case MYFUNC is a straight line between $(0, 0)$ and $(1, 3)$, it is obvious that the average value was correctly calculated as 1.5. ●

6.6.2   Passing Subroutine Names as Arguments

If a subroutine name is included as a calling argument, then a *pointer to that subroutine* is passed to the subprogram being called. If the corresponding formal argument in the subprogram is used in a **CALL** statement, then when the subprogram is executed, the subroutine in the calling argument list will be used in place of the dummy subroutine in the subprogram. Consider the following example:

```
           PROGRAM TEST1
           REAL X, Y, OUTPUT
           EXTERNAL MYSUB
           . . .
           CALL EVAL1 ( MYSUB, X, Y, OUTPUT )
           . . .
           END
   *
           SUBROUTINE EVAL1 ( SUBX, A, B, RESULT )
           REAL A, B, RESULT
           REAL TEMP
           CALL SUBX ( A, B, TEMP )
           RESULT = B * TEMP
           RETURN
           END
   *
           SUBROUTINE MYSUB ( P, Q, R )
           REAL P, Q, R
           R = P * SIN (Q )
           RETURN
           END
```

When program TEST1 calls subroutine EVAL1, it passes the name of subroutine MYSUB as a calling argument. Therefore, when the statement "CALL SUBX" is reached in routine EVAL1, subroutine MYSUB will be called in place of the dummy subroutine SUBX. Note that the subroutine name being passed must appear in an **EXTERNAL** statement in the calling program.[6]

6.6.3   Passing Intrinsic Function Names as Arguments

It is also possible to pass a *specific intrinsic function* as a calling argument to another subprogram. If the name of an intrinisc function is included as a calling argument, then a pointer to that function is passed to the subprogram. If the corresponding formal argument in the subprogram is used as a function, then when the subprogram is executed, the intrinsic function in the calling argument list will be used in place of the dummy function in the subprogram. Note that generic intrinsic functions may not be used as calling arguments—only specific intrinsic functions may be used.

Before it can be used as a calling argument to a subprogram, a specific intrinsic function must be declared in an **INTRINSIC** statement in the calling program. The **INTRINSIC** statement is a specification statement of the form

```
INTRINSIC name1, name2, ...
```

It states that *name1, name2,* etc. are names of intrinsic functions. The **INTRINSIC** statement must appear in the declaration section of a routine, before the first executable statement. The reason that an **INTRINSIC** statement is required is the same as the reason that an **EXTERNAL** statement is required: it permits the compiler to distinguish between a variable and an intrinsic function of the same type.

■ **EXAMPLE   6-9**   *Passing Intrinsic Functions to Subprograms in an Argument List*
We will illustrate the use of intrinsic functions in an argument list by modifying the test driver program TAVEVL to pass the intrinsic function SIN(X) to AVEVAL. The modified program is shown in Figure 6-24. Note that SIN is declared in an **INTRINSIC** statement. The function SIN is averaged over 101 samples in the interval [0, 2π], and the results are printed out.

```
      PROGRAM TAVEV2
C
C  Purpose:
C    To test the AVEVAL function by calling it with the intrinsic
C    function SIN.
C
C  Record of revisions:
C      Date       Programmer          Description of change
C      ====       ==========          =====================
C    08/01/91   S. J. Chapman        Original code
C
```

---

[6] User-defined functions and subroutines can appear in **EXTERNAL** statements even if they are not being passed as calling arguments to a subprogram. In fact, the software standards applied to many large programming projects *require* that every subprogram called by a routine be included in an **EXTERNAL** statement within the routine. This procedure improves software maintenance, since any programmer inspecting a subprogram can tell immediately just what subprograms are required by that subprogram.

```
      IMPLICIT NONE
C
C     Declare functions.
C
      REAL       AVEVAL
      INTRINSIC SIN
C
C     Declare parameters.
C
      REAL        TWOPI
      PARAMETER ( TWOPI = 6.283185 )
C
C     Declare local variables.
C
      REAL    AVE
C
C     Call function with FUNC=SIN.
C
      AVE = AVEVAL ( SIN, 0., TWOPI, 101 )
      WRITE (*,1000) 'SIN', AVE
 1000 FORMAT (1X,'The average value of ',A,' between 0. and TWOPI is ',
     *        F16.6,'.')
C
      STOP
      END
```

FIGURE 6-24   Test driver program for function AVEVAL, illustrating how to pass an intrinsic function as a calling argument.

When program TAVEV2 is executed, the results are

```
C:\BOOK\FORT>tavev2
The average value of SIN between 0. and TWOPI is      .000000.
```

Since the average of a sinusoid between 0 and 2π is 0.0, we can see that the average value was correctly calculated. ●

The passing of subprogram names as calling arguments to other subprograms is one of the most confusing parts of the FORTRAN language for both neophyte and experienced FORTRAN programmers. This feature should be avoided unless there is a good reason for using it.

■
GOOD PROGRAMMING PRACTICE

Avoid passing subprogram names to other subprograms as calling arguments unless there is a good reason for doing so, since this practice makes the programs more confusing and harder to maintain.

6.7   SUMMARY

In Chapter 6, we presented an introduction to FORTRAN subprograms. Subprograms are independently compiled FORTRAN routines with their own declaration sections, execution sections, and termination sections. They are extremely important to the design, coding, and maintenance of large programs. Subprograms permit the independent testing of subtasks as a project is being built, allow time savings through reusable code, and improve reliability through variable hiding.

There are two types of subprograms: subroutines and functions. Subroutines are subprograms whose results include more than one variable. A subroutine is defined using a **SUBROUTINE** statement, and is executed using a **CALL** statement. Input data is passed to a subroutine and results are returned from the subroutine through argument lists on the **SUBROUTINE** statement and **CALL** statement. When a subroutine is called, pointers is passed to the subroutine pointing to the memory locations of each argument in the argument list. The subroutine reads from and writes to those memory locations.

Data can also be passed to subroutines through **COMMON** blocks. A **COMMON** block refers to a particular area of a computer's memory, and every main program and subroutine that contains the **COMMON** block has access to the common memory. Therefore, a main program can set a variable which can be read by a subroutine, and vice versa. **COMMON** blocks are less flexible than calling arguments, but are sometimes used to exchange large amounts of data between routines.

Variables in **COMMON** blocks may not be initialized with **DATA** statements in programs or subprograms that include the blocks, since doing so might result in conflicting definitions for the initial value of the variables (one routine might initialize a variable to be one value, while another routine might try to initialize it to be a different value). Instead, variables in **COMMON** blocks must be initialized with **DATA** statements in a separate **BLOCK DATA** subprogram. Since they can only be initialized in one location, there can be no conflict as to the initial value of the variable.

FORTRAN functions are subprograms whose results are a single number, logical value, or character string. There are two types of FORTRAN functions: intrinsic (built-in) functions and user-defined functions. Intrinsic functions were discussed in Chapter 2. User-defined functions are declared using the **FUNCTION** statement, and are executed by naming the function as a part of a FORTRAN expression. Data may be passed to a user-defined function through calling arguments or via **COMMON** blocks.

A properly designed FORTRAN function should not change its input arguments. It should *only* change the single output value.

It is possible to pass a function to a subprogram via a calling argument, provided that the function is declared with either an **EXTERNAL** or an **INTRINSIC** statement in the calling program. However, this feature makes programs more complicated and harder to maintain, so it should be avoided.

6.7.1 Summary of Good Programming Practice

The following guidelines should be adhered to when working with subroutines and functions.

1. Break large program tasks into smaller, more understandable subprograms whenever possible.
2. You may use either a subroutine or a function subprogram when the desired result is a single value. If more than one output value is required, always use a subroutine.
3. Make sure that the argument lists in all subroutine or function calls match the routine's declared dummy parameters in *number, type,* and *order.* Otherwise, the input data may be misinterpreted by the subroutine or function.
4. Test for possible error conditions within a subroutine, and set an error flag to be returned to the calling routine. The calling routine should test for error conditions after the subroutine call, and take appropriate actions if an error occurs.
5. If a subroutine or function requires that the value of a local variable not change between successive calls to the subprogram, include the variable in a **SAVE** statement.
6. **COMMON** blocks may be used to pass large amounts of data between routines within a program. Always declare the **COMMON** blocks identically in every routine containing them, so that the variables always have the same name and type in each routine. This greatly reduces confusion when moving from routine to routine within the program.
7. Use **BLOCK DATA** subprograms to initialize data in **COMMON** blocks.
8. Be sure to declare the type of any function subprograms both in the function itself and in any routines that call the function.

CHAPTER 6 KEY WORDS

Argument list	Pass-by-reference
Calling arguments	Subprogram
Dummy arguments	Subroutine
Function	Test driver program
Intrinsic function	Unit testing
Local variables	User-defined function
Main program	

CHAPTER 6 SUMMARY OF FORTRAN STATEMENTS AND STRUCTURES

BLOCK DATA Statement:

```
BLOCK DATA name
```

Example:

```
BLOCK DATA MYDATA
INTEGER I(12)
COMMON /BLOCK/ I
DATA I / 1, 2, 3, 4, 5, 6, 6, 5, 4, 3, 2, 1 /
END
```

Description: The **BLOCK DATA** statement defines the beginning of a **BLOCK DATA** subprogram, which is used to initialize data in a **COMMON** block. The *name* is optional.

CALL Statement:

```
CALL subname ( arg1, arg2, ... )
```

Example:

```
CALL SORT ( NUM, DATA1 )
```

Description: This statement transfers execution from the current routine to subroutine *subname*, passing pointers to the calling arguments *arg1*, *arg2*, ... to the subroutine. The subroutine executes until either a **RETURN** or an **END** statement is encountered, and then execution continues in the calling routine at the next executable statement following the **CALL** statement.

COMMON Statement:

```
COMMON / blknam / var1, var2, ...
```

Example:

```
COMMON / COMDAT / A, I(-3:3), L
```

Description: This statement defines a **COMMON** block with the name *blknam*. The variables declared in the block will be allocated consecutively starting at a specific memory location. They will be accessible to any routine in which **COMMON** block *blknam* is declared.

There can be any number of **COMMON** blocks in a program. Each block with a different name will be allocated to a different region of memory.

In standard FORTRAN 77, character variables may not be mixed with other types of variables in the same **COMMON** block.

EXTERNAL Statement:

EXTERNAL *name1, name2, ...*

Example:
EXTERNAL MYFUNC

Description: This statement declares that a particular name is an externally defined function or subroutine. It must be used in a calling program if the subprogram name is to appear in the argument list of a subroutine or function subprogram.

FUNCTION Statement:

[*type*] FUNCTION *name(arg1, arg2, ...)*

Examples:
INTEGER FUNCTION MAXVAL (NUM, IARRAY)

FUNCTION GAMMA(X)

Description: This statement declares a user-defined FORTRAN function. The type of the function may be declared on the **FUNCTION** statement, or it may be declared in a separate type declaration statement. The function is executed by including *name(arg1, arg2, ...)* in an expression in the calling program. The dummy arguments *arg1, arg2, ...* are placeholders for the calling arguments passed when the function is executed.

   If a function has no arguments, then it must be declared with an empty pair of parentheses [*name*()].

INTRINSIC Statement:

INTRINSIC *name1, name2, ...*

Example:
INTRINSIC SIN, ABS

Description: This statement declares that a particular name is a specific intrinsic function. It must be used in a calling program if the subprogram name is to appear in the argument list of a **CALL** statement or function subprogram.

RETURN Statement:

RETURN

Example:
RETURN

Description: When this statement is executed in a subprogram, control returns to the routine that called the subprogram. This statement is optional at the end of a subroutine or function, since execution automatically returns to the calling routine whenever an **END** statement is reached.

SAVE Statement:

```
SAVE [var1, var2, ...]
```

Examples:
```
SAVE COUNT, INDEX

SAVE
```

Description: This statement declares that a *local variable* in a subroutine or function must remain unchanged between successive calls to the subroutine or function. If a list of variables is included, only those variables will be saved. If no list is included, every local variable in the subroutine or function will be saved.

Note that the **SAVE** statement is only required to save local variables. The contents of variables in **COMMON** are automatically preserved between calls to a subprogram, unless they are modified by some other routine accessing the same **COMMON** block.

SUBROUTINE Statement:

```
SUBROUTINE name( arg1, arg2, ... )
```

Example:
```
SUBROUTINE SORT ( NUM, DATA1 )
```

Description: This statement declares a FORTRAN subroutine. The subroutine is executed with a **CALL** statement. The dummy arguments *arg1, arg2, ...* are placeholders for the calling arguments passed when the subroutine is executed.

CHAPTER 6 EXERCISES

1. What is the difference between a subroutine and a function subprogram?
2. When a subroutine is called, how is data passed from the calling program to the subroutine, and how are the results of the subroutine returned to the calling program?
3. What are the advantages and disadvantages of the pass-by-reference scheme used in FORTRAN?
4. What is the purpose of declaring the length of an array in a subroutine argument list with an asterisk? What are the advantages and disadvantages of doing so?
5. Suppose that a 15-element array A is passed to a subroutine as a calling argument. What will happen if the subroutine attempts to write to element A(16)?

6. Suppose that a real value is passed to a subroutine in an argument that is declared to be an integer in the subroutine. Is there any way for the subroutine to tell that the argument type is mismatched? What happens on your computer when the following code is executed?

```
PROGRAM MAIN
IMPLICIT NONE
REAL X
X = -5.
CALL SUB1 ( X )
END
SUBROUTINE SUB1 ( I )
INTEGER I
WRITE (*,*) ' I = ', I
RETURN
END
```

7. Determine whether the following subroutine calls are correct or not. If they are in error, specify what is wrong with them.

 (*a*)
```
PROGRAM MAIN
IMPLICIT NONE
INTEGER I, J(3), K
REAL A(4), B, C(2)
...
CALL SUB1 ( A, I, B, J, C, K )
...
END
SUBROUTINE SUB1 ( A, I, B, J, C, K )
IMPLICIT NONE
REAL I, J(3), K
INTEGER A(4), B, C(2)
...
RETURN
END
```

 (*b*)
```
PROGRAM TEST
IMPLICIT NONE
INTEGER N, IRES, FACT
READ (*,*) N
IRES = FACT(N)
WRITE (*,*) N,'! = ', IRES
END
FUNCTION FACT(N)
IMPLICIT NONE
INTEGER FACT, N
IF ( N .LE. 1 ) THEN
FACT = 1
ELSE
FACT = N * FACT(N-1)
END IF
END
```

(c)
```
        PROGRAM BOUNDS
        IMPLICIT NONE
        INTEGER LEN, I, J
        PARAMETER ( LEN = 20)
        REAL TEST(LEN)
        DATA TEST /  1., 2., 3., 4., 5., 6., 7., 8., 9.,10.,
     *              11.,12.,13.,14.,15.,16.,17.,18.,19.,20. /
C
        CALL TSTSUB ( I, TEST, J )
        ...
        END
        SUBROUTINE TSTSUB ( LEN, ARRAY, IRES )
        IMPLICIT NONE
        INTEGER LEN, IRES
        INTEGER ARRAY(LEN)
C
        DO 10 I = 1, LEN
            IRES = IRES + SQRT(ARRAY(I))
     10 CONTINUE
        END
```

8. What is the purpose of the **SAVE** statement? When should it be used?

9. What values will be printed out by the following program?

```
        PROGRAM MAIN
        IMPLICIT NONE
        REAL    A, B(2), C(4)
        COMMON / DATA1 / A, B, C
        CALL SUB1
        END
        SUBROUTINE SUB1
        IMPLICIT NONE
        REAL    L, M(4), N(2)
        COMMON / DATA1 / L, M, N
        WRITE (*,*) L, M(2), N(2)
        RETURN
        END
        BLOCK DATA MYBLK
        REAL    A, B(2), C(4)
        COMMON / DATA1 / A, B, C
        DATA A, B, C / 1., 2., 3., 4., 1., 2., 3. /
        END
```

10. Modify the selection sort subroutine developed in this chapter to sort integer values.

11. Modify the selection sort subroutine developed in this chapter so that it sorts real values in *descending* order.

12. Write a driver program to test the statistical subroutines developed in Example 6-3. Be sure to test the routines with a variety of input data sets. Did you discover any problems with the subroutines?

13. Write a subroutine that uses subroutine RAN0 to generate a set of random numbers in the range $[-1.0, 1.0)$.

14. It is often useful to be able to simulate the throw of a fair die. Write a FORTRAN function DICE() that simulates the throw of a fair die by returning some random integer between 1 and 6 every time that it is called. (*Hint:* Call RAN0 to generate a random number sequence. Divide the possible values out of RAN0 into six equal intervals, and return the number of the interval that a given random number falls into.)

15. What is the purpose of a **BLOCK DATA** subprogram? Why do we need to use it?

16. Write three FORTRAN functions to calculate the hyperbolic sine, cosine, and tangent functions:

$$\sinh(x) = \frac{e^x - e^{-x}}{2}$$

$$\cosh(x) = \frac{e^x + e^{-x}}{2}$$

$$\tanh(x) = \frac{e^x - e^{-x}}{e^x + e^{-x}}$$

Use your functions to calculate the hyperbolic sines, cosines, and tangents of the following values: $-2, -1.5, -1.0, -0.5, -0.25, 0.0, 0.25, 0.5, 1.0, 1.5,$ and 2.0. Sketch the shapes of the hyperbolic sine, cosine, and tangent functions.

17. Write a FORTRAN function to calculate the dot product of two vectors $\mathbf{V}_1$ and $\mathbf{V}_2$:

$$\mathbf{V}_1 \cdot \mathbf{V}_2 = V_{x1}V_{x2} + V_{y1}V_{y2} + V_{z1}V_{z2}$$

where $\mathbf{V}_1 = V_{x1}\mathbf{i} + V_{y1}\mathbf{j} + V_{z1}\mathbf{k}$ and $\mathbf{V}_2 = V_{x2}\mathbf{i} + V_{y2}\mathbf{j} + V_{z2}\mathbf{k}$. Use the function to calculate the dot product of the two vectors $\mathbf{V}_1 = [-2, 4, .5]$ and $\mathbf{V}_2 = [.5, 3, 2]$.

18. Write a subroutine to calculate the cross-product of two vectors $\mathbf{V}_1$ and $\mathbf{V}_2$:

$$\mathbf{V}_1 \times \mathbf{V}_2 = (V_{y1}V_{z2} - V_{y2}V_{z1})\mathbf{i} + (V_{z1}V_{x2} - V_{z2}V_{x1})\mathbf{j} + (V_{x1}V_{y2} - V_{x2}V_{y1})\mathbf{k}$$

where $\mathbf{V}_1 = V_{x1}\mathbf{i} + V_{y1}\mathbf{j} + V_{z1}\mathbf{k}$ and $\mathbf{V}_2 = V_{x2}\mathbf{i} + V_{y2}\mathbf{j} + V_{z2}\mathbf{k}$. Use the function to calculate the cross product of the two vectors $\mathbf{V}_1 = [-2, 4, 0.5]$ and $\mathbf{V}_2 = [0.5, 3, 2]$.

19. The *size* of a matrix is specified by the number of rows and columns in the matrix. For example, an $N \times M$ matrix has N rows and M columns. Matrix addition and subtraction are only defined for two matrices of the same size. If two matrices are of the same size, then the sum of the two matrices is just the sum

of the corresponding components in each matrix. For example, if matrices A and B are 2×2 matrices

$$A = \begin{bmatrix} a_{11} & a_{12} \\ a_{21} & a_{22} \end{bmatrix} \quad \text{and} \quad B = \begin{bmatrix} b_{11} & b_{12} \\ b_{21} & b_{22} \end{bmatrix}$$

then their sum $C = A + B$ is

$$C = \begin{bmatrix} a_{11} + b_{11} & a_{12} + b_{12} \\ a_{21} + b_{21} & a_{22} + b_{22} \end{bmatrix}$$

Write two subroutines to calculate the sum and difference of two matrices if they are of the same size. If they are of different sizes, the subroutines should set an error flag and return to the calling program. The dimensions of all three arrays A, B, and C should be passed to the subroutines from the calling program so that size checking can be done. Check your subroutines by adding and subtracting the following two arrays:

$$A = \begin{bmatrix} 2 & -1 & 2 \\ -1 & -3 & 4 \\ 2 & 4 & 2 \end{bmatrix} \quad B = \begin{bmatrix} 1 & 2 & 3 \\ 2 & 1 & 2 \\ 3 & 2 & 1 \end{bmatrix}$$

20. Matrix multiplication is only defined for two matrices in which *the number of columns in the first matrix is equal to the number of rows in the second matrix.* If matrix A is an $N \times L$ matrix, and matrix B is an $L \times M$ matrix, then the product $C = A \times B$ is an $N \times M$ matrix whose elements are given by the equation

$$c_{ik} = \sum_{j=1}^{L} a_{ij} b_{jk}$$

For example, if matrices A and B are 2×2 matrices

$$A = \begin{bmatrix} 3.0 & -1.0 \\ 1.0 & 2.0 \end{bmatrix} \quad \text{and} \quad B = \begin{bmatrix} 1.0 & 4.0 \\ 2.0 & -3.0 \end{bmatrix}$$

then the elements of matrix C are

$$c_{11} = a_{11} b_{11} + a_{12} b_{21} = (3.0)(1.0) + (-1.0)(2.0) = 1.0$$

$$c_{12} = a_{11} b_{12} + a_{12} b_{22} = (3.0)(4.0) + (-1.0)(-3.0) = 15.0$$

$$c_{21} = a_{21} b_{11} + a_{22} b_{21} = (1.0)(1.0) + (2.0)(2.0) = 5.0$$

$$c_{22} = a_{21} b_{12} + a_{22} b_{22} = (1.0)(4.0) + (2.0)(-3.0) = -2.0$$

Write a subroutine to calculate the product of two matrices if they are of compatible sizes. If they are not of compatible sizes, set an error flag and return to the calling program. The dimensions of all three arrays A, B, and C should be passed to the subroutines from the calling program so that size checking can be done. Check your subroutines by multiplying the following two pairs arrays:

$$(a) \quad A = \begin{bmatrix} 2 & -1 & 2 \\ -1 & -3 & 4 \\ 2 & 4 & 2 \end{bmatrix} \quad B = \begin{bmatrix} 1 & 2 & 3 \\ 2 & 1 & 2 \\ 3 & 2 & 1 \end{bmatrix}$$

$$(b) \quad A = \begin{bmatrix} 1 & -1 & -2 \\ 2 & 2 & 0 \\ 3 & 3 & 3 \\ 5 & 4 & 4 \end{bmatrix} \quad B = \begin{bmatrix} -2 \\ 5 \\ 2 \end{bmatrix}$$

21. It is often useful to sort an array ARR1 into ascending order, while simultaneously carrying along a second array ARR2. In such a sort, each time an element of array ARR1 is exchanged with another element of ARR1, the corresponding elements of array ARR2 are also swapped. When the sort is over, the elements of array ARR1 are in ascending order, while the elements of array ARR2 that were associated with particular elements of array ARR1 are still associated with them. For example, suppose we have the following two arrays:

```
Element    ARR1    ARR2
    1.      6.      1.
    2.      1.      0.
    3.      2.     10.
```

After sorting array ARR1 while carrying along array ARR2, the contents of the two arrays are:

```
Element    ARR1    ARR2
    1.      1.      0.
    2.      2.     10.
    3.      6.      1.
```

Write a subroutine to sort one real array into ascending order while carrying along a second one. Test the subroutine with the following two 9-element arrays:

```
DATA A /  1., 11.,  -6., 17.,-23.,  0.,  5.,  1., -1. /
DATA B / 31.,101., 36.,-17.,  0., 10., -8., -1., -1. /
```

22. Write a subroutine that attempts to locate the maximum and minimum values of an arbitrary function $f(x)$ over a certain range. The function being evaluated should be passed to the subroutine as a calling argument. The subroutine should have the following input arguments:

```
FSTVAL — The first value of x to search
LSTVAL — The last value of x to search
NSTEPS — The number of steps to include in the search
FUNC   — The name of the function to search
```

The subroutine should have the following output arguments:

```
XMIN   – The value of x at which the minimum was found
MINVAL – The minimum value of f(x) found
XMAX   – The value of x at which the maximum was found
MAXVAL – The maximum value f(x) found
```

23. Write a test driver program for the subroutine generated in the previous problem. The test driver program should pass to the subroutine the user-defined function $f(x) = x^2 - 3x - 3$, and search for the minimum and maximum in 200 steps over the range $-10 \le x \le 10$. It should print out the resulting minimum and maximum values.

24. Write a test driver program for the subroutine generated in exercise 22. The test driver program should pass to the subroutine the intrinsic function EXP(X), and search for the minimum and maximum in 101 steps over the range $-10 \le x \le 10$. It should print out the resulting minimum and maximum values.

25. The *derivative* of a continuous function $f(x)$ is defined by the equation

$$f'(x) = \frac{d}{dx} f(x) = \lim_{x \to 0} \frac{f(x + \Delta x) - f(x)}{\Delta x}$$

In a sampled function, this definition becomes

$$f'(x_i) = \frac{f(x_{i+1}) - f(x_i)}{\Delta x}$$

where $\Delta x = x_{i+1} - x_i$. Assume that a vector VECT contains NSAMP samples of a function taken at a spacing of DX per sample. Write a subroutine that calculates the derivative of this vector. The routine should check to make sure that DX is greater than zero to prevent divide-by-zero errors in the subroutine.

To check your subroutine, you should generate a data set whose derivative is known, and compare the result of the subroutine with the known correct answer. A good choice for a test function is sin x. From elementary calculus, we know that d/dx (sin x) = cos x. Generate an input vector containing 100 values of the function sin x starting at $x = 0$, and using a step size Δx of 0.05. Take the derivative of the vector with your subroutine, and then compare the resulting answers to the known correct answer. How close did your routine come to calculating the correct value for the derivative?

26. We will now explore the effects of input noise on the quality of a numerical derivative. First, generate an input vector containing 100 values of the function sin x starting at $x = 0$, and using a step size Δx of 0.05, just as you did in the previous problem. Next, use subroutine RAN0 to generate a small amount of random noise with a maximum amplitude of ± 0.02, and add that random noise to the samples in your input vector. Note that the peak amplitude of the noise is only 2% of the peak amplitude of your signal, since the maximum value of sin x is 1. Now take the derivative of the function using the derivative

subroutine that you developed in the last problem. How close to the theoretical value of the derivative did you come? (See Figure 6-25.)

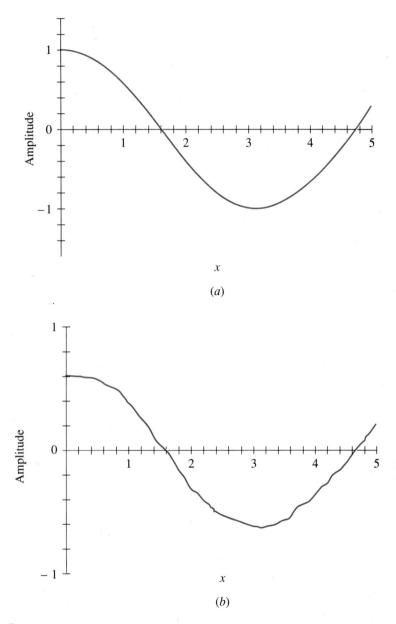

(a)

(b)

FIGURE 6-25   (a) A plot of sin x as a function of x with no noise added to the data. (b) A plot of sin x as a function of x with a 2% peak amplitude uniform random noise added to the data.

27. The subroutine RAN0 created in Example 6-6 generates a set of uniformly distributed random numbers in the range between 0 and 1, producing one number for each call to the subroutine. Any subroutine that produces only one output value each time it is called can also be written as a function. Create a function RAN1 that generates a set of uniformly distributed random numbers in the same manner as subroutine RAN0. Function RAN1 should use the existing subroutine SEED to specify the starting point of the sequence.

28. Develop a subroutine that will calculate slope m and intercept b of the least-squares line that best fits an input data set. The input data points (x, y) will be passed to the subroutine in two input arrays, X and Y. The equations describing the slope and intercept of the least-squares line are

$$y = mx + b \qquad (4\text{-}4)$$

$$m = \frac{(\Sigma xy) - (\Sigma x)\bar{y}}{(\Sigma x^2) - (\Sigma x)\bar{x}} \qquad (4\text{-}5)$$

and

$$b = \bar{y} - m\bar{x} \qquad (4\text{-}6)$$

where

Σx	is the sum of the x values
Σx^2	is the sum of the squares of the x values
Σxy	is the sum of the products of the corresponding x and y values
$\bar{x}$	is the mean (average) of the x values
$\bar{y}$	is the mean (average) of the y values

Test your routine using a test driver program and the following 20-point input data set:

Sample Data to Test Least-Squares Fit Routine

No.	x	y	No.	x	y
1	−4.91	−8.18	11	−0.94	0.21
2	−3.84	−7.49	12	0.59	1.73
3	−2.41	−7.11	13	0.69	3.96
4	−2.62	−6.15	14	3.04	4.26
5	−3.78	−5.62	15	1.01	5.75
6	−0.52	−3.30	16	3.60	6.67
7	−1.83	−2.05	17	4.53	7.70
8	−2.01	−2.83	18	5.13	7.31
9	0.28	−1.16	19	4.43	9.05
10	1.08	0.52	20	4.12	10.95

29. Develop a subroutine that will calculate both the slope m and intercept b of the least-squares line that best fits an input data set, and also the correlation coefficient of the fit. The input data points (x, y) are passed to the subroutine in two input arrays, X and Y. The equations describing the slope and intercept of the least-squares line are given in the previous problem, and the equation for the correlation coefficient is

$$r = \frac{n(\Sigma xy) - (\Sigma x)(\Sigma y)}{\sqrt{[(n\Sigma x^2) - (\Sigma x)^2][(n\Sigma y^2) - (\Sigma y)^2]}}$$

where

Σx	is the sum of the x values
Σy	is the sum of the y values
Σx^2	is the sum of the squares of the x values
Σy^2	is the sum of the squares of the y values
Σxy	is the sum of the products of the corresponding x and y values n is the number of points included in the fit

Test your routine using a test driver program and the 20-point input data set given in the previous problem.

30. The *determinant* of a matrix is a mathematical operation that is defined for square (N × N) matrices. If A is a 3 × 3 matrix,

$$A = \begin{bmatrix} a_{11} & a_{12} & a_{13} \\ a_{21} & a_{22} & a_{23} \\ a_{31} & a_{32} & a_{33} \end{bmatrix}$$

then the determinant of matrix A is defined by the following equation:

$$|A| = a_{11}a_{22}a_{33} + a_{12}a_{23}a_{31} + a_{13}a_{21}a_{32} - a_{31}a_{22}a_{13} - a_{32}a_{23}a_{11}$$
$$- a_{33}a_{21}a_{12}$$

Write a FORTRAN function that will calculate the determinant of a 3 × 3 matrix. Test your function by writing a test driver program and calculating the determinant of the following two arrays:

$$(a) \quad A1 = \begin{bmatrix} 5 & -2 & 0 \\ 3 & 2 & 2 \\ 1 & 2 & -1 \end{bmatrix}$$

$$(b) \quad A2 = \begin{bmatrix} -6 & -4 & -4 \\ 3 & 2 & 2 \\ 1 & 2 & -1 \end{bmatrix}$$

31. When testing the operation of subprograms or portions of a program, it is very useful to have an set of *elapsed time subroutines*. By starting a timer running before a subroutine or a particular part of a program executes, and then checking the time after the execution is completed, we can see how fast or slow the subroutine is. In this manner, a programmer can identify the time-consuming portions of his or her program, and rewrite them if necessary to make them faster.

Write a pair of subroutines named SET and ETIME to calculate the elapsed time in seconds between the last time that subroutine SET was called and the time that subroutine ETIME is being called. When subroutine SET is called, it should get the current time and store it into a variable in a **COMMON** block. When subroutine ETIME is called, it should get the current time, and then calculate the difference between the current time and the time that was stored in the **COMMON** block the last time that subroutine SET was called. The elapsed time in seconds between the two calls should be returned to the calling routine in an argument of subroutine ETIME.

Note: To make these subroutines, you will have to read the system clock on your particular computer system. Every computer has a different way to read the values in its system clock, so you will have to either ask your instructor or else look in your computer manuals to find the proper subroutine names and calling sequence to read the clock on your particular computer.

32. Use subroutine RAN0 to generate a set of five arrays of random numbers. The five arrays should be 10, 100, 1000, and 10,000 elements long. Then, use your elapsed time subroutines to determine the time that it takes subroutine **SORT** to sort each array. How does the elapsed time to sort increase as a function of the number of elements being sorted? *Hint:* On a fast computer, you may not be able to calculate the elapsed time required to sort the 10- and 100-element arrays—it may be too small for the quantization of your computer's system clock. If you have this problem, you can sort small arrays many times between calls to routines SET and ETIME, and get the average time for all calls. For example, the following code would calculate the time it takes to sort a 10-element array 100 times, and then get the average time per sort.

```
      PROGRAM TSTSRT
      INTEGER I, J, ISIZE, NLOOPS
      PARAMETER ( ISIZE = 10 )
      PARAMETER ( NLOOPS = 100 )
      REAL A(ISIZE), B(ISIZE)
C
C     Calculate random values
C
      DO 10 I = 1, ISIZE
         CALL RAN0 ( A(I) )
   10 CONTINUE
C
```

```
C       Start the timer.
C
        CALL SET
C
C       Main loop.
C
        DO 30 I = 1, NLOOPS
C
C          Copy array A to B
C
           DO 20 J = 1, ISIZE
              B(J) = A(J)
   20      CONTINUE
C
C          Sort array B.
C
           CALL SORT ( B, ISIZE )
C
   30   CONTINUE
C
C       Get elapsed time...
C
        CALL TIMER ( SEC )
C
C       Write out average time.
C
        WRITE (*,*) 'Average sort time = ', SEC / REAL(NLOOPS)
C
        END
```

33. The value of the exponential function e^x can be calculated by evaluating the following infinite series:

$$e^x = \sum_{n=0}^{\infty} \frac{x^n}{n!}$$

Write a FORTRAN function that calculates e^x using the first 12 terms of the infinite series. Compare the result of your function with the result of the intrinsic function EXP(X) for $x = -10, -5., -1., 0., 1., 5., 10.,$ and 15.

34. Use subroutine SIMUL to calculate the point at which the following lines intersect.

```
 W + 2X - 3Y + 2Z =  2
2W -  X      + 3Z = -4
-2W - 2X +  Y +  Z =  0
3W +  X +  Y - 2Z = -3
```

Check the answer produced by the subroutine by substituting the values for W, X, Y, and Z back into the equations.

35. Use subroutine RAN0 to generate an array containing 10,000 random numbers between 0.0 and 1.0. Then, use the statistics subroutines developed in this chapter to calculate the average and standard deviation of values in the array. The theoretical average of a uniform random distribution in the range $[0, 1)$ is 0.5, and the theoretical standard deviation of the uniform random distribution is $1/\sqrt{12}$. How close does the random array generated by RAN0 come to behaving like the theoretical distribution?

Character Variables

A **character variable** is a variable that contains character information. In this context, a "character" is any symbol found in a **character set.** There are two basic character sets in common use in the United States: EBCDIC and ASCII. The EBCDIC character set is used in IBM mainframes and compatibles, while the ASCII character set is used on essentially all of the other computers in the world. Both character sets include the digits 0-9, the uppercase letters A-Z, the lowercase letters a-z, and other specialized symbols such as +, -, *, /, !, etc. Most symbols appear in both of the character sets, but they are represented by different patterns of bits in each set. The ASCII and EBCDIC character sets are shown in Appendix A.

In many countries outside the United States, an extended ASCII character set is popular. The first 128 symbols of this character set are identical to ASCII. The next 128 symbols include the special letters and diacritical marks needed to write most European languages.

FORTRAN generally does not care about the difference between character sets. It takes each symbol and stores it in 1 byte of computer memory, whether that symbol is from an ASCII or an EBCDIC character set. All reads, writes, and assignments are the same regardless of character set. However, *some character comparisons and manipulations are character-set dependent.* If not handled properly, these dependencies could cause trouble when we try to move our code from one computer to another one. We will point out these dependencies and how to avoid them whenever we come to them.

7.1 DECLARING AND INITIALIZING CHARACTER VARIABLES

A character variable is declared using the **CHARACTER** type statement:

```
CHARACTER*<len> var1, ...
```

or

```
CHARACTER var1*<len>, ...
```

where len is the number of characters that can be stored in the character variable. The following are examples of legal character variable declarations:

```
CHARACTER*20 FILENM
CHARACTER FILEXT*3, DATE*8, TIME*8
```

Character variables may be initialized by assignment statements, by **DATA** statements, or by **READ** statements. A *character expression* may be assigned to a character variable with an assignment statement. If the character expression is *shorter* than the length of the character variable to which it is assigned, then the rest of the variable is padded out with blanks. For example, the statements

```
CHARACTER FILEXT*3
FILEXT = 'F'
```

store the value 'Fᵇᵇ' into variable FILEXT. If the character expression is *longer* than the length of the character variable to which it is assigned, then the portion of the expression that is longer than the length of the character variable is discarded. For example, the statements

```
CHARACTER FILEX1*3
FILEX1 = 'FILE01'
```

store the value 'FIL' into variable FILEX1, and the characters 'E01' are discarded. Character variables may also be initialized with **DATA** statements. The same rules apply here as for assignment statements:

```
CHARACTER FILEXT*3, FILEX1*3
DATA FILRXT, FILEX1 / 'F', FILE01' /
```

The above lines initialize FILEXT to 'Fᵇᵇ' and FILEX1 to 'FIL'.

The rules for reading and writing with character variables were explained in Chapter 4.

7.2   CHARACTER STRING MANIPULATIONS

FORTRAN 77 character strings can be manipulated in many different ways. A string may be subdivided into substrings using **substring specifications.** Conversely, two or more strings may be combined into a single larger string using a **concatenation operator.** Two strings may also be compared using **relational operators** or **lexical functions** to determine whether one of them is "greater than" the other one (we will define "greater than" for character strings later in the chapter).

7.2.1 Substring Specifications

A **substring specification** selects a portion of a character variable, and treats that portion as if it were an independent character variable. If the variable STR1 is a

CHARACTER*6 variable containing the string '123456', then the substring STR1(2:4) would be a three-character variable containing the string '234'. Note that the substring STR1(2:4) really refers to the same memory locations as characters 2–4 of STR1, so if the contents of STR1(2:4) are changed, the characters in the middle of variable STR will also be changed.

A character substring is denoted by placing integer values representing the starting and stopping character numbers in parentheses following the variable name (never use real values for this purpose). The starting and stopping character numbers must be separated by a colon. The stopping character number must always be greater than or equal to the starting number, or an error will be generated. For example, an expression like STR(4:3) is illegal, and will produce an error when the program is executed.

The following example illustrates the use of substrings.

EXAMPLE 7-1 *Substring Assignments* What will be the contents of variables B and C at the end of the following program?

```
PROGRAM TEST
CHARACTER*8 A, B, C
DATA B / '12345678' /
A = 'ABCDEFGHIJ'
C = A(5:7)
B(7:8) = A(2:6)
END
```

SOLUTION Initially, variable A contains 'ABCDEFGH', and variable B contains '12345678'. Line 5 assigns A(5:7) to variable C. Since C is eight characters long, five blanks are padded into variable C, and C will contain 'EFGbbbbb'. Line 6 assigns A(2:6) to B(7:8). Since B(7:8) is only two characters long, only the first two characters of A(2:6) are used. Therefore, variable B contains '123456BC'. ●

7.2.2 The Concatenation (//) Operator

It is also possible to combine two or more strings or substrings into a single large string. This operation is known as **concatenation.** The concatenation operator in FORTRAN is represented by a double slash with no space between the slashes (//). After the following lines are executed:

```
PROGRAM TEST
CHARACTER A*10, B*8, C*8
A = 'ABCDEFGHIJ'
B = '12345678'
C = A(1:3) // B(4:5) // A(6:8)
END
```
variable C will contain the string 'ABC45FGH'.

When using the concatenation operator, *you should be careful not to use the same variable on both sides of an assignment statement.* Consider the following code:

```
CHARACTER A*9
A = '12345678'
A = A(1:4) // '-' // A(5:8)
END
```

After these statements, A should contain '1234-5678'. Some FORTRAN compilers produce the correct answer, while others produce incorrect answers or abort when the statement is executed. The *safe* way to insert the dash into the middle of variable A is to *use a temporary variable to store the intermediate result* after the concatenation operation, and then to transfer the intermediate result back into A. The following code works correctly on all compilers:

```
CHARACTER A*9, TEMP*9
A = '12345678'
TEMP = A(1:4) // '-' // A(5:8)
A = TEMP
END
```

PROGRAMMING PITFALLS

Be careful not to use the same character variable on both sides of an assignment statement. If you do, your code may execute incorrectly on some computers. Use an intermediate temporary variable to avoid this problem.

7.3   CHARACTER COMPARISON OPERATIONS

Character strings may be compared to each other using either the relational operators that were introduced in Chapter 2, or some special character comparison functions that we will meet in this chapter. The character comparison functions, which are also called *lexical functions,* have an advantage over the relational operators when program portability is considered. We will now discuss both ways of comparing character strings.

7.3.1   The Relational Operators with Character Data

Character strings can be compared in logical expressions using the relational operators **.EQ., .NE., .LT., .LE., .GT.,** and **.GE.**. The result of the comparison is a logical value that is either TRUE or FALSE. For instance, the expression '123' **.EQ.** '123' is TRUE, while the expression '123' **.EQ.** '1234' is FALSE.

In standard FORTRAN 77, character strings may be compared with character strings, and numbers may be compared with numbers, but *character strings may not be compared to numbers*. Therefore, the expression

```
INTEGER I
I .EQ. '123'
```

will produce an error at compilation time.[1]

How are two characters compared to determine if one is greater than the other? The comparison is based on the **collating sequence** of the characters. The collating sequence of the characters is the order in which they occur within a specific character set. For example, the character 'A' is character number 65 in the ASCII character set, while the character 'B' is character number 66 in the set (see Appendix A). Therefore, the logical expression A **.LT.** B is TRUE in the ASCII character set. On the other hand, the character 'a' is character number 97 in the ASCII set, so 'a' is greater than 'A'.

Comparisons based on collating sequence are inherently dangerous, since different character sets have different collating sequences. For example, in the EBCDIC character set, 'a' is less than 'A', just the opposite of the ASCII character set. Code that depends on collating sequence is likely to fail when moved between computers!

We can make some comparisons safely regardless of character set. The FORTRAN 77 standard specifies that the letters 'A' to 'Z' must always be in alphabetical order, that the numbers '0' to '9' must always be in numerical sequence, and that the letters and numbers must not be intermingled in the collating sequence. Beyond that, however, all bets are off. The relationships among the special symbols and the relationship between the uppercase and lowercase letters may differ for different character sets and collating sequences. We must be very careful comparing strings! (There is a safe machine- and character set-independent way to compare characters, which we will introduce in a few moments).

How are two strings compared to determine if one is greater than the other? The comparison begins with the first character in each string. If they are the same, then the second two characters are compared. This process continues until the first difference is found between the strings. For example, 'AAAAAB' **.GT.** 'AAAAAA'.

What happens if the strings are different lengths? The comparison begins with the first letter in each string, and progresses through each letter until a difference is found. If the two strings are the same all the way to the end of one of them, then the other string is considered the larger of the two. Therefore

```
'AB' .GT. 'AAAA'   and   'AAAAA' .GT. 'AAAA'
```

EXAMPLE 7-2 *Alphabetizing Words*   It is often necessary to alphabetize lists of character strings (names, places, etc.). Write a subroutine that will accept a character array and alphabetize the data in the array.

---

[1]Some compilers permit such comparisons as an extension to standard FORTRAN 77, but *do not use this extension* if it is available to you. It makes your code nonportable between computers.

SOLUTION Since relational operators work for character strings the same way that they work for real values, it is easy to modify the sorting subroutine that we developed in the last chapter to alphabetize an array of character variables. All we have to do is to substitute character array declarations and I/O statements for the real declarations in the sorting routines. The rewritten program is shown in Figure 7-1:

```
      PROGRAM SORT4
C
C  Purpose:
C    To read in a CHARACTER input data set, sort it into ascending order
C    using the selection sort algorithm, and to write the sorted data
C    to the standard output device.  This program calls subroutine
C    SORTC to do the actual sorting.
C
C  Record of revisions:
C      Date        Programmer          Description of change
C      ====        ==========          =====================
C    07/03/91    S. J. Chapman         Original code
C
C  List of variables:
C    A       -- CHARACTER data array to sort.
C    EXCEED  -- Logical indicating that array limits are exceeded.
C    FILENM  -- Name of input data file to read.
C    I       -- Index variable.
C    ISTAT   -- I/O status variable:  0 for success
C    NVALS   -- Number of data values to sort.
C
      IMPLICIT NONE
C
C    Parameters
C
      INTEGER   MAXSIZ
      PARAMETER ( MAXSIZ = 10 )
C
C    Declare the variables used in this program.
C
      INTEGER      I, ISTAT, NVALS
      LOGICAL      EXCEED
      CHARACTER*20 A(MAXSIZ), TEMP
      CHARACTER*20 FILENM
C
C    Get the name of the file containing the input data.
C
      WRITE (*,1000)
 1000 FORMAT(1X,'Enter the file name containing the data to be sorted:')
      READ (*,1010) FILENM
 1010 FORMAT ( A20 )
C
C    Open input data file.  Status is OLD because the input data must
C    already exist.
C
      OPEN ( UNIT=9, FILE=FILENM, STATUS='OLD', IOSTAT=ISTAT )
C
C    Was the OPEN successful?
C
      IF ( ISTAT .EQ. 0 ) THEN
C
```

```
C          The file was opened successfully, so read the data to sort
C          from it, sort the data, and write out the results.
C
           READ (9, 1010, IOSTAT=ISTAT) TEMP
C
C          Begin WHILE loop.  Did we read the value successfully?
C
   10      IF ( ISTAT .EQ. 0 ) THEN
C
C             Yes.  Increment number of values.
C
              NVALS = NVALS + 1
C
C             Is NVALS <= MAXSIZ?  If so, store the value in array A.
C             If not, set the array size exceeded flag to .TRUE.
C
              IF ( NVALS .LE. MAXSIZ ) THEN
                 A(NVALS) = TEMP
              ELSE
                 EXCEED = .TRUE.
              END IF
C
C             Read next value.
C
              READ (9, 1010, IOSTAT=ISTAT) TEMP
              GO TO 10
C
C             End of WHILE Loop
C
           END IF
C
C          Was the array size exceeded?  If so, tell user and quit.
C
           IF ( EXCEED ) THEN
              WRITE (*,1020) NVALS, MAXSIZ
 1020         FORMAT (' Maximum array size exceeded: ', I6, '.', I6 )
           ELSE
C
C             Array size not exceeded.  Sort the data.
C
              CALL SORTC ( A, NVALS )
C
C             Now write out the sorted data.
C
              WRITE (*,1030) ' The sorted output data values are: '
 1030         FORMAT (A)
              WRITE (*,1040) ( A(I), I = 1, NVALS )
 1040         FORMAT (4X,A20)
           END IF
C
C          END of IF OPEN successful...
C
        END IF
C
        END
        SUBROUTINE SORTC ( ARRAY, N )
C
C Purpose:
C   To sort CHARACTER array ARRAY into ascending order using a selection
C   sort.
C
```

```
C  Record of revisions:
C      Date         Programmer          Description of change
C      ====         ==========          =====================
C   07/03/91     S. J. Chapman          Original code
C
C  List of calling arguments:
C     NAME    I/O  TYPE               DESCRIPTION
C     ====    ===  ====               ===========
C     ARRAY   IO   CHAR ARRAY    Input:  array to be sorted.
C                                Output: sorted array.
C     N       I    INTEGER       Number of values in array ARRAY.
C
C  List of local variables:
C     I      -- Index variable.
C     IPTR   -- Pointer to the smallest value found during a search.
C     J      -- Index variable.
C     TEMP   -- Temporary variable used to swap values in array.
C
      IMPLICIT NONE
C
C  Declare calling parameters.
C
      CHARACTER*20  ARRAY(*)
      INTEGER       N
C
C  Declare local variables.
C
      INTEGER I,. IPTR, J
      CHARACTER*80 TEMP
C
      DO 20 I = 1, N-1
C
C        Find the minimum value in ARRAY(I) through ARRAY(N)
C
         IPTR = I
         DO 10 J = I+1, N
            IF ( ARRAY(J) .LT. ARRAY(IPTR) ) THEN
               IPTR = J
            END IF
10       CONTINUE
C
C        IPTR now points to the minimum value, so swap A(IPTR) with A(I)
C        if I <> IPTR.
C
         IF ( I .NE. IPTR ) THEN
            TEMP        = ARRAY(I)
            ARRAY(I)    = ARRAY(IPTR)
            ARRAY(IPTR) = TEMP
         END IF
C
20    CONTINUE
C
C     Termination section.
C
      RETURN
      END
```

FIGURE 7-1 A program to alphabetize character strings using a version of the selection sort algorithm adapted for character strings.

To test this program, we will place the following character values in file INPUTC:

```
FORTRAN
fortran
ABCD
ABC
XYZZY
9.0
A9IDL
```

If we compile and execute the program on a computer with an ASCII collating sequence, the results of the test run are:

```
C:\BOOK\FORT>sort4
Enter the file name containing the data to be sorted:
inputc
The sorted output data values are:
   9.0
   A9IDL
   ABC
   ABCD
   FORTRAN
   XYZZY
   fortran
```

Note that the number 9 was placed before any of the letters, and that the lowercase letters were placed after the uppercase letters. These locations are in accordance with the ASCII table in Appendix A.

If this program were executed on a computer with the EBCDIC character set and collating sequence, the answer would have been different than the one given above. In exercise 7, at the end of this chapter, you will be asked to work out the expected output of this program if it were executed in an EBCDIC computer. ●

7.3.2 The **LLT**, **LLE**, **LGT**, and **LGE** Functions

The result of the program in the previous example depended on the character set and collating sequence of the characters in the computer on which it was executed. This dependence is bad, since it makes our FORTRAN program nonportable between computers. We need some way to ensure that programs produce the *same answer* regardless of the computer on which they are compiled and executed.

Fortunately, the FORTRAN 77 language includes a set of four logical intrinsic functions for just this purpose: **LLT** (lexically less than), **LLE** (lexically less than or equal to), **LGT** (lexically greater than), and **LGE** (lexically greater than or equal to). These functions are the exact equivalent of the relational operators .LT., .LE., .GT., and .GE., except that *they always compare characters according to the ASCII collating sequence, regardless of the computer they are running on*. If these functions are used instead of the relational operators to compare character strings, the results will be the same on every computer!

A simple example using the **LLT** function is shown below. Here, character variables STR1 and STR2 are being compared using the relational operator **.LT.** and the logical function **LLT.** The value of RES1 varies from computer to computer, but the value of RES2 is always TRUE on any computer.

```
LOGICAL RES1, RES2
CHARACTER*6 STR1, STR2
STR1 = 'A1'
STR2 = 'a1'
RES1 = STR1 .LT. STR2
RES2 = LLT ( STR1, STR2 )
END
```

■
GOOD PROGRAMMING PRACTICE

If there is any chance that your program will have to run on computers with both ASCII and EBCDIC character sets, use the logical functions **LLT, LLE, LGT,** and **LGE** to test for inequality between two character strings. *Do not use* the relational operators **.LT., .LE., .GT.,** and **.GE.** with character strings, since their results may vary from computer to computer.

■
EXAMPLE 7-3 *Using the Lexical Functions* Convert the character sorting subroutine SORTC from Example 7-2 to use the **LLT, LLE, LGT,** and **LGE** functions for string comparison in a computer-independent fashion.

SOLUTION   The rewritten subroutine is shown in Figure 7-2:

```
      SUBROUTINE SORTC ( ARRAY, N )
C
C  Purpose:
C    To sort CHARACTER array ARRAY into ascending order using a selection
C    sort.  This version of the SORT routine uses the lexical functions
C    for comparisons.
C
C  Record of revisions:
C      Date        Programmer          Description of change
C      ====        ==========          =====================
C    07/04/91    S. J. Chapman         Original code
C
C  List of calling arguments:
C    NAME    I/O  TYPE          DESCRIPTION
C    ====    ===  ====          ===========
C    ARRAY   IO   CHAR ARRAY    Input:  array to be sorted.
C                               Output: sorted array.
C    N       I    INTEGER       Number of values in array ARRAY.
C
C  List of local variables:
C    I       -- Index variable.
C    IPTR    -- Pointer to the smallest value found during a search.
```

```
C     J        -- Index variable.
C     TEMP     -- Temporary variable used to swap values in array.
C
      IMPLICIT NONE
C
C     Declare calling parameters.
C
      CHARACTER*20  ARRAY(*)
      INTEGER       N
C
C     Declare local variables.
C
      INTEGER I, IPTR, J
      CHARACTER*80 TEMP
C
      DO 20 I = 1, N-1
C
C        Find the minimum value in ARRAY(I) through ARRAY(N)
C
         IPTR = I
         DO 10 J = I+1, N
            IF ( LLT( ARRAY(J), ARRAY(IPTR) ) ) THEN
               IPTR = J
            END IF
10       CONTINUE
C
C        IPTR now points to the minimum value, so swap A(IPTR) with A(I)
C        if I <> IPTR.
C
         IF ( I .NE. IPTR ) THEN
            TEMP        = ARRAY(I)
            ARRAY(I)    = ARRAY(IPTR)
            ARRAY(IPTR) = TEMP
         END IF
C
20    CONTINUE
C
C     Termination section.
C
      RETURN
      END
```

FIGURE 7-2 The character sorting subroutine rewritten to use lexical functions.

Testing this subroutine is left as an exercise to the user. If you have access to a computer with an EBCDIC character set, try substituting this subroutine for the one in Example 7-2, and see what happens to the output data. ●

7.4 INTRINSIC CHARACTER FUNCTIONS

The FORTRAN language contains four other intrinsic functions which are important for manipulating character data. These functions are CHAR, ICHAR, LEN, and INDEX. We will now discuss these functions and describe their use.

The CHAR function converts an input integer value into a corresponding output character. An example of the CHAR function is shown below:

```
CHARACTER*1 OUT
INTEGER INPUT
INPUT = 65
OUT = CHAR(INPUT)
```

The input to the CHAR function is a single integer argument, and the output from the function is *the single character whose collating sequence number matches the input argument* for the particular computer. For example, if a computer uses the ASCII collating sequence, then CHAR(65) is the character 'A'.

The ICHAR function converts an input character into a corresponding output integer. An example of the ICHAR function is shown below:

```
CHARACTER*1 INPUT
INTEGER OUT
INPUT = 'A'
OUT = ICHAR(INPUT)
```

The input to the ICHAR function is a single character, and the output from the function is *the integer whose collating sequence number matches the input character* for the particular computer. For example, if a computer uses the ASCII collating sequence, then ICHAR('A') is the integer 65.

Function LEN returns the declared length of a character string. The input to LEN is a character string STR1, and the output from it is an integer containing the number of characters in STR1. An example of the LEN function is shown below:

```
CHARACTER*20 STR1
INTEGER OUT
STR1 = 'ABC'
OUT = LEN(STR1)
```

The output from LEN is 20. Note that the output of LEN is the declared size of the string, and *not* the number of nonblank characters in the string.

The INDEX function searches for a pattern in a character string. The inputs to the function are two strings: STR1 containing the characters to search, and STR2 containing the pattern that we are looking for. The output from the function is an integer containing the position in the character string STR1 at which the pattern was found. If no match is found, INDEX returns a 0. An example of the CHAR function is shown below:

```
CHARACTER STR1*20, STR2*6
INTEGER OUT
STR1 = 'THIS IS A TEST!'
STR2 = 'TEST'
OUT = INDEX(STR1,STR2)
```

The output of this function is the integer 11, since TEST begins at character 11 in the input character string.

TABLE 7-1 Some Common Character Intrinsic Functions

Function Name and Argument(s)	Argument Types	Result Type	Comments
LLT(STR1,STR2)	CHARACTER	LOGICAL	TRUE if STR1 < STR2 according to the ASCII collating sequence
LLE(STR1,STR2)	CHARACTER	LOGICAL	TRUE if STR1 ≤ STR2 according to the ASCII collating sequence
LGT(STR1,STR2)	CHARACTER	LOGICAL	TRUE if STR1 > STR2 according to the ASCII collating sequence
LGE(STR1,STR2)	CHARACTER	LOGICAL	TRUE if STR1 ≥ STR2 according to the ASCII collating sequence
CHAR(IVAL)	INTEGER	CHARACTER	Returns character corresponding to IVAL
ICHAR(CHAR)	CHARACTER	INTEGER	Returns integer corresponding to CHAR.
LEN(STR1)	CHARACTER	INTEGER	Returns length of STR1.
INDEX(STR1,STR2)	CHARACTER	INTEGER	Returns the character number of the first location in STR1 to contain the pattern in STR2. (0 =no match)

If STR2 were 'IS', then what would the value of INDEX(STR1,STR2) be? The answer is 3, since 'IS' occurs within the word 'THIS'. The INDEX function never sees the word 'IS' because it stops searching at the first occurrence of the search pattern in the string.

7.5 USER-DEFINED CHARACTER FUNCTIONS

User-defined functions may return character values. If a function returns a character value, it must be declared to be of type **CHARACTER** both in the function itself and in any routine that calls the function. Once the type declaration has been made, user-defined character functions are just like any other user defined function.

EXAMPLE 7-4 *Converting Numerical Representations of Months into Character Strings* Write a user-defined function that accepts a numerical representation of a month of the year (1–12), and converts it into a three-character string ('JAN' to 'DEC') describing the month.

SOLUTION   The function that converts the number of the month into a character string must be declared as **CHARACTER*3** both in the function itself and in any calling routines. A simple function to perform this task is shown in Figure 7-3:

```
      CHARACTER*3 FUNCTION MONTH ( IMONTH )
C
C Purpose:
C   To convert the numerical representation of a month into a 3-
C   character string representing the month.
C
C Record of revisions:
C     Date        Programmer           Description of change
C     ====        ==========           =====================
C   07/03/93    S. J. Chapman          Original code
C
C List of calling arguments:
C   NAME     I/O  TYPE       DESCRIPTION
C   ====     ===  ====       ===========
C   IMONTH    I   INTEGER    Number of month to convert.
C   MONTH     O   CHAR*3     Character string for month.
C
C List of local variables:
C   MONTHS -- Array of legal months
C
      IMPLICIT NONE
C
C   Declare calling parameters.
C
      INTEGER IMONTH
C
C   Declare local variables.
C
      CHARACTER*3 MONTHS(12)
C
C   Data
C
      DATA MONTHS / 'JAN', 'FEB', 'MAR', 'APR', 'MAY', 'JUN',
     *              'JUL', 'AUG', 'SEP', 'OCT', 'NOV', 'DEC' /
C
      IF ( ( IMONTH .GE. 1 ) .AND. ( IMONTH .LE. 12 ) ) THEN
C
C     Set character string for month.
C
         MONTH = MONTHS ( IMONTH )
C
      ELSE
C
C     Month out of range--return blanks.
C
         MONTH = '   '
C
      END IF
C
      RETURN
      END
```

FIGURE 7-3   A function that returns a character string corresponding to a particular month.

A test driver program for function MONTH is shown in Figure 7-4:

```
      PROGRAM TMONTH
C
C  Purpose:
C    To test function MONTH.
C
C  Record of revisions:
C      Date        Programmer         Description of change
C      ====        ==========         =====================
C    07/03/93    S. J. Chapman        Original code
C
C  List of local variables:
C    IMONTH -- Numerical representation of month
C    CMONTH -- Character representation of month
C
      IMPLICIT NONE
C
C  Declare external functions:
C
      CHARACTER*3 MONTH
C
C  Declare local variables.
C
      INTEGER IMONTH
C
C  Get number of month.
C
      WRITE (*,*) 'Enter number of month:'
      READ (*,*) IMONTH
C
C  Write character representation of month.
C
      WRITE (*,1000) IMONTH, MONTH(IMONTH)
 1000 FORMAT (1X,'The string for month number ',I2,' is ',A3,'.')
C
      END
```

FIGURE 7-4   Test driver program for function MONTH.

If the test driver program is executed, the results are

```
C:\BOOK\FORT>tmonth
Enter number of month:
4
The string for month number 4 is APR.

C:\BOOK\FORT>tmonth
Enter number of month:
10
The string for month number 10 is OCT.
```

Note that the function is correctly converting the number of a month into a character string corresponding to the month. ●

7.6   PASSING CHARACTER VARIABLES TO SUBROUTINES AND FUNCTIONS

In Example 7-2, we wrote a subroutine to alphabetize an array of character variables. The character array in that subroutine was declared as

```
INTEGER N
CHARACTER*20 ARRAY(N)
```

The subroutine sorts character arrays with any number of elements, as long as each element in the array is 20 characters long. If we wanted to sort data in an array whose elements were 21 characters long, then we would need a whole new subroutine to do it! This behavior is unreasonable. It should be possible to write a single subroutine to process character data in a given fashion, and allow that subroutine to use character array elements of whatever length is available.

FORTRAN contains just such a feature. The language allows a special form of the character type declaration for dummy character arguments in subprograms. This special declaration takes the form

```
CHARACTER*(*) string
```

where *string* is the name of a dummy character argument. This declaration says that dummy argument *string* is a character variable, but the length of the character variable is not explicitly known at compilation time. If the subroutine or function using *string* needs to know its length, it can call function LEN to get that information. The dummy arguments in subroutine SORTC could have been declared as

```
INTEGER N
CHARACTER*(*) ARRAY(N)
```

If they were declared in this manner, the subroutine would work equally well for arrays of character variables containing 1, 20, or even 80 characters per element.

Remember that *subroutine arguments are just placeholders* for the variables that will be passed to the subroutine when it is called. No actual memory is allocated in the subroutine for the dummy arguments. Since no memory is being allocated in the subroutine, the FORTRAN compiler does not need to know the length of the strings that will be passed to the subroutine when it executes. It needs to know that a character variable will be passed in a given argument, but not the length of the variable. Therefore, we can use the **CHARACTER*(*)** type declaration statement for dummy character arguments in a subroutine.

On the other hand, any character variables that are local to the subroutine must be declared with ordinary **CHARACTER*len** statements. Memory will be allocated in the subroutine for these local variables, and we must explicitly specify the length of each one for the compiler to know how much memory to allocate for it. In Example 7-2, TEMP is a local character variable in subroutine SORTC, and ARRAY is a dummy character argument in subroutine SORTC. Since TEMP is local to the subroutine, it must be declared with an explicit length. Since ARRAY is a dummy character argument, it could be declared with the **CHARACTER*(*)** statement.

If ARRAY is declared with the **CHARACTER * (*)** statement, subroutine SORTC will work correctly with character arrays containing up to 80 characters per element. The limitation on element size is caused by variable TEMP. Note that variable TEMP is declared to be an 80-character variable in subroutine SORTC. Since the temporary swap variable is 80 characters long, this subroutine will only work properly with a character array ARRAY whose elements are less than or equal to 80 characters long.

EXAMPLE 7-5 *Changing Case* We saw in Example 7-2 that lowercase character strings were not alphabetized properly with uppercase strings, since the collating sequence numbers of the lowercase letters were different from the collating sequence numbers of the corresponding uppercase letters. The difference between uppercase and lowercase letters also causes a problem when we are attempting to match a pattern within a character variable, since 'STRING' is not the same as 'string' or 'String'. It is often desirable to shift all character variables to uppercase to make matching and sorting easier. Write a subroutine to convert all of the lowercase letters in a character string to uppercase, while leaving any other characters in the string unaffected.

SOLUTION This problem is made more complicated by the fact that we don't know which collating sequence is used by the computer that the subroutine will be running on. Appendix A shows the two common collating sequences, ASCII and EBCDIC. If we look at Appendix A, we can see that *there is a fixed offset* between an uppercase letter and the corresponding lowercase letter in each collating sequence. However, that offset is different for the two sequences. Furthermore, the EBCDIC sequence complicates matters by inserting some non-alphabetical characters into the middle of the alphabet. These characters should not be affected by the uppercase shift. The ASCII character set is much simpler, since all letters are in order, and there are no nonalphabetical characters mixed into the middle of the alphabet. For simplicity in this example, we will assume that the ASCII collating sequence is used. (In exercise 17 at the end of this chapter, you will write a subroutine that works correctly in either the ASCII or the EBCDIC collating sequences.)

1. State the problem.
Write a subroutine to convert all of the lower case letters in a character string to upper case, while not affecting numeric and special characters. Design the subroutine to work properly in computers with the ASCII collating sequence.

2. Define the inputs and outputs.
The input to the subroutine is the character argument STRING. The output from the subroutine is also in STRING. STRING can be of arbitrary length.

3. Describe the algorithm.
If we look at the ASCII table in Appendix A, we note that the uppercase letters begin at sequence number 65, while the lowercase letters begin at sequence number

97. There are exactly 32 numbers between each uppercase letter and its lowercase equivalent.

This fact gives us our basic algorithm for shifting strings to uppercase. We determine if a character is lowercase. If it is, we subtract 32 from its sequence number to convert it to uppercase. The initial pseudocode for this algorithm is

```
Determine if character is lower case. If so,
   Convert to integer form
   Subtract 32 from the integer
   Convert back to character form
End of IF
```

The final pseudocode for this subroutine is

```
*   Get length of STRING
*
LENGTH ← LEN(STRING)
*
DO for I = 1 to LENGTH
   IF (STRING(I:I) >= 'a') .AND. (STRING(I:I) <= 'z') THEN
      S ← CHAR ( ICHAR (STRING(I:I) - 32 ) )
      STRING(I:I) ← S
   END of IF
END of DO
*
RETURN
END
```

where LENGTH is the length of the input character string. Note that we are using an intermediate character variable S to avoid using STRING(I:I) on both sides of an assignment statement. This is a safety precaution, since some compilers have problems with the same character string on both sides of an assignment statement. By writing the code this way, it should work on all computers.

4. Turn the algorithm into FORTRAN statements.

The resulting FORTRAN subroutines are shown in Figure 7-5.

```
      SUBROUTINE UCASE ( STRING )
C
C  Purpose:
C    To shift a character string to UPPER case (ASCII only)
C
C  Record of revisions:
C     Date        Programmer           Description of change
C     ====        ==========           =====================
C   07/05/91    S. J. Chapman          Original code
C
C  List of calling arguments:
C    NAME    I/O  TYPE          DESCRIPTION
C    ====    ===  ====          ===========
C    STRING  IO   CHARACTER     Input/output character string
C
```

```
C  List of local variables:
C     I       -- Index variable.
C     LENGTH -- Length of STRING
C     S       -- Converted character.
C
C     IMPLICIT NONE
C
C     Declare calling parameters
C
      CHARACTER*(*)  STRING
C
C     Declare local variables
C
      INTEGER     I, LENGTH
      CHARACTER*1 S
C
C     Get the length of the input STRING
C
      LENGTH = LEN ( STRING )
C
C     Now shift lower case letters to upper case.
C
      DO 10 I = 1, LENGTH
         IF ( ( STRING(I:I) .GE. 'a' ) .AND.
     *        ( STRING(I:I) .LE. 'z' ) ) THEN
            S = CHAR ( ICHAR ( STRING(I:I) ) - 32 )
            STRING(I:I) = S
         END IF
   10 CONTINUE
C
      RETURN
      END
```

FIGURE 7-5 Subroutine UCASE.

5. Test the resulting FORTRAN program.

To test this subroutine, it is necessary to write a driver program to read a character string, call the subroutine, and write out the results. A test driver program is shown in Figure 7-6:

```
      PROGRAM TUCASE
C
C  Purpose:
C    To test subroutine UCASE.
C
      IMPLICIT NONE
      CHARACTER*20 STRING
      WRITE (*,*) ' Enter test string (up to 20 characters): '
      READ (*,100) STRING
  100 FORMAT (A20)
      CALL UCASE(STRING)
      WRITE (*,*) ' The shifted string is: ', STRING
      END
```

FIGURE 7-6 Test driver program for subroutine UCASE.

The results from the test program for two input strings are

```
C:\BOOK\FORT>tucase
 Enter test string (up to 20 characters):
This is a test!...
 The shifted string is: THIS IS A TEST!...

C:\BOOK\FORT>tucase
 Enter test string (up to 20 characters):
abcf1234^&*$po()-
 The shifted string is: ABCF1234^&*$PO()-
```

The subroutine is shifting all lowercase letters to upper case, while leaving everything else alone. It appears to be working correctly. ●

QUIZ 7-1

This quiz provides a quick check to see if you have understood the concepts introduced in Sections 7.1 through 7.6. If you have trouble with the quiz, reread the sections, ask your instructor, or discuss the material with a fellow student. The answers to this quiz are found in the back of the book.

For questions 1–3, state the result of the following expressions. If the results depend on the character set used, state the result for both the ASCII and EBCDIC character sets.

1. `'abcde' .LT. 'ABCDE'`
2. `LLT ('abcde' , 'ABCDE')`
3. `'1234' .EQ. '1234 '`

For questions 4 and 5, state whether each of the following statements is legal or not. If they are legal, tell what they do. If they are not legal, state why they are not legal.

4.
```
CHARACTER STRING(20)
INTEGER I, J
DATA STRING / 'SOME DATA' /
DATA I / 37 /
J = I / 2 + 10
WRITE (*,*) STRING(I:J)
```

5.
```
FUNCTION DAY(IDAY)
IMPLICIT NONE
CHARACTER*3 DAY, DAYS(7)
INTEGER IDAY
DATA DAYS /'SUN', 'MON', 'TUE', 'WED', 'THU', 'FRI', 'SAT'/
IF ( ( IDAY .GE. 1 ) .AND. ( IDAY .LE. 7 ) ) THEN
   DAY = DAYS(IDAY)
END IF
RETURN
END
```

For questions 6–10, state the contents of each variable after the code has been executed.

6.
```
CHARACTER LAST*20, FIRST*20, MI*1
CHARACTER NAME*41
DATA LAST  / 'JOHNSON' /
DATA FIRST / 'JAMES' /
DATA MI    / 'R' /
NAME = LAST // ',' // FIRST // MI
```

7.
```
CHARACTER A*3, B*12
DATA A / '123' /
B = 'ABCDEFGHIJKLMNOPQRSTUVWXYZ'
B(5:8) = A(2:3)
```
8.
```
CHARACTER A1*4, A2*4 B*12, C*12
DATA A1, A2 / '1A', '1z' /
IF ( A1 .GT. A2 ) THEN
   B = 'A1 > A2'
ELSE
   B = 'A1 <= A2'
END IF
IF ( LGT (A1, A2 ) ) THEN
   C = 'A1 LGT A2'
ELSE
   C = 'A1 LLE A2'
END IF
```
9.
```
CHARACTER A1*4, C*12
INTEGER I, J
DATA A1, C / '1A', ' ' /
CALL SUB1 (A1, C, I, J)
END
SUBROUTINE SUB1 (STR1, STR2, LEN1, LEN2 )
CHARACTER*(*) STR1, STR2
INTEGER LEN1, LEN2
LEN1 = LEN(STR1)
LEN2 = LEN(STR2)
RETURN
END
```
10.
```
CHARACTER LINE*80
INTEGER IPOS1, IPOS2, IPOS3
LINE = 'This is a test line containing some input data!'
IPOS1 = INDEX (LINE, 'in')
IPOS2 = INDEX (LINE, 'Test')
IPOS3 = INDEX (LINE, 't l')
```

7.7 INTERNAL FILES

In the previous chapters of this book, we learned how to manipulate numeric data. So far in this chapter, we have learned how to manipulate character data. What we have *not* learned yet is how to convert numeric data into character data, and vice versa. There is a special mechanism in FORTRAN 77 for such conversions, known as **internal files.**

Internal files are a special extension of the FORTRAN I/O system in which the **READs** and **WRITEs** occur to internal character buffers (internal files) instead of disk files (external files). Anything that can be written to an external file can also be written to an internal file, where it will be available for further manipulation. Likewise, anything that can be read from an external file can be read from an internal file.

The general form of a **READ** from an internal file is

```
READ (buffer, format) arg1, arg2, ...
```

where *buffer* is the input character string, *format* is the format for the **READ,** and *arg1, arg2,* etc. are the values to be read from the buffer. The general form of a **WRITE** to an internal file is

```
WRITE (buffer,format) arg1, arg2, ...
```

where *buffer* is the output character string, *format* is the format for the **WRITE,** and *arg1, arg2,* etc. are the values to be written to the buffer.

A common use of internal files is to convert character data into numeric data, and vice versa. For example, if the character variable INPUT contains the string '135.4', the following code converts the character data into a real value:

```
      CHARACTER*5 INPUT
      REAL VALUE
      DATA INPUT / ' 135.4' /
      READ (INPUT,100) VALUE
100   FORMAT (F5.0)
```

Certain I/O features are not available with internal files. List-directed I/O statements may not be used with internal files, so if INPUT is a character variable, a statement like the following is illegal, and will produce an error at compilation time:

```
READ (INPUT,*) VALUE
```

The format of the conversions must be explicitly specified with internal files. Also, the **OPEN, CLOSE, BACKSPACE,** and **REWIND** statements may not be used with them.

■ **GOOD PROGRAMMING PRACTICE**

Use internal files to convert data from character format to numeric format, and vice versa.

7.8 CHARACTER STRINGS IN FORTRAN I/O STATEMENTS

In Chapter 4, we learned that the general form of a FORTRAN **WRITE** statement is

```
WRITE (lu,label) output list
```

where *lu* is the logical unit number to write the data to, and *label* is the label number of the **FORMAT** statement describing how the data is to be written out. To direct the output data to a specific location (screen, file, etc.), we would associate that location with an LU number, and then write to that LU. To output data in a specific format, we would place the format descriptors in a **FORMAT** statement and include the label of that statement in the **WRITE.**

Now that we have learned about character strings and variables, we can discuss some generalizations of FORTRAN I/O statements. We already know that we can substitute a character variable for the logical unit number in a **WRITE** statement. If we do so, then we are writing to an internal file, which is just a character variable within the program's memory.

It is also possible to substitute a character expression or variable for the **FORMAT** statement number in a **WRITE** statement. Recall that a **FORMAT** statement is just a character string describing how the data is to be formatted. FORTRAN permits us to place the character string directly in the *format* location of the **WRITE** statement, instead of writing it in a separate **FORMAT** statement. The following three **WRITE** statements are all equivalent:

```
      WRITE (*,100) A, B
  100 FORMAT (1X,2F10.4)

      CHARACTER*12 FMT
      FMT = '(1X,2F10.4)'
      WRITE (*,FMT) A, B

      WRITE (*,'(1X,2F10.4)') A, B
```

The first **WRITE** statement uses a conventional **FORMAT** statement to describe the format of the output data. In the second example, we are storing the format information in a character variable, and then naming that variable in the **WRITE** statement. This second approach is very useful, since we can modify the contents of the format *while the program is executing,* and adapt our format information to the type of data received by the program. In the third example, the character string is included directly in the **WRITE** statement (note that the string must be in single quotes). This type of format is convenient for small I/O statements, since all of the information is on a single line, and the programmer doesn't have to go look for a **FORMAT** statement before he or she can figure out what the **WRITE** statement is doing.

All of these formatting options are valid for both **READ** and **WRITE** statements.

■
EXAMPLE 7-6 *Varying a FORMAT to Match the Data to Be Output* So far, we have seen two ways to write out a real data value. The first way uses the F*w.d* format descriptor to display the data in a format with a fixed decimal point, and the second way uses the E*w.d* format descriptor to display the data in exponential notation. The F format descriptor displays data in a manner that is easier for a person to understand quickly, but it will fail to display the number correctly if the absolute value of the number is either too small or too large. The E format descriptor displays the number correctly regardless of size, but it is harder for a person to read at a glance.

Write a FORTRAN function that will convert a real number into characters for display in a 12-character-wide field. The function should check the size of the number to be printed out, and modify the format statement to display the data in F12.4 format for as long as possible until the absolute value of the number either gets too big or too small. When the number is out of range for the F format, the function should switch to E format.

SOLUTION In the F12.4 format, the function displays four digits to the right of the decimal place. One additional digit is required for the decimal point, and another one is required for the minus sign, if the number is negative. After subtracting those characters, there are seven characters left over for positive numbers, and six characters left over for negative numbers. Therefore, we must convert the number to exponential notation for any positive number larger than 9,999,999, and any negative number smaller than −999,999.

If the absolute value of the number to be displayed is smaller than 0.01, then the display should shift to E format, because there will not be enough significant digits displayed by the F12.4 format. However, an exact zero value should be displayed in normal F notation rather than exponential notation.

When it is necessary to switch to exponential format, we will use the 1PE12.5 format, since having a significant digit to the left of the decimal point makes the number appear in ordinary scientific notation. It also saves one character in the display, because we will not be wasting a character displaying a 0 to the left of the decimal point.

1. State the problem.

Write a function to convert a real number into 12 characters for display in a 12-character-wide field. Display the number in F12.4 format if possible, unless the number overflows the format descriptor or gets too small to display with enough precision in an F12.4 field. When it is not possible to display the number in F12.4 format, switch to the 1PE12.5 format. However, display an exact zero in F12.4 format.

2. Define the inputs and outputs.

The input to the function is a real number passed through the argument list. The function returns a 12-character expression containing the number in a form suitable for displaying.

3. Describe the algorithm.

The basic requirements for this function were discussed above. The pseudocode to implement these requirements is shown below:

```
IF VALUE > 9999999. THEN
    Use 1PE12.5 format
ELSE IF VALUE < -999999. THEN
    Use 1PE12.5 format
ELSE IF VALUE = 0. THEN
    Use F12.4 format
ELSE IF ABS(VALUE) < 0.01
    Use 1PE12.5 format
ELSE
    USE F12.4 format
END of IF
WRITE value to buffer using specified format
```

4. Turn the algorithm into FORTRAN statements.

The resulting FORTRAN function is shown in Figure 7-7. Function RE2CHR illustrates both how to use internal files and how to use a character variable to contain format descriptors. The proper format descriptor for the real-to-character conversion is stored in variable FMT, and an internal **WRITE** operation is used to write the character string into buffer STRING.

```
      FUNCTION RE2CHR ( VALUE )
C
C  Purpose:
C    To convert a real value into a 13-character string, with the number
C    printed in as readable a format as possible considering its range.
C    This routine prints out the number according to the following rules:
C       1.  VALUE > 9999999.           1PE12.5
C       2.  VALUE < -999999.           1PE12.5
C       3.  0.   < ABS(VALUE) < 0.01   1PE12.5
C       5.  VALUE = 0.0                F12.4
C       6.  Otherwise                  F12.4
C
C  Record of revisions:
C     Date       Programmer          Description of change
C     ====       ==========          =====================
C    07/11/91    S. J. Chapman       Original code
C
C  List of calling arguments:
C     NAME    I/O  TYPE           DESCRIPTION
C     ====    ===  ====           ===========
C     VALUE    I   REAL           Value to convert to character form.
C     RE2CHR   O   CHARACTER*12   Output character string.
C
C  List of local variables:
C     FMT    -- Variable containing format.
C     STRING -- Buffer to hold output characters.
C
      IMPLICIT NONE
C
C     Declare calling parameters.
C
```

```
      REAL         VALUE
      CHARACTER*12  RE2CHR
C
C     Declare local variables.
C
      CHARACTER FMT*9, STRING*12
C
C     Select proper format
C
      IF ( VALUE .GT. 9999999. ) THEN
         FMT = '(1PE12.5)'
      ELSE IF ( VALUE .LT. -999999. ) THEN
         FMT = '(1PE12.5)'
      ELSE IF ( VALUE .EQ. 0. ) THEN
         FMT = '(F12.4)'
      ELSE IF ( ABS(VALUE) .LT. 0.01 ) THEN
         FMT = '(1PE12.5)'
      ELSE
         FMT = '(F12.4)'
      END IF
C
C     Convert to character form.
C
      WRITE (STRING,FMT) VALUE
      RE2CHR = STRING
C
      RETURN
      END
```

FIGURE 7-7   Character function RE2CHR.

5. Test the resulting FORTRAN program.

To test this function, it is necessary to write a driver program to read a real number, call the subroutine, and write out the results. A test driver program is shown in Figure 7-8:

```
      PROGRAM TRE2CH
C
C  Purpose:
C    To test function RE2CHR.
C
C  Record of revisions:
C      Date        Programmer           Description of change
C      ====        ==========           =====================
C    07/11/91    S. J. Chapman          Original code
C
C  External routines:
C    RE2CHR -- Convert real to character string
C    UCASE  -- Shift string to upper case
C
C  List of local variables:
C    CH     -- Character variable to hold Y/N response.
C    CONV   -- Logical flag to control WHILE loop.
C    VALUE  -- Value to be converted.
C
```

```
      IMPLICIT NONE
C
      REAL      VALUE
      CHARACTER RE2CHR*12, CH*1
      LOGICAL   CONV
C
C     Begin WHILE loop.
C
      CONV = .TRUE.
    1 IF ( CONV ) THEN
C
C        Prompt for input value.
C
         WRITE (*,'(1X,A)') 'Enter value to convert:'
         READ (*,*) VALUE
C
C        Write converted value, and see if we want another.
C
         WRITE (*,'(1X,A,A,A)') 'The result is ', RE2CHR(VALUE),
     *                          ': Convert another one? (Y/N) [N]'
C
C        Get answer.
C
         READ (*,'(A)') CH
C
C        Convert answer to upper case to make match.
C
         CALL UCASE ( CH )
C
C        Do another?
C
         IF ( CH .EQ. 'Y' ) THEN
            CONV = .TRUE.
         ELSE
            CONV = .FALSE.
         END IF
C
         GO TO 1
      END IF
C
      END
```

FIGURE 7-8   Test driver program for function RE2CHR.

To verify that this function is working correctly for all cases, we must feed it values that fall within each of the ranges that it is designed to test for. Therefore, we will test it with the following numbers:

```
0.
0.001234567
1234.567
12345678.
-123456.7
-1234567.
```

The results from the test program for the six input values are

```
C:\BOOK\FORT>tre2ch
Enter value to convert:
0.
The result is        .0000: Convert another one? (Y/N) [N] .
y
Enter value to convert:
0.001234567
The result is 1.23457E-03: Convert another one? (Y/N) [N]
Y
Enter value to convert:
1234.567
The result is   1234.5670: Convert another one? (Y/N) [N]
Y
Enter value to convert:
12345678.
The result is 1.23457E+07: Convert another one? (Y/N) [N]
y
Enter value to convert:
-123456.7
The result is -123456.7000: Convert another one? (Y/N) [N]
y
Enter value to convert:
-1234567.
The result is -1.23457E+06: Convert another one? (Y/N) [N]
n
```

The function appears to be working correctly for all possible input values.   ●

The test program TRE2CH also contains a few interesting features. Since we would normally use the program to test more than one value, it is structured as a while loop. The user is prompted by the program to determine whether or not to repeat the loop. The first character of the user's response is stored in variable CH, and is compared to the character 'Y'. If the user responded with a 'Y', the loop is repeated; otherwise, it is terminated. Note that subroutine UCASE is called to shift the contents of CH to uppercase, so that both 'y' and 'Y' are interpreted as yes answers. This form of repetition control is very useful in interactive FORTRAN programs.

EXAMPLE   7-7   *Plotting Data* It is often useful for an engineer to get a plot of a data set, so that he or she can see just what it looks like. A plot will show patterns in the data that are not obvious when a person is just scanning a column of numbers.

The best plots available are the high-resolution plots generated by plotters, laser printers, and similar devices, using special programs to generate control codes used by the devices. These devices and programs are expensive and may not always be available. If they are not available, it is still possible for anyone with access to a computer to plot a data set by creating a *line printer plot* with a simple FORTRAN subroutine.

A line printer plot is a plot composed of characters placed in specific columns corresponding to the values in the data set. It is low resolution, because the number of columns on a line printer are limited. However, it does have the advantage that it doesn't cost anything!

We will write a subroutine to make a line printer plot of a data set whose samples were taken at regular intervals. (Exercise 27, at the end of the chapter, asks us to write a more general plotting subroutine that supports samples taken at arbitrary intervals.) The upper and lower limits of the plot should be under user control, and it should be possible to calculate default limits based on the values in the data set.

SOLUTION The plot subroutine will need to plot the data in a fixed number of columns small enough to fit on the line printer that the plot will be printed on. Since we do not know how wide a particular printer will be, this plot will be designed to fit on an 80-column printer, which is the smallest size that we will normally encounter. If we allocate 15 characters for printing out the values of the data points, then the plotting area can be 65 characters wide.

The plotting routine will first need to determine the minimum and maximum values to plot. These values can either be passed from the calling program, or they can be calculated from the largest and smallest numbers in the data set. Once we know what the largest and smallest values to plot are, we can divide the difference between those numbers into 65 evenly spaced bins. For each data point, if the point falls within a specific bin, then an asterisk will be printed out in that bin.

1. State the problem.

Write a subroutine that will generate an 80-character-wide line printer plot on a user-specified LU number for an input data set containing values sampled at regular intervals. The maximum and minimum values to plot may either be specified by the calling routine, or they may be calculated by default in the plot subroutine. The subroutine should also write out the actual values being plotted.

2. Define the inputs and outputs.

The inputs to this subroutine are:

a. A real array Y containing the data to plot.
b. The number of points NPTS in the array.
c. The minimum value MINVAL and the maximum value MAXVAL to plot.
d. A default flag DEFALT to tell the subroutine to calculate its own plotting limits.
e. The logical unit number LU to send the plot to.

The outputs from the program are the individual lines of the plot, sent to logical unit LU.

3. Describe the algorithm.
The basic pseudocode for this program is

```
IF DEFALT THEN
    Calculate the limits of the plot
End of IF
Write out an upper border for the plot
DO for I = 1 to NPTS
    Set left & right borders of plot
    Set zero position for plot
    Place asterisk in col corresponding to Y(I)
    Write out Y(I) and plot line
End of DO
Write out a lower border for the plot
Write out number of points plotted
```

4. Turn the algorithm into FORTRAN statements.
The resulting FORTRAN subroutine is shown in Figure 7-9. Note that we are using subroutines RMIN and RMAX from Chapter 6 to determine the smallest and largest values in the input array, and function RE2CHR to print out the values of the data points in an easy-to-read manner that works for all possible input values. We are taking advantage of our previous work, and not having to reinvent the wheel!

```
      SUBROUTINE PLOT ( Y, NPTS, MINVAL, MAXVAL, DEFALT, LU )
C
C Purpose:
C   Subroutine to plot the points in array Y.  The data in the
C   array is assumed to be at a uniform spacing.
C
C Record of revisions:
C     Date        Programmer          Description of change
C     ====        ==========          =====================
C   07/01/91    S. J. Chapman         Original code
C
C List of calling arguments:
C   NAME     I/O  TYPE         DESCRIPTION
C   ====     ===  ====         ===========
C   DATA1    I    REAL ARRAY   Data to plot.
C   NPTS     I    INTEGER      Number of points to plot.
C   MINBIN   I    REAL         Smallest value to plot.
C   MAXBIN   I    REAL         Largest value to plot.
C   DEFALT   I    LOGICAL      Flag to set default bins.
C   LU       I    INTEGER      Output LU to plot on.
C
C List of external references:
C   RE2CHR -- Function to convert real data to character format
C   RMAX   -- Subroutine to find the max value in an array
C   RMIN   -- Subroutine to find the min value in an array
C
C List of parameters:
C   NBINS  -- Number of bins over which to plot Y
C
C List of local variables:
C   ANNOT  -- Char variable to contain annotation (Y-amplitude)
C   I      -- Loop index
C   IBIN   -- Bin number for current Y value
C   IBIN0  -- Bin number for zero-crossing
C   IMAX   -- Location of max value in input array
```

```
C       IMIN    -- Location of min value in input array
C       FRAC    -- Fraction of plot width at which to position data
C       MAXAMP  -- Amplitude of max sample in Y array
C       MINAMP  -- Amplitude of min sample in Y array
C       PLTBUF  -- Plotting buffer
C       SCL   . -- Scale on border of plot
C
        IMPLICIT NONE
C
C       Calling arguments.
C
        INTEGER NPTS, LU
        REAL    Y(NPTS), MINVAL, MAXVAL
        LOGICAL DEFALT
C
C       Declare external function.
C
        CHARACTER*12 RE2CHR
C
C       Parameters
C
        INTEGER    NBINS
        PARAMETER ( NBINS = 65 )
C
C       Local variables.
C
        CHARACTER PLTBUF*65, ANNOT*14
        CHARACTER SCL*65
        SAVE      SCL
        REAL      MAXAMP, MINAMP, FRAC
        INTEGER   I, IMAX, IMIN, IBIN, IBINO
C
C       Data
C
        DATA SCL( 1:30) /'+-----------------------------' /
        DATA SCL(31:60) /'------------------------------' /
        DATA SCL(61:65) /'----+' /
C
C       If the scales are defaulted, set min and max of Y axis.
C
        IF ( DEFALT ) THEN
C
C          Get the largest and smallest values in the data array.
C
           CALL RMAX ( Y, NPTS, MAXAMP, IMAX )
           CALL RMIN ( Y, NPTS, MINAMP, IMIN )
C
C          Set default values for range of Y axis.
C
           MAXVAL = MAXAMP
           MINVAL = MINAMP
        END IF
C
C       We will divide MINVAL to MAXVAL into 65 bins for
C       plotting purposes.  Locate the zero bin, if it is
C       between MINVAL and MAXVAL.
C
        IF ( (MAXVAL .GT. 0.) .AND. (MINVAL .LT. 0) ) THEN
           FRAC = ( 0. - MINVAL) / (MAXVAL - MINVAL )
           IBINO = NINT ( (NBINS-1) * FRAC ) + 1
```

```
            ELSE
                IBINO = 0
            END IF
C
C       Set zero into border of plot, if it is within
C       the limits of the plot.
C
            ANNOT = ' '
            IF ( IBINO .GT. 0 ) THEN
                SCL(IBINO:IBINO) = '+'
            END IF
C
C       Print upper border.
C
            WRITE (LU,1000) RE2CHR(MINVAL), RE2CHR(MAXVAL)
   1000 FORMAT (10X,A,46X,A)
            WRITE (LU,'(A,1X,A)') ANNOT, SCL
C
C       Plot data points.
C
            DO 40 I = 1, NPTS
C
C           Clear line
C
                PLTBUF = ' '
                ANNOT  = ' '
C
C           Set value of Y data point.
C
                ANNOT(2:13) = RE2CHR ( Y(I) )
C
C           Set min and max borders.
C
                PLTBUF(1:1)   = '|'
                PLTBUF(65:65) = '|'
C
C           Set zero line, if within borders.
C
                IF ( IBINO .GT. 0 ) THEN
                    PLTBUF(IBINO:IBINO) = '|'
                END IF
C
C           Plot point on array.
C
                FRAC = ( Y(I) - MINVAL ) / ( MAXVAL - MINVAL )
                IBIN = NINT ( (NBINS-1) * FRAC ) + 1
                IF ( (IBIN .GE. 1) .AND. (IBIN .LE. NBINS) ) THEN
                    PLTBUF(IBIN:IBIN) 5 '*'
                END IF
C
C           Write out line.
C
                WRITE (LU,'(A,1X,A)') ANNOT, PLTBUF
C
     40 CONTINUE
C
C       Print amplitude scale at bottom of plot.
C
            ANNOT = ' '
            WRITE (LU,'(A,1X,A)') ANNOT, SCL
            WRITE (LU,1000) RE2CHR(MINVAL), RE2CHR(MAXVAL)
```

```
C
C      Print out summary info.
C
       WRITE (LU,'(/,10X,A,I12)' ) 'Number of Points = ', NPTS
C
       RETURN
       END
```

FIGURE 7-9   Subroutine PLOT.

5. Test the resulting FORTRAN program.

To test this subroutine, we will write a driver program that generates a data set based on the function

$$y(t) = 10\ e^{-0.2t}\ \sin t$$

and call the plot subroutine with that data. The test driver program TPLOT is shown in Figure 7-10.

```
       PROGRAM TPLOT
C
C  Purpose:
C    Program to test subroutine PLOT.  This program generates
C    a data set based on the function:
C       Y(T) =  10. * EXP (-T/5) * SIN (T)
C    starting at T = 0 for 12 seconds, with a step size DT = 1/3.
C
       IMPLICIT NONE
C
       REAL     Y(0:36), MINVAL, MAXVAL
       INTEGER NPTS, LU, I
       LOGICAL DEFALT
C
C      Generate function.
C
       DO 10 I = 0, 36
          Y(I) = 10. * EXP ( -REAL(I) / 15. ) * SIN ( REAL(I) / 3. )
    10 CONTINUE
C
C      Set up call to plot.
C
       NPTS   = 37
       MINVAL = 0.
       MAXVAL = 0.
       DEFALT = .TRUE.
       LU     = 6
C
       CALL PLOT ( Y, NPTS, MINVAL, MAXVAL, DEFALT, LU )
C
       END
```

FIGURE 7-10   Test driver program for subroutine PLOT.

A plot of the input function is shown in Figure 7-11(a), and the output of the line printer plot is shown in Figure 7-11(b). The line printer plot gives us a good idea of the overall behavior of the data set. ●

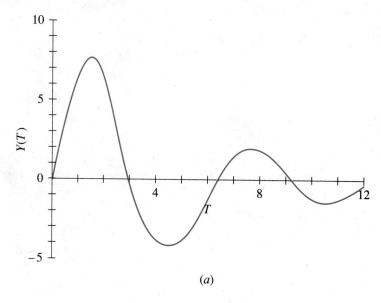

(a)

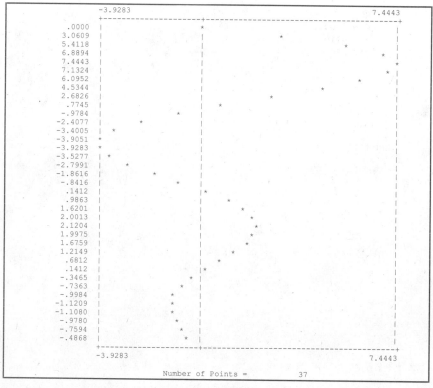

(b)

FIGURE 7-11 (a) Plot of function $y(t) = 10e^{-0.2t} \sin t$. (b) Line printer plot of the function produced by subroutine PLOT.

QUIZ 7-2

This quiz provides a quick check to see if you have understood the concepts introduced in Sections 7.7 and 7.8. If you have trouble with the quiz, reread the sections, ask your instructor, or discuss the material with a fellow student. The answers to this quiz are found in the back of the book.

For questions 1–4, state whether each of the following groups of statements is correct or not. If correct, describe the results of the statements.

1.
```
REAL         VALUE
CHARACTER IDENT*11
VALUE = -333.4
IDENT = '999-99-9999'
WRITE (*,'(1X,A15,3X,F10.4)') VALUE, IDENT
```

2.
```
CHARACTER BUFF*24, BUFF1*24
INTEGER I
DATA BUFF / '(T20,'OUTPUT:',/,T20,I6)'/
DATA BUFF1 / 'ABCDEFGHIJKLMNOPQRSTYVWX'/
DATA I / -1234 /
IF ( BUFF1(20:20) .EQ. 'S' ) THEN
    BUFF(20:20) = '3'
END IF
WRITE (*,BUFF) I
```

3.
```
CHARACTER OUTBUF*80
INTEGER I, J, K
I = 123
J = 1023 / 1024
K = -11
WRITE (OUTBUF,*) I, J, K
```

4.
```
CHARACTER LINE*30, FMT*30
INTEGER IVAL1, IVAL2
REAL RVAL3
DATA LINE / '123456789012345678901234567890'/
DATA FMT  / '(3X,I6,12X,I3,F6.2)            '/
READ (LINE,FMT) IVAL1, IVAL2, RVAL3
```

7.9   SUMMARY

A character variable is a variable that contains character information. Character variables are declared using the **CHARACTER** type definition statement, and initialized using assignment statements, **DATA** statements, or FORTRAN **READ** statements.

A substring of a character variable may be selected using a substring specification, such as STR1(1:6). Here, STR1(1:6) refers to the first six characters of character variable STR1.

Two or more character strings may be combined using the concatenation operator (//).

Two character strings may be compared using the relational operators. However, the result of the comparison may differ depending on the collating sequence of the characters on a particular computer. It is safer to test character strings for inequality using the lexical functions, which always return the same value on any computer regardless of collating sequence.

Internal files provide a means to convert data from character form to numeric form and vice versa within a FORTRAN program. They involve writes to and reads from a character variable within the program.

Character strings and variables may also be used to contain format information for I/O operations. The major advantage of storing the formatting information in a character variable is that it can be modified during program execution, if necessary.

7.9.1   Summary of Good Programming Practice

The following guidelines should be adhered to when working with character variables:

1. Do not use the same character variable on both sides of an assignment statement. Instead, use a temporary character variable to store an intermediate result before assigning it back to the character variable. This action helps make your code more portable, since not all compilers can handle such assignments properly.

2. Use the lexical functions rather than the relational operators to compare two character strings for inequality. This action avoids potential problems when a program is moved from a computer with an ASCII character set to a computer with an EBCDIC character set.

3. Use the **CHARACTER*(*)** type statement to declare character variables in subprograms. This feature allows the program to work with strings of arbitrary lengths. If the subroutine needs to know the actual length of a particular variable, it may call the LEN function with that variable as a calling argument.

CHAPTER 7 KEY WORDS

ASCII character set	Concatenation
Character set	EBCDIC character set
Character variable	Substring specification
Collating sequence	

CHAPTER 7 SUMMARY OF FORTRAN STATEMENTS AND STRUCTURES

Internal READ Statement:

```
READ (buffer,label) output list
```

Example:

```
        READ (LINE,100) I, J, SLOPE
100 FORMAT ( 1X, 2I10, F10.2 )
```

Description: The internal **READ** statement reads the data in the input list according to the formats specified in the **FORMAT** statement with statement label *label.* The data is read from the internal character variable *buffer.*

Internal WRITE Statement:

```
WRITE (buffer,label) output list
```

Example:

```
        WRITE (LINE,100) I, J, SLOPE
100 FORMAT ( 1X, 2I10, F10.2 )
```

Description: The internal **WRITE** statement writes the data in the output list according to the formats specified in the **FORMAT** statement with statement label *label.* The data is written to the internal character variable *buffer.*

CHAPTER 7 EXERCISES

1. Determine the contents of each variable in the following code fragment after the code has been executed:

```
CHARACTER A*16, B*16, C*16
DATA A /'1234567890123456'/
DATA B /'ABCDEFGHIJKLMNOP'/
C = A(6:8)
C(10:12) = B(9:11)
```

2. Determine the contents of each variable in the following code fragment after the code has been executed:

```
CHARACTER A*16, B*16, C*16
DATA A /'1234567890123456'/
DATA B /'ABCDEFGHIJKLMNOP'/
C = A(3:8) // '-' // B(9:12)
C(8:11) = B(2:4)
```

3. Determine the contents of each variable in the following code fragment after the code has been executed:

```
CHARACTER A*16, B*16, C*16
DATA A /'1234567890123456'/
DATA B /'ABCDEFGHIJKLMNOP'/
IF ( A .GT. B ) THEN
    C = A(1:6) // B(7:12) // A(13:16)
ELSE
    C = B(7:12) // A(1:6) // A(13:16)
END IF
A(7:9) = '='
B(10:12) = C(1:3)
```

4. Determine the contents of each variable in the following code fragment after the code has been executed. How does the behavior of this code fragment differ from the behavior of the one in exercise 3?

```
CHARACTER A*16, B*16, C*16
DATA A /'1234567890123456'/
DATA B /'ABCDEFGHIJKLMNOP'/
IF ( LGT(A,B) ) THEN
    C = A(1:6) // B(7:12) // A(13:16)
ELSE
    C = B(7:12) // A(1:6) // A(13:16)
END IF
A(7:9) = '='
B(10:12) = C(1:3)
```

5. Determine the contents of each variable in the following code fragment after the code has been executed:

```
CHARACTER A*16, B*16, C*2
DATA A /'1234567890123456'/
DATA B /'ABCDEFGHIJKLMNOP'/
C = A(1:8) // B(9:12)
A = C // B
```

6. Determine the contents of each variable in the following code fragment after the code has been executed. Will the results of this code fragment be the same on computers with both ASCII and EBCDIC collating sequences, or will the results differ?

```
CHARACTER STR1*9, STR2*18, TEMP*6
INTEGER BASE1, BASE2
BASE1 = ICHAR ( 'A' ) - 1
BASE2 = ICHAR ( 'a' ) - 1
DO 10 I = 1, 10
    STR1(I:I) = CHAR(I+BASE1)
    STR2(I:I) = CHAR(I+BASE2)
10 CONTINUE
TEMP = STR2(6:20)
STR2 = STR1 // TEMP
```

7. Determine the order in which the character strings in Example 7-2 would be sorted by the subroutine SORTC, if executed in a computer using the EBCDIC collating sequence.

8. Rewrite subroutine UCASE as a character function.

9. Write a subroutine that will properly alphabetize an array of character strings *without regard to the case of the letters* on a computer with an ASCII collating sequence. The subroutine must preserve the actual input data as a part of the sorting process. (In other words, the subroutine cannot modify the input strings to make them all uppercase or all lowercase.)

10. Write a subroutine LCASE that converts an ASCII string to lowercase.

11. Write a subroutine LCASE that converts an EBCDIC string to lowercase.

12. Determine the order in which the following character strings will be sorted by the subroutine SORTC of Example 7-2(*a*) according to the ASCII collating sequence, and (*b*) according to the EBCDIC collating sequence.

```
'This is a test!'
'?well?'
'AbCd'
'aBcD'
'1DAY'
'2nite'
'/DATA/'
'quit'
```

13. Determine the contents of each variable in the following code fragment after the return from the subroutine call:

```
CHARACTER*10 I, J, K*20, L*2
INTEGER LENC, I1, I2
DATA I1, I2 /7, 9/
I = '0987654321'
J = 'ABCDEFGHIJ'
L = J(I1:I2)
CALL CSUB (I, J, K, LENC)
END
SUBROUTINE CSUB (A, B, C, LENC )
CHARACTER*(*) A, B, C
INTEGER LENC
C = A(LEN(A)-2:LEN(A)) // B(3:LEN(B))
LENC = LEN ( C )
RETURN
END
```

14. Determine the contents of each variable in the following code fragment after the code has been executed:

```
      CHARACTER*132 BUFFER
      REAL A, B
      INTEGER I, J
      I = 1700
      J = 2400
      A = REAL ( 1700 / 2400 )
      B = REAL ( 1700 ) / 2400
      WRITE (BUFFER,100) I, J, A, B
100 FORMAT ( T11,I10,T31,I10,T51,F10.4,T28,F10.4)
```

15. Determine the contents of each variable in the following code fragment after the code has been executed:

```
      CHARACTER BUFFER*80, SCRTCH*30
      INTEGER I, J
      REAL    A, B
      DATA BUFFER / '12345678901234567890123456789012345678901234567890'/
      DATA SCRTCH / '(T6,I6,T10,I7,T10,F7.3,F6.0)  '/
      READ (BUFFER,SCRTCH) I, J, A, B
```

16. Determine the contents of each variable in the following code fragment after the code has been executed:

```
      CHARACTER BUFFER*80, FMT*20
      INTEGER I, BASE
      REAL    A(3)
      A(1) = 10010.
      A(2) = 0.0332
      A(3) = A(1) * A(2)
      BASE = ICHAR ( '1' ) - 1
      FMT = ' '
      BUFFER = ' '
      DO 10 I = 6, 0, -1
         IF ( NINT(ABS(A(3))) .GT. 10**I ) THEN
            FMT(1:12) = '('' A(3) = '','
            ITEMP = MAX ( 6-I, 0 )
            FMT(13:19) = 'F14.' // CHAR(ITEMP + BASE)
            FMT(20:20) = ')'
            GO TO 20
         END IF
10 CONTINUE
      FMT = '('' A(3) = '',F14.7)'
20 CONTINUE
      WRITE (BUFFER,FMT) A(3)
```

17. Write a version of subroutine UCASE that will correctly shift lowercase letters to uppercase regardless of whether it is run on an ASCII or an EBCDIC computer.

18. Write a subroutine LCASE that will correctly shift uppercase letters to lowercase regardless of whether it is run on an ASCII or an EBCDIC computer.

19. Write a subroutine CAPS that searches for all of the words within a character variable, and capitalizes the first letter of each word, while shifting the remainder of the word to lowercase. Assume that all nonalphabetical and nonnumeric characters can mark the boundaries of a word within the character variable (e.g., periods, commas, etc.). Nonalphabetical characters should be left unchanged. Test your routine on the following character variables:

```
CHARACTER*40 A, B, C
DATA A /'this is a test--does it work?'/
DATA B /'this iS the 2nd test!'/
DATA C /'123 WHAT NOW?!?  xxxoooxxx.'/
```

20. The intrinsic function LEN returns the number of characters that a character variable can store, *not* the number of characters actually stored in the variable. Write a function LENU that returns the number of characters actually used within a variable. The function should determine the number of characters actually used by determining the positions of the first and last nonblank characters in the variable, and performing the appropriate math. Test your function with the following variables.

```
CHARACTER*30 A(3)
DATA A(1) /'How many characters are used?'  /
DATA A(2) /'  ...and how about this one?  '/
DATA A(3) /'  !  !                         '/
```

21. When a relatively short character string is assigned to a longer character variable, the extra space in the variable is filled with blanks. In many circumstances, we would like to use a substring consisting of only the *nonblank* portions of the character variable. To do so, we need to know where the nonblank portions are within the variable. Write a subroutine that will accept a character variable of arbitrary length, and return two integers containing the numbers of the first and last nonblank characters in the variable. Test your subroutine with several character variables of different lengths and with different contents.

22. A common feature of large programs is an *input parameter file* in which the user can specify certain values to be used during the execution of the program. In simple programs, the values in the file must be listed in a specific order, and none of them may be skipped. These values may be read with a series of con-

secutive **READ** statements. If a value is left out of the input file or an extra value is added to the input file, all subsequent **READ** statements are misaligned, and the numbers go into the wrong locations in the program.

In more sophisticated programs, default values are defined for the input parameters in the file. In such a system, *only the input parameters whose defaults need to be modified need to be included in the input file*. Furthermore, the values that do appear in the input file may occur in any order. Each parameter in the input file is recognized by a corresponding *keyword* indicating what that parameter is for.

For example, a numerical integration program might include default values for the starting time of the integration, the ending time of the integration, the step size to use, and whether or not to plot the output. These values could be overridden by lines in the input file. An input parameter file for this program might contain the following items:

```
START = 0.0
STOP = 10.0
DT = 0.2
PLOT OFF
```

These values could be listed in any order, and some of them could be omitted if the default values are acceptable. In addition, the keywords might appear in uppercase, lowercase, or mixed case. The program reads this input file a line at a time, and updates the variable specified by the keyword with the value on the line.

Write a subroutine that accepts an input character argument containing a line from the input parameter file, and has the following output arguments:

```
REAL START, STOP, DT
LOGICAL PLOT
```

The subroutine should check for a keyword in the line, and update the variable that matches that keyword. It should recognize the keywords 'START', 'STOP', 'DT', and 'PLOT'. If the keyword 'START' is recognized, the subroutine should check for an equal sign, and use the value to the right of the equal sign to update variable START. It should behave similarly for the other keywords with real values. If the keyword 'PLOT' is recognized, the subroutine should check for 'ON' or 'OFF', and update the logical accordingly. (*Hint:* Use subroutine UCASE to shift each line to all uppercase for easy recognition. Then, use function INDEX to identify keywords.)

23. A *histogram* is a plot that shows how many times a particular measurement falls within a certain range of numbers. For example, consider the students in

this class. Suppose that there are 30 students in the class, and that their scores on the last exam fell within the following ranges:

Range	Number of Students
100–95	3
94–90	6
89–85	9
84–80	7
79–75	4
74–70	2
69–65	1

A plot of the number of students scoring in each range of numbers is a histogram (Figure 7-12).

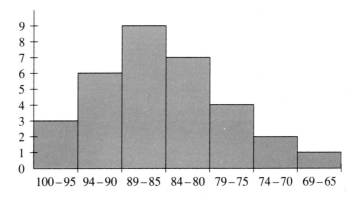

FIGURE 7-12   Histogram of student scores on last test.

In this case, we started with a set of data consisting of 30 student grades. We divided all possible grades on the test into 20 bins that covered the range of possible scores (0–100), and then counted how many student scores fell within each bin. After adding up the number of scores that fell within each bin, we plotted the result. (Since no one scored below 65, we didn't bother to plot all of the empty bins between 0 and 64 in Figure 7-12.)

Write a subroutine that will accept an array of real input data values, divide them into a user-specified number of bins over a user-specified range, and accumulate the number of samples that fall within each bin. The subroutine should then plot a histogram of the data values using a line-printer plot.

24. Use the random-number generation subroutine RAN0 that was developed in Chapter 6 to generate an array of 20,000 random numbers in the range [0, 1). Use the histogram subroutine developed in the previous exercise to divide the range between 0 and 1 into 20 bins, and to plot a histogram of the 20,000 random numbers. How uniform was the distribution of the numbers generated by the random number generator?

25. A polynomial is a function of the form

$$y(x) = a_0 + a_1 x + a_2 x^2 + a_3 x^3 + \ldots$$

Write a program that can read a parameter file containing a polynomial in standard FORTRAN notation, as well as START, STOP, and INCR keywords. Then, plot the function from $x =$ START to $x =$ STOP in increments of $\Delta x =$ INCR. The function should support reading and plotting polynomials of up to ninth order. A typical parameter file for this program would be

```
Y(X)   = -2. * X**2 + 3.0 * X + 7
START = -2.
STOP  = 2.
INCR  = 0.2
```

26. Write a subroutine that can plot a series of (x, y) pairs of points over a user-specified range of x and y values. Test your subroutine by plotting the points generated by the following code fragment.

```
     REAL X(40), Y(40), PI
     PARAMETER ( PI = 3.141592 )
     DO 10 I = 1, 40
        X(I) = COS(REAL(I)*(PI/20.))
        Y(I) = SIN(REAL(I)*(PI/20.))
10 CONTINUE
```

27. Write a program that will open a user-specified disk file containing the source code for a FORTRAN program. The program should copy the source code from the input file to a user-specified output file, stripping out any comment lines during the copying process.

28. *Run-length encoding* consists of replacing long sequences of the same character with a single copy of that character followed by a repetition count. For example, the string 'AAAAAAAcccccYYYYY11111' could be run length encoded as '\A7\c4\Y5\14'. Note that the backslash character is a *flag* that indicates that the following character is repeated, and the number is the repetition count. For simplicity, we will assume that there are no backslashes in the string to be processed. Write two FORTRAN functions to convert a string into its run-length encoded equivalent, and to convert a run-length encoded string back into a normal string. Test the functions on the following three 50-character strings.

```
     5    10   15   20   25   30   35   40   45   50
----|----|----|----|----|----|----|----|----|----|
     jjjjjGGGGG 0000000ssss...33333-----%%%%%!!#LL
This is a test of text with very little repetition
     abcd aabbccdd aaabbbcccddd aaaabbbbccccdddd
----|----|----|----|----|----|----|----|----|----|
     5    10   15   20   25   30   35   40   45   50
```

Are the run-length encoded strings shorter or longer than the original strings? Why?

29. Note from the previous example that run-length encoding actually increases the length of a string if there are fewer than three of a character to be repeated. Write a modified pair of encoding and decoding functions that do not encode repeated characters if there are fewer than three consecutive identical characters. Identify sequences of uncoded characters by preceding them with a vertical bar character (|). For example, the string 'AAAAAbcdEEEEff' could be run-length encoded as '\A5 | bcd\E4 | ff'. Assume that neither the backslash nor the vertical bar appears in any text to be processed. Test your functions on the three 50-character strings given in the previous example.

8 Advanced I/O Concepts

In Chapter 4, we learned the basics of FORTRAN input and output statements. We learned how to read in data using the formatted **READ** statement, and to write out data using the formatted **WRITE** statement. We also learned about the most common format descriptors: **A, E, F, I, L, P, T, X,** and /. Finally, we learned how to open, close, read, write, and position sequential disk files.

This chapter deals with the more advanced features of the FORTRAN I/O system. It includes additional format descriptors and more details about the use of sequential disk files, unformatted disk files, and direct access disk files for data storage.

8.1 ADDITIONAL FORMAT DESCRIPTORS

A complete list of all FORTRAN 77 FORMAT descriptors is shown in Table 8-1. Seven of the format descriptors describe output data types: **I** for integer values, **E, F,** and **G** for real values, **D** for double-precision values[1]; **L** for logical values, and **A** for character values. Five of them control the horizontal and vertical position of data: **X,** /, **T, TL,** and **TR.** The **P** descriptor is a scale factor that controls the position of the decimal point when displaying real and double-precision data. The **S, SP,** and **SN** descriptors control whether or not positive signs are displayed before positive numbers. The **BN** (Blank Null) and **BZ** (Blank Zero) descriptors control the way blanks are interpreted when reading an input data field. The ':' character controls the way that **FORMAT** statements associated with **WRITE** statements are scanned after the last variable in the **WRITE** statement has been written out.

We will now describe the format descriptors that were not described in Chapter 4 (except for the **D** descriptor, which will be put off until the discussion of double-precision variables in Chapter 9).

---

[1]Double-precision variables are described in Chapter 9.

TABLE 8-1 Complete List of FORTRAN 77 Format Descriptors

FORMAT *Descriptors*		*Usage*
A	**A***w*	Character data
BN		Blank Null: ignore blanks in numerical input fields
BZ		Blank Zero: interpret blanks in a numerical input field as zeros
D*w.d*		**DOUBLE PRECISION** data in exponential notation (will be discussed in Chapter 9)
E*w.d*	**E***w.d***E***e*	**REAL** data in exponential notation
F*w.d*		**REAL** data in decimal notation
G*w.d*		**REAL** data displayed in either exponential or decimal notation, depending on the value
I*w*	**I***w.m*	**INTEGER** data
L*w*		**LOGICAL** data
*k***P**		Scale factor for display of **REAL** data
T*c*		TAB: move to column c of current line
TL*n*		TAB: move left *n* columns in current line
TR*n*		TAB: move right *n* columns in current line
*n***X**		Horizontal spacing: skip *n* spaces
S		Sign control: use default system convention
SP		Sign control: display "+" before positive numbers
SS		Sign control: suppress "+" before pos numbers
'*x . . . x*'	*n***H***x . . . x*	Character strings (the *n*H*x . . . x* form is obsolete)
/		Vertical spacing: move down 1 line
:		Format scanning control character
O*w*		Display integer data in octal format[2]
Z*w*		Display integer data in hexadecimal format[2]

where

c	column number
d	number of digits to right of decimal place
e	number of digits in exponent
k	scale factor (number of places to shift decimal point)
m	minimum number of digits to be displayed
w	field width in characters

[2]The **O** and **Z** format descriptors are common extensions to FORTRAN 77 that have been incorporated into the FORTRAN 90 standard.

8.1.1   Real Output—the G Descriptor

The **F** format descriptor is used to display real values in a fixed format. For example, the descriptor **F7.3** displays a real value in the format *ddd.ddd* for positive numbers, or *-dd.ddd* for negative numbers. The **F** descriptor produces output data in an easy-to-read format. Unfortunately, if the number to be displayed with an **F7.3** descriptor is ≥ 1000 or ≤ -100, then the output data is replaced by a field of asterisks: ***********. By contrast, the **E** format descriptor displays a number regardless of its range. However, numbers displayed in the **E** format are not as easy to interpret as numbers displayed in the **F** format. Although the following two numbers are identical, the one displayed in the **F** format is easier to understand:

```
    225.671    0.225671E+03
```

Because the **F** format is easier to read, it would be really nice to have a format descriptor which displays numbers in the **F** format whenever possible, but then switches to the **E** format when they become too big or too small. The **G** (general) format descriptor behaves in just this fashion.

The **G** format descriptor has the form

$$r\mathrm{G}w.d \qquad \text{or} \qquad r\mathrm{G}w.d\mathrm{E}e$$

where

- **G**   indicates real (floating-point) data presented in either standard notation or exponential notation, depending upon the value of the number.
- *w*   is the field width in which the data is to be displayed.
- *d*   is the number of digits to the right of the decimal point.
- *e*   is the number of digits to use to display the exponent.
- *r*   is the **repetition indicator**. It indicates the number of times this descriptor is used. This value is optional; if it is absent, the format descriptor is used only once.

A real value displayed with a **G** format descriptor will either be displayed in **F** or **E** format, depending on the size of the number. The format used depends on the exponent associated with the number. If the real value to be displayed is represented as $\pm 0.dddddd \times 10^{k}$ and the format descriptor to be used for the display is **G**$w.d$, then the relationship between d and k determines how the data is displayed. If $0 \leq k \leq d$, the value is output in **F** format with a field width of $w - 4$ characters followed by four blanks. *The decimal point will be adjusted (within the $w - 4$ characters) as necessary to display as many significant digits as possible.* If the exponent is negative or is greater than d, the value is output in **E** format. In either case, a total of d significant digits are displayed.

The operation of the **G** format descriptor is illustrated below. In the first example, k is -1, so the output comes out in **E** format. For the last example, k is 6 and d is 5, so the output again comes out in **E** format. For all of the examples in between,

$0 \le k \le d$, so the output comes out in **F** format with the decimal point adjusted to display as many significant digits as possible.

Value	Exponent	G Descriptor	Output
0.012345	−1	**G11.5**	0.12345E-01
0.123450	0	**G11.5**	0.12345ƀƀƀƀ
1.234500	1	**G11.5**	1.23450ƀƀƀƀ
12.34500	2	**G11.5**	12.3450ƀƀƀƀ
123.4500	3	**G11.5**	123.450ƀƀƀƀ
1234.500	4	**G11.5**	1234.50ƀƀƀƀ
12345.00	5	**G11.5**	12345.0ƀƀƀƀ
123450.0	6	**G11.5**	0.12345E+06

8.1.2 The TAB Descriptors

There are three **TAB format descriptors**: **T**c, **TL**n, and **TR**n. We saw the **T**c descriptor in Chapter 4. In a formatted **WRITE** statement, it makes the output of the descriptor following it begin at column c in the output buffer. In a formatted **READ** statement, it makes the field of the following descriptor begin at column c in the input buffer. For example, the following code prints the letter 'Z' in column 30 of the output line (remember that column 1 is used for carriage control and is not printed).

```
        WRITE (*,100) 'Z'
100 FORMAT (T31,A)
```

The **T**c descriptor performs an *absolute* tab function, in the sense that the output moves to column c regardless of where the previous output was. By contrast, the **TL**n and **TR**n descriptors are *relative* tab functions. **TL**n moves the output left by n columns, and **TR**n moves the output right by n columns. Where the next output occurs depends on the location of the previous output on the line. For example, the following code prints a 100 in columns 10–12 and a 200 in columns 17–19:

```
        WRITE (*,100) 100, 200
100 FORMAT (T11,I3,TR4,I3)
```

8.1.3 The SIGN Descriptors

The **SIGN format descriptors** control the display of positive signs before positive numbers in an output line. There are three SIGN format descriptors: **S, SP,** and **SS.** The **SP** descriptor causes positive signs to be displayed before all positive numerical values following it in the same format statement, while the **SS** descriptor suppresses positive signs before all positive numerical values following it in the same format statement. The **S** descriptor restores the system default behavior for all positive numerical values following it (the system default may vary from system to system, but it is usual not to display positive signs).

In the following example, the system default applies to the first and last numbers displayed, while the second number is always displayed with a positive sign, and the third number is always displayed without a positive sign.

```
      PROGRAM SIGN
      I = 100
      WRITE (*,100) I, I, I, I
100   FORMAT (1X,I10,SP,I10,SS,I10,S,I10)
      END
```

The system default for Microsoft FORTRAN is to display positive numbers without signs. Therefore, if this code is compiled using the Microsoft FORTRAN compiler, the output is

```
C:\BOOK\FORT>SIGN
          100       +100        100         100
```

8.1.4 Blank Interpretation—the BN and BZ Descriptors

The **BN** (Blank Null) and **BZ** (Blank Zero) descriptors control the way in which blanks are interpreted in input data fields. If the **BN** descriptor is in effect, blanks are ignored. If the **BZ** descriptor is in effect, blanks are treated as zeros. In either case, if an entire input data field is blank, then the field is interpreted as 0.

To understand the difference between the **BN** and **BZ** options, consider the following input data line:

```
      5    10   15   20   25   30
  ----|----|----|----|----|----|
    3     6.7
  ----|----|----|----|----|----|
      5    10   15   20   25   30
```

If this line is read with the **BN** option,

```
      READ (*,100) I, A
100   FORMAT (BN,I5,F5.0)
```

then I is assigned a value of 3 and A is assigned a value of 6.7. If the line is read with the **BZ** option

```
      READ (*,100) I, A
100   FORMAT (BZ,I5,F5.0)
```

then I is assigned a value of 300, and A is assigned a value of 6.7. Note that the blanks in the **I5** input field were interpreted as if they were zeros.

The FORTRAN 77 standard states that blanks should be ignored by default in **READ** statements. The standard behavior in FORTRAN 66 and earlier versions was to treat blanks as zeros. With the **BN** and **BZ** descriptors, a programmer can specify whether a particular input statement should behave according to the FORTRAN 77 standard, or according to the older standards.

8.1.5 The Colon (:) Descriptor

In Chapter 4, we learned that if a **WRITE** statement runs out of variables before the end of its corresponding **FORMAT** statement, the use of the **FORMAT** statement stops at the first format descriptor without a corresponding variable, or at the end of the **FORMAT** statement, whichever comes first. For example, the statements

```
   M = 1
   WRITE (*,40) M
40 FORMAT (1X, 'M = ', I3, ' N = ', I4, ' O = ', F7.2)
```

produce the output

```
    5    10   15   20   25   30
----|----|----|----|----|----|
M =    1 N =
----|----|----|----|----|----|
    5    10   15   20   25   30
```

since the use of the **FORMAT** statement stops at **I4**, which is the first unmatched format descriptor. Similarly, the statements

```
   VOLTAGE = 13800.
   WRITE (*,50) VOLTAGE / 1000.
50 FORMAT (1X, 'VOLTAGE = ', F8.1, ' kV')
```

produce the output

```
    5    10   15   20   25   30
----|----|----|----|----|----|
VOLTAGE =    13.8 kV
----|----|----|----|----|----|
    5    10   15   20   25   30
```

since there are no unmatched descriptors, and the use of the **FORMAT** statement stops at the end of the statement.

The colon descriptor (**:**) permits a user to modify the normal behavior of **FOR-MAT** descriptors with **WRITE** statements. The colon descriptor serves as a *conditional stopping point* for the **WRITE** statement. If there are more values to print out, the colon is ignored, and the execution of the formatted **WRITE** statement continues according to the normal rules for using **FORMAT** statements. However, if a colon is encounted in the **FORMAT** and there are no more values to write out, execution of the **WRITE** statement stops at the colon.

To help understand the use of the colon, let's examine the simple program shown in Figure 8-1.

```
      PROGRAM TEST
      IMPLICIT NONE
      REAL    X(8)
      INTEGER I
      DATA X / 1.1, 2.2, 3.3, 4.4, 5.5, 6.6, 7.7, 8.8 /
C
      WRITE (*,100) (I, X(I), I = 1, 8)
  100 FORMAT (/,1X,'The output values are: '/,
     *        3(5X,'X(',I2,') = ',F10.4))
C
      WRITE (*,200) (I, X(I), I = 1, 8)
  200 FORMAT (/,1X,'The output values are: '/,
     *        3(:,5X,'X(',I2,') = ',F10.4))
C
      END
```

FIGURE 8-1   Program illustrating the use of the colon format descriptor.

This program contains an eight-element array whose values we wish to print out three-abreast across the page. Note that the portion of the format descriptors inside the parentheses has a repeat count of three, so each line will contain three values printed in identical format before the program advances to the next line. If the program is compiled and executed, the result is

```
C:\BOOK\FORT>test

The output values are:
      X( 1) =      1.1000    X( 2) =      2.2000    X( 3) =      3.3000
      X( 4) =      4.4000    X( 5) =      5.5000    X( 6) =      6.6000
      X( 7) =      7.7000    X( 8) =      8.8000    X(

The output values are:
      X( 1) =      1.1000    X( 2) =      2.2000    X( 3) =      3.3000
      X( 4) =      4.4000    X( 5) =      5.5000    X( 6) =      6.6000
      X( 7) =      7.7000    X( 8) =      8.8000
```

The first **WRITE** statement and **FORMAT** statement run out of values to output after X(8) is written, but since it is in the middle of a format, the **WRITE** continues to execute until it comes to the first output descriptor without a corresponding variable. As a result, an extra 'X(' is printed out. The second **WRITE** statement and **FORMAT** are identical to the first pair, except that there is a colon at the beginning of the repeated portion of the **FORMAT** statement. This pair also runs out of values to output after X(8) is written. Since it is in the middle of a format, the **WRITE** continues to execute, but immediately bumps into the colon, and stops. In this case, the extra 'X(' is not printed out.

The colon descriptor is most commonly used to terminate output cleanly in the middle of a line, as it was in the example above.

8.1.6 Integer Output—the O and Z Descriptors

There are two additional format descriptors that may be used to display integer data: the **O** and **Z** descriptors. The **O** descriptor displays the contents of an integer variable in octal format, and the **Z** descriptor displays the contents of an integer variable in hexadecimal format. *These format descriptors are not a part of the* FORTRAN 77 *standard.* However, they are common extensions to FORTRAN 77 which are also a part of the FORTRAN 90 standard. They may or may not be supported by your particular compiler. These descriptors have the general form

$$r\text{O}w \quad \text{or} \quad r\text{Z}w$$

where

O   indicates integer data displayed in octal format.
Z   indicates integer data displayed in hexadecimal format.
w   is the number of characters to use to display the integer data. This parameter is known as the **field width** of the descriptor.
r   is the **repetition indicator.** It indicates the number of times this descriptor will be used. This field is optional; if it is absent, the format descriptor is used only once.

Integer values are *right-justified* in their fields. This means that integers are printed out so that the last digit of the integer occupies the rightmost column of the field. If an integer is too large to fit into the field in which it is to be printed, then the field is filled with asterisks. For example, if the values of the integer variables I1 and I2 are

```
I1 = 12
I2 = 255
```

then the following statements

```
        WRITE (*,200) I1, I1, I1
        WRITE (*,200) I2, I2, I2
200 FORMAT (' ','I1 = ' I6,' OCTAL = ',O6,' HEX = ',Z6)
```

will produce the output

```
        5    10   15   20   25   30   35   40
    ----|----|----|----|----|----|----|----|
    I1 =       12 OCTAL = 000014 HEX = 00000C
    I2 =      255 OCTAL = 000377 HEX = 0000FF
    ----|----|----|----|----|----|----|----|
        5    10   15   20   25   30   35   40
```

The **O** and **Z** format descriptors are extensions to the FORTRAN 77 language, so not every compiler will support them. If you use these descriptors, you may be certain that your programs will continue to run under FORTRAN 90, but you may be restricting your portability among FORTRAN 77 compilers.

■
8.2   DEFAULTING VALUES IN LIST-DIRECTED INPUT

List-directed input has the advantage of being very simple to use, since no **FORMAT** statements need be written for it. For example, a list-directed **READ** statement is very useful for getting input information from a user at a terminal. The user may type the input data in any column, and the **READ** statement will still interpret it properly.

Furthermore, list-directed **READ** statements support **null values.** If an input data line contains two consecutive commas, then the corresponding variable in the input list is left unchanged. This behavior permits a user to default one or more input data values to their previously defined values. Consider the following example:

```
PROGRAM TEST
I = 1
J = 2
K = 3
WRITE (*,*) 'Enter I, J, and K:'
READ (*,*) I, J, K
WRITE (*,*) 'I, J, K = ', I, J, K
END
```

When this program is compiled and executed, the results are

```
C:\BOOK\FORT>test
Enter I, J, and K:
1000,,-2002
I, J, K =         1000           2        -2002
```

Note that the value of J was defaulted to 2, while new values were assigned to I and K. It is also possible to default all of the remaining variables on a line by concluding it with a slash.

```
C:\BOOK\FORT>test
Enter I, J, and K:
1000 /
I, J, K =         1000           2           3
```

Quiz 8-1

This quiz provides a quick check to see if you have understood the concepts introduced in Sections 8.1 and 8.2. If you have trouble with the quiz, reread the sections, ask your instructor, or discuss the material with a fellow student. The answers to this quiz are found in the back of the book.

For questions 1–5, determine what will be written out when the statements are executed.

```
  1.    INTEGER I, J
        REAL A
        I = 100
        J = 2
        A = 6.4
        WRITE (*,1) I, J, A
      1 FORMAT (1X, T30, I5, TL20, I5, TR20, F8.2)
```

2.
```
       REAL A
       DATA A / 4096.07 /
       WRITE (*,1) A, A, A, A, A
     1 FORMAT (1X, F10.1, F9.2, E12.5, G12.5, G11.4)
```

3.
```
       INTEGER I
       REAL DATA1(5)
       DATA DATA1 / -17.2, 2*4.0, .3, -2.22 /
       WRITE (*,1) (I, DATA1(I), I=1, 5)
     1 FORMAT (2(10X,'DATA1(',I3,') = ',F10.4,:,',,'))
```

4.
```
       INTEGER I, J
       READ (*,1) I, J
     1 FORMAT (BZ,I10,T1,BN,I10)
       WRITE (*,2) I, J
     2 FORMAT (' I = ',I10,' J = ',I10)
```

where the input line is

```
        5    10   15   20
    ----|----|----|----|
        25        56
    ----|----|----|----|
        5    10   15   20
```

5.
```
       INTEGER I, J, K
       I = -2002
       J = 1776
       K = -3
       WRITE (*,*) 'Enter I, J, & K:'
       READ (*,*) I, J, K
       WRITE (*,1) I, J, K
     1 FORMAT (' I = ',I10,' J = ',I10,' K = ',I10)
```

where the input line is

```
        5    10   15   20
    ----|----|----|----|
       /
    ----|----|----|----|
        5    10   15   20
```

6.
```
       INTEGER I, J, K
       I = -2002
       J = 1776
       K = -3
       WRITE (*,*) 'Enter I, J, & K:'
       READ (*,*) I, J, K
       WRITE (*,1) I, J, K
     1 FORMAT (' I = ',I10,' J = ',I10,' K = ',I10)
```

where the input line is

```
        5    10   15   20
    ----|----|----|----|
       ,          -1001/
    ----|----|----|----|
        5    10   15   20
```

8.3   ADVANCED DISK FILE I/O

A summary of FORTRAN 77 I/O statements is shown in Table 8-2. The statements permit us to open and close files, check the status of the files, go to a specific position within the files, and to read from or write to them.

In this section, we will learn about all of the statements found in the table. Some of them were introduced in simplified form in Chapter 4, but even the statements that we are already familiar with have many additional options to learn about.

TABLE 8-2   FORTRAN 77 I/O Statements

Statement	*Function*
OPEN	Open a file (connect it to an LU)
CLOSE	Close a file (disconnect it from an LU)
INQUIRE	Check on properties of a file
READ	Read data from a file (via an LU)
WRITE	Write data to a file (via an LU)
REWIND	Rewind a sequential file to the beginning
BACKSPACE	Move back one record in a sequential file
ENDFILE	Move to the end of a sequential file

8.3.1   The OPEN Statement

A disk file must be connected to an LU before data can be read from or written to the file. This connection is established using the **OPEN** statement. Once we are through reading from or writing to the file, the file should be disconnected from the LU using the **CLOSE** statement. After the **CLOSE** statement has been executed, the LU will no longer be connected to the file, and it may be connected to some other file using another **OPEN** statement.

The **OPEN** statement has the general form

```
OPEN (open list)
```

where *open list* consists of two or more clauses separated by commas. The possible clauses in an **OPEN** statement are:

1. A **UNIT**= clause specifying the logical unit that is to be connected to the file
2. A **FILE**= clause specifying the name of the file to open
3. A **STATUS**= clause specifying whether the file is new, old, scratch, or unknown
4. An **IOSTAT**= clause returning the status of the **OPEN** operation
5. An **ERR**= clause specifying the statement label of a statement to be executed if the file open fails

6. An **ACCESS**= clause specifying whether to use sequential or direct access
7. A **FORM**= clause specifying whether the file is formatted or unformatted
8. A **BLANK**= clause specifying whether blank columns in numeric fields are to be treated as zeros or to be ignored
9. A **RECL**= clause specifying the record length if the file is opened with direct access

The above clauses may be included in the **OPEN** statement in any order. Not all of the clauses will be included in any given **OPEN** statement. Some of the clauses are only meaningful for specific types of files. For example, the **RECL**= clause is only meaningful for direct access files. Also, some combinations of clauses have contradictory meanings, and produce errors at compilation time. We will point out some examples of these contradictions as we discuss the details of the clauses below.

The UNIT= Clause
This clause has the form

```
UNIT= integer
```

where *integer* is an integer constant, variable, or expression containing the **logical unit** number to be associated with the file. The range of integers that may be used for LUs will vary from computer to computer, so you should check with your instructor or with a manual for your specific computer to determine the legal LU numbers for that system. Almost all computers will accept logical unit numbers in the range 1–99, so it is generally safe to use those values. *The* **UNIT**=lu *clause must be present in any* **OPEN** *statement.* The LU number specified here is used in later **READ** and **WRITE** statements to access the file.

The **UNIT**=lu clause may be abbreviated to just the lu number if it appears as the first clause in an **OPEN** statement. This feature is included in FORTRAN 77 for backward compatibility with earlier versions of FORTRAN. Therefore, the following two statements are equivalent:

```
OPEN ( UNIT=10, ... )
OPEN ( 10, ... )
```

The FILE= Clause
This clause has the form

```
FILE= string
```

where *string* is a character string, variable, or expression containing the name of the file to connect to the specified logical unit. *A file name must be supplied for all files* except for scratch files.

The STATUS= Clause

This clause has the form

```
STATUS= string
```

where *string* is a character string, variable, or expression containing the status of the file to connect to the specified LU. There are four possible file statuses: **'OLD'**, **'NEW'**, **'SCRATCH'**, and **'UNKNOWN'**.

If the file status is **'OLD'**, then the file must already exist on the system when the **OPEN** statement is executed, or the **OPEN** will fail with an error. This is a useful feature to use with input data files, since those files should already exist or there would be no data to read. If an input file is opened with the **'OLD'** status and the **IOSTAT**= clause is used, the programmer can test for a problem with the input data file, and tell the user about the problem in a graceful manner.

If the file status is **'NEW'**, the file must *not* already exist on the system when the **OPEN** statement is executed, or the **OPEN** will fail with an error. This is a useful feature to use with output data files when you want to be careful not to overwrite existing data.

If the file status is **'SCRATCH'**, a **scratch file** will be created on the computer and attached to the logical unit. A scratch file is a temporary file that is created by the computer, and which the program can use for temporary data storage while it is running. When a scratch file is closed or when the program ends, the file is automatically deleted from the system. Note that *the* **FILE**= *clause is not used with a scratch file,* since no permanent file is created. It is an error to specify a file name for a scratch file.

If the file status is **'UNKNOWN'**, then the file is not known to be either new or old. In that case, the computer will first look for an existing file with the specified name, and open it if it exists. If the file does not exist, then the computer will create a new file with that name and open it. The **'UNKNOWN'** status can be used for output files if you are certain that it is OK to overwrite output files from an earlier run of the program.

If there is no **STATUS**= clause in an **OPEN** statement, the default status is **'UNKNOWN'**.

The IOSTAT= Clause

This clause has the form

```
IOSTAT= integer variable
```

where *integer variable* is an integer variable that will contain the status after the **OPEN** statement is executed. If the file is opened successfully, the status variable will contain a zero. If the open failed, then the status variable will contain a positive value corresponding to the type of error which occurred. Since the meanings of the error codes vary from computer to computer, you must look them up in the appropriate manuals for your computer system.

The ERR= Clause

This clause has the form

```
ERR= statement label
```

where *statement label* is the label of an executable statement. If the file open fails, then the program will jump to the statement specified and execute it. The **ERR=** clause thus provides a way to add special code to handle file open errors.

The ACCESS= Clause

This clause has the form

```
ACCESS= string
```

where *string* is a character string, variable, or expression containing the access method to be used with the file. There are two types of access methods, **'SEQUEN-TIAL'** and **'DIRECT'**. **Sequential access** involves opening a file and reading or writing its records in order from beginning to end. Sequential access is the default access mode in FORTRAN, and all files that we have seen so far have been sequential files. The records in a file opened with sequential access do not have to be any particular length.

If a file is opened with **direct access**, it is possible to jump directly from one record to another within the file at any time without having to read any of the records in between. Every record in a file opened with direct access must be of the same length.

The FORM= Clause

This clause has the form

```
FORM= string
```

where *string* is a character string, variable, or expression containing the format of the file. There are two file formats, **'FORMATTED'** and **'UNFORMATTED'**. The data in **formatted files** consists of recognizable characters, numbers, etc. These files are called formatted because we must use FORMAT statements (or list-directed I/O statements) to convert their data into a form usable by the computer whenever we read them in or write them out. When we write to a formatted file, the bit patterns stored in the computer's memory are translated into a series of ASCII or EBCDIC characters that we can read, and those characters are written to the file. The instructions for the translation process are included in the **FORMAT** statement. All of the disk files that we have used so far have been formatted files.

By contrast, **unformatted files** contain data which is an exact copy of the data stored in the computer. When we write to an unformatted file, the exact bit patterns in the computer's memory are copied into the file. Unformatted files are much smaller than the corresponding formatted files, but the information in an unformatted file is coded into bit patterns that cannot be easily examined or used by people. Furthermore, the bit patterns corresponding to particular values vary among different types of computer systems, so unformatted files cannot easily be moved from one type of computer to another one.

If a file uses sequential access, the default file format is **'FORMATTED'**. If the file uses direct access, the default file format is **'UNFORMATTED'**.

The BLANK= Clause

This clause has the form

```
BLANK= string
```

where *string* is a character string, variable, or expression containing either **'ZERO'** or **'NULL'**. This clause specifies whether blank columns in numerical fields are to be treated as blanks or zeros. It is the equivalent of the **BN** and **BZ** format descriptors, except that the value specified here applies to the entire file. A **BN** or **BZ** format descriptor in a particular **FORMAT** statement overrides the setting of the **BLANK=** clause for that particular statement. The default condition is **'NULL'**, meaning that blanks are ignored.

The RECL= Clause

This clause has the form

```
RECL= integer
```

where *integer* is an integer constant, variable, or expression containing the length of each record in a direct access file. For formatted files opened with direct access, this clause contains the length of each record in characters. For unformatted files, this clause contains the length of each record in machine-dependent units.

The Importance of Using IOSTAT= or ERR= Clauses

If a file open fails, and there is no **IOSTAT=** clause or **ERR=** clause in the **OPEN** statement, the FORTRAN program prints out an error message and aborts. This behavior is very inconvenient in a large program that runs for a long period of time, since large amounts of work can be lost if the program aborts. It is much better to trap such errors, and let the user tell the program what to do about the problem. The user could specify a new disk file, or he or she could let the program shut down, gracefully saving all the work done so far.

If either the **IOSTAT=** clause or **ERR=** clause are present in the **OPEN** statement, the FORTRAN program will *not* abort when an open error occurs. If the **ERR=** clause is present, then execution transfers to the statement specified in the clause. An example of such an operation is shown below.

```
OPEN ( UNIT=8, FILE='TEST.DAT', STATUS='OLD', ERR=9998 )
READ (8,100) ...
...
...
...
OPEN ( UNIT=9, FILE='OUTPUT.DAT', STATUS='NEW', ERR=9998 )
WRITE (9,100) ...
```

```
      ...
      ...
      ...
      GO TO 9999
C
 9998 CONTINUE
      WRITE (*,*) ' Error opening file. Program shutting down!'
      ...
      ... (Shutdown code here)
      ...
C
 9999 CONTINUE
      END
```

This approach permits the program to shut down gracefully, but does not tell the user just which file open failed or why it failed. A better approach would be to use the **IOSTAT**= clause to report the exact reason for the failure. For example

```
      OPEN ( UNIT=8, FILE='TEST.DAT', STATUS='OLD', IOSTAT=ISTAT )
C
C     Check for OPEN error
C
      IF ( ISTAT .NE. 0 ) THEN
         WRITE (*,*) 'Input file OPEN failed: ISTAT = ', ISTAT
         GO TO 9998
      END IF
C
      READ (8,100) ...
      ...
      ...
      ...
      OPEN ( UNIT=9, FILE='OUTPUT.DAT', STATUS='NEW', IOSTAT=ISTAT )
C
C     Check for OPEN error
C
      IF ( ISTAT .NE. 0 ) THEN
         WRITE (*,*) 'Output file OPEN failed: ISTAT = ', ISTAT
         GO TO 9998
      END IF
C
      WRITE (9,100) ...
      ...
      ...
      ...
      GO TO 9999
C
 9998 CONTINUE
      WRITE (*,*) ' Error opening file. Program shutting down!'
      ...
      ... (Shutdown code here)
      ...
C
 9999 CONTINUE
      END
```

Further enhancements permit the user to specify new file names and try again, etc.

■ GOOD PROGRAMMING PRACTICE

Always use the **IOSTAT**= clause in **OPEN** statements to trap file open errors. When an error is detected, tell the user all about the problem before shutting down gracefully or requesting an alternate file.

Examples

Some example **OPEN** statements are shown below

1. **OPEN (UNIT=9, FILE='X')**
   This statement opens a file named X and attaches it to logical unit 9. The status of the file is **'UNKNOWN',** so the program opens an existing file named X if one already exists, or create a file named X if one doesn't already exist. The file is opened for sequential access. It is a formatted file, with blanks in numerical fields treated as nulls. Since there is no **IOSTAT**= or **ERR**= clause, an open error would abort the program containing this statement.

2. **OPEN (22, STATUS='SCRATCH')**
   This statement creates a scratch file, and attaches it to LU 22. The scratch file is automatically given some unique name by the system, and is automatically deleted when the file is closed or the program ends. The file is opened for sequential access. It is a formatted file, with blanks in numerical fields treated as nulls. Since there is no **IOSTAT**= or **ERR**= clause, an open error would abort the program containing this statement.

3. **OPEN (FILE='INPUT', UNIT=LU, STATUS='OLD', IOSTAT=ISTAT)**
   This statement opens an existing file named INPUT, and attaches it to the logical unit corresponding to the value of variable LU. The status of the file is **'OLD',** so this **OPEN** statement will fail if the file does not already exist. The file is opened for sequential access. It is a formatted file, with blanks in numerical fields treated as nulls. An operation status code is returned in variable ISTAT. It is 0 for a successful file open, and positive for an unsuccessful file open. Since the **IOSTAT**= clause is present in this statement, an open error would not abort the program containing this statement.

8.3.2 The CLOSE Statement

Once we are through using a file, the file should be disconnected from its LU using the **CLOSE** statement. After the **CLOSE** statement has been executed, the LU is no longer connected to the file, and may be connected to some other file using another **OPEN** statement.

A FORTRAN program will automatically update and close any open files whenever the program ends. Therefore, a **CLOSE** statement is not actually required unless we want to attach more than one file to the same logical unit. However, it is good practice to close any file with a **CLOSE** statement just as soon as the program is finished using it. When a file has been opened by one program, no other program may have access to it at the same time. By closing the file as soon as possible, we can make it available for other programs to use. This is especially important for files that are shared by many people.

■

GOOD PROGRAMMING PRACTICE

Always explicitly close each disk file with a **CLOSE** statement as soon as possible after a program is finished using it, so that it may be available for use by others.

The **CLOSE** statement has the general form

```
CLOSE (close list)
```

where *close list* consists of one or more clauses separated by commas. The possible clauses in an **CLOSE** statement are

1. **UNIT**= clause specifying the logical unit of the file to be closed
2. A **STATUS**= clause specifying whether the file is to be kept or deleted
3. An **IOSTAT**= clause returning the status of the close operation
4. An **ERR**= clause specifying the statement label of a statement to be executed if the file close fails

The above clauses may be included in the **CLOSE** statement in any order.

The UNIT= Clause

This clause has the form

```
UNIT= integer
```

where *integer* is an integer constant, variable, or expression containing the LU number associated with the file. *The **UNIT**= clause must be present in any **CLOSE** statement.*

The **UNIT**=**lu** clause may be abbreviated to just the lu number if it appears as the first clause in a **CLOSE** statement. This feature is included in FORTRAN 77 for backward compatibility with earlier versions of FORTRAN. Therefore, the following two statements are equivalent:

```
CLOSE ( UNIT=10, IOSTAT=I )
CLOSE ( 10, IOSTAT=I )
```

The STATUS= Clause

This clause has the form

```
STATUS= string
```

where *string* is a character string, variable, or expression containing the status of the file connected to the specified LU. There are two possible file statuses: **'KEEP'** and **'DELETE'**.

If the file status is **'KEEP'**, the file is kept on the file system after it is closed. If the file status is **'DELETE'**, the file is deleted after it is closed. A scratch file is always deleted when it is closed. For any other type of file, the default status is **'KEEP'**.

The IOSTAT= Clause

This clause has the form

```
IOSTAT= integer variable
```

where *integer variable* is an integer variable which will contain the status after the **CLOSE** statement is executed. If the file is closed successfully, the status variable contains a zero. If the close failed, then the status variable will contain a positive value corresponding to the type of error that occurred. Since the meanings of the error codes vary from computer to computer, you must look them up in the appropriate manuals for your computer system.

The ERR= Clause

This clause has the form

```
ERR= statement label
```

where *statement label* is the label of an executable statement. If the file close fails, the program jumps to the statement specified and executes it. The **ERR=** clause thus provides a way to handle close errors.

Examples

Some example **CLOSE** statements are shown below:

1. **CLOSE (9)**
    This statement closes the file attached to LU 9. If the file is a scratch file, it will be deleted; otherwise, it will be kept. Since there is no **IOSTAT=** or **ERR=** clause, a close error would abort the program containing this statement.
2. **CLOSE (UNIT=22, STATUS='DELETE', IOSTAT=ISTAT)**
    This statement closes and deletes the file attached to LU 22. An operation status code is returned in variable ISTAT. It is 0 for a successful close, and positive for an unsuccessful close. Since the **IOSTAT=** clause is present in this statement, a close error would not abort the program containing this statement.

8.3.3 The INQUIRE Statement

It is often necessary to check on the status or properties of a file which we want to use in a FORTRAN program. The **INQUIRE** statement is used for this purpose. It is designed to provide detailed information about a file, either before or after the file has been opened.

The input to the **INQUIRE** statement is either a **FILE**= clause or a **UNIT**= clause (but not both simultaneously!). If a file has not yet been opened, it must be identified by name. If the file is already open, it may be identified by either name or LU. There are 15 possible output clauses in the **INQUIRE** statement. To find out a particular piece of information about a file, just include the appropriate clause in the statement. A complete list of all clauses is given in Table 8-3.

TABLE 8-3   Clauses Allowed in the INQUIRE Statement

Clause	Input or Output	Variable Type	Possible Values and Their Meanings
FILE= *filename*	Input	Character	Name of file to check[1]
UNIT= *lu*	Input	Integer	LU of file to check[1]
EXIST= *variable*	Output	Logical	TRUE if file with specified name or LU exists; FALSE otherwise
OPENED= *variable*	Output	Logical	TRUE if file with specified name or LU is opened; FALSE otherwise
NAMED= *variable*	Output	Logical	TRUE if file has a name; FALSE otherwise (scratch files are unnamed)
NUMBER= *variable*	Output	Integer	LU number of file, if opened. If file is not opened, this value is undefined.
RECL= *variable*	Output	Integer	The record length of a direct access file; undefined for sequential files
NEXTREC= *variable*	Output	Integer	For a direct access file, one more than the number of the last record read from or written to the file; undefined for sequential files
NAME= *variable*	Output	Character	Name of file if file has a name (see **NAMED**= above); undefined otherwise
ACCESS= *variable*	Output	Character	'SEQUENTIAL' if file is opened for sequential access; 'DIRECT' if opened for direct access[2]
SEQUENTIAL= *variable*	Output	Character	'YES' if file can be opened for sequential access; 'NO' if it cannot; 'UNKNOWN' if we cannot tell[2]
DIRECT= *variable*	Output	Character	'YES' if file can be opened for direct access; 'NO' if it cannot; 'UNKNOWN' if we cannot tell[2]

TABLE 8-3   Clauses Allowed in the INQUIRE Statement, Continued

Clause	Input or Output	Variable Type	Possible Values and Their Meanings
FORM= *variable*	Output	Character	'FORMATTED' if the file is opened for formatted I/O; 'UNFORMATTED' if the file is opened for unformatted I/O; undefined if file is not opened[3]
FORMATTED= *variable*	Output	Character	'YES' if file can be connected for formatted I/O; 'NO' if it cannot be connected for formatted I/O; 'UNKNOWN' if we cannot tell[3]
UNFORMATTED= *variable*	Output	Character	'YES' if file can be connected for unformatted I/O; 'NO' if it cannot be connected for unformatted I/O; 'UNKNOWN' if we cannot tell[3]
BLANK= *variable*	Output	Character	'ZERO' if blanks in numeric fields are to be interpreted as zeros; 'NULL' if blanks are to be ignored; undefined if the file is not opened[4]

[1]One and only one of the **FILE**= and **UNIT**= clauses may be included in any **INQUIRE** statement.
[2]The difference between the **ACCESS**= clause and the **SEQUENTIAL**= and **DIRECT**= clauses is that the **ACCESS**= clause tells what sort of access is being used, while the other two clauses tell what sort of access can be used.
[3]The difference between the **FORM**= clause and the **FORMATTED**= and **UNFORMATTED**= clauses is that the **FORM**= clause tells what sort of I/O is being used, while the other two clauses tell what sort of I/O can be used.
[4]The **BLANK**= clause is only defined for files connected for formatted I/O.

EXAMPLE   8-1   *Preventing Output Files from Overwriting Existing Data*   In many programs, the user is asked to specify an output file into which the results of the program are written. It is good programming practice to check to see if the output file already exists before opening it and writing into it. If it already exists, the user should be asked if he or she really wants to destroy the data in the file before the program overwrites it. If so, the program can open the file and write into it. If not, the program should get a new output file name and try again. Write a program that demonstrates a technique for protection against overwriting existing files.

SOLUTION   The pseudocode for an algorithm of this sort is

```
WHILE file not open yet DO
    Prompt user for the output file name FILENM
    Read file name FILENM
    INQUIRE: Does the file already exist?
```

```
            IF file does not exist THEN
                Open file FILENM
            ELSE file already exists
                Prompt user about overwriting
                Read answer (Y/N)
                IF answer is yes THEN
                    Open file FILENM
                END of IF
            END of IF
        END of WHILE loop
        Write output data
```

The resulting FORTRAN program is shown in Figure 8-2.

```
1           PROGRAM OPEN
2   C
3   C  Purpose:
4   C    To illustrate the process of checking before overwriting an
5   C    output file.
6   C
7   C  Record of revisions:
8   C      Date       Programmer         Description of change
9   C      ====       ==========         =====================
10  C    09/27/91    S. J. Chapman       Original code
11  C
12  C  List of local variables:
13  C    FEXIST -- Logical .TRUE. if file exists.
14  C    FILENM -- Output file name.
15  C    LOPEN  -- Logical .TRUE. if output file is open
16  C    YN     -- Character variable for Yes/No test
17  C
18          IMPLICIT NONE
19  C
20  C    Declare local variables.
21  C
22          CHARACTER FILENM*12, YN*1
23          LOGICAL   FEXIST, LOPEN
24  C
25  C    Initialize output data flag to .FALSE.
26  C
27          LOPEN = .FALSE.
28  C
29  C    Begin output WHILE loop
30  C
31     10 CONTINUE
32        IF ( .NOT. LOPEN ) THEN
33  C
34  C       Get output file name.
35  C
36            WRITE (*,*) 'Enter output file name: ',
37            READ (*,100) FILENM
38     100    FORMAT (A)
39  C
40  C       Does this file already exist?
41  C
42            INQUIRE ( FILE=FILENM, EXIST=FEXIST )
43            IF ( .NOT. FEXIST ) THEN
44  C
```

```
45  C           It's OK, the file didn't already exist.  Open file.
46  C
47                  OPEN ( UNIT=9, FILE=FILENM )
48                  LOPEN = .TRUE.
49  C
50            ELSE
51  C
52  C              File exists.  Should we replace it?
53  C
54                  WRITE (*,*) 'Output file exists.  Overwrite it? (Y/N)'
55                  READ (*,100) YN
56  C
57  C              Yes or no?
58  C
59                  CALL UCASE ( YN )
60                  IF ( YN .EQ. 'Y' ) THEN
61  C
62  C                  It's OK.  Open file.
63  C
64                      OPEN ( UNIT=9, FILE=FILENM )
65                      LOPEN = .TRUE.
66  C
67                  ELSE
68  C
69  C                  Go get another file name.
70  C
71                      GO TO 10
72                  END IF
73              END IF
74        END IF
75  C
76  C     Now write output data.
77  C
78        WRITE (9,*) 'This is the output file!'
79  C
80  C     Close and save file.
81  C
82        CLOSE (9,STATUS='KEEP')
83  C
84        END
```

FIGURE 8-2   Program illustrating how to prevent an output file from accidentally overwriting data.

Test this program for yourself. Can you suggest additional improvements to make this program work better? (*Hint*: What about the **OPEN** statements?)   ●

GOOD PROGRAMMING PRACTICE

It is good practice to check to see if your output file is overwriting an existing data file. If it is, make sure that the user really wants to do that before destroying the data in the file.

8.3.4 The READ Statement

The **READ** statement reads data from the file associated with the specified logical unit, converts its format according to the specified **FORMAT** descriptors, and stores it into the variables in the I/O list. A **READ** statement keeps reading input lines until all of the variables in *iolist* have been filled, the end of the input file is reached, or an error occurs.

The **READ** statement has the general form

```
READ (control list) iolist
```

where *control list* consists of one or more clauses separated by commas. The possible clauses in an **READ** statement are:

1. A **UNIT**= clause specifying the logical unit from which data is read.
2. An **FMT**= clause specifying the format of the data. This is either the statement label of a **FORMAT** statement, or a character string containing the format itself.
3. An **IOSTAT**= clause returning the status of the read operation
4. An **END**= clause specifying the statement label of a statement to be executed if the end of the input file is reached
5. An **ERR**= clause specifying the statement label of a statement to be executed if the read fails
6. A **REC**= clause specifying the record number to read if the file is opened with direct access

The above clauses may be included in the **READ** statement in any order. Not all of the clauses are included in any given **READ** statement.

The UNIT= Clause
This clause has the form

```
UNIT= integer    or    UNIT= *
```

where *integer* is an integer constant, variable, or expression containing the LU number from which to read the data, or * indicates reading data from the standard input device. *The* **UNIT**= *clause must be present in any* **READ** *statement.*

The LU may also be specified by just naming it in the **READ** statement without the **UNIT**= clause. This feature is included in FORTRAN 77 for backward compatibility with earlier versions of FORTRAN. If the logical unit is specified in this alternate form, it must be the first clause in the **READ** statement. The following two statements are equivalent:

```
READ ( UNIT=10, ... )
READ ( 10, ... )
```

The FMT= Clause

This clause has the form

    FMT= *statement label*   **or**   FMT= *string*   or   FMT= *

where *statement label* is the label of a **FORMAT** statement, *string* is a character string containing the format information, or * indicates list-directed I/O. A **FMT=** clause must be supplied for all formatted **READ** statements.

   If the **FMT=** clause is the *second* clause in a **READ** statement, then it may be abbreviated by just naming the statement number, character variable, or * containing the format. This feature is included in FORTRAN 77 for backward compatibility with earlier versions of FORTRAN. Therefore, the following two statements are equivalent:

    READ (UNIT=10, FMT=100) DATA
    READ (10, 100) DATA

   Note that a format may be specified in either a **FORMAT** statement or a character string. Therefore, the following three sets of statements are equivalent to each other.

        READ (UNIT=21, FMT=100) I, J, K
    100 FORMAT (3I10)

        STR = '(3I10)'
        READ (21, STR) I, J, K

        READ (21, '(3I10)') I, J, K

The IOSTAT= Clause

This clause has the form

    IOSTAT= *integer variable*

where *integer variable* is an integer variable that will contain the status after the **READ** statement is executed. If the read is successful, then the status variable will contain a zero. If an end-of-file condition is detected, then the status variable will contain a -1. If the read fails, the status variable will contain a positive value corresponding to the type of error that occurred. Since the meanings of the error codes vary from computer to computer, you must look them up in the appropriate manuals for your computer system.

The END= Clause

This clause has the form

    END= *statement label*

where *statement label* is the label of an executable statement. If the end of the input file is reached, the program jumps to the statement specified and executes it. The **END=** clause provides a way to handle unexpected end-of-file conditions.

The ERR= Clause

This clause has the form

```
ERR= statement label
```

where *statement label* is the label of an executable statement. If an error occurs during a file read, then the program jumps to the statement specified and executes it. (The most common read error is a mismatch between the type of the input data in a field and the format descriptors used to read it. For example, if the characters 'A123' appeared by mistake in a field read with the **I4** descriptor, an error would be generated.) The **ERR=** clause provides a way to handle read errors.

The REC= Clause

This clause has the form

```
REC= integer
```

where *integer* is an integer constant, variable, or expression containing the number of the record to read in a direct access file. It only applies to files opened with direct access.

The Importance of Using IOSTAT= or END= and ERR= Clauses

If a read fails, and there is no **IOSTAT=** clause or **ERR=** clause in the **READ** statement, then the FORTRAN program prints out an error message and aborts. Similarly, if the end of the input file is reached, and there is no **IOSTAT=** clause or **END=** clause in the **READ** statement, the FORTRAN program will abort. If either the **IOSTAT=** clause or **ERR=** and **END=** clauses are present in the **READ** statement, the FORTRAN program will not abort when read errors or end-of-file conditions occur. Instead, the programmer can do something to handle those conditions and allow the program to continue running.

The following example shows how to use the **IOSTAT=** message to read an unknown number of input values without aborting when the end of the input file is reached. It uses a while loop to read data until the end of the input file is reached.

```
      OPEN ( UNIT=8, FILE='TEST.DAT', STATUS='OLD' )
C
C     Read input data
C
      NVALS = 0
   10 CONTINUE
      NVALS = NVALS + 1
      READ (8,100,IOSTAT=ISTAT) ARRAY(NVALS)
C
C     Check for end of data
C
      IF ( ISTAT .EQ. -1 ) THEN
C
```

```
C              End of data
C
               GO TO 20
C
         ELSE
C
C              Get more data
C
             , GO TO 10
C
               END IF
C
      20 CONTINUE
         NVALS = NVALS - 1
```

A similar loop using the **END**= clause to accomplish the same purpose is shown below.

```
      OPEN ( UNIT=8, FILE='TEST.DAT', STATUS='OLD' )
C
C     Read input data
C
      NVALS = 0
   10 CONTINUE
      NVALS = NVALS + 1
      READ (8,100,END=20) ARRAY(NVALS)
C
C     Get more data
C
      GO TO 10
C
C     End of data reached
C
   20 CONTINUE
      NVALS = NVALS - 1
```

GOOD PROGRAMMING PRACTICE

Use the **IOSTAT**= clause (or the **END**= and **ERR**= clauses) on **READ** statements to prevent programs from aborting on errors or end-of-file conditions. When an error or end-of-file condition is detected, the program can take appropriate actions to continue processing or to shut down gracefully.

8.3.5   The WRITE Statement

The **WRITE** statement takes data from the variables in the I/O list, converts its format according to the specified **FORMAT** descriptors, and writes it out to the file associated with the specified LU. The **WRITE** statement has the general form

```
WRITE (control list) iolist
```

where *control list* consists of one or more clauses separated by commas. The possible clauses in a **WRITE** statement are the same as those in the **READ** statement, except that there is no **END**= clause.

8.3.6 File Positioning Statements

There are two file positioning statements in FORTRAN 77: **REWIND** and **BACK-SPACE.** The **REWIND** statement positions the file so that the next **READ** statement will read the first line in the file. The **BACKSPACE** statements move the file back by one line.These statements have the general form

```
REWIND (control list)
BACKSPACE (control list)
```

where *control list* consists of one or more clauses separated by commas. The possible clauses in a file positioning statement are

1. **UNIT**= clause specifying the logical unit to act on (*required*)
2. An **IOSTAT**= clause returning the status of the file positioning operation
3. An **ERR**= clause specifying the statement label of a statement to be executed if the positioning operation fails

The meanings of these clauses are the same as in the other I/O statements described above. Also, the LU may be specified without the **UNIT**= clause if it is in the first position of the control list.

The following statements are examples of legal file positioning statements:

```
REWIND (LU)
BACKSPACE (UNIT=12, IOSTAT=ISTAT)
BACKSPACE (8, ERR=9999)
```

For compatibility with earlier versions for FORTRAN, a file positioning statement containing only an LU number can also be specified without parentheses:

```
REWIND 6
BACKSPACE LU
```

8.3.7 The ENDFILE Statement

The **ENDFILE** statement writes an end-of-file record at the current position in a file, and then positions the file after the end-of-file record. After executing an **END-FILE** statement on a file, no further **READ**s or **WRITE**s are possible until either a **BACKSPACE** or a **REWIND** statement is executed. Until then, any further **READ** or **WRITE** statements will produce an error. This statement has the general form

```
ENDFILE (control list)
```

where *control list* consists of one or more clauses separated by commas. The possible clauses in an **ENDFILE** statement are

1. **UNIT**= clause specifying the LU to act on (required)
2. An **IOSTAT**= clause returning the status of the operation
3. An **ERR**= clause specifying the statement label of a statement to be executed if an error occurs

The meanings of these clauses are the same as in the other I/O statements described earlier. Also, the LU may be specified without the **UNIT**= clause if it is in the first position of the control list.

For compatibility with earlier versions of FORTRAN, an **ENDFILE** statement containing only an LU number can also be specified without parentheses. The following statements are examples of legal file positioning statements:

```
ENDFILE (UNIT=12, IOSTAT=ISTAT)
ENDFILE 6
```

8.4 UNFORMATTED FILES

All of the files that we have used so far in this book have been **formatted files.** The data in a formatted file consists of recognizable characters, numbers, etc. stored in a standard coding scheme such as ASCII or EBCDIC. These files are easy to distinguish, because we can see the characters and numbers in the file when we display them on the screen or print them on the printer. However, to use data in a formatted file, a computer program must translate the characters in the file into the internal integer or real format used by that particular computer. The instructions for this translation are provided by format descriptors.

Formatted files have the advantage that we can readily see what sort of data they contain. However, they also have disadvantages. A computer must do a great deal of work to convert a number between the computer's internal representation and that used in the file. All of this work is just wasted effort if we are going to be reading the data back into another program on the same computer. Also, the internal representation of a number usually requires much less space than the corresponding ASCII or EBCDIC representation of the number found in a formatted file. For example, the internal representation of a 32-bit real value requires 4 bytes of space. The ASCII representation of the same value would be $\pm 0.dddddddE\pm ee$, which requires 14 bytes of space (1 byte per character). Thus, storing data in ASCII or EBCDIC format is inefficient and wasteful of disk space.

Unformatted files overcome these disadvantages by copying the information from the computer's memory directly to the disk file with no conversions at all. Since no conversions occur, no computer time is wasted formatting the data. Furthermore, the data occupies a much smaller amount of disk space. On the other hand, unformatted data cannot be examined and interpreted directly by humans. In addition, it cannot usually be moved between different types of computers, because those types of computers have different internal ways to represent integers and real values.

Formatted and unformatted files are compared in Table 8-4. In general, formatted files are best for data that people must examine, or data that may have to be moved between different types of computers. Unformatted files are best for storing information that will not need to be examined by human beings, and that will be used on the same type of computer on which it was created. Under those circumstances, unformatted files are both faster and occupy less disk space.

Unformatted I/O statements look just like formatted I/O statements, except that the **FMT=** clause is left out of the control list in the **READ** and **WRITE** statements. For example, the following two statements perform formatted and unformatted writes of array A:

```
      WRITE (UNIT=10,FMT=100,IOSTAT=ISTAT) ( A(I), I = 1, 1000 )
100 FORMAT ( 1X, 5E13.6 )
      WRITE (UNIT=10,IOSTAT=ISTAT) ( A(I), I = 1, 1000 )
```

A file may be either **FORMATTED** or **UNFORMATTED,** but not both. Therefore, we cannot mix formatted and unformatted I/O statements within a single file. The **INQUIRE** statement can be used to determine the formatting status of a file.

TABLE 8-4   Comparison of Formatted and Unformatted Files

Formatted Files	*Unformatted Files*
Can display data on output devices	Cannot display data on output devices
Can easily transport data between different computers	Cannot easily transport data between computers with different internal data representations
Requires a relatively large amount of disk space	Requires relatively little disk space
Slow: requires a lot of computer time	Fast: requires little computer time

GOOD PROGRAMMING PRACTICE

Use formatted files to create data that must be readable by humans, or that must be transferable between different types of computers. Use unformatted files to efficiently store large quantities of data that do not have to be directly examined, and that will remain on only one type of computer. Also, use unformatted files when I/O speed is critical.

8.5   DIRECT ACCESS FILES

Direct access files are files that are written and read using direct access. Records in a sequential access file must be read in order from beginning to end. By contrast, records in a direct access file may be read in arbitrary order. Direct access files are especially useful for information that may need to be accessed in any order, such as database files.

The key to the operation of a direct access file is that *every record in a direct access file must be of the same length.* If each record is the same length, then it is a simple matter to calculate exactly how far the ith record is into the disk file, and to read that disk sector directly without reading all of the sectors before it in the file. For example, suppose that we want to read the 120th record in a direct access file with 100-byte records. The 120th record is located between bytes 11,901 and 12,000 of the file. The computer can calculate the disk sector containing those bytes, and read it directly.

A direct access file is opened by specifying **ACCESS**=**'DIRECT'** in the **OPEN** statement. The length of each record in a direct access file must be specified in the **OPEN** statement using the **RECL**= clause. A typical **OPEN** statement for a direct access formatted file is shown below.

```
      OPEN ( UNIT=8, FILE='DIRIO', ACCESS='DIRECT', FORM='FORMATTED',
     *       RECL=40 )
```

Note that the **FORM**= clause had to be specified, since the default form for direct access is **'UNFORMATTED'**.

For formatted files, the length of each record in the **RECL**= clause is specified in units of characters. Therefore, each record in file DIRIO above is 40 characters long. For unformatted files, the length specified in the **RECL**= clause may be in units of bytes, words, or some other machine-dependent quantity. You will have to check the documentation for your computer to determine the units that it uses.

READ and **WRITE** statements for direct access files look like ones for sequential access files, except that the **REC**= clause may be included to specify the particular record to read or write (if the **REC**= clause is left out, then the next record in the file will be read or written). A typical **READ** statement for a direct access formatted file is shown below.

```
      READ ( 8, 100, REC=IREC ) IVAL
  100 FORMAT ( I6 )
```

Direct access, unformatted files whose record length is a multiple of the sector size of a particular computer are the most efficient FORTRAN *files possible on that computer.* Because they are direct access, it is possible to read any record in such a file directly. Because they are unformatted, no computer time is wasted in format conversions during reads or writes. Finally, because each record is exactly one disk sector long, only one disk sector needs to be read or written for each record. (Shorter records which are not multiples of the disk sector size might stretch across two disk sectors, forcing us to read both sectors to recover the information in the record.) Because these files are so efficient, many large programs written in FORTRAN are designed to use them.

A simple example program using a direct access, formatted file is shown in Figure 8-3. This program creates a direct access, formatted file named DIRIO with 40 characters per record. It fills the first 100 records with information, and then directly recovers whichever record the user specifies.

```
      PROGRAM DIRECT
C
C  Purpose:
C    To illustrate the use of direct access FORTRAN files.
C
C  Record of revisions:
C     Date       Programmer          Description of change
C     ====       ==========          =====================
C    10/05/91    S. J. Chapman       Original code
C
C  List of local variables:
C     I      -- Index variable.
C     IREC   -- Record number in file.
C     LINE   -- String containing current line.
C
      IMPLICIT NONE
C
      INTEGER I, IREC
      CHARACTER LINE*40
C
C    Open a direct access formatted file with 40 characters per record.
C
      OPEN ( UNIT=8, FILE='DIRIO', ACCESS='DIRECT', FORM='FORMATTED',
     *       RECL=40 )
C
C    Insert 100 records into this file.
C
      DO 100 I = 1, 100
         WRITE ( 8, '(A,I3,A)', REC=I ) 'This is record ', I, '.'
  100 CONTINUE
C
C    Find out which record the user wants to retrieve.
C
      WRITE (*,*) 'Which record would you like to see?'
      READ (*,'(I3)') IREC
C
C    Retrieve the desired record.
C
      READ ( 8, '(A)', REC=IREC ) LINE
C
C    Display the record.
C
      WRITE (*, '(A,/,5X,A)' ) ' The record is: ', LINE
C
      END
```

FIGURE 8-3 An example program using a direct access, formatted file.

When the program is compiled and executed on a PC, the results are

```
C:\BOOK\FORT>direct
Which record would you like to see?
34
The record is:
    This is record  34.
```

■ **GOOD PROGRAMMING PRACTICE**

Use sequential access files for data that is normally read and processed sequentially. Use direct access files for data that must be read and written in any arbitrary order.

■ **GOOD PROGRAMMING PRACTICE**

Use direct access, unformatted files for applications where large quantities of data must be manipulated quickly. If possible, make the record length of the files a multiple of the basic disk sector size for your computer.

Quiz 8-2

This quiz provides a quick check to see if you have understood the concepts introduced in Sections 8.3–8.5. If you have trouble with the quiz, reread the sections, ask your instructor, or discuss the material with a fellow student. The answers to this quiz are found in the back of the book.

For questions 1–6, determine whether the following statements are valid. If not, specify what is wrong with them.

1.
```
      INTEGER I
      I = 29
      OPEN (UNIT=I,FILE='TEMP',STATUS='SCRATCH')
      WRITE (FMT=100,UNIT=I) I
100   FORMAT (1X,'The LU is ',I3)
```

2.
```
      INTEGER I
      I = 7
      OPEN (UNIT=I,STATUS='SCRATCH',ACCESS='DIRECT')
      WRITE (FMT=100,UNIT=I) I
100   FORMAT (1X,'The LU is ',I3)
```

3.
```
      INTEGER I, J
      I = 7
      OPEN (UNIT=I,STATUS='SCRATCH',ACCESS='DIRECT',RECL=80)
      WRITE (FMT=100,UNIT=I) I
100   FORMAT (I10)
      CLOSE (I)
```

4.
```
      INTEGER I, J
      I = 7
      OPEN (UNIT=I,STATUS='SCRATCH',ACCESS='DIRECT',RECL=80)
```

```
              READ (UNIT=I,REC=37) J
              CLOSE (I)
5.            REAL A(9)
              DATA A / 5*-100., 4*100. /
              OPEN (8,FILE='MYDATA',STATUS='UNKNOWN',IOSTAT=ISTAT)
              WRITE (8,10) ( A(I), I = 1, 3 )
        10 FORMAT ( 1X, 3E14.7 )
              WRITE (8,*) ( A(I), I = 4, 6 )
              WRITE (UNIT=8) ( A(I), I = 7, 9 )
              CLOSE ( 8 )
6.            REAL A(3)
              LOGICAL EXISTS
              INTEGER LU
              DATA LU / 11 /
              INQUIRE (FILE='MYDATA',EXIST=EXISTS,UNIT=LU)
              IF ( EXISTS ) THEN
                 OPEN (UNIT=LU,FILE='MYDATA',STATUS='OLD',IOSTAT=ISTAT)
                 READ (LU,10) ( A(I), I = 1, 3 )
        10       FORMAT ( 1X, 3E14.7 )
                 CLOSE (UNIT=LU,STATUS='DELETE')
              END IF
```

EXAMPLE 8-2 *Spare Parts Inventory* Any engineering organization that maintains computers or test equipment needs to keep a supply of spare parts and consumable supplies on hand for use when equipment breaks, printers run out of paper, etc. They need to keep track of these supplies to determine how many of each type are being used in a given period of time, how many are in stock, and when to order more of a particular item. In actual practice, these functions are usually implemented with a database program. Here, we will write a simple FORTRAN program to keep track of stockroom supplies.

A program to keep track of stockroom supplies needs to maintain a database of all available supplies, their descriptions, and their quantities. A typical database record consists of

1. **Stock Number** A unique number by which the item is known. Stock numbers start at 1 and go up to however many items are carried in the stockroom.
2. **Description** Description of item (30 characters)
3. **Vendor** The company that makes or sells the item (10 characters)
3. **Vendor number** The number by which the item is known to the vendor (20 characters)
4. **Number in stock** (6 characters)
5. **Minimum quantity** If fewer than this number of the item are in stock, it should be reordered (6 characters)

We will create a database in which the number of each record corresponds to the stock number of the item in the record. There will need to be as many records as there are items in stock, and each record will be 72 bytes long. Furthermore, it may be necessary to withdraw items from stock in any order, so we should have direct access to any record in the database. We will implement the database using a direct access, formatted FORTRAN file with a record length of 72 bytes.

In addition, we will need a file containing information about the withdrawals from stock of various parts and supplies, and their replenishment by purchases from vendors. This transaction file consists of stock numbers and quantities purchased or withdrawn (purchases of supplies are indicated by positive numbers, and withdrawals from stock are indicated by negative numbers). Since the transactions in the transaction file are read in chronological sequence, it is OK to use a sequential file for the transaction file.

Finally, we need a file for reorders and error messages. This output file contains reordering messages whenever the quantity of a stock item falls below the minimum quantity. It also contains error messages if someone tries to withdraw an item which is not currently in stock.

1. State the problem.

Write a program to maintain a database of stockroom supplies for a small computer company. The program accepts inputs describing the issues from the stockroom and replenishments of the stocks, and constantly updates the database of stockroom supplies. It will also generate reorder messages whenever the supply of an item gets too low.

2. Define the inputs and outputs.

The input to the program will be a sequential transaction file describing the issues from the stockroom and replenishments of the stocks. Each purchase or issue will be a separate line in the transaction file. Each record consists of a *stock number* and *quantity* in free format.

There are two outputs from the program. One will be the database itself, and the other consists of a message file containing reordering and error messages. The database file consists of 72-byte records structured as described above.

3. Describe the algorithm.

When the program starts, it opens the database file, transaction file, and message file. It then processes each transaction in the transaction file, updating the database as necessary, and generating required messages. The high-level pseudocode for this program is

```
Open the three files
WHILE transactions file is not at end-of-file DO
   Read transaction
   Apply to database
   IF error or limit exceeded THEN
      Generate error / reorder message
   END of IF
End of WHILE
Close the three files
```

The final pseudocode for this program is

```
*
*    Open files
*
Open database file for DIRECT access
Open transaction file for SEQUENTIAL access
Open message file for SEQUENTIAL access
Position message file at end of current messages
*
*     Process transactions
*
Read the first transaction
WHILE transactions file is not at end-of-file DO
   Add / subtract quantities from database
   IF quantity < 0 THEN
      Generate error message
   END of IF
   IF quantity < minimum THEN
      Generate reorder message
   END of IF
   Read the next transaction
End of WHILE
*
*     Close files
*
Close database file
Close transaction file
Close message file
```

4. Turn the algorithm into FORTRAN statements.
The resulting FORTRAN subroutines are shown in Figure 8-4.

```
      PROGRAM STOCK
C
C Purpose:
C    To maintain an inventory of stockroom supplies, and generate
C    warning messages when supplies get low.
C
C Record of revisions:
C      Date       Programmer          Description of change
C      ====       ==========          =====================
C    11/01/91   S. J. Chapman         Original code
C
C List of local variables:
C    DBFILE -- Name of database file
C    DESCR  -- Description of item
C    IQUAN  -- Quantity in transaction
C    ISTAT  -- Status variable
C    ISTOCK -- Stock number of item in transaction
C    LUDB   -- Logical unit of database file
C    LUM    -- Logical unit of message file
C    LUT    -- Logical unit of transactions file
C    MFILE  -- Name of message file
C    MIN    -- Minimum quantity to keep in stock
C    NUMBER -- Number of an item in stock
```

```
C     TFILE  -- Name of transaction file
C     VENDOR -- Vendor of item
C     VENNUM -- Vendor's stock number
C
      IMPLICIT NONE
C
C     Declare local variables
C
      INTEGER      IQUAN, ISTAT, ISTOCK, LUDB, LUM, LUT, NUMBER, MIN
      CHARACTER*24 DBFILE, MFILE, TFILE
      CHARACTER    DESCR*30, VENDOR*10, VENNUM*20
C
C     Data
C
      DATA DBFILE / 'STOCK.DB'  /
      DATA MFILE  / 'STOCK.MSG' /
      DATA TFILE  / 'STOCK.TRN' /
      DATA LUDB   / 7 /
      DATA LUM    / 8 /
      DATA LUT    / 9 /
C
C     Open database file.
C
      OPEN (LUDB, FILE=DBFILE, STATUS='OLD', ACCESS='DIRECT',
     *      FORM='FORMATTED', RECL=72, IOSTAT=ISTAT )
C
C     Check for error.
C
      IF ( ISTAT .NE. 0 ) THEN
         WRITE (*,'(A,A,A,I6)') ' Open failed on file ', DBFILE,
     *                          '. ISTAT = ', ISTAT
         STOP
      END IF
C
C     Open transaction file.
C
      OPEN (LUT, FILE=TFILE, STATUS='OLD', ACCESS='SEQUENTIAL',
     *      IOSTAT=ISTAT )
C
C     Check for error.
C
      IF ( ISTAT .NE. 0 ) THEN
         WRITE (*,'(A,A,A,I6)') ' Open failed on file ', TFILE,
     *                          '. ISTAT = ', ISTAT
         STOP
      END IF
C
C     Open message file.
C
      OPEN (LUM, FILE=MFILE, STATUS='UNKNOWN', ACCESS='SEQUENTIAL',
     *      IOSTAT=ISTAT )
C
C     Check for error.
C
      IF ( ISTAT .NE. 0 ) THEN
         WRITE (*,'(A,A,A,I6)') ' Open failed on file ', MFILE,
     *                          '. ISTAT = ', ISTAT
         STOP
      END IF
C
```

```
C     Read transaction.
C
      READ (LUT,*,IOSTAT=ISTAT) ISTOCK, IQUAN
C
C     Process transaction (beginning of WHILE loop).
C
   10 CONTINUE
      IF ( ISTAT .EQ. 0 ) THEN
C
C        Get database record
C
         READ (LUDB,'(A30,A10,A20,I6,I6)',REC=ISTOCK,IOSTAT=ISTAT)
     *        DESCR, VENDOR, VENNUM, NUMBER, MIN
C
C        Check for error.
C
         IF ( ISTAT .NE. 0 ) THEN
            WRITE (*,'(A,I6,A,I6)')
     *        ' Read failed on database file record ', ISTOCK,
     *        ' ISTAT = ', ISTAT
            STOP
         END IF
C
C        Update record.
C
         NUMBER = NUMBER + IQUAN
C
C        Check for errors.
C
         IF ( NUMBER .LT. 0 ) THEN
C
C           Write error message to message file.
C
            WRITE (LUM,'(A,I6,A)') ' ERROR: Stock number ', ISTOCK,
     *                             ' has quantity < 0! '
C
C           Reset quantity to 0.
C
            NUMBER = 0
C
         END IF
C
C        Check for quantities < minimum.
C
         IF ( NUMBER .LT. MIN ) THEN
C
C           Write reorder message to message file.
C
            WRITE (LUM,100) ' Reorder stock number ', ISTOCK,
     *                      ' from vendor ', VENDOR,
     *                      ' Description: ', DESCR
  100       FORMAT (A,I6,A,A,/,A,A)
         END IF
C
C        Update database record
C
         WRITE (LUDB,'(A30,A10,A20,I6,I6)',REC=ISTOCK,IOSTAT=ISTAT)
     *        DESCR, VENDOR, VENNUM, NUMBER, MIN
C
```

```
C          READ next transaction, and go to beginning of WHILE loop.
C
           READ (LUT,*,IOSTAT=ISTAT) ISTOCK, IQUAN
           GO TO 10
C
       END IF
C
C      End of updates.  Close files and exit.
C
       CLOSE ( LUDB )
       CLOSE ( LUT )
       CLOSE ( LUM )
C
       END
```

FIGURE 8-4   Program **STOCK**.

5. Test the resulting FORTRAN program.

To test this subroutine, it is necessary to create a sample database file and transaction file. The following simple database file has only four stock items:

```
     5    10   15   20   25   30   35   40   45   50   55   60   65   70
----|----|----|----|----|----|----|----|----|----|----|----|----|----|---
Paper, 8.5 x 11", 500 sheets  MYNEWCO   111-345                  12     5
Toner, Laserjet IIP           HP        92275A                    2     2
Disks, 3.5 in Floppy, 1.44 MB MYNEWCO   54242                    10    10
Cable, Parallel Printer       MYNEWCO   11-32-J6                   1     1
----|----|----|----|----|----|----|----|----|----|----|----|----|----|---
     5    10   15   20   25   30   35   40   45   50   55   60   65   70
```

The following transaction file contains records of the dispensing of three reams of paper and five floppy disks. In addition, two new toner cartridges arrive and are placed in stock.

```
     1    -3
     3    -5
     2     2
```

If the program is run against this transaction file, the new database becomes

```
     5    10   15   20   25   30   35   40   45   50   55   60   65   70
----|----|----|----|----|----|----|----|----|----|----|----|----|----|---
Paper, 8.5 x 11", 500 sheets  MYNEWCO   111-345                   9     5
Toner, Laserjet IIP           HP        92275A                    4     2
Disks, 3.5 in Floppy, 1.44 MB MYNEWCO   54242                     5    10
Cable, Parallel Printer       MYNEWCO   11-32-J6                   1     1
----|----|----|----|----|----|----|----|----|----|----|----|----|----|---
     5    10   15   20   25   30   35   40   45   50   55   60   65   70
```

and the message file contains the following lines:

```
Reorder stock number      3 from vendor MYNEWCO
    Description:  Disks, 3.5 in Floppy, 1.44 MB
```

By comparing the before-and-after values in the database, we can see that the program is functioning correctly. ●

This example illustrated several different advanced I/O features. The files that had to exist in order for the program to work are opened with the **'OLD'** status, while the output message file may or may not previously exist. It is opened with the **'UNKNOWN'** status. The example uses both direct access and sequential access files. The direct access file was used in the database, where it is necessary to be able to access any record in any order. The sequential files were used for simple input and output lists that were processed in sequential order. Many of the format descriptors were in the form of strings embedded in **READ** and **WRITE** statements, rather than being included in separate **FORMAT** statements.

Note that a real database would have probably used direct access *unformatted* files, instead of formatted files. We used formatted files here to make it easy to see the before-and-after effects on the database.

8.6   SUMMARY

In this chapter, we covered the additional format descriptors[3] **G, TL, TR, S, SP, SN, BN, BZ,** and **:.** The **G** descriptor provides a way to display real data in either **E** or **F** format, depending on the value being displayed. The **TL***n* and **TR***n* descriptors shift the position of output data in the current line left and right by *n* characters. The **S, SP,** and **SN** descriptors control the display of positive signs on positive integers or real numbers, and the **BN** and **BZ** descriptors control the interpretation of blanks in input numerical fields. The colon descriptor (:) serves as a conditional stopping point for a **WRITE** statement. If there are more values to print out, the colon is ignored, and the execution of a formatted **WRITE** statement continues according to the normal rules for using **FORMAT** statements. However, if a colon is encountered in the **FORMAT** and there are no more values to write out, execution of a **WRITE** statement stops at the colon.

Next we covered advanced FORTRAN I/O features. The **INQUIRE** and **END-FILE** statements were introduced, and all possible options were explained for all FORTRAN I/O statements.

We emphasized the importance of using **IOSTAT=, END=,** and/or **ERR=** clauses in I/O statements to control the actions taken by a program when an I/O error is encountered. A large robust program should be able to recover from an error without losing everything it has done so far. It should tell the user what the problem is, and ask for possible solutions (specify a new file name, new disk, etc.). At a minimum, it should save partial results before shutting down gracefully.

We introduced two file forms: *formatted* and *unformatted*. Formatted files contain data in the form of ASCII or EBCDIC characters, while unformatted files con-

---

[3]Also the **O** and **Z** descriptors, which are extensions to FORTRAN 77.

tain data that is a direct copy of the bit images stored in the computer's memory. Formatted I/O requires a large amount of computer time, since the data must be translated every time a read or write occurs. However, formatted files can be easily moved between computers. Unformatted I/O is very quick, since no translation occurs. However, unformatted files cannot be easily inspected by humans, and cannot be easily moved between computers of different types.

We introduced two access methods: *sequential* and *direct*. Sequential access files are files intended to be read or written in sequential order. There is a limited ability to move around within a sequential file using the **REWIND** and **BACK-SPACE** commands, but the records in these files must basically be read one after another. Direct access files are files intended to be read or written in any arbitrary order. To make this possible, each record in a direct access file must be of a fixed length. If the length of each record is known, then it is possible to directly calculate where to find any specific record in the disk file, and to read or write only that record. Direct access files are especially useful for large blocks of identical records which might need to be accessed in any order. A common application for them is in databases.

8.6.1 Summary of Good Programming Practice

The following guidelines should be adhered to when working with FORTRAN I/O:

1. Always use the **IOSTAT**= clause on **OPEN** statements to trap file open errors. When an error is detected, tell the user all about the problem before shutting down gracefully or requesting an alternate file.
2. Always explicitly close each disk file with a **CLOSE** statement as soon as possible after a program is finished using it, so that it may be available for use by others.
3. Check to see if your output file is overwriting an existing data file. If it is, make sure that the user really wants to do that before destroying the data in the file.
4. Use the **IOSTAT**= clause (or the **END**= and **ERR**= clauses) on **READ** statements to prevent programs from aborting on errors or end-of-file conditions. When an error or end-of-file condition is detected, the program can take appropriate actions to continue processing or to shut down gracefully.
5. Use formatted files to create data that must be readable by humans, or must be transferable between different types of computers. Use unformatted files to efficiently store large quantities of data that do not have to be directly examined, and that will remain on only one type of computer. Also, use unformatted files when I/O speed is critical.
6. Use sequential access files for data which is normally read and processed sequentially. Use direct access files for data which must be read and written in any arbitrary order.
7. Use direct access, unformatted files for applications where large quantities of data must be manipulated quickly. If possible, make the record length of the files a multiple of the basic disk sector size for your computer.

CHAPTER 8 KEY WORDS

Direct access	Sequential access
Formatted files	SIGN format descriptors
Logical unit number	TAB format descriptors
Null values	Unformatted files
Scratch file	

CHAPTER 8 SUMMARY OF FORTRAN STATEMENTS AND STRUCTURES

BACKSPACE Statement:

```
BACKSPACE (control list)
```
or
```
BACKSPACE (lu)
```
or
```
BACKSPACE lu
```

Possible clauses in the cortrol list are **UNIT=**, **IOSTAT=**, and **ERR=**.

Example:
```
BACKSPACE (8)
BACKSPACE (LU,IOSTAT=ISTAT)
BACKSPACE 11
```

Description: The **BACKSPACE** statement moves the current position of a file back by one record.

CLOSE Statement:

```
CLOSE (close list)
```
or
```
CLOSE (LU)
```

Possible clauses in the close list are **UNIT=**, **STATUS=**, **IOSTAT=**, and **ERR=**.

Example:
```
CLOSE (UNIT=8, IOSTAT=ISTAT)
CLOSE (8)
```

Description: The **CLOSE** statement closes the file associated with an LU number.

ENDFILE Statement:

```
ENDFILE (control list)
```
or
```
ENDFILE (lu)
```
or
```
ENDFILE lu
```

Possible clauses in the control list are **UNIT=**, **IOSTAT=**, and **ERR=**.

Example:
```
ENDFILE (8)
ENDFILE ( UNIT=LU, IOSTAT=ISTAT )
```
Description: The **ENDFILE** statement writes an end-of-file record to a file, and positions the file beyond the end-of-file record.

INQUIRE Statement:

```
INQUIRE (control list)
```

Example:
```
LOGICAL LNAMED
CHARACTER FNAME*24, ACCTYP*10
INQUIRE (UNIT=22, NAMED=LNAMED, NAME=FNAME, ACCESS=ACCTYP)
```
Description: The **INQUIRE** statement permits a user to determine the properties of a file. The file may be specified either by its file name, or (after the file is opened) by its LU number. The 16 possible clauses in the **INQUIRE** statement are described in Table 8-3.

OPEN Statement:

```
OPEN (open list)
```

Possible clauses in the open list are **UNIT=**, **FILE=**, **STATUS=**, **IOSTAT=**, and **ERR=**, **ACCESS=**, **FORM=**, **BLANK=**, and **RECL=**.

Example:
```
OPEN (UNIT=8, FILE='X', STATUS='OLD', IOSTAT=IER)
```
Description: The **OPEN** statement associates a file with an LU number, so that it can be accessed by **READ** or **WRITE** statements.

READ Statement:

```
READ (control list) output list
```
or
```
READ (lu,label) output list
```

Possible clauses in the control list are **UNIT=**, **FMT=**, **IOSTAT=**, **END=**, **ERR=**, and **REC=**.

Example:
```
      READ (*,*) DIST
      READ (*,100) TIME, SPEED
100 FORMAT ( F10.4, F18.4 )
      READ (UNIT=9,FMT=200,IOSTAT=I) TIME, SPEED
100 FORMAT ( F10.4, F18.4 )
```

Description: The formatted **READ** statement reads data from an input buffer according to the formats specified in the **FORMAT** statement with statement label *label*.

REWIND Statement:

```
     REWIND (control list)
or
     REWIND (lu)
or
     REWIND lu
```

Possible clauses in the control list are **UNIT=, IOSTAT=,** and **ERR=.**

Example:

```
     REWIND (8)
     REWIND (LU,IOSTAT=ISTAT)
     REWIND 12
```

Description: The **REWIND** statement moves the current position of a file back to the beginning of the file.

WRITE Statement:

```
     WRITE (control list) output list
or
     WRITE (lu,label) output list
```

Possible clauses in the control list are **UNIT=, FMT=, IOSTAT=, ERR=,** and **REC=.**

Example:

```
         WRITE (*,*) INICPT
         WRITE (6,100) I, J, SLOPE
     100 FORMAT ( 1X, 2I10, F10.2 )
         READ (UNIT=10,FMT=200,IOSTAT=I) TIME, SPEED
     100 FORMAT ( F10.4, F18.4 )
```

Description: The formatted **WRITE** statement outputs the data in the output list according to the formats specified in the **FORMAT** statement with statement label *label*.

◼ CHAPTER 8 EXERCISES

1. Both the **BN / BZ** format descriptors and the **BLANK=** clause control the manner in which blanks are interpreted in **READ** statements. What are the relationships between these two methods of blank interpretation control? If the **BLANK=** clause says to interpret blanks as nulls, and a **READ** of the file uses

the **BZ** descriptor, which one wins? Will the blanks be interpreted as nulls or zeros in that **READ** statement?

2. Write the form of the **G** format descriptor that will display 7 significant digits of a number. What is the minimum width of this descriptor?

3. Write out the following integers with the **I8** and **I8.8** format descriptors. How do the outputs compare?
   (*a*) 1024
   (*b*) −128
   (*c*) 30,000

4. Write out the integers from the previous exercise with the **Z8** (hexadecimal) and **O11** (octal) format descriptors, if they are supported by your compiler.

5. Use subroutine RAN0 developed in Chapter 6 to generate nine random numbers in the range [−100000, 100000). Display the numbers with the **G11.5** and **SP** format descriptors.

6. Suppose that you wanted to display the nine random numbers generated in the previous exercise in the following format:

```
    5   10   15   20   25   30   35   40   45
----|----|----|----|----|----|----|----|----|-
VALUE(1) = ±xxxxxx.xx    VALUE(2) = ±xxxxxx.xx
VALUE(3) = ±xxxxxx.xx    VALUE(4) = ±xxxxxx.xx
VALUE(5) = ±xxxxxx.xx    VALUE(5) = ±xxxxxx.xx
VALUE(7) = ±xxxxxx.xx    VALUE(8) = ±xxxxxx.xx
VALUE(9) = ±xxxxxx.xx
----|----|----|----|----|----|----|----|----|-
    5   10   15   20   25   30   35   40   45
```

Write a single format descriptor that would generate this output. Use the colon descriptor appropriately in the format statement.

7. Suppose that the following numbers were to be displayed with a **G10.4** format descriptor. What form would each number take?
   (*a*) -6.38765×10^{10}
   (*b*) -6.38765×10^{2}
   (*c*) -6.38765×10^{-1}
   (*d*) 2345.6

8. Are the following statements equivalent or not? What are the advantages and disadvantages of each form?

```
      WRITE (3,100) A, B, I
  100 FORMAT (6X,F10.2,5X,F10.2,5X,I10)

      CHARACTER*60 FMT
      FMT = '(6X,F10.2,5X,F10.2,5X,I10)'
      WRITE (3,FMT) A, B, I

      WRITE (3,'(6X,F10.2,5X,F10.2,5X,I10)') A, B, I
```

9. What is the difference between using the **TR***n* format descriptor and the *n***X** format descriptor to move 10 characters to the right in an output format statement?

10. What is printed out by the following FORTRAN statements?

(a)
```
          INTEGER I, J
          REAL    DT
          I = -123456
          J = 2
          DT = 1.2E-3
          WRITE (*,1000) I, DT, J, DT
     1000 FORMAT ('1',SP,'I = ', I8,TR5,G10.4,T45,I8,TL20,F10.4)
```

(b)
```
          REAL VALUE
          INTEGER I
          VALUE = 356.248
          WRITE (*,200) 'VALUE = ', (VALUE, I = 1,5)
      200 FORMAT ('0',A,F10.4,G10.2,G11.5,G11.6,1PE10.3)
```

(c)
```
          REAL    DB(10)
          INTEGER I
          DO 10 I = 1, 10
          DB(I) = 10. * ALOG10( REAL(I) )
       10 CONTINUE
          WRITE (*,'(T22,A)') 'Amplitude versus dB:'
          WRITE (*,'(T22,A)') '===================='
          WRITE (*,11) (I, DB(I), I = 1, 10)
       11 FORMAT (T10,'DB(',I2,') = ',F5.2,2X,:,
          *              'DB(',I2,') = ',F5.2,2X,:,
          *              'DB(',I2,') = ',F5.2,2X,:)
```

(d)
```
          INTEGER I(5), J
          DO 10 J = 1, 5
            I(J) = J**2
       10 CONTINUE
          READ (*,*) I
          WRITE (*,500) I
      500 FORMAT (3(10X,I5))
```

Input Data:
```
          5    10   15   20   25   30
       ----|----|----|----|----|----|
            -101   ,,   17              /
             20         71         ,,
       ----|----|----|----|----|----|
          5    10   15   20   25   30
```

11. Assume that a file is opened with the following statement:

```
      OPEN ( UNIT = 71, FILE = 'MYFILE')
```

What is the status of the file when it is opened this way? Will the file be opened for sequential or direct access? Will it be formatted or unformatted? How will blanks be interpreted in the file? How long will each record be? What will happen if the file is not found? What will happen if an error occurs during the open process?

12. Answer the questions of the previous exercise for the following files.

    (*a*)
    ```
         OPEN ( UNIT=21, FILE='MYFILE', ACCESS='DIRECT',
       *     FORM='FORMATTED', RECL=80, IOSTAT=ISTAT )
    ```
    (*b*)
    ```
         OPEN ( UNIT=10, FILE='YOURFILE', ACCESS='DIRECT',
       *     STATUS='OLD', RECL=80, IOSTAT=ISTAT )
    ```
    (*c*)
    ```
         OPEN ( UNIT=21, FILE='MYFILE', ACCESS='SEQUENTIAL',
       *     BLANK='ZERO', STATUS='UNKNOWN' )
    ```
    (*d*)
    ```
         OPEN ( UNIT=1, STATUS='SCRATCH', IOSTAT=ISTAT )
    ```

13. The **IOSTAT=** clause in a **READ** statement can return positive, negative, or zero values. What do positive values mean? Negative values? Zero values?

14. Write a FORTRAN program that generates 100 random values in the range [0, 100), and writes them out, one per line, to a user-specified output file. After writing out the values, the program should use the **ENDFILE** statement to write an end-of-file marker at the end of the file. Finally, it should rewind the file, read record 27, and print out the value contained in that record.

15. Write a FORTRAN program that prompts the user for an input file name and an output file name, and then copies the input file to the output file, trimming trailing blanks off of the end of each line before writing it out. The program should use the **STATUS=** and **IOSTAT=** clauses in the **OPEN** statement to confirm that the input file already exists, and use the **STATUS=** and **IOSTAT=** clauses in the **OPEN** statement to confirm that the output file does not already exist. If the output file is already present, prompt the user to see if it should be overwritten. If so, overwrite it, and if not, stop the program. After the copy process is completed, the program should ask the user whether or not to delete the original file. The program should set the proper status in the input file's **CLOSE** statement if the file is to be deleted.

16. Write a FORTRAN program that prompts the user for an input file name and an output file name, and then copies the input file to the output file, trimming trailing blanks off of the end of each line before writing it out. This version of the copy program should use the **INQUIRE** statement to verify the existence of the input file before it is opened, and should use the **INQUIRE** statement to verify that the output file does not exist before it is opened. If the output file is already present, then prompt the user to see if it should be overwritten. If so, overwrite it, and if not stop the program.

17. Determine whether or not each of the following sets of FORTRAN statements is valid. If not, explain why not. If so, describe the output from the statements.
    (*a*) Statements:
    ```
              CHARACTER LINE*80
              INTEGER LU1, LU2
              DATA LU1, LU2 / 35, 36 /
              OPEN (LU1, FILE='INPUT', STATUS='OLD')
         OPEN (UNIT=LU2, FILE='MYSCR', STATUS='SCRATCH')
         READ (LU1,'(A)') LINE
         WRITE (LU2,*) LINE
    ```

Contents of file INPUT:

```
     5    10   15   20   25   30   35   40   45   50
----|----|----|----|----|----|----|----|----|----|
This is line 1 of the file.
These are miscellaneous numbers:  1, -17, 35, -101
This is line 3 of the file.
----|----|----|----|----|----|----|----|----|----|
     5    10   15   20   25   30   35   40   45   50
```

(b) Statements:

```
      CHARACTER LINE*80, ACC*10, FMT*10, BLK*10
      INTEGER LU1
      LOGICAL LEXIST, LNAMED, LOPEN
      DATA LU1/ 35 /
      INQUIRE (FILE = 'INPUT',EXIST = LEXIST)
      IF ( LEXIST ) THEN
         OPEN (LU1, FILE = 'INPUT', STATUS = 'OLD')
         INQUIRE (UNIT = LU1,OPENED = LOPEN,EXIST = LEXIST,
     *           NAMED = LNAMED,ACCESS = ACC,FORM = FMT, BLANK=BLK)
         WRITE (*,100) LEXIST, LOPEN, LNAMED, ACC, FMT, BLK
100      FORMAT (1X,' File status:  Exists = ',L1,
     *           ' Opened = ', L1, ' Named = ',L1,
     *           ' Access = ', A,/,' Format = ',A,
     *           ' Blanks = ', A)
      END IF
```

Contents of File INPUT:

```
     5    10   15   20   25   30   35   40   45   50
----|----|----|----|----|----|----|----|----|----|
This is line 1 of the file.
These are miscellaneous numbers:  1, -17, 35, -101
This is line 3 of the file.
----|----|----|----|----|----|----|----|----|----|
     5    10   15   20   25   30   35   40   45   50
```

(c) Statements:

```
      CHARACTER LINE*80, ACC*10, FMT*10, BLK*10
      INTEGER LU1
      LOGICAL LEXIST, LNAMED, LOPEN
      DATA LU1/ 35 /
      OPEN (LU1, STATUS = 'SCRATCH')
      INQUIRE (UNIT = LU1,OPENED = LOPEN,EXIST = LEXIST,
     *         NAMED = LNAMED,ACCESS = ACC,FORM = FMT, BLANK = BLK)
      WRITE (*,100) LEXIST, LOPEN, LNAMED, ACC, FMT, BLK
100 FORMAT (1X,' File status:  Exists = ',L1,
     *           ' Opened = ', L1, ' Named = ',L1,
     *           ' Access = ', A,/,' Format = ',A,
     *           ' Blanks = ', A)
```

(**d**)   Statements:

```
INTEGER I1
I1 = 10
OPEN (9, FILE = 'FILE1', ACCESS = 'DIRECT', FORM = 'FORMATTED',
*       STATUS = 'NEW')
WRITE (9,'(I6)') I1
END
```

18.   Write a FORTRAN program that prompts the user for an input file name and an output file name, and then copies the input file to the output file *in reversed order*. That is, the *last record* of the input file is the first record of the *output file*. The program should use the **STATUS=** and **IOSTAT=** clauses in the **OPEN** statement to confirm that the input file already exists, and use the **STATUS=** and **IOSTAT=** clauses in the **OPEN** statement to confirm that the output file does not already exist. If the output file is already present, then prompt the user to see if it should be overwritten. If so, overwrite it, and if not stop the program. (*Hint*: Use **READ** statements to move to the end of the input file, and **BACKSPACE** statements to work backward through it. Be careful of the **IOSTAT** values!)

19.   Write a FORTRAN program containing a real array with 1000 values in it. Fill the array with the numbers 1000–1,000,000, increasing by 1000 with each element in the array. Then perform the following actions:

(**a**)   Open a formatted sequential file and write the numbers out to the file preserving the full seven significant digits of the numbers. (Use the **E** format so that numbers of any size will be properly represented.) Write 10 numbers per line to the file, so that there are 100 lines in the file. How big is the resulting file (in characters, words, blocks, or whatever measure is used by your computer system)?

(**b**)   Open an unformatted sequential file and write the numbers out to the file. Write 10 numbers per line to the file, so that there are 100 lines in the file. How big is the resulting file?

(**c**)   Which file was smaller, the formatted file or the unformatted file? Was there a large difference between size of the two files?

(**d**)   Use the subroutines SET and ETIME created in exercise 31 in Chapter 6 to time the formatted and unformatted writes. Which one is faster? (*Note*: If you cannot tell the timing difference between the two programs while only writing 1000 values to the files, modify the programs to write the entire 1000 value-set 10 times or 100 times.)

20.   Write a FORTRAN program containing a real array with 10,000 values in it. Fill the array with 1000 random numbers in the range $[-100{,}000, 100{,}000)$. Then perform the following actions:

(**a**)   Open a formatted sequential file, and write the numbers out to the file preserving the full seven significant digits of the numbers. (Use the **E14.7** format so that numbers of any size will be properly represented.)

How big is the resulting file (in characters, words, blocks, or whatever measure is used by your computer system)?

(b) Open a formatted direct access file with 14 characters per record, and write the numbers out to the file preserving the full seven significant digits of the numbers. (Use the **E14.7** format so that numbers of any size will be properly represented.) How big is the resulting file (in characters, words, blocks, or whatever measure is used by your computer system)?

(c) Open an unformatted direct access file and write the numbers out to the file. Make the record length of each record large enough to hold one number. (This parameter is computer dependent; you will have to ask your instructor for the proper value for the **RECL=** clause.) How big is the resulting file (in characters, words, blocks, or whatever measure is used by your computer system)?

(d) Which file was smaller, the formatted direct access file or the unformatted direct access file? Was there a large difference between size of the two files? How do they compare to the files sizes in the previous example?

(e) Now, retrieve 100 records from each file in the following order: Record 1, Record 1000, Record 2, Record 999, Record 3, Record 998, etc. Use the subroutines SET and ETIME created in exercise 31 in Chapter 6 to time the reads from each of the files. Which one is fastest? (*Note*: If you cannot tell the timing difference among the three programs while only reading 100 values from the files, modify the programs to read 1000 values.)

(f) How did the sequential access file compare to the random access file when reading data in this order?

21. It is often necessary to open an existing sequential file and to append new lines to the text already in the file. For example, the file containing an error log for a program should be opened each time the program starts, and any new errors that occur during execution should be added to the file without deleting the older errors. Write a subroutine APPEND that will perform the following functions:

(a) If the user-specified file does not exist, create it, and open it for sequential access on the user-specified LU number.

(b) If the file does exist, open it for sequential access on the user-specified LU number. Then, read forward through the file until the end-of-file record is detected. Finally, backspace one record so that the file points just before the end-of-file mark.

Test your subroutine in two steps:

1. Use it to create a new file. Write two lines to the file, and close the file. Examine it after the program completes to see if it behaved properly.

2. Use it to open an existing file. Write two lines to the file, and close the file. Examine it after the program completes to see if the lines were properly appended to the previously existing data.

22. Write a program that will open a user-specified disk file containing the source code for a FORTRAN program. The program should copy the source code from the input file to a user-specified output file, stripping out any comment lines during the copying process. The program should detect the presence of the specified input file using an **INQUIRE** statement. If the file is not present, the program should offer the user the choice of either changing to a new file name or aborting the operation. It should also detect the presence of the specified output file using an **INQUIRE** statement. If the output file is already present, the program should offer the user the choice of either overwriting the file, changing to a new file name, or aborting the operation. Test your code for all combinations of input and output files present or missing.

9 Additional Data Types

So far, we have used four FORTRAN data types: **INTEGER, REAL, LOGICAL,** and **CHARACTER.** The FORTRAN 77 language includes two additional data types: **DOUBLE PRECISION** and **COMPLEX.** We will study these additional types in this chapter.

9.1 THE **DOUBLE PRECISION** DATA TYPE

The real data type is used to represent numbers containing decimal points. A real variable (also called a **single-precision** or **floating-point** variable) is usually 4 bytes (or 32 bits) long. It is divided into two parts, a **mantissa** and an **exponent.** In a typical implementation, 24 bits of the number are devoted to the mantissa, and 8 bits are devoted to the exponent. The 24 bits devoted to the mantissa are enough to represent six to seven significant decimal digits, so a real number can have up to about seven significant digits.[1] Similarly, the 8 bits of the exponent are enough to represent numbers as large as 10^{38} and as small as 10^{-38}.

The use of the bits in a floating-point number varies slightly from computer to computer, so the range of possible exponents and the number of significant digits in a real number will vary slightly. However, on a typical system,[2] the real variable type can represent numbers in the range -10^{38} to -10^{-38}, the number 0.0, and numbers in the range 10^{-38} to 10^{38} with about seven significant digits' accuracy.

---

[1] One bit is used to represent the sign of the number, and 23 bits are used to represent the magnitude of the mantissa. Since $2^{23} = 8,388,608$, it is possible to represent between six and seven significant digits with a real number.

[2] When we say "typical" here, we are describing the Institute of Electrical and Electronics Engineers (IEEE) Standard for single precision numbers. Most new computer systems conform to this standard, but some older systems allocate their bits in a different fashion. For example, IBM mainframes allocate 23 bits to the mantissa and 9 bits to the exponent, giving them a range of about 10^{-76} to 10^{76}, and about six significant digits of accuracy.

There are times when a 4-byte real number cannot adequately express a value that we need to use in solving a problem. In scientific and engineering work, it is sometimes necessary to express a number to more than seven significant digits of accuracy. Also, scientists and engineers sometimes work with numbers larger than 10^{38} or smaller than 10^{-38}. In either case, we cannot use a single-precision variable to represent the number. FORTRAN 77 includes a **DOUBLE PRECISION** data type for use in these circumstances.

A double-precision variable is usually 8 bytes (or 64 bits) long. In a typical implementation,[3] 53 bits of the number are devoted to the mantissa, and 11 bits are devoted to the exponent. The 53 bits devoted to the mantissa are enough to represent 15 to 16 significant decimal digits. Similarly, the 11 bits of the exponent are enough to represent numbers as large as 10^{308} and as small as 10^{-308}.

9.1.1 Double-Precision Constants and Variables

A double-precision constant looks just like a single-precision constant with an exponent, except that the **E** in the exponent is replaced by a **D**. If a decimal point is present in the number without an exponent, the number is interpreted as single precision. For example,

```
3.0       is a single-precision constant
3.0E0     is a single-precision constant
3.0D0     is a double-precision constant
```

A double-precision variable is declared using a **DOUBLE PRECISION** type statement. The form of this statement is

```
DOUBLE PRECISION var1, var2, etc.
```

The following example illustrates the use of double-precision variables and constants.

```
      PROGRAM DOUBLE
C
      IMPLICIT NONE
C
      REAL R
      DOUBLE PRECISION D
C
      R = 1. / 3.E0
      D = 1.D0 / 3.D0
C
      WRITE (*,*) R
      WRITE (*,*) D
C
      END
```

---

[3]When we say "typical" here, we are describing the IEEE Standard for double-precision numbers. Most new computer systems conform to this standard, but some older systems allocate their bits in a different fashion. When older systems differ from the standard, they usually do so by making the size of the exponent the same in both single-precision and double-precision numbers. For example, VAX computers allocate 56 bits to the mantissa and 8 bits to the exponent of their double-precision numbers, giving them a range of 10^{-38} - 10^{38}, and 16 - 17 significant digits of accuracy.

Here, R contains 1/3 calculated with single-precision arithmetic, while D contains 1/3 calculated with double-precision arithmetic. The output of this program is

```
C:\BOOK\FORT>double
  3.333333E-01
  3.333333333333333E-001
```

Note that R contains 7 significant digits, while D contains 16 significant digits.

9.1.2   Format Descriptors for DOUBLE PRECISION Data

There is a special format descriptor for use with double-precision data: the **D** format descriptor. The **D** format descriptor has the form

> *r***D***w.d*

where

D	indicates double-precision data in exponential notation
w	is the field width in which the data is to be displayed
d	is the number of digits to the right of the decimal point
r	is the repetition indicator. It indicates the number of times this descriptor is used. This value is optional; if it is absent, the format descriptor is used only once.

The **D** format descriptor displays double-precision data in exponential format, just as the **E** format descriptor displays single-precision data in exponential format.

Note that it is also possible to read and write double-precision data using the **E, F,** and **G** format descriptors normally associated with single-precision numbers. The following example illustrates the use of these descriptors with double-precision data.

```
      PROGRAM TEST
      DOUBLE PRECISION X
      X = 1234567.89D0
      WRITE (*,100) X, X, X, X
  100 FORMAT (1X, E18.9, 1X, F16.4, 1X, G18.9, 1X, D18.9 )
      END
```

The output from this program is

```
     5    10   15    20   25    30   35    40   45    50   55    60   65    70   75
  ----|----|----|----|----|----|----|----|----|----|----|----|----|----|----|
     .123456789E+07       1234567.8900       1234567.89          .123456789D+07
  ----|----|----|----|----|----|----|----|----|----|----|----|----|----|----|
     5    10   15    20   25    30   35    40   45    50   55    60   65    70   75
```

Note that the **D** and **E** format descriptors produced identical output when used with the double-precision variable **X.** In FORTRAN 77, **D** and **E** are identical, and can be used interchangeably for double-precision data. The **D** format descriptor only exists for backward compatibility with earlier versions of FORTRAN.

9.1.3 Mixed-Mode Arithmetic

When an arithmetic operation is performed between a double-precision number and another number, FORTRAN converts the other number to double-precision, and then performs the operation, with a double-precision result. However, note that the automatic mode conversion *does not occur* until the double-precision number and the other number both appear in the same operation. Therefore, it is possible for a portion of an expression to be evaluated in integer or real arithmetic, followed by another portion evaluated in double-precision arithmetic.

For example, suppose that we want to add 1/3 to 1/3, and get the answer to 15 significant digits. We might try to calculate the answer with any of the following expressions:

Expression	*Result*
1.D0/3. + 1/3	3.333333333333333E-001
1./3. + 1.D0/3.	6.666666333333333E-001
1.D0/3. + 1./3.D0	6.666666666666666E-001

1. In the first expression, the single-precision constant 3. is converted to double precision before dividing into the double-precision constant 1.D0, producing the result 3.333333333333333E-001. Next, the integer constant 1 is divided by the integer constant 3, producing an integer 0. Finally, the integer 0 is converted into double precision and added to the first number, producing the final value of 3.333333333333333E-001.

2. In the second expression, 1./3. is evaluated in single precision producing the result 3.333333E-01, and 1.D0/3. is evaluated in double precision, producing the result 3.333333333333333E-001. Then, the single-precision result is converted to double precision and added to the double-precision result to produce the final value of 6.666666333333333E-001.

3. In the third expression, both terms are evaluated in double precision, leading to a final value of 6.666666666666666E-001.

As we can see, adding 1/3 + 1/3 produces significantly different answers depending on the type of numbers used in each part of the expression. The third expression shown above yields the answer that we really wanted, while the first two are inaccurate to a greater or lesser degree. This result should serve as a warning: if you really need double-precision arithmetic, you should be careful to ensure that *all* intermediate portions of a calculation are performed with double-precision arithmetic, and that all intermediate results are stored in double-precision variables.

The best way to ensure that all parts of a calculation are performed in double precision is to explicitly convert integer and real values to double precision before they are used. FORTRAN includes a generic function **DBLE()** to convert integer or single-precision values into double precision. A programmer should use **DBLE()** to explicitly convert numbers to double precision, rather than relying on mixed-mode arithmetic to do the job.

PROGRAMMING PITFALLS

Mixed-mode expressions are dangerous because they are hard to understand and may produce misleading results. Avoid them whenever possible.

GOOD PROGRAMMING PRACTICE

Use the **DBLE()** function to convert integer or single-precision numbers to double precision when they are needed in double-precision calculations.

9.1.4 DOUBLE PRECISION Intrinsic Functions

FORTRAN contains many specific functions to support double-precision calculations. In addition, generic functions that support single-precision (**REAL**) inputs also support double-precision inputs. If the input value is single precision, the function is calculated with a single-precision result. If the input value is double precision, the function is calculated with a double-precision result. Table 9-1 contains a list of some generic functions and specific functions that support double-precision calculations.

9.1.5 When to Use DOUBLE PRECISION Numbers

We have seen that double-precision numbers are better than single-precision (**REAL**) numbers, offering more precision and greater range. If they are so good, why bother with single-precision numbers at all? Why don't we just use double-precision numbers all the time?

There are a couple of good reasons for not using double-precision numbers all the time. For one, every double-precision number requires twice as much memory as a single-precision number. This extra size makes programs using them much larger, and computers with more memory are required to run the programs. Another important consideration is speed. Double-precision calculations are normally *much* slower than single-precision calculations, so computer programs using double-precision calculations run much slower than computer programs using single-

TABLE 9-1   Intrinsic Functions that Support Double Precision

Generic Function	Specific Function	Function Value	Comments
SQRT(X)	DSQRT(X)	$\sqrt{x}$	Square root of x for $x \geq 0$
ABS(X)	DABS(X)	$|x|$	Absolute value of x
SIN(X)	DSIN(X)	$\sin(x)$	Sine of x (x must be in *radians*)
COS(X)	DCOS(X)	$\cos(x)$	Cosine of x (x must be in *radians*)
TAN(X)	DTAN(X)	$\tan(x)$	Tangent of x (x must be in *radians*)
EXP(X)	DEXP(X)	e^x	e raised to the xth power
LOG(X)	DLOG(X)	$\log_e(x)$	Natural logarithm of x for $x > 0$
LOG10(X)	DLOG10(X)	$\log_{10}(x)$	Base-10 logarithm of x for $x > 0$
DBLE(X)	DBLE(X)		Convert argument to double precision
	DPROD(X1,X2)		Calculate double-precision product of two real (single-precision) numbers x_1 and x_2
ASIN(X)	DASIN(X)	$\sin^{-1}(x)$	Inverse sine of x ($-1 \leq x \leq 1$, results in *radians*)
ACOS(X)	DACOS(X)	$\cos^{-1}(x)$	Inverse cosine of x ($-1 \leq x \leq 1$, results in *radians*)
ATAN(X)	DATAN(X)	$\tan^{-1}(x)$	Inverse tangent of x (results in *radians*)

precision calculations.[4] Because of these disadvantages, we should only use double-precision numbers when they are actually needed.

When are double-precision numbers actually needed? There are three general cases:

1. *When the dynamic range of the calculation requires numbers whose absolute values are smaller than 10^{-38} or larger than 10^{38}.* In this case, the problem must either be rescaled, or double-precision variables must be used.[5]
2. *When the problem requires numbers of very different sizes to be added to or subtracted from one another.* If two numbers of very different sizes must be

[4]Intel-based PC compatibles (286, 386, etc.) with a math coprocessor are an exception to this general rule. The math coprocessor performs hardware calculations with 80-bit accuracy regardless of the precision of the data being processed. As a result, there is little speed penalty for double-precision operations on a PC.

[5]If the double-precision variables on your computer only have 8-bit exponents, this case does not apply to you.

added or subtracted from one another, the resulting calculation will lose a great deal of precision. For example, suppose we wanted to add the number 3.25 to the number 1000000.0. In single precision, the calculation would be 1000003.0. In double precision, the number would be 1000003.25.

3. *When the problem requires two numbers of nearly equal size to be subtracted from one another.* When two numbers of very nearly equal size must be subtracted from each other, small errors in the last digits of the two numbers become greatly exaggerated.

   For example, consider two nearly equal numbers that are the result of a series of single-precision calculations. Because of the roundoff error in the calculations, each of the numbers is accurate to 0.0001%. The first number A1 should be 1.0000000, but through roundoff errors in previous calculations is actually 1.0000010, while the second number A2 should be 1.0000005, but through roundoff errors in previous calculations is actually 1.0000000. The difference between these numbers should be

$$\text{DTRUE} = \text{A1} - \text{A2} = -0.0000005$$

but the actual difference between them is

$$\text{DACT} = \text{A1} - \text{A2} = 0.0000010$$

Therefore, the error in the subtracted number is

$$\% \text{ ERROR} = \frac{\text{DACT} - \text{DTRUE}}{\text{DTRUE}} \times 100\%$$

$$\% \text{ ERROR} = \frac{0.0000010 - (-0.0000005)}{-0.0000005} \times 100\% = -300\%$$

Notice that the single-precision math created a 0.0001% error in A1 and A2, and then the subtraction blew that error up into a 300% error in the final answer! When two nearly equal numbers must be subtracted as a part of a calculation, the entire calculation should be performed in double precision to avoid roundoff error problems.

EXAMPLE 9-1 *Numerical Calculation of Derivatives*   The derivative of a function is defined mathematically as

$$\frac{d}{dx} f(x) = \lim_{\Delta x \to 0} \frac{f(x + \Delta x) - f(x)}{\Delta x} \tag{9-1}$$

The derivative of a function is a measure of the instantaneous slope of the function at the point being examined. In theory, the smaller Δx, the better the estimate of the derivative is. However, the calculation can go bad if there is not enough precision to avoid roundoff errors. Note that as Δx gets small, we will be subtracting two numbers that are nearly equal, and the effect of roundoff errors is multiplied.

To test the effects of precision on our calculations, we will calculate the derivative of the function

$$f(x) = \frac{1}{x}$$

(9-2)

for the location $x = 0.15$.

SOLUTION From elementary calculus, we can analytically calculate the derivative of $f(x)$ to be

$$\frac{d}{dx} f(x) = \frac{d}{dx} \frac{1}{x} = \frac{-1}{x^2}$$

For $x = 0.15$,

$$\frac{d}{dx} f(x) = \frac{-1}{x^2} = -44.44444444444444...$$

We will now attempt to evaluate the derivative of Equation (9-2) for sizes of Δx from 10^{-1} to 10^{-10} using both single- and double-precision mathematics. We will print out the results for each case, together with the true analytical solution and the resulting error.

A FORTRAN program to evaluate the derivative of Equation (9-2) is shown in Figure 9-1.

```
      PROGRAM DIFF
C
      IMPLICIT NONE
C
C
C  Purpose:
C    To test the effects of finite precision by differentiating
C    a function with 10 different step sizes, both with single
C    precision and double precision.  The test will be based upon
C    the function F(X) = 1./X.
C
C  Record of revisions:
C       Date        Programmer          Description of change
C       ====        ==========          =====================
C     02/02/92    S. J. Chapman         Original code
C
C  List of local variables:
C     ANS     -- True (analytic) answer
C     DANS    -- Double precision answer
C     DERPCT  -- Double precision percent error
C     DPX     -- Double precision F(X)
C     DPXPDX  -- Double precision F(X+DX)
C     DX      -- Step size
C     I       -- Index variable.
C     SANS    -- Single precision answer
C     SERPCT  -- Single precision percent error
C     SPX     -- Single precision F(X)
C     SPXPDX  -- Single precision F(X+DX)
C     X       -- Point at which to evaluate function dF(X)/dt
```

```
C
C       Declare local variables
C
        DOUBLE PRECISION ANS, DANS, X, DX, DPX, DPXPDX
        INTEGER          I
        REAL             SANS, SERPCT, DERPCT, SPX, SPXPDX
C
C       Print headings.
C
        WRITE (*,1)
      1 FORMAT ( 1X, '    DX        TRUE ANS      SP ANS         DP ANS ',
       *         '                 SP ERR    DP ERR  ')
C
C       Calculate analytic solution at X=0.15.
C
        X = 0.15D0
        ANS = - ( 1.D0 / X**2 )
C
C       Calculate answer from definition of differentiation
C
        DO 10 I = 1, 10
C
C          Get delta X.
C
           DX = 1.D0 / 10.D0**I
C
C          Calculate single precision answer.
C
           SPXPDX = 1./(REAL(X)1REAL(DX))
           SPX    = 1./REAL(X)
           SANS   = ( SPXPDX - SPX ) / REAL(DX)
C
C          Calculate single precision error, in percent.
C
           SERPCT 5 ( SANS - REAL(ANS) ) / REAL(ANS) * 100.
C
C          Calculate double precision answer.
C
           DPXPDX = 1.D0/(X+DX)
           DPX    = 1.D0/X
           DANS   = ( DPXPDX - DPX ) / DX
C
C          Calculate double precision error, in percent.
C
           DERPCT = ( DANS - ANS ) / ANS * 100.
C
C          Tell user.
C
           WRITE (*,100) DX, ANS, SANS, DANS, SERPCT, DERPCT
    100    FORMAT (1X, 1PE10.3, 0PF12.7, F12.7, 1PD22.14, 0PF9.3, F9.3)
C
     10 CONTINUE
C
        END
```

FIGURE 9-1   Program to evaluate the derivative of the function $f(x) = 1/x$ at $x = 0.15$ using both single-precision and double-precision arithmetic.

When this program is compiled and executed on a PC, the following results are obtained:

```
C:\BOOK\FORT>diff
   DX        TRUE ANS      SP ANS           DP ANS            SP ERR    DP ERR
1.000E-01  -44.4444444  -26.6666600  -2.66666666666667D+01  -40.000   -40.000
1.000E-02  -44.4444444  -41.6666500  -4.16666666666667D+01   -6.250    -6.250
1.000E-03  -44.4444444  -44.1498800  -4.41501103752762D+01    -.663     -.662
1.000E-04  -44.4444444  -44.4126100  -4.44148345547379D+01    -.072     -.067
1.000E-05  -44.4444444  -44.4412200  -4.44414816790584D+01    -.007     -.007
1.000E-06  -44.4444444  -44.3458600  -4.44441815019120D+01    -.222     -.001
1.000E-07  -44.4444444  -42.9153400  -4.44444148151035D+01   -3.440     .000
1.000E-08  -44.4444444  -47.6837200  -4.44444414604561D+01    7.288     .000
1.000E-09  -44.4444444    .0000000   -4.44444445690806D+01 -100.000     .000
1.000E-10  -44.4444444    .0000000   -4.44444481217943D+01 -100.000     .000
```

Note that when Δx was fairly large, both the single-precision and double-precision results give essentially the same answer. In that range, the accuracy of the result is only limited by the step size. As Δx gets smaller and smaller, the single-precision answer gets better and better until $\Delta x \approx 10^{-5}$. For step sizes smaller than 10^{-5}, roundoff errors start to dominate the solution. The double-precision answer gets better and better until $\Delta x \approx 10^{-9}$. For step sizes smaller than 10^{-9}, double-precision roundoff errors start to get progressively worse.

In this problem, the use of double precision allowed us to improve the quality of our answer from four to eight correct significant digits. The problem also points out the critical importance of a proper Δx size in producing a right answer. Such concerns occur in all computer programs performing scientific and engineering calculations. In all such programs, there are parameters that *must* be chosen correctly, or roundoff errors will result in bad answers. The design of proper algorithms for use on computers is a whole discipline in itself, known as **numerical analysis.** ●

9.1.6 Solving Large Systems of Simultaneous Linear Equations

In Chapter 6, we introduced the method of Gaussian elimination to solve systems of simultaneous linear equations of the form

$$a_{11}x_1 + a_{12}x_2 + \ldots + a_{1n}x_n = b_1$$
$$a_{21}x_1 + a_{22}x_2 + \ldots + a_{2n}x_n = b_2$$
$$\ldots$$
$$a_{n1}x_1 + a_{n2}x_2 + \ldots + a_{nn}x_n = b_n$$

The method of Gaussian elimination works as follows:

1. Find the largest absolute value among the coefficients $a_{11}, a_{21}, a_{31}, \ldots, a_{n1}$.
2. Swap the equation containing the coefficient with the maximum value to be the first equation in the set.

3. Multiply the first equation by the ratio $-a_{i1}/a_{11}$ and add it to equation i to eliminate x_1 in all equations except the first one.

4. Find the largest absolute value among the coefficients $a_{22}, a_{32}, \ldots, a_{n2}$.

5. Swap the equation containing the coefficient with the maximum value to be the second equation in the set.

6. Multiply the second equation by the ratio $-a_{i2}/a_{22}$ and add it to equation i to eliminate x_2 in all equations except the second one.

7. Repeat steps 4 through 6 until every equation contains only one unknown x_i.

8. Divide each equation by the coefficients a_{ii} of x_i. The B vector will then contain the solution to the simultaneous equations.

In this process, the first equation in the set is multiplied by constants and added to all of the other equations in the set to eliminate x_1, and then the process is repeated with the second equation in the set multiplied by constants and added to all of the other equations in the set to eliminate x_2, and so forth for all of the equations. *This type of solution is subject to cumulative roundoff errors that eventually make the answers unusable.* Any roundoff errors in eliminating the coefficients of x_1 are propagated into even bigger errors when eliminating the coefficients of x_2, which are propagated into even bigger errors when eliminating the coefficients of x_3, *etc.* For a large enough system of equations, the cumulative roundoff errors produce unacceptably bad solutions.

How big must a system of equations be before roundoff error makes it impossible to solve them using Gaussian elimination? There is no easy answer to this question. Some systems of equations are more sensitive to slight roundoff errors than others are. To understand why this is so, let's look at the two simple sets of simultaneous equations shown in Figure 9-1. Figure 9-1(a) shows a plot of the two simultaneous equations

$$3.0\,x - 2.0\,y = 3.0 \qquad\qquad\qquad \text{(9-3)}$$
$$5.0\,x + 3.0\,y = 5.0$$

The solution to this set of equations is $x = 1.0$ and $y = 0.0$. The point $(1.0, 0.0)$ is the intersection of the two lines on the plot in Figure 9-2(a). Figure 9-2(b) shows a plot of the two simultaneous equations

$$1.00\,x - 1.00\,y = -2.00 \qquad\qquad\qquad \text{(9-4)}$$
$$1.03\,x - 0.97\,y = -2.03$$

The solution to this set of equations is $x = -1.5$ and $y = 0.5$. The point $(-1.5, 0.5)$ is the intersection of the two lines on the plot in Figure 9-2(b).

Now let's compare the sensitivity of Equations 9-3 and 9-4 to slight errors in the coefficients of the equations. (A slight error in the coefficients of the equations is similar to the effect of roundoff errors on the equations.) Assume that coefficient a_{11} of Equations (9-3) is in error 1%, so that a_{11} is really 3.03 instead of 3.00. Then the solution to the equations becomes $x = 0.995$ and $y = 0.008$, which is almost the

Plot of a Well-Conditioned Set of Simultaneous Equations

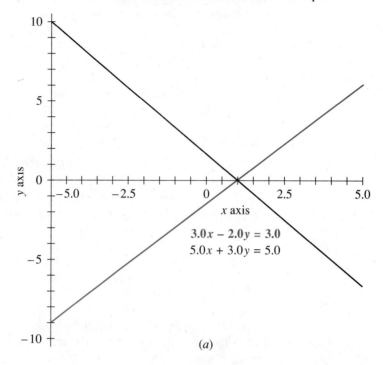

$$3.0x - 2.0y = 3.0$$
$$5.0x + 3.0y = 5.0$$

(a)

Plot of an Ill-Conditioned Set of Simultaneous Equations

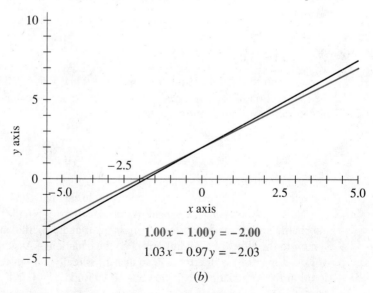

$$1.00x - 1.00y = -2.00$$
$$1.03x - 0.97y = -2.03$$

(b)

FIGURE 9-2   (a) Plot of a well-conditioned 2 × 2 set of equations.
(b) Plot of an ill-conditioned 2 × 2 set of equations.

same as the solution to the original equations. Now, let's assume that coefficient a_{11} of Equations (9-4) is in error by 1%, so that a_{11} is really 1.01 instead of 1.00. Then the solution to the equations becomes $x = 1.789$ and $y = 0.193$, which is a major shift compared to the previous answer. Equations (9-3) were relatively insensitive to small coefficient errors, while Equations (9-4) were *very* sensitive to small coefficient errors.

If we examine Figure 9-2(*b*) closely, it is obvious why Equations (9-4) are so sensitive to small changes in coefficients. The lines representing the two equations are almost parallel to each other, so a tiny change in one of the equations moves their intersection point by a large distance. If the two lines had been exactly parallel to each other, then the system of equations would either have had no solutions or an infinite number of solutions. In the case where the lines are nearly parallel, there is a single unique solution, but its location is sensitive to slight changes in the coefficients. Therefore, systems like Equations (9-4) are very sensitive to accumulated roundoff noise during Gaussian elimination.

Systems of simultaneous equations that behave well like Equations (9-3) are called *well-conditioned systems,* and systems of simultaneous equations that behave poorly like Equations (9-4) are called *ill-conditioned systems.* Well-conditioned systems of equations are relatively immune to roundoff error, while ill-conditioned systems are very sensitive to roundoff error.

When working with large systems of equations or ill-conditioned systems of equations, it is helpful to work in double-precision arithmetic. Double-precision arithmetic dramatically reduces roundoff errors, allowing Gaussian elimination to produce correct answers even for difficult systems of equations.

EXAMPLE   9-2   *Solving Large Systems of Linear Equations*   For large and/or ill-conditioned systems of equations, Gaussian elimination only produces a correct answer if double-precision arithmetic is used to reduce roundoff error. Write a subroutine that uses double-precision arithmetic to solve a system of simultaneous linear equations. Test your subroutine by comparing it to the single-precision subroutine SIMUL created in Chapter 6. Compare the two subroutines on both well-defined and ill-defined systems of equations.

SOLUTION   The double-precision subroutine DSIMUL is essentially identical to the single-precision subroutine SIMUL that we developed in Chapter 6.

1.   State the problem.

Write a subroutine to solve a system of *N* simultaneous equations in *N* unknowns using Gaussian elimination, double-precision arithmetic, and the maximum pivot technique to avoid roundoff errors. The subroutine must be able to detect singular sets of equations, and set an error flag if they occur.

2.   Define the inputs and outputs.

The input to the subroutine consists of an $N \times N$ double-precision matrix A with the coefficients of the variables in the simultaneous equations, and a double-precision vector B with the contents of the right-hand sides of the equations. The outputs from the subroutine are the solutions to the set of equations (in vector B), and an error flag. Note that the matrix of coefficients A is destroyed during the solution process.

3. Describe the algorithm.

The pseudocode for this subroutine is

```
      DO for IROW = 1 to N
*
*         Find peak pivot for column IROW in rows I to N
*
          IPEAK = IROW
          DO for JROW = IROW to N
              IF |A(JROW,IROW)| > |A(IPEAK,IROW)| then
                  IPEAK ← JROW
              END of IF
          END of DO
*
*         Check for singular equations
*
          IF |A(IPEAK,IROW)| < EPSLON THEN
              Equations are singular; set error code & exit
          END of IF
*
*         Otherwise, if IPEAK <> IROW, swap equations IROW & IPEAK
*
          IF IPEAK <> IROW
              DO for KCOL = 1 to N
                  TEMP ← A(IPEAK,KCOL)
                  A(IPEAK,KCOL) ← A(IROW,KCOL)
                  A(IROW,KCOL) ← TEMP
              END of DO
              TEMP ← B(IPEAK)
              B(IPEAK) ← B(IROW)
              B(IROW) ← TEMP
          END of IF
*
*         Multiply equation IROW by -A(JROW,IROW)/A(IROW,IROW), and
*         add it to Eqn JROW
*
          DO for JROW = 1 to N except for IROW
              FACTOR ← -A(JROW,IROW)/A(IROW,IROW)
              DO for KCOL = 1 to N
                  A(JROW,KCOL) ← A(IROW,KCOL) * FACTOR + A(JROW,KCOL)
              END of DO
              B(JROW) ← B(IROW) * FACTOR + B(JROW)
          END of DO
      END of DO
*
*     End of main loop over all equations.  All off-diagonal
*     terms are now zero.  To get the final answer, we must
*     divide each equation by the coefficient of its on-diagonal
*     term.  End of main loop over all equations
*
```

```
              DO for IROW = 1 to N
                 B(IROW) ← B(IROW) / A (IROW,IROW)
                 A(IROW,IROW) ← 1.
              END of DO
         *
              RETURN
              END
```

4. Turn the algorithm into FORTRAN statements.

The resulting FORTRAN subroutine is shown in Figure 9-3.

```
      SUBROUTINE DSIMUL ( A, B, NDIM, N, ERROR )
C
C  Purpose:
C    Subroutine to solve a set of N linear equations in N
C    unknowns using Gaussian elimination and the maximum
C    pivot technique.  This subroutine uses double precision
C    arithmetic to avoid cumulative roundoff errors.
C
C  Record of revisions:
C      Date        Programmer          Description of change
C      ====        ==========          =====================
C 0. 06/11/91  S. J. Chapman      Original code (real)
C 1. 11/03/91  S. J. Chapman      Modified for double precsision
C
C  List of calling arguments:
C     NAME   I/O  TYPE       DIM     DESCRIPTION
C     ====   ===  ====       ===     ===========
C     A      I    DBLE ARR NDIMxNDIM Array of coefficients (N x N).
C                                    This array is of size NDIM x
C                                    NDIM, but only N x N of the
C                                    coefficients are being used.
C                                    The declared dimension NDIM
C                                    must be passed to the sub, or
C                                    it won't be able to interpret
C                                    subscripts correctly.  (This
C                                    array is destroyed during
C                                    processing.)
C     B      IO   DBLE ARR   NDIM    Input: Right-hand side of eqns.
C                                    Output: Solution vector.
C     N      I    INTEGER            Number of equations to solve.
C     ERROR  O    INTEGER            Error flag:
C                                    0 -- No error
C                                    1 -- Singular equations
C
C  List of local parameters:
C     EPSLON -- A "small" number for comparison when determining that
C               a matrix is singular.
C
C  List of local variables:
C     FACTOR -- Factor to multiply eqn IROW by before adding to
C               eqn JROW
C     IROW   -- Number of equation currently being processed
C     IPEAK  -- Pointer to equation containing maximum pivot value
C     JROW   -- Number of equation compared to current equation
C     KCOL   -- Index over all columns of equation
C     TEMP   -- Scratch real variable
C
```

```
        IMPLICIT NONE
C
C       Calling arguments.
C
        INTEGER NDIM, N, ERROR
        DOUBLE PRECISION A(NDIM,NDIM), B(NDIM)
C
C       Parameters.
C
        REAL            EPSLON
        PARAMETER       ( EPSLON = 1.0E-12 )
C
C       Local variables.
C
        INTEGER IROW, JROW, KCOL, IPEAK
        DOUBLE PRECISION FACTOR, TEMP
C
C       Process N times to get all equations...
C
        DO 50 IROW = 1, N
C
C           Find peak pivot for column IROW in rows I to N
C
            IPEAK = IROW
            DO 10 JROW = IROW+1, N
               IF (ABS(A(JROW,IROW)) .GT. ABS(A(IPEAK,IROW))) THEN
                  IPEAK = JROW
               END IF
   10       CONTINUE
C
C           Check for singular equations.
C
            IF ( ABS(A(IPEAK,IROW)) .LT. EPSLON ) THEN
               ERROR = 1
               RETURN
            END IF
C
C           Otherwise, if IPEAK <> IROW, swap equations IROW & IPEAK
C
            IF ( IPEAK .NE. IROW ) THEN
               DO 20 KCOL = 1, N
                  TEMP         = A(IPEAK,KCOL)
                  A(IPEAK,KCOL) = A(IROW,KCOL)
                  A(IROW,KCOL)  = TEMP
   20          CONTINUE
               TEMP     = B(IPEAK)
               B(IPEAK) = B(IROW)
               B(IROW) = TEMP
            END IF
C
C           Multiply equation IROW by -A(JROW,IROW)/A(IROW,IROW), and
C           add it to Eqn JROW (for all eqns except IROW itself).
C
            DO 40 JROW = 1, N
               IF ( JROW .NE. IROW ) THEN
                  FACTOR = -A(JROW,IROW)/A(IROW,IROW)
                  DO 30 KCOL = 1, N
                     A(JROW,KCOL) = A(IROW,KCOL)*FACTOR + A(JROW,KCOL)
```

```
   30        CONTINUE
             B(JROW) = B(IROW)*FACTOR + B(JROW)
          END IF
   40   CONTINUE
   50 CONTINUE
C
C     End of main loop over all equations.  All off-diagonal
C     terms are now zero.  To get the final answer, we must
C     divide each equation by the coefficient of its on-diagonal
C     term.
C
      DO 60 IROW = 1, N
         B(IROW)      = B(IROW) / A (IROW,IROW)
         A(IROW,IROW) = 1.
   60 CONTINUE
C
C     Set error flag to 0 and return.
C
      ERROR = 0
      RETURN
      END
```

FIGURE 9-3   Subroutine DSIMUL.

5. Test the resulting FORTRAN programs.

To test this subroutine, it is necessary to write a driver program. The driver program opens an input data file to read the equations to be solved. The first line of the file will contain the number of equations N in the system, and each of the next N lines will contain the coefficients of one of the equations. The coefficients are stored in a single-precision array and sent to subroutine SIMUL for solution, and are also stored in a double-precision array and sent to subroutine DSIMUL for solution. To verify that the solutions are correct, they are plugged back into the original equations, and the resulting errors are calculated. The solutions and errors for single-precision and double-precision arithmetic are displayed in a summary table.

The test driver program for subroutine DSIMUL is shown in Figure 9-4.

```
      PROGRAM TDSIMU
C
C  Purpose:
C    To test subroutine DSIMUL, which solves a set of N linear
C    equations in N unknowns.  This test driver calls subroutine
C    SIMUL to solve the problem in single precision, and subrou-
C    tine DSIMUL to solve the problem in double precision.  The
C    results of the two solutions together with their errors are
C    displayed in a summary table.
C
C  Record of revisions:
C      Date        Programmer          Description of change
C      ====        ==========          =====================
C    09/19/92    S. J. Chapman         Original code
C
C  Parameters:
C    MAXSIZ — Maximum size of system to solve
C
```

```
C   List of local variables:
C      A       -- Single-precision coefficients
C      A1      -- Copy of single-precision coefficients used to check
C                 solution
C      B       -- Single precision constant values
C      B1      -- Copy of single precision constant values used to
C                 check solution
C      DA      -- Double-precision coefficients
C      DA1     -- Copy of double-precision coefficients used to check
C                 solution
C      DB      -- Double precision constant values
C      DB1     -- Copy of double precision constant values used to
C                 check solution
C      DERR    -- Array of double-precision errors
C      ERR     -- Array of single-precision errors
C      ERROR   -- Error flag returned by subroutines
C      I       -- DO loop variable
C      ISTAT   -- I/O status
C      J       -- DO loop variable
C      N       -- Size of system of equations to solve
C
       IMPLICIT NONE
C
       INTEGER     MAXSIZ
       PARAMETER ( MAXSIZ = 40 )
C
       INTEGER    I, J, N, ISTAT, ERROR
       REAL              A(MAXSIZ,MAXSIZ),   B(MAXSIZ)
       REAL              A1(MAXSIZ,MAXSIZ),  B1(MAXSIZ)
       REAL              ERR(MAXSIZ), ERRMX
       DOUBLE PRECISION DA(MAXSIZ,MAXSIZ),   DB(MAXSIZ)
       DOUBLE PRECISION DA1(MAXSIZ,MAXSIZ), DB1(MAXSIZ)
       DOUBLE PRECISION DERR(MAXSIZ), DERRMX
       CHARACTER FILENM*20
C
C   Get the name of the disk file containing the equations.
C
       WRITE (*,1000)
 1000 FORMAT (' Enter the file name containing the eqns: ')
       READ (*,1010) FILENM
 1010 FORMAT ( A20 )
C
C   Open input data file.  Status is OLD because the input data must
C   already exist.
C
       OPEN ( UNIT=1, FILE=FILENM, STATUS='OLD', IOSTAT=ISTAT )
C
C   Was the OPEN successful?
C
       IF ( ISTAT .EQ. 0 ) THEN
C
C      The file was opened successfully, so read the number of
C      equations in the system.
C
          READ (1,*) N
C
C      If the number of equations is <= MAXSIZ, read them in
C      and process them.
C
```

```
          IF ( N .LE. MAXSIZ ) THEN
             DO 10 I = 1, N
                READ (1,*) (DA(I,J), J=1,N), DB(I)
   10        CONTINUE
C
C            Save copies of the original equations in both single
C            and double precision.
C
             DO 30 I = 1, N
                DO 20 J = 1, N
                   DA1(I,J) = DA(I,J)
                   A(I,J)   = DA(I,J)
                   A1(I,J)  = DA(I,J)
   20           CONTINUE
                DB1(I) = DB(I)
                B(I)   = DB(I)
                B1(I)  = DB(I)
   30        CONTINUE
C
C            Display coefficients.
C
             WRITE (*,1020)
 1020        FORMAT (/,1X,'Coefficients before calls:')
             DO 40 I = 1, N
                WRITE (*,1030) (A(I,J), J=1,N), B(I)
 1030           FORMAT (1X,7F11.4)
   40        CONTINUE
C
C            Solve equations.
C
             CALL SIMUL  (A,  B,  MAXSIZ, N, ERROR )
             CALL DSIMUL (DA, DB, MAXSIZ, N, ERROR )
C
C            Check for error.
C
             IF ( ERROR .NE. 0 ) THEN
                WRITE (*,1040)
 1040           FORMAT (/1X,'Zero pivot encountered!',
     *                  //1X,'There is no unique solution to this system.')
             ELSE
C
C               No errors.  Check for roundoff by substituting into
C               the original equations, and calculate the differences.
C
                ERRMX  = 0.
                DERRMX = 0.
                DO 60 I = 1, N
                   ERR(I)  = 0.
                   DERR(I) = 0.
                   DO 50 J = 1, N
                      ERR(I)  = A1(I,J)  * B(J)  + ERR(I)
                      DERR(I) = DA1(I,J) * DB(J) + DERR(I)
   50              CONTINUE
                   ERR(I)  =  ERR(I) - B1(I)
                   DERR(I) = DERR(I) - DB1(I)
                   ERRMX  = MAX ( ERRMX,  ABS(ERR(I))  )
                   DERRMX = MAX ( DERRMX, ABS(DERR(I)) )
   60           CONTINUE
C
```

```
C           Tell user about it.
C
            WRITE (*,1050)
 1050       FORMAT (/1X,' I      SP X(I)        DP X(I)      ',
     *           '     SP ERR         DP ERR  ')
            WRITE (*,1052)
 1052       FORMAT ( 1X,' ===    =========      =========    ',
     *           '    =======        ======== ')
            DO 70 I = 1, N
               WRITE (*,1060) I, B(I), DB(I), ERR(I), DERR(I)
 1060          FORMAT (1X, I3, 2X, G15.6, G15.6, F15.8, F15.8)
   70       CONTINUE
C
C           Write maximum errors.
C
            WRITE (*,1070) ERRMX, DERRMX
 1070       FORMAT (/,1X,'Max single-precision error:',F15.8,
     *             /,1X,'Max double-precision error:',F15.8)
C
         END IF
       END IF
     END IF
     END
```

FIGURE 9-4   Test driver program for subroutine DSIMUL.

To test the subroutine, we call it with three different data sets. The first of them should be a well-conditioned system of equations, the second one should be an ill-conditioned system of equations, and the third should have no unique solution. The first system of equations that we will use to test the subroutine is the 6 × 6 system of equations shown below:

$$
\begin{aligned}
-2.0\,X_1 + 5.0\,X_2 + 1.0\,X_3 + 3.0\,X_4 + 4.0\,X_5 - 1.0\,X_6 &= 0.0 \\
2.0\,X_1 - 1.0\,X_2 - 5.0\,X_3 - 2.0\,X_4 + 6.0\,X_5 + 4.0\,X_6 &= 1.0 \\
-1.0\,X_1 + 6.0\,X_2 - 4.0\,X_3 - 5.0\,X_4 + 3.0\,X_5 - 1.0\,X_6 &= -6.0 \\
4.0\,X_1 + 3.0\,X_2 - 6.0\,X_3 - 5.0\,X_4 - 2.0\,X_5 - 2.0\,X_6 &= 10.0 \\
-3.0\,X_1 + 6.0\,X_2 + 4.0\,X_3 + 2.0\,X_4 - 6.0\,X_5 + 4.0\,X_6 &= -6.0 \\
2.0\,X_1 + 4.0\,X_2 + 4.0\,X_3 + 4.0\,X_4 + 5.0\,X_5 - 4.0\,X_6 &= -2.0
\end{aligned}
$$

(9-5)

If this system of equations is placed in a file called SYS6.WEL, and program TDSIMU is run on this file, the results are

```
C:\BOOK\FORT>tdsimu
Enter the file name containing the eqns:
sys6.wel
Coefficients before calls:
-2.0000     5.0000     1.0000     3.0000     4.0000    -1.0000      .0000
 2.0000    -1.0000    -5.0000    -2.0000     6.0000     4.0000     1.0000
-1.0000     6.0000    -4.0000    -5.0000     3.0000    -1.0000    -6.0000
 4.0000     3.0000    -6.0000    -5.0000    -2.0000    -2.0000    10.0000
-3.0000     6.0000     4.0000     2.0000    -6.0000    -4.0000    -6.0000
 2.0000     4.0000     4.0000     4.0000     5.0000    -4.0000    -2.0000
```

I	SP X(I)	DP X(I)	SP ERR	DP ERR
1	.662556	.662556	.00000125	.00000000
2	-.132567	-.132567	.00000072	.00000000
3	-3.01373	-3.01373	.00000238	.00000000
4	2.83548	2.83548	.00000095	.00000000
5	-1.08520	-1.08520	-.00000095	.00000000
6	-.836043	-.836043	-.00000119	.00000000

Max single-precision error: .00000238
Max double-precision error: .00000000

For this well-conditioned system, the results of single-precision and double-precision calculations are essentially identical. The second system of equations that we use to test the subroutine is the 6×6 system of equations shown below.

$$
\begin{aligned}
-2.0\ X_1 + 5.0\ X_2 \quad & + 1.0\ X_3 + 3.0\ X_4 + 4.0\ X_5 - 1.0\ X_6 = \quad 0.0 \\
2.0\ X_1 - 1.0\ X_2 \quad & - 5.0\ X_3 - 2.0\ X_4 + 6.0\ X_5 + 4.0\ X_6 = \quad 1.0 \\
-1.0\ X_1 + 6.0\ X_2 \quad & - 4.0\ X_3 - 5.0\ X_4 + 3.0\ X_5 - 1.0\ X_6 = -6.0 \\
4.0\ X_1 + 3.0\ X_2 \quad & - 6.0\ X_3 - 5.0\ X_4 - 2.0\ X_5 - 2.0\ X_6 = 10.0 \\
-3.0\ X_1 + 6.0\ X_2 \quad & + 4.0\ X_3 + 2.0\ X_4 - 6.0\ X_5 + 4.0\ X_6 = -6.0 \\
2.0\ X_1 - 1.00001\ X_2 \quad & - 5.0\ X_3 - 2.0\ X_4 + 6.0\ X_5 + 4.0\ X_6 = \quad 1.0001
\end{aligned}
$$

(9-6)

If this system of equations is placed in a file called SYS6.ILL, and program TDSIMU is run on this file, the results are

```
C:\BOOK\FORT>tdsimu
Enter the file name containing the eqns:
sys6.ill

Coefficients before calls:
    -2.0000    5.0000    1.0000    3.0000    4.0000   -1.0000     .0000
     2.0000   -1.0000   -5.0000   -2.0000    6.0000    4.0000    1.0000
    -1.0000    6.0000   -4.0000   -5.0000    3.0000   -1.0000   -6.0000
     4.0000    3.0000   -6.0000   -5.0000   -2.0000   -2.0000   10.0000
    -3.0000    6.0000    4.0000    2.0000   -6.0000    4.0000   -6.0000
     2.0000   -1.0000   -5.0000   -2.0000    6.0000    4.0000    1.0001
```

I	SP X(I)	DP X(I)	SP ERR	DP ERR
1	-47.1687	-38.5295	1.17031000	.00000000
2	-11.9188	-10.0000	-12.03978000	.00000001
3	-54.1493	-47.1554	-4.66129700	.00000000
4	30.3244	26.1372	-10.90311000	.00000001
5	-19.1049	-15.8502	10.58505000	-.00000001
6	-6.02235	-5.08561	-12.03976000	.00000001

Max single-precision error: 12.03978000
Max double-precision error: .00000001

For this ill-conditioned system, the results of the single-precision and double-precision calculations are dramatically different. The single-precision numbers X(I)

differ from the true answers by almost 20%, while the double-precision answers are almost exactly correct. Double-precision calculations are essential for a correct answer to this problem! The third system of equations that we use to test the subroutine is the 6 × 6 system of equations shown below.

$$
\begin{aligned}
-2.0\ X_1 + 5.0\ X_2 + 1.0\ X_3 + 3.0\ X_4 + 4.0\ X_5 - 1.0\ X_6 &= 0.0 \\
2.0\ X_1 - 1.0\ X_2 - 5.0\ X_3 - 2.0\ X_4 + 6.0\ X_5 + 4.0\ X_6 &= 1.0 \\
-1.0\ X_1 + 6.0\ X_2 - 4.0\ X_3 - 5.0\ X_4 + 3.0\ X_5 - 1.0\ X_6 &= -6.0 \\
4.0\ X_1 + 3.0\ X_2 - 6.0\ X_3 - 5.0\ X_4 - 2.0\ X_5 - 2.0\ X_6 &= 10.0 \\
-3.0\ X_1 + 6.0\ X_2 + 4.0\ X_3 + 2.0\ X_4 - 6.0\ X_5 + 4.0\ X_6 &= -6.0 \\
2.0\ X_1 - 1.0\ X_2 - 5.0\ X_3 - 2.0\ X_4 + 6.0\ X_5 + 4.0\ X_6 &= 1.0
\end{aligned}
$$

(9-7)

If this system of equations is placed in a file called SYS6.SNG, and program TDSIMU is run on this file, the results are

```
C:\BOOK\FORT>tdsimu
Enter the file name containing the eqns:
sys6.sng

Coefficients before calls:
   -2.0000     5.0000     1.0000     3.0000     4.0000    -1.0000      .0000
    2.0000    -1.0000    -5.0000    -2.0000     6.0000     4.0000     1.0000
   -1.0000     6.0000    -4.0000    -5.0000     3.0000    -1.0000    -6.0000
    4.0000     3.0000    -6.0000    -5.0000    -2.0000    -2.0000    10.0000
   -3.0000     6.0000     4.0000     2.0000    -6.0000     4.0000    -6.0000
    2.0000    -1.0000    -5.0000    -2.0000     6.0000     4.0000     1.0000

Zero pivot encountered!

There is no unique solution to this system.
```

Since the second and sixth equations of this set are identical, there is no unique solution to this system of equations. The subroutine correctly identified and flagged this situation.

Subroutine DSIMUL seems to be working correctly for all three cases: well-conditioned systems, ill-conditioned systems, and singular systems. Furthermore, these tests showed the clear advantage of the double-precision routine over the single-precision routine for ill-conditioned systems. ●

9.2   THE **COMPLEX** DATA TYPE

Complex numbers occur in many problems in science and engineering. For example, complex numbers are used in electrical engineering to represent alternating current voltages, currents, and impedances. The differential equations that describe the behavior of most electrical and mechanical systems also give rise to complex numbers. Because they are so ubiquitous, it is impossible to work as an engineer without a good understanding of the use and manipulation of complex numbers.

A complex number has the general form

$$c = a + bi \tag{9-8}$$

where c is a complex number, a and b are both real numbers, and i is $\sqrt{-1}$. The number a is called the **real part** and b is called the **imaginary part** of the complex number c. Since a complex number has two components, it can be plotted as a point on a plane (see Figure 9-5). The horizontal axis of the plane is the real axis, and the vertical axis of the plane is the imaginary axis, so that any complex number $a + bi$ can be represented as a single point a units along the real axis and b units along the imaginary axis. A complex number represented this way is said to be in **rectangular coordinates,** since the real and imaginary axes define the sides of a rectangle.

A complex number can also be represented as a vector of length z and angle θ pointing from the origin of the plane to the point P (see Figure 9-6). A complex number represented this way is said to be in **polar coordinates.**

$$c = a + bi = z \, \underline{/\theta}$$

The relationships among the rectangular and polar coordinate terms a, b, z, and θ are:

$$a = z \cos \theta \tag{9-9}$$
$$b = z \sin \theta \tag{9-10}$$
$$z = \sqrt{a^2 + b^2} \tag{9-11}$$
$$\theta = \tan^{-1} \frac{b}{a} \tag{9-12}$$

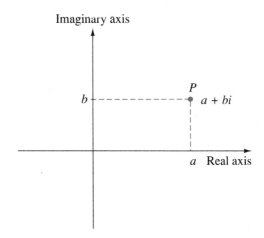

FIGURE 9-5   Representing a complex number in rectangular coordinates.

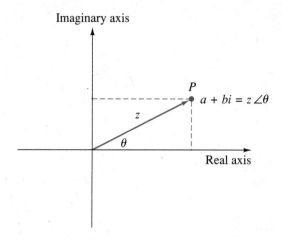

FIGURE 9-6   Representing a complex number in polar coordinates.

FORTRAN uses rectangular coordinates to represent complex numbers. Each complex number consists of a pair of single-precision real numbers (a, b) occupying successive locations in memory. The first number (a) is the real part of the complex number, and the second number (b) is the imaginary part of the complex number.

If complex numbers c_1 and c_2 are defined as $c_1 = a_1 + b_1 i$ and $c_2 = a_2 + b_2 i$, then the addition, subtraction, multiplication, and division of c_1 and c_2 are defined as

$$c_1 + c_2 = (a_1 + a_2) + (b_1 + b_2)i \tag{9-13}$$

$$c_1 - c_2 = (a_1 - a_2) + (b_1 - b_2)i \tag{9-14}$$

$$c_1 \times c_2 = (a_1 a_2 - b_1 b_2) + (a_1 b_2 + b_1 a_2)i \tag{9-15}$$

$$\frac{c_1}{c_2} = \frac{a_1 a_2 + b_1 b_2}{a_2^2 + b_2^2} + \frac{b_1 a_2 - a_1 b_2}{a_2^2 + b_2^2} i \tag{9-16}$$

When two complex numbers appear in a binary operation, FORTRAN performs the required additions, subtractions, multiplications, or divisions between the two complex numbers using the above formulas.

9.2.1   Complex Constants and Variables

A **complex constant** consists of two real constants separated by commas and enclosed in parentheses. The first real constant is the real part of the complex number, and the second real constant is the imaginary part of the complex number. For example, the following complex constants are equivalent to the complex numbers shown next to them:

```
(1., 0.)                       1 + 0i
(0.7071,0.7071)                0.7071 + 0.7071i
(0.,  -1.)                      - i
(1.01E6, 0.5E2)                1010000 + 50i
```

A complex variable is declared using a **COMPLEX** type declaration statement. The form of this statement is

```
COMPLEX var1, var2, etc.
```

For example, the following statement declares a 256-element complex array. Remember that we are actually allocating 512 thirty-two-bit values, since two real values are required for each complex number.

```
COMPLEX ARRAY(256)
```

9.2.2 Initializing Complex Variables

Like other variables, complex variables may be initialized by assignment statements, by **DATA** statements, or by **READ** statements. The following code initializes array ARRAY to (0.,0.) using an assignment statement.

```
        COMPLEX ARRAY(256)
        DO 10 I = 1, 256
           ARRAY(I) = (0.,0.)
10 CONTINUE
```

When a complex number is initialized with a **DATA** statement, it should be initialized with a complex constant. The first value in the complex constant is assigned to the real part of the variable, and the second value in the constant is assigned to the imaginary part of the variable. The following code initializes variable A1 to $(3.14159, -3.14159)$ using a **DATA** statement:

```
COMPLEX A1
DATA A1 / (3.14159, -3.14159) /
```

When a complex number is read or written with a formatted I/O statement, the first format descriptor encountered is used for the real part of the complex number, and the second format descriptor encountered is used for the imaginary part of the complex number. The following code initializes variable A1 using a formatted **READ** statement.

```
COMPLEX A1
READ (*,'(F10.2,F10.2)') A1
```

The value in the first 10 characters of the input line is placed in the real part of variable A1, and the value in the second 10 characters of the input line is placed in the imaginary part of variable A1. Note that no parentheses are included on the input line when we read a complex number using formatted I/O. By contrast, when we read a complex number with a *free format* I/O statement, the complex number must be typed exactly like a complex constant, parentheses and all. The following read statement

```
COMPLEX A1
READ (*,*) A1
```

requires that the input value be typed: (1.0,0.25).

9.2.3 Mixed-Mode Arithmetic

When an arithmetic operation is performed between a complex number and another number (real, integer, or double precision), FORTRAN converts the other number into a complex number, and then performs the operation, with a complex result. Real, integer, and double-precision numbers are converted to complex form by (1) converting the number to type real and assigning that value to the real part of the complex number, and (2) assigning 0.0 to the imaginary part of the complex number. For example, the following code will produce an output of $(300., -300.)$:

```
COMPLEX C1, C2
INTEGER I
DATA C1, I / (100., -100.), 3 /
C2 = C1 * I
WRITE (*,*) C2
```

Initially, C1 is a complex variable containing the value $(100., -100.)$, and I is an integer containing the value 3. When the fourth line is executed, the integer I is converted into the complex number (3.,0.), and that number is multiplied by C1 to give the result $(300., -300.)$.

If a real expression is assigned to a complex variable, the value of the expression is placed in the real part of the complex variable, and the imaginary part of the complex variable is set to zero. If two real expressions need to be assigned to the real and imaginary parts of a complex variable, then the CMPLX function (described next) must be used.

When a complex value is assigned to a real or double-precison variable, *the real part of the complex number is placed in the variable, and the imaginary part is discarded.* For example, the value stored in the variable A below is 3.14.

```
REAL A
COMPLEX C
C = (3.14,-6.28)
A = C
```

9.2.4   Using Complex Numbers with Relational Operators

It is possible to compare two complex numbers with the **.EQ.** relational operator to see if they are equal to each other, and to compare them with the **.NE.** operator to see if they are not equal to each other. However, they *cannot be compared with the* **.GT., .LT., .GE.,** *or* **.LE.** *operators.* The reason for this is that complex numbers consist of two separate parts. Suppose that we have two complex numbers $c_1 = a_1 + b_1 i$ and $c_2 = a_2 + b_2 i$, with $a_1 > a_2$ and $b_1 < b_2$. How can we possibly say which of these numbers is larger?

On the other hand, it is possible to compare the *magnitudes* of two complex numbers. The magnitude of a complex number can be calculated with the CABS intrinsic function (see below), or directly from Equation (9-11).

$$|c| = \sqrt{a^2 + b^2} \qquad \text{(9-11)}$$

Since the magnitude of a complex number is a real value, two magnitudes can be compared with any of the relational operators.

9.2.5   COMPLEX Intrinsic Functions

FORTRAN contains many specific and generic functions that support complex calculations. These functions fall into three general categories:

1. **Type conversion functions**   These functions convert data to and from the complex data type. Function CMPLX(a,b) is a generic function that converts numbers *a* and *b* into a complex number whose real part has value *a* and whose imaginary part has value *b*. Functions REAL(), DBLE(), and INT() convert the *real part* of a complex number into the corresponding data type, and throw away the imaginary part of the complex number. Function AIMAG() converts the *imaginary part* of a complex number into a real number.

2. **Absolute value function**   This function calculates the absolute value of a number. Function CABS(c) is a function that calculates the absolute value of a complex number using the equation

    $$\text{CABS}(c) = \sqrt{a^2 + b^2}$$

    where $c = a + bi$

3. **Mathematical functions**   These functions include exponential functions, logarithms, trigonometric functions, and square roots. The generic functions SIN, COS, LOG10, SQRT, etc. work as well with complex data as they do with real (single-precision) or double-precision data. However, you should be aware that the definition of these functions is different for complex numbers than it is for real numbers, so the results may surprise you.

A summary of the FORTRAN intrinsic functions supporting complex numbers is given in Table 9-2.

TABLE 9-2   Intrinsic Functions that Support **COMPLEX** Numbers

Generic Function	Specific Function	Function Value	Comments
CMPLX(a,b)			Combines a and b into a complex number $a + bi$ (a, b may be integer, real, or double precision)
REAL(c)			Convert real part of complex number c into a real number
DBLE(c)			Convert real part of complex number c into a double-precision number
INT(c)			Convert real part of complex number c into an integer
ABS(c)	CABS(c)	$\sqrt{a^2 + b^2}$	Calculate magnitude of a complex number (result is **REAL**)
	CONJG(c)	$c*$	Calculate the complex conjugate of c. If $c = a + bi$, then $c* = a - bi$.
SQRT(c)	CQRT(c)	$\sqrt{c}$	Square root of c
SIN(c)	CSIN(c)	$\sin(c)$	Sine of c
COS(c)	CCOS(c)	$\cos(c)$	Cosine of c
TAN(c)	CTAN(c)	$\tan(c)$	Tangent of c
EXP(c)	CEXP(c)	e^c	e raised to the cth power
LOG(c)	CLOG(c)	$\log_e(c)$	Natural logarithm of c
LOG10(c)	CLOG10(c)	$\log_{10}(c)$	Base-10 logarithm of c

It is important to be careful when converting a complex number to a real or double-precison number. If we use the REAL() or DBLE() functions to do the conversion, only the *real* portion of the complex number is translated. In many cases, what we really want is the *magnitude* of the complex number. If so, we must use CABS() instead of REAL() to do the conversion.

PROGRAMMING PITFALLS

Be careful when converting a complex number to a real or double-precision number. Find out whether the real part of the number or the magnitude of the number is needed, and use the proper function to do the conversion.

■
EXAMPLE   9-3   *The Quadratic Equation (Revisited)*   Write a general program to solve for the roots of a quadratic equation, regardless of type. Use complex variables so that no branches will be required based on the value of the discriminant.

SOLUTION

1. State the problem.

Write a program that solves for the roots of a quadratic equation, whether they are distinct real roots, repeated real roots, or complex roots, without requiring tests on the value of the discriminant.

2. Define the inputs and outputs.

The inputs required by this program are the coefficients a, b, and c of the quadratic equation

$$ax^2 + bx + c = 0 \qquad (3\text{-}1)$$

The output from the program is the roots of the quadratic equation, whether they are real, repeated, or complex.

3. Describe the algorithm.

This task can be broken down into three major sections, whose functions are input, processing, and output:

```
Read the input data
Calculate the roots
Write out the roots
```

We will now break each of the above major sections into smaller, more detailed pieces. In this algorithm, the value of the discriminant is unimportant in determining how to proceed. The resulting pseudocode is

```
Write 'Enter the coefficients A, B, and C: '
Read in A, B, C
DISCR ← CMPLX( B**2 - 4. * A * C, 0. )
X1 ← ( -B + SQRT(DISCR) ) / ( 2. * A )
X2 ← ( -B - SQRT(DISCR) ) / ( 2. * A )
Write 'The roots of this equation are: '
Write 'X1 = ', REAL(X1), ' +i ', AIMAG(X1)
Write 'X2 = ', REAL(X2), ' +i ', AIMAG(X2)
```

4. Turn the algorithm into FORTRAN statements.

The final FORTRAN code is shown in Figure 9-7.

```
       PROGRAM ROOTS2
C
C  Purpose:
C    To find the roots of a quadratic equation using complex numbers
C    to eliminate the need to branch based on the value of the
C    discriminant.
C
```

```
C  Record of revisions:
C       Date        Programmer           Description of change
C       ====        ==========           =====================
C     11/15/92    S. J. Chapman          Original code
C
C  List of variables:
C     A       -- The coefficient of X**2.
C     B       -- The coefficient of X.
C     C       -- The constant coefficient.
C     DISCR   -- The discriminant of the quadratic equation.
C     X1      -- The first root of the equation.
C     X2      -- The second root of the equation.
C
      IMPLICIT NONE
C
C     Declare the variables used in this program.
C
      REAL        A, B, C, DISCR
      COMPLEX     X1, X2
C
C     Get the name of the file containing the input data.
C
      WRITE (*,1000)
 1000 FORMAT (' Program to solve for the roots of a quadratic equation',
     *         /,' of the form A * X**2 + B * X + C. ' )
      WRITE (*,1005)
 1005 FORMAT (' Enter the coefficients A, B, and C: ')
      READ (*,*) A, B, C
C
C     Calculate the discriminant
C
      DISCR = B**2 - 4. * A * C
C
C     Calculate the roots of the equation
C
      X1 = ( -B + SQRT( CMPLX(DISCR,0.) ) ) / (2. * A )
      X2 = ( -B - SQRT( CMPLX(DISCR,0.) ) ) / (2. * A )
C
C     Tell user.
C
      WRITE (*,*) 'The roots are: '
      WRITE (*,100) '   X1 = ', REAL(X1), ' + i ', AIMAG(X1)
      WRITE (*,100) '   X2 = ', REAL(X2), ' + i ', AIMAG(X2)
  100 FORMAT (A,F10.4,A,F10.4)
C
      END
```

FIGURE 9-7   A program to solve the quadratic equation using complex numbers.

5. Test the program.

Next we must test the program using real input data. We will test cases in which the discriminant is greater than, less than, and equal to 0 to be certain that the program is working properly under all circumstances. From Equation (3-1), it is possible to verify the solutions to the equations given below.

$$x^2 + 5x + 6 = 0 \qquad x = -2, \text{ and } x = -3$$
$$x^2 + 4x + 4 = 0 \qquad x = -2$$
$$x^2 + 2x + 5 = 0 \qquad x = -1 \pm 2i$$

When the above coefficients are fed into the program, the results are

```
C:\BOOK\FORT>roots2
Program to solve for the roots of a quadratic equation
of the form A * X**2 + B * X + C.
Enter the coefficients A, B, and C:
1,5,6
The roots are:
   X1 =    -2.0000 + i      .0000
   X2 =    -3.0000 + i      .0000

C:\BOOK\FORT>roots2
Program to solve for the roots of a quadratic equation
of the form A * X**2 + B * X + C.
Enter the coefficients A, B, and C:
1,4,4
The roots are:
   X1 =    -2.0000 + i      .0000
   X2 =    -2.0000 + i      .0000

C:\BOOK\FORT>roots2
Program to solve for the roots of a quadratic equation
of the form A * X**2 + B * X + C.
Enter the coefficients A, B, and C:
1,2,5
The roots are:
   X1 =    -1.0000 + i     2.0000
   X2 =    -1.0000 + i    -2.0000
```

The program gives the correct answers for our test data in all three possible cases. Note how much simpler this program is compared to the quadratic root solver found in Example 3-1. The use of the complex data type has greatly simplified our program. ●

Quiz 9-1

This quiz provides a quick check to see if you have understood the concepts introduced in Sections 9.1 and 9.2. If you have trouble with the quiz, reread the sections, ask your instructor, or discuss the material with a fellow student. The answers to this quiz are found in the back of the book.

For questions 1–5, determine the type of the data produced by each expression, and also how many digits are significant in the final answer.

1. `1.D0 / 6.D0 + 2 * (1/11.D0) ** 5`
2. `4 * 2.**5 + NINT ( CABS((3.,4.)) )`

3. `4 * 2**5 + NINT ( CABS((3.,4.)) )`

4. `5 * CMPLX ( COS(0.7853981633974), SIN(0.7853981633974) )`

5.
```
REAL THETA
DOUBLE PRECISION SINTH
THETA = 0.78539816339745D0
SINTH = SIN( THETA )
```

6. Write a simple program to determine the number of bits of precision available in the single-precision data type on your computer.

7. What will be written out by the code shown below?

```
COMPLEX A, B, C, D
A = ( 1.,  -1. )
B = ( -1., -1. )
C = ( 10.,  1. )
D = ( A + B ) / C
WRITE (*,*) D
```

8. Use the definitions in Equations (9-13) through (9-16) to write a computer program that evaluates D in the problem above *without using complex numbers.* How much harder is it to evaluate this expression without the benefit of complex numbers?

For question 9, determine the values written out by the following statements.

9.
```
COMPLEX B
REAL A, C
DATA A, B, C / 1.,(2., 3.)., 4. /
WRITE (*,*) A, B, C
```

9.3 SUMMARY

In this chapter, we introduced the double-precision and complex data types. Double-precision numbers are essentially the same as single-precision numbers, except that they contain twice as many bits (64 bits for double precision versus 32 bits for single precision on most computers). Double-precision numbers have more significant digits than single-precision numbers, since they have more bits in their mantissas, and they have a greater range, since they have more bits in their exponents.

Double-precision variables are declared using a **DOUBLE PRECISION** type statement. They may be read in and written out using the **D, E, F,** or **G** format descriptors.

In a binary operation involving a double-precision number and an integer or real number, the integer or real number is first converted into double precision, and then the operation is performed in double precision. However, this conversion does not occur until the double-precision number appears in the same operation as the other number. Therefore, it is possible for a part of an expression to be evaluated in integer or real arithmetic before the conversion, with a consequent loss of accuracy. For example, the second part of the expression shown below is evaluated in real arithmetic, so the final answer is only valid to seven significant digits, even though it is stored in a double-precision variable.

```
DOUBLE PRECISION D
INTEGER I
REAL A
DATA I, A / 17, 3. /
D = 1.D0 / 7.D0 + I / A
```

A programmer should use the DBLE() function as necessary to ensure that all portions of a double-precision calculation are in fact done with double-precision arithmetic. For example, the following code is evaluated entirely in double-precision arithmetic.

```
DOUBLE PRECISION D
INTEGER I
REAL A
DATA I, A / 17, 3. /
D = 1.D0 / 7.D0 + DBLE(I) / DBLE(A)
```

Double-precision numbers take up more space and require more computer time to calculate than single-precision numbers, so they should not be used indiscriminately. In general, they should be used when.

1. A problem requires many significant digits or a large range of numbers
2. Numbers of dramatically different sizes must be added or subtracted
3. Two nearly equal numbers must be subtracted, and the result used in further calculations

Complex numbers consist of two single-precision (real) numbers in successive locations in memory. These two numbers are treated as though they were the real and imaginary parts of a single complex number expressed in rectangular coordinates. They are processed according to the rules for complex addition, subtraction, multiplication, division, etc.

Complex constants are written as two real numbers in parentheses, separated by commas (e.g., (1.,-1.)). Complex variables are declared using a **COMPLEX** type statement. They may be read in and written out using the **E, F,** or **G** format descriptors. When reading or writing complex numbers, the real and imaginary parts of the number are processed separately. To read in a complex number, we need two successive format descriptors and two successive numbers on the input line. The first number becomes the real part and the second number becomes the imaginary part of the complex number. If list-directed input is used with complex numbers, the input value must be typed as a complex constant, complete with parentheses.

In a binary operation involving a complex number and an integer, real number, or double-precision number, the other is first converted to complex, and then the operation is performed using complex arithmetic.

9.3.1   Summary of Good Programming Practice

The following guidelines should be adhered to when working with double-precision and complex numbers:

1. Use double-precision numbers instead of real numbers whenever
    (a) A problem requires many significant digits or a large range of numbers
    (b) Numbers of dramatically different sizes must be added or subtracted
    (c) Two nearly equal numbers must be subtracted, and the result used in further calculations
2. Avoid mixed-mode arithmetic whenever possible by explicitly converting values to double precision with the DBLE() function. When an expression is partially evaluated in integer or real arithmetic and then converted to double precision, some precision may be lost. This sort of behavior can introduce subtle bugs into a program which are almost impossible to find.
3. Be careful when you are converting a complex number to a real or double-precision number. If you use the REAL() or DBLE() functions, only the *real* portion of the complex number is translated. In many cases, what we really want is the *magnitude* of the complex number. If so, we must use CABS() instead of REAL() to do the conversion.

CHAPTER 9 KEY WORDS

Complex	Mantissa
Double precision	Polar coordinates
Exponent	Real
Floating-point	Rectangular coordinates
Imaginary	Single precision

CHAPTER 9 SUMMARY OF FORTRAN STATEMENTS AND STRUCTURES

COMPLEX Statement:

```
COMPLEX var1(, var2, etc.)
```

Example:

```
COMPLEX VOLTS, I11
```

Description:

The **COMPLEX** statement is a specification statement that declares variables of the complex data type. This statement overrides the default typing specified in FORTRAN.

DOUBLE PRECISION Statement:

```
DOUBLE PRECISION var1(, var2, etc.)
```

Example:
```
DOUBLE PRECISION DIST, TIME
```

Description:
The **DOUBLE PRECISION** statement is a specification statement that declares variables of the double-precision data type. This statement overrides the default typing specified in FORTRAN.

CHAPTER 9 EXERCISES

1. What are the advantages and disadvantages of double-precision numbers compared to single-precision numbers? When should double-precision numbers be used instead of single-precision numbers?

2. What is an ill-conditioned system of equations? Why is it hard to find the solution to an ill-conditioned set of equations?

3. The following arithmetic expression contains a mixture of real, integer, double-precision, and complex constants. What is the final type and precision of the value produced by this expression?

```
(15 / 3) * 11. / 3.333333333333D0 + (1.,0.)
```

4. State whether each of the following sets of FORTRAN statements are legal or illegal. If they are illegal, what is wrong with them? If they are legal, what do they do?

(*a*) *Statements:*
```
        DOUBLE PRECISION A
        REAL B
        READ (*,100) A, B
100 FORMAT (E18.2)
        WRITE (*,*) A, B
```

Input Data:
```
      5    10   15   20   25   30   35   40   45   50
   ----|----|----|----|----|----|----|----|----|----|
   111111111111111111111111111111111111111111111
   222222222222222222222222222222222222222222222
   333333333333333333333333333333333333333333333
   ----|----|----|----|----|----|----|----|----|----|
      5    10   15   20   25   30   35   40   45   50
```

(**b**)   *Statements:*

```
     COMPLEX A1(5)
     INTEGER I
     DO 10 I = 1, 10
        A1(I) = CMPLX ( I, -2*I )
 10  CONTINUE
     IF (A1(5) .GT. ABS(A1(3))) THEN
        WRITE (*,100) (I, A1(I), I = 1, 5)
100     FORMAT (3X,'A(',I2,') = (',F10.4,',',F10.4,')')
     END IF
```

5. Determine the type of the data produced by each expression, and also how many digits are significant in the final answer.
   (**a**) `2.0 ** (1.E0 / 3.D0)`
   (**b**) `NINT (2 * 3.14159265359 * 100.D0)`
   (**c**) `EXP ( CMPLX ( -2., 3.14159265359D0 / 2.0D0 ) )`
   (**d**) `LOG ( CMPLX ( REAL(4 / 3), 0.D0 ) )`
   (**e**) `10. ** (1.,0.)`
   (**f**) `NINT(CABS(1.D2*EXP ( CMPLX ( -2., 3.14159265359D0 / 2.0D0 ) )))`

6. Write a subroutine to calculate the derivative of a double-precision function $f(x)$ at position $x = x_0$. The calling arguments to the subroutine should be the function $f(x)$, the location x_0 at which to evaluate the function, and the step size Δx to use in the evaluation. The output from the subroutine will be the derivative of the function at point $x = x_0$. Note that the function to be evaluated should be passed to the subroutine as a calling argument! Test your subroutine by evaluating the function $f(x) = 10 \sin 20x$ at position $x = 0$.

7. If you have not done so previously, write a set of elapsed time subroutines for your computer, as described in exercise 31 in Chapter 6. Use the elapsed time subroutines to compare the time required to solve a 10×10 system of simultaneous equations in single precision and in double precision. To do this, you will need to write two test driver subroutines (one single precision and one double precision) that read in the coefficients of the equations, start the timer running, solve the equations, and then calculate the elapsed time. How much slower is the double-precision solution than the single-precision solution on your computer? (*Hint*: If you have a fast computer, you might have to create an inner loop and solve the system of equations 10 or more times to get a meaningful elapsed time.)

   Test your program on the system of equations shown below (this set of equations is contained in file SYS10 on the disk accompanying this book):

$$
\begin{aligned}
-2x_1 + 5x_2 + x_3 + 3x_4 + 4x_5 - x_6 + 2x_7 - x_8 - 5x_9 - 2x_{10} &= -5 \\
6x_1 + 4x_2 - x_3 + 6x_4 - 4x_5 - 5x_6 + 3x_7 - x_8 + 4x_9 + 3x_{10} &= -6 \\
-6x_1 - 5x_2 - 2x_3 - 2x_4 - 3x_5 + 6x_6 + 4x_7 + 2x_8 - 6x_9 + 4x_{10} &= -7 \\
2x_1 + 4x_2 + 4x_3 + 4x_4 + 5x_5 - 4x_6 + 0x_7 + 0x_8 - 4x_9 + 6x_{10} &= 0 \\
-4x_1 - x_2 + 3x_3 - 3x_4 - 4x_5 - 4x_6 - 4x_7 + 4x_8 + 3x_9 + 3x_{10} &= 5
\end{aligned}
$$

$$
\begin{array}{r}
4x_1 + 3x_2 + 5x_3 + x_4 + x_5 + x_6 + 0x_7 + 3x_8 + 3x_9 + 6x_{10} = -8 \\
x_1 + 2x_2 - 2x_3 + 0x_4 + 3x_5 - 5x_6 + 5x_7 + 0x_8 + x_9 - 4x_{10} = 1 \\
-3x_1 - 4x_2 + 2x_3 - x_4 - 2x_5 + 5x_6 - x_7 - x_8 - 4x_9 + x_{10} = -4 \\
5x_1 + 5x_2 - 2x_3 - 5x_4 + x_5 - 4x_6 - x_7 + 0x_8 - 2x_9 - 3x_{10} = -7 \\
-5x_1 - 2x_2 - 5x_3 + 2x_4 + x_5 - 3x_6 + 4x_7 - x_8 - 4x_9 + 4x_{10} = 6
\end{array}
$$

8. Create a subroutine CSIMUL to solve for the unknowns in a system of simultaneous linear equations that have complex coefficients. Test your subroutine by solving the system of equations shown below.

$$
\begin{array}{r}
(-2+i5)\ x_1 + (1+i3)\ x_2 + (4-i1)\ x_3 = (7+i5) \\
(2-i1)\ x_1 + (-5-i2)\ x_2 + (6+i4)\ x_3 = (-10-i8) \\
(-1+i6)\ x_1 + (-4-i5)\ x_2 + (3-i1)\ x_3 = (-3-i3)
\end{array}
$$

9. Write a subroutine that accepts a complex number $c = a + ib$ stored in a variable of type **COMPLEX,** and returns the amplitude C and the phase θ of the number in two real variables.

10. Write a FORTRAN function that accepts two real arguments containing the amplitude C and the phase θ of a complex number, converts the number to rectangular form, and then returns the rectangular value to the calling program as a standard complex number.

11. Euler's equation defines e raised to an imaginary power in terms of sinusoidal functions as follows:

$$
e^{i\theta} = \cos\theta + i\sin\theta
$$

Write a function to evaluate $e^{i\theta}$ for any θ using Euler's equation. Also, evaluate $e^{i\theta}$ using the intrinsic complex exponential function CEXP. Compare the answers you get by the two methods for the cases where $\theta = 0$, $\pi/2$, and π.

10

Introduction to Numerical Methods

Most FORTRAN programs are written to solve some sort of mathematical problem. The name FORTRAN itself comes from FORmula TRANslation, implying that the language is designed to translate mathematical formulas for solution on a computer. Normally, we can take any mathematical formula that works on paper (an **algorithm**), convert it into FORTRAN statements, and solve the problem on a computer.

However, this statement is only true within limits. Computers are wonderful devices, but they are *not* perfect. If we do not consider the real-world limitations of our computers when we implement algorithms, we can wind up with programs that take too long to run. Worse, we can get programs that give incorrect answers even though *every mathematical equation within the program is correct!* We have already seen a few examples of this effect when we solved for the derivative of a function and examined ill-conditioned systems of equations in Chapter 9.

The first section of this chapter explains some of the limitations of computers for solving numerical problems. It describes the major types of errors that can occur during computer calculations and problem solving.

After explaining the limitations of computer mathematics, we introduce a number of examples illustrating the proper use of computers to solve typical problems important in many areas of science and engineering. These examples illustrate the thought involved in designing a practical application.

The study of solution techniques for use on computers is a branch of mathematics known as **numerical analysis,** and the individual techniques used to solve problems on computers are called **numerical methods.** The study of numerical methods is a separate course in itself, with whole textbooks devoted to that topic alone. This chapter barely scratches the surface of the numerical methods, but it should give you some feel for the limitations of computers and the techniques used to avoid them.

10.1 THE TYPES OF ERRORS FOUND IN COMPUTER CALCULATIONS

There are two major classes of errors that are common in computer calculations. One of them is intrinsic to the nature of the computer itself, and the other one is due to programmer errors caused by the selection of an inappropriate model for the data being analyzed.

10.1.1 Errors Intrinsic to the Nature of a Computer

The errors intrinsic to the nature of the computer itself are due to the fact that any computer has a *finite precision*. A single-precision number typically has 6 to 7 significant digits, and a double-precision number typically has 14 to 15 significant digits. Many real numbers cannot be represented exactly on a computer. For example, the fraction 2/3 may be represented on a computer as 0.666667 in single precision, or as 0.66666666666667 in double precision, but it can never be *exactly* correct: 0.666666666 . . . . This failure to represent a number exactly is the first source of error that occurs in our calculations.

The Distinction Between Truncation and Rounding

Whenever two numbers are added, subtracted, multiplied, or divided, there are inevitable **truncation** or **roundoff** errors associated with the operations. There is an important distinction between truncation and roundoff. When a number is truncated to n significant digits, the first n significant digits are preserved, and all other digits are thrown away. By contrast, when a number is rounded off to n significant digits, the n significant digits that most closely represent the original number are preserved. For example, consider the number 2/3, which is equivalent to 0.666666666 . . . . If this number is *truncated* to three significant digits, the result is 0.666. If it is *rounded* to three significant digits, the result is 0.667, since 0.667 is closer to the original number than 0.666.

Some computers truncate the results of their mathematical operations, while other computers round the results of their operations. In general, computers that employ rounding will have smaller numerical errors than the computers that employ truncation. This difference between rounding and truncation may cause slight differences in numerical accuracy as a program is moved from one type of computer to another one.

To better understand the effects of limited precision, truncation, and roundoff on numerical calculations, let's consider a fictitious computer that has only three significant digits of accuracy. This computer can perform addition, subtraction, multiplication, and division on any two numbers, but each number can only have three significant digits, and the result will have three significant digits. This computer will exhibit the same types of errors that we would find in a real computer, but they will be greatly exaggerated, and so much easier for us to see.

First, let's consider the difference between truncation and roundoff on calculations in this computer. For example, suppose that we wish to add the two numbers 0.123 and 0.0456 together. Each of these numbers can be represented on the computer, since they have only three significant digits of precision. The correct sum of these numbers is

```
0.123
0.0456
0.1686
```

If the computer employs truncation, then the 0.0456 will be truncated to 0.045 before it is added to 0.123, and the result will be

```
0.123
0.045
0.168
```

If the computer employs rounding, then the 0.0456 will be rounded to 0.046 before it is added to 0.123, and the result will be

```
0.123
0.046
0.169
```

The answer using rounding is closer to the truth than the answer using truncation.

Errors in Adding Series of Numbers

Suppose that we have a long series of numbers to add up. On computers with finite precision, *the order in which the numbers are added affects the final answer that we get.* To understand this effect, let's use our hypothetical computer with truncation to add the following series of numbers.

```
0.0488
0.0958
0.3370
0.3690
```

The true sum of these numbers is 0.8506. If the numbers are added starting with the *largest number first* and adding successively smaller ones while truncating results at three significant digits, the result is

```
0.369
0.337
0.706
0.095    Number truncated to three digits for addition
0.801
0.048    Number truncated to three digits for addition
0.849
```

If the numbers are added starting with the *smallest number first* and adding successively larger ones while truncating results at three significant digits, the result is

```
0.0488
0.0958
0.144     Result truncated to three digits
0.337
0.481
0.369
0.850
```

The answer that we get depends on the order in which the numbers are added! Note that the answer that we get when adding the smallest numbers first is closer to the truth than the answer that we get when adding the largest numbers first. This happens because fewer truncations occur when we add the numbers from smallest to largest than when we add the numbers from largest to smallest.

In general, if we are adding a series of numbers together, we should add them in order from smallest numbers to the largest numbers to minimize the inaccuracies due to truncation and roundoff errors.[1] This effect has practical implications for the design of many FORTRAN functions. Most trigonometric and transcendental functions are actually calculated as the sum of the first few terms of an infinite series. For example, the transcendental function e^x can be calculated from the infinite series

$$e^x = 1 + \frac{x}{1} + \frac{x^2}{2!} + \frac{x^3}{3!} + \frac{x^4}{4!} + \frac{x^5}{5!} + \frac{x^6}{6!} + \ldots \qquad (10\text{-}1)$$

or

$$e^x = \sum_{n=0}^{\infty} \frac{x^n}{n!} \qquad (10\text{-}2)$$

A computer implementation of this function would include only the first few terms—just enough to attain the desired precision. Let's calculate the first few terms of this infinite series and see what they look like. If $x = 1$, then the series would reduce to

$$e^1 = 1 + \frac{1}{1} + \frac{1}{2!} + \frac{1}{3!} + \frac{1}{4!} + \frac{1}{5!} + \frac{1}{6!} + \ldots$$

$$e^1 = 1 + 1 + 0.5 + 0.166667 + 0.0416667 + 0.008333333$$
$$+ 0.001388889 + \ldots$$

As you can see, these terms decrease in size rapidly as n increases. If we evaluate the first 12 terms of this series to calculate the value of e^1, we will be adding together numbers of dramatically different sizes. The error in the resulting answer will be minimized if we add the smallest one first, and then work back toward the largest ones.

---

[1] A similar but smaller effect occurs on a computer that rounds off numbers instead of truncating them. It is still better to add the smaller numbers first, but the difference between adding the larger numbers first and adding the smaller numbers first will be much smaller on a machine that rounds.

In terms of FORTRAN code, the following two calculations of e^x are *not* identical. The second one is better than the first because it minimizes truncation errors.

```
REAL EXP1, X
X = 1.
EXP1 = 0.
DO 10 I = 0, 11
    EXP1 = EXP1 + X**I / FACT(I)
10 CONTINUE

REAL EXP1, X
X = 1.
EXP1 = 0.
DO 10 I = 11, 0, -1
    EXP1 = EXP1 + X**I / FACT(I)
10 CONTINUE
```

GOOD PROGRAMMING PRACTICE

When adding a large series of real numbers, add them from smallest to largest to minimize truncation errors.

Errors Due to Subtracting Nearly Equal Numbers

A second source of error occurs when subtracting two numbers with nearly equal values. If two nearly equal numbers are subtracted from each other, the resulting number will have less precision than either of the original values, and that loss of precision can produce larger errors in later calculations. For example, suppose that we wish to evaluate the following expression with our three-significant-digit computer:

$$w - x + y + z$$

where $w = 0.0256$, $x = 0.0224$, $y = 0.939$, and $z = 0.879$. The correct result of this expression is 1.8212, which to three significant digits is 1.82. On our computer, the result of this expression depends on the order in which it is evaluated. In theory, this expression could be evaluated as either

$$(w - x) + (y + z)$$

or

$$(y - x) + (w + z)$$

The result of the first expression is

```
  0.0256    w
 -0.0224    x
  0.0032

  0.939     y
  0.879     z
  1.81      Result truncated to three significant digits
```

```
1.81
0.0032     = 0 when truncated to three significant digits
1.81
```

The result of the second expression is

```
 0.939   y
-0.022   x  Truncated to three digits for addition
 0.917
```

```
 0.025   w  Truncated to three digits for addition
 0.879   z
 0.904
```

```
 0.917   y − x
 0.904   w + z
 1.82    Result truncated to three significant digits
```

The answer differed depending on the order of the operations! The results were worse when two nearly equal numbers were subtracted and that result was used in further calculations.

In general, the accuracy of an answer drops when we must subtract two nearly equal numbers. This is especially obvious when the difference between the two numbers will be used in the denominator of an expression. We saw that effect dramatically in Example 9-1 while we were solving for the numerical derivative of a function.

■ **GOOD PROGRAMMING PRACTICE**

Precision is lost whenever two nearly equal numbers must be subtracted and the result used in further calculations. If an algorithm requires you to subtract two nearly equal numbers at an intermediate point in the calculation, it may be necessary to perform the calculation in double-precision arithmetic.

Cumulative Errors Due to Multiple Cascaded Operations

A third source of error occurs when the errors in one operation are propagated into a later operation, producing an even larger error in that operation. That error in turn produces even larger errors in later operations in the chain. In other words, the error *propagates* and *grows* during the calculations. Because errors increase with each operation, it pays to keep the number of operations in your algorithms as small as possible.

For example, consider the two expressions 4 * A * B and (A + A + A + A) * B, where A = 0.568 and B = 0.502. These expressions are theoretically equal to 1.140554, which is 1.14 when truncated to three significant digits. However, when we evaluate them with our three-significant-digit truncating computer, the results are different. The first expression becomes

```
    4.00
x  0.568
    2.27        Result truncated to three significant digits


    2.27
x  0.502
    1.13        Result truncated to three significant digits
```

The second expression becomes

```
    0.568
+  0.568
    1.13        Result truncated to three significant digits
+  0.56         Truncated to three significant digits for addition
    1.69
+  0.56         Truncated to three significant digits for addition
    2.25


    2.25
x  0.502
    1.12        Result truncated to three significant digits
```

Here, the expression containing more operations had a larger error than the expression containing fewer operations. It pays to simplify your expressions to contain as few operations as possible.

■ GOOD PROGRAMMING PRACTICE

Wherever possible, simplify your expressions to contain as few operations as possible. The fewer the cascaded operations you perform, the more accurate your final answer will be. You will get the answer faster, too!

We observed the propagation of small errors into successively larger ones when we solved the simultaneous equations in Chapter 9. Single-precision arithmetic generally worked well for well-conditioned systems containing a small number of equations in a small number of unknowns. However, for larger systems and for ill-conditioned systems, the answers became progressively worse. The larger systems of equations required more arithmetic operations to find solutions than the smaller ones did, so there was more chance for errors to build up during the solution process.

10.1.2 Errors Due to Incorrect Models

Another common source of errors in computer programs is the use of *inappropriate models* to analyze data. For example, consider least squares fits. We learned in earlier chapters how to calculate the line that "best fits" a data set. But what if the behavior of the input data set is not linear? In that case, the least squares fit line will be meaningless.

A falling ball provides a good illustration of this problem. Suppose that we make noisy measurements of the position and velocity of a ball as it falls after it has been thrown downward from a 50-m height. Since the measurements are noisy, we would like to perform a fit to the data to get a better feel for the position and velocity of the ball as a function of time. The following measurements are made as the ball falls to the ground:

TABLE 10-1 Measured Position and Velocity of Ball Versus Time

Time (sec)	Position (m)	Velocity (m/s)
0.167	49.9	−5.1
0.333	52.2	−12.9
0.500	50.6	−15.1
0.667	47.0	−6.8
0.833	47.7	−12.3
1.000	42.3	−18.0
1.167	37.9	−5.7
1.333	38.2	−6.3
1.500	38.0	−12.7
1.667	33.8	−13.7
1.833	26.7	−26.7
2.000	24.8	−31.3
2.167	22.0	−22.9
2.333	16.5	−25.6
2.500	14.0	−25.7
2.667	5.6	−25.2
2.833	2.9	−35.0
3.000	0.8	−27.9

Note that the velocity values appear to be noisier than the position measurements. This is true because the instrument used to measure velocity was not as accurate as the instrument used to measure position.

The velocity data is plotted as a function of time in Figure 10-1(a). (See Figure 10-1 on pages 518 and 519.) There is a lot of scatter in this data set, but it does appear to follow a roughly linear trend. More importantly, we *know* from elementary physics that the velocity of a ball thrown in the presence of a uniform gravitational field should be given by the equation

$$v(t) = at + v_0 \tag{10-3}$$

If we do a linear least-squares fit to this data, the resulting fit is

$$v(t) = -8.69t - 4.53 \qquad \textbf{(10-4)}$$

which, considering the high noise level on the data, is in fairly good agreement with the actual conditions under which the ball was dropped (the actual acceleration was -10 m/s^2 and the actual initial velocity was -2 m/s).

The measured position data is plotted as a function of time in Figure 10-1(b). There is somewhat less noise on this data set, since it is easier for us to measure position than it is to measure velocity. If we do a linear least squares fit to this data, the resulting fit is

$$y(t) = -18.87t + 60.47 \qquad \textbf{(10-5)}$$

This fit is shown in Figure 10-1(b), and it even looks reasonable. However, it is complete garbage!

We know from elementary physics that the position of a ball thrown in the presence of a uniform gravitational field is given by the equation

$$y(t) = \frac{1}{2}at^2 + v_0t + y_0 \qquad \textbf{(10-6)}$$

The position of the ball as a function of time is a *quadratic* function, not a linear function. Therefore, fitting a straight line to the data is both meaningless and misleading. It is a case of garbage in, garbage out!

To properly analyze this data set, we must fit it to a parabola instead of a straight line. We will develop a technique to perform a least squares fit to a parabola in an example later in this chapter. The position data is shown together with a best-fit parabola in Figure 10-1(c).

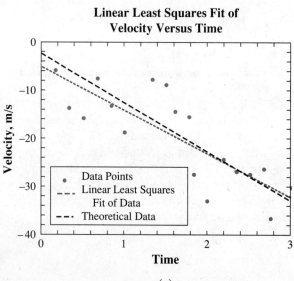

(a)

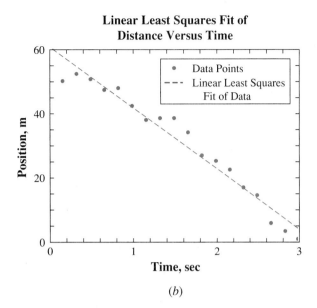

(b)

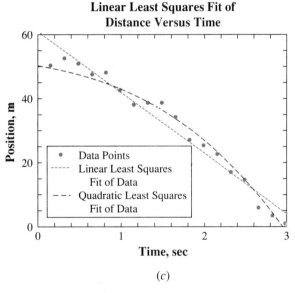

(c)

FIGURE 10-1   (a) Measured velocity of a ball as a function of time after it is thrown. Both the line corresponding to theoretical velocity of the ball and the least squares fit of the velocity are shown. (b) Measured position of the ball as a function of time after it is thrown, together with a linear least squares fit through the data. (c) Measured position of the ball as a function of time after it is thrown, together with a quadratic least squares fit through the data.

The linear least squares fit to the position data in Equation (10-5) is invalid. If we used it to estimate the position of the ball at time $t = 1.2$ s, we would add an additional error to our estimate due to the fact that the model itself is inaccurate. Programmers must be constantly alert to recognize problems of this sort. Before attempting to write any program, they should be certain that they understand the theory behind the program well enough to detect model-based flaws of this sort.

GOOD PROGRAMMING PRACTICE

Think carefully about what you want to do *before* you start programming. Pay attention to the types of models appropriate to the data that you are working with. Otherwise, garbage in will yield garbage out!

EXAMPLE 10-1 *Higher-Order Least Square Fits* As we saw above, it does not make sense to perform a linear least squares fit on a data set when we know in advance that the data is not linear. Instead, we need to fit the data to the shape that we theoretically expect the data to have. For example, the positions of a falling ball as a function of time should be fitted to a parabola, since we know from elementary physics that the position of the ball will change quadratically with time.

It is possible to extend the idea of least squares fits to find the best (least squares) fit to a polynomial more complicated than a straight line. Any polynomial may be represented by an equation of the form

$$y(x) = c_0 + c_1 x + c_2 x^2 + c_3 x^3 + c_4 x^4 + \ldots \tag{10-7}$$

where the order of the polynomial corresponds to the highest power of x appearing in the polynomial. To perform a least squares fit to a polynomial of order n, we must solve for the coefficients $c_0, c_1, \ldots, c_n$ that minimize the error between the polynomial and the data points being fit.

The polynomial being fitted to the data may be of any order as long as there are at least as many data points as there are coefficients to solve for. For example, the data may be fitted to a first-order polynomial of the form

$$y(x) = c_0 + c_1 x$$

as long as there are at least two data points in the fit. This is a straight line, where c_0 is the intercept of the line, and c_1 is the slope of the line. Similarly, the data may be fitted to a second-order polynomial of the form

$$y(x) = c_0 + c_1 x + c_2 x^2$$

as long as there are at least three data points in the fit. This is a quadratic expression whose shape is parabolic.

It can be shown[2] that the coefficients of a linear least squares fit to the polynomial $y(x) = c_0 + c_1 x$ are the solutions of the following system of equations:

$$N c_0 + \left(\sum x \right) c_1 = \sum y$$
$$\left(\sum x \right) c_0 + \left(\sum x^2 \right) c_1 = \sum xy$$

(10-8)

where

(x_i, y_i)	is the ith sample measurement
N	is the number of sample measurements included in the fit
$\sum x$	is the sum of the x_i values of all measurements
$\sum x^2$	is the sum of the squares of the x_i values of all measurements
$\sum xy$	is the sum of the products of the corresponding x_i and y_i values

Any number of sample measurements (x_i, y_i) may be used in the fit, as long as the number of measurements is greater than or equal to 2. In a problem at the end of this chapter, you will be asked to prove that the solution to Equations (10-8) is identical to Equations (4-5) and (4-6), which we have been using to perform linear least square fits.

The formulation shown above can be extended to fits of higher-order polynomials. For example, it can be shown that the coefficients of a least squares fit to the second-order polynomial $y(x) = c_0 + c_1 x + c_2 x^2$ are the solutions of the following system of equations

$$N c_0 + \left(\sum x \right) c_1 + \left(\sum x^2 \right) c_2 = \sum y$$
$$\left(\sum x \right) c_0 + \left(\sum x^2 \right) c_1 + \left(\sum x^3 \right) c_2 = \sum xy$$
$$\left(\sum x^2 \right) c_0 + \left(\sum x^3 \right) c_1 + \left(\sum x^4 \right) c_2 = \sum x^2 y$$

(10-9)

where the various terms have meanings similar to the ones described above. Any number of sample measurements (x_i, y_i) may be used in the fit, as long as the number of measurements is greater than or equal to 3. The least squares fit of the data to a parabola can be found by solving Equations (10-9) for c_0, c_1, and c_2.

The same idea can be extended to fitting polynomials of any order. To fit data to a polynomial of order n, the user must solve an $n \times n$ set of simultaneous equations, and must have at least n sample measurements (x_i, y_i). The general case of fitting an nth order polynomial to a data set is considered in exercise 6 at the end of this chapter.

---

[2]*Probability and Statistics,* by Athanasios Papoulis, Prentice-Hall, 1990, pp. 392–93.

For this example, we will write a subroutine to perform a least squares fit to a second-order polynomial (a parabola), and we will use that subroutine to fit a parabola to the position data contained in Table 10-1.

SOLUTION   The least squares fit subroutine will have to calculate the coefficients of c_0, c_1, and c_2 and the constants on the right side of Equations (10-9). It can then call subroutine SIMUL to actually solve for the coefficients c_0, c_1, and c_2. The subroutine will have to check for two possible error conditions: not enough input data, and singular equations.

1.   State the problem.
Write a subroutine to perform a least squares fit to a second-order polynomial (a parabola) of the form

$$y(x) = c_0 + c_1 x + c_2 x^2$$

The subroutine should accept an array of input points (x_i, y_i) to be fit. The input points will be divided into separate x and y arrays. It should test to ensure that there are at least three points in the input array, and report an error if insufficient data is available. The subroutine should also report an error if the set of simultaneous equations is singular.

2.   Define the inputs and outputs.
The inputs to this subroutine are

   (*a*) Two arrays of input points X and Y to be fit.

   (*b*) The number of values NVALS in the X and Y arrays.

   The outputs from this subroutine are an array C containing the coefficients of the polynomial C(0), C(1), and C(2), and an error flag IERROR. If the fit is successful, IERROR should be 0. If simultaneous equations are singular, IERROR should be 1, and if there are fewer than three input points, IERROR should be 2.

3.   Describe the algorithm.
This program can be broken down into four major steps:

```
Check to see that there is sufficient input data.
Build the coefficients of the simultaneous equations.
Solve the simultaneous equations.
Return the coefficients of the polynomial.
```

The first step of the program is to check that there is enough data to perform the fit. If there are not three points available, then we will set the error flag to 2 and get out now. If there is enough data, then we must build the coefficients for the simultaneous equations. This step is divided into two parts: calculating the sums used as coefficients, and assigning the proper sum to each coefficient. Next, we will call subroutine SIMUL to solve for the coefficients of the equation. Finally, those coefficients will be returned to the calling program.

The detailed pseudocode for the subroutine is

```
      IF NVALS < 3 Then
          IERROR ← 2
      ELSE
  *       Build sums as follows:
          Clear SUMX, SUMX2, SUMX3, SUMX4, SUMY, SUMXY, SUMX2Y
          DO for I = 1 to NVALS
              SUMX   ← SUMX   + X(I)
              SUMX2  ← SUMX2  + X(I)**2
              SUMX3  ← SUMX3  + X(I)**3
              SUMX4  ← SUMX4  + X(I)**4
              SUMXY  ← SUMXY  + X(I)*Y(I)
              SUMX2Y ← SUMX2Y + X(I)**2*Y(I)
              SUMY   ← SUMY   + Y(I)
          END of DO
  *       Now assign sums to coefficients of equations
          A(1,1) ← REAL(N)
          A(2,1) ← SUMX
          A(3,1) ← SUMX2
          A(1,2) ← SUMX
          A(2,2) ← SUMX2
          A(3,2) ← SUMX3
          A(1,3) ← SUMX2
          A(2,3) ← SUMX3
          A(3,1) ← SUMX4
          B(1)   ← SUMY
          B(2)   ← SUMXY
          B(3)   ← SUMX2Y
          CALL SIMUL ( A, B, 3, 3, IERROR )
  *       Was the solution successful?
          IF IERROR = 0 then
              C(0) ← B(1)
              C(1) ← B(2)
              C(2) ← B(3)
          ELSE
              C(0) ← 0.
              C(1) ← 0.
              C(2) ← 0.
          END of IF
      END of IF
      RETURN
```

4. Turn the algorithm into FORTRAN statements.

The resulting FORTRAN subroutine is shown in Figure 10-2. Note that this subroutine calls subroutine SIMUL, which we wrote in Chapter 6.

```
      SUBROUTINE LSQFT2 ( X, Y, NVALS, C, IERROR )
C
C  Purpose:
C    To perform a least-squares fit of an input data set
C    to the parabola
C        Y(X) = C(0) + C(1) * X + C(2) * X**2,
C    and print out the resulting coefficients.  The input
C    data set consists of NVALS (X,Y) pairs contained in
C    arrays X and Y.  The output coefficients of the
C    quadratic fit C0, C1, and C2 are placed in array C.
C
C  Record of revisions:
C      Date        Programmer          Description of change
C      ====        ==========          =====================
C    02/01/93    S. J. Chapman        Original code
C
C  List of calling arguments:
C    NAME     I/O  TYPE      DIM    DESCRIPTION
C    ====     ===  ====      ===    ===========
C    X        I    REAL ARR   N     Array of X data values.
C    Y        I    REAL ARR   N     Array of Y data values.
C    NVALS    I    INT              Number of values in arrays
C                                   X and Y.
C    C        0    REAL ARR   3     Coefficients C0, C1, and C2
C    IERROR   0    INT              Error flag:
C                                   0 - No error.
C                                   1 - Singular equations
C                                   2 - Not enough input values
C
C  List of local variables:
C    A        -- Array of coefficients of C
C    B        -- Right side of coefficient equations
C    I        -- Index variable
C    SUMX     -- The sum of all input X values
C    SUMX2    -- The sum of all input X**2
C    SUMX3    -- The sum of all input X**3
C    SUMX4    -- The sum of all input X**4
C    SUMXY    -- The sum of all X*Y values
C    SUMX2Y   -- The sum of all X**2*Y values
C    SUMY     -- The sum of all input Y values
C
      IMPLICIT NONE
C
C    Declare the dummy arguments for this subroutine.
C
      INTEGER NVALS, IERROR
      REAL    X(NVALS), Y(NVALS), C(0:2)
C
C    Declare local variables.
C
      INTEGER I
      REAL    SUMX, SUMX2, SUMX3, SUMX4
      REAL    SUMY, SUMXY, SUMX2Y
      REAL    A(3,3), B(3)
C
C    First, check to make sure that we have enough input data.
C
      IF ( NVALS .LT. 3 ) THEN
C
C       Insufficient data.  Set IERROR = 2, and get out.
C
         IERROR = 2
      ELSE
```

```
C
C           Zero the sums used to build the equations.
C
            SUMX   = 0.
            SUMX2  = 0.
            SUMX3  = 0.
            SUMX4  = 0.
            SUMY   = 0.
            SUMXY  = 0.
            SUMX2Y = 0.
C
C           Build the sums required to solve the equations.
C
            DO 10 I = 1, NVALS
               SUMX   = SUMX   + X(I)
               SUMX2  = SUMX2  + X(I)**2
               SUMX3  = SUMX3  + X(I)**3
               SUMX4  = SUMX4  + X(I)**4
               SUMY   = SUMY   + Y(I)
               SUMXY  = SUMXY  + X(I) * Y(I)
               SUMX2Y = SUMX2Y + X(I)**2 * Y(I)
      10    CONTINUE
C
C           Set up the coefficients of the equations.
C
            A(1,1) = REAL(NVALS)
            A(2,1) = SUMX
            A(3,1) = SUMX2
            A(1,2) = SUMX
            A(2,2) = SUMX2
            A(3,2) = SUMX3
            A(1,3) = SUMX2
            A(2,3) = SUMX3
            A(3,3) = SUMX4
            B(1)   = SUMY
            B(2)   = SUMXY
            B(3)   = SUMX2Y
C
C           Solve for the LSQFIT coefficients.  They will
C           be returned in array B if IERROR = 0.
C
            CALL SIMUL ( A, B, 3, 3, IERROR )
C
C           If IERROR = 0, return the coefficients to the
C           user.
C
            IF ( IERROR .EQ. 0 ) THEN
               C(0) = B(1)
               C(1) = B(2)
               C(2) = B(3)
            ELSE
               C(0) = 0.
               C(1) = 0.
               C(2) = 0.
            END IF
      END IF
C
      RETURN
      END
```

FIGURE 10-2   Subroutine LSQFT2.

5. Test the program.

We must develop a test driver program to test this subroutine. The program should read the input points from a data file, call subroutine LSQFT2, and report the results of the fit. A suitable test driver program is shown in Figure 10-3.

```
      PROGRAM TLSQF2
C
C  Purpose:
C    To test subroutine LSQFT2, which performs a least-
C    squares fit to a parabola.  The input data for this fit
C    comes from a user-specified input data file.
C
C  Record of revisions:
C     Date       Programmer          Description of change
C     ====       ==========          =====================
C    02/01/93   S. J. Chapman        Original code
C
C  List of parameters:
C     LU     -- The logical unit number to use for file I/O
C     MAXINP -- The maximum number of data points to include
C               in the fit
C
C  List of variables:
C     C        -- Coefficients of the polynomial:
C                   Y(X) = C(0) + C(1) * X + C(2) * X**2
C     FILENM -- The input file name (<= 24 characters)
C     I      -- Do loop index
C     IERROR -- The status flag returned by LSQFT2
C     ISTAT  -- The status flag returned by the I/O statements
C               and subroutine calls
C     NVALS  -- The number of input data pairs (x,y)
C
      IMPLICIT NONE
C
C     Declare parameters.
C
      INTEGER    LU, MAXINP
      PARAMETER ( LU     = 12   )
      PARAMETER ( MAXINP = 1000 )
C
C     Declare the variables used in this program.
C
      CHARACTER*24 FILENM
      INTEGER NVALS, IERROR, ISTAT, I
      REAL    C(0:2), X(MAXINP), Y(MAXINP)
C
C     Prompt user and get the name of the input file.
C
      WRITE (*,1000)
 1000 FORMAT (1X,'This program performs a least-squares fit of an ',/,
     *           1X,'input data set to a parabola.  Enter the name',/,
     *           1X,'of the file containing the input (x,y) pairs:' )
      READ (*,1010) FILENM
 1010 FORMAT (A)
C
C     Open the input file
C
      OPEN (UNIT=LU, FILE=FILENM, STATUS='OLD', IOSTAT=ISTAT )
C
```

```
C      Was the OPEN successful?
C
       IF ( ISTAT .EQ. 0 ) THEN
C
C          The file was opened successfully, so read the data to fit
C          from it, do the fit, and write out the coefficients.
C
           I = 1
           READ (LU,*,IOSTAT=ISTAT) X(I), Y(I)
C
C          Begin WHILE loop.  Did we read the value successfully?
C
   10      IF ( ISTAT .EQ. 0 ) THEN
C
C              Yes.  Increment pointer for next value.
C
               I = I + 1
C
C              Is I > MAXINP?  If so, tell user and quit.
C
               IF ( I .GT. MAXINP ) THEN
                  WRITE (*,1020) MAXINP
 1020             FORMAT (' ','Maximum input values exceeded: ', I6 )
                  GO TO 9999
               END IF
C
C              Otherwise, read next value.
C
               READ (LU,*,IOSTAT=ISTAT) X(I), Y(I)
               GO TO 10
C
C              End of WHILE Loop
C
           END IF
C
C      When we get here, the last READ was bad, so the number of values
C      we have is one less than I.
C
       NVALS = I - 1
C
C      Now, fit the data to a parabola.
C
       CALL LSQFT2 ( X, Y, NVALS, C, IERROR )
C
C      Tell user about results of fit.
C
       IF ( IERROR .EQ. 0 ) THEN
C
           WRITE (*, 1030 ) C, NVALS
 1030      FORMAT ('0','Regression coefficients for the least-',
      *                 'squares fit parabola:',
      *             /,1X,'  C(0)  = ', F12.3,
      *             /,1X,'  C(1)  = ', F12.3,
      *             /,1X,'  C(2)  = ', F12.3,
      *             /,1X,'  NVALS = ', I12 )
C
       ELSE
           WRITE (*,1040) IERROR
 1040      FORMAT (' Error returned from LSQFT2: ', I6 )
C
```

```
            END IF
C
C           Close input file.
C
            CLOSE (LU)
C
        END IF
C
 9999 CONTINUE
      END
```

FIGURE 10-3   Test driver program for subroutine LSQFT2.

To properly test subroutine LSQFT2, we need to call it with three different data sets:

1. A valid data set with a known answer
2. An invalid data set that produces a singular set of equations
3. An invalid data set with too few input data points

The program must be able to correctly handle all three cases. For the first data set, let's place five points exactly fitting the equation $y(x) = 1 + x + \frac{1}{2} x^2$ into a file called LSQFT21:

```
       -1.0          0.5
        0.0          1.0
        1.0          2.5
        3.0          8.5
        2.0          5.0
```

If we call program TLSQF2 with this data set, the results are

```
C:\BOOK\FORT>TLSQF2
This program performs a least-squares fit of an
input data set to a parabola. Enter the name
of the file containing the input (x,y) pairs:
LSQFT21

Regression coefficients for the least-squares fit parabola:
   C(0)  =         1.000
   C(1)  =         1.000
   C(2)  =          .500
   NVALS =             5
```

For the second data set, let's place three points in a file LSQFT22, but make two of them duplicates of each other. In this case, there will be three input points, but they will represent only two distinct locations along the parabola. Since a minimum of three independent variables are required to solve a set of three equations in three unknowns, this data set should produce a singular set of equations:

```
1.1        4.4
1.1        4.4
3.0        4.0
```

If we call program TLSQF2 with this data set, the results are

```
C:\BOOK\FORT>TLSQF2
This program performs a least-squares fit of an
input data set to a parabola.  Enter the name
of the file containing the input (x,y) pairs:
LSQFT22
Error returned from LSQFT2:     1
```

Finally, let's place two points in file LSQFT23. Since there is not enough data to fit the parabola, the program ought to return with the error code set to 2.

```
0.0        0.5
3.0        1.0
```

If we call program TLSQF2 with this data set, the results are

```
C:\BOOK\FORT>TLSQF2
This program performs a least-squares fit of an
input data set to a parabola. Enter the name
of the file containing the input (x,y) pairs:
LSQFT23
Error returned from LSQFT2:     2
```

The program seems to be working correctly for all possible input cases.   ●

We can use this program to properly fit the time and position data from Table 10-1 to a parabola, which we know physically should be the proper shape for this data set. If the time and position data in Table 10-1 are placed in file LSQPOS and the program is run, the results are

```
C:\BOOK\FORT>TLSQF2
This program performs a least-squares fit of an
input data set to a parabola. Enter the name
of the file containing the input (x,y) pairs:
LSQPOS

Regression coefficients for the least-squares fit parabola:
   C(0)  =       53.133
   C(1)  =       -5.618
   C(2)  =       -4.189
   NVALS =           18
```

This curve is plotted in Figure 10-1(c). As you can see, it does fit the data pretty well.

10.2   NUMERICAL APPLICATIONS

In this section, we will design a number of subroutines that have practical engineering and scientific applications. We have already seen a number of such subroutines and functions. In Chapter 6, we developed statistics subroutines, sorting subroutines, simultaneous equation solvers, and random number generators. In Chapter 7, we introduced plotting programs. In Chapter 9, we developed routines to take the derivative of a function, and also routines to solve larger or ill-conditioned systems of simultaneous equations. We will now develop two additional subroutines to integrate user-specified functions and to find the real roots of equations.

10.2.1   Numerical Integration—Finding the Area Under a Curve

We learned how to take the numerical derivative of a function in Chapter 9. The derivative of a function is defined by the equation

$$\frac{d}{dx}f(x) = \lim_{\Delta x \to 0} \frac{f(x + \Delta x) - f(x)}{\Delta x} \qquad \text{(9-1)}$$

As we mentioned, the derivative of a function $f(x)$ at a point x_0 may be interpreted as the slope of the function at that point.

By contrast, the *integral* of a function $f(x)$ may be interpreted as the total area under the curve of the function between a starting point and an ending point. Figure 10-4(a) shows a function $f(x)$ plotted as a function of x. The area under this curve between points x_1 and x_2 is equal to the integral of the function $f(x)$ with respect to x between points x_1 and x_2. How can we find this area?

In general, we don't know the area under a curve of arbitrary shape. However, we *do* know the area of a rectangle. The area of a rectangle is just equal to the length of the rectangle times its width:

Area = length × width

Suppose that we fill the entire area under the curve between points x_1 and x_2 with a series of small rectangles, and then add up the areas of each of the rectangles. If we do this, then we will have an estimate of the area under the curve $f(x)$. Figure 10-4(b) shows the area under the curve filled with many small rectangles, each of width Δx and length $f(x_i)$, where x_i is the position of the rectangle along the x axis. Adding up the area in these rectangles gives us an approximate equation for the area under the curve

$$A \approx \sum_{x_1}^{x_2} f(x)\,\Delta x \qquad \textbf{(10-10)}$$

The area calculated by Equation (10-10) is only approximate, since the rectangles do not exactly match the shape of the curve that they are approximating. However,

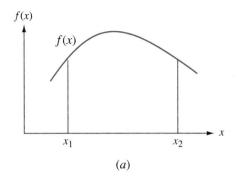

(a)

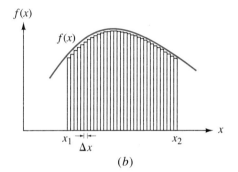

(b)

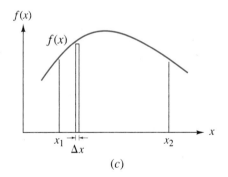

(c)

FIGURE 10-4 (a) A plot of $f(x)$ versus x. The area under this curve between points x_1 and x_2 is equal to $\int_{x_1}^{x_2} f(x)\, dx$. (b) The area under the curve between points x_1 and x_2 divided into many small rectangles. (c) Each rectangle is Δx wide and $f(x_i)$ high, where x_i is the center of rectangle i. The area of the rectangle is Area $= f(x_i)\, \Delta x$.

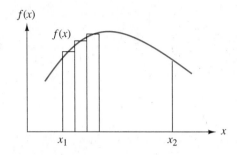

FIGURE 10-5   When the area under the curve is divided into only a few rectangles, the rectangles do not match the shape of the curve as closely as when the area under the curve is divided into many rectangles. Compare to Figure 10-4(*b*).

the more rectangles that the area under the curve is divided into, the better the resulting fit will be (see Figure 10-5). If we use an infinite number of infinitely thin rectangles, we would calculate the area under the curve precisely. In fact, we have just defined integration! An integral is the sum given by Equation (10-10) in the limit as Δx gets very small and the number of rectangles gets very large.

$$\int f(x)\, dx = \lim_{x \to 0} \sum f(x)\, \Delta x \qquad \text{(10-11)}$$

EXAMPLE 10-2 *Numerical Integration*   Write a subroutine to find the area under a curve $f(x)$ between two points x_1 and x_2, where $x_1 \le x_2$. (Or expressed in terms of calculus, write a subroutine to calculate the definite integral of the function $f(x)$ between two points x_1 and x_2.) The subroutine should allow the user to specify the function to be integrated and the step size Δx as calling arguments.

SOLUTION   This subroutine should divide the area under the curve into N rectangles, each of which is Δx wide and $f(x_c)$ tall (where x_c is the value of x at the center of the rectangle). It should then sum up the areas of all of the rectangles, and return the result. The number of rectangles N is given by

$$N = \frac{x_2 - x_1}{\Delta x} \qquad \text{(10-12)}$$

The value of N should be rounded up to the next whole integer. If N is rounded up, then the last interval will be less than Δx wide.

1. State the problem.
Write a subroutine to find the area under a curve (integrate) $f(x)$ between two points x_1 and x_2, where $x_1 \le x_2$, using rectangles to approximate the area under the curve. The subroutine should allow the user to specify the function to be integrated, the step size Δx, and the starting and ending values of the integral as calling arguments.

2. Define the inputs and outputs.

The inputs to this subroutine are

    (*a*) The function $f(x)$ to integrate

    (*b*) The step size Δx

    (*c*) The starting value x_1

    (*d*) The ending value x_2.

The outputs from this subroutine are

    (*a*) The area AREA under the curve.

    (*b*) An error flag IERROR.

3. Describe the algorithm.

This subroutine can be broken down into three major steps:

```
Check to see that x₁ ≤ x₂.
Calculate the number of rectangles to use.
Add up the area of the rectangles.
```

The first step of the program is to check that $x_1 \leq x_2$. If it is not, an error flag should be set, and the subroutine should return to the calling program. The second step is to calculate the number of rectangles to use using Equation (10-12). The third step is to calculate the area of each rectangle, and to add all of the areas up. The detailed pseudocode for these steps is

```
IF X1>X2 Then
    IERROR ← 1
ELSE
    IERROR ← 0
    AREA ← 0.
    N ← INT( (X2-X1) / DX + 1.)
    DO for I = 1 to N
        XSTART ← X1 + REAL(I-1) * DX
        WIDTH  ← MIN ( DX, X2 - XSTART )
        HEIGHT ← F( XSTART + WIDTH/2. )
        AREA   ← AREA + WIDTH * HEIGHT
    END of DO
END of IF
```

Note that the starting position XSTART of rectangle I can be found from the starting position of the integration plus I − 1 steps, since I − 1 rectangles have preceded rectangle I. The width of each rectangle is DX except for the last one, which may be smaller (the MIN function ensures that the last rectangle will have the proper width). Finally, the height of the rectangle is calculated to be the size of function F at the center of the rectangle.

4. Turn the algorithm into FORTRAN statements.

The resulting FORTRAN subroutine is shown in Figure 10-6.

```
      SUBROUTINE INTEG1 ( F, X1, X2, DX, AREA, IERROR )
C
C  Purpose:
C    To integrate function F(X) between X1 and X2 using
C    rectangles of width DX to approximate the area
C    under the curve F(X).
C
C  Record of revisions:
C      Date        Programmer           Description of change
C      ===         =======              =================
C    03/04/93    S. J. Chapman          Original code
C
C  List of calling arguments:
C    NAME    I/O  TYPE     DIM     DESCRIPTION
C    ===     ==   ===      ==      ========
C    F        I   REAL FUN         Function to integrate.
C    X1       I   REAL            Starting point for integral.
C    X2       I   REAL            Ending point for integral.
C    DX       I   REAL            Step size.
C    AREA     O   REAL            Area under the curve.
C    IERROR   O   INT             Error flag:
C                                 0 - No error.
C                                 1 - X1 > X2
C
C  List of local variables:
C    HEIGHT = Height of rectangle
C    I      = Index variable
C    N      = Number of rectangles to integrate
C    WIDTH  = Width of rectangle
C    XSTART = Starting position of rectangle
C
      IMPLICIT NONE
C
C  Declare the dummy arguments for this subroutine.
C
      INTEGER  IERROR
      REAL     F, X1, X2, DX, AREA
      EXTERNAL F
C
C  Declare local variables.
C
      INTEGER I, N
      REAL    XSTART, HEIGHT, WIDTH
C
C  First, check to make sure that we have enough input data.
C
      IF ( X1 .GT. X2 ) THEN
C
C    Error.
C
         IERROR = 1
      ELSE
C
```

```
C         Clear error flag and area.
C
          IERROR = 0
          AREA   = 0
C
C         Calculate the number of intervals to use.
C
          N = INT( (X2-X1) / DX + 1. )
C
C         Calculate and sum the areas of each rectangle.
C
          DO 10 I = 1, N
             XSTART = X1 + REAL(I-1) * DX
             WIDTH  = MIN ( DX, X2 - XSTART )
             HEIGHT = F( XSTART + WIDTH/2. )
             AREA   = AREA + WIDTH * HEIGHT
   10     CONTINUE
       END IF
C
       RETURN
       END
```

FIGURE 10-6   Subroutine INTEG1.

5.   Test the program.

We must develop a test driver program and a test function to integrate in order to test this subroutine. The test function should be something whose integral can be calculated analytically for comparison with the subroutine output. For this case, we integrate the function $f(x) = 3x^2 + 0.5$ from $x_1 = 0$ to $x_2 = 3$. The test driver program and function are shown in Figure 10-7:

```
      PROGRAM TINTG1
C
C  Purpose:
C    To test subroutine INTEG1, which integrates a function.
C    The function to be integrated is passed to the subroutine
C    as a calling argument.  This driver routine will integrate
C    the function with step sizes DX of 1.0, 0.5, 0.1, 0.05,
C    and 0.01.
C
C  Record of revisions:
C      Date        Programmer          Description of change
C      ===         =======             ================
C    03/04/93    S. J. Chapman         Original code
C
C  List of variables:
C     AREA    -- Area under the curve.
C     DX      -- Step size.
C     I       -- Index variable.
C     IERROR  -- Error flag.
C     X1      -- Starting point for integral.
C     X2      -- Ending point for integral.
C
      IMPLICIT NONE
C
```

```
C      Declare the external function being passed to subroutine
C      INTEG1.
C
       REAL    FUN
       EXTERNAL FUN
C
C      Declare the variables used in this program.
C
       INTEGER I, IERROR
       REAL    DX(7), AREA(7), X1, X2
C
C      Data
C
       DATA DX / 1., 0.5, 0.1, 0.05, 0.01, 0.005, 0.001 /
       DATA X1 / 0. /
       DATA X2 / 3. /
C
C      Call routine INTEG1 with each step size, and print out
C      the results.
C
       DO 10 I = 1, 7
           CALL INTEG1 ( FUN, X1, X2, DX(I), AREA(I), IERROR )
    10 CONTINUE
C
C      Write out results.
C
       WRITE (*,1000)
  1000 FORMAT ('0','  Step Size',5X,'Area',/,
      *         ' ',' =========',5X,'====')
       DO 20 I = 1, 7
           WRITE (*,1010) DX(I), AREA(I)
  1010 FORMAT (1X,F9.4,3X,F9.4)
    20 CONTINUE
C
       END
       FUNCTION FUN(X)
C
C  Purpose:
C    Function to be integrated.
C
       IMPLICIT NONE
C
       REAL FUN, X
C
C      Evaluate function.
C
       FUN = 3 * X**2 + 0.5
C
       RETURN
       END
```

FIGURE 10-7 Test driver program for subroutine INTEG1.

The analytic solution to this problem is

$$\int_0^3 (3x^2 + 0.5)dx = (x^3 + 0.5x) \Big|_0^3 = 27 + 1.5 = 28.5$$

If we call program TINTG1, the results are

```
C:\BOOK\FORT>TINTG1
   Step Size      Area
   =======       ====
    1.0000      27.7500
     .5000      28.3125
     .1000      28.4925
     .0500      28.4981
     .0100      28.4999
     .0050      28.5000
     .0010      28.5000
```

Notice that the smaller the step size became, the closer the final answer was to the truth. However, the smaller the step size, the longer it takes to calculate the integral. At some point, a smaller step size no longer makes sense. For example, changing the step size from 0.01 to 0.005 doubled the work required to calculate the answer, but only changed the least significant digit of the number! A step size of 0.01 would have been good enough for this function.   ●

10.2.2   Finding the Roots of Equations

Computers are often used to find the **roots of an equation.** The roots of an equation such as

$$f(x) = 0 \qquad\qquad \textbf{(10-13)}$$

are those values of x that satisfy the equation. There are explicit formulas for finding the roots of some simple functions like quadratic equations. However, *there is no simple closed-form way to calculate the roots of most equations.*

If there is no standard closed-form way to calculate the roots of an equation, we must find the roots by searching for them using some trial-and-error method. First, we will pick a trial value for x, and evaluate the function $f(x)$ for that x to see how close to zero it is. Then we will pick a new trial value for x based on the results of the first value, and repeat the process over and over until we come up with a value for x for which $f(x)$ is acceptably close to zero. This trial-and-error process is known as **iteration.** It is a common technique used to solve many classes of computer problems.

Let's examine a sample function to help us understand how we can apply iteration to find the roots of an equation. Suppose that we wish to find the roots to the equation

$$\cos x = x \qquad\qquad \textbf{(10-14)}$$

In other words, we wish to find those values of x for which $\cos x = x$. The first step in finding the roots of the equation is to rewrite it in the form $f(x) = 0$ so that solving for the roots becomes a matter of searching for zero crossings in the function $f(x)$.

$$f(x) = \cos x - x = 0 \tag{10-15}$$

A plot of the function $f(x) = \cos x - x$ is shown in Figure 10-8. As you can see, it has one zero crossing in the range of the function plotted. How can we find that zero crossing with a computer? What clue tells us that a zero crossing has occurred? The answer is simple. If we evaluate a function at one point x_1 and get a positive value, and then evaluate the function at another point x_2 and get a negative value, then there must have been a zero crossing somewhere between x_1 and x_2! For example, if we evaluate the function $f(x) = \cos x - x$ at $x = 0$, we find that $f(0) = 1.0$. If we then evaluate the function at $x = 1$, we find that $f(1) = -0.4597$. Since the sign of the function changed between 0 and 1, there must be a zero crossing (and therefore a root of the equation) somewhere between 0 and 1.

Now suppose that we know that a root is located between two values x_1 and x_2. How do we close in on the actual value of the root? A good way to do this is by calculating the value of the function at the point x_m exactly half way between $f(x_1)$ and $f(x_2)$, and comparing the sign of $f(x_m)$ with the signs of $f(x_1)$ and $f(x_2)$. The sign of $f(x_m)$ will differ from the sign of one of the other two values, and we will know that the root lies somewhere between x_m and that value. We can repeat this process (iterate) over and over until we have located the root as accurately as we wish to.

For example, consider the function $f(x) = \cos x - x$. We know that $f(0) = 1.0$ and $f(1) = -0.4597$, so a root of this function lies somewhere between 0 and 1.

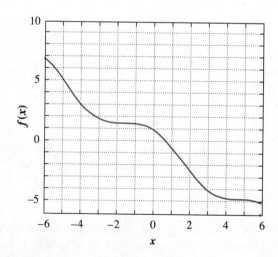

FIGURE 10-8   Plot of the function $f(x) \cos x - x$.

Let's iterate. The first five steps that we take while closing in on the root are shown below.

Iteration	x_1	x_m	x_2	$f(x_1)$	$f(x_m)$	$f(x_2)$	Result
1	0.0	0.5	1.0	1.0	0.338	−0.460	$0.5 < x < 1.0$
2	0.5	0.75	1.0	0.338	−0.018	−0.468	$0.5 < x < 0.75$
3	0.5	0.625	0.75	0.338	0.186	−0.018	$0.625 < x < 0.75$
4	0.625	0.6875	0.75	0.186	0.085	−0.018	$0.6875 < x < 0.75$
5	0.6875	0.71875	0.75	0.085	0.034	−0.018	$0.71875 < x < 0.75$

After five iterations, we know that the root lies somewhere between 0.71875 and 0.7500. If we continue this process, we can find the root to any desired accuracy.

The process of solving for the roots of an equation involves three steps:

1. Express the equation in the form $f(x) = 0$, so that roots of the equation will occur at zero-crossing of the function $f(x)$.
2. Scan the function at a regular spacing until two adjacent samples have a different sign. When that happens, there must be a zero-crossing somewhere in between the two samples.
3. Calculate the value of the function at a point halfway through the region in which we know there is a zero crossing to determine in which half of the region the zero crossing occurs. Repeat this process over and over until the location of the zero crossing (root) is known to the desired accuracy.

EXAMPLE 10-3 *Finding the Roots of an Equation*   Write a subroutine to find a root of a user-supplied equation. The equation must be in the form $f(x) = 0$, where $f(x)$ is a FORTRAN function passed to the subroutine as a calling argument. The subroutine will work by evaluating the function $f(x)$ starting at a position x_1 and at intervals of Δx thereafter until either position x_2 is reached or the sign of $f(x)$ changes. If the sign of $f(x)$ never changes, no root was found in the interval. If the sign does change, the subroutine will locate the position of the root by repeatedly bisecting the interval where the sign of $f(x)$ changes. The root will be considered correct when $|f(x)|$ is less than 10^{-5}.

SOLUTION   This subroutine will have two basic parts. The first part will be a **DO** loop that goes from x_1 to x_2 in steps of Δx, looking for a point where $f(x)$ changes sign. Once it finds an interval in which $f(x)$ changes sign, it will locate the position of the root by repeatedly bisecting the interval until $|f(x)|$ is less than 10^{-5}. When it finds the root, it will return to the calling program.

1. State the problem.

Write a subroutine to find a root of a user-supplied equation. The equation must be in the form $f(x) = 0$, where $f(x)$ is a FORTRAN function passed to the subroutine as a calling argument. The subroutine will search for a root between positions x_1 and x_2 in intervals of Δx.

2. Define the inputs and outputs.

The inputs to this subroutine are

    (*a*) The function $f(x)$ to check for roots

    (*b*) The starting value to search x_1

    (*c*) The ending value to search x_2

    (*d*) The step size Δx

The outputs from this subroutine are

    (*a*) The root ROOT

    (*b*) An error flag IERROR

3. Describe the algorithm.

This subroutine can be broken down into three major steps:

```
Check to see that x₁ ≤ x₂.
Scan to find a zero crossing.
Bisect the vicinity of the zero crossing until |F(X)| < EPSLON.
```

The first step of the program is to check that $x_1 \leq x_2$. If it is not, an error flag should be set, and the subroutine should return to the calling program. The second step is to search from x_1 to x_2 in steps of Δx to find a zero crossing. If no zero crossing is found, set an error flag and return. If one is found, then locate the position of the root by repeatedly bisecting the interval until $|f(x)|$ is less than 10^{-5}.

How can we detect a sign change? We will create two logicals LVALA and LVALB. They will be TRUE when the function values are > 0, and FALSE otherwise. Then we can test to see if LVALA is equivalent to LVALB. If so, there has been no sign change between points XA and XB. If not, a sign change has occurred, so we know that a root exists between XA and XB.

The detailed pseudocode for these steps is

```
IF X1 > X2 Then
    IERROR ← 1
    AROOT ← 0.
ELSE
    IERROR ← 0
    AROOT ← 0.
*
*      Get number of steps to search
*
       N ← NINT( (X2-X1) / DX + 1.)
*
*      Get value at first step
*
```

```
          XA ← X1
          VALA ← F(XA)
          LVALA ← VALA > 0.
          DO for I = 1 to N
*
*             Get value of next step.
*
              XB ← MIN ( X1 + REAL(I-1) * DX, X2 )
              VALB ← F(XB)
              LVALB ← VALB > 0.
*
*             See if there was a sign change in this interval.
*
              IF LVALA <> LVALB Then
*
*                 There was a sign change in the interval.  Process
*                 it in a WHILE loop.  Get first value at midpoint.
*
                  XM ← (XA + XB) / 2.
                  VALM ← F(XM)
                  LVALM ← VALM > 0.
*
*                 While loop.
*
                  WHILE ABS(VALM) > EPSLON do
                     IF LVALA = LVALM THEN
*
*                         The sign change was in the 2nd half.
*
                          XA ← XM
                          VALA ← VALM
                          LVALA ← LVALM
                     ELSE
*
*                         The sign change was in the 1st half.
*
                          XB ← XM
                          VALB ← VALM
                          LVALB ← LVALM
                     END of IF
*
*                     Get value at midpoint of new interval.
*
                      XM ← (XA + XB) / 2.
                      VALM ← F(XM)
                      LVALM ← VALM .GT. 0.
                  END of WHILE
*
*                 We reach here when ABS(VALM) < = EPSLON.
*
                  AROOT ← XM
                  IERROR ← 0
                  EXIT here
              END of IF LVALA <> LVALB
*
```

```
*        We are still searching for a sign change here
*
            XA ← XB
            VALA ← VALB
            LVALA ← LVALB
         END of DO
      END of IF
```

Note that this subroutine *returns with the first root that it finds* while scanning be-tween x_1 and x_2. If you want to continue searching for more roots, you must call the subroutine again with a new x_1 that is slightly larger than the root discovered in the previous call to the subroutine.

4. Turn the algorithm into FORTRAN statements.

The resulting **FORTRAN** subroutine is shown in Figure 10-9.

```
      SUBROUTINE ROOT ( F, X1, X2, DX, AROOT, IERROR )
C
C  Purpose:
C    To find a root of function F(X) between X1 and
C    X2, searching with step sizes of DX.
C
C  Record of revisions:
C      Date        Programmer        Description of change
C      ===         =======           =================
C    03/04/93    S. J. Chapman       Original code
C
C  List of calling arguments:
C    NAME     I/O  TYPE      DIM      DESCRIPTION
C    ===      ==   ===       ==       ========
C    F        I    REAL FUN           Function to integrate.
C    X1       I    REAL              Starting point for integral.
C    X2       I    REAL              Ending point for integral.
C    DX       I    REAL              Step size.
C    AROOT    O    REAL              Root of the function.
C    IERROR   O    INT               Error flag:
C                                    0 - No error.
C                                    1 - X1 > X2
C                                    2 - No root found.
C
C  List of parameters:
C    EPSLON -- Convergence criterion for root solution
C
C  List of local variables:
C    LVALA -- Logical value .TRUE. if F(XA) > 0.
C    LVALB -- Logical value .TRUE. if F(XB) > 0.
C    LVALM -- Logical value .TRUE. if F(XM) > 0.
C    I     -- Index variable
C    N     -- Number of steps in search
C    VALA  -- F(XA)
C    VALB  -- F(XB)
C    VALC  -- F(XM)
C    XA    -- Start of current interval
C    XB    -- End of current interval
C    XM    -- Midpoint of current interval
C
      IMPLICIT NONE
C
```

```
C       Declare the dummy arguments for this subroutine.
C
        INTEGER  IERROR
        REAL     F, X1, X2, DX, AROOT
        EXTERNAL F
C
C       Declare local parameters.
C
        REAL          EPSLON
        PARAMETER ( EPSLON = 1.0E-5 )
C
C       Declare local variables.
C
        INTEGER I, N
        REAL    XA,    XB,    XM
        REAL    VALA,  VALB,  VALM
        LOGICAL LVALA, LVALB, LVALM
C
C       First, check to make sure that we have enough input data.
C
        IF ( X1 .GT. X2 ) THEN
C
C          Error.
C
           IERROR = 1
           AROOT  = 0.
        ELSE
C
C          Get number of steps to search over for sign change.
C
           N = NINT( (X2-X1) / DX + 1. )
C
C          Get first F(XA) and the sign of F(XA).
C
           XA    = X1
           VALA  = F(XA)
           LVALA = VALA .GT. 0.
C
C          Search for a sign change between X1 and X2.
C
           DO 30 I = 1, N
C
C             Get value and sign of function at end of interval.
C
              XB    = MIN ( X1 + REAL(I-1) * DX, X2 )
              VALB  = F(XB)
              LVALB = VALB .GT. 0.
C
C             Is there a sign change in this interval?
C
              IF ( LVALA .NEQV. LVALB ) THEN
C
C                Yes!  We found a sign change interval.  Process it!
C                First, get the value at the midpoint of interval.
C
                 XM    = (XA + XB) / 2.
                 VALM  = F(XM)
                 LVALM = VALM .GT. 0.
C
```

```
C              Begin While loop.  End when we get close enough
C              to the root.
C
   10          IF ( ABS(VALM) .GE. EPSLON ) THEN
C
C                  Not close enough to root.  Decide which half
C                  of interval to continue processing.      '
C
               IF ( LVALA .EQV. LVALM ) THEN
C
C                      Sign change in second half.  The midpoint of
C                      the old interval becomes the beginning of the
C                      new one.
C
                   XA    = XM
                   VALA  = VALM
                   LVALA = LVALM
               ELSE
C
C                      Sign change in first half.  The midpoint of
C                      the old interval becomes the endpoint of the
C                      new one.
C
                   XB    = XM
                   VALB  = VALM
                   LVALB = LVALM
               END IF
C
C                  Get the value at the midpoint of new interval.
C
               XM    = (XA + XB) / 2.
               VALM  = F(XM)
               LVALM = VALM .GT. 0.
C
               GO TO 10
            ELSE
C
C                  We have the root to the desired tolerances.
C                  Reset error flag and get out.
C
               IERROR = 0
               AROOT  = XM
               GO TO 9999
            END IF
         END IF
C
C          We are still in DO loop searching for a sign change.
C          The endpoint of the last unsuccessful interval will be
C          the start of the next one.
C
         XA    = XB
         VALA  = VALB
         LVALA = LVALB
C
   30    CONTINUE
C
C          If we get here, no sign changes were found.  Set error
C          flag.
C
```

```
          IERROR = 2
          AROOT  = 0.
C
       END IF
C
 9999 CONTINUE
       RETURN
       END
```

FIGURE 10-9   Subroutine ROOT.

     5. Test the program.

We must develop a test driver program and a test function to solve for to test this subroutine. The test driver program is shown in Figure 10-10. Note that the function to be tested must be declared in a separate function subprogram.

```
       PROGRAM TROOT
C
C  Purpose:
C    To test subroutine ROOT, which locates the roots of
C    function FUN that fall between X=X1 and X=X2.
C
C  Record of revisions:
C      Date         Programmer         Description of change
C      ===          =======            ================
C    03/04/93     S. J. Chapman        Original code
C
C  List of variables:
C    AROOT  -- Resulting root.
C    DX     -- Step size.
C    I      -- Index variable.
C    IERROR -- Error flag.
C    X1     -- Starting point to search for root.
C    X2     -- Ending point to search for root.
C
       IMPLICIT NONE
C
C    Declare the external function being passed to subroutine
C    ROOT.
C
       REAL    FUN
       EXTERNAL FUN
C
C    Declare the variables used in this program.
C
       INTEGER IERROR
       REAL    DX, AROOT, X1, X2
C
C    Data
C
       DATA DX / 0.1 /
       DATA X1 / -6. /
       DATA X2 /  6. /
C
C    Tell user what we are doing.
C
```

```
       WRITE (*,1000) X1, X2
 1000 FORMAT ('0','Searching for roots between ',F14.5,' and ',F14.5,'.')
C
C      Begin WHILE loop.
C
   10 IF ( X1 .LT. X2 ) THEN
C
C          Call routine ROOT with each step size, and print out
C          the results.
C
           CALL ROOT ( FUN, X1, X2, DX, AROOT, IERROR )
C
C          Write out results.
C
           IF ( IERROR .EQ. 0 ) THEN
              WRITE (*,1010) AROOT
 1010         FORMAT (' ','There is a root is at ',F14.5, '.')
              X1 = AROOT + 0.00005
           ELSE IF ( IERROR .EQ. 2 ) THEN
              WRITE (*,1020) X1, X2
 1020         FORMAT (' ','No root found between ',F14.5,' and ',F14.5,'.')
           END IF
C
           GO TO 10
       END IF
C
       END
```

FIGURE 10-10   Test driver program for subroutine ROOT.

We will test this subroutine with several different functions. First, let's use the function in Equation (10-15) that we worked with above.

$$f(x) = \cos x - x = 0 \qquad (10\text{-}15)$$

The corresponding function subprogram would be

```
       FUNCTION FUN(X)
C
C  Purpose:
C      Function used to test subroutine ROOT.
C
       IMPLICIT NONE
       REAL FUN, X
       FUN = COS(X) - X
       RETURN
       END
```

and the result of running the test driver program with this function would be

```
C:\BOOK\FORT>TROOT

Searching for roots between      -6.00000 and      6.00000.
There is a root is at        .73909.
No root found between        .73909 and      6.00000.
```

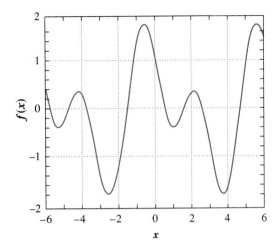

FIGURE 10-11   Plot of the function $f(x) = \cos x - \sin 2x$. This function is used to test subroutine ROOT.

This answer is consistent with our hand calculations above, when we found that the root was somewhere between 0.71875 and 0.75.

Now let's try a function with more than one root between −6 and 6. The function

$$f(x) = \cos x - \sin 2x = 0 \qquad \text{(10-16)}$$

is periodic, and has many roots within the range we are examining. This function is shown in Figure 10-11. When we implement this equation as a function subprogram and call subroutine ROOT with it function, the results are

```
C:\BOOK\FORT>TROOT

Searching for roots between      -6.00000 and        6.00000.
There is a root is at      -5.75958.
There is a root is at      -4.71239.
There is a root is at      -3.66519.
There is a root is at      -1.57080.
There is a root is at        .52360.
There is a root is at       1.57080.
There is a root is at       2.61800.
There is a root is at       4.71239.
No root found between       4.71239 and        6.00000.
```

Finally, let's try the a function with no roots between −6 and 6. The function

$$f(x) = x^4 + 1 = 0 \qquad \text{(10-17)}$$

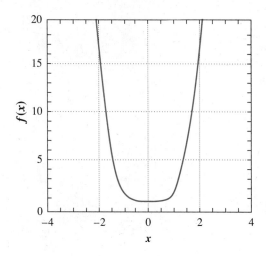

FIGURE 10-12   Plot of the function $f(x) = x^4 + 1$. This function is used to test subroutine ROOT.

has no real roots at all. It is shown in Figure 10-12. When we call subroutine ROOT with this function, the results are

```
C:\BOOK\FORT>TROOT

Searching for roots between        -6.00000 and        6.00000.
No root found between        -6.00000 and        6.00000.
```

The subroutine ROOT appears to be working correctly.   ●

Finding the roots of an equation can be much more complicated than we have shown here. For example, this routine would never detect an even number of repeated roots, and it could also miss roots if two of them are closer together than the step size Δx used in the search. Furthermore, if the slope of the function $f(x)$ were very steep in the vicinity of the root, it might take a long time for the solution to converge to within the limits $|f(x)| < 10^{-5}$. Under those circumstances, a better convergence criterion might be to stop processing when the interval XB − XA gets below some acceptable accuracy limit.

There are many other techniques available to help solve for the roots of equations. One of these techniques, the Newton-Raphson method, is the subject of exercise 10 at the end of this chapter. The details of other root-solving techniques may be found in advanced numerical methods textbooks.

10.3   SUMMARY

Computer calculations are generally not perfect. Because of the finite precision of computer floating-point values, there is always some truncation or roundoff error in any sequence of calculations. If the sequence of calculations is long enough, the output from the program can be meaningless even though every equation in the program is correct. Eventually, the error will come to dominate the solution.

Some problems are more sensitive to the effects of truncation or roundoff errors than others. For example, roundoff errors can have a serious effect on the solution of ill-conditioned systems of equations, while having relatively little effect on the solution of well-conditioned systems of equations. In general, problems which involve subtracting two nearly equal numbers are very sensitive to roundoff errors. (This is the basic problem associated with solving ill-conditioned systems.) If a problem requires you to subtract nearly equal numbers at some point in the solution process, you should consider using double-precision numbers for the problem.

Another common source of error in computer programs is using an inappropriate model to analyze a particular problem. For example, it makes no sense at all to try to fit a straight line to data that is not straight. Linear regression only makes sense if the process being modeled exhibits linear behavior. If not, modeling should be done with an equation that matches the theoretical behavior of the data.

The study of mathematical methods for use on computers is a branch of mathematics known as numerical analysis. It is normally the subject of one or more separate courses following this course.

Several subroutines with practical engineering and scientific applications were developed in this chapter. These routines illustrate the thought process that an engineer applies to the design of his or her applications, and also provide some useful subroutine to serve as building blocks in other programs.

10.3.1 Summary of Good Programming Practice

The following guidelines should be adhered to when working with computer programs.

1. When adding a large series of numbers, add the smallest numbers first and the larger ones later in order to minimize truncation and rounding errors.
2. Whenever possible, simplify your expressions to contain as few operations as possible. The fewer the operations that you perform, the smaller cumulative errors will be, and the faster the program will run.
3. Think carefully about what you want to do *before* you start programming. Pay attention to the types of models appropriate to the data that you are working with. Otherwise, garbage in will yield garbage out!

CHAPTER 10 KEY WORDS

Algorithm	Roundoff
Numerical analysis	Truncation
Numerical methods	

CHAPTER 10 EXERCISES

1. The function $\sin x$ may be evaluated by the infinite series

    $$\sin x = x - \frac{x^3}{3!} + \frac{x^5}{5!} - \frac{x^7}{7!} + \dots$$

    Calculate $\sin \pi/2$ twice using the first eight terms of this series, first adding the numbers from largest to smallest, and then adding the numbers from smallest to largest. Do you get the same answer either way on your computer?

2. The derivative of a function $f(x)$ is defined by Equation (9-1).

    $$\frac{d}{dx} f(x) = \lim_{\Delta x \to 0} \frac{f(x + \Delta x) - f(x)}{\Delta x} \qquad \text{(9-1)}$$

    It is a way of calculating the slope (or tangent) of a curve at a particular point. In Chapter 9, we calculated the derivative of the function $f(x) = 1/x$ for the location $x_0 = 0.15$ directly from this definition. Figure 10-13 shows the calculation of the derivative of $f(x)$ directly from Equation (9-1).

    If we examine Figure 10-13, we can see that the slope of the expression $(f(x + \Delta x) - f(x))/\Delta x$ is significantly different from the actual tangent to the curve at x_0, and will remains so until Δx gets to be very small. This is true because we are looking at the curve $f(x)$ on only one side of the point we are evaluating. If instead we subtract two points at equal distances on either side of x_0, the difference $(f(x + \Delta x/2) - f(x - \Delta x/2))/\Delta x$ has a slope that is more nearly equal to the tangent of the curve at the point we are evaluating (see Figure 10-14). Therefore the numerical approximation of the derivative should be better if we express the definition of the derivative as

    $$\frac{d}{dx} f(x) = \lim_{\Delta x \to 0} \frac{f(x + \Delta x/2) - f(x - \Delta x/2)}{\Delta x} \qquad \textbf{(10-18)}$$

    Write a subroutine to calculate the derivative from Equation (10-18), and test the routine by evaluating the function $f(x) = 1/x$ for the location $x_0 = 0.15$. Compare the results derived from Equations (9-1) and (10-18) for a series of step sizes. How do the two numbers compare? Which is more accurate? (Equation (9-1) is known as a *forward difference* equation, while Equation (10-18) is known as a *central difference* equation.)

3. Create a test data set by calculating points (x_i, y_i) along the curve $y(x) = x^2 - 4x + 3$ for $x_i = 0, 0.1, 0.2, \dots, 5.0$. Next, use subroutine RAN0 to add random noise to each of the y_i values. Then, use subroutine LSQFT2 to try to estimate the coefficients of the original function that generated the data set. Try this when the added random noise has the range:
    (*a*) 0.0 (no added noise)
    (*b*) $[-0.1, 0.1]$
    (*c*) $[-0.5, 0.5]$
    (*d*) $[-1.0, 1.0]$
    (*e*) $[-1.5, 1.5]$
    (*f*) $[-2.0, 2.0]$
    How did the quality of the fit change as the amount of noise in the data increased?

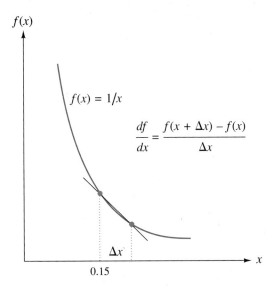

$f(x)$

$f(x) = 1/x$

$$\frac{df}{dx} = \frac{f(x + \Delta x) - f(x)}{\Delta x}$$

Δx

x

0.15

FIGURE 10-13 Calculation of the derivative directly from Equation (9-1). This is called a forward difference equation, since it compares the values at the point being evaluated (x_0) and a point beyond the point being evaluated $(x_0 + \Delta x)$ to determine the slope df/dx.

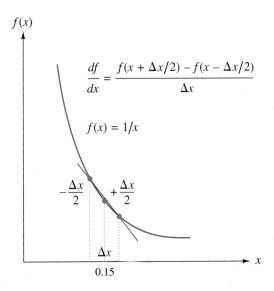

$f(x)$

$$\frac{df}{dx} = \frac{f(x + \Delta x/2) - f(x - \Delta x/2)}{\Delta x}$$

$f(x) = 1/x$

$-\frac{\Delta x}{2}$ $+\frac{\Delta x}{2}$

Δx

x

0.15

FIGURE 10-14 Calculation of the derivative from Equation (10-18). This is called a central difference equation, since it compares the values at two points equal distances before $(x_0 - \frac{\Delta x}{2})$ and after $(x_0 + \frac{\Delta x}{2})$ the point being evaluated to determine the slope df/dx at x_0.

4. Repeat exercise 3, except this time use a data set containing all the points (x_i, y_i) along the curve $y(x) = x^2 - 4x + 3$ for $x_i = 0, 0.1, 0.2, \ldots, 10.0$. How does the longer data set affect the quality of the fit?

5. In this chapter, we stated that the coefficients of a linear least squares fit to the polynomial $y(x) = c_0 + c_1 x$ are the solutions of the following system of equations

$$N c_0 + \left(\sum x\right) c_1 = \sum y$$

$$\left(\sum x\right) c_0 + \left(\sum x^2\right) c_1 = \sum xy \qquad \text{(10-8)}$$

where

(x_i, y_i)	is the ith sample measurement
N	is the number of sample measurements included in the fit
$\sum x$	is the sum of the x_i values of all measurements
$\sum x^2$	is the sum of the squares of the x_i values of all measurements
$\sum xy$	is the sum of the products of the corresponding x_i and y_i values

Prove that the solutions of Equations (10-8) are identical to Equations (4-5) and (4-6) if $c_1 = m$ and $c_0 = b$.

$$m = \frac{\left(\sum xy\right) - \left(\sum x\right)\bar{y}}{\left(\sum x^2\right) - \left(\sum x\right)\bar{x}} \qquad \text{(4-5)}$$

$$b = \bar{y} - m\bar{x} \qquad \text{(4-6)}$$

where $\bar{x}$ is the mean (average) of the $\bar{x}$ values, and $\bar{y}$ is the mean (average) of the y values.

6. It can be shown that the coefficients of a least squares fit to the nth-order polynomial $y(x) = c_0 + c_1 x + c_2 x^2 + \ldots + c_n x^n$ are the solutions of the following system of $n + 1$ equations in $n + 1$ unknowns

$$N c_0 + \left(\sum x\right) c_1 + \left(\sum x^2\right) c_2 + \ldots + \left(\sum x^n\right) c_n = \sum y$$

$$\left(\sum x\right) c_0 + \left(\sum x^2\right) c_1 + \left(\sum x^3\right) c_2 + \ldots + \left(\sum x^{n+1}\right) c_n = \sum xy$$

$$\left(\sum x^2\right) c_0 + \left(\sum x^3\right) c_1 + \left(\sum x^4\right) c_2 + \ldots + \left(\sum x^{n+2}\right) c_n = \sum x^2 y$$

$$\vdots \qquad \vdots \qquad \vdots \qquad \vdots \qquad \vdots$$

$$\left(\sum x^n\right) c_0 + \left(\sum x^{n+1}\right) c_1 + \left(\sum x^{n+2}\right) c_2 + \ldots + \left(\sum x^{2n}\right) c_n = \sum x^n y$$

Write a subroutine that implements a least squares fit to any polynomial of up to 10th order. (*Note:* As order of the polynomial being fitted increases, the size of the system of simultaneous equations to be solved increases, and the system of equations becomes progressively less well-conditioned. You may wish to use the double-precision subroutine DSIMUL to solve your system of simultaneous equations!)

7. In Example 10-2, we approximated the area under a curve by filling the area with a series of rectangles whose width was Δx and whose height was the value of the function at the center of the rectangle (see Figure 10-5). An alternate way to fill the space under the curve is with trapezoids, as shown in Figure 10-15. Write a subroutine to calculate the area under a function using trapezoids to sum up the area instead of rectangles. Test the two routines by integrating the function $f(x) = \sin^2 x$ from $x_1 = 0$ to $x_2 = 3$ using a variety of step sizes Δx. How do the results of the two methods compare for a given function and step size?

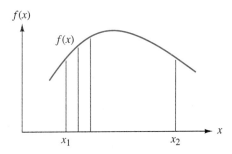

FIGURE 10-15   Filling the area under a curve $f(x)$ with trapezoids.

8. When a data set is analyzed, it is common to see most of the data behaving approximately as expected, but with a few really "wild" points thrown into the middle of the data set. These "wild" points are often so far away from the rest of the data that it is obvious that they are not real. If those data points are left in the data set when it is analyzed, they can distort the results of the analysis. For example, examine Figure 10-16(*a*). Most of the data points in Figure 10-16(*a*) appear to lie roughly along a straight line, but two of the points are really far away from the line. Those points are "wild" points. If a linear least squares fit is performed on the data with the wild points present, they distort the fit (Figure 10-16(*b*)). If the wild points are eliminated from the data set, a least squares fit produces much better results (Figure 10-16(*c*)).

It is common for a user to edit wild points out of a data set as a part of the analysis process. How can wild points be edited out of a data set? The most common approach to such editing is to reject points that are more than a cer-

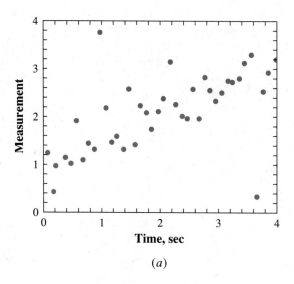

(*a*)

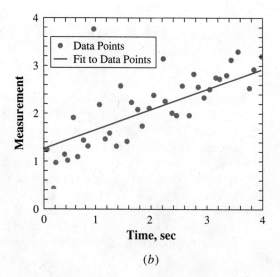

(*b*)

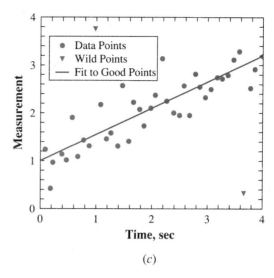

(c)

FIGURE 10-16 (a) A sample data set containing "wild" points. (b) A linear least squares fit with "wild" points included. (c) A linear least squares fit with "wild" points excluded.

tain number of standard deviations away from the rest of the data in the set. One possible procedure is described below:

1. If the data is expected to behave in a linear fashion, perform a linear least squares fit to the entire data set.
2. Calculate the distance of each data point from the fitted line, and determine the standard deviation of the distance of the data points from the line. The distance of a data point (x_i, y_i) from the line may be calculated as follows:

   Expected value of y_i: $\quad \hat{y}_i = mx_i + b$
   Distance of point from line: $\quad d = y_i - \hat{y}_i$

   where $\hat{y}_i$ is the expected value of y_i, m is the slope of the fitted line, and b is the intercept of the fitted line. Then calculate the standard deviation using the equations presented in earlier chapters.
3. Reject as "wild" any points that are more than *thresh* standard deviations away from the rest of the data set, where *thresh* is a user-specifiable quantity. (*Note: thresh* is a real quantity, not an integer.)
4. Re-fit the data without the wild points to update the slope and intercept of the line fitted to the data.

Write a subroutine that will perform a least-squares fit to a data set, reject any points more than *thresh* standard deviations away from the rest of the data, and then perform a new fit with the remainder of the data. The quantity *thresh* should be specified by the user in a calling argument, and the number of points actually rejected should be returned in an argument to the calling routine.

When the subroutine is written, test it on the following data set using a threshold of 3:

Table of Measurements

Time, s	Measurement	Time, s	Measurement
0.1	1.2528	2.1	2.3929
0.2	0.4373	2.2	3.1488
0.3	0.9886	2.3	2.2762
0.4	1.1365	2.4	2.0197
0.5	1.0393	2.5	1.9674
0.6	1.9057	2.6	2.5918
0.7	1.0968	2.7	1.9639
0.8	1.4423	2.8	2.8846
0.9	1.3135	2.9	2.5716
1.0	3.7680	3.0	2.3368
1.1	2.1781	3.1	2.5031
1.2	1.4717	3.2	2.7563
1.3	1.5945	3.3	2.7283
1.4	1.3275	3.4	2.8041
1.5	2.6522	3.5	3.1251
1.6	1.4280	3.6	3.2839
1.7	2.2315	3.7	0.3361
1.8	2.0951	3.8	2.5426
1.9	1.7505	3.9	2.9296
2.0	2.1190	4.0	3.1786

9. Find the real roots of the following equations in the range $-10 \le x \le 10$.
   (a) $\sin^2 x = 0.25$
   (b) $f(x) = x^4 - 5x^2 + 5 = 0$
   (c) $0.1x^3 - 2x^2 + 3x + 3 = 0$
   (d) $\text{sinc } x = 0.1$ (*Note*: $\text{sinc } x = \sin x / x$)

10. The Newton-Raphson method is an alternate technique for finding the roots of the equation $f(x) = 0$. In the bisection algorithm that we used in this chapter, we located a zero crossing by calculating the value of $f(x)$ at the midpoint of an interval containing a zero crossing, and then repeating the process with the half of the original interval that still contained the zero crossing. The process was repeated until the function $f(x)$ was within an acceptable distance of zero. By contrast, the Newton-Raphson method uses the slope of the curve near the zero crossing of the function to make a more intelligent estimate of the location of the zero crossing. Because each guess made by the Newton-Raphson method is better than each guess made by the bisection method, it is possible to find the zero crossing in fewer iterations.

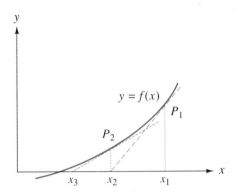

FIGURE 10-17

To understand the Newton-Raphson method, examine Figure 10-17. Figure 10-17 shows a function $f(x)$ near a zero-crossing (and therefore, near a root of the original equation). Suppose that we start at point on the function $P_1 = (x_1, y_1)$. If we calculate the slope of the function at P_1 and project that slope down to $y = 0$, then we will be at point x_2, which is closer to the zero crossing than x_1. The value of the function at x_2 is $y_2 = f(x_2)$. Now let's calculate the slope of the function at $P_2 = (x_2, y_2)$, and project that slope down to $y = 0$. Then we will be at point x_3, which is even closer to the zero crossing than x_2. This process converges to the location of the zero crossing in just a few iterations.

How can we find the slope m_1 of the function at point P_1? The slope of a curve at any given point is the derivative of the curve at that point, so we can use our derivative calculating subroutine from exercise 2 to get the slope of the function at the point. How can we find point x_2 given a knowledge of point $P_1 = (x_1, y_1)$ and the slope of the tangent line m_1? We can get it directly from the equation for a straight line $y = mx + b$. Since we know x_1, y_1, and m_1, we can solve for b_1.

$$b_1 = y_1 - m_1 x_1 \tag{10-19}$$

Since $y = 0$ at the zero crossing, we can calculate a value for x_2.

$$x_2 = -\frac{b_1}{m_1} \tag{10-20}$$

Finally, substituting Equation (10-19) into Equation (10-20) yields

$$x_2 = x_1 - \frac{y_1}{m_1} \tag{10-21}$$

Write a subroutine to find a root of a user-supplied equation of the form $f(x) = 0$, where $f(x)$ is a FORTRAN function passed to the subroutine as a calling argument. The subroutine searches for a root between positions x_1 and x_2 in intervals of Δx, and uses the Newton-Raphson method to zero in on the location of the root once it has discovered a zero-crossing interval. Test the subroutine on the four equations given in exercise 9.

11. Write a modified version of the bisection subroutine in Example 10-3 that returns the number of iterations required to zero in on the root within a sign-change interval. Also, write a modified version of the Newton-Raphson method subroutine in exercise 10 that returns the number of iterations required to zero in on the root within a sign-change interval. Use both modified subroutines to find the root of the function

$$f(x) = \sin x - x^2 = 0$$

between 0.5 and 1.0 with a step size Δx of 0.5. How many iterations were required by each technique to find the root of the function to the accuracy $|f(x)| < 10^{-5}$?

12. Write a modified version of the bisection subroutine in Example 10-3 that considers a root to be found when the interval size XB $-$ XA gets smaller than a user-specified limit. Make the acceptable limit a calling argument of the subroutine. Also, your subroutine should return the number of iterations required to zero in on the root within a sign-change interval. Test your code on the function

$$f(x) = \sin x - x^2 = 0$$

with the convergence criterion $|XB - XA| < 0.001$. How many iterations were required to find the root?

FORTRAN Libraries

One of the greatest advantages of FORTRAN subprograms is that they are *reusable*. Once a subprogram has been written to perform a particular task, we can use that subprogram over and over again whenever we need to perform that task. For example, in Example 6-1, we wrote a subroutine to sort an array of real values into ascending order. That subroutine can now be used to sort arrays of real values in a totally different program at any time in the future.

A FORTRAN programmer does not have to constantly "reinvent the wheel." Once one programmer has created a working, debugged subprogram to perform a particular task, any other programmer can perform the same function simply by calling that subroutine.

Let's suppose that you are a programmer working on a large project, one portion of which requires you to solve a system of simultaneous linear equations. You happen to know that another programmer, Susan Jones, has already written and debugged a subroutine to solve a system of simultaneous linear equations. What can you do? There are at least three possibilities. First, you could write your own subroutine to solve the system of linear equations, but that would be a stupid waste of time. Second, you could get the *source code* to Susan's subroutine and *compile* it together with your own program. This approach would work, but Susan would have to agree to give you her source code, and you would waste time recompiling code that has already been compiled. Finally, you could get the compiled *object module* for her subroutine, and *link* it with your code. This option is the best choice, since you will not waste time recompiling her subroutine when it has already been compiled.

To make FORTRAN subprograms available for easy reuse, their object modules are often collected into **libraries**. A *library* is a collection of compiled FORTRAN object modules organized into a single disk file, which is indexed for easy recovery. When a FORTRAN program calls subroutines that are located in a library, the linker searches the library to get the object modules for the subroutines being called, and includes them in the final program.

Object module libraries are very useful. Subroutine object modules in a library do not have to be recompiled for use, so it is quicker to compile and link programs using library subroutines. In addition, libraries can be distributed in object form only, protecting the source code which someone invested so much time writing.

With libraries, FORTRAN is almost infinitely extensible. For example, if you are writing programs to perform statistical analyses, you can purchase an off-the-shelf statistical subroutine library that will perform extremely complicated statistical processes with a single subroutine call. The subroutine library will make your program easier and quicker to write and debug. The hardest part of the analysis is performed in the subroutine library, and that portion of the code has already been debugged!

■ **GOOD PROGRAMMING PRACTICE**

Place the object modules of any subroutines that you may wish to reuse into a library. The routines in a library are easy to keep track of, and may be linked quickly into any new programs that you may write.

■
11.1   TYPES OF FORTRAN LIBRARIES

There is an enormous market for FORTRAN subroutine libraries to perform various special functions. There are specialized libraries for calculating statistical functions, solving mathematical equations, signal processing, plotting data, analyzing seismic data, and many more functions. When a user needs to write a sophisticated program in some specialized area, he or she can purchase a subroutine package to make the task easier.

Some libraries are provided free by the computer makers themselves. These libraries usually contain subroutines and functions (called **system utilities**) permitting a programmer to perform simple but useful tasks on the computer. For example, some routines in the library permit the programmer to get the current date and time, the name of the computer on which the program is being run, the amount of memory available, the priority of the program, etc. *A programmer should be careful when using routines from these libraries.* These routines usually differ from computer to computer, so using them will make a computer program less portable. If they must be used, it is best to include each one in a special user-written interface routine, and to call the system routine through the user-written interface routine everywhere in the program. For example, a programmer might define an interface subroutine TIMSEC that gets the current time from the system library subroutine and returns it to the calling program in a standard format. If the program is moved to another computer, subroutine TIMSEC would have to be rewritten to use the system library routine on the new computer, but none of the routines calling TIMSEC would have to be modified at all! If a program is written in this fashion, then when it is moved between computers, only the interface routines have to be rewritten.

EXAMPLE 11-1 *Interface to a System Time Subroutine* There is no standard FORTRAN 77 subroutine or function that returns time of day information to a user. Instead, time of day information is available from subroutines or functions contained in the system libraries supplied by each computer and/or compiler vendor. The calling sequence of these time routines will probably differ from computer to computer, so using them will make your programs nonportable.

However, sometimes we *must* have the time of day for a computer program to work properly. If we do need time information in a program, then the call to the system time of day routine should be encapsulated inside an interface routine with a standard calling sequence, and all of the routines in the program that need time information should call the interface routine. If the program is later moved from one computer to another one, only the interface routine will have to be rewritten. The other subroutines in the program will not have to change, since they only called the interface subroutine, and not the system library routine. The interface routine itself may have to be totally rewritten for the new computer, but as long as the calling sequence of the routine is unchanged, the rest of the program will be unaffected by the change.

To illustrate this idea, we will now write an interface subroutine TIMSEC that returns the elapsed time in seconds since the beginning of the day. This example is written for Microsoft FORTRAN; you should write a version of the interface routine with the same calling sequence on whatever computer you are using to run FORTRAN programs.

SOLUTION The system library function in Microsoft FORTRAN that returns time of day information is called GETTIM. Its calling sequence is

```
CALL GETTIM ( HOUR, MINUTE, SECOND, HNDRTH )
```

where

HOUR	is the integer variable containing the current hour
MINUTE	is the integer variable containing the current minute
SECOND	is the integer variable containing the current second
HNDRTH	is the integer variable containing the current hundredth of a second

This is the system library routine that is not the same from computer to computer. We will hide this routine inside the interface subroutine TIMSEC.

1. State the problem.
Write an interface subroutine TIMSEC to fetch the elapsed time in seconds since the beginning of the day. A double-precision variable will be used to hold the elapsed time value to preserve full accuracy down to the millisecond level.

2. Define the inputs and outputs.
There are no inputs to this subroutine. The output from this program is a double-precision variable containing the elapsed time in seconds since the beginning of the day.

3. Describe the algorithm.

This program can be broken down into two major steps:

```
Get the current time from the system library routine.
Convert the time into double precision seconds.
```

The first step of the program is to get the current time in the form supplied by the system routine. For Microsoft **FORTRAN**, this is the current time in units of hours, minutes, seconds, and hundredths of seconds. The next step is to multiply the values together appropriately to produce an output in double-precision seconds. The detailed pseudocode for this subroutine is

```
CALL GETTIM ( HOUR, MINUTE, SECOND, HNDRTH)
SEC ← 3600.0D0 * DBLE(HOUR) + 60.0D0 * DBLE(MINUTE) + DBLE(SECOND)
        + DBLE(HNDRTH) / 100.0D0
RETURN
```

4. Turn the algorithm into FORTRAN statements.

The resulting FORTRAN subroutine is shown in Figure 11-1. Note that it calls subroutine GETTIM from the Microsoft **FORTRAN** system library.

```
      SUBROUTINE TIMSEC ( SEC )
C
C Purpose:
C   To return the elapsed time in seconds since the start
C   of the day.  This routine is an interface routine intended
C   to isolate the calling program from the details of the
C   system library call used to get the time.
C
C Record of revisions:
C     Date        Programmer          Description of change
C     ====        ==========          =====================
C   07/21/92    S. J. Chapman         Original code
C
C List of calling arguments:
C   NAME    I/O  TYPE        DIM     DESCRIPTION
C   ====    ===  ====        ===     ===========
C   SEC      O   DBLE                Time of day in seconds.
C
C List of local variables:
C   HOUR   -- Current hour.
C   MINUTE -- Current minute.
C   SECOND -- Current second.
C   HNDRTH -- Current hundredth of a second.
C
      IMPLICIT NONE
C
C Declare the dummy arguments for this subroutine.
C
      DOUBLE PRECISION SEC
C
C Declare local variables.
C
      INTEGER HOUR, MINUTE, SECOND, HNDRTH
C
```

```
C     Call the system library routine.
C
      CALL GETTIM ( HOUR, MINUTE, SECOND, HNDRTH )
C
C     Convert to double precision seconds.
C
      SEC = 3600.0D0 * DBLE ( HOUR ) + 60.0D0 * DBLE ( MINUTE )
     *    + DBLE ( SECOND ) + DBLE ( HNDRTH ) / 100.0D0
C
      RETURN
      END
```

FIGURE 11-1   Subroutine TIMSEC (version for Microsoft FORTRAN).

5. Test the program.

To test this subroutine, we need to write a test driver program. The test driver program will get the system time using subroutine TIMSEC and then convert the result back into a time of day readable by humans. The test driver program is shown in Figure 11-2.

```
      PROGRAM TTIMSC
C
C Purpose:
C    To test subroutine TIMSEC.  This routine gets the current
C    time in seconds from TIMSEC, and reconstructs the time in
C    hours, minutes, and seconds to make sure that interface
C    routine worked correctly.
C
C Record of revisions:
C    Date        Programmer          Description of change
C    ====        ==========          =====================
C    07/21/92    S. J. Chapman       Original code
C
C List of local variables:
C    HOUR    — Current hour.
C    MINUTE  — Current minute.
C    SEC     — Total time in seconds.
C    SECOND  — Current second.
C    HNDRTH  — Current hundredth of a second.
C
      IMPLICIT NONE
C
C     Declare local variables.
C
      INTEGER HOUR, MINUTE, SECOND, HNDRTH
      DOUBLE PRECISION SEC
C
C     Get system time in seconds since start of day.
C
      CALL TIMSEC ( SEC )
C
C     Unpack this time.  First, get current hour.
C
      HOUR = INT ( SEC / 3600.0D0 )
      SEC  = SEC - DBLE (HOUR ) * 3600.0D0
C
```

```
C     Get current minute.
C
      MINUTE = INT ( SEC / 60.0D0 )
      SEC    = SEC - DBLE ( MINUTE ) * 60.0D0
C
C     Get current second.
C
      SECOND = INT ( SEC )
      SEC    = SEC - DBLE ( SECOND )
C
C     Get current hundredth.
C
      HNDRTH = INT ( SEC * 100.0D0 )
C
C     Tell user.
C
      WRITE (*,1000) HOUR, MINUTE, SECOND, HNDRTH
 1000 FORMAT ('0','The current time is: ', I2.2, ':', I2.2, ':',
     *         I2.2, '.', I2.2)
C
      END
```

FIGURE 11-2   Test driver program for subroutine TIMSEC.

Since current time is a moving target, we will test this routine by displaying the current time with the DOS command TIME before and after running program TTIMSC.

```
C:\BOOK\FORT>time
Current time is 11:08:06.98a
Enter new time:

C:\BOOK\FORT>ttimsc

The current time is: 11:08:09.50

C:\BOOK\FORT>time
Current time is 11:08:11.70a
Enter new time:
```

Since the output from TTIMSC appears in between the two times produced by the TIME command, subroutine TTIMSC appears to be working correctly. You should now write a version of TTIMSC that works properly on your own computer. ●

■ GOOD PROGRAMMING PRACTICE

Use interface subroutines and functions to hide calls to computer-dependent system libraries. By restricting computer-dependent calls to a few interface subroutines, it is much easier to move the program between computers.

Many different third-party vendors sell subroutine libraries to perform specific functions. The disadvantage of using one of these libraries is that you must purchase it first. Offsetting this disadvantage are many advantages. First and foremost, a company can save programming and debugging effort by purchasing and using the library. Programmer time is so expensive that a company almost always wins by purchasing off-the-shelf routines if they are available. Another major advantage is **host computer independence.** The vendor of a subroutine library usually supports versions of the library on many different computers. If you write a program that uses the library on one computer, and then it becomes necessary to make it work on another computer, all you have to do is to purchase a copy of the library for the new computer. The vendor of the library has done all the hard work of translating the library routines for you!

Subroutine libraries also support **device independence.** A properly designed subroutine library permits a programmer to work with many different types of devices without changing his or her source code. The best example of this use occurs in plotting graphical data on an output device (laser printer, plotter, CRT terminal, etc.). The FORTRAN language contains no standard method for plotting graphics on an output device. The reason for this lack is that there are literally *hundreds* of different graphical output devices, each with its own special commands and control codes. It is impossible to build standard support for all possible devices into a general-purpose language.

A number of subroutine library vendors have stepped into this breach. They sell libraries that permit a programmer to generate graphics output in a *device-independent* manner, and then to plot it on whatever output device is desired at the moment. These libraries include special interface subroutines that are called by the programmer. The format of the calls is the same regardless of the computer on which the program is running or the output device on which the data is to be plotted. The interface routines produce a device-independent intermediate file (called a **metafile**) containing the graphical data in a standard format. Then, a special program is run to translate the device-independent graphical data into the commands required for the particular output device being used at the moment. *The graphical output from these libraries may be redirected to different types of devices without changing the original computer program at all.* With these libraries, a programmer can plot his or her output interactively on a terminal while a program is being tested and debugged, and then send the output to a hardcopy device once the program is working correctly.

11.2 USING FORTRAN LIBRARIES

The general principles of how to build and use libraries are the same for all libraries on all computers. However, the specific details differ from computer to computer. We will now describe the general principles of library use, and your instructor will provide you with the information required to make and use libraries on your particular computer.

11.2.1   Making Libraries and Linking Programs with Libraries

A library may contain any number of subroutines and function subprograms. Each subroutine or function is first compiled with the FORTRAN compiler to produce an object module. Then, the object module is added to the library using a special program called the **librarian.** The librarian places all of the object modules into a single large file, and generates a table of contents describing each module in the library and where to find it within the file.

To use subroutines from the library in one of your programs, you must include the appropriate subroutine calls in the program, and compile the program with the FORTRAN compiler. Next, you must link the program with the **linker** to produce an executable file. If you specify the name of your library when you run the linker, the linker searches the table of contents in the library to see if any of the subroutines you need are present in the library. If they are, then the linker extracts those subroutines from the library and include them in your final executable program.

Remember that *the procedures for compiling subprograms, placing them in libraries, and using the libraries vary from computer to computer.* You must ask your instructor or a knowledgeable user for the proper procedures on your particular computer.

11.2.2   Selecting and Using Library Routines

Suppose that we are working on a programming project, and that we wish to use library routines to make our job easier. How do we identify the proper routines to use, and how do we apply them properly? A good place to start is with the library's index.

Normally, any FORTRAN library will come with an index that classifies the routines in the library by function. If we know what we wish to do, it is a simple matter to look into the index to find one or more routines that are candidates to do the job. Once these candidates are identified, then we can turn to the manual pages describing the routines to confirm that they do what we want. The manual pages will tell us exactly how to call the subroutines or functions, including the calling sequence, the type and dimension of each calling argument, and the possible error codes, if any.

We will illustrate this procedure with the library BOOKLIB that comes with this book. As an example, suppose that we wish to add two matrices together using the routines in the BOOKLIB library. If we check the library index in Appendix D, we see that subroutines MMADD and DMMADD add two matrices together. Let's turn to the manual page for these routines.

The manual page for subroutines MMADD and DMMADD is reproduced in Figure 11-3 for convenience. Let's look at that page now. From it, we can see that MMADD adds two matrices in single precision, while DMMADD adds two matrices in double precision. If we are interested in single precision, then the subroutine that we want is MMADD. Note that the manual page shows the calling sequence required by this subroutine, including the type of each calling argument, the dimension of each array, the direction (input or output) of the argument, and a description of its contents. The arguments passed from the calling routine must match this list in type and size, or the results of the call to the subroutine will be unpredictable. The page also includes a description of the algorithm implemented by the subroutine, and an example of how to use the subroutine.

MMADD/DMMADD (SINGLE/DOUBLE PRECISION)
MMSUB/DMMSUB (SINGLE/DOUBLE PRECISION)

Purpose To add (subtract) two-dimensional matrices A and B of the same size, and store the result in a third matrix C (matrix C may be the same as either A or B).

Usage

```
CALL MMADD ( A, B, C, IDROW, IDCOL, NROW, NCOL )
CALL MMSUB ( A, B, C, IDROW, IDCOL, NROW, NCOL )
```

Arguments

Name	Type	Dim	I/O	Description
A	R/D	IDROW × IDCOL	I	First matrix to add/subtract
B	R/D	IDROW × IDCOL	I	Second matrix to add/subtract
C	R/D	IDROW × IDCOL	O	Resulting matrix
IDROW	I		I	Declared size of matrices (rows)
IDCOL	I		I	Declared size of matrices (columns)
NROW	I		I	Number of rows to add/subtract
NCOL	I		I	Number of columns to add/subtract

Algorithm

MMADD: $c_{ij} = a_{ij} + b_{ij}$ $i = 1$ to NROW, $j = 1$ to NCOL

MMSUB: $c_{ij} = a_{ij} - b_{ij}$ $i = 1$ to NROW, $j = 1$ to NCOL

Example

This example declares two 10 × 10 arrays A and B, initializes them with 2 × 2 matrices, and adds the matrices using subroutine MMADD.

```
      REAL A(10,10), B(10,10), C(10,10)
      INTERGER I, J, NROW, NCOL
      DATA NROW, NCOL / 2, 2 /
      DATA A(1,1), A(2,1), A(1,2), A(2,2) / 1., 2., 3., 4. /
      DATA B(1,1), B(2,1), B(1,2), B(2,2) / 5., 6., 7., 8./
      CALL MMADD ( A, B, C, 10, 10, 2, 2 )
      WRITE (*,1000) ((I,J,C(I,J), I=1, NROW), J=1, NCOL)
 1000 FORMAT (' C(',I2,',',I2,') = ',F10.4)
```

Result

```
C( 1, 1) =       6.0000
C( 2, 1) =       8.0000
C( 1, 2) =      10.0000
C( 2, 2) =      12.0000
```

FIGURE 11-3   Manual page for subroutines MMADD and DMMADD.

In the argument list for this subroutine, *the sizes of the matrices* A, B, *and* C *are declared by arguments* IDROW *and* IDCOL, while the numbers of rows and columns to add are declared by arguments NROW and NCOL. Why is there a distinction between the declared size of the matrices and the size of the data to be added together? Matrices A, B, and C must be declared large enough to contain the largest-sized problems that the program will ever need to handle. For example, matrices A, B, and C may be declared as 4×4 matrices in order to support problems of up to that size, but the current problem may only require 2×2 matrices. We must tell the subroutine that the matrices are 4×4, so that it will know how to locate a term like A(1,2). Therefore, we pass IDROW and IDCOL to the subroutine. On the other hand, we must also tell it that we only want to add a 2×2 portion of the matrices. If we just let the subroutine add all of the values declared in the matrices, then 3/4 of the operations performed by the subroutine would be on unused portions of the matrices, and would be wasted! For this reason, we also pass NROW and NCOL.

Recall from Chapter 5 that arrays are allocated in memory *column order*. All of column 1 is allocated, and then all of column 2, etc. Because of this allocation scheme, a subroutine using a two-dimensional array must know the number of rows in the array in order to calculate the memory location of any element in that array. If we again consider the 4×4 array A, we can see that element A(1,2) is the fifth element in the array, since the entire first column is allocated in memory before the first element in the second column. The routine must know that there are four rows in the array!

EXAMPLE 11-2   *Adding Matrices*   Let's illustrate the effect of passing incorrect array sizes to subroutines by adding two 2×2 matrices that are stored in arrays of size 4×4 with the BOOKLIB library routine MMADD. We will do this addition three times:

1. Once with the correct array sizes (4×4) and correct number of rows and columns to add (2×2).

Two-dimensional 4 × 4 array A:

$$A = \begin{bmatrix} A(1,1) & A(1,2) & A(1,3) & A(1,4) \\ A(2,1) & A(2,2) & A(2,3) & A(2,4) \\ A(3,1) & A(3,2) & A(3,3) & A(3,4) \\ A(4,1) & A(4,2) & A(4,3) & A(4,4) \end{bmatrix}$$

Memory allocation for the 4 × 4 array A:

A(1,1)
A(2,1)
A(3,1)
A(4,1)
A(1,2)
A(2,2)
A(3,2)
A(4,2)
A(1,3)
A(2,3)
A(3,3)
A(4,3)
A(1,4)
A(2,4)
A(3,4)
A(4,4)

FIGURE 11-4   Memory allocation for a 4 × 4 array A.

2. Once with incorrect array sizes (2 × 2), but with the correct number of rows and columns to add (2 × 2). (This is the most common mistake made by a novice programmer using a library for the first time.)
3. Once with correct array sizes (4 × 4), but with an incorrect number of rows and columns to add (4 × 4).

SOLUTION   A program to add two 2 × 2 matrices A and B and store the result in matrix C is shown in Figure 11-5. Matrices A, B, and C are each sized to hold 4 × 4 values. Note that the elements of matrix A are initialized with values of 1. through 16., and the elements of matrix B are initialized with values of 100. through 1600., while all of matrix C is initialized with zeros. With this combination, it will be possible to determine from matrix C whether or not the addition worked correctly.

```fortran
      PROGRAM MATADD
C
C  Purpose:
C    To illustrate the use of library subroutine MMADD, and
C    also to illustrate the errors caused by passing incorrect
C    array sizes to MMADD.
C
C  Record of revisions:
C      Date         Programmer          Description of change
C      ====         ==========          =====================
C    03/21/93     S. J. Chapman         Original code
C
C  List of local variables:
C    A       -- Input matrix.
C    B       -- Input matrix.
C    C       -- Output matrix.
C    I       -- Index variable.
C    IDCOL   -- Number of columns declared in matrices A, B, and C.
C    IDROW   -- Number of rows declared in matrices A, B, and C.
C    J       -- Index variable.
C    NCOL    -- Number of columns used in matrices A, B, and C.
C    NROW    -- Number of rows used in matrices A, B, and C.
C
      IMPLICIT NONE
C
C     Declare local variables.
C
      REAL A(4,4), B(4,4), C(4,4)
      INTEGER IDCOL, IDROW, NCOL, NROW, I, J
C
C     Data
C
      DATA A / 1.,    2.,    3.,    4.,    5.,    6.,    7.,    8.,
     *         9.,   10.,   11.,   12.,   13.,   14.,   15.,   16. /
      DATA B / 100., 200.,  300.,  400.,  500.,  600.,  700.,  800.,
     *         900., 1000., 1100., 1200., 1300., 1400., 1500., 1600. /
      DATA C / 16*0. /
C
C     Call MMADD subroutine correctly to add 2 x 2 matrices A and B
C     and place the result in C.
C
      IDROW = 4
      IDCOL = 4
      NROW  = 2
```

```
          NCOL  = 2
          CALL MMADD ( A, B, C, IDROW, IDCOL, NROW, NCOL )
C
C         Print out matrix C.
C
          WRITE (*,'(/1X,A)')
     *          Result with matrix sizes declared correctly:'
          WRITE (*,'(3X,4F10.2)') ((C(I,J), J=1,4), I=1,4)
C
C         Clear array C.
C
          DO 20 I = 1, 4
             DO 10 J = 1, 4
                C(I,J) = 0.
      10     CONTINUE
      20 CONTINUE
C
C         Call MMADD subroutine with all parameters equal to 2.
C
          IDROW = 2
          IDCOL = 2
          NROW  = 2
          NCOL  = 2
          CALL MMADD ( A, B, C, IDROW, IDCOL, NROW, NCOL )
C
C         Print out matrix C.
C
          WRITE (*,'(/1X,A)')
     *          'Result with matrix sizes declared incorrectly:'
          WRITE (*,'(3X,4F10.2)') ((C(I,J), J=1,4), I=1,4)
C
C         Call MMADD subroutine with all parameters equal to 4.
C
          IDROW = 4
          IDCOL = 4
          NROW  = 4
          NCOL  = 4
          CALL MMADD ( A, B, C, IDROW, IDCOL, NROW, NCOL )
C
C         Print out matrix C.
C
          WRITE (*,'(/1X,A)')
     *          'Result with NROW & NCOL declared incorrectly:'
          WRITE (*,'(3X,4F10.2)') ((C(I,J), J=1,4), I=1,4)
C
          END
```

FIGURE 11-5 Program to test subroutine MMADD.

When this program is executed, the results are

```
C:\BOOK\FORT>matadd
Result with matrix sizes declared correctly:
     101.00    505.00       .00       .00
     202.00    606.00       .00       .00
        .00       .00       .00       .00
        .00       .00       .00       .00
```

```
Result with matrix sizes declared incorrectly:
    101.00       .00       .00       .00
    202.00       .00       .00       .00
    303.00       .00       .00       .00
    404.00       .00       .00       .00

Result with NROW & NCOL declared incorrectly:
    101.00    505.00    909.00   1313.00
    202.00    606.00   1010.00   1414.00
    303.00    707.00   1111.00   1515.00
    404.00    808.00   1212.00   1616.00
```

When both the sizes of the arrays and the number of rows and columns to add are correct, the output from the subroutine is correct. If the size of the arrays were specified incorrectly to be 2×2, then the subroutine will not be able to index into the arrays properly. It will believe that the third memory location in array A is A(1,2), when in fact it is A(3,1). This confusion causes the wrong array elements to be added together, and the results are stored in the wrong locations in C. Finally, if the sizes of the arrays are specified correctly but the number of rows and columns to add are incorrectly specified as 4, all elements of arrays A and B will be added, and the result will be stored in array C. The data that we want is indeed present in the upper left corner of C, but a lot of unnecessary work was done as well while getting the answer. ●

A subroutine does not actually need to know how many columns there are in a two-dimensional array, since the number of columns does not affect the way that an array element is accessed in memory. Therefore, many library routines are written so that only IDROW is passed when two-dimensional arrays are passed to subroutines. However, if we pass IDCOL as well as IDROW, and if the subroutine is compiled with the bounds-checking option turned on, then it will be able to perform bounds checking while we are debugging programs that use these routines.

In fact, it is possible to make two libraries with the same subroutines: a debugging library and a standard library. The routines in the debugging library will be compiled with all of the checking options turned on. They will run slowly, but they will tell a user if any out-of-bounds references occur. The routines in the standard library will be compiled with all of the checking options turned off. They will run very quickly, but the user will not be informed if an error occurs. Normally, a programmer would link with the debugging library while testing a new program to ensure that any errors in the program are caught. Once the program has been debugged, he or she will link to the standard library so that the program will run faster.

Quiz 11-1

This quiz provides a quick check to see if you have understood the concepts introduced in Sections 11.1 and 11.2. If you have trouble with the quiz, reread the sections, ask your instructor, or discuss the material with a fellow student. The answers to this quiz are found in the back of the book.

1. Determine how to create libraries and place subroutines into libraries on your computer.
2. Determine how to link with libraries on your computer.
3. Find a subroutine or function in library BOOKLIB that will take the dot product of two vectors. Write a program that uses that routine to calculate the dot product of the vectors VA = [10. −2. 40. 3.] and VB = [7. −10. −4. 6.] Compile the program, link it with BOOKLIB, execute it. What is the result of the program?

11.3   EXAMPLE PROBLEMS

The diskette that accompanies the instructors manual for this book contains a number of the useful subroutines and functions that we have developed in the book, as well as some others of general interest. Your instructor will probably have compiled the routines and generated a BOOKLIB library on the computer that you are using with this course. He or she will be able to tell you how to access this library.

The subroutines and functions contained in the library are described in Appendix D. The purpose of each routine is given in the appendix, together with a description of its calling sequence, arguments, and algorithm. To use the library, you should look through the descriptions of the routines to locate one that performs the function you need, and then check to see what its calling sequence is. Once you know which routine you would like to use and how it is called, you can add the appropriate calls to your program as you write it. Finally, you should search the BOOKLIB library when you compile and link the program.

When you go to work in industry, you will probably be using routines from much larger libraries for some of the functions in your programs. The procedure will be exactly the same in that case as it is with our simple library:

1. Search the library documentation for the routines to perform the task you need
2. Check the documentation for the proper calling sequence for your routines
3. Insert calls to the routines in your program
4. Link the program with the library containing the desired routines

The following three examples illustrate the use of routines from the BOOKLIB library in the solution of practical problems.

EXAMPLE 11-3 *Interpolating Between Data Points*   When engineers or scientists make measurements in the real world, they usually record the data only at discrete intervals. For example, the voltage in a sensing circuit might be measured and recorded only once a second during an experiment. What happens if, after the experiment, it is necessary to know the voltage at some point *between* the recorded measurements? Then the user must *interpolate* between the measured values to estimate the unknown voltage.

In this example, we will write a program to interpolate a data value at a user-specified point within a data set, using BOOKLIB routines to do the hard work.

SOLUTION The input measurements must be in the form of (x, y) pairs, where x is the independent variable (such as the time at which a measurement is made) and y is the dependent variable (the measurement itself). The input measurements will be read from a user-specified input file, where each (x, y) pair occupies a separate line in the file. The data in the file must be ordered in terms of increasing values of x. The program must be able to ask the user for the input file name, to read the measurement data, and then to ask the user for the point x_0 at which to interpolate a value y_0.

If we check Appendix D, we see that there is an interpolation routine included in BOOKLIB. It is called INTERP, and it performs a linear interpolation between points in the input data set.

Subroutine INTERP returns an error if the point to be interpolated is outside the range of the input data set, so the program we write must handle that situation.

1. State the problem.

Write a program to read an input data set, and to interpolate a measured value at a user-specified point within the data set.

2. Define the inputs and outputs.

The inputs to this program are:

(*a*) The file name of the file containing the data set.
(*b*) A file containing the data set, organized in (x, y) pairs in order of increasing x, with one (x, y) pair per line.
(*c*) The point x_0 at which to estimate the value y_0.

The output from this program is the value y_0.

3. Describe the algorithm.

This program will have to read in the input data set and the desired position at which to interpolate the value y_0. It will have to present the data to subroutine INTERP, and display the results. Note that the program will also have to handle error codes returned by INTERP. The pseudocode for this program is shown below.

```
Prompt user for the input file name FILNAM
Read FILNAM
Prompt user for the desired point X0
Read X0
Open File FILNAM
IF Open successful THEN
   Read data values from file
   If Read successful then
      CALL INTERP to interpolate the point Y0
      Check for errors in subroutine INTERP
      IF no errors THEN
         Write out Y0
      ELSE
         Tell user of INTERP failure
      End of IF
   ELSE
      Tell user of read failure
   End of IF
END of IF
```

4. Turn the algorithm into FORTRAN statements.

The resulting FORTRAN program is shown in Figure 11-6. Note that this program calls subroutine INTERP from the BOOKLIB library.

```
      PROGRAM INTTST
C
C  Purpose:
C    To interpolate the value Y0 at position X0, given a set of
C    (X,Y) measurements organized in increasing order of X.
C
C  Record of revisions:
C      Date        Programmer         Description of change
C      ====        ==========         =====================
C    08/22/93    S. J. Chapman        Original code
C
C  List of local variables:
C    ERROR  -- Error flag: 0 = No error
C    EXCEED -- Logical variable indicating array sizes exceeded
C    FILNAM -- File name to write test signal to.
C    ISTAT  -- I/O status flag.
C    MAXLEN -- Maximum number of input values.
C    NPTS   -- Number of points in input data set.
C    TEMP1  -- Temporary variable for reading X values
C    TEMP2  -- Temporary variable for reading Y values
C    X      -- Values of independent variable X.
C    X0     -- Position at which to interpolate Y0.
C    Y      -- Values of dependent variable Y.
C    Y0     -- Interpolated value.
C
      IMPLICIT NONE
C
C    Declare parameters.
C
      INTEGER    MAXLEN
      PARAMETER ( MAXLEN = 100 )
C
C    Declare local variables.
C
      REAL    X(MAXLEN), Y(MAXLEN), X0, Y0, TEMP1, TEMP2
      INTEGER ISTAT, ERROR, NPTS
      LOGICAL EXCEED
      CHARACTER FILNAM*32
C
      NPTS = 0
C
C    Get input file name.
C
      WRITE (*,*) 'Enter input file name:'
      READ (*,'(A)') FILNAM
C
C    Get point X0 at which to interpolate data.
C
      WRITE (*,*) 'Enter point X0 at which to interpolate Y0:'
      READ (*,*) X0
C
C    Open input file on LU 7.
C
```

```
      OPEN ( UNIT=7, FILE=FILNAM, STATUS='OLD', IOSTAT=ISTAT )
C
C     Was the file open successful?
C
      IF ( ISTAT .EQ. 0 ) THEN
C
C        The file was opened successfully, so read the data set.
C
         READ (7, *, IOSTAT=ISTAT) TEMP1, TEMP2
C
C        Begin WHILE loop.  Did we read the value successfully?
C
   10    IF ( ISTAT .EQ. 0 ) THEN
C
C           Yes.  Increment number of points.
C
            NPTS = NPTS + 1
C
C           Is NPTS <= MAXLEN?  If so, store the value in array A.
C           If not, set the array size exceeded flag to .TRUE.
C
            IF ( NPTS .LE. MAXLEN ) THEN
               X(NPTS) = TEMP1
               Y(NPTS) = TEMP2
            ELSE
               EXCEED = .TRUE.
            END IF
C
C           Read next value.
C
            READ (7, *, IOSTAT=ISTAT) TEMP1, TEMP2
            GO TO 10
C
C           End of WHILE Loop
C
         END IF
C
C        Was the array size exceeded?  If so, tell user and quit.
C
         IF ( .NOT. EXCEED ) THEN
C
C           Array size not exceeded.  Interpolate the data.
C
            CALL INTERP ( X, Y, NPTS, X0, Y0, ERROR )
C
C           Display results.
C
            IF ( ERROR .EQ. 0 ) THEN
               WRITE (*,1030) X0, Y0
 1030          FORMAT (1X,'The interpolated value at X ',1PE14.6,' is ',
     *                 E14.6,'.')
            ELSE
               WRITE (*,1040)
 1040          FORMAT (1X,'ERROR—Point X0 is outside the range of X.')
            END IF
         ELSE
            WRITE (*,1020) NPTS, MAXLEN
```

```
 1020        FORMAT (' Maximum number of points exceeded: ', I6,
     *               ' > ', I6 )
            END IF
C
C           END of IF OPEN successful...
C
        END IF
        END
```

FIGURE 11-6   A program to interpolate values in a data set, using BOOKLIB routine INTERP.

5. Test the program.

To test this program, we will create an input data file INTDAT containing the following (x, y) data pairs (note that $y = x^2$ for this data set):

.0	.0
.5	.3
1.0	1.0
1.5	2.3
2.0	4.0
2.5	6.3
3.0	9.0
3.5	12.3
4.0	16.0
4.5	20.3
5.0	25.0

We will test the program using the values $x_0 = 3.1$ and $x_0 = 5.5$.

```
C:\BOOK\FORT>inttst
Enter input file name:
intdat
Enter point X0 at which to interpolate Y0:
3.1
The interpolated value at X   3.100000E+00 is   9.660000E+00.

C:\BOOK\FORT>inttst
Enter input file name:
intdat
Enter point X0 at which to interpolate Y0:
5.5
ERROR—Point X0 is outside the range of X.
```

The correct value of y_0 for $x_0 = 3.1$ is 9.61. As you can see, the interpolation program came pretty close to the correct answer. Also, the program correctly identified $x_0 = 5.5$ as being outside the range of the input data set. ●

Note: Examples 11-4 and 11-5 involve more complex mathematics than the other examples presented in this book. If they are too difficult for your current mathematical background, they may be skipped with no loss of continuity.

■
EXAMPLE   11-4 *Generating Noisy Simulated Data*   It is common in engineering or scientific applications to simulate the operation of a large system (such as an airplane) *before* it is built. It is *much* cheaper to find and correct design errors in simulations before a piece of hardware is built than it is to fix the thing afterward. The simulated system is fed input data typical of that the real system would see, and the engineers observe the response of the simulation to the inputs. If an error is found, the simulation is modified, and the process is repeated until a successful design has been found.

To make certain that a design works, the input data fed to it must be typical of the data that the system would see in the real world. Since all real-world measurements are noisy, the simulated input data must also be corrupted by some random noise to make the inputs realistic. These noisy input data sets are often generated by special simulation subroutines.

In this example, we will develop a subroutine to generate a simulated input signal consisting of a sine wave corrupted by a known amount of noise. The equation for a sinusoidal signal is:

$$y(t) = \sqrt{2}A \sin 2\pi f t \tag{11-1}$$

where A is the root-mean-square (rms) amplitude of the sinusoid, f is the frequency of the sinusoid in hertz, and t is time in seconds. We generate our test signal by calculating the values of $y(t)$ at specific times separated by Δt seconds. The output values from the test sinusoid will be

$y_0 = y(0)$

$y_1 = y(\Delta t)$

$y_2 = y(2\Delta t)$

$\cdots$

$y_i = y(i\Delta t)$

etc.

If the spacing between each sample of the waveform is Δt seconds, then there will be $1/\Delta t$ samples per second. If the sampling frequency is defined as

$$f_s = \frac{1}{\Delta t} \tag{11-2}$$

the expression for the test sinusoid in Equation (11-1) becomes

$$y_i = \sqrt{2}A \sin \left(2\pi \frac{f}{f_s} i \right) \tag{11-3}$$

To make our simulated input signal, we will corrupt this sinusoid with noise. Let's check the BOOKLIB library to see what sort of noise generation routines are available. A quick check of Appendix D shows that there are two random-number-generating functions: function RAN1, which generates a uniform random noise sequence whose amplitude varies between 0 and 1, and function GRAN1, which generates a Gaussian random noise sequence centered at 0 with a standard deviation of 1. The distribution of samples produced by the uniform random noise routine RAN1 is shown in Figure 11-7(*a*). As you can see, there is an equal probability that any

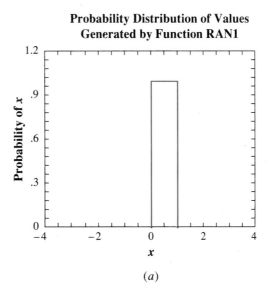

(*a*)

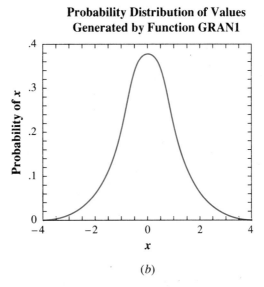

(*b*)

FIGURE 11-7   (*a*) Probability distribution of values generated by function RAN1. (*b*) Probability distribution of values generated by function GRAN1.

number between 0 and 1 will be produced by the function. The distribution of samples produced by the Gaussian random noise routine GRAN1 is shown in Figure 11-7(*b*). It is the classic bell-shaped curve that describes so many phenomena in nature (including, probably, the distribution of grades in this class!). The distribution of samples produced by the GRAN1 routine is more representative of the types of noise that might corrupt our real signals, so we will use the GRAN1 routine to simulate the noise on our test signal.

How much noise should be combined with the sinusoid? For some tests, we would like to have very little noise added to the simulated input signal, while for others, we would like to have a lot of noise added to the signal. The amount of noise mixed in with the desired signal is specified by a quantity called the **signal to noise ratio** (SNR). The SNR is the ratio of the desired signal amplitude to the noise amplitude. It is usually expressed on a logarithmic scale in decibels (dB). The SNR of a signal is given by the equation

$$SNR = 20 \log_{10} \left(\frac{A_{signal}}{A_{noise}} \right) \qquad (11\text{-}4)$$

where A_{signal} is the rms amplitude of the signal, and A_{noise} is the rms amplitude of the noise. For this example, we should be able to specify the desired SNR of the test signal, and the program should be able to use Equation (11-4) to add the proper amount of noise to the desired sinusoidal signal.

With this background, let's formally state the problem we are trying to solve: *Write a program that will generate a simulated input signal consisting of a sinusoid corrupted by a specified amount of Gaussian noise. The amplitude and frequency of the sinusoid, the sampling frequency f_s, and the SNR of the signal should be under user control. Also, the user should be able to specify the duration of the test signal in seconds. The subroutine that generates the test signal should place the resulting output signal in an array so that it may be easily fed into a system to be tested. The calling program should also write the test signal to disk.*

We will also plot the output signal generated by this program for several different SNRs. These plots will make obvious the corrupting effect of noise on the simulated input data.

SOLUTION   The program must be able to ask the user for the critical information, calculate a sinusoidal signal corrupted by noise, and output the test signal in a user-specified array.

1.   State the problem.
The problem has been succinctly stated above.

2.   Define the inputs and outputs.
The inputs to this program are:

(*a*) The desired rms amplitude A of the sinusoid.
(*b*) The desired frequency f of the sinusoid in hertz (Hz).
(*c*) The desired sampling frequency f_s in Hz.

(*d*) The duration of the signal (TOTLEN) in seconds.
(*e*) The desired signal-to-noise ratio in dB.
(*f*) The name of a file to which the simulated data may be written.

The output from this program is an array containing the desired test signal. Note that the array must be able to hold the entire test signal. Since the length of the signal is TOTLEN seconds and there are f_s samples per second, the number of samples required is

$$NSAMP = (TOTLEN)(f_s) + 1 \qquad\qquad \textbf{(11-5)}$$

where the 1 is for the extra sample at time zero. Therefore the output array must be at least NSAMP samples long.

3. Describe the algorithm.

This program can be broken down into four major steps:

```
Get the input parameters from the user.
Calculate the desired signal plus noise.
Return the result in the output array.
Write the data to disk.
```

The first step of the program is to get the desired input parameters from the user. Next, the desired signal corrupted by the specified amount of noise must be calculated. This step should properly be done in a subroutine, since it is a logically separate function. Furthermore, if we write the test generator as a subroutine, we will be able to include that subroutine directly into the programs written for the system we are trying to test. Finally, we return the results in the output array, and write them out to a disk file so that we can see what we have done.

The detailed pseudocode for the main program is

```
Prompt user for the desired rms amplitude AMP
READ AMP
Prompt user for the desired frequency FREQ
READ FREQ
Prompt user for the desired sampling frequency FS
READ FS
Prompt user for the total signal length TOTLEN
READ TOTLEN
Prompt user for the desired SNR
READ SNR
Prompt user for FILNAM
READ FILNAM
OPEN File FILNAM
IF OPEN successful THEN
   CALL TSTSIG to calculate signal
   Check for errors in subroutine TSTSIG
   IF no errors THEN
      WRITE out results to disk
```

```
        ELSE
            Tell user of TSTSIG failure
        END of IF
    ELSE
        Tell user of OPEN failure
    END of IF
```

Subroutine TSTSIG performs the actual work of calculating the test signal. The user-specified input parameters AMP, FREQ, FS, TOTLEN, and SNR must be passed to the subroutine, as well as an output array to put the results in. The subroutine calculates the number of samples required in the output signal, and determines if enough space is available in the output array. If so, it will calculate the desired signal from Equation (11-3)

$$y_i = \sqrt{2}A \sin\left(2\pi\frac{f}{f_s}i\right) \qquad \text{(11-3)}$$

for $i = 0$ to NSAMP $- 1$. The required amplitude of the noise may be derived by solving for the noise amplitude in Equation (11-4).

$$A_{noise} = \frac{A_{signal}}{10^{\left(\frac{SNR}{20}\right)}} \qquad \textbf{(11-6)}$$

The detailed pseudocode for subroutine TSTSIG is

```
NSAMP ← NINT (TOTLEN / DT ) + 1
AMPNOI ← AMP / ( 10.**(SNR/20.))
IF NSAMP > array length
    Set error code
ELSE
    Calculate FACTOR ← 2 * PI * FREQ / FS
    Calculate PKAMP ← SQRT(2.) * AMP
    DO for I = 1 to NSAMP
        Calculate sinusoid:
        OUTPUT(I)← PKAMP * SIN (FACTOR * REAL(I))
        Calculate total signal
        OUTPUT(I) ← OUTPUT(I) + AMPNOI * GRAN1()
    END of DO loop
END of IF
RETURN
```

4. Turn the algorithm into FORTRAN statements.

The resulting FORTRAN program is shown in Figure 11-8. Note that this program calls function GRAN1 from the BOOKLIB library.

```
    PROGRAM GETSIG
C
C  Purpose:
C    To generate a test signal consisting of a user-specified sinusoidal
C    signal corrupted by noise.
C
```

```
C  List of local variables:
C      AMP    -- RMS amplitude of sinusoid.
C      FILNAM -- File name to write test signal to.
C      FREQ   -- Frequency of sinusoid in Hz.
C      FS     -- Sampling frequency in Hz.
C      I      -- Index variable.
C      ISTAT  -- I/O status flag.
C      SNR    -- Desired signal to noise ratio.
C      MAXLEN -- Length of array OUTPUT.
C      OUTPUT -- Output signal.
C      NSAMP  -- Number of samples in the output signal.
C      ERROR  -- Error flag: 0 = No error
C
       IMPLICIT NONE
C
C      Declare parameters.
C
       INTEGER    MAXLEN
       PARAMETER ( MAXLEN = 10000 )
C
C      Declare local variables.
C
       REAL    AMP, FREQ, FS, TOTLEN, SNR, OUTPUT(MAXLEN)
       INTEGER I, ISTAT, ERROR, NSAMP
       CHARACTER FILNAM*32
C
C      Get sinusoid amplitude.
C
       WRITE (*,*) 'Enter the desired amplitude of the sinusoid:'
       READ (*,*) AMP
C
C      Get sinusoid frequency.
C
       WRITE (*,*) 'Enter the desired frequency of the sinusoid, in Hz:'
       READ (*,*) FREQ
C
C      Get sampling interval.
C
       WRITE (*,*) 'Enter sampling frequency in Hz: '
       READ (*,*) FS
C
C      Get total signal length, in seconds.
C
       WRITE (*,*) 'Enter total signal length in seconds: '
       READ (*,*) TOTLEN
C
C      Get SNR in dB.
C
       WRITE (*,*) 'Enter desired SNR in dB:'
       READ (*,*) SNR
C
C      Get output file name.
C
       WRITE (*,*) 'Enter output file name:'
       READ (*,'(A)') FILNAM
C
C      Open output file on LU 7.
C
```

```
      OPEN ( UNIT=7, FILE=FILNAM, STATUS='UNKNOWN', IOSTAT=ISTAT )
C
C     Was the file open successful?
C
      IF ( ISTAT .EQ. 0 ) THEN
C
C         Yes.  Calculate the resulting test data set.
C
          CALL TSTSIG ( AMP, FREQ, FS, TOTLEN, SNR, MAXLEN,
     *                  OUTPUT, NSAMP, ERROR )
C
C         Check for errors in subroutine TSTSIG.
C
          IF ( ERROR .NE. 0 ) THEN
             WRITE (*,*) 'Error in subroutine TSTSIG: no data available.'
          ELSE
C
C            Data is OK.  Write out results.
C
             DO 10 I = 1, NSAMP
                WRITE (7, '(1X,F14.6,3X,F14.6)') REAL(I-1)/FS, OUTPUT(I)
   10        CONTINUE
C
          END IF
C
      ELSE
C
C         A file OPEN error occurred.
C
          WRITE (*,'(3A,I6)') 'Open error in file ', FILNAM, ' ISTAT = ',
     *                  ISTAT
      END IF
      END
      SUBROUTINE TSTSIG ( AMP, FREQ, FS, TOTLEN, SNR, MAXLEN,
     *                  OUTPUT, NSAMP, ERROR )
C
C Purpose:
C   To generate a test signal consisting of a user-specified sinusoidal
C   signal corrupted by noise.
C
C List of calling arguments:
C   NAME      I/O  TYPE        DESCRIPTION
C   ====      ===  ====        ===========
C   AMP       I    REAL        RMS amplitude of sinusoid.
C   FREQ      I    REAL        Frequency of sinusoid in Hz.
C   FS        I    REAL        Sampling frequency of the signal, in Hz.
C   SNR       I    REAL        Desired signal to noise ratio.
C   MAXLEN    I    INTEGER     Length of array OUTPUT.
C   OUTPUT    O    REAL ARRAY  Output signal.
C   NSAMP     O    INTEGER     Number of samples in the output signal.
C   ERROR     O    INTEGER     Error flag: 0 = No error
C
C List of local variables:
C   AMPNOI -- RMS amplitude of the noise.
C   FACTOR -- 2 * PI * FREQ / FS
C   I      -- Index variable.
C   PKAMP  -- Peak amplitude of the sinusoid.
C
```

```
      IMPLICIT NONE
C
C     Declare calling parameters.
C
      REAL      AMP
      REAL      FREQ
      REAL      FS
      REAL      TOTLEN
      REAL      SNR
      INTEGER MAXLEN
      REAL      OUTPUT(MAXLEN)
      INTEGER NSAMP
      INTEGER ERROR
C
C     Declare function name.
C
      REAL      GRAN1
C
C     Declare parameters.
C
      REAL        PI
      PARAMETER ( PI = 3.14159265359 )
C
C     Declare local variables.
C
      INTEGER I
      REAL      AMPNOI, FACTOR, PKAMP
C
C     Calculate NSAMP and noise amplitude
C
      NSAMP  = NINT ( TOTLEN * FS ) + 1
      AMPNOI = AMP / ( 10.**(SNR/20.) )
C
C     Is there enough room to place the data in the output array?
C
      IF ( NSAMP .GT. MAXLEN ) THEN
C
C        No!  Set error condition and get out.
C
         ERROR = 1
         NSAMP = 0
C
      ELSE
C
C        Yes! Calculate the output data array.
C
         FACTOR = 2. * PI * FREQ / FS
         PKAMP  = SQRT(2.) * AMP
         DO 20 I = 1, NSAMP
            OUTPUT(I) = PKAMP * SIN ( FACTOR * REAL(I-1) )
            OUTPUT(I) = OUTPUT(I) + AMPNOI * GRAN1()
   20    CONTINUE
      END IF
C
      RETURN
      END
```

FIGURE 11-8   The program of Example 11-4.

5. Test the program.

To test this program, we can run it with the following parameters, and plot the output signals:

```
AMP    = 10
FREQ   = 1 Hz
FS     = 100 Hz
TOTLEN = 2 seconds
SNR    = 0, 10, 20, and 30 dB
```

The output from this program is plotted in Figure 11-9 on pages 587–588. The effect of differing amounts of noise on the test data set are obvious in this plot. ●

EXAMPLE 11-5 *Detecting Signals in the Presence of Noise* A common problem faced by engineers throughout the world is the *detection of signals buried in noise*. In a communications system, an engineer might try to extract a transmitted radio signal from a background of random noise. To do so, he or she must process the received signal in some fashion that enhances the desired signal while suppressing the undesired noise which was received at the same time. The detection of signals buried in noise is also important to mechanical engineers. For example, excessive vibrations occurring at certain frequencies in mechanical turbines indicate bearing wear and the need for maintenance. In this case, the signal that the engineer wants to detect is the vibration associated with worn bearings, and the noise is all of the other sound produced by the turbine. Sonar systems are another example of the need to detect signals buried in noise. The power systems aboard Russian (and other European) ships run at a frequency of 50 Hz, while the power systems aboard U.S. ships run at a frequency of 60 Hz. Therefore, the detection of a 50-Hz sonar signal might indicate the presence of a potential adversary, while the detection of a 60-Hz signal might indicate the presence of a potential friend. In this case, the engineer is trying to detect the 50- or 60-Hz tones against the background of the general sea noise.

There are many ways of detecting signals in the presence of noise. One very common approach, which works for *narrowband signals,* is to analyze the frequency content of the received signal plus noise. If a signal is *narrowband,* then it occupies only a small range of frequencies, and all of its energy will be concentrated there. Random noise, on the other hand, is typically *broadband,* occupying a wide range of frequencies. Because the energy of the noise is spread over a large band of frequencies, the energy *at any particular frequency* will be relatively small. The energy of the narrowband signal is all concentrated at one frequency, so even a relatively weak signal can be stronger than the portion of the noise energy occurring at the same frequency. This comparison can be done by examining the **spectrum** of the signal plus the noise.

This process is illustrated in Figure 11-10 on pages 589–591. Figure 11-10(*a*) shows a 10-Hz sinusoid with an rms amplitude of 1 volt (V). Figure 11-10(*b*) shows

Test Signal at 0 dB SNR

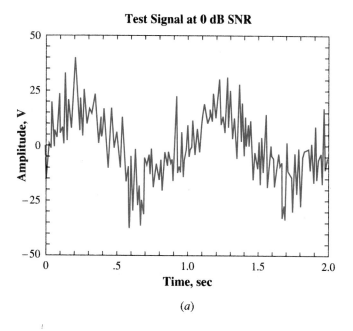

(*a*)

Test Signal at 10 dB SNR

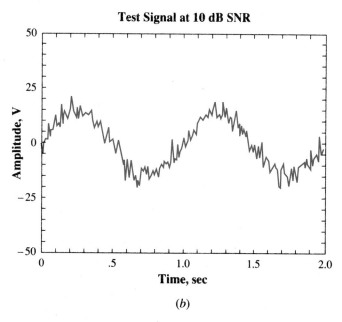

(*b*)

FIGURE 11-9 Sample output from the TSTSIG subroutine for (*a*) 0 dB SNR, (*b*) 10 dB SNR, (*c*) 20 dB SNR, and (*d*) 30 dB SNR. For all cases, AMP = 10, FREQ = 1 Hz, DT = 0.01 seconds, and TOTLEN = 2 seconds.

Test Signal at 20 dB SNR

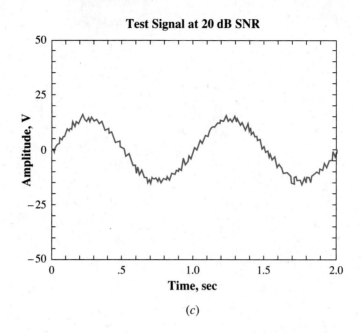

(*c*)

Test Signal at 30 dB SNR

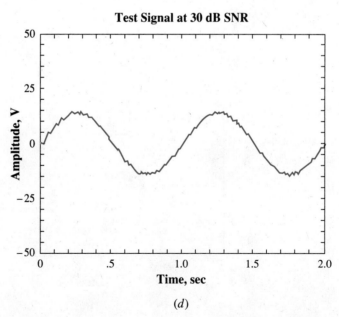

(*d*)

FIGURE 11-9   Continued.

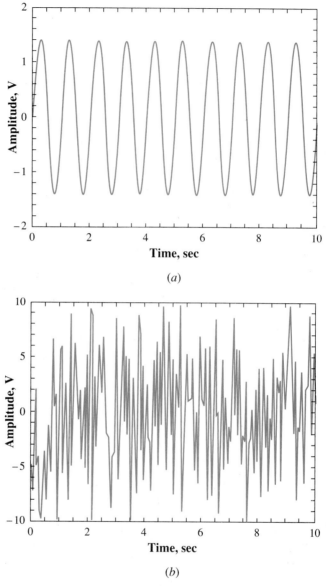

FIGURE 11-10 Detecting a narrowband signal in the presence of noise: (*a*) A
10-Hz sinusoidal signal with an amplitude of 1 V. (*b*) Gaussian
random noise with an rms amplitude of 5 V. (*c*) The sum of the
signal in (*a*) with the noise in (*b*). Note that no trace of the signal is visible to the naked eye. (*d*) The frequency spectrum of
the 10-Hz, 1-V sinusoidal signal. (*e*) The frequency spectrum
of the Gaussian random noise. (*f*) The frequency spectrum associated with the signal in (*c*), which contains both the signal
and the noise. Note that the 1-V signal is detectable out of a
background noise that is five times as strong.

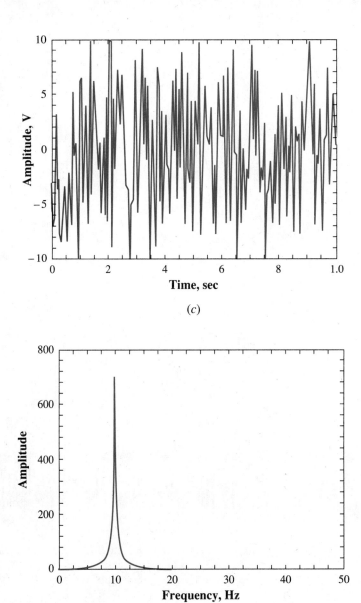

(c)

(d)

FIGURE 11-10   Continued.

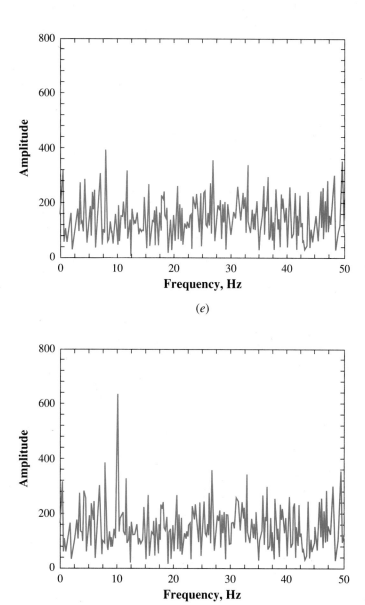

(e)

(f)

FIGURE 11-10 Continued.

a Gaussian random noise with an rms amplitude five times larger than that of the sinusoid. Finally, Figure 11-10(c) shows the sinusoidal signal plus the random noise added together. From Equation (11-4), this waveform has an SNR of

$$\text{SNR} = 20 \log_{10} \left(\frac{A_{\text{signal}}}{A_{\text{noise}}} \right) = 20 \log_{10} \left(\frac{1}{5} \right) = -14 \text{ dB}$$

You can't even see the sinusoidal signal in the presence of all of that noise!

Now, let's look at the frequency spectra of the these three signals. The frequency spectrum of the pure sinusoid is shown in Figure 11-10(d). Notice that all of the energy in the signal is concentrated in a narrow band of frequencies around 10 Hz. The frequency spectrum of the random noise is shown in Figure 11-10(e). Notice that the energy in the noise is scattered more or less evenly throughout all frequencies. Finally, the frequency spectrum of the sinusoidal signal plus the noise is shown in Figure 11-10(f). In this figure, the signal can be picked out of the noise even though the rms amplitude of the noise was five times greater than the rms amplitude of the signal!

Examining the frequency spectra of signals is a very good way to detect narrowband signals in the presence of noise. How can we determine the frequency content of a signal? The standard way to determine the frequency content of a time signal is to calculate the *discrete Fourier transform* (DFT) of that signal. The DFT is defined by the equation

$$F_n = \sum_{k=0}^{N-1} t_k e^{2\pi i k n T / f_s} \tag{11-7}$$

where

t_k	= the kth time sample of the signal being analyzed
N	= the total number of samples in the signal being analyzed
T	= the duration of the signal being analyzed in seconds
f_s	= the sampling frequency of the signal being analyzed
F_n	= the nth frequency component of the output spectrum (a complex number).

There are N components in the complete output spectrum.

The relationship between the length of the signal being analyzed T, the sampling frequency f_s, and number of samples N is

$$N = f_s T \tag{11-8}$$

There is also a fixed relationship between the sampling frequency f_s and the spacing ΔF between components of the output frequency spectrum. This relationship is

$$\Delta F = \frac{f_s}{N} = \frac{1}{T} \tag{11-9}$$

Therefore, the longer the signal being analyzed, the greater the density of samples in the resulting spectrum.

The detailed theory of the DFT is far beyond the scope of this book. It is normally discussed during graduate-level digital signal processing courses. Fortunately, we don't have to worry about that! The beauty of having a subroutine library available is that *someone else* studied the theory and wrote and checked the subroutine implementing the algorithm. All that we users have to know is the calling sequence of the subroutine, and just enough theory to use the subroutine intelligently.

The BOOKLIB library included with this book contains an implementation of the DFT known as the *fast Fourier transform* (FFT). The FFT is just a fast implementation of the DFT algorithm given in Equation (11-7). It has the special restriction that the number of samples in the time series being analyzed must be a power of 2 (16, 32, 64, 128, 256, etc.). If the number of samples in the series is not a power of 2, then trailing zeros must be added at the end of the series until the total number of samples is a power of 2. This process is called **zero padding.**

With this background, let's state the problem that we would like to solve: *Write a program that can analyze a time sequence to determine if any narrowband signals are buried within the data. Plot the output frequency spectrum of the time series, and determine by inspection whether or not a signal was present.*

SOLUTION   Since the times series to be analyzed can be quite long, they should be read from an input disk file. For compatibility with the test data generator created in the previous example, we will assume that the input data file contains two values per line, with the first one being the time of the sample and the second one being the value of the sample. (This program does not need the times of each sample, so it will have to be designed to skip over that data.)

The program will need to know the name of the input disk file, and also the sampling frequency of the input data set. It will open the input file and read in all of the data samples. If necessary, the program will zero pad end of the data until it is a power of 2 long, and then calculate the complex frequency spectrum of the signal by calling BOOKLIB routine FFT. The program must then calculate the amplitude of the frequency spectrum. The amplitude of the spectrum can then be displayed with BOOKLIB routine PLOTXY.

1. State the problem.
The problem has been succinctly stated above.

2. Define the inputs and outputs.
The inputs to this program are:

  (*a*) The name of a file containing the input data.
  (*b*) The input data in the file.
  (*c*) The sampling frequency f_s of the data.

The output from this program is a plot of the amplitude spectrum of the input time series.

3.   Describe the algorithm.

This program can be broken down into four major steps:

```
Read the input data.
Calculate the complex amplitude spectrum using routine FFT.
Calculate the magnitude of the amplitude spectrum.
Plot the magnitude of the amplitude spectrum.
```

The first step of the program is to get the desired input data from the user. The program should open a user-supplied file containing an unknown number of data points in the form of (time, value) pairs, with one pair per line. The program will read in all of the data, stopping when the end of the file is detected. The detailed pseudocode for this step is

```
Prompt user for the input file name FILNAM
READ FILNAM
Prompt user for sampling frequency FS
READ FS
OPEN file FILNAM
IF OPEN is successful THEN
   I ← 0
   Read TIME, TEMP (TIME is a dummy variable—we don't need it.)
   WHILE Read successful
      I ← I + 1
      DATA1(I) ← TEMP
      READ next TIME, TEMP
   End of WHILE
   . . .
   . . .
   . . .
End of IF
```

If we examine the description of subroutine FFT found in Appendix D, we see that the input data must be of type COMPLEX, and the length of the array must be a power of 2. Therefore, we must transfer the input data from real array DATA1 into the complex array CDATA1, and then zero pad the length array CDATA1 up to the next power of two before calling subroutine FFT. The next power of two can be calculated by subroutine NXTMUL, which is also found in BOOKLIB. Subroutine FFT can then be called to calculate the complex amplitude spectrum. The detailed pseudocode for these steps is

```
DO from I = 1 to NVALS
   CDATA(I) ← CMPLX( DATA(I), 0. )
End of DO
*
*   Zero pad data.
*
CALL NXTMUL ( NVALS, 2, IEXP, FFTSIZ )
```

```
        DO from I = NVALS+1 to FFTSIZ
           CDATA(I) ← ( 0., 0. )
        End of DO
        *
        *  Call FFT to calculate complex spectrum
        *
        CALL FFT ( CDATA, FFTSIZ, IERROR )
```

Finally, we would like to plot the magnitude of the amplitude spectrum of the data. If the spectrum can be presented as a series of (frequency, value) pairs, then we can use BOOKLIB subroutine PLOTXY to do the plotting. Subroutine PLOTXY can handle up to a maximum of 65 data bins, so there will be many frequency samples in each bin plotted. We will plot the maximum value for any frequency sample falling in a given bin. The detailed pseudocode for this step is

```
        *
        *  Generate (freq, value) pairs to plot at a spacing DF of 1 Hz.
        *
        *  Frequency values in each bin
        DO from I = 0 to NINT(FS)
           XPLOT(I) ← REAL(I)
        End of DO
        *
        *  Calculate maximum spectral amplitudes in each plotting bin
        *
        DO from I = 1 to FFTSIZ
        *    Calculate frequency of data point to nearest Hz
           IFREQ ← NINT ( ( FS / FFTSIZ ) * ( I - 1) )
           YPLOT(IFREQ) ← MAX ( YPLOT(IFREQ), CABS(CDATA(I)) )
        End of DO
        *
        *  Plot data.
        *
        CALL PLOTXY ( XPLOT, YPLOT, NINT(FS), MINX, MAXX, MINY, MAXY,
                      NINT(FS)+1, 65, .TRUE., LU )
```

   4. Turn the algorithm into FORTRAN statements.
   The resulting FORTRAN program is shown in Figure 11-11. Note that this program calls functions FFT, NXTMUL, and PLOTXY from the BOOKLIB library.

```
      PROGRAM SPCTRM
C
C  Purpose:
C    To calculate and plot the spectrum of an input data set.
C
C  Record of revisions:
C     Date        Programmer          Description of change
C     ====        ==========          =====================
C    04/20/93    S. J. Chapman        Original code
C
```

```
C   List of variables:
C      DATA1  -- Real array containing input time data.
C      CDATA  -- Complex array containing input time data, and
C                later the output complex spectrum.
C      FILNAM -- Name of input data file to read.
C      FFTSIZ -- Size of FFT to perform (power of 2)
C      FS     -- Sampling frequency in Hz.
C      I      -- Index variable.
C      IEXP   -- The exponent 2**IEXP corresponding to the next power
C                of 2.
C      IFREQ  -- Frequency of a spectral sample to the nearest Hz.
C      ISTAT  -- I/O status variable:  0 for success
C      LU     -- Logical unit to plot output on.
C      MEDIAN -- The median of the input samples.
C      MAXX   -- Maximum X value to plot.
C      MINX   -- Minimum X value to plot.
C      MAXY   -- Maximum Y value to plot.
C      MINY   -- Minimum Y value to plot.
C      NVALS  -- Number of data values to sort.
C      XPLOT  -- Array of frequency points to plot.
C      YPLOT  -- Amplitude values corresponding to each point in XPLOT.
C
       IMPLICIT NONE
C
C      Parameters
C
       INTEGER    MAXSIZ
       PARAMETER ( MAXSIZ = 8192 )
C
C      Declare the variables used in this program.
C
       INTEGER      I, ISTAT, NVALS, IEXP, FFTSIZ, LU, IFREQ
       REAL         DATA1(MAXSIZ), TIME, FS, XPLOT(0:64), YPLOT(0:64)
       REAL         MAXX, MINX, MAXY, MINY
       COMPLEX      CDATA(MAXSIZ)
       CHARACTER*20 FILNAM
C
C      Data
C
       DATA LU / 6 /
C
C      Get the name of the file containing the input data.
C
       WRITE (*,1000)
 1000  FORMAT (' Enter the file name containing the input data: ')
       READ (*,1010) FILNAM
 1010  FORMAT ( A20 )
C
C      Get the sampling frequency of the input data.
C
       WRITE (*,*) 'Enter the sampling frequency of the input data:'
       READ (*,*) FS
C
C      Open input data file.  Status is OLD because the input data must
C      already exist.
C
       OPEN ( 9, FILE=FILNAM, STATUS='OLD', IOSTAT=ISTAT )
C
```

```
C     Was the OPEN successful?
C
      IF ( ISTAT .EQ. 0 ) THEN
C
C         The file was opened successfully, so read the data to process
C         from it, process the data, and plot the results.
C
          I = 1
          READ (9, *, IOSTAT=ISTAT) TIME, DATA1(I)
C
C         Begin WHILE loop.  Did we read the value successfully?
C
   10     IF ( ISTAT .EQ. 0 ) THEN
C
C             Yes.  Increment pointer for next value.
C
              I = I + 1
C
C             Is I > MAXSIZ?  If so, tell user and quit.
C
              IF ( I .GT. MAXSIZ ) THEN
                 WRITE (*,1020) MAXSIZ
 1020            FORMAT (' Maximum array size exceeded: ', I6 )
                 GO TO 9999
              END IF
C
C             Otherwise, read next value.
C
              READ (9, *, IOSTAT=ISTAT) TIME, DATA1(I)
              GO TO 10
C
C         End of WHILE Loop
C
          END IF
C
C         When we get here,, the last READ was bad, so the number of values we
C         have is one less than I.
C
          NVALS = I - 1
C
C         Now, convert the data to complex form.
C
          DO 20 I = 1, NVALS
             CDATA(I) = CMPLX ( DATA1(I), 0. )
   20     CONTINUE
C
C         Zero pad the data.
C
          CALL NXTMUL ( NVALS, 2, IEXP, FFTSIZ )
          DO 30 I = NVALS+1, FFTSIZ
             CDATA(I) = (0.,0.)
   30     CONTINUE
C
C         Call FFT to calculate complex spectrum.
C
          CALL FFT ( CDATA, FFTSIZ, ISTAT )
C
```

```
C         Generate (freq, value) pairs to plot at a frequency spacing of
C         1 Hz.  First, place the frequency values in each bin.
C
          DO 40 I = 0, NINT(FS)
             XPLOT(I) = REAL(I)
   40     CONTINUE
C
C         Calculate the maximum spectral amplitudes for each plotting
C         bin.
C
          DO 50 I = 1, FFTSIZ
C
C            Calculate the frequency of the data point to nearest Hz.
C
             IFREQ = NINT ( (FS / REAL(FFTSIZ)) * REAL(I-1) )
             YPLOT(IFREQ) = MAX ( YPLOT(IFREQ), CABS(CDATA(I)) )
   50     CONTINUE
C
C         Plot spectrum.
C
          CALL PLOTXY ( XPLOT, YPLOT, NINT(FS), MINX, MAXX, MINY,
     *                  MAXY, NINT(FS), 65, .TRUE., LU )
C
       ELSE
C
C         If we get here, the open failed.
C
          WRITE (*,'(1X,A,A)') 'Open failed on file: ', FILNAM
C
       END IF
C
 9999 CONTINUE
       END
```

FIGURE 11-11   Program SPCTRM of Example 11-4.

5. Test the program.

To test this program, we will run program GETSIG with the following parameters:

```
AMP    = 2.
FREQ   = 12 Hz
FS     = 50 Hz
TOTLEN = 10 seconds
SNR    = -5 dB
FILNAM = EX11-4.DAT
```

A plot of the output test data from program GETSIG is shown in Figure 11-12 (on page 600). Note that the signal is hidden within the random noise. If we now feed the file EX11-4.DAT to program SPCTRM, the results are:

```
C:\BOOK\FORT>SPCTRM
Enter the file name containing the input data:
EX11-4.DAT
Enter the sampling frequency of the input data:
50
```

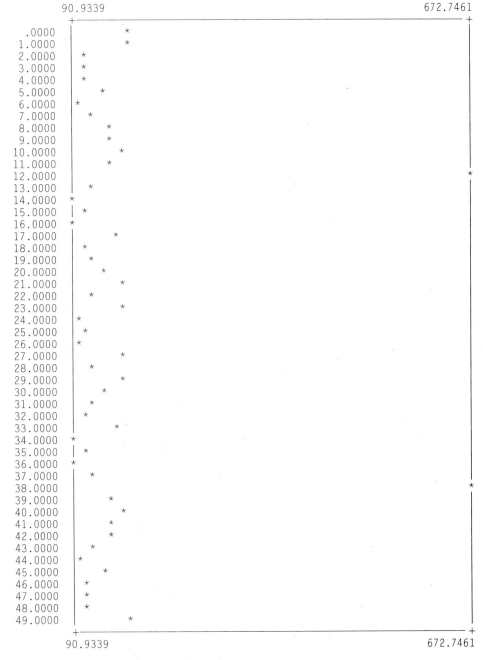

```
              90.9339                                          672.7461
              +---------------------------------------------------+
    .0000     |               *                                   |
   1.0000     |               *                                   |
   2.0000     |  *                                                |
   3.0000     |  *                                                |
   4.0000     |  *                                                |
   5.0000     |      *                                            |
   6.0000     | *                                                 |
   7.0000     |   *                                               |
   8.0000     |     *                                             |
   9.0000     |     *                                             |
  10.0000     |       *                                           |
  11.0000     |     *                                             |
  12.0000     |                                                 * |
  13.0000     |   *                                               |
  14.0000     |*                                                  |
  15.0000     |  *                                                |
  16.0000     |*                                                  |
  17.0000     |        *                                          |
  18.0000     |  *                                                |
  19.0000     |   *                                               |
  20.0000     |     *                                             |
  21.0000     |       *                                           |
  22.0000     |   *                                               |
  23.0000     |       *                                           |
  24.0000     |*                                                  |
  25.0000     |  *                                                |
  26.0000     |*                                                  |
  27.0000     |       *                                           |
  28.0000     |    *                                              |
  29.0000     |       *                                           |
  30.0000     |     *                                             |
  31.0000     |    *                                              |
  32.0000     |  *                                                |
  33.0000     |     *                                             |
  34.0000     |*                                                  |
  35.0000     |  *                                                |
  36.0000     |*                                                  |
  37.0000     |   *                                               |
  38.0000     |                                                 * |
  39.0000     |     *                                             |
  40.0000     |      *                                            |
  41.0000     |    *                                              |
  42.0000     |    *                                              |
  43.0000     |   *                                               |
  44.0000     |*                                                  |
  45.0000     |    *                                              |
  46.0000     |  *                                                |
  47.0000     |  *                                                |
  48.0000     |  *                                                |
  49.0000     |       *                                           |
              +---------------------------------------------------+
              90.9339                                          672.7461

         Number of Points =            50
```

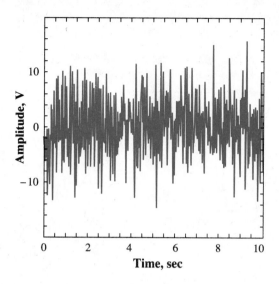

FIGURE 11-12   Plot of test data generated by program GETSIG and used to test program SPCTRM.

The peak of the spectrum occurs at 12 Hz, so we have properly detected the 12-Hz signal embedded in the noise. A detailed plot of the output spectrum is shown in Figure 11-13. As you can see, the detailed spectrum matches the results of our line printer plot. ●

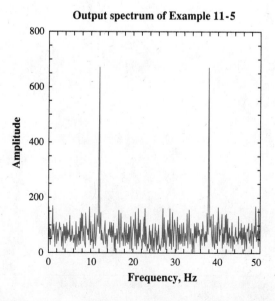

FIGURE 11-13   The output spectrum produced by program SPCTRM.

Notice that in addition to the signal peak at 12 Hz, there is also a peak at 38 Hz. In fact, the entire spectrum is symmetrical about the 25 Hz point! A point at 25 Hz $+ \Delta f$ has exactly the same amplitude as the point at 25 Hz $- \Delta f$. This effect always occurs when working with FFTs and sampled data systems. In fact, the data below 25 Hz is a valid picture of the frequency content at those frequencies, while the data above 25 Hz is just a mirror image of the data below 25 Hz. The data above 25 Hz is said to be *aliased*. Aliasing is the effect that causes wagon wheels to appear to be rotating backward in old Western movies.

What is special about 25 Hz in the above data set? The answer is that it is *half of the sampling frequency* f_s. In general, all frequencies greater than half the sampling frequency will be aliased, and all frequencies below that point will be valid. Half of the sampling frequency f_s has a special name: the Nyquist frequency $f_{nyquist}$. If you intend to analyze the frequency content of a data set, you must make certain that the Nyquist frequency of the data set is higher than the highest frequency that you are looking for.

11.4   SUMMARY

Libraries are a convenient mechanism for storing the object modules from subroutines and functions that you may want to reuse in the future. When a routine is placed in a library, it is stored in the library's file, and an entry is made in the library's table of contents to tell the linker where to find the routine.

Some libraries are available directly from computer vendors. These libraries typically contain utilities to return important system or program information, or to interface with specific pieces of hardware attached to the computers. The format of the routines in these libraries varies from one computer to another, so calling these routines will make your code nonportable. To keep your code as portable as possible, you should call system library routines through an *interface subroutine* or *function*. If you later want to move the program to another computer, only the interface routines will need to be rewritten.

Many pre-built libraries are available from commercial software vendors. These third-party libraries provide routines to solve problems in specific areas such as engineering, signal processing, plotting, statistics, etc. Using these libraries can save a great deal of time when you are writing a new program, since many of the hardest functions have already been programmed and debugged for you. They can also improve the portability of your code, since it is possible to buy these libraries for many different computers.

11.4.1   Summary of Good Programming Practice

The following guidelines should be adhered to when working with libraries:

1.   Use libraries to store and keep track of the subroutines and functions which you may be able to reuse in more than one program.

2. Purchase and use appropriate third-party libraries to make the development of complex programs in specialized areas easier. It is almost always easier and cheaper to buy an off-the-shelf product to perform a specific function than it is to develop and debug the function for yourself.

3. Always use interface routines between your code and system libraries supplied by your computer's maker. All of the machine-specific code in your program will be concentrated in the interface routines, so only the interface routines will need to be modified when the program is moved to another computer.

CHAPTER 11 KEY WORDS

Device independence   Linker
Host computer independence   Metafile
Librarian   System utilities
Library

CHAPTER 11 EXERCISES

1. List the advantages of using libraries.

2. What are system libraries? Why should they be used with caution? If you are going to use a system library routine, how should you use it?

3. Write a form of the interface subroutine TIMSEC that works correctly for your computer.

4. Build a library called MYLIB, and insert subroutines SORT (Example 6-1) and RAN0 (Example 6-6) into it.

5. Write a test program that generates 1000 random numbers between 0 and 10, and then sorts them into ascending order. Use subroutines RAN0 and SORT in the program. Link the program with library MYLIB to access subroutines RAN0 and SORT.

6. Use subroutines in the BOOKLIB library to calculate and plot the function sinc (x) between -2π and 2π. Then, calculate the derivative of sinc (x) with respect to x, and plot the derivative between -2π and 2π.

7. Multiply 4×4 arrays A and B together using the matrix multiplication routine in library BOOKLIB. Write out the resulting array, and check your results by calculating a few elements by hand.

$$A = \begin{bmatrix} 4 & 2 & 8 & -6 \\ 2 & -4 & 3 & -5 \\ 8 & 3 & 1 & -2 \\ -6 & -5 & -2 & 2 \end{bmatrix} \quad B = \begin{bmatrix} -5 & 7 & 2 & 3 \\ 7 & 4 & 5 & 1 \\ 2 & 5 & -3 & -2 \\ 3 & 1 & -2 & -2 \end{bmatrix}$$

8. Add the 4×4 arrays A and B shown in exercise 7 using the matrix addition subroutine in library BOOKLIB. Write out the resulting array, and check your results by calculating a few elements by hand.

9. Subtract the 4 × 4 arrays A and B shown in exercise 7 using the matrix subtraction subroutine in library BOOKLIB. Write out the resulting array, and check your results by calculating a few elements by hand.
10. Explain the distinction between IDROW and NROW in Example 11-2.
11. The selection sort algorithm that we introduced in Chapter 5 is by no means the only type of sorting algorithm available. One alternate possibility is the *heapsort* algorithm, the description of which is beyond the scope of this book. However, an implementation of the heap sort algorithm is included in BOOK-LIB.

    If you have not done so previously, write a set of elapsed time subroutines for your computer, as described in exercise 31 in Chapter 6. Generate an array containing 2,000 random values. Use the elapsed time subroutines to compare the time required to sort these 2,000 values using the selection sort and the heapsort. Which algorithm is faster? (*Note*: Be sure that you are sorting the same array each time. The best way to do this is to make a copy of the original array before sorting, and then sort the two arrays with the different subroutines.)
12. The inverse A^{-1} of an n × n matrix A is the matrix such that

    A A⁻¹ = I

    where I is the identity matrix. Note that the identity matrix I has all ones along the diagonal, and zeros everwhere else.

    $$I = \begin{bmatrix} 1 & 0 & \dots & 0 \\ 0 & 1 & \dots & 0 \\ \dots & \dots & \dots & \dots \\ 0 & 0 & \dots & 1 \end{bmatrix}$$

    Find the inverse of the 5 × 5 matrix C using the routines available in BOOK-LIB.

    $$C = \begin{bmatrix} -2 & 5 & 1 & 3 & 4 \\ -1 & 2 & -1 & -5 & -2 \\ 6 & 4 & -1 & 6 & -4 \\ -5 & 3 & -1 & 4 & 3 \\ -6 & -5 & -2 & -2 & -3 \end{bmatrix}$$

    Prove that the inverse is correct by multiplying C and C^{-1} to get the identity matrix, using routines from BOOKLIB.
13. The principal difference between the two random number generating subroutines RAN0 and GRAN0 is the distribution of the data values produced by each of the routines. Generate a 10,000-element array of random numbers produced by each of the random number generators, and use the histogram subroutine built into BOOKLIB to plot a histogram of the noise distributions produced by the RAN0 and GRAN0 subroutines. How do they compare?

14. The BOOKLIB library contains two subroutines to perform least squares fits to a polynomial of user-specified order: LSQFT and DLSQFT. Write two programs that read (x, y) values from an input data file and fit a polynomial of user-specified order to the data. To test your programs, generate a file containing 21 (x, y) values from the equation

$$y(x) = 1 + 2x - x^2 + 4x^3 + 8x^4$$

for $x = 0.0, 0.25, 0.50, \ldots, 5.0$.

   (a) Perform a fourth-order fit to the data set using both LSQFT and DLSQFT. How do the resulting coefficients compare to the known values in the equation that generated the data?

   (b) Perform a *ninth*-order fit to the data set using both LSQFT and DLSQFT. How do the resulting coefficients compare to the known values in the equation coefficients? (In this case, the coefficients of x^5, x^6, etc. should all turn out to be zero, since they were not in the equation that generated the input data.)

   (c) What is the difference between the performance of LSQFT and DLSQFT on higher-order fits?

15. Use a BOOKLIB subroutine to plot the function $y(x) = e^x$ from $x = 0$ to $x = 3$ in steps of 0.1. Next, take the derivative of the function $y(x) = e^x$ at $x = 0$, $0.1, \ldots, 3.0$, and plot the derivative of the function. Compare the function to its derivative. How do they look?

16. The DFT is defined in Equation (11-7). The FFT is a special algorithm for calculating the DFT in cases where the number of data points is a power of 2. Compare the DFT and the FFT in the following steps:

   (a) Create a 512-point data set containing the function sin (x) sampled at 1/16 second intervals as follows:

```
      COMPLEX CDATA(512)
      DT = 1. / 16.
      DO 10 I = 1, 512
         CDATA(I) = SIN(REAL(I-1)*DT)
   10 CONTINUE
```

   (b) Take the DFT of these samples using the routines in BOOKLIB. Time the DFT routine execution with subroutine TIMSEC.

   (c) Take the FFT of these samples using the routines in BOOKLIB. Time the FFT routine execution with subroutine TIMSEC.

   (d) How much difference in speed is there between the DFT and FFT algorithms?

17. Integrate the function $f(x) = 1 + 4x - 2x^2$ from $x_1 = 0$ to $x_2 = 3$ using a step size of Δx of 0.05.

18. Create a data set consisting of 40 (x, y) pairs of values, where $x(t) = \sin(t)$ and $y(t) = \sin(2t + \pi/6)$ for $t = 0$ to 2π in steps of $\pi/20$. Plot the data set using routines in BOOKLIB.

12 Miscellaneous FORTRAN Features

There are a number of odds and ends in the FORTRAN 77 language that have not fit logically into our discussions in the previous chapters. These miscellaneous features of the language are described here.

The features we describe in this chapter date from the early days of the FORTRAN language. They are the skeletons in FORTRAN's closet. For the most part, they are either incompatible with good structured programming or are obsolete. As such, they should not be used in new programs that you write. However, you may see them in existing programs that you are required to maintain or modify, so you should be familiar with them.

When a feature should not be used in your programs, it will be flagged with a GOOD PROGRAMMING PRACTICE note.

12.1 OBSOLETE AND/OR UNDESIRABLE DECLARATION STATEMENTS

There are four obsolete and/or undesirable FORTRAN statements that may appear in the declaration section of a FORTRAN program. They are:

1. The **IMPLICIT** statement
2. The **DIMENSION** statement
3. The Unlabeled **COMMON** Statement
4. The **EQUIVALENCE** statement

These statements are described below.

12.1.1 The IMPLICIT Statement

We introduced the **IMPLICIT** statement in Chapter 2 as a way of overriding the default typing convention built into FORTRAN. By default, parameters and variables whose names begin with the letters I through N are integers, while all other parameters and variables are reals. The **IMPLICIT** statement permits us to override these defaults.

The general form of the **IMPLICIT** statement is

IMPLICIT *type1* (a_1, a_2, a_3, ...), *type2* (b_1, b_2, b_3, ...), ...

where *type1*, *type2*, etc. are any legal data types: **INTEGER, REAL, LOGICAL, CHARACTER, DOUBLE PRECISION,** or **COMPLEX.** The letters a_1, a_2, a_3, etc. are the first letters whose type will be *type1*, and so forth for the other types. If a range of letters is to be declared as the same type, then the range may be indicated by the first and last letters separated by a dash (-). For example, the following statements declare that variables starting with the letters A, B, C, I, and Z are **COMPLEX,** and variables beginning with the letter D are **DOUBLE PRECISION.** Variables beginning with other letters retain their default types. Finally, the variables I1 and I2 are explicitly declared to be integers, overriding the **IMPLICIT** statement.

```
IMPLICIT COMPLEX (A-C, I, Z), DOUBLE PRECISION D
INTEGER I1, I2
```

The **IMPLICIT NONE** statement was described in Chapter 2 and has been used throughout the book. It cancels all default types. When the **IMPLICIT NONE** statement is used in a program, every parameter, variable, and function name in the program must be declared explicitly. Remember that the **IMPLICIT NONE** statement is an extension to standard FORTRAN 77, so it may not work with all compilers. However, it is supported by all of the most popular compilers, and it is included in the new FORTRAN 90 standard.

Since every parameter and variable in your program should be declared explicitly, there is no need for the standard **IMPLICIT** statement in any well-designed program. Only the **IMPLICIT NONE** statement should be used. However, you must be familiar with it, since you will encounter it in older FORTRAN programs.

■ **GOOD PROGRAMMING PRACTICE**

Do not use **IMPLICIT** statements in your programs, except for **IMPLICIT NONE.** All of your programs should include the **IMPLICIT NONE** statement if your compiler supports it, and all parameters, variables, and functions in your programs should be explicitly typed.

12.1.2   The DIMENSION Statement

The **DIMENSION** statement is a declaration statement used to declare the *length* of arrays. The general form of a **DIMENSION** statement is

DIMENSION *array([i1:]i2, [j1:]j2, ...), ...*

where *array* is an array name, and i_1, i_2, j_1, j_2, etc. are the dimensions of the arrays. For example, a six-element array ARR could be declared with the following statement:

DIMENSION ARR(6)

Notice that the **DIMENSION** statement declares the length of an array, but not its type. If ARR is not included in any type specification statement, then its type will default to real because the name begins with the letter A. If we wish to declare both the type and the length of the array, then we would have to use one of the following sets of statements.

```
REAL ARR
DIMENSION ARR(6)
```

or

```
REAL ARR(6)
```

The **DIMENSION** statement is only needed when we declare the length of an array while using default typing. Since we never use default typing in good FORTRAN programs, there is no need to ever use this statement. It is a holdover from earlier versions of FORTRAN.

■ GOOD PROGRAMMING PRACTICE

Do not use **DIMENSION** statements in your programs. Since all variables and arrays in your programs will be explicitly typed, the lengths of the arrays can be declared in the type declaration statements. There is never a need for **DIMENSION** statements in well-designed programs.

12.1.3 The Unlabeled COMMON Statement

There is an alternate form of the **COMMON** statement which is called the **unlabeled COMMON statement.** An unlabeled **COMMON** statement has the form

```
COMMON var1, var2, var3, ...
```

where *var1*, *var2*, etc. are variables or arrays allocated in successive memory locations starting at the beginning of the common block. The unlabeled **COMMON** statement is exactly like an ordinary **COMMON** block, except that this block has no name.

The unlabeled **COMMON** statement is a relic left over from earlier versions of FORTRAN. Before FORTRAN IV, it was only possible to declare one **COMMON** area in any given program, and all the common variables in the program had to be declared in that single area. Any program including any of the common variables had to include all of them. By contrast, in modern FORTRAN 77 we can have as many common areas as we need in a program, with the areas distinguished from one another by having different names. As a matter of good practice, you should always use named common blocks in your programs.

GOOD PROGRAMMING PRACTICE

Avoid the unlabeled **COMMON** statement. Always use named **COMMON** statements in your programs.

12.1.4 The EQUIVALENCE Statement

It is sometimes useful to refer to a particular location in computer memory by more than one name. In the past, computer memory was a limited and very expensive item. Because computer memory was so expensive, it was common for large computer programs to reuse portions of memory for scratch calculations over and over again in different routines within the program. If a very large amount of scratch memory were needed several times within a program, only one scratch array would be allocated, and it would be used over and over wherever scratch memory was needed. The scratch memory would often be referred to by different names in different portions of the program, but the same physical memory would be used each time.

To support such applications, FORTRAN provides a mechanism for assigning two or more names to the same physical memory location: the **EQUIVALENCE statement**. The **EQUIVALENCE** statement appears in the declaration section of a program after all type declaration statements and before any **DATA** statements. The form of the **EQUIVALENCE** statement is

```
EQUIVALENCE ( var1, var2, var3, ...)
```

where *var1*, *var2*, etc. are variables or array elements. *Every variable appearing within the parentheses in an* **EQUIVALENCE** *statement is assigned to the same memory location by the* FORTRAN *compiler*. If some of the variables are array elements, then this statement also fixes the relative relationships of all elements within the arrays. Consider the following example:

```
INTEGER I1(2,2)
INTEGER J1(5)
EQUIVALENCE ( I1(2,1), J1(4) )
```

Here, I1(2,1) and J1(4) occupy the same memory location. Because of the way arrays are laid out in memory, I1(1,2) and J1(5) also occupy a single memory location (see Figure 12-1).

EQUIVALENCE statements are inherently dangerous and should only be used if *absolutely* required by a particular program. A common problem occurs when we first perform some calculation using an equivalenced array under one name (say, ARRAY1) in a program, and then perform a different calculation using the same equivalenced array under another name (say, ARRAY2) in another part of the program. If we then try to access values in ARRAY1, we will find that they have all been destroyed by the operations on ARRAY2. This can be an especially big problem if the program is being modified by some person other than the original pro-

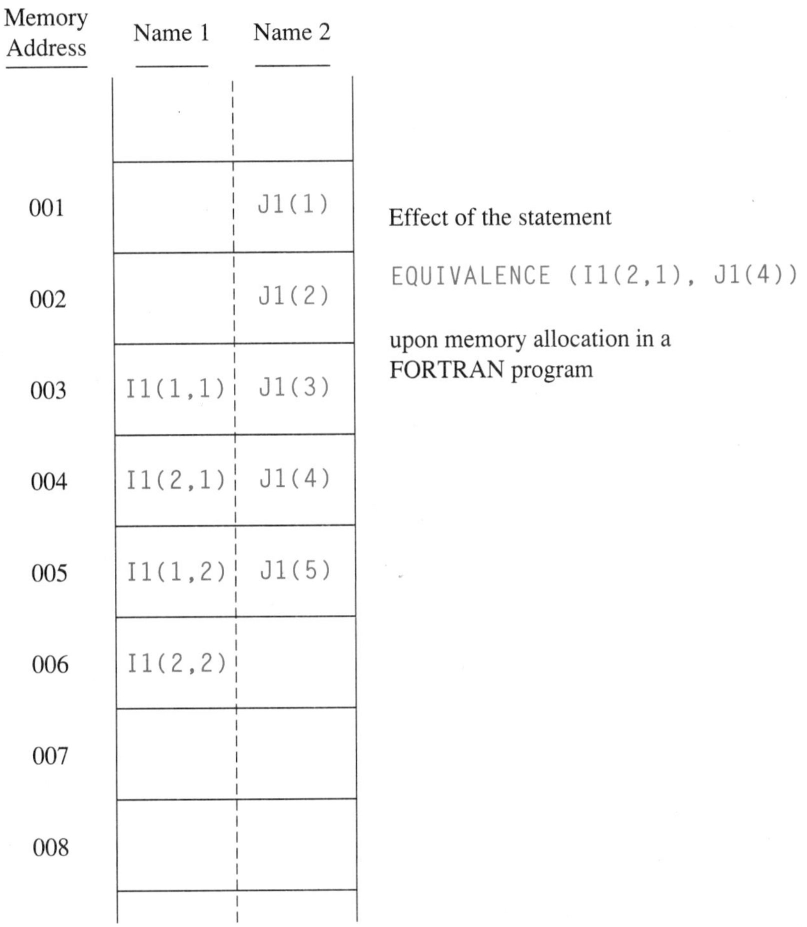

Memory Address	Name 1	Name 2
001		J1(1)
002		J1(2)
003	I1(1,1)	J1(3)
004	I1(2,1)	J1(4)
005	I1(1,2)	J1(5)
006	I1(2,2)	
007		
008		

Effect of the statement

```
EQUIVALENCE (I1(2,1), J1(4))
```

upon memory allocation in a FORTRAN program

FIGURE 12-1   The effect of the **EQUIVALENCE** statement on memory allocation in a FORTRAN program. Because I1(2,1) and J1(4) must be the same physical location, arrays I1 and J1 overlap in the computer's memory.

grammer. Since the data in array ARRAY1 has been destroyed without ARRAY1 ever appearing in an assignment statement, it can be very hard to track down this bug.

Since computer memory has gotten both cheaper and more plentiful over the years, the need for equivalencing arrays and reusing computer memory has decreased dramatically. You should not equivalence variable names in your programs unless you have a very good reason to do so. If you do need to reuse scratch memory arrays in your program, it is better to use the *same name* at each use to make it clear that the contents of the arrays have been modified (since you are using the same name, no **EQUIVALENCE** statement is required, and anyone debugging the program later can see that the memory is being reused). The only time that you might need an **EQUIVALENCE** statement is when the scratch array must be used with variables of *different types* at different points within the program. In that case, you should declare two different arrays with different types but with similar names, and equivalence them. Also, carefully comment your actions to make it clear that the two arrays really occupy the same memory locations. For example

```
C       The following two scratch arrays occupy the same memory
C       in the computer, and so overwrite each other...
        INTEGER ISIZE
        PARAMETER ( ISIZE = 1000000 )
        INTEGER ISCR(ISIZE)
        REAL    RSCR(ISIZE)
        EQUIVALENCE ( ISCR, RSCR )
        ...
```

Finally, note that the **EQUIVALENCE** statement effectively assigns two or more different names to the same *memory location*. From this statement, it follows that names must be associated with memory locations, or they may not be equivalenced. Names that are not associated with a specific memory location (e.g., dummy subroutine arguments and function names) may not be used in an **EQUIVALENCE** statement.

■ **GOOD PROGRAMMING PRACTICE**

Do not use **EQUIVALENCE** statements in your programs unless you absolutely must do so. If you do need to reuse scratch memory arrays in your program, it is better to use the same name at each use to make it clear that the contents of the arrays have been modified.

■ **12.2**   UNDESIRABLE SUBPROGRAM FEATURES

There are three subprogram features that are undesirable and should never be used in modern FORTRAN programs. They are:

1. Alternate subroutine returns
2. Alternate entry points
3. The statement function

12.2.1   Alternate Subroutine Returns

When a FORTRAN program calls a normal subroutine, the subroutine is executed, and then control returns to the first executable statement following the subroutine call.

It is sometimes useful to execute different code in the calling routine depending on the results of the subroutine call. FORTRAN supports such operation by providing **alternate subroutine returns.** Alternate subroutine returns are statement labels passed as calling arguments to the subroutine. When the subroutine executes, it can decide to return control to any of the statement labels specified in the argument list. Alternate subroutine returns are specified in the following manner:

1. The statement labels associated with all possible alternate returns are specified as arguments in the **CALL** statement by preceding each label with an asterisk:

   ```
   CALL SUB1 (A, B, C, *n1, *n2, *n3)
   ```

   where n1, n2, and n3 are the statement numbers to which execution may be transferred.
2. The alternate returns are specified in the subroutine statement by asterisks:

   ```
   SUBROUTINE SUB1 (A, B, C, *, *, *)
   ```

   where the asterisks correspond to the locations of the alternate returns in the calling statement.
3. The particular alternate return to be executed is specified by a parameter on the **RETURN** statement:

   ```
   RETURN k
   ```

   where k is the *position* of the alternate return to be executed. In the above example, there are three possible alternate returns, so k could take on a value from 1 to 3.

In the following example, there are two possible returns. The first return is for normal completion, and the second one is for error conditions.

```
      CALL CALC ( A1, A2, RESULT, *100, *999 )
C
C     Normal return—continue execution.
C
  100 ...
      ...
      ...
      STOP
C
C     Error in subroutine call—process error and stop.
C
  999 WRITE (*,*) 'Error in subroutine CALC.  Execution aborted.'
      STOP 999
      END
      SUBROUTINE CALC ( A1, A2, RESULT, *, * )
      REAL A1, A2, RESULT, TEMP
C
C     Calculate SQRT ( (A1 * A2) / (A1 + A2) ), if possible
C
```

```
      IF ( ABS(A1 + A2) .GT. 1.0E-10 ) THEN
         TEMP = (A1 * A2) / (A1 + A2)
      ELSE
         RETURN 2
      END IF
C
      IF ( TEMP .GE. 0. ) THEN
         RESULT = SQRT ( TEMP )
      ELSE
         RETURN 2
      END IF
C
      RETURN 1
      END
```

Alternate subroutine returns should never be used in modern FORTRAN code. They make program maintenance and debugging much harder by making it difficult to follow the execution path through the program. They contribute to the "spaghetti code" so commonly found in older programs. There are other, much better ways to provide for different program execution paths depending upon the results of a subroutine call. The simplest and best approach is to include a logical **IF** structure that tests the subroutine return parameters immediately after the subroutine call, and then takes action depending on the status returned by the subroutine.

■ **GOOD PROGRAMMING PRACTICE**

Do not use alternate subroutine returns in your programs. They make programming debugging and maintenance much harder, and simple, structured alternatives are available.

12.2.2   Alternate Entry Points

The normal entry point for a FORTRAN subroutine or function is the first executable statement in the subprogram. However, it is possible to get program execution to start at a different point within subprogram if that point is specified with an **ENTRY statement.** An **ENTRY** statement has the form

```
      ENTRY name ( arg1, arg2, ...)
```

where ***name*** is the name of the entry point, and *arg1*, *arg2*, etc. are the dummy arguments passed to the subroutine at the entry point. When a subprogram is called by the name specified in the **ENTRY** statement, execution begins at the first executable statement following the **ENTRY** statement instead of the first executable statement in the subprogram.

A common use of the **ENTRY** statement occurs when a subprogram must be initialized the first time it is used but not thereafter. In that case, a special initialization entry point may be included in the subprogram. For example, consider the following FORTRAN subroutine, which evaluates a third-order polynomial for a specific input value X. Before the polynomial can be evaluated, the coefficients of the polynomial must be specified. If the coefficients of the polynomial change infrequently, we could specify them in a special **ENTRY** to the subroutine.

```
          PROGRAM TEST
          REAL A, B, C, D
          A = 1.
          B = 2.
          C = 1.
          D = 2.
          CALL INITL ( A, B, C, D )
          DO 10 I = 1, 10
             CALL EVAL3 ( REAL(I), RES )
             WRITE (*,*) 'EVAL3(',I,') = ', RES
       10 CONTINUE
          END
          SUBROUTINE EVAL3 ( X, RES )
C
C         Evaluates a third order polynomial of the form:
C             RES = A + B*X + C*X**2 + D*X**3
C
C         Declare calling arguments
C
          IMPLICIT NONE
          REAL A1, B1, C1, D1, X, RES
C
C         Declare local variables
C
          REAL A, B, C, D
          SAVE A, B, C, D
C
C         Calculate RES
C
          RES = A + B**X + C*X**2 + D*X**3
C
          RETURN
C
C         Entry INITL specifies the values of A, B, C, and D
C         to be used when evaluating the polynomial.
C
          ENTRY INITL (A1, B1, C1, D1)
C
          A = A1
          B = B1
          C = C1
          D = D1
C
          RETURN
          END
```

Note from the above example that the various entry points in a subroutine do not have to have the same calling sequence. However, we must be sure to call each entry point with the proper argument list for that particular entry point.

The use of entry points should be discouraged. The implementation of subroutine **ENTRY** statements differs slightly from FORTRAN compiler to FORTRAN compiler, and it is possible to get unpredictable results when moving a working program containing **ENTRY** statements from one computer to another one.

Another disadvantage of **ENTRY** statements occurs when we need to modify the code of a subroutine containing multiple entry points. If there are any code segments or variables in common to the different entry points, we can get in serious trouble. In the process of changing the subroutine to make one entry point work correctly, we can inadvertently screw up the operation of another entry point. After a subroutine containing multiple entry points is modified, it must be tested *very* carefully, both the entry point being modified and all other entry points.

The original reason for using multiple entry points in a subroutine was to share segments of code for multiple purposes, thus reducing the size of the completed program. This reason no longer makes sense today. As cheap as memory is now, there is no good reason to *ever* use an entry point. If you write separate routines for each function you need, your code will be much more maintainable.

If you do need to share data between multiple subprograms, the data should be included in a **COMMON** block instead of being local to a subroutine with multiple entry points. The previous example can be rewritten without entry points as follows:

```
            PROGRAM TEST
            REAL A, B, C, D
            A = 1.
            B = 2.
            C = 1.
            D = 2.
            CALL INITL ( A, B, C, D )
            DO 10 I = 1, 10
               CALL EVAL3 ( REAL(I), RES )
               WRITE (*,*) 'EVAL3(',I,') = ', RES
        10 CONTINUE
            END
            SUBROUTINE EVAL3 ( X, RES )
C
C
C       Evaluates a third order polynomial of the form:
C           RES = A + B*X + C*X**2 + D*X**3
C
C       Declare calling arguments
C
            IMPLICIT NONE
            REAL X, RES
C
C       Declare common block /PARMS/
C
```

```
        REAL              A, B, C, D
        COMMON / PARMS / A, B, C, D
C
C       Calculate RES
C
        RES = A + B**X + C*X**2 + D*X**3
C
        RETURN
        END
C
C       Subroutine INITL specifies the values of A, B, C, and D
C       for the polynomial
C          RES = A + B*X + C*X**2 + D*X**3
C
        SUBROUTINE INITL (A1, B1, C1, D1)
C
C       Declare calling parameters.
C
        IMPLICIT NONE
        REAL A1, B1, C1, D1
C
C       Declare common block /PARMS/
C
        REAL              A, B, C, D
        COMMON / PARMS / A, B, C, D
C
        A = A1
        B = B1
        C = C1
        D = D1
C
        RETURN
        END
```

■ **GOOD PROGRAMMING PRACTICE**

Avoid alternate entry points in your programs. There is no good reason to use them
in a modern FORTRAN program.

In Chapter 6, we introduced the function subprogram. A function subprogram is a
subprogram that returns a single value to the calling program. Its input values are
passed via an argument list. A function subprogram is called by being named as a
part of a FORTRAN expression.

There is another type of FORTRAN function: the **statement function.** A statement function consists of a *single statement*. It must be defined in the declaration section of a FORTRAN program before the first executable statement in the program. An example of a statement function is shown in the example below:

```
      PROGRAM POLYFN
C
C     This program evaluates a third order polynomial
C     of the form:
C         RES = A + B*X + C*X**2 + D*X**3
C     using a statement function.
C
      IMPLICIT NONE
C
C     Declare local variables.
C
      REAL    A, B, C, D, X, Y
      INTEGER I
C
C     Declare dummy arguments of the statement function.
C
      REAL A1, B1, C1, D1, X1, RES
C
C     Declare statement function RES.
C
      RES(A1,B1,C1,D1,X1) = A1 + B1**X1 + C1*X1**2 + D1*X1**3
C
C     Set up coefficients of polynomial RES.
C
      A = 1.
      B = 2.
      C = 1.
      D = 2.
C
C     Evaluate polynomial for X values of 1 through 10.
C
      DO 10 I = 1, 10
         X = REAL(I)
         Y = RES(A,B,C,D,X)
         WRITE (*,*) 'Y(',I,') = ', Y
   10 CONTINUE
      END
```

In this example, real statement function RES is defined as

```
      RES(A1,B1,C1,D1,X1) = A1 + B1**X1 + C1*X1**2 + D1*X1**3
```

where A1, B1, C1, D1, and X1 are *dummy arguments*. Note that the types of the function and its dummy arguments must all be declared or defaulted before the function is defined. The dummy arguments are placeholders for the actual values that are used when the function is executed later in the program. The dummy arguments must agree in type and number with the actual arguments which are used when the function is executed. At execution time, the value in the first argument of the function is used instead of A1 wherever A1 appears in the statement function, and so forth for all other arguments.

If you take a close look at the statement function, you will notice that a statement function looks exactly like an assignment statement that assigns a value to an array element. Since this is so, how can the FORTRAN compiler tell the difference between them? To make it possible to tell the difference between them, FORTRAN requires that *all statement functions must be defined in the declaration section of a program,* before the first executable statement.

Unlike function subprograms, statement functions can only be used in the program or subprogram in which they are declared. They are limited to functions that can be evaluated in a single expression with no branches or loops. In addition, the calling arguments must be variables, constants, or array elements. Unlike a function subprogram, it is not possible to pass whole arrays to a statement function.

Statement functions can lead to another sort of confusion, too. If a variable name appears in the argument list of a statement function, and again elsewhere in the program, *the same variable name represents two totally different things in a single program unit.* In the statement function, it is a dummy argument, while elsewhere in the program, the exact same symbol is a variable! To make things more confusing, any variables that are used in a statement function and do not appear in the argument list take on the same values as they have within the program at the point where the statement function is executed. For example, consider the program shown below:

```
      PROGRAM CONFUS
C
C  Purpose:
C    To illustrate the double use of a symbol in a statement function
C    and in the rest of a program.
C
      IMPLICIT NONE
C
      REAL F, X, Y, Z
C
C    Declare statement function.
C
      F(X) = X**2 + Z
C
C    Data
C
      DATA X, Y, Z / 1., 2., 3. /
C
C    Write output.
C
      WRITE (*,1000) X, F(X)
      WRITE (*,1000) Y, F(Y)
      WRITE (*,1000) Z, F(Z)
 1000 FORMAT (' ','VAL = ',F10.2,' F(VAL) = ',F10.2)
C
      END
```

In the statement function, X is a dummy argument and Z is a real variable. Elsewhere in the program, X is a variable containing the value 1.0. The results of executing this program are

```
C:\BOOK\FORT>confus
VAL =        1.00 F(VAL) =         4.00
VAL =        2.00 F(VAL) =         7.00
VAL =        3.00 F(VAL) =        12.00
```

Note that the X in the statement function took on the values 1.0, 2.0, and 3.0 as the program executed, while the X in the main program remained 1.0 all the time. The Z in the statement function and the Z in the main program were 3.0 at all times. This can be very confusing to an inexperienced programmer!

Statement functions are a very old feature of FORTRAN, dating all the way back to FORTRAN 1 in 1954. They are considered an obsolescent part of the language, and have been replaced by function subprograms. Function subprograms can do anything a statement function can do, and much more besides. There is no reason to ever use statement functions in your programs.

■

GOOD PROGRAMMING PRACTICE

Never use statement functions in your programs. Use function subprograms instead.

■
12.3   MISCELLANEOUS EXECUTION CONTROL FEATURES

There are two statements that pause or stop the execution of a program: the **PAUSE** and **STOP** statements. The **PAUSE** statement is rarely used in a modern FORTRAN program, since the same function can be done more flexibly with a combination of **WRITE** and **READ** statements. The **STOP** statement is more common, but it is not always necessary either, since program execution will terminate when the **END** statement is reached. However, it is sometimes useful to have multiple stopping points in a program. In that case, each stopping point will need a **STOP** statement. If there are multiple **STOP** statements in a program, each one should be labeled with a unique argument (as explained below) so that the user can tell which **STOP** statement was executed.

When we write FORTRAN programs whose results are meant to be viewed from a terminal, it is necessary to pause the program at certain points while the user examines the results displayed on the terminal. Otherwise, the information may scroll off the top of the display before it can be read. After the user reads the output data on the terminal, he or she can either continue the program or abort it.

FORTRAN includes a special statement designed to pause the execution of a program until the user starts it up again: the **PAUSE statement.** The general form of the **PAUSE** statement is

```
PAUSE prompt
```

where *prompt* is an optional value to be displayed when the **PAUSE** statement is executed. The prompt may be either a character constant or an integer between 0 and 99,999. When the **PAUSE** statement is executed, the value of *prompt* is displayed on the terminal, and execution stops until the user restarts the program. When the program is restarted, execution will begin at the statement following the **PAUSE** statement.

The **PAUSE** statement is not particularly common, since it is possible to perform the same function with **WRITE** and **READ** statements with much more flexibility.

12.3.2   Arguments Associated with the STOP Statement

Like the **PAUSE** statement described above, it is possible to include an argument with the **STOP** statement. The general form of the **STOP** statement is

```
STOP output argument
```

where *output argument* is an optional value to be displayed when the **STOP** statement is executed. The output argument may be either a character constant or an integer between 0 and 99,999. It is mainly used when there are multiple **STOP** statements in a program. If there are multiple **STOP** statements and a separate output argument is associated with each one, then the programmer and user can tell which of the **STOP** statements was executed when the program quit.

If there are multiple **STOP** statements in a program, it is a good idea to use either a separate output argument on each one or a separate **WRITE** statement before each one, so that a user can tell which **STOP** a program halted on. An example program with multiple **STOP** statements is shown in Figure 12-2. The first **STOP** occurs if the file specified by the user does not exist. It is clearly marked by the **WRITE** statement that occurs just before it. The second **STOP** occurs when the program completes normally. If this stop is executed, the message 'Normal Completion.' will be printed out when the program terminates.

```
      PROGRAM STPTST
C
C  Purpose:
C    To illustrate multiple STOP statements in a program.
C
C  List of variables:
C    FILENM -- The input file name (<= 24 characters)
C    IERROR -- The status flag returned by the I/O statements
C    LU     -- The logical unit number to use for file I/O
C    N      -- The number of input data pairs (x,y)
```

```
C     SLOPE  -- The slope of the line
C     SUMX   -- The sum of all input X values
C     SUMX2  -- The sum of all input X values squared
C     SUMXY  -- The sum of all X*Y values
C     SUMY   -- The sum of all input Y values
C     X      -- An input X value
C     XBAR   -- The average X value
C     Y      -- An input Y value
C     YBAR   -- The average Y value
C     YINT   -- The Y-axis intercept of the line
C
      IMPLICIT NONE
C
C     Declare the variables used in this program.
C
      CHARACTER*24 FILENM
      INTEGER N, IERROR, LU
C
C     Use LU 12 for the input file
C
      PARAMETER ( LU = 12 )
C
C     Prompt user and get the name of the input file.
C
      WRITE (*,1000)
 1000 FORMAT (1X,'Enter file name: ')
      READ (*,1010) FILENM
 1010 FORMAT (A)
C
C     Open the input file
C
      OPEN (UNIT=LU, FILE=FILENM, STATUS='OLD', IOSTAT=IERROR )
C
C     Check to see of the OPEN failed.
C
      IF ( IERROR .GT. 0 ) THEN
         WRITE (*,1020) FILENM
 1020    FORMAT (1X,5'ERROR: File ',A,' does not exist!')
         STOP
      END IF
C
C     Normal processing...
C
      ...
      ...
      ...
C
C     Close input file, and quit.
C
      CLOSE (LU)
C
      STOP 'Normal completion.'
      END
```

FIGURE 12-2   A program to illustrate the use of multiple **STOP** statements in a single program unit.

Quiz 12-1

This quiz provides a quick check to see if you have understood the concepts introduced in Sections 12.1 through 12.3. If you have trouble with the quiz, reread the sections, ask your instructor, or discuss the material with a fellow student. The answers to this quiz are found in the back of the book.

For questions 1–5, determine whether the following code fragments are correct or not. If not, indicate what is wrong with them.

1.
```
       PROGRAM MYTEST
       IMPLICIT NONE
       REAL A1, B1, C1, X, QUAD
       QUAD(A1,B1,C1,X) = A1*X**2 + B1*X + C1
       DATA A1, B1, C1 / 1., 2., 1. /
       X = QUAD(-3.)
       WRITE (*,*) 'QUAD(-3) = ', X
       END
```

2.
```
       PROGRAM MYTEST
       IMPLICIT DOUBLE PRECISION (C), LOGICAL(L), COMPLEX(C,Z)
       INTEGER M
       DATA A1, B1, C1, D1 / 1., 2., 1., 1. /
       DATA L, M, N / 1, 2, 3 /
       DO 10 LOOP = 1, 5
          Z1 = SQRT ( A1**2 + B1**2 + C1**2 ) / D1
    10 CONTINUE
       END
```

3.
```
       PROGRAM MYPROG
C
C      Calculate the hypotenuse of a right triangle
C
       IMPLICIT NONE
       REAL SIDE1, SIDE2, HYPOT
       WRITE (*,*) 'Enter lengths of Sides 1 and 2:'
       READ (*,*) SIDE1, SIDE2
       HYPOT(SIDE1,SIDE2) = SQRT(SIDE1**2 + SIDE2**2)
       WRITE (*,*) 'The hypotenuse is ', HYPOT(SIDE1,SIDE2)
       END
```

4.
```
       REAL FUNCTION FACT(N)
C
C      Function to calculate and return N factoral as a REAL
C
       IMPLICIT NONE
       INTEGER N
       REAL    TEMP
       EQUIVALENCE ( TEMP, FACT )
C
       TEMP = 1.
       DO 10 I = N, 1, -1
          TEMP = TEMP * REAL(I)
    10 CONTINUE
       RETURN
       END
```

5.

```
        PROGRAM MYTEST
        REAL A, B, C
        COMMON / MYDATA / A, B, C
        CALL SUB3 (A, B, C, *10, *20, *30)
    10  WRITE (*,*) 'Return 1'
        STOP 1
    20  WRITE (*,*) 'Return 2'
        STOP 'TWO'
    30  WRITE (*,*) 'Return 3'
        STOP 3
        END
        SUBROUTINE SUB3 (A, B, C, *, *, *)
        REAL A, B, C
        IF ( A .GT. B ) THEN
            RETURN 1
        ELSE IF ( B .GT. C ) THEN
            RETURN 2
        ELSE IF ( C .GT. A ) THEN
            RETURN 3
        END IF
        END
        BLOCK DATA MYBLK
        IMPLICIT NONE
        REAL A, B, C
        COMMON / MYDATA / A, B, C
        DATA A, B, C / 1., 2., 3. /
        RETURN
        END
```

For questions 6–8, write the statement function that would perform the following calculations.

6. The kinetic energy of an object $KE = \frac{1}{2}mv^2$

7. The potential energy of an object $PE = mgh$

8. The area of a circle $A = \pi r^2$

12.4   OBSOLETE BRANCHING STRUCTURES

In Chapter 3, we described the logical **IF** structure, which is the standard way to implement branches in modern FORTRAN. This section describes several additional ways to produce branches. They are all archaic survivals from earlier versions of FORTRAN that are still supported for backward compatibility. These features should *never* be used in any new FORTRAN program. However, you may run into them if you ever have to work with old FORTRAN programs. They are described here for possible future reference.

12.4.1   The Arithmetic IF Statement

The **arithmetic IF statement** goes all the way back to the origins of FORTRAN in 1954. The structure of an arithmetic **IF** statement is

```
IF (arithmetic expression) label1, label2, label3
```

where *arithmetic expression* is any integer, real, or double-precision arithmetic expression, and *label1*, *label2*, and *label3* are labels of executable FORTRAN statements. When the arithmetic **IF** statement is executed, the arithmetic expression is evaluated. If the resulting value is negative, execution transfers to the statement at *label1*. If the value is zero, execution transfers to the statement at *label2*. If the value is positive, execution transfers to the statement at *label3*.

To illustrate the use of an arithmetic **IF** statement, let's compare the evaluation of the roots of a quadratic equation using both logical **IF** structures and the arithmetic **IF** structure. The code for the logical **IF** structure (reproduced from Chapter 3) is shown in Figure 12-3, and the corresponding code for the arithmetic **IF** structure is shown in Figure 12-4. As you can see, the logical **IF** structure is much easier to understand.

```
      PROGRAM QUAD4
C
C
C     This program reads the coefficients of a quadratic equation of the form
C           A * X**2 + B * X + C = 0,
C     and solves for the roots of the equation.
C
C
C     Get the coefficients of the quadratic equation.
C
      WRITE (*,*) ' Enter the coefficients A, B and C: '
      READ (*,*) A, B, C
C
C     Echo the coefficients to make sure they are entered correctly.
C
      WRITE (*,*) ' The coefficients are : ', A, B, C
C
C     Check the discriminant and calculate its roots.
C
      DISCR = B**2 - 4*A*C
      IF ( DISCR .LT. 0) THEN
         WRITE (*,*) ' This equation has complex roots:'
         WRITE (*,*) ' X = ', -B/2*A, ' +i ', SQRT(ABS(DISCR))/2*A
         WRITE (*,*) ' X = ', -B/2*A, ' -i ', SQRT(ABS(DISCR))/2*A
      ELSE IF ( (B**2 - 4.*A*C) .EQ. 0) THEN
         WRITE (*,*) ' This equation has a single repeated real root:'
         WRITE (*,*) ' X = ', -B/2*A
      ELSE
         WRITE (*,*) ' This equation has two distinct real roots:'
         WRITE (*,*) ' X = ', (-B + SQRT(ABS(DISCR)))/2*A
         WRITE (*,*) ' X = ', (-B - SQRT(ABS(DISCR)))/2*A
      END IF
C
      END
```

FIGURE 12-3   Program solving for the roots of a quadratic equation using a logical **IF** structure.

```
      PROGRAM QUAD5
C
C     This program reads the coefficients of a quadratic equation of the form
C           A * X**2 + B * X + C = 0,
C     and solves for the roots of the equation using an arithmetic IF
C     structure.
C
C     Get the coefficients of the quadratic equation.
C
      WRITE (*,*) ' Enter the coefficients A, B and C: '
      READ (*,*) A, B, C
C
C     Echo the coefficients to make sure they are entered correctly.
C
      WRITE (*,*) ' The coefficients are : ', A, B, C
C
C     Check the discriminant and calculate its roots.
C
      DISCR = B**2 - 4*A*C
      IF ( DISCR ) 10, 20, 30
C
   10 WRITE (*,*) ' This equation has complex roots:'
      WRITE (*,*) ' X = ', -B/2*A, ' +i ', SQRT(ABS(DISCR))/2*A
      WRITE (*,*) ' X = ', -B/2*A, ' -i ', SQRT(ABS(DISCR))/2*A
      GO TO 40
C
   20 WRITE (*,*) ' This equation has a single repeated real root:'
      WRITE (*,*) ' X = ', -B/2*A
      GO TO 40
C
   30 WRITE (*,*) ' This equation has two distinct real roots:'
      WRITE (*,*) ' X = ', (-B + SQRT(ABS(DISCR)))/2*A
      WRITE (*,*) ' X = ', (-B - SQRT(ABS(DISCR)))/2*A
C
   40 CONTINUE
      END
```

FIGURE 12-4   Program solving for the roots of a quadratic equation using an arithmetic IF structure.

The arithmetic **IF** should never be used in any modern FORTRAN program.

■ **GOOD PROGRAMMING PRACTICE**

Never use arithmetic **IF** statement in your programs. Use the logical **IF** structure instead.

12.4.2   The Computed GO TO Statement

The computed GO TO statement has the form

        GO TO (*label1, label2, label3,..., labelk*), *integer expression*

where *label1* through *labelk* are labels of executable FORTRAN statements, and the *integer expression* evaluates to an integer between 1 and k. If the integer expression evaluates to 1, then the statement at *label1* is executed. If the integer expression evaluates to 2, then the statement at *label2* is executed, and so forth up to k. If the integer expression is less than 1 or greater than k, this is an error condition, and the behavior of the statement will vary from computer to computer.

An example of a computed **GO TO** statement is shown below. In this example, the number 2 would be printed out when the program is executed.

```
      PROGRAM TEST
      I = 2
      GO TO (10, 20), I
10    WRITE (*,*) '1'
      GO TO 30
20    WRITE (*,*) '2'
30    STOP
      END
```

The computed **GO TO** should never be used in any modern FORTRAN program.

■ **GOOD PROGRAMMING PRACTICE**

Never use the computed **GO TO** statement in your programs. Use the logical **IF** structure instead.

12.4.3 The Assigned GO TO Statement

The assigned **GO TO** statement has two possible forms:

```
GO TO integer variable, (label1, label2, label3, ... , labelk)
```

or

```
GO TO integer variable
```

where *integer variable* contains the statement number of the statement to be executed next, and *label1* through *labelk* are labels of executable FORTRAN statements. Before this statement is executed, a statement label must be assigned to the integer variable using the **ASSIGN** statement:

```
ASSIGN label TO integer variable
```

When the first form of the assigned **GO TO** is executed, the program checks the value of the integer variable against the list of statement labels. If the value of the variable is in the list, then execution branches to the statement with that label. If the value of the variable is not in the list, an error occurs.

When the second form of the assigned **GO TO** is executed, no error checking is done. If the value of the variable is a legal statement label in the program, control branches to the statement with that label. If the value of the variable is not a legal statement label, execution continues with the next executable statement after the **GO TO.**

An example of an assigned **GO TO** statement is shown below. In this example, the number 1 would be printed out when the program is executed.

```
      PROGRAM TEST
      ASSIGN 10 TO I
      GO TO I (10, 20)
10    WRITE (*,*) '1'
      GO TO 30
20    WRITE (*,*) '2'
30    END
```

The assigned **GO TO** should never be used in any modern FORTRAN program.

■ **GOOD PROGRAMMING PRACTICE**

Never use the assigned **GO TO** statement in your programs. Use the logical **IF** structure instead.

Quiz 12-2

This quiz provides a quick check to see if you have understood the concepts introduced in Section 12.4. If you have trouble with the quiz, reread the section, ask your instructor, or discuss the material with a fellow student. The answers to this quiz are found in the back of the book.

For questions 1–5, determine whether the following code fragments are correct or not. If they are correct, indicate what ouput is expected from them. If not, indicate what is wrong with them.

1.
```
      PROGRAM TEST1
      IMPLICIT NONE
      REAL A1, B1, C1, X
      DATA A1, B1, C1 / 10., 20., 10. /
      X = A1 - B1 - C1
   1  IF ( X ) 10, 20, 30
  10  X = X + 11.
      GO TO 1
  20  X = X / 2.
      GO TO 1
  30  X = X + 11.
      WRITE (*,*) 'X = ', X
      END
```

```
2.        PROGRAM INTRPT
          IMPLICIT NONE
          CHARACTER*6 C
          REAL A1, B1, C1, X
          DATA A1, B1, C1 / 10., 20., 10. /
          WRITE (*,*) 'Enter test value: '
          READ (*,*) C
          GO TO (10, 20, 10, 20) C
      10  X = A1 - 2.*B1 + C1
          GO TO 999
      20  X = -A1 + 2*B1 - C1
          WRITE (*,*) 'X = ', X
          END
```

The input data is

```
0     5    10    15    20
|----|----|----|-    |
      3
0     5    10    15    20
|----|----|----|----|
```

```
3.        PROGRAM ASGOTO
          REAL A, B, C
          A = 30.
          B = 40.
          INTEGER I
          IF (A-B) 10, 20, 30
          C = 2.
      10  ASSIGN 15 TO I
          GO TO I
      20  ASSIGN 20 TO I
          GO TO I
      30  ASSIGN 10 TO I
          GO TO I (20, 30)
          END
```

12.5   OBSOLETE I/O STATEMENTS

There are two obsolete I/O statements that work only with the standard input and output devices. They are equivalent to subsets of some of the I/O statements that we have already studied. These statements are the **PRINT** statement and a special form of the **READ** statement.

12.5.1   The PRINT Statement

The **PRINT** statement is a special output statement that writes only the the standard output device. The general form of a **PRINT** statement is

```
PRINT fmt, val1, val2, val3, ...
```

where *fmt* is the format to use for printing, and *val1*, *val2*, *val3*, etc. are the values to be printed to the standard output device. It is completely equivalent to the **WRITE** statement shown below:

```
WRITE (*,fmt) val1, val2, val3, ...
```

It is preserved for backward compatibility with earlier versions of FORTRAN, and should never be used in any modern program.

■
GOOD PROGRAMMING PRACTICE

Never use the **PRINT** statement in your programs. Use the **WRITE** statement instead.

12.5.2 The Obsolete Form of the READ Statement

The obsolete form of the **READ** statement is the input analog to the **PRINT** statement. It is a special input statement that reads only from the standard input device. This statement has the form

```
READ fmt, val1, val2, val3, ...
```

where *fmt* is the format to use for for reading data, and *val1*, *val2*, *val3*, etc. are the variables to be read from the standard input device. It is completely equivalent to the **READ** statement shown below.

```
READ (*,fmt) val1, val2, val3, ...
```

It is preserved for backward compatibility with earlier versions of FORTRAN, and should never be used in any modern program.

■
GOOD PROGRAMMING PRACTICE

Never use obsolete form of the **READ** statement in your programs. Use the modern form of the **READ** statement instead.

12.6 SUMMARY

In this chapter, we introduced a variety of miscellaneous FORTRAN features. Most of these features are either obsolete, unnecessary, or incompatible with modern structured programming. They are maintained for backward compatibility with older versions of FORTRAN, and should not be used in new programs.

The **IMPLICIT** statement provides a way to override the default typing convention built into FORTRAN. With the **IMPLICIT** statement, it is possible to define all parameters, variables, and functions whose names begin with a specific letter as being of a specific type. Since we should always explicitly declare every variable in a modern program, there is no place for the standard **IMPLICIT** statement in a well-designed FORTRAN program.

The **IMPLICIT NONE** statement is an extension of the **IMPLICIT** statement that cancels all default typing and forces every variable in a program to be explicitly typed. It is not included in the FORTRAN 77 standard, but it is supported by almost all modern FORTRAN 77 compilers. If your compiler supports it, use it! Also, **IMPLICIT NONE** is a part of the FORTRAN 90 standard.

The unlabeled **COMMON** statement is an alternate form of the **COMMON** statement in which the common block does not have a name. It is a feature left over from earlier version for FORTRAN, and should not be used in modern programs.

The **EQUIVALENCE** statement assigns two different names to the same memory location. It has limited use in modern FORTRAN programs, but there are times when it is important. The main use of the **EQUIVALENCE** statement is to make a large scratch memory array usable with more than one type of data.

The **PAUSE** statement pauses the execution an interactive FORTRAN program until the user resumes it. It is of limited use, since a combination of **WRITE** and **READ** statements can perform the same function more flexibly.

It is possible to add an argument to the **STOP** statement. The argument may be either a character constant or an integer constant between 0 and 99,999. When the **STOP** statement is executed, its argument is printed out. The principal use of this feature is for debugging. If there is more than one **STOP** statement in the program, the user can tell which one was executed by which argument was printed out. Alternately, the user can place a **WRITE** statement before each **STOP** statement to give more detailed information about why the program quit.

It is possible to specify alternate subroutine returns, in which program execution continues at an alternate location in the calling program after a subroutine call. This feature is incompatible with good programming design, and should not be used.

It is possible to specify alternate entry points into subroutines or function subprograms. If a subroutine or function is called by a given entry point name, then execution will begin at the first executable statement following that entry point. Multiple entry points are incompatible with good programming design, and should not be used.

The statement function is an older type of function which consists of a single statement. It looks like an assignment statement, and can only be distinguished from an assignment statement by its location in the declaration section of a program. The statement function has been superseded by the function subprogram, and should not be used in new programs.

The arithmetic **IF** statement, computed **GO TO** statement, and assigned **GO TO** statement are all old branching structures. They have been superseded by the logical **IF** structure, and should never be used.

There are two obsolete I/O statements that work only with the standard input and output devices. They are the **PRINT** statement and the obsolete form of the **READ** statement. These statements should never be used in a modern FORTRAN program.

12.6.1   Summary of Good Programming Practice

The following guidelines should be adhered to when writing FORTRAN programs.

1. Always use the **IMPLICIT NONE** statement in your programs if it is supported by your compiler. Never use any other form of the **IMPLICIT** statement. Instead, always explicitly type every variable in your programs.

2. Do not use **DIMENSION** statements in your programs. Since all variables and arrays in your programs will be explicitly typed, the lengths of the arrays can be declared in the type declaration statements. There is never a need for **DIMENSION** statements in well-designed programs.

3. Avoid the unlabeled **COMMON** statement. Always use named **COMMON** statements in your programs.

4. Use the **EQUIVALENCE** statement sparingly, and only when you absolutely need it. The principal use of the **EQUIVALENCE** statement is to make large scratch memory arrays usable with more than one type of data.

5. Never use alternate subroutine returns or multiple entry points in your programs. Alternate subroutine returns make it hard to follow the flow of execution in a program, and therefore make debugging harder. Multiple entry points within a single subroutine make your code less modular, and changes to the code for one entry point could inadvertently affect the other entry points.

6. Do not use statement functions. Anything that can be accomplished with a statement function can be accomplished much better with a function subprogram, and the confusion of a single symbol being used for two different purposes can be avoided.

7. The **PAUSE** statement may be used to temporarily halt the execution of a program until the user restarts it. However, a combination of **WRITE** and **READ** statements can do the job better, so you never actually need to use the **PAUSE** statement.

8. Use arguments on the **STOP** statement to distinguish among multiple **STOP** statements if more than one is present in a program. Ideally, there should be only one **STOP** statement in a well-designed program (or none at all, if the **END** statement is used to stop the program). However, if more than one statement is present, add an argument to each one so that you can tell which one is executed when the program runs. Alternately, you can place a **WRITE** statement before each **STOP** statement to give more detailed information about why the program quit.

9. Never use the arithmetic **IF** statement, computed **GO TO** statement, or assigned **GO TO** statement. They have all been replaced by the logical **IF** structure.

10. Never use the **PRINT** statement in your programs. Use the **WRITE** statement instead.

11. Never use the obsolete form of the **READ** statement in your programs. Use the modern form of the **READ** statement instead.

CHAPTER 12 KEY WORDS

Alternate subroutine returns	**IMPLICIT** statement
Arithmetic **IF** statement	Local variables
Assigned **GO TO** statement	**PAUSE** statement
Computed **GO TO** statement	**PRINT** statement
ENTRY statement	Statement function
EQUIVALENCE statement	Unlabeled **COMMON** statement

CHAPTER 12 SUMMARY OF FORTRAN STATEMENTS AND STRUCTURES

Arithmetic IF Statement:

```
IF (arithmetic expression) label1, label2, label3
```

Examples:

```
IF (B**2-4.*A*C) 10, 20, 30
```

Description: The arithmetic **IF** statement is an obsolete conditional branching statement. If the arithmetic expression is negative, control will be transferred to statement with label *label1*. If the arithmetic expression is zero, control will be transferred to statement with label *label2*, and if the arithmetic expression is positive, control will be transferred to statement with label *label3*.

Assigned GO TO Statement:

```
ASSIGN label TO integer variable
GO TO integer variable
```

or

```
GO TO integer variable, (label1, label2, ... labelk)
```

Examples:

```
      ASSIGN 100 TO I
      ...
      GO TO I
      ...
100 ... (execution continues here)
```

Description: The assigned **GO TO** statement is an obsolete branching structure. A statement label is first assigned to an integer variable using the **ASSIGN**

statement. When the assigned **GO TO** statement is executed, control branches to the statement whose label was assigned to the integer variable.

Computed GO TO Statement:

```
GO TO (label1, label2, ... labelk), integer variable
```

Examples:

```
GO TO (100, 200, 300, 400), I
```

Description: The computed **GO TO** statement is an obsolete branching structure. Control is transferred to one of the statements whose label is listed, depending on the value of the integer variable. If the variable is 1, then control is transferred to the first statement in the list, etc.

DIMENSION Statement:

```
DIMENSION array( [i1:]i2, [j1:]j2, ... ), ...
```

Example:

```
DIMENSION A1(100), A2(-5:5), I(2)
```

Description: This statement declares the size of an array but *not* its type. Either the type must be declared in a separate type declaration statement, or else it will be defaulted. **DIMENSION** statements are not required in well-written code, since type declaration statements perform the same purpose.

ENTRY Statement:

```
ENTRY name ( arg1, arg2, ... )
```

Example:

```
ENTRY SORTI ( NUM, DATA1 )
```

Description: This statement declares an entry point into a FORTRAN subroutine or function subprogram. The entry point is executed with a **CALL** statement. The dummy arguments *arg1, arg2, . . .* are placeholders for the calling arguments passed when the subprogram is executed. This statement should be avoided in modern programs.

EQUIVALENCE Statement:

```
EQUIVALENCE ( var1, var2, ...)
```

Examples:

```
EQUIVALENCE ( SCR1, ISCR1 )
```

Description: The **EQUIVALENCE** statement is a specification statement that specifies that all of the variables in the parentheses occupy the same location in memory.

IMPLICIT Statement:

```
IMPLICIT type1 (a₁, a₂, a₃, ...), type2 (b₁, b₂, b₃, ...), ...
```

Examples:

```
IMPLICIT COMPLEX (C,Z), LOGICAL (L)
```

Description: The **IMPLICIT** statement is a specification statement that overrides the default typing built into FORTRAN. It specifies the default type to assume for parameters and variables whose names begin with the specified letters.

IMPLICIT NONE Statement:

```
IMPLICIT NONE
```

Examples:

```
IMPLICIT NONE
```

Description: The **IMPLICIT NONE** statement is a specification statement that cancels all default typing. When the **IMPLICIT NONE** statement is used, every parameter, variable, and function name in the program must be explicitly typed. **This is an extension to standard FORTRAN 77.**

PAUSE Statement:

```
PAUSE prompt
```

Examples:

```
PAUSE 12
```

Description: The **PAUSE** statement is an executable statement that temporarily stops the execution of the FORTRAN program, until the user resumes it. The prompt is either an integer between 0 and 99,999 or a character constant. It is displayed when the **PAUSE** statement is executed.

PRINT Statement:

```
PRINT fmt, value1, value2, ...
```

Examples:

```
PRINT *, 'X = ', X
```

Description: The **PRINT** statement is an obsolete output statement that writes out values only to the standard output device. It is equivalent to a **WRITE (*,fmt)** statement. There is no need for this statement in a modern FORTRAN program.

READ Statement (obsolete form):

```
READ fmt, value1, value2, ...
```

Examples:

```
    READ 9, X
9 FORMAT (F10.4)
```

Description: The obsolete form of the **READ** statement is an obsolete input statement that reads in values only from the standard input device. It is equivalent to a **READ (*,fmt)** statement. There is no need for this form of the **READ** statement in a modern FORTRAN program.

Statement Function:

```
    name(arg1,arg2,...) = expression containing arg1, arg2, ...
```

Examples:

Definition:
```
    QUAD(A,B,C,X) = A * X**2 + B * X + C
```
Use:
```
    RESULT = 2. * PI * QUAD(A1,B1,C1,1.5*T)
```

Description: The statement function is an older structure which has been replaced by the function subprogram. It is defined in the declaration section of a program, and may be used only within that program. The arguments *arg1*, *arg2*, etc., are dummy arguments which are replaced by actual values when the function is used.

Unlabeled COMMON Statement:

```
    COMMON var1, var2, ...
```

Example:

```
    COMMON A, I(-3:3)
```

Description: This statement defines an unlabeled **COMMON** block. The variables declared in the block will be allocated consecutively starting at a specific memory location. They will be accessible to any routine in which an unlabeled **COMMON** block is declared.

    The unlabeled **COMMON** structure has been replaced by the labeled block **COMMON** in modern FORTRAN 77.

CHAPTER 12 EXERCISES

WARNING: In the following problems, you will be asked to create programs that solve problems using specific features described in this chapter. The purpose of these exercises is to familiarize yourself with these features so that you will recognize them if you see them in an old program. The programs you will be creating are *not* examples of good programming practice.

1. Which of the features described in this chapter would you expect to find in a well-designed program? Why?
2. What is the order in which default typing, the **IMPLICIT** statement, and explicit type declarations are applied? If more than one appears in a single program, which one is actually applied? What is the type of variable C1 if:

   (*a*)   C1 appears in a program without being typed at all?

   (*b*)   C1 appears in a program with the following statement:

   ```
   IMPLICIT COMPLEX A-F
   ```

   (*c*)   C1 appears in a program with the following statements:

   ```
   IMPLICIT COMPLEX (A-F)
   INTEGER C1
   ```

3. Write a program that can read and sort a very large amount (up to 100,000 values) of either real or integer data. The user will provide the program with the name of a file containing the data to sort, and a flag to indicate whether the input data is integer or real. The program will read in the data in the correct format, call the appropriate heap sort routine from library BOOKLIB to sort it, and write the sorted data out to a user-specified file. To save space in this program, use the **EQUIVALENCE** statement to make the 100,000 value integer and real arrays overlay each other.
4. Rewrite the third-order least squares fit subroutine and the test driver program of Example 10-1 to use alternate subroutine returns for the two error conditions recognized by the subroutine. Test your program with the same test data sets that were used in Example 10-1.
5. Rewrite the random number generator of Example 6-6 so that it uses an **ENTRY** statement to initialize the seed of the random number generator.
6. Write a program that solves for the roots of a statement function using the bisection method described in Chapter 10. What are the disadvantages of using a statement function instead of an external function, as we did in Example 10-3?
7. Write statement functions to perform the following calculations:

   (*a*)   Power supplied to an AC load: $P = V I \cos \theta$

   (*b*)   The area of a triangle: $A = \dfrac{1}{2} b h$

   (*c*)   Angle θ in a triangle (from the law of cosines): $\theta = \cos^{-1}\left(\dfrac{a^2 + b^2 - c^2}{2ab}\right)$

8. Write a program that reads a list of real values from a disk file, and then writes them out onto the CRT screen, using the **PAUSE** statement to pause the output after every 22 lines.

9. Write a program to calculate the roots of a quadratic equation, using the arithmetic **IF** to determine the types of roots present in the equation. Terminate each possible path through the code with its own **STOP** statement, and add an informative message to each **STOP** statement. Use the **PRINT** statement to output your results. Test the program on the following quadratic equations:

   (a) $x^2 + 5x + 6 = 0$
   (b) $x^2 + 4x + 4 = 0$
   (c) $x^2 + 2x + 5 = 0$

10. Write a program to calculate the roots of a quadratic equation, using the arithmetic **IF** to determine the types of roots present in the equation. Use the obsolete form of the **READ** statement to read in the coefficients of the quadratic equation. Use the **ASSIGN** statement to assign a different statement number in each branch of the arithmetic **IF,** and then use an assigned **GO TO** statement to make the program execution branch in different directions depending on the value of the discriminant. Use the **PRINT** statement to output your results.

11. Write a program to calculate the roots of a quadratic equation, using the arithmetic **IF** to determine the types of roots present in the equation. Use the obsolete form of the **READ** statement to read in the coefficients of the quadratic equation. Store a different value into an integer variable in each branch of the arithmetic **IF,** and then use a computed **GO TO** statement to make the program execution branch in different directions depending on the value of the discriminant. Use the **PRINT** statement to output your results.

Introduction To FORTRAN 90

The most exciting recent event to happen in the world of FORTRAN programming is the adoption of the new FORTRAN 90 standard.[1] The new standard is a major improvement over the FORTRAN 77 language, with many new and useful features. Although it will be years before FORTRAN 90 compilers are universally available, we will introduce the language here to show you how the FORTRAN language is evolving between FORTRAN 77 and FORTRAN 90.

The first and most important point to make about FORTRAN 90 is that *almost the entire* FORTRAN 77 *language is included as a subset of the new language.* Therefore, everything you have learned in this book and all of the programs you have written in FORTRAN 77 will still work in FORTRAN 90.

FORTRAN 90 has been improved in so many ways that describing it would require a whole new book. In this chapter, we will content ourselves with summarizing some of the major differences between the two languages to give you a flavor of the changes. A version of this book devoted entirely to the FORTRAN 90 language will appear when appropriate compilers are more readily available.

NOTE: The description of FORTRAN 90 contained in this chapter is very brief, and many important features of the language are never mentioned. This introduction will give you some examples of the changes between FORTRAN 77 and FORTRAN 90. However, you will have to consult a FORTRAN 90 book for the details.

13.1 NEW SOURCE FORMAT

One major disadvantage of FORTRAN 77 was the old source format, which specified that columns 1 through 5 were for statement labels, column 6 was for continuation, and columns 7 through 72 were for source code. This source format was estab-

---

[1] American National Standard Programming Language FORTRAN, ANSI X3.198-1992; and International Standards Organization ISO/IEC 1539: 1991, Information Technology—Programming Languages—FORTRAN.

lished back in the days of punched computer cards, when column counting was relatively easy. The old source format is very inconvenient for code entered on today's computer terminals, since the user must carefully count by hand to ensure that his or her source code is in the right columns.

The limitations of the old source format have been so severe that many vendors have offered free-format options with their compilers. Unfortunately, these options were nonstandard and not portable from computer to computer. To ensure portability, programmers have been forced to rely on the old fixed source format.

FORTRAN 90 frees us from the old source format by defining a new standard **free format** for source code. Each line in FORTRAN 90 may be up to 132 characters long, and source code may appear in any column on the line. If present, statement labels must still precede the source code on a line, but they do not have to occupy any particular columns. Continuation lines are indicated by an ampersand (&) at the end of the line to be continued, and (optionally) by an ampersand at the beginning of the continuation line. Samples of FORTRAN 90 statements that are continued to the next line are shown below. The following three source statements are equivalent.

```
ROOT1 = ( -B + SQRT (B**2 - 4. * A * C) ) / ( 2. * A )

ROOT1 = ( -B + SQRT (B**2 - 4. * A * C) )       &
        / ( 2. * A )

ROOT1 = ( -B + SQRT (B**2 - 4. * A * C) )       &
      & / ( 2. * A )
```

Another nice feature of FORTRAN 90 is the inclusion of **in-line comments.** The exclamation mark (!) has been reserved as the marker of in-line comments. Any characters between the exclamation mark and the end of the line are treated as comments and not processed by the compiler. The exclamation mark is the only comment indicator that is valid with free source format, and it can also be used with the fixed source format. For example

```
DISCRIMINANT = B**2 - 4. * A * C           ! Get discriminant
IF ( DISCRIMINANT > 0. ) THEN              ! Two real roots
   ! Solve for the two real roots...
   ROOT1 = ( -B + SQRT(DISCRIMINANT) ) / ( 2. * A )
   ROOT2 = ( -B - SQRT(DISCRIMINANT) ) / ( 2. * A )
END IF
```

Incidentally, the use of the exclamation point to indicate an in-line comment is supported by most modern FORTRAN 77 compilers. If you have access to this feature, you may take advantage of it today with confidence that your code will still run under FORTRAN 90.

Finally, FORTRAN 90 supports a mechanism to include multiple statements in a single line of source code by separating the statements with semicolons. Thus, the following two sets of statements are equivalent in FORTRAN 90:

```
X = 1. ; Y = 1.25 ; I = 7    ! Three statements on one line
```

and

```
X = 1.                       ! One statement per line
Y = 1.25
I = 7
```

13.2   NEW VARIABLE NAMES AND TYPES

13.2.1   FORTRAN 90 Names

Parameter, variable, function, and program names in FORTRAN 90 may be up to 31 characters long, and may contain any combination of letters, numbers, and the underscore character. The only restriction on names is that they must begin with a letter. No embedded blanks are permitted in a name. For example, the following names are legal in FORTRAN 90:

```
TIME_OF_DAY
DISTANCE
ABCDEFGHIJKLMNOPQRSTUVWXYZ01234
```

and the following names are illegal in FORTRAN 90:

```
3_DAYS                              ! Begins with a number
A DOG                              ! Embedded space
TIME_TO_TARGET_INTERCEPT_IN_MSEC   ! Too long
OK?                               ! Illegal character
```

The 31-character variable names are supported by most modern FORTRAN 77 compilers. If your compiler supports this feature, you may use it freely knowing that your code will still run under FORTRAN 90.

13.2.2   FORTRAN 90 Variable Types

All of the standard types in FORTRAN 77 are available in FORTRAN 90: INTEGER, REAL, DOUBLE PRECISION, COMPLEX, CHARACTER, and LOGICAL. However, the method of declaring them has changed. FORTRAN 90 has only five declared data types: **INTEGER, REAL, COMPLEX, CHARACTER,** and **LOGICAL,** but it supports multiple KINDs of each data type. A KIND is a version of a data type that is stored in a specific amount of memory, and has a specific range and precision. For example, a FORTRAN 90 compiler might support two KINDs of real numbers, 4-byte real numbers and 8-byte real numbers. The 4-byte real numbers would correspond to the FORTRAN 77 real data type, and the 8-byte real numbers would correspond to the FORTRAN 77 double-precision data type. Each KIND of a data type is assigned a number to identify it. On many computers, KIND = 1 of the real data type will correspond to the FORTRAN 77 real data type, and KIND = 2 of the real data type will correspond to the FORTRAN 77 double-precision data type. Therefore, single-precision real variables can be declared as

```
REAL ( KIND = 1 )          name        ! single precision
```

and double-precision real variables can be declared as

```
REAL ( KIND = 2 )          name        ! double precision
```

Since the KIND associated with a specific precision might vary from computer to computer, it is customary to declare the KIND number by an easy-to-change parameter.

```
REAL ( KIND = SHORT )   name     ! REAL variables
REAL ( KIND = LONG  )   name     ! DOUBLE PRECISION variables
```

where SHORT and LONG are previously defined parameters. If the KIND parameter is left off of a declaration, a default length is assumed. The default length varies from computer to computer, but is typically the same as the length of the FORTRAN 77 **REAL** type on that computer.

The **CHARACTER** variable type now includes provisions for languages written in non-roman alphabets. Different alphabets are declared using the KIND parameter, and different lengths are declared using the LENGTH parameter. If the KIND parameter is missing, ASCII characters are assumed. If a number appears in parentheses without either the KIND or LEN keywords, it is assumed to be the length of the variable. Some examples of character declarations are

```
CHARACTER ( LEN = 20, KIND = 1)   name ! 20 English characters
CHARACTER ( LEN = 20 )            name ! 20 English characters
CHARACTER ( 20 )                  name ! 20 English characters
CHARACTER ( LEN = 20, KIND = KANJI) name ! 20 Kanji characters
```

13.2.3   FORTRAN 90 Parameters and Data Initialization

Parameters in FORTRAN 90 are the same as parameters in FORTRAN 77, but the way they are defined has changed. Parameters may now be entirely defined on a single line. For example, a FORTRAN 77 parameter might be declared as

```
INTEGER      MAXSIZ
PARAMETER ( MAXSIZ = 100 )
```

The corresponding parameter in FORTRAN 90 is

```
INTEGER, PARAMETER :: MAXSIZ = 100
```

Variables may also be initialized in the same manner. In FORTRAN 77, a variable would be declared and initialized as follows:

```
REAL PI
DATA PI / 3.141592 /
```

The corresponding FORTRAN 90 statement is

```
REAL (KIND=SHORT) :: PI = 3.141592
```

13.2.4 Derived Data Types and Structures

A very exciting change to the language is the inclusion of **derived data types** and **structures.** A derived data type is a type composed of one or more standard data types (or possibly previously defined user data types). The information stored in the various components of the derived data type usually describes information about a particular object. For example, suppose that we are interested in collecting information about a number of people. In this case, we can create a derived data type PERSON which describes an individual. Each element in type PERSON will contain some type of information about the person. If we would like to have the name, address, and ID number of each individual, we could define type PERSON as follows:

```
TYPE PERSON
    CHARACTER(LEN=16) LAST_NAME
    CHARACTER(LEN=16) FIRST_NAME
    CHARACTER(LEN=1)  MIDDLE_INITIAL
    CHARACTER(LEN=48) ADDRESS_LINE_1
    CHARACTER(LEN=48) ADDRESS_LINE_2
    CHARACTER(LEN=20) CITY
    CHARACTER(LEN=2)  STATE
    CHARACTER(LEN=10) ZIP
    INTEGER ID
END TYPE PERSON
```

Every object that is declared to be of type PERSON will have the nine elements shown above, and the elements can be used to store information about a particular individual.

A *structure* is an object that is declared to be of a derived data type. We could define a structure STUDENT which would contain information about a particular student as follows:

```
TYPE (PERSON) STUDENT
```

The structure STUDENT would consist of the nine different elements described in the derived type declaration statement.

As you can see, a structure is a generalization of the idea of an array. An array consists of many elements, *each one of which must be of identically the same type.* By contrast, a structure consists of many elements, *any of which may be of different types.* Each individual element of a structure may be used just like any other variable of the same type. An individual element is addressed by naming the structure and the element with a percent sign (%) between them. For example, a last name could be assigned to element LAST_NAME of structure STUDENT as follows

```
STUDENT%LAST_NAME = 'JOHNSON'
```

The structure element STUDENT%LAST_NAME is a 16-character variable that can be used like any other character variable in your programs.

13.3   EXPRESSIONS AND RELATIONAL OPERATORS

Most FORTRAN 90 expressions and relational operators are identical to those in FORTRAN 77. The major differences are that there are new symbols for the relational operators, and there is a provision to allow the programmer to create new user-defined operators.

The new symbols for the relational operators are shown in Table 13-1 below. Note that both the old and the new symbols are fully supported, and they may be used interchangeably within a program. Be careful to maintain a careful distinction between = and ==. A single equal sign is the assignment operator, while a double equal sign represents the logical operator "is equal to."

TABLE 13-1   Old and New Symbols for Relational Operators

Operator	*Old Symbol*	*New Symbol*
Less than	.LT.	<
Less than or equal to	.LE.	<=
Greater than	.GT.	>
Greater than or equal to	.GE.	>=
Equal to	.EQ.	==
Not equal to	.NE.	/=

It is possible for a user to create additional operators to meet some specific need, and to use them within a program just like the ones built into the language. The details of how to do this are somewhat involved, so they will not be described here.

QUIZ 13-1

This quiz provides a quick check to see if you have understood the concepts introduced in Sections 13.1 through 13.3. If you have trouble with the quiz, reread the sections, ask your instructor, or discuss the material with a fellow student. The answers to this quiz are found in the back of the book.

Questions 1–3 contain a list of valid and invalid FORTRAN 90 program names. State whether or not each program name is valid. If it is invalid, say why it is invalid.

1. `PROGRAM MY_FIRST_PROGRAM`
2. `PROGRAM SECOND-PROGRAM`
3. `PROGRAM 3RD*PROGRAM`

Questions 4–7 contain a list of valid and invalid FORTRAN 90 variable names. State whether or not each variable name is valid. If the variable name is valid, specify its type (assume default typing). If it is invalid, say why it is invalid.

4. `DISTANCE`

5. `_UPPER_CASE`

6. `lower_case`

7. `I_WANT_TO_GET_OUT_OF_THIS_CLASS`

In questions 8–12, answer the question and / or perform the action specified.

8. Write a statement to declare variable LOOP_COUNT as a 2-byte integer, assuming that 2-byte integers are KIND=2 on a particular computer. What is the largest integer that can be stored in this variable?

9. Write a statement to declare variable INDEX as a 4-byte integer, assuming that 4-byte integers are KIND=3 on a particular computer. What is the largest integer that can be stored in this variable?

10. Write a statement to declare a double-precision variable MICROSECONDS using FORTRAN 90 syntax.

11. Write statements to declare a user-defined type STATE_VECTOR containing the following elements: a double-precision variable RANGE, a single-precision variable RANGE_RATE, a single-precision variable AZIMUTH, a single-precision variable ELEVATION, and a double-precision variable TIME_OF_VALIDITY. Declare a structure TARGET to be of type STATE_VECTOR.

12. Write a statement to store the value 40.0D6 into element RANGE of structure TARGET.

Write the following expressions in FORTRAN 90 syntax.

13. START_TIME is greater than or equal to 0.

14. If A1 is equal to A2 then CALL SUBROUTINE_1

13.4 BRANCHING AND LOOPING STRUCTURES

Several new branching and looping structures are included in FORTRAN 90. Together, they provide much more flexibility in program design, and lead to clearer, easier-to-understand programs. We will introduce the major features of these new structures, but you should be aware that this brief treatment ignores some of the details of their use. You should consult a FORTRAN 90 textbook for a full treatment of these features.

13.4.1 Branching Structures

FORTRAN 90 supports the logical **IF** structure found in FORTRAN 77, with the additional feature that each structure can be named. Names are optional, but if they are used, they can help avoid confusion in large, nested **IF** structures. The general form of the logical **IF** structure is

```
[name:] IF (logical expression 1) THEN
          ...
        ELSE IF (logical expression 2) THEN [name]
          ...
        ELSE IF (logical expression 3) THEN [name]
          ...
        ELSE [name]
          ...
        END IF [name]
```

where *name* is the optional name of the structure (name is shown in brackets because it is optional). Although **IF** structure names are optional, you should use them. They make it very obvious which **IF** a particular **ELSE IF, ELSE,** or **END IF** clause is associated with when **IF** structures are nested one inside another.

To illustrate the changes described so far, the quadratic equation solving program from Example 3-1 has been rewritten in FORTRAN 90, and is presented in Figure 13-1.

```
PROGRAM NEW_ROOTS

!  Purpose:
!    This program solves for the roots of a quadratic equation of the form
!    A * X**2 + B * X + C = 0.  It calculates the answers regardless of the
!    type of roots that the equation possesses.
!
!  Record of revisions:
!     Date        Programmer          Description of change
!     ====        ==========          =====================
!    07/21/93   S. J. Chapman         Original code

IMPLICIT NONE

!  Declare parameters.

INTEGER, PARAMETER :: SHORT = 1    ! Single precision is KIND=1 for this machine

!  Declare the variables used in this program.

REAL (KIND=SHORT) A                ! Coefficient of X**2 term of equation
REAL (KIND=SHORT) B                ! Coefficient of X term of equation
REAL (KIND=SHORT) C                ! Constant term of equation
REAL (KIND=SHORT) DISCRIMINANT     ! Discriminant of the equation
REAL (KIND=SHORT) COMPLEX_ROOT_IM  ! Imaginary part of equation (for complex roots)
REAL (KIND=SHORT) COMPLEX_ROOT_RE  ! Real part of equation (for complex roots)
REAL (KIND=SHORT) REAL_ROOT_1      ! First solution of equation (for real roots)
REAL (KIND=SHORT) REAL_ROOT_2      ! Second solution of equation (for real roots)
!
!  Prompt the user for the coefficients of the equation
!
WRITE (*,*) ' This program solves for the roots of a quadratic '
WRITE (*,*) ' equation of the form A * X**2 + B * X + C = 0. '
WRITE (*,*) ' Enter the coefficients A, B, and C:'
READ  (*,*) A, B, C

!  Calculate discriminant

DISCRIMINANT = B**2 - 4. * A * C
```

```
!  Solve for the roots, depending upon the value of the discriminant

SOLVE: IF ( DISCRIMINANT > 0. ) THEN            ! There are 2 real roots, so...
          REAL_ROOT_1 = ( -B + SQRT(DISCRIMINANT) ) &
                        / ( 2. * A )
          REAL_ROOT_2 = ( -B - SQRT(DISCRIMINANT) ) &
                        / ( 2. * A )
          WRITE (*,*) ' This equation has two real roots:'
          WRITE (*,*) ' X1 = ', REAL_ROOT_1
          WRITE (*,*) ' X2 = ', REAL_ROOT_2
       ELSE IF ( DISCRIMINANT == 0. ) THEN   ! There are repeated roots, so...
          REAL_ROOT_1 = ( -B ) / ( 2. * A )
          WRITE (*,*) ' This equation has repeated real roots:'
          WRITE (*,*) ' X1 = ', REAL_ROOT_1
       ELSE
         COMPLEX_ROOT_RE = ( -B ) / ( 2. * A )
         COMPLEX_ROOT_IM = SQRT ( ABS ( DISCRIMINANT ) ) &
                           / ( 2. * A )
          WRITE (*,*) ' This equation has complex roots:'
          WRITE (*,*) ' X1 = ', COMPLEX_ROOT_RE, ' +i ', COMPLEX_ROOT_IM
          WRITE (*,*) ' X2 = ', COMPLEX_ROOT_RE, ' -i ', COMPLEX_ROOT_IM
       END IF SOLVE

!  Finish up.

END PROGRAM
```

FIGURE 13-1   The quadratic equation solving program of Example 3-1 rewritten to illustrate
FORTRAN 90 features.

A new branching structure has also been defined: the **SELECT CASE** structure. The **SELECT CASE** structure executes different code based on the result of
an arithmetic expression. It has the form

```
[name:]   SELECT CASE (case expression)
          CASE (low1:high1)
             Statements
          CASE (low2:high2)
             Statements
          CASE (low3:high3)
             Statements
          ...
          ...
          CASE DEFAULT
             Statements
          END SELECT [name]
```

where *case expression* is an integer, logical, or character expression. If the result of
the expression is between *low1* and *high1,* then the statements in the first block will
be executed. If the result of the expression is between *low2* and *high2,* then the statements in the second block will be executed, and so forth for all the other blocks. If
the result of the expression does not lie within any of the specified ranges, then the
statements in **CASE DEFAULT** will be executed. Note that the ranges associated
with each case must not overlap.

The function of the **SELECT CASE** structure can also be performed with a logical **IF** structure. However, in the situation in which all the branches of the logical **IF** structure depend on the results of the same expression, the **SELECT CASE** structure can produce more compact and easily understandable results.

Figure 13-2 shows the quadratic equation program rewritten to use the **SELECT CASE** structure. In this example, the case expression is -1, 0, or 1 depending on the value of the discriminant.

```
PROGRAM NEW_ROOTS2

!  Purpose:
!    This program solves for the roots of a quadratic equation of the form
!    A * X**2 + B * X + C = 0.  It calculates the answers regardless of the
!    type of roots that the equation possesses.  This program also illustrates
!    the use of the SELECT CASE structure.
!
!  Record of revisions:
!      Date         Programmer          Description of change
!      ====         ==========          =====================
!    07/21/93     S. J. Chapman         Original code

IMPLICIT NONE

!  Declare parameters.

INTEGER, PARAMETER :: SHORT = 1     ! Single precision is KIND=1 for this machine

!  Declare the variables used in this program.

REAL (KIND=SHORT) A                ! Coefficient of X**2 term of equation
REAL (KIND=SHORT) B                ! Coefficient of X term of equation
REAL (KIND=SHORT) C                ! Constant term of equation
INTEGER (KIND=0)  CASE_EXPR        ! Case expression (KIND=0 means default type)
REAL (KIND=SHORT) DISCRIMINANT     ! Discriminant of the equation
REAL (KIND=SHORT) COMPLEX_ROOT_IM  ! Imaginary part of equation (for complex roots)
REAL (KIND=SHORT) COMPLEX_ROOT_RE  ! Real part of equation (for complex roots)
REAL (KIND=SHORT) REAL_ROOT_1      ! First solution of equation (for real roots)
REAL (KIND=SHORT) REAL_ROOT_2      ! Second solution of equation (for real roots)
!
!  Prompt the user for the coefficients of the equation
!
WRITE (*,*) ' This program solves for the roots of a quadratic '
WRITE (*,*) ' equation of the form A * X**2 + B * X + C = 0. '
WRITE (*,*) ' Enter the coefficients A, B, and C:'
READ  (*,*) A, B, C

!  Calculate discriminant

DISCRIMINANT = B**2 - 4. * A * C

!  Solve for the roots, depending upon the value of the discriminant.
!    If DISCRIMINANT < 0, CASE_EXPR = -1
!    If DISCRIMINANT = 0, CASE_EXPR =  0
!    If DISCRIMINANT > 0, CASE_EXPR =  1
```

```
IF ( DISCRIMINANT .NE. 0 ) THEN
   CASE_EXPR = NINT ( DISCRIMINANT / ABS(DISCRIMINANT) )
ELSE
   CASE_EXPR = 0
END IF

SOLVE: SELECT CASE ( CASE_EXPR )
      CASE ( 1: )   ! POS: There are 2 real roots, so...
         REAL_ROOT_1 = ( -B + SQRT(DISCRIMINANT) ) &
                     / ( 2. * A )
         REAL_ROOT_2 = ( -B - SQRT(DISCRIMINANT) ) &
                     / ( 2. * A )
         WRITE (*,*) ' This equation has two real roots:'
         WRITE (*,*) ' X1 = ', REAL_ROOT_1
         WRITE (*,*) ' X2 = ', REAL_ROOT_2
      CASE ( 0 )       ! ZERO: There are repeated roots, so...
         REAL_ROOT_1 = ( -B ) / ( 2. * A )
         WRITE (*,*) ' This equation has repeated real roots:'
         WRITE (*,*) ' X1 = ', REAL_ROOT_1
      CASE ( : -1 ) ! NEG: There are two complex roots, so...
         COMPLEX_ROOT_RE = ( -B ) / ( 2. * A )
         COMPLEX_ROOT_IM = SQRT ( ABS ( DISCRIMINANT ) ) &
                         / ( 2. * A )
         WRITE (*,*) ' This equation has complex roots:'
         WRITE (*,*) ' X1 = ', COMPLEX_ROOT_RE, ' +i ', COMPLEX_ROOT_IM
         WRITE (*,*) ' X2 = ', COMPLEX_ROOT_RE, ' -i ', COMPLEX_ROOT_IM
      END SELECT SOLVE

! Finish up.

END PROGRAM
```

FIGURE 13-2   The quadratic equation solving program of Example 3-1 rewritten to use the **SELECT CASE** structure.

13.4.2   Looping Structures

The standard iterative **DO** structure in FORTRAN 90 has the form

```
[name:]  DO INDEX = ISTART, IEND, INCR
            Statement 1        ⎫
            Statement 2        ⎪
            Statement 3        ⎬ Body
            ...                ⎪
            Statement n        ⎭
         END DO [name]
```

It looks similar to the **DO** structure in FORTRAN 77, except that the terminal statement in the loop is **END DO** instead of **CONTINUE**. Note that no statement label is required in this form of a **DO** loop.

The standard **WHILE** loop in FORTRAN 90 has the form

```
[name:]  DO
            IF (logical expr) EXIT
            Statement 1
            Statement 2        ⎫
            Statement 3        ⎬ Body
            ...                ⎭
            Statement n
         END DO [name]
```

When the **IF** statement is executed with the logical expression TRUE, control is transferred to the first executable statement following the **END DO.**

An alternate form of the **WHILE** statement also exists. It works in a slightly different manner than the previous example. In this form of the loop, the logical expression is evaluated before the beginning of each loop. While the logical expression is TRUE, the loop will continue executing. When the logical expression becomes FALSE, the loop will no longer execute, and control will be transferred to the first executable statement following the **END DO.**

```
[name:]  DO WHILE (logical expr)
            Statement 1
            Statement 2        ⎫
            Statement 3        ⎬ Body
            ...                ⎭
            Statement n
         END DO [name]
```

Figure 13-3 contains a rewritten version of the statistics program from Example 3-3. This program illustrates the use of the **WHILE** loop in a real example.

```
PROGRAM NEW_STAT2

!  Purpose:
!    To calculate mean and the standard deviation of an input
!    data set.

!  Record of revisions:
!     Date        Programmer         Description of change
!     ====        ==========         =====================
!    07/23/93    S. J. Chapman       Original code

IMPLICIT NONE

!  Declare parameters.

INTEGER, PARAMETER :: SHORT = 1    ! Single precision is KIND=1 on this machine
INTEGER, PARAMETER :: INT32 = 3    ! 32-bit integers are KIND=3 on this machine

!  Declare the variables used in this program.

INTEGER (KIND=INT32) N       ! The number of input samples.
REAL    (KIND=SHORT) X       ! An input data value.
REAL    (KIND=SHORT) STD_DEV ! The standard deviation of the input samples.
REAL    (KIND=SHORT) SUMX    ! The sum of the input values.
```

```
REAL    (KIND=SHORT) SUMX2     ! The sum of the squares of the input values.
REAL    (KIND=SHORT) XBAR      ! The average of the input samples.

! Initialize the counter and sums to zero.

N = 0;   SUMX = 0.;   SUMX2 = 0.;   X = 0.

! Get first number.

WRITE (*,*) ' Enter first number: '
READ  (*,*) X
WRITE (*,*) ' The number is ', X

! Loop to read input values.

DO WHILE ( X >= 0. )

   !Accumulate sums.

   N     = N + 1
   SUMX  = SUMX + X
   SUMX2 = SUMX2 + X**2

   !Get next number.

   WRITE (*,*) ' Enter next number: '
   READ  (*,*) X
   WRITE (*,*) ' The number is ', X

END DO

! Check to see if we have enough input data.

IF ( N .LT. 2 ) THEN ! Insufficient data...

   WRITE (*,*) ' At least 2 values must be entered.'

ELSE ! Enough data is available, so...

   ! Calculate the mean and standard deviation

   XBAR    = SUMX / REAL(N)
   STD_DEV = SQRT( (REAL(N) * SUMX2 - SUMX**2) &
             / (REAL(N) * REAL(N-1)) )

   ! Tell user.

   WRITE (*,*) ' The mean of this data set is:', XBAR
   WRITE (*,*) ' The standard deviation is:   ', STD_DEV

END IF

END PROGRAM
```

FIGURE 13-3   Statistics program from Example 3-3 modified to use FORTRAN 90 features.

The **DO WHILE** structure is supported by most modern FORTRAN 77 compilers. If your compiler supports this feature, you may use it freely knowing that your code will still run under FORTRAN 90.

Both the **DO** loop and the **WHILE** loop end on an **END DO** statement, and not on a **CONTINUE** statement with a statement label attached to it. This design substantially improves the structure of a program by eliminating the need for statement numbers. Statement numbers can be a significant source of error in FORTRAN 77. If a statement number is typed incorrectly in a FORTRAN 77 **DO** statement, the **DO** loop could suddenly include code that should not be repeated. For example, consider the following code fragment.

```
    DO 10 I = 1, 10
        Statement 1
        Statement 2
10  CONTINUE
        Statement 3
        Statement 4
20  CONTINUE
```

If the **DO** statement were incorrectly typed as **DO 20 I = 1, 10,** the **DO** loop would execute Statements 3 and 4 ten times instead of once. This problem does not occur with FORTRAN 90 structures.

13.4.3 The WHERE Structure

The **WHERE** structure is a new looping structure that does not correspond to anything in FORTRAN 77. It is a special looping structure designed to apply only to the elements of an array. The general form of a **WHERE** structure is

```
WHERE (logical expr)
    Statement 1      ⎫
    Statement 2      ⎪
    Statement 3      ⎬ Block 1
    ...              ⎪
    Statement n      ⎭
ELSEWHERE
    Statement 1      ⎫
    Statement 2      ⎪
    Statement 3      ⎬ Block 2
    ...              ⎪
    Statement n      ⎭
END WHERE
```

This statement is designed to apply the operation or set of operations in Block 1 to all of the elements of an array that satisfy *logical expr,* and to apply the operation or set of operations in Block 2 to all the elements of the array that do *not* satisfy *logical expr.* For example, suppose that array A1 is defined by the statement

```
REAL (KIND=SHORT) A1(3,3)
```

and that we have the following **WHERE** structure:

```
WHERE ( A1 > 0. )
   A1 = LOG10(A1)
ELSEWHERE
   A1 = 0.
END WHERE
```

This structure will take the logarithm of each element of array A1 that is greater than zero, and will set each element of array A1 that is less than or equal to zero. The equivalent FORTRAN 77 code that would perform this function is

```
REAL A1(3,3)
...
DO 20 I = 1, 3
   DO 10 J = 1, 3
      IF ( A1(I,J) .GT. 0. ) THEN
         A1'I,J) = LOG10(A1(I,J))
      ELSE
         A1(I,J) = 0.
      END IF
10    CONTINUE
20 CONTINUE
```

13.5 ARRAY OPERATIONS

In FORTRAN 77, array elements were always operated on as individual units. For example, if we wanted to add two arrays together, it was necessary to add every element of the two arrays individually. To add two arrays A and B of dimension (3,3,3), we would execute the following FORTRAN 77 code.

```
REAL A(3,3,3), B(3,3,3), C(3,3,3)
...
DO 30 I = 1, 3
   DO 20 J = 1, 3
      DO 10 K = 1, 3
         C(I,J,K) = A(I,J,K) + B(I,J,K)
10       CONTINUE
20    CONTINUE
30 CONTINUE
```

In FORTRAN 90, *entire arrays may be operated on with a single assignment statement* provided that they are of compatible dimensions. For matrix addition, two arrays may be added provided that they are of the same size, and each array element in the output array is just the sum of the corresponding elements in the two arrays being added. Therefore, the following lines perform the same function as the FORTRAN 77 example above.

```
REAL(KIND=SHORT) A(3,3,3), B(3,3,3), C(3,3,3)
...
C = A + B
```

On the other hand, the following code would produce a compilation error, since the arrays are not of compatible dimensions.

```
REAL(KIND=SHORT) A(3,3,3), B(2,2,2), C(3,3,3)
...
C = A + B
```

Array operations are *much* easier to implement in FORTRAN 90!

QUIZ 13-2

This quiz provides a quick check to see if you have understood the concepts introduced in Sections 13.4 through 13.5. If you have trouble with the quiz, reread the sections, ask your instructor, or discuss the material with a fellow student. The answers to this quiz are found in the back of the book.

In questions 1–7, answer the question and / or perform the action specified.

1. Write a FORTRAN 90 logical **IF** structure that assigns letter grades based on a student's average in a course as follows:

100–95	A
94–90	B
80–89	C
70–79	D
0–69	F

2. Write a FORTRAN 90 **CASE** structure that assigns letter grades based on a student's average in a course as shown above.
3. Write an iterative loop to sum up the values in array C(1000) in variable SUM using FORTRAN 90 syntax.
4. Write a **WHILE** loop to read values from a disk file until the end of file is reached. Use FORTRAN 90 syntax.

5. Write a **WHERE** structure to take the square root of all elements of array CO-VARIANCE that are greater than zero, and to do nothing to the elements of the array that are less than or equal to zero.
6. Write a FORTRAN 90 program to read two m × n arrays A and B from a disk file, and then to subtract array B from array A.

13.6   SUBPROGRAMS

FORTRAN 90 contains five basic types of subprograms:

1. External subroutines
2. External functions
3. Internal subroutines
4. Internal functions
5. Modules

13.6.1   External Subroutines

External subroutines are the same as the subroutines in FORTRAN 77. Each external subroutine is an independent program unit that is defined outside of all other program units. It starts with a **SUBROUTINE** statement and ends with an **END SUBROUTINE** statement. A subroutine declared in this fashion can be called from any other routine in the program using a **CALL** statement.

13.6.2   External Functions

External functions are the same as the function subprograms in FORTRAN 77. Each external function is an independent program unit that is defined outside of all other program units. It starts with a **FUNCTION** statement and ends with an **END FUNCTION** statement. A function declared in this fashion can be called from any other routine in the program by naming the function as a part of an executable statement.

13.6.3   Internal Subroutines

Internal subroutines are subroutines that are defined entirely within the body of another program or subprogram. *Internal subroutines are like ordinary subroutines, except that they can only be called from within the program unit in which they are defined.* No other program units may call these subroutines. They start with a **SUBROUTINE** statement and end with an **END SUBROUTINE** statement, but both the start and the end of the subroutine lie entirely within another program unit. The declaration of an internal subroutine within a program unit is preceded by a **CONTAINS** statement.

```
PROGRAM TEST
...
...
CONTAINS
   SUBROUTINE SUB1(A, B, C)
   ...
   ...
   END SUBROUTINE SUB1
...
...
CALL SUB1 (X, Y, Z)
...
END
```

13.6.4   Internal Functions

Internal functions are like a hybrid between a FORTRAN 77 function subprogram and a statement function. The structure of an internal function is like that of a function subprogram, except that it is defined entirely within the body of another program unit. Like a statement function, *an internal function can only be called from within the program unit in which it is defined.* No other program units may call it. Like external functions, internal functions start with a **FUNCTION** statement and end with an **END FUNCTION** statement. The declaration of an internal function within a program unit is preceded by a **CONTAINS** statement.

```
PROGRAM TEST
...
...
CONTAINS
   FUNCTION MYFUNC(Z)
   ...
   ...
   END FUNCTION
...
...
OUTPUT = 2. * PI * MYFUNC (X)
...
END PROGRAM
```

13.6.5   Modules

The final type of FORTRAN 90 program unit is the **module.** A module is a program unit that is used to package data definitions and operations that will be used in other program units. The data definitions and operations are defined only once in the module, and then the module is referenced by name in any program unit that needs it.[2] Modules begin with the **MODULE** statement, and end with an **END MODULE** statement.

An example module is shown in Figure 13-4. This module is named F90_KIND. It declares names for the KINDs of data types supported on the FORTRAN 90 compiler that I used while preparing this text.

```
MODULE F90_KIND

!  Purpose:
!     To declare and name the KINDs of variables supported by
!     this FORTRAN 90 compiler.

!  Record of revisions:
!      Date          Programmer          Description of change
!      ====          ==========          =====================
!    08/31/93     S. J. Chapman          Original code

IMPLICIT NONE

! Supported Real and Complex kinds
!     Single precision
      integer, parameter :: short = 1
!     Double precision
      integer, parameter :: long  = 2

! Supported Integer kinds
!     Single byte integer
      integer, parameter :: int8   = 1
!     Two byte integer
      integer, parameter :: int16  = 2
!     Four byte integer
      integer, parameter :: int32  = 3

! Supported Logical kinds
!     Single byte logical
      integer, parameter :: byte   = 1
!     Four byte logical
      integer, parameter :: word   = 2

! Character type
!     Normal single byte character (ASCII sequence)
      integer, parameter :: ascii  = 1

END MODULE F90_KIND
```

FIGURE 13-4   Module declaring and naming the KINDs of variables supported on a particular FORTRAN 90 compiler.

Modules are referenced in other program units by naming them in a **USE** statement. To use the KIND definitions given in module F90_KIND, a program would include the line

```
USE F90_KIND
```

at the beginning of its declaration section before any other type declarations.

---

[2] In this role, the **MODULE** statement is a replacement for the **INCLUDE** statement, which is a nonstandard extension to FORTRAN 77.

Modules are actually more sophisticated than they appear from this cursory overview, but we will have to postpone their advanced features to a separate FOR-TRAN 90 textbook.

13.6.6   Recursion

FORTRAN 90 subprograms can be declared to be **recursive,** which means that the subroutine or function can call itself. FORTRAN 77 subprograms are not recursive. If a FORTRAN 77 subprogram tries to call itself, unpredictable (but generally bad) behavior will result.

FORTRAN 90 subprograms are declared to be recursive by adding a RECUR-SIVE clause to SUBROUTINE or FUNCTION statement that declares the subprogram. If the subprogram is function, there must also be a RESULT clause in the function declaration to specify the name under which the values in the function are returned. For example, subroutine MYSUB can be declared recursive as follows:

```
RECURSIVE SUBROUTINE MYSUB (A, B)
...
...
...
END SUBROUTINE
```

Similarly, recursive function MYFUN can be declared as follows:

```
RECURSIVE FUNCTION MYFUN (A, B) RESULT (RETURN_VALUE)
...
...
RETURN_VALUE = ...
END SUBROUTINE
```

■
EXAMPLE   13-1   *The Factorial Function*   The function N! is defined as

```
N! = 1                                 N = 0
N! = N * (N-1) * (N-2) * ... * 3 * 2 * 1   N > 0
```

In Example 3-5, we used a **DO** loop to calculate this function:

```
NFAC = 1
DO 10 I = 1, N
   NFAC = NFAC * I
10 CONTINUE
```

However, we can also write the factorial function in recursive form as follows:

```
N! = 1              N = 0
N! = N * (N-1)!     N > 0
```

If $N > 0$, then N! is just N times (N-1)!. Therefore, we should be able to write a recursive function that can be used to calculate N!.

SOLUTION The recursive function FACTORIAL(N) should return a value of 1.0 if N = 0, and should return N * FACTORIAL(N-1) if N > 0. The code to calculate this function is shown in Figure 13-5, and a test driver routine for the function is shown in Figure 13-6. Note that the function declaration contains a RESULT clause, and the name in the RESULT clause is used to return a value from the function.

```
RECURSIVE FUNCTION FACTORIAL(N) RESULT (NFACT)

!  Purpose:
!     To calculate the factorial function using recursive
!     calls to this function.

!  Record of revisions:
!     Date        Programmer          Description of change
!     ====        ==========          =====================
!     09/02/93    S. J. Chapman       Original code

USE F90_KIND

IMPLICIT NONE

!  List of calling arguments:
!     NAME        I/O  TYPE      DIM      DESCRIPTION
!     ====        ===  ====      ===      ===========
!     N           I    INT32              Value to calculate factorial for.
!     FACTORIAL   O    INT32              Factorial function.
!     NFACT       O    INT32              Result of function.

INTEGER (KIND=INT32) N
INTEGER (KIND=INT32) NFACT

IF ( N > 0 ) THEN
   NFACT = N * FACTORIAL(N-1)
ELSE
   NFACT = 1
END IF

RETURN
END FUNCTION FACTORIAL
```

FIGURE 13-5 The factorial function.

```
PROGRAM T_FACT

!  Purpose:
!     To test the recursive factorial function FACTORIAL.

!  Record of revisions:
!     Date        Programmer          Description of change
!     ====        ==========          =====================
!     09/02/93    S. J. Chapman       Original code

!  Include the KINDs defined for this compiler
USE F90_KIND

IMPLICIT NONE
```

```
!  List of local variables:
!      N           --   Number to calculate factorial of
!      FACTORIAL --   Factorial function

!  Declare local variables
INTEGER (KIND=INT32) N
INTEGER (KIND=INT32) FACTORIAL

!  Get value to calculate factorial of.
WRITE (*,*) 'Please enter N: '
READ (*,*) N

!  Calculate and write out answer.
WRITE (*,100) FACTORIAL(N)
100 FORMAT (1X,'N! = ',I10)

END PROGRAM
```

FIGURE 13-6   A test driver routine for the factorial function.

When program T_FACT is executed on a PC with N = 0 and N = 5, the results are

```
C:\BOOK\FORT>t_fact
 Please enter N:
0
 N! =            1

C:\BOOK\FORT>t_fact
 Please enter N:
5
 N! =          120
```

We can see by inspection that the results are correct.   ●

13.7   DYNAMIC MEMORY ALLOCATION AND POINTERS

All memory in FORTRAN 77 is **static memory.** With static memory, the size of every array in a program must be declared when the program is compiled, and can only be changed by recompiling and relinking the program. This can be a very serious limitation, since the arrays in any application that we write must be made large enough to handle the largest problem that we will ever attempt to solve. If the arrays are made large, we will be wasting a lot of memory most of the time, and the program may not run at all on some computers with small memories. On the other hand, if the arrays are made small, then we cannot solve large problems at all.

FORTRAN 90 includes a better way to handle the memory problem: **dynamic memory.** With dynamic memory, the program can decide at run time how much memory it will need and allocate only that amount. The same program will be able to run on small computers and large computers without recompiling and without wasting memory.

An array using dynamic memory is declared using the **ALLOCATABLE** statement, and is actually allocated with the **ALLOCATE** statement. When the program is through using the memory, it can free it up for other uses with the **DEALLO-**

CATE statement. An example illustrating the use of these statements is shown in Figure 13-7. In this program, we solve a system of N simultaneous equations in N unknowns. Unlike the FORTRAN 77 examples in Chapter 6, this program only allocates the memory actually required to solve the problem. Any other memory in the computer remains free for use by other programs.

```
PROGRAM SOLVE

! Purpose:
!    Solves a system of linear equations of the form
!       A x = B
!    where A is an N x N matrix, and B is an N x 1 vector.  The
!    number of equations N is specified by the user.

! Record of revisions:
!     Date        Programmer         Description of change
!     ====        ==========         =====================
!    09/11/93    S. J. Chapman       Original code
!

USE F90_KIND   ! Kind declarations for this compiler

IMPLICIT NONE

! Declare variables...
REAL (KIND=SHORT)              A         ! Coefficient matrix A (N x N)
REAL (KIND=SHORT)              B         ! Value matrix B (N x 1)
INTEGER ( KIND=INT32)         ERROR      ! Error flag
INTEGER ( KIND=INT32)         I          ! Index variable
INTEGER ( KIND=INT32)         ISTAT      ! I/O status
INTEGER ( KIND=INT32)         J          ! Index variable
INTEGER (KIND=INT32)          N          ! Dimension of system of equations.
CHARACTER (KIND=ASCII,LEN=20) FILENM     ! File name to open for coefficients
ALLOCATABLE A(:,:), B(:)

! Get the name of the disk file containing the equations.
WRITE (*,*) 'Enter the file name containing the eqns: '
READ (*,'(A20)') FILENM

! Open input data file.  Status is OLD because the input data must
! already exist.
!
OPEN ( UNIT=1, FILE=FILENM, STATUS='OLD', IOSTAT=ISTAT )

! Was the OPEN successful?

OPEN: IF ( ISTAT == 0 ) THEN

        !The file was opened successfully, so read the number of
        !equations in the system.
        READ (1,*) N

        !Allocate memory for A and B.
        ALLOCATE ( A(N,N), B(N) )

        !Read in equations.
        DO I = 1, N
           READ (1,*) (A(I,J), J=1,N), B(I)
        END DO
```

```
          !Display coefficients.
          WRITE (*,1020)
          1020 FORMAT (/,1X,'Coefficients before call:')
          DO I = 1, N
             WRITE (*,1030) (A(I,J), J=1,N), B(I)
             1030 FORMAT (1X,7F11.4)
          END DO

          !Solve equations.
          CALL SIMUL (A, B, N, N, ERROR )

          !Check for error.
          IF ( ERROR /= 0 ) THEN
             WRITE (*,1040)
             1040 FORMAT (/1X,'Zero pivot encountered!', &
                          //1X,'There is no unique solution to this system.')
          ELSE

             !No errors. Display coefficients.
             WRITE (*,1050)
             1050 FORMAT (/,1X,'Coefficients after call:')
             DO I = 1, N
                WRITE (*,1030) (A(I,J), J=1,N), B(I)
             END DO

             !Write final answer.
             WRITE (*,1060)
             1060 FORMAT (/,1X,'The solutions are:')
             DO I = 1, N
                WRITE (*,1070) I, B(I)
                1070 FORMAT (3X,'X(',I2,') = ',F16.6)
             END DO
          END IF
       END IF OPEN

! Deallocate dynamic arrays.
DEALLOCATE ( A, B )

END PROGRAM
```

FIGURE 13-7 A program to solve a system of simultaneous equations. This program illustrates the use of dynamic memory allocation in a FORTRAN 90 program.

It is also possible to declare **pointers** to dynamic memory, and to address the memory indirectly via the pointers. The details of using pointers are a bit complex, and must be postponed to a book actually dealing with FORTRAN 90.

13.8   I/O System Improvements

Several enhancements have been added to the I/O system in FORTRAN 90. The most important of these enhancements are **nonadvancing I/O operations** and **NAMELIST I/O operations**.

13.8.1   Nonadvancing I/O Operations

In FORTRAN 77, every **READ** statement uses at least one line in the input data file. Any data left over at the end of the line is ignored, and the next **READ** statement will begin at the start of the next line in the input file. Similarly, every **WRITE** statement writes at least one complete line to the output file, and the data in the next **WRITE** statement will start at the beginning of the next line in the output file.

This behavior is somewhat limiting, especially when we are working with I/O to computer terminals. For example, there is no way in FORTRAN 77 to write out a prompt to a terminal, and then read in a response from the same line. FORTRAN 90 overcomes this limitation by adding an ADVANCE= clause to **READ** and **WRITE** statements. If ADVANCE='NO', the program will not advance to the next line at the end of the **READ** or **WRITE.**

It is easy to create prompts using this feature. For example, the following code produces the prompt 'Enter the number of students in the class: ', and the user's answer is typed on the same line as the prompt just after the colon.

```
WRITE (*,*,ADVANCE='NO') 'Enter the number of students in the class: '
READ (*,'(I6)') NO_OF_STUDENTS
```

13.8.2   Namelist I/O

Namelist I/O is a convenient way to write out a list of variable names and values, or to read in a list of variable names and values. A **namelist** is just a list of variable names. The general form of a namelist is:

```
NAMELIST / list_name / var1, var2, ...
```

where *list_name* is the name of the namelist, and *var1, var2,* etc. are the variables in the list. **NAMELIST** is a specification statement, and must appear before the first executable statement in a program. The variables listed in a namelist may be read in or written out as a unit using namelist-directed **READ** or **WRITE** statements.

The general form of a namelist-directed **WRITE** statement is:

```
WRITE (UNIT=unit, NML=list_name)
```

where *unit* is the logical unit to which the data will be written, and *list_name* is the name of the namelist to be written out. When a namelist-directed **WRITE** statement is executed, all of the variables named in the namelist are printed out together with their values. For example, consider the code shown in Figure 13-8.

```
PROGRAM WRITE_NAMELIST

!  Purpose:
!    To illustrate a NAMELIST-directed WRITE statement.

USE F90_KIND

IMPLICIT NONE
```

```
! Declare variables
INTEGER (KIND=INT32) I, J        ! Integer variables
REAL (KIND=SHORT)    A, B        ! Real variables

! Declare namelist
NAMELIST /MYLIST/ I, J, A, B

! Initialize variables
DATA I, J, A, B / 1, 2, -999., 0. /

! Write NAMELIST
WRITE (UNIT=6, NML=MYLIST)

END
```

FIGURE 13-8   A simple program using a **NAMELIST**-directed **WRITE** statement.

When this code is executed, the following list of variable names and values is printed out.

```
&MYLIST I = 1, J = 2, A =  -9.9900000E+02, B =   0.0000000E+00/
```

Note that the namelist output begins with an ampersand and the list name, and concludes with a slash.

The general form of a namelist-directed **READ** statement is

```
READ (UNIT=unit, NML=list_name)
```

where *unit* is the logical unit from which the data will be read, and *list_name* is the name of the namelist to be read in. When a namelist-directed **READ** statement is executed, the program searches the input file for the marker *&list_name,* which indicates the beginning of the namelist. It then reads in all of the values in the namelist until a */* is encountered to terminate the **READ.** The values in the input list may appear on any line within the input file, as long as they are between the markers *&list_name* and */.* The values are assigned to the namelist variables according to the names given in the input list.

Namelist-directed **READ** statements are *very* useful. Suppose that you are writing a program containing 100 important input variables. The variables will be initialized to their usual values by default in the program. During any particular run of the program, anywhere from 1 to 10 of these default values may need to be changed, but the others would remain the same. In this case, you should include all 100 values in a namelist and include a namelist-directed **READ** in the program. Whenever a user runs the program, he or she can just list the few values to be changed in the namelist input file, and all of the other input variables will remain unchanged. This approach is much better than using an ordinary **READ** statement, since all 100 values would need to be listed in the ordinary **READ**'s input file, even if they were not being changed in a particular run.

Consider the example in Figure 13-9, which illustrates how a namelist **READ** can update selected values in the namelist.

```
PROGRAM READ_NAMELIST

!  Purpose:
!    To illustrate a NAMELIST-directed READ statement.

USE F90_KIND

IMPLICIT NONE

! Declare variables
INTEGER (KIND=INT32) I, J        ! Integer variables
REAL (KIND=SHORT)    A, B        ! Real variables

! Declare namelist
NAMELIST /MYLIST/ I, J, A, B

! Initialize variables
DATA I, J, A, B / 1, 2, -999., 0. /

! Write NAMELIST before update
WRITE (UNIT=6, NML=MYLIST)

! Read NAMELIST update
READ (UNIT=5, NML=MYLIST)

! Write NAMELIST after update
WRITE (UNIT=6, NML=MYLIST)

END
```

FIGURE 13-9   A simple program using a **NAMELIST**-directed **READ** statement.

If the input file on unit 5 contains the following data,

```
&MYLIST
  B =         2000.,
  I =            17,
  /
```

then variable B is assigned the value 2000., and variable I is assigned the value 17. The values of all other variables in the namelist will not be changed. The result of executing this program will be

```
C:\BOOK\FORT>nml_read
&MYLIST I = 1, J = 2, A =  -9.9900000E+02, B =   0.0000000E+00/
&MYLIST
  B = 2000.,
  I = 17,
  /
&MYLIST I = 17, J = 2, A =  -9.9900000E+02, B =   2.0000000E+03/
```

Note that the values of I and B were updated during the namelist read, while the values of J and A remained unchanged.

The **NAMELIST** statement is supported by many of the current FORTRAN 77 compilers. If your compiler supports it, you may use it freely knowing that your code will still work in FORTRAN 90.

Quiz 13-3

This quiz provides a quick check to see if you have understood the concepts introduced in Sections 13.6 through 13.8. If you have trouble with the quiz, reread the sections, ask your instructor, or discuss the material with a fellow student. The answers to this quiz are found in the back of the book.

In questions 1–3, answer the question and/or perform the action specified.

1. Explain the difference between an internal subroutine and an external subroutine.
2. What are the advantages of using dynamic memory instead of static memory in a FORTRAN progam? What are the disadvantages?
3. Write a FORTRAN 90 program that initializes values I, J, K, and L to 1, 2, 3, and 4, respectively. Then use a namelist-directed READ statement to update values I and L only, and print out the values of I, J, K, and L.

13.9   SUMMARY

FORTRAN 90 is a great improvement over FORTRAN 77. It introduces many new features designed to make it easier to write readable, structured programs. However, essentially all of FORTRAN 77 is included in FORTRAN 90, so your existing programs will continue to run under FORTRAN 90.

The major improvements in FORTRAN 90 include:

1. *A new free source format* that eliminates column counting. The new format supports 132 column lines, in-line comments, and multiple statements per line.
2. *Longer names.* Variable, parameter, and function names may now be up to 31 characters long, and may include underscore (_) characters.
3. *New type declaration statements* that include a KIND clause to support multiple sizes of integer and real variables.
4. *New user defined types and structures.* Users may create data types designed to match the problem being solved.
5. *A new branching structure.* The **SELECT CASE** structure can be used to specify different actions based on the range of an arithmetic expression.
6. *New looping structures.* There are now two standard ways to implement a **WHILE** loop: the **DO WHILE** structure and the **DO** loop with a conditional **EXIT** statement. All **DO** loops may now terminate on an **END DO** statement. In addition, the **WHERE** structure is a special-purpose structure that loops through all of the elements of an array that satisfy a particular condition.
7. *Array operations.* Arithmetic operations can be applied to entire arrays with a single assignment statement, provided that the arrays are of compatible sizes for the operations being performed.
8. *New subprogram types.* FORTRAN 90 includes three new subprogram types: internal subroutines, internal functions, and modules. Internal subroutines and

internal functions are similar to the subroutines and functions in FORTRAN 77, except that they are local to the routines in which they are defined. Modules are convenient ways to encapsulate data and possibly operations defined on the data so that they will only need to be declared once in a program.

9. *Dynamic memory allocation.* FORTRAN 90 supports the dynamic allocation of array memory, so that only the amount of memory actually required is used. Dynamic memory may be allocated at any time when it is needed, and may be freed up after it is used. FORTRAN 90 also supports pointers to dynamic memory structures.

10. *Nonadvancing I/O operations.* New nonadvancing **READ** and **WRITE** statements permit us to read and/or write several times to the same line.

11. *Namelist I/O.* Namelists permit variables to be read in or printed out keyed by their variable names.

13.9.1 Summary of Good Programming Practice

Some of the features of FORTRAN 90 are quite common in good FORTRAN 77 compilers. If you use them, you may be sure that your code will still be compatible with the new FORTRAN 90 compilers. However, you will reduce the portability of your code to other FORTRAN 77 compilers. If portability to other FORTRAN 77 compilers is important to you, you should *not* use any of the features described in this chapter.

If you are not concerned about portability to other FORTRAN 77 compilers, you may use any of the features described in this chapter that may be supported in your current compiler. You will not need to worry about FORTRAN 90 compatibility in the future. The FORTRAN 90 features that are most commonly found in FORTRAN 77 compilers are

1. Long variable names
2. **DO WHILE** loops
3. The **END DO** statement
4. Namelist I/O
5. Dynamic memory allocation

CHAPTER 13 KEY WORDS

Derived data types
Dynamic memory
External function
External subroutine
Free format
Internal function
Internal subroutine

Module
Namelist
Nonadvancing I/O operations
Pointer
Static memory
Structure

CHAPTER 13 EXERCISES

1. How long may a FORTRAN 90 source line be? How do you indicate continuation to another line in FORTRAN 90?

2. Name three ways to mark comment lines in FORTRAN 90. Which of them work with fixed-format source code? Which of them work with free format source code?

3. State whether each of the following variable names are legal or illegal under FORTRAN 90.
   - (a) LOGICAL_SORT_DATA
   - (b) DAY&NIGHT
   - (c) IS_PRESENT?
   - (d) 12345

4. Write FORTRAN 90 statements to declare a double-precision variable DETERMINANT and a 2-byte integer INDEX. (Assume that the KINDs supported by your FORTRAN compiler are those given in Figure 13-4.)

5. Create a user-defined data type called BOOK. Type BOOK should consist of the following elements: TITLE (36 characters), AUTHOR (36 characters), PUBLISHER (20 characters), COPYRIGHT (4 characters), and PAGE_COUNT (integer). Declare a structure MY_LIB consisting of 1000 elements of type BOOK.

6. Write the old and new symbols for the relational operators. Why does the symbol for "is equal to" have *two* equal signs?

7. Use a **SELECT CASE** statement to implement an algorithm that shifts uppercase letters to lowercase.

8. Rewrite the linear least squares fit program of Example 4-5 in FORTRAN 90, using the **DO WHILE** structure to implement the **WHILE** loop.

9. Rewrite the linear least squares fit program of Example 4-5 in FORTRAN 90, using the **DO** structure with an **IF () EXIT** statement to implement the **WHILE** loop.

10. Use a **WHERE** structure to implement the algorithm

$$a_{ij} = \frac{a_{ij}}{b_{ij}} \text{ for } i = 1 \text{ to M and } j = 1 \text{ to N}$$

    where A and B are M $\times$ N matrices and $b_{ij} \neq 0$.

11. What conditions are required before two matrices can be added together? Write the FORTRAN 90 equations that would add two compatible arrays A and B and store the result in C.

12. Write a piece of FORTRAN 90 code that prompts a user for a file name, and then reads the file name from the same line as the input prompt.

13. Write a program that reads in a real data set and calculates its median. Use allocatable arrays to hold the input data set.

ASCII and EBCDIC Coding Systems

Each character in FORTRAN is stored in one byte of memory, so there are 256 possible values for each character variable. The table shown below contains the characters corresponding to each possible decimal and binary value in both the ASCII and the EBCDIC coding systems. Where characters are blank, they either correspond to control characters or are not defined.

Decimal	Binary	Octal	Hexadecimal	ASCII Character	EBCDIC Character
0	00000000	0	0	NUL	NUL
. . .	. . .	. . .	. . .	. . .	. . .
32	00100000	40	20	Space	
33	00100001	41	21	!	
34	00100010	42	22	"	
35	00100011	43	23	#	
36	00100100	44	24	$	
37	00100101	45	25	%	
38	00100110	46	26	&	
39	00100111	47	27	'	
40	00101000	50	28	(	
41	00101001	51	29	)	
42	00101010	52	2A	*	
43	00101011	53	2B	+	
44	00101100	54	2C	,	
45	00101101	55	2D	-	

Decimal	Binary	Octal	Hexadecimal	ASCII Character	EBCDIC Character
46	00101110	56	2E	.	
47	00101111	57	2F	/	
48	00110000	60	30	0	
49	00110001	61	31	1	
50	00110010	62	32	2	
51	00110011	63	33	3	
52	00110100	64	34	4	
53	00110101	65	35	5	
54	00110110	66	36	6	
55	00110111	67	37	7	
56	00111000	70	38	8	
57	00111001	71	39	9	
58	00111010	72	3A	:	
59	00111011	73	3B	;	
60	00111100	74	3C	<	
61	00111101	75	3D	=	
62	00111110	76	3E	>	
63	00111111	77	3F	?	
64	01000000	100	40	@	Space
65	01000001	101	41	A	
66	01000010	102	42	B	
67	01000011	103	43	C	
68	01000100	104	44	D	
69	01000101	105	45	E	
70	01000110	106	46	F	
71	01000111	107	47	G	
72	01001000	110	48	H	
73	01001001	111	49	I	
74	01001010	112	4A	J	¢
75	01001011	113	4B	K	.
76	01001100	114	4C	L	<
77	01001101	115	4D	M	(
78	01001110	116	4E	N	+
79	01001111	117	4F	O		
80	01010000	120	50	P	&
81	01010001	121	51	Q	

Decimal	Binary	Octal	Hexadecimal	ASCII Character	EBCDIC Character
82	01010010	122	52	R	
83	01010011	123	53	S	
84	01010100	124	54	T	
85	01010101	125	55	U	
86	01010110	126	56	V	
87	01010111	127	57	W	
88	01011000	130	58	X	
89	01011001	131	59	Y	
90	01011010	132	5A	Z	!
91	01011011	133	5B	[	$
92	01011100	134	5C	\	*
93	01011101	135	5D	]	)
94	01011110	136	5E	^ (or ↑)	;
95	01011111	137	5F	_	¬
96	01100000	140	60	`	-
97	01100001	141	61	a	/
98	01100010	142	62	b	
99	01100011	143	63	c	
100	01100100	144	64	d	
101	01100101	145	65	e	
102	01100110	146	66	f	
103	01100111	147	67	g	
104	01101000	150	68	h	
105	01101001	151	69	i	
106	01101010	152	6A	j	
107	01101011	153	6B	k	,
108	01101100	154	6C	l	%
109	01101101	155	6D	m	_
110	01101110	156	6E	n	>
111	01101111	157	6F	o	?
112	01110000	160	70	p	
113	01110001	161	71	q	
114	01110010	162	72	r	
115	01110011	163	73	s	
116	01110100	164	74	t	
117	01110101	165	75	u	
118	01110110	166	76	v	

Decimal	Binary	Octal	Hexadecimal	ASCII Character	EBCDIC Character
119	01110111	167	77	w	
120	01111000	170	78	x	
121	01111001	171	79	y	
122	01111010	172	7A	z	:
123	01111011	173	7B	{	#
124	01111100	174	7C	|	@
125	01111101	175	7D	}	'
126	01111110	176	7E	~	=
127	01111111	177	7F	DEL	"
128	10000000	200	80		
129	10000001	201	81		a
130	100000010	202	82		b
131	100000011	203	83		c
132	100000100	204	84		d
133	100000101	205	85		e
134	100000110	206	86		f
135	100000111	207	87		g
136	100001000	210	88		h
137	100001001	211	89		i
. . .	. . .	. . .	. . .	. . .	. . .
145	10010001	221	91		j
146	10010010	222	92		k
147	10010011	223	93		l
148	10010100	224	94		m
149	10010101	225	95		n
150	10010110	226	96		o
151	10010111	227	97		p
152	10011000	230	98		q
153	10011001	231	99		r
. . .	. . .	. . .	. . .	. . .	. . .
162	10100010	242	A2		s
163	10100011	243	A3		t
164	10100100	244	A4		u
165	10100101	245	A5		v
166	10100110	246	A6		w
167	10100111	247	A7		x

Decimal	Binary	Octal	Hexadecimal	ASCII Character	EBCDIC Character
168	10101000	250	A8		y
169	10101001	251	A9		z
. . .	. . .	. . .	. . .	. . .	. . .
192	11000000	300	C0		}
193	11000001	301	C1		A
194	11000010	302	C2		B
195	11000011	303	C3		C
196	11000100	304	C4		D
197	11000101	305	C5		E
198	11000110	306	C6		F
199	11000111	307	C7		G
200	11001000	310	C8		H
201	11001001	311	C9		I
. . .	. . .	. . .	. . .	. . .	. . .
208	11010000	320	D0		}
209	11010001	321	D1		J
210	11010010	322	D2		K
211	11010011	323	D3		L
212	11010100	324	D4		M
213	11010101	325	D5		N
214	11010110	326	D6		O
215	11010111	327	D7		P
216	11011000	330	D8		Q
217	11011001	331	D9		R
. . .	. . .	. . .	. . .	. . .	. . .
224	11100000	340	E0	\	
225	11100001	341	E1		
226	11100010	342	E2		S
227	11100011	343	E3		T
228	11100100	344	E4		U
229	11100101	345	E5		V
230	11100110	346	E6		W
231	11100111	347	E7		X
232	11101000	350	E8		Y
233	11101001	351	E9		Z
. . .	. . .	. . .	. . .	. . .	. . .

Decimal	Binary	Octal	Hexadecimal	ASCII Character	EBCDIC Character
240	11110000	360	F0		0
241	11110001	361	F1		1
242	11110010	362	F2		2
243	11110011	363	F3		3
244	11110100	364	F4		4
245	11110101	365	F5		5
246	11110110	366	F6		6
247	11110111	367	F7		7
248	11111000	370	F8		8
249	11111001	371	F9		9
...	...	...	...	...	...
255	11111111	377	FF		

FORTRAN 77 Intrinsic Functions

This appendix describes the intrinsic functions built into the FORTRAN 77 language, and provides some suggestions for their proper use.

B.1 SPECIFIC VERSUS GENERIC INTRINSIC FUNCTIONS

Many common functions are built directly into the FORTRAN language. They are called *intrinsic functions*. There are two types of intrinsic functions: *specific functions* and *generic functions*. Specific functions require input data to be of a specific type, and produce output values of a specific type. By contrast, generic functions may take data of more than one type, and produce output values whose type depends on the type of the input data.

To illustrate this point, let's consider the specific function ALOG(X) and the generic function LOG(X). The specific function ALOG(X) requires that its input value X be of type **REAL,** and produces an output value of type **REAL**. If an input value of a type other than **REAL** is supplied to the function, the output of the function is undefined and varies from computer to computer. By contrast, the generic function LOG(X) accepts input values of types **REAL, DOUBLE PRECISION,** and **COMPLEX**, and produces a result of the same type as the input value.

FORTRAN compilers contain built-in routines for each specific function, but *do not* contain routines for generic functions. When a FORTRAN compiler encounters a generic function, it examines the arguments of the function, and calls the proper specific function to match the input arguments. For example, if the generic function LOG(X) is included in a program and X is double precision, the FORTRAN compiler will automatically include a call to the specific function DLOG(X) at that point. If X had been complex instead, the compiler would have included a call to the specific function CLOG(X).

If you have a choice between using a generic function and using a specific function for a particular application, you should normally use the generic function. If you use the generic function, it will be easier to modify the program later. For example, a program written in single-precision arithmetic could be converted to double precision without having to explicitly change every function within the program.

■
GOOD PROGRAMMING PRACTICE

Use generic functions rather than specific functions whenever possible to make your programs easier to modify.

The only time that a specific function is actually required is when the function is passed as a calling argument to another function or subroutine. When a specific function name is declared in an **INTRINSIC** statement and included as a calling argument to a subprogram, then a pointer to that function is passed to the subprogram. If the corresponding formal argument is used as a function within the subprogram, then when the subprogram is executed, the specific function in the calling argument list will be executed in place of the dummy function in the subprogram. Generic functions cannot be used in this manner, since there are no actual intrinsic routines corresponding to the generic function names.

The example shown below illustrates the use of a specific function as a calling argument in a subroutine call. The example finds a root of the function ALOG(X) between 0.1 and 10.0 using the subroutine ROOT developed in Chapter 10.

■
EXAMPLE B-1 *Passing a Specific Function to a Subroutine*   The specific function ALOG(X) computes the natural logarithm of X for any X > 0. A plot of the function ALOG(X) is shown in Figure B-1. As you can see, this function has a root at X = 1.

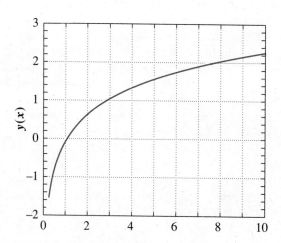

FIGURE B-1   Plot of the function $y(x) = \ln x$.

Suppose that we wish to find the roots of this function in the range $0.1 \le X \le 10.0$. We can find the roots of the function using the subroutine ROOT developed in Chapter 10. To use this subroutine, we must pass the name of the function ALOG as a command line argument in the call to subroutine ROOT, and we must declare the function ALOG in an **INTRINSIC** statement within the calling program. A program that performs these functions is shown in Figure B-2.

```
      PROGRAM INTRIN
C
C  Purpose:
C     To find a root of the specific intrinsic function
C     ALOG(), between the limits of 0.1 and 10.0.
C
C  Record of revisions:
C       Date        Programmer          Description of change
C       ====        ==========          =====================
C     05/04/93    S. J. Chapman         Original code
C
C  Intrinsic function declared:
C     ALOG - Natural logarithm
C
C  List of variables:
C     X1      -- Starting point to search for root
C     X2      -- Ending point to search for root
C     DX      -- Step size.
C     AROOT   -- Root (returned from subroutine ROOT)
C     IERROR  -- Error flag.
C
      IMPLICIT NONE
C
      REAL       ALOG, X1, X2, DX, AROOT
      INTEGER    IERROR
      INTRINSIC  ALOG
C
C     Set of calling parameters.
C
      X1 = 0.1
      X2 = 10.0
      DX = 0.5
C
C     Call ROOT to find a root.
C
      CALL ROOT ( ALOG, X1, X2, DX, AROOT, IERROR )
C
C     Display result.
C
      IF ( IERROR .EQ. 0 ) THEN
         WRITE (*,'(1X,A,F12.6)') 'Root found at ', AROOT
      ELSE
         WRITE (*,'(1X,A,I6)') ' Error: IERROR = ', IERROR
      END IF
      END
```

FIGURE B-2   Program to calculate the roots of the specific intrinsic function ALOG(X). This program illustrates the passing of intrinsic functions as arguments to subprograms.

When the program is executed, the result is

```
C:\BOOK\FORT>intrin
Root found at        .999994
```

This answer is correct to the accuracy specified in subroutine ROOT. ●

If the generic function LOG had been passed as a calling argument instead of the specific function ALOG, a compile-time error would have occurred.

B.2   MATHEMATICAL INTRINSIC FUNCTIONS

Table B-1 contains an alphabetical listing of the mathematical intrinsic functions included in FORTRAN 77. The table describes each function first by its generic name (if one exists), and then by the specific names associated with each data type. Note that sometimes a generic and specific function have the same name (e.g., the generic function SIN(X) has the same name as the specific function SIN(X)). In these cases, the difference between the generic function and the specific function are only important if the function is to be passed as a calling argument to a subprogram.

The meanings of the symbols used in the table are

X, Y	A value whose type is not specified.
RX, RY	Values of type REAL
IX, IY	Values of type INTEGER
DX, DY	Values of type DOUBLE PRECISION
CX, CY	Values of type COMPLEX
CR	Real portion of a complex value
CI	Imaginary part of a complex value
CHX, CHY	Values of type CHARACTER

TABLE B-1   Mathematical Functions

Generic Name	Specific Name	Function Type	Argument Type(s)	Description	Note
ABS(X)				Absolute value of X	
	ABS(RX)	REAL	REAL	$\lvert RX \rvert$	
	IABS(RX)	INTEGER	INTEGER	$\lvert IX \rvert$	
	DABS(DX)	DBLE	DBLE	$\lvert DX \rvert$	
	CABS(CX)	CMPL	CMPL	$\lvert CX \rvert = \sqrt{CR^2 + CI^2}$	

TABLE B-1   Continued

Generic Name	Specific Name	Function Type	Argument Type(s)	Description	Note
ACOS(X)				Inverse cosine of X for $(-1.0 \le X \le 1.0)$. The result is in *radians*, in the range $0 \le ACOS(X) \le \pi$	1
	ACOS(RX)	REAL	REAL	$\cos^{-1}(RX)$	
	DACOS(DX)	DBLE	DBLE	$\cos^{-1}(DX)$	
AINT(X)				Truncate X to a whole number	2
	AINT(RX)	REAL	REAL	Truncate RX to a whole number	
	DINT(DX)	DBLE	DBLE	Truncate DX to a whole number	
ANINT(X)				Round X to nearest whole number	
	ANINT(RX)	REAL	REAL	Round RX to nearest whole number (produces a REAL result)	
	DNINT(DX)	DBLE	DBLE	Round DX to nearest whole number (produces a DOUBLE PRECISION result)	
ASIN(X)				Inverse sine of X for $(-1.0 \le X \le 1.0)$. The result is in *radians*, in the range $-\dfrac{\pi}{2} \le ASIN(X) \le \dfrac{\pi}{2}$	1
	ASIN(RX)	REAL	REAL	$\sin^{-1}(RX)$	
	DASIN(DX)	DBLE	DBLE	$\sin^{-1}(DX)$	
ATAN(X)				Inverse tangent of X for any X. The result is in *radians*, in the range $-\dfrac{\pi}{2} \le ATAN(X) \le \dfrac{\pi}{2}$	
	ATAN(RX)	REAL	REAL	$\tan^{-1}(RX)$	
	DATAN(DX)	DBLE	DBLE	$\tan^{-1}(DX)$	

TABLE B-1   Continued

Generic Name	Specific Name	Function Type	Argument Type(s)	Description	Note
ATAN2(X,Y)				Inverse tangent of X/Y, valid in any quadrant. The result is in *radians*, in the range $-\pi < \text{ATAN2(X,Y)} \le \pi$	
	ATAN2(RX,RY)	REAL	REAL	$\tan^{-1}\left(\dfrac{RX}{RY}\right)$	
	DATAN2(DX,DY)	DBLE	DBLE	$\tan^{-1}\left(\dfrac{DX}{DY}\right)$	
(None)	CONJG(CX)	CMPL	CMPL	Conjugate of CX: If CX = CR + i CI, then CONJG(CX) = CR − i CI	
(None)	DPROD(RX,RY)	DBLE	REAL	The DOUBLE PRECISION product of two single-precision numbers.	
COS(X)				cosine of X (X must be in *radians*)	
	COS(RX)	REAL	REAL	cos (RX)	
	DCOS(DX)	DBLE	DBLE	cos (DX)	
	CCOS(CX)	CMPL	CMPL	cos (CX)	
COSH(X)				Hyperbolic cosine of X	
	COSH(RX)	REAL	REAL	cosh (RX)	
	DCOSH(DX)	DBLE	DBLE	cosh (DX)	
DIM(X,Y)				X − (minimum of X and Y)	
	DIM(RX,RY)	REAL	REAL	RX − (minimum of RX and RY)	
	IDIM(IX,IY)	INTEGER	INTEGER	IX − (minimum of IX and IY)	
	DDIM(DX,DY)	DBLE	DBLE	DX − (minimum of DX and DY)	
EXP(X)				e^X	
	EXP(RX)	REAL	REAL	e^{RX}	
	DEXP(DX)	DBLE	DBLE	e^{DX}	
	CEXP(CX)	CMPL	CMPL	e^{CX}	

TABLE B-1   Continued

Generic Name	Specific Name	Function Type	Argument Type(s)	Description	Note
LOG(X)				$\log_e(x)$ or $\ln(x)$ for $X \geq 0$	
	ALOG(RX)	REAL	REAL	$\log_e$ (RX)	
	DLOG(DX)	DBLE	DBLE	$\log_e$ (DX)	
	CLOG(CX)	CMPL	CMPL	$\log_e$ (CX)	
LOG10(X)				$\log_{10}(x)$ for $X \geq 0$	
	ALOG10(RX)	REAL	REAL	$\log_{10}$ (RX)	
	DLOG10(DX)	DBLE	DBLE	$\log_{10}$ (DX)	
MAX(X,Y,...)				Maximum of X, Y, ... (Supports any number of arguments)	
	AMAX0(IX,IY,...)	REAL	INTEGER	Maximum of IX, IY, ... (output converted from INTEGER to REAL)	
	AMAX1(RX,RY,...)	REAL	REAL	Maximum of RX, RY, ...	
	MAX0(IX,IY,...)	INTEGER	INTEGER	Maximum of IX, IY, ...	
	MAX1(RX,RY,...)	INTEGER	REAL	Maximum of RX, RY, ... (output converted from REAL to INTEGER)	
	DMAX1(RX,RY,...)	DBLE	DBLE	Maximum of DX, DY, ...	
MIN(X,Y,...)				Minimum of X, Y, ... (Supports any number of arguments)	
	AMIN0(IX,IY,...)	REAL	INTEGER	Minimum of IX, IY, ... (output converted from INTEGER to REAL)	
	AMIN1(RX,RY,...)	REAL	REAL	Minimum of RX, RY, ...	
	MIN0(IX,IY,...)	INTEGER	INTEGER	Minimum of IX, IY, ...	
	MIN1(RX,RY,...)	INTEGER	REAL	Minimum of RX, RY, ... (output converted from REAL to INTEGER)	
	DMIN1(RX,RY,...)	DBLE	DBLE	Minimum of DX, DY, ...	

TABLE B-1   Continued

Generic Name	Specific Name	Function Type	Argument Type(s)	Description	Note
MOD(X,Y)				Remainder or modulo function: X modulo Y	
	AMOD(RX,RY)	REAL	REAL	RX modulo RY	
	MOD(IX,IY)	INTEGER	INTEGER	IX modulo IY	
	DMOD(DX,DY)	DBLE	DBLE	DX modulo DY	
SIGN(X,Y)				Transfer sign of Y to $\lvert X \rvert$	3
	SIGN(RX,RY)	REAL	REAL	Transfer sign of RY to $\lvert IX \rvert$	
	ISIGN(IX,IY)	INTEGER	INTEGER	Transfer sign of IY to $\lvert IX \rvert$	
	DSIGN(DX,DY)	DBLE	DBLE	Transfer sign of DY to $\lvert DX \rvert$	
SIN(X)				sine of X (X must be in *radians*)	
	SIN(RX)	REAL	REAL	sin (RX)	
	DSIN(DX)	DBLE	DBLE	sin (DX)	
	CSIN(CX)	CMPL	CMPL	sin (CX)	
SINH(X)				Hyperbolic sine of X	
	SINH(RX)	REAL	REAL	sinh (RX)	
	DSINH(DX)	DBLE	DBLE	sinh (DX)	
SQRT(X)				Square root of X for $X \geq 0$	
	SQRT(RX)	REAL	REAL	$\sqrt{RX}$	
	DSQRT(DX)	DBLE	DBLE	$\sqrt{DX}$	
	CSQRT(CX)	CMPL	CMPL	$\sqrt{CX}$	
TAN(X)				tangent of X (X must be in *radians*)	
	TAN(RX)	REAL	REAL	tan (RX)	
	DTAN(DX)	DBLE	DBLE	tan (DX)	

TABLE B-1 Continued

Generic Name	Specific Name	Function Type	Argument Type(s)	Description	Note
TANH(X)				Hyperbolic tangent of X	
	TANH(RX)	REAL	REAL	tanh (RX)	
	DTANH(DX)	DBLE	DBLE	tanh (DX)	

1. If an argument is passed to this function that is outside the defined range of the function, then a run-time error will occur. For example, ACOS(-1.2) will produce a run-time error.
2. The AINT function truncates a number to its integer portion without regard to sign, and outputs it as a REAL value. For example, AINT(2.2) is equal to 2.0, and AINT(-2.2) is equal to -2.0.
3. The SIGN function applies the sign of value Y to the magnitude of value X. For example, SIGN($-45.2,2.12$) is 45.2, and SIGN($-45.2,-100.34$) is -45.2.

B.3 TYPE CONVERSION INTRINSIC FUNCTIONS

Table B-2 contains an alphabetical listing of the intrinsic functions that convert values from one type to another one. The table describes each function first by its generic name, and then by the specific names associated with different data types. The meanings of the symbols in the table are the same as those in Table B-1.

TABLE B-2 Table of Type Conversion Functions

Generic Name	Specific Name	Function Type	Argument Type(s)	Description	Note
(None)	AIMAG(CX)	REAL	CMPL	Convert imaginary part of CX to type REAL	
CMPLX(X)		CMPL	REAL or DBLE	Convert X to COMPLEX, placing X in the real part of the complex number: CX = X + i 0	

TABLE B-2   Continued

Generic Name	Specific Name	Function Type	Argument Type(s)	Description	Note
CMPLX(X,Y)		CMPL	REAL or DBLE	Convert X and Y to COMPLEX, placing X in the real part of the complex number and Y in the imaginary part of the complex number: CX = X + i Y	
DBLE(X)		DBLE	INTEGER REAL, or CMPL	Convert X to DOUBLE PRECISION	
INT(X)				Truncate X to an integer	1
	IFIX(RX)	INTEGER	REAL	Truncate RX to an integer	
	IDINT(DX)	INTEGER	DBLE	Truncate DX to an integer	
NINT(X)				Round X to nearest integer	
	NINT(RX)	INTEGER	REAL	Round RX to nearest integer	
	IDNINT(DX)	INTEGER	DBLE	Round DX to nearest integer	
REAL(X)				Convert X to type REAL	
	FLOAT(IX)	REAL	INTEGER	Convert IX to type REAL	
	SNGL(IX)	REAL	DBLE	Convert DX to type REAL	
	REAL(CX)	REAL	CMPL	Convert real part of CX to type REAL	

1. The INT function truncates a number to its integer portion without regard to sign, and outputs it as an INTEGER value. For example, INT(2.2) is equal to 2, and INT(−2.2) is equal to −2.

B.4   CHARACTER INTRINSIC FUNCTIONS

Table B-3 contains an alphabetical listing of the character intrinsic functions included in FORTRAN 77. The meanings of the symbols in the table are the same as those in Table B-1. Note that the character functions only have specific names, not generic names. The use of these functions is described in Chapter 7.

TABLE B-3   Character Intrinsic Functions

Specific Name	Function Type	Argument Type(s)	Description	Note
CHAR(IX)	CHARACTER	INTEGER	The result of this function is the character in the IXth position in the collating sequence for the character set being used on the computer.	1
ICHAR(CHX)	INTEGER	CHARACTER	The result of this function is the collating position of character CHX in the character set being used on the computer.	2
INDEX(CHX,CHY)	INTEGER	CHARACTER	Starting position of substring CHY within string CHX. For example, the result of INDEX('TEST','ST') = 3.	
LEN(CHX)	INTEGER	CHARACTER	Length of character string CHX.	3
LGE(CHX,CHY)	LOGICAL	CHARACTER	Function is TRUE if CHX $\geq$ CHY according to the ASCII collating sequence	4
LGT(CHX,CHY)	LOGICAL	CHARACTER	Function is TRUE if CHX > CHY according to the ASCII collating sequence	4
LLE(CHX,CHY)	LOGICAL	CHARACTER	Function is TRUE if CHX $\leq$ CHY according to the ASCII collating sequence	4

TABLE B-3   Continued

Specific Name	Function Type	Argument Type(s)	Description	Note
LLT(CHX,CHY)	LOGICAL	CHARACTER	Function is TRUE if CHX < CHY according to the ASCII collating sequence	4

1. The result of this function depends on the character set being used on a particular computer. For example, the function CHAR(80) produces a 'P' on a machine using the ASCII collating sequence, and an '&' on a machine using the EBCDIC collating sequence.

2. The result of this function depends on the character set being used on a particular computer. For example, the function ICHAR('A') produces the integer 65 on a machine using the ASCII collating sequence, and the integer 193 on a machine using the EBCDIC collating sequence.

3. The function LEN returns the *declared length* of a character string, not the actual number of characters stored in it. In the following example, the function LEN will return a value of 80, not a value of 3.

```
CHARACTER*80 STRING
STRING = 'ABC'
LENSTR = LEN(STRING)
```

4. This function produces the same result regardless of the collating sequence used on a particular computer.

Bit Manipulation Functions

Standard FORTRAN 77 does not include intrinsic functions to manipulate the individual bits of a word. This lack is a significant problem, since many applications require that a program check the status of individual bits to determine how to process a data set. For example, if we are processing data read in from a hardware device of some sort, there will often be a *status word* included in the data set. Each bit in the status word serves as a flag for a particular event. The program using the data will have to check individual bits of the status word to determine whether or not particular events have occurred.

Since bit manipulation functions are very important, each compiler vendor provided its own set of functions to perform these manipulations. Unfortunately, these functions were not always compatible with each other, since there was no standard. The result was that FORTRAN programs were less portable, since moving a program from a computer of one type to a computer of another type might involve rewriting all bit-manipulation functions.

This was an intolerable situation for any large user who maintained many different types of computers, and one of the largest users of all did something about it. The U.S. military defined a standard set of bit manipulation functions and published it in MIL-STD 1753. It then required all vendors selling to the military to support those functions. The result is that we now have a standard set of functions that are supported by almost all FORTRAN 77 compilers, even though they are not a part of the actual standard. In addition, these functions have been incorporated into the FORTRAN 90 standard, so all code employing them will continue to work in the future.

There are nine standard bit manipulation intrinsic functions. They fall into three basic groups.

1. Functions that set, clear, and test individual bits within a word
2. Functions that perform logical operations on individual bits within a word
3. Functions that shift the bits around within a word

The functions are shown in Table C-1.

TABLE C-1   Bit Manipulation Intrinsic Functions

Specific Name	Function Type	Argument Type(s)	Description	Note
Functions that Set, Clear, and Test Bits				
IBCLR(IX,IPOS)	INTEGER	INTEGER	Clear bit IPOS in word IX to 0. Note that IPOS must be a number between 1 and the maximum number of bits in a word in the particular computer.	1
IBSET(IX,IPOS)	INTEGER	INTEGER	Set bit IPOS in word IX to 1. Note that IPOS must be a number between 1 and the maximum number of bits in a word in the particular computer.	1
BTEST(IX,IPOS)	LOGICAL	INTEGER	Check the status of bit IPOS in word IX. If the bit is 1, then the function returns TRUE. If the bit is 0, then the function returns FALSE.	1
Logical Operations on Bits				
IAND(IX,IY)	INTEGER	INTEGER	Bit-by-bit logical AND of all bits in IX and IY	2
IEOR(IX,IY)	INTEGER	INTEGER	Bit-by-bit logical Exclusive OR of all bits in IX and IY	3
IOR(IX,IY)	INTEGER	INTEGER	Bit-by-bit logical Inclusive OR of all bits in IX and IY	4
NOT(IX)	INTEGER	INTEGER	Bit-by-bit logical NOT of all bits in IX	5
Functions that Shift Bits				
ISHFT(IX,ISH)	INTEGER	INTEGER	The bits in word IX are shifted left by ISH bits. (If ISH is negative, the bits are shifted right.) Zeros are shifted in from the other end.	
ISHFTC(IX,ISH)	INTEGER	INTEGER	ISHFTC is a *circular* shift. The bits in word IX are shifted left by ISH bits. The bits that are shifted off of the left end of the word reappear at the right end of the word. (If ISH is negative, the bits are shifted right.)	

TABLE C-1 Continued

1. In the above functions, IPOS is the position of a bit within a word. A value of 1 corresponds to the least significant bit of a word (2^0), a value of 2 corresponds to the next least significant bit of the word (2^1), and so on up to the maximum number of bits in the word.

2. The function IAND implements the logical AND on a bit-by-bit basis according to the following truth table.

IX	0	0	1	1
IY	0	1	0	1
IAND(IX,IY)	0	0	0	1

3. The function IEOR implements the logical exclusive OR on a bit-by-bit basis according to the following truth table.

IX	0	0	1	1
IY	0	1	0	1
IEOR(IX,IY)	0	1	1	0

4. The function IOR implements the logical inclusive OR on a bit-by-bit basis according to the following truth table.

IX	0	0	1	1
IY	0	1	0	1
IOR(IX,IY)	0	1	1	1

5. The function NOT implements the logical NOT on a bit-by-bit basis according to the following truth table.

IX	0	1
NOT(IX)	1	0

To illustrate the use of these functions, we will consider two simplified 8-bit integers IX and IY (integers will have 32 or more bits on most computers, but the functions will still work as described below). Suppose that integers IX and IY have the values shown in Table C-2. Then the output of each of the bit manipulation functions will be as shown in the table. Make sure that you understand the reasons that each function produces the result shown.

TABLE C-2   Sample Output from Manipulation Intrinsic Functions

Function	IX	IY	IPOS	Result
IBCLR(IX,IPOS)	11111111		3	11111011
IBSET(IX,IPOS)	00000000		7	01000000
BTEST(IX,IPOS)	10000010		2	.TRUE.
IAND(IX,IY)	10101100	10010011		10000000
IEOR(IX,IY)	10101100	10010011		00111111
IOR(IX,IY)	10101100	10010011		10111111
NOT(IX)	10101100			01010011
ISHFT(IX,2)	10101100			10110000
ISHFT(IX,−2)	10101100			00101011
ISHFTC(IX,2)	10101100			10110010

BOOKLIB Routine Descriptions

The BOOKLIB library contains a number of useful subroutines and functions that are intended to be used with this book. The library may be used to teach the general principles of FORTRAN library use. These routines are distributed on a disk along with the Instructors Manual that accompanies this book. Your instructor will probably have generated a library containing them on the computer that you are using in this course.

The routines in BOOKLIB are indexed by name and by function in Table D-1.

TABLE D-1 Routines Included in Library BOOKLIB

Name	*Function*	*Page*
AVESD	Calculate average and standard deviation of a data set	A-25
CSIMUL	Solve a system of simultaneous equations (complex)	A-57
DDERIV	Calculate derivative of a user-supplied function (double precision)	A-26
DERIV	Calculate derivative of a user-supplied function	A-26
DFT	Calculate discrete Fourier transform from its definition	A-27
DLSQFT	Perform a least-squares fit of an input data set to the nth-order polynomial (double precision)	A-43
DMINV	Invert an $N \times N$ matrix using Gaussian elimination and the maximum pivot technique (double precision)	A-45
DMMADD	Add two-dimensional matrices A and B (double precision)	A-46
DMMMUL	Multiply two-dimensional matrices A and B (double precision)	A-47
DMMSUB	Subtract two-dimensional matrices A and B (double precision)	A-46
DSIMUL	Solve a system of simultaneous equations (double precision)	A-57
FFT	Calculate fast discrete Fourier transform	A-28
GRAN0	Gaussian random number generator (subroutine)	A-29
GRAN1	Gaussian random number generator (function)	A-29
HIST	Print a histogram of an input data set on a line printer	A-30
HSORTC	Sort a character array into ascending order using the heapsort algorithm	A-32

TABLE D-1   Continued

Name	Function	Page
HSORTI	Sort an integer array into ascending order using the heapsort algorithm	A-32
HSORTR	Sort a real array into ascending order using the heapsort algorithm	A-32
HSRTI2	Sort an integer array into ascending order while carrying along a second array, using the heapsort algorithm	A-33
HSRTR2	Sort a real array into ascending order while carrying along a second array, using the heapsort algorithm	A-33
IDFT	Calculate inverse discrete Fourier transform from its definition	A-35
IFFT	Calculate inverse fast discrete Fourier transform	A-36
IMAX	Return the magnitude and location of the maximum value in an integer array	A-37
IMIN	Return the magnitude and location of the minimum value in an integer array	A-37
INTEG	Integrate a user-supplied function $f(x)$ between points x_1 and x_2 using rectangles of width Δx	A-38
INTEGD	Integrate a descrete function specified by a series of (x, y) values between points x_1 and x_2, where x_1 and x_2 both lie within the range of input values in the (x, y) pairs	A-39
INTERP	Linearly interpolate the value y_0 at position x_0, given a set of (x, y) measurements organized in increasing order of x	A-40
LCASE	Shift a character string to lowercase	A-41
LENU	Return the position of the last non-blank character in a string	A-42
LSQFT	Perform a least squares fit of an input data set to the nth-order polynomial	A-43
MEDIAN	Calculate the median of a real input data set	A-44
MINV	Invert an N $\times$ N matrix using Gaussian elimination and the maximum pivot technique	A-45
MMADD	Add two-dimensional matrices A and B	A-46
MMMUL	Multiply two-dimensional matrices A and B	A-47
MMSUB	Subtract two-dimensional matrices A and B	A-46
NXTMUL	Calculate the next power of a base above a specific number	A-49
PLOT	Print a line printer plot of a function	A-50
PLOTXY	Print a line printer cross-plot of a set of (x, y) data points	A-51
RE2CHR	Convert a real value into a 13-character string, with the number printed in as readable a format as possible considering its range	A-54
RMAX	Return the magnitude and location of the maximum value in a real array	A-54
RMIN	Return the magnitude and location of the minimum value in a real array	A-54
RAN0	Uniform random number generator (subroutine)	A-55
RAN1	Uniform random number generator (function)	A-55
SEED	Set the starting point for the pseudorandom sequences generated by routines RAN0, RAN1, GRAN0, and GRAN1	A-56
SIMUL	Solve a system of simultaneous equations	A-57

TABLE D-1 Continued

Name	Function	Page
SINC	Calculate the sinc function: sinc $(x) = \sin(x)/x$	A-58
SSORTC	Sort a character array into ascending order using the selection sort algorithm	A-59
SSORTI	Sort an integer array into ascending order using the selection sort algorithm	A-59
SSORTR	Sort a real array into ascending order using the selection sort algorithm	A-59
UCASE	Shift a character string to uppercase	A-60

AVESD

Purpose

To calculate the average and standard deviation of an input data set.

Usage

```
CALL AVESD ( RA, N, AVE, SD, IERROR )
```

Arguments

Name	Type	Dim	I/O	Description
RA	R	N	I	Data set to analyze
N	I		I	Number of data points
AVE	R		O	Average of data set
SD	R		O	Standard deviation of data set
IERROR	I		O	Error flag: 0 = No error
				1 = SD invalid (N = 1)
				2 = AVE and SD invalid (N < 1)

Algorithm:

This subroutine calculates the average and standard deviation according to the formulas:

$$\bar{x} = \frac{1}{N}\sum_{i=1}^{N} x_i$$

and

$$\sigma = \sqrt{\frac{N\sum_{i=1}^{N} x_i^2 - \left(\sum_{i=1}^{N} x_i\right)^2}{N(N-1)}}$$

Example

This example calculates average and standard deviation of a small data set.

```
        REAL RA(6)
        DATA RA / 1., 4., 1., -4., 0., 2. /
        CALL AVESD ( RA, 6, AVE, SD, IERROR )
        WRITE (*,1000) AVE, SD
   1000 FORMAT (' AVE = ', F10.4,'    SD = ',F10.4)
```

Result

```
   AVE =      .6667    SD =      2.6583
```

DERIV/DDERIV (SINGLE/DOUBLE PRECISION)

Purpose

To calculate the derivative of a function $f(x)$ at point x_0 using step size Δx. If $\Delta x = 0.0$, then take the derivative with as much accuracy as possible. This subroutine expects the function $f(x)$ to be passed as a calling argument.

Usage

```
     CALL DERIV ( F, X0, DX, DFDX, IERROR )
```

Arguments

Name	Type	Dim	I/O	Description
F	R/D FUN		I	Function to take derivative of
X0	R/D		I	Point at which to take derivative
DX	R/D		I/O	Step size to use when taking derivative (≥ 0.0). If DX = 0.0, then the routine calculates an optimal step size, and returns that step size in this variable.
DFDX	R/D		O	The derivative $df(x)/dx$
IERROR	I		O	Error flag: 0 = No error
				1 = DX < 0.

Algorithm

This subroutine calculates the derivative using the central difference method:

$$\frac{d}{dx}f(x) \approx \frac{f(x + \Delta x/2) - f(x - \Delta x/2)}{\Delta x}$$

The subroutine uses the user-specified Δx if it is > 0. Otherwise, it tries values of $\Delta x = 0.1, 0.01$, etc. until roundoff errors start to dominate in the solution. If Δx is zero, then the actual Δx used to calculate the derivative is returned in variable DX.

Example

This example calculates derivative of function sin (x) at $x_0 = 1.0$ using the default step size.

```
      INTRINSIC SIN
      INTEGER ERROR
      REAL    DFDX, DX
      CALL DERIV ( SIN, 1.0, DX, DFDX, ERROR )
      WRITE (*,1000) DFDX
 1000 FORMAT (' The derivative of SIN(X) at X0 = 1.0 is: ', F10.6)
      WRITE (*,1010) COS(1.0)
 1010 FORMAT (' The theoretical value is:                ', F10.6)
      WRITE (*,1020) DX
 1020 FORMAT (' The step size used is:                   ', F10.6)
```

Result

```
The derivative of SIN(X) at X0 = 1.0 is:    .540316
The theoretical value is:                   .540302
The step size used is:                      .001000
```

DFT

Purpose

To perform a discrete Fourier transform on complex array CIN with the result returned in array COUT. This routine calculates the DFT directly from its definition.

Usage

```
CALL DFT ( CIN, COUT, NPTS )
```

Arguments

Name	Type	Dim	I/O	Description
CIN	**C**	**NPTS**	**I**	Input: time series to analyze
COUT	**C**	**NPTS**	**O**	Output: frequency spectrum of data set
NPTS	**I**		**I**	Number of data points

Algorithm

This subroutine calculates the DFT directly from its definition. It is very slow compared to subroutine FFT for large arrays of data. Unlike subroutine FFT, it does not require that the number of input points be a power of 2. If there are N input values, t_k is the kth value in the input time sequence, and F_n is the nth component in the output frequency spectrum, then

$$F_n = \sum_{k=0}^{N-1} t_k\, e^{-2\pi i k n / N}$$

WARNING: This routine is very slow for large array sizes. It is included in the library to support homework problems only. For real work, use subroutine FFT instead.

Example

This example calculates the frequency spectrum of a 16-point complex data set consisting of all (1.0, 0.0). Because this data set is constant, the peak of the frequency spectrum of the data should be 0 Hz (DC).

```
      COMPLEX CIN(16), COUT(16)
      DATA CIN / 16*(1.0,0.0)/
      CALL DFT ( CIN, COUT, 16 )
      WRITE (*,1000) (I,COUT(I), I=1, 16)
 1000 FORMAT (' COUT(',I2,') = (',F10.4,',',F10.4,')')
```

Result

```
CARR( 1) = (  16.0000,    .0000)  CARR( 9) = (    .0000,    .0000)
CARR( 2) = (    .0000,    .0000)  CARR(10) = (    .0000,    .0000)
CARR( 3) = (    .0000,    .0000)  CARR(11) = (    .0000,    .0000)
CARR( 4) = (    .0000,    .0000)  CARR(12) = (    .0000,    .0000)
CARR( 5) = (    .0000,    .0000)  CARR(13) = (    .0000,    .0000)
CARR( 6) = (    .0000,    .0000)  CARR(14) = (    .0000,    .0000)
CARR( 7) = (    .0000,    .0000)  CARR(15) = (    .0000,    .0000)
CARR( 8) = (    .0000,    .0000)  CARR(16) = (    .0000,    .0000)
```

FFT

Purpose

To perform an in-place fast DFT on complex array CARR. The size of the data set in array CARR must be a power of 2 (32, 64, 128, etc., up to 65,536). Before the call to FFT, array CARR will contain the time sequence to analyze. After the call to FFT, array CARR will contain the frequency spectrum of the data.

Usage

```
      CALL FFT ( CARR, NFFT, IERROR )
```

Arguments

Name	Type	Dim	I/O	Description
CARR	C	NFFT	I/O	Input: time series to analyze
				Output: frequency spectrum of data set
NFFT	I		I	Number of data points (must be a power of 2)
IERROR	I		O	Error flag: 0 = No error
				1 = NFFT not a power of 2

Algorithm

This subroutine employs a Radix 2, in-place, decimation in frequency algorithm. For details, see Oppenheim and Shaffer, *Digital Signal Processing,* Prentice-Hall, 1975. If there are N input values, t_k is the kth value in the input time sequence, and F_n is the nth component in the output frequency spectrum, then

$$F_n = \sum_{k=0}^{N-1} t_k e^{-2\pi i k n/N}$$

Example

This example calculates the frequency spectrum of a 16-point complex data set consisting of all (1.0, 0.0). Because this data set is constant, the peak of the frequency spectrum of the data should be 0 Hz (DC).

```
      COMPLEX CARR(16)
      DATA CARR / 16*(1.0,0.0)/
      CALL FFT ( CARR, 16, IERROR )
      WRITE (*,1000) (I,CARR(I), I=1, 16)
 1000 FORMAT (' CARR(',I2,') = (',F10.4,',',F10.4,')')
```

Result

```
CARR( 1) = (  16.0000,    .0000)  CARR( 9) = (    .0000,    .0000)
CARR( 2) = (    .0000,    .0000)  CARR(10) = (    .0000,    .0000)
CARR( 3) = (    .0000,    .0000)  CARR(11) = (    .0000,    .0000)
CARR( 4) = (    .0000,    .0000)  CARR(12) = (    .0000,    .0000)
CARR( 5) = (    .0000,    .0000)  CARR(13) = (    .0000,    .0000)
CARR( 6) = (    .0000,    .0000)  CARR(14) = (    .0000,    .0000)
CARR( 7) = (    .0000,    .0000)  CARR(15) = (    .0000,    .0000)
CARR( 8) = (    .0000,    .0000)  CARR(16) = (    .0000,    .0000)
```

GRAN0/GRAN1 (Subroutine/REAL Function)

Purpose

These routines generate a sequence of Gaussian (or normal) pseudorandom numbers with a mean of 0 and a standard deviation of 1. Both routines perform the same function: GRAN0 is a subroutine, and GRAN1 is a real function.

Usage

```
CALL GRAN0 ( VALUE )
VALUE = GRAN1()
```

Arguments

Name	Type	Dim	I/O	Description
VALUE	**R**		**O**	A value in the random number sequence
GRAN1	**R**		**O**	Function: GRAN1 returns a value in the random number sequence

Algorithm

Subroutine GRAN0 and function GRAN1 generate Gaussian or normal pseudoran-dom number sequences with a mean of 0 and a standard deviation of 1. One value in the sequence is returned for each call to the routines. The sequence of numbers will be the same every time a program is run with a given seed value. If it is important to vary the random sequence generated in different runs of a program, use subroutine SEED to change the starting value for the sequence.

Example

This example uses function GRAN1 to generate 20 random numbers with a normal distribution.

```
      REAL GRAN1
      CALL SEED(156977)
      WRITE (*,*) 'Normal distribution random number sequence:'
      DO 10 I = 1, 4
         WRITE (*,1000) GRAN1(), GRAN1(), GRAN1(), GRAN1(), GRAN1()
1000     FORMAT (1X,5F10.6)
   10 CONTINUE
```

Result

```
      Normal distribution random number sequence:
       -.790328  -.581786  -.791403  1.378180  1.186708
      -2.622262  -.493331   .308717   .321949   .396289
      -1.079518   .264666  -.192846   .359310   .151070
       1.578430 -1.048197   .191992  1.298939   .686792
```

HIST

Purpose

Subroutine to print a histogram of an input data set on a line printer.

Usage:

```
CALL HIST (DATA1, NPTS, NBINS, MINBIN, MAXBIN, DEFALT, LU, IERROR)
```

Arguments

Name	Type	Dim	I/O	Description
DATA1	R	NPTS	I	Data set to analyze
NPTS	I		I	Number of points in input data set
NBINS	I		I	Number of bins to accumulate statistics in. The range is $1 \leq NBINS \leq 100$, with a default value of 20.
MINBIN	R		I	Value of the smallest bin in the histogram. The default value is the smallest number in the data set.
MAXBIN	R		I	Value of the largest bin in the histogram. The default value is the largest number in the data set.
DEFALT	L		I	If TRUE, default choice of bins.
LU	I		I	Logical unit to print histogram on.
IERROR	I		O	Error flag: 0 = No error 1 = Too many bins requested (>100) 2 = Too few bins requested (<1) 3 = MAXBIN = MINBIN. These values must differ.

Algorithm

This subroutine calculates the range of values associated with each bin, and then accumulates statistics on the input data set. It then prints the resulting histogram on the device specified by logical unit LU.

Example

This example uses function GRAN1 to generate 10,000 random numbers with a normal distribution, and then plots a histogram of the data using subroutine HIST. Note that the values of NBINS, MINBIN, and MAXBIN are defaulted.

```
      REAL GRAN1, DATA1(10000)
      INTEGER NBINS, MINBIN, MAXBIN
      DO 10 I = 1, 10000
         DATA1(I) = GRAN1()
10    CONTINUE
      CALL HIST (DATA1, 10000, NBINS, MINBIN, MAXBIN, .TRUE., 6, IERROR )
```

Result

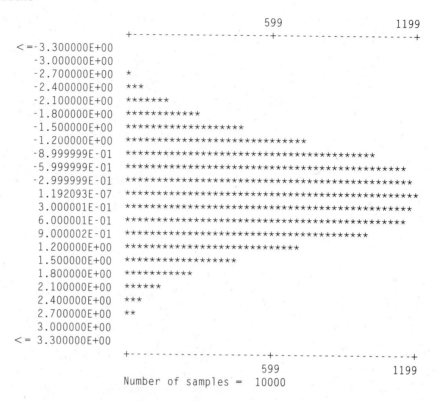

```
                                                 599                    1199
                            +---------------------+--------------------+
  < =-3.300000E+00
    -3.000000E+00
    -2.700000E+00          *
    -2.400000E+00          ***
    -2.100000E+00          *******
    -1.800000E+00          ************
    -1.500000E+00          ******************
    -1.200000E+00          ****************************
    -8.999999E-01          ******************************************
    -5.999999E-01          **********************************************
    -2.999999E-01          ***********************************************
     1.192093E-07          *************************************************
     3.000001E-01          **********************************************
     6.000001E-01          *********************************************
     9.000002E-01          **************************************
     1.200000E+00          ****************************
     1.500000E+00          ******************
     1.800000E+00          ************
     2.100000E+00          ******
     2.400000E+00          ***
     2.700000E+00          **
     3.000000E+00
  < = 3.300000E+00
                            +---------------------+--------------------+
                                                 599                    1199
                            Number of samples =   10000
```

HSORTI/HSORTR/HSORTC (INTEGER/REAL/CHARACTER)

Purpose:

To sort an array into ascending order using the heapsort algorithm.

Usage

```
CALL HSORTI ( IARRAY, N, IERROR )
CALL HSORTR ( RARRAY, N, IERROR )
CALL HSORTC ( CARRAY, N, IERROR )
```

Arguments

Name	Type	Dim	I/O	Description
IARRAY	I	N	I/O	Integer array
RARRAY	R/D	N	I/O	Real array
CARRAY	CHAR	N	I/O	Character array
N	I		I	Number of elements in array
IERROR	I		O	Error flag: 0 = No error
				1 = N <= 0

Algorithm

These subroutines sort arrays into ascending order using the heapsort algorithm. This algorithm is much more efficient than the selection sort algorithm. It should be used instead of the selection sort whenever arrays of any size are to be sorted.

Example

This example declares an integer array IARRAY and initializes with 15 values. It uses subroutine HSORTI to sort the array into ascending order.

```
      INTEGER IARRAY(15), N, IERROR
      DATA N / 15 /
      DATA IARRAY / -100,    0,  -20,    1,  -20,
     *               90, -123,  602,    5,   17,
     *               91,   -4,    0,   37,  -11 /
      WRITE (*,*) ' IARRAY before sorting: '
      WRITE (*,1000) IARRAY
 1000 FORMAT (3X,5I6)
      CALL HSORTI ( IARRAY, N, IERROR )
      WRITE (*,*) ' IARRAY after sorting: '
      WRITE (*,1000) IARRAY
```

Result

```
IARRAY before sorting:
  -100     0   -20     1   -20
    90  -123   602     5    17
    91    -4     0    37   -11
IARRAY after sorting:
  -123  -100   -20   -20   -11
    -4     0     0     1     5
    17    37    90    91   602
```

HSRTI2/HSRTR2 (INTEGER/REAL)

Purpose

To sort an array into ascending order while carrying along a second array, using the heapsort algorithm.

Usage

```
CALL HSRTI2 ( IAR1, IAR2, N, IERROR )
CALL HSRTR2 ( RAR1, RAR2, N, IERROR )
```

Arguments

Name	Type	Dim	I/O	Description
IARR1	I	N	I/O	Integer array to sort
IARR2	I	N	I/O	Integer array carry along
RARR1	R/D	N	I/O	Real array to sort
RARR2	R/D	N	I/O	Real array to carry along
N	I		I	Number of elements in array
IERROR	I		O	Error flag: 0 = No error
				1 = N < = 0

Algorithm

These subroutines sort arrays into ascending order using the heapsort algorithm, and carry along a second array. For example, if IARR1(I) is moved to the top of array IARR1, then IARR2(I) is moved to the top of array IARR2. These routines permit a user to sort the contents of one array according to the values in another one.

Example

This example declares two integer arrays IARRAY and IPOINT. It initializes IAR-RAY with 15 arbitrary values, and IPOINT with the numbers 1 through 15. After sorting the arrays with subroutine HSRTI2, the values in IPOINT are pointers to the original locations of the values in IARRAY.

```
      INTEGER IARRAY(15), IPOINT(15), N, IERROR
      DATA N / 15 /, IARRAY / -100,    0,  -20,    1,  -20,
     *                         90, -123,  602,    5,   17,
     *                         91,   -4,    0,   37,  -11 /
      DATA IPOINT / 1, 2, 3, 4, 5, 6, 7, 8, 9, 10, 11, 12, 13, 14, 15 /
      CALL HSRTI2 ( IARRAY, IPOINT, N, IERROR )
      WRITE (*,*) ' Sorted array and original locations: '
      WRITE (*,1000) (IARRAY(I), IPOINT(I), I = 1, 15)
 1000 FORMAT (3X,2I6,8X,2I6,8X,2I6)
```

Result

```
      Sorted array and original locations:
      -123      7        -100      1         -20      3
       -20      5         -11     15          -4     12
         0     13           0      2           1      4
         5      9          17     10          37     14
        90      6          91     11         602      8
```

IDFT

Purpose
To perform an inverse DFT on complex array CIN with the result returned in array COUT. This routine calculates the inverse DFT directly from its definition.

Usage

```
CALL IDFT ( CIN, COUT, NPTS )
```

Arguments

Name	Type	Dim	I/O	Description
CIN	C	NPTS	I	Input: Frequency spectrum of data set
COUT	C	NPTS	O	Output: Resulting time series
NPTS	I		I	Number of data points

Algorithm
This subroutine calculates the inverse DFT directly from its definition. It is very slow compared to subroutine IFFT for large arrays of data. Unlike subroutine IFFT, it does not require that the number of input points be a power of 2. If there are N input values, t_k is the kth value in the input time sequence, and F_n is the nth component in the output frequency spectrum, then

$$F_n = \frac{1}{N} \sum_{k=0}^{N-1} t_k \, e^{2\pi i k n/N}$$

WARNING: This routine is very slow for large array sizes. It is included in the library to support homework problems only. For real work, use subroutine IFFT instead.

Example
This example calculates the frequency spectrum of a 16-point complex data set consisting of all (1.0, 0.0). Because this data set is constant, the peak of the frequency spectrum of the data should be 0 Hz (DC).

   This example shows that IDFT is the inverse of DFT. Here, we take both the DFT and the inverse DFT of a data set, and wind up with the data we started with.

```
COMPLEX CIN(16), CINTER(16), COUT(16)
DATA CIn  / (0.,0.), (1.,0.),  (2.,0.),  (1.,0.),
     *      (0.,0.), (-1.,0.), (-2.,0.), (-1.,0.),
     *      (0.,0.), (1.,0.),  (2.,0.),  (1.,0.),
     *      (0.,0.), (-1.,0.), (-2.,0.), (-1.,0.) /
```

```
          CALL DFT ( CIN, CINTER, 16 )
          CALL IDFT ( CINTER, COUT, 16 )
          WRITE (*,1000) (COUT(I), I=1, 16)
     1000 FORMAT '' COUT = ',/,4('  (',F4.1,',',F4.1,')'))
```

Result

```
COUT =
(  .0,  .0) ( 1.0,  .0) ( 2.0,  .0) ( 1.0,  .0)
(  .0,  .0) (-1.0,  .0) (-2.0,  .0) (-1.0,  .0)
(  .0,  .0) ( 1.0,  .0) ( 2.0,  .0) ( 1.0,  .0)
(  .0,  .0) (-1.0,  .0) (-2.0,  .0) (-1.0,  .0)
```

IFFT

Purpose

To perform an in-place inverse FFT on complex array CARR. The size of the data set in array CARR must be a power of 2 (32, 64, 128, etc., up to 65,536). Before the call to FFT, array CARR will contain the frequency spectrum of a data set. After the call to FFT, array CARR will contain the corresponding time sequence.

Usage:

```
          CALL FFT ( CARR, NFFT, IERROR )
```

Arguments

Name	Type	Dim	I/O	Description
CARR	C	NFFT	I/O	Input: Frequency spectrum of data set
				Output: Resulting time series
NFFT	I		I	Number of data points (must be a power of 2)
IERROR	I		O	Error flag: 0 = No error
				1 = NFFT not a power of 2

Algorithm

This subroutine employs a Radix 2, in-place, decimation in frequency algorithm. For details, see Oppenheim and Shaffer, *Digital Signal Processing,* Prentice-Hall, 1975. If there are N input values, F_n is the nth component in the input frequency spectrum, and t_k is the kth value in the output time sequence, then

$$t_k = \frac{1}{N} \sum_{n=0}^{N-1} F_n e^{2\pi i k n/N}$$

Example

This example shows that IFFT is the inverse of FFT. Here, we take both the FFT and the inverse FFT of a data set, and wind up with the data we started with.

```
      COMPLEX CARR(16)
      DATA CARR / (0.,0.), (1.,0.),  (2.,0.),  (1.,0.),
     *            (0.,0.), (-1.,0.), (-2.,0.), (-1.,0.),
     *            (0.,0.), (1.,0.),  (2.,0.),  (1.,0.),
     *            (0.,0.), (-1.,0.), (-2.,0.), (-1.,0.) /
      CALL FFT ( CARR, 16, IERROR )
      CALL IFFT ( CARR, 16, IERROR )
      WRITE (*,1000) (CARR(I), I=1, 16)
 1000 FORMAT (' CARR = ',/,4(' (',F4.1,',',F4.1,')'))
```

Result

```
CARR =
(  .0,   .0) ( 1.0,   .0) ( 2.0,   .0) ( 1.0,   .0)
(  .0,   .0) (-1.0,   .0) (-2.0,   .0) (-1.0,   .0)
(  .0,   .0) ( 1.0,   .0) ( 2.0,   .0) ( 1.0,   .0)
(  .0,   .0) (-1.0,   .0) (-2.0,   .0) (-1.0,   .0)
```

IMAX/IMIN

Purpose

To return the magnitude and location of the maximum (minimum) value in an integer array.

Usage

```
CALL IMAX ( IA, N, MAXVAL, INDEX )
CALL IMIN ( IA, N, MINVAL, INDEX )
```

Arguments

Name	Type	Dim	I/O	Description
IA	I	N	I	Input array
N	I		I	Number of elements in array IA
MAXVAL	I		O	Maximum value in array IA
MINVAL	I		O	Minimum value in array IA
INDEX	I		O	Index of array element containing min/max value

Algorithm

```
INDEX   ← 1                      INDEX   ← 1
MAXVAL  ← IA(I)                  MINVAL  ← IA(I)
DO for I = 2 to N               DO for I = 2 to N
   IF IA(I) > MAXVAL Then          IF IA(I) < MINVAL Then
      MAXVAL  ← IA(I)                 MINVAL  ← IA(I)
      INDEX   ← I                     INDEX   ← I
   END of IF                       END of IF
END of DO                       END of DO
```

Example

This example uses IMAX to find the maximum value in a 10-element array IA.

```
      INTEGER IA(10), MAXVAL
      INTEGER N, INDEX
      DATA N /10/, IA / 1, -5, 11, -17, 2, 22, -1, 0, 11, 1 /
      CALL IMAX ( IA, N, MAXVAL, INDEX )
      WRITE (*,1000) INDEX, MAXVAL
 1000 FORMAT (' IA(',I2,') = ',I6)
```

Result

```
      IA( 6) =       22
```

INTEG

Purpose

To integrate a function $f(x)$ between points x_1 and x_2 using rectanges of width Δx. This subroutine expects the function $f(x)$ to be passed as a calling argument.

Usage

```
      CALL INTEG ( F, X1, X2, DX, AREA, IERROR )
```

Arguments

Name	Type	Dim	I/O	Description
F	R FUN		I	Name of function to integrate
X1	R		I	Starting point for integration
X2	R		I	Ending point for integration
DX	R		I	Step size for integration
AREA	R		O	Integrated value
IERROR	I		O	Error flag: 0 = No error
				1 = X1 > X2

Algorithm

This subroutine calculates the area under the curve $f(x)$ by dividing the distance between x_1 and x_2 into steps of size Δx and calculating the area under the curve for each step. The area calculation is done by approximating the area under the curve as a rectangle whose height is the value of $f(x)$ at the center of the step interval.

Example

This example uses INTEG to integrate the intrinsic function sin (x) from 0 to π. (The theoretical area of this integral is 2.0.)

```
      INTRINSIC SIN
      INTEGER IERROR
      REAL X1, X2, DX, AREA
      DATA X1, X2 , DX / 0., 3.141592, 0.05 /
      CALL INTEG ( SIN, X1, X2, DX, AREA, IERROR )
      WRITE (*,1000) AREA
1000  FORMAT (' The area under curve SIN(X) from 0. to PI is: ', F10.6)
```

Result

```
      The area under curve SIN(X) from 0. to PI is:   2.000208
```

INTEGD

Purpose

To integrate a descrete function specified by a series of (x, y) values between points x_1 and x_2, where x_1 and x_2 both lie within the range of input values in the (x, y) pairs. The (x, y) pairs must be passed to this subroutine in increasing order of x.

Usage

```
      CALL INTEGD ( X, Y, NPTS, X1, X2, AREA, IERROR )
```

Arguments

Name	Type	Dim	I/O	Description
X	R	NPTS	I	Values of independent variable x
Y	R	NPTS	I	Values of dependent variable y
NPTS	I		I	Number of (x, y) values passed to the subroutine
X1	R		I	Starting point for integration
X2	R		I	Ending point for integration
AREA	R		O	Integrated value
IERROR	I		O	Error flag: 0 = No error
				1 = X1 > X2
				2 = X1 < X(1)
				3 = X1 > X(NPTS)

Algorithm

This subroutine calculates the area under a curve specified by a series of discrete (x, y) points by calculating the area under the trapezoids formed by adjacent pairs of (x, y) values.

Example

This example uses INTEGD to integrate the intrinsic function sin (x) from 0 to π. Note that sin (x) is specified by (x, y) values in a pair of arrays. (The theoretical area of this integral is 2.0.)

```
      INTEGER I, NPTS, IERROR
      REAL X(101), Y(101), X1, X2, DX, AREA
      DATA NPTS, X1, X2 / 101, 0., 3.141592 /
      DX = ( X2 - X1 ) / REAL(NPTS - 1)
      DO 10 I = 1, NPTS
         X(I) = DX * REAL(I-1)
         Y(I) = SIN(X(I))
   10 CONTINUE
      CALL INTEGD ( X, Y, NPTS, X1, X2, AREA, IERROR )
      WRITE (*,1000) AREA
 1000 FORMAT (' The area under curve SIN(X) from 0. to PI is: ', F10.6)
```

Result

```
      The area under curve SIN(X) from 0. to PI is:   1.999836
```

INTERP

Purpose

To linearly interpolate the value y_0 at position x_0, given a set of (x, y) measurements organized in increasing order of x.

Usage

```
      CALL INTERP ( X, Y, NPTS, X0, Y0, IERROR )
```

Arguments

Name	Type	Dim	I/O	Description
X	R	NPTS	I	Values of independent variable x
Y	R	NPTS	I	Values of dependent variable y
NPTS	I		I	Number of (x, y) measurements
X0	R		I	Point at which to interpolate Y0
Y0	R		O	Interpolated value at point X0
IERROR	I		O	Error flag: $0 =$ No error
				$-1 = X0 < X(1)$
				$1 = X0 > X(NPTS)$

Algorithm

```
Find points X(I) and X(I+1) that straddle X0
SLOPE ← ( Y(I+1)-Y(I) ) / ( X(I+1)-X(I) )
Y0 ← SLOPE * ( X0 - X(I) ) + Y(I)
```

This routine requires that X0 fall between two points in array X. If X0 is outside the range of the points in X, the subroutine returns an error.

Example

This example interpolates the value at X0 = 5.2.

```
      INTEGER NPTS, IERROR
      REAL X(4), Y(4), X0, Y0
      DATA X / 3., 4., 5., 6. /, Y / 2.0, 0.9, 0.0, -0.9 /
      DATA NPTS / 4 /, X0 / 5.2 /
      CALL INTERP ( X, Y, NPTS, X0, Y0, IERROR )
      WRITE (*,1000) ' X0 = ', X0, ' Y0 = ', Y0
 1000 FORMAT (1X,A,F8.3,A,F8.3)
```

Result

```
X0 =     5.200  Y0 =     -.180
```

LCASE

Purpose

Subroutine to shift a character string to lowercase.

Usage

```
CALL LCASE ( STRING )
```

Arguments

Name	Type	Dim	I/O	Description
STRING	**CHAR**		**I/O**	Input: input character string Output: character string shifted to lowercase

Algorithm

Subroutine LCASE shifts all uppercase letters in an input character string to lowercase, and leaves all other letters unchanged. It works for both ASCII and EBCDIC collating sequences.

Example

```
CHARACTER*30 STRING
STRING = 'This is a Test: 12345%!?''
WRITE (*,'(A,A)') ' Before LCASE: ', STRING
CALL LCASE ( STRING )
WRITE (*,'(A,A)') ' After LCASE:  ', STRING
```

Result

```
Before LCASE: This is a Test: 12345%!?.
After LCASE:  this is a test: 12345%!?.
```

LENU

Purpose

Function to return the position of the last non-blank character in a string.

Usage

```
LENGTH = LENU ( STRING )
```

Argument

Name	Type	Dim	I/O	Description
STRING	**CHAR**		**I**	Input character string
LENU	**I**		**O**	Position of last non-blank character in string If the string is entirely blank, LENU returns a 0.

Algorithm

Function LENU returns the position of the last non-blank character in a string. This function differs from the intrinsic function LEN in that LEN returns the number of characters that can fit into a string, while LENU returns the number of characters actually being used in the string. LENU is especially useful for determining the portion of a character string to print out. The function starts at the last character in the string, and works backwards until it encounters a non-blank character. It returns the position of the first non-blank character encountered.

Example

```
CHARACTER*25 STRING
STRING = 'This is a Test.'
WRITE (*,'(A,I2)') ' String Length = ', LEN(STRING)
WRITE (*,'(A,I2)') ' Length used   = ', LENU(STRING)
```

Result

```
String Length = 25
Length used   = 15
```

■ LSQFT/DLSQFT (Single/Double Precision)

Purpose

Subroutine to perform a least squares fit of an input data set to the nth-order polynomial

$$y(x) = c_0 + c_1 x + c_2 x^2 + \ldots + c_n x^n.$$

Usage

```
CALL LSQFT ( X, Y, NVALS, ORDER, C, IERROR )
CALL DLSQFT ( X, Y, NVALS, ORDER, C, IERROR )
```

Arguments

Name	Type	Dim	I/O	Description
X	R/D	NVALS	I	Values of independent variable x
Y	R/D	NVALS	I	Values of dependent variable y
NVALS	I		I	Number of (x, y) measurements
ORDER	I		I	Order (highest power) of polynomial to fit (1–9 for LSQFT; 1–20 for DLSQFT)
C	R/D	0:ORDER	I	Coefficients of fit
IERROR	I		O	Error flag: 0 = no error
				1 = singular equations
				2 = not enough input values
				3 = illegal polynomial order specified

Algorithm

Subroutine LSQFT/DLSQFT performs a least squares fit of an input data set consiting of (x, y) pairs of data points to an nth-order polynomial, where n can be 1–9 for LSQFT and 1–20 for DLSQFT. The algorithm implemented is described in exercise 6 in Chapter 10.

Example

```
C     This code fits a 3rd order polynomial to 6 input data points.  The data points
C     were produced by the eqn:
C        Y(X) = 1. - X + X**2 - X**3
      REAL X(6), Y(6), C(0:3)
      INTEGER NVALS, ORDER, IERROR
      DATA NVALS / 6 /, ORDER / 3 /
      DATA X / 0., 1., 2., 3., 4., 5. /
      DATA Y / 1., 0., -5., -20., -51., -104. /
      CALL LSQFT ( X, Y, NVALS, ORDER, C, IERROR )
      WRITE (*,'(A,4(F10.5,1X))') ' The coefficients are:  ', C
```

Result

```
          The coefficients are:   1.00004   -1.00014    1.00007   -1.00001
```

MEDIAN

Purpose

To calculate the median of a real input data set.

Usage

```
          CALL MEDIAN ( RA, N, MED )
```

Arguments

Name	Type	Dim	I/O	Description
RA	**R**	**N**	**I**	Data set to analyze. The contents of this array are sorted into ascending order during the call to subroutine MEDIAN.
N	**I**		**I**	Number of data points
MED	**R**		**O**	Median of data set

Algorithm

This subroutine calculates the median of a data set by first sorting it into ascending order. After sorting, it returns the middle value as the median. If there are an odd number of elements in the data set, the middle one is returned. If there are an even number of elements, the average of the middle two elements is returned.

Example

This example calculates median of a small data set.

```
          REAL RA(7), MED
          DATA RA / -1., 4., 1., -4., 0., 2., 3., /
          CALL MEDIAN ( RA, 7, MED )
          WRITE (*,1000) MED
     1000 FORMAT (' MEDIAN = ', F10.4)
```

Result

```
MEDIAN =     1.0000
```

MINV/DMINV (Single/Double Precision)

Purpose

To invert an N × N matrix using Gaussian elimination and the maximum pivot technique.

Usage

```
CALL MINV ( A, B, NDIM, N, IERROR )
CALL DMINV ( A, B, NDIM, N, IERROR )
```

Arguments

Name	Type	Dim	I/O	Description
A	R/D	NDIM × NDIM	I	Matrix to invert (Note that A is destroyed during the inversion process.)
B	R/D	NDIM × NDIM	O	Inverse matrix A^{-1}
NDIM	I		I	Declared size of matrices
N	I		I	No. of rows and columns actually used in A
IERROR	I		O	Error flag: 0 = no error 1 = no inverse found (pivot too small)

Algorithm

This subroutine uses Gaussian elimination and the maximum pivot technique to construct the inverse of an N × N matrix. It initializes matrix B to the identity matrix, and then performs Gaussian elimination on matrix A, applying exactly the same operations to matrix B that were applied to matrix A. When the operation is over and A contains the identity matrix, B contains matrix A^{-1}. These matrix inversion routines suffer from the same conditioning problems as Gaussian elimination routines, so the double-precision version will be required for large and/or ill-conditioned matrices.

Example

This example declares two 10 × 10 arrays A and B, initializes array A with a 2 × 2 matrix, and inverts the matrix using subroutine MINV.

```
REAL A(10,10), B(10,10)
INTEGER I, J, NDIM, N
DATA NDIM, N / 10, 2 /
```

```
       DATA A(1,1), A(2,1), A(1,2), A(2,2) / 1., 2., 3., 4. /
       CALL MINV ( A, B, NDIM, N, IERROR )
       WRITE (*,1000) ((B(I,J), J=1, N), I=1, N)
  1000 FORMAT (1X,'B = ',/,(4X,F10.4,4X,F10.4))
```

Result

```
   B =
         -2.0000          1.5000
          1.0000          -.5000
```

MMADD/DMMADD (SINGLE/DOUBLE PRECISION)
MMSUB/DMMSUB (SINGLE/DOUBLE PRECISION)

Purpose

To add (subtract) two-dimensional matrices A and B of the same size, and store the result in a third matrix C (matrix C may be the same as either A or B).

Usage

```
    CALL MMADD ( A, B, C, IDROW, IDCOL, NROW, NCOL )
    CALL MMSUB ( A, B, C, IDROW, IDCOL, NROW, NCOL )
```

Arguments

Name	Type	Dim	I/O	Description
A	R/D	IDROW × IDCOL	I	First matrix to add/subtract
B	R/D	IDROW × IDCOL	I	Second matrix to add/subtract
C	R/D	IDROW × IDCOL	O	Resulting matrix
IDROW	I		I	Declared size of matrices (rows)
IDCOL	I		I	Declared size of matrices (columns)
NROW	I		I	Number of rows to add/subtract
NCOL	I		I	Number of columns to add/subtract

Algorithm

MMADD: $c_{ij} = a_{ij} + b_{ij}$ $i = 1$ to NROW, $j = 1$ to NCOL

MMSUB: $c_{ij} = a_{ij} - b_{ij}$ $i = 1$ to NROW, $j = 1$ to NCOL

Example

This example declares two 10 × 10 arrays A and B, initializes them with 2 × 2 matrices, and adds the matrices using subroutine MMADD.

```
    REAL A(10,10), B(10,10), C(10,10)
    INTEGER I, J, NROW, NCOL
    DATA NROW, NCOL / 2, 2 /
```

```
      DATA A(1,1), A(2,1), A(1,2), A(2,2) / 1., 2., 3., 4. /
      DATA B(1,1), B(2,1), B(1,2), B(2,2) / 5., 6., 7., 8. /
      CALL MMADD ( A, B, C, 10, 10, 2, 2 )
      WRITE (*,1000) ((I,J,C(I,J), I=1, NROW), J=1, NCOL)
 1000 FORMAT (' C(',I2,',',I2,') = ',F10.4)
```

Result

```
C( 1, 1) =      6.0000
C( 2, 1) =      8.0000
C( 1, 2) =     10.0000
C( 2, 2) =     12.0000
```

MMMUL/DMMMUL (Single/Double Precision)

Purpose

To multiply two-dimensional matrices A and B of sizes (NROW1 × NCOL1) and (NCOL1 × NCOL2) respectively, and store the result in a third matrix C of size (NROW1 × NCOL2) (matrix C may not be the same as either A or B).

Usage

```
      CALL MMMUL  ( A, IDROW1, IDCOL1, B, IDROW2, IDCOL2,
     *              C, IDROW3, IDCOL3, NROW1, NCOL1, NCOL2 )
      CALL DMMMUL ( A, IDROW1, IDCOL1, B, IDROW2, IDCOL2,
     *              C, IDROW3, IDCOL3, NROW1, NCOL1, NCOL2 )
```

Arguments

Name	Type	Dim	I/O	Description
A	R/D	IDROW1 × IDCOL1	I	First matrix to multiply
B	R/D	IDROW2 × IDCOL2	I	Second matrix to multiply
C	R/D	IDROW3 × IDCOL3	O	Result of A × B
IDROW1	I		I	Declared size of matrix A (rows)
IDCOL1	I		I	Declared size of matrix A (columns)
IDROW2	I		I	Declared size of matrix A (rows)
IDROW2	I		I	Declared size of matrix A (columns)
IDCOL3	I		I	Declared size of matrix A (rows)
IDCOL3	I		I	Declared size of matrix A (columns)
NROW1	I		I	Number of actual rows in matrix A
NCOL1	I		I	Number of actual columns in matrix A, and Number of actual rows in matrix B
NCOL2	I		I	Number of actual columns in matrix B

Algorithm

These subroutines multiply two matrices of compatible sizes, and store the result in a third matrix. They keep track of the actual numbers of rows and columns declared for each array, so they can be used to multiply matrices that occupy only a portion of the declared size of an array.

$$\text{MMMUL:} \quad c_{ik} = \sum_{j=1}^{L} a_{ij} b_{jk} \qquad i = 1 \text{ to } \texttt{NROW1}, \quad k = 1 \text{ to } \texttt{NCOL2}$$

Example

This example declares three arrays A, B, and C of sizes 2×2, 4×5, and 3×3, respectively. It defines two 2×2 matrices in A and B as follows:

$$A = \begin{bmatrix} 3.0 & -1.0 \\ 1.0 & 2.0 \end{bmatrix} \qquad B = \begin{bmatrix} 3.0 & 4.0 \\ 2.0 & -3.0 \end{bmatrix}$$

Note that all of the space in array A is used, but much of the space in array B is unused. This will not cause a problem because subroutine MMMUL keeps track of where each element is stored within array B.

```
      INTEGER IDROW1, IDCOL1, IDROW2, IDCOL2, IDROW3, IDCOL3
      INTEGER NROW1, NCOL1, NCOL2
      PARAMETER ( IDROW1 = 2 )
      PARAMETER ( IDCOL1 = 2 )
      PARAMETER ( IDROW2 = 4 )
      PARAMETER ( IDCOL2 = 5 )
      PARAMETER ( IDROW3 = 3 )
      PARAMETER ( IDCOL3 = 3 )
      REAL A(IDROW1,IDCOL1), B(IDROW2,IDCOL2), C(IDROW3,IDCOL3)
      DATA NROW1, NCOL1, NCOL2 / 2, 2, 2 /
      DATA A(1,1), A(2,1), A(1,2), A(2,2) / 3., 1., -1., 2. /
      DATA B(1,1), B(2,1), B(1,2), B(2,2) / 3., 2., 4., -3. /
      CALL MMMUL ( A, IDROW1, IDCOL1, B, IDROW2, IDCOL2,
     *               C, IDROW3, IDCOL3, NROW1, NCOL1, NCOL2 )
      WRITE (*,1000) ((I,J,C(I,J), I=1, NROW1), J=1, NCOL2)
 1000 FORMAT (' C(',I2,',',I2,') = ',F10.4)
```

Result

```
C( 1, 1) =      7.0000
C( 2, 1) =      7.0000
C( 1, 2) =     15.0000
C( 2, 2) =     -2.0000
```

■ NXTMUL

Purpose

Subroutine to calculate the smallest exponent EXP that satisfies the expression VALUE <= MUL (= BASE**EXP). This calculation is useful for sizing FFTs, etc.

Usage

```
CALL NXTMUL ( VALUE, BASE, EXP, MUL )
```

Arguments

Name	Type	Dim	I/O	Description
VALUE	I		I	First matrix to multiply
BASE	I		I	Base value for the exponent
EXP	I		O	Smallest exponent satisfying the inequality given above
MUL	I		O	The next power of BASE that is greater than VALUE: MUL = BASE**EXP

Algorithm

This subroutine calculates successive powers of the base number BASE until one of them exceeds the value VALUE. When that happens, the subroutine returns both the exponent EXP and the base raised to the exponent MUL. The subroutine is useful for calculating the next power of 2 when working with FFTs. For example, the call

```
CALL NXTMUL ( 48, 2, EXP, MUL )
```

would return with EXP = 6 and MUL = 64, since 2**6 = 64, which is greater than 48.

Example

This example calculates the next power of 2 greater than the number 997:

```
      INTEGER EXP, MUL
      CALL NXTMUL ( 997, 2, EXP, MUL )
      WRITE (*,1000) EXP, MUL
1000 FORMAT (' EXP = ', I6, '   MUL = ', I6 )
```

Result

```
EXP =     10   MUL =    1024
```

PLOT

Purpose

Subroutine to print a line printer plot of a function.

Usage

```
CALL PLOT ( DATA1, NPTS, MINVAL, MAXVAL, DEFALT, LU )
```

Arguments

Name	Type	Dim	I/O	Description
DATA1	R	NPTS	I	Data set to plot
NPTS	I		I	Number of points in input data set
MINVAL	R		I	Smallest value to plot. The default value is the smallest number in the data set.
MAXVAL	R		I	Largest value to plot. The default value is the largest number in the data set.
DEFALT	L		I	If TRUE, default choice of MINVAL and MAXVAL
LU	I		I	Logical unit to print plot on

Algorithm

This subroutine makes a line printer plot of an input data set on the device specified by logical unit LU.

Example

This example plots the function sin (x) for 0–10 in steps of 0.5. Note that the values of MINVAL and MAXVAL are defaulted.

```
      REAL DATA1(20)
      INTEGER MINVAL, MAXVAL
      DO 10 I = 1, 20
         DATA1(I) = SIN(REAL(I)/2.)
   10 CONTINUE
      CALL PLOT (DATA1, 20, MINVAL, MAXVAL, .TRUE., 6 )
```

Result

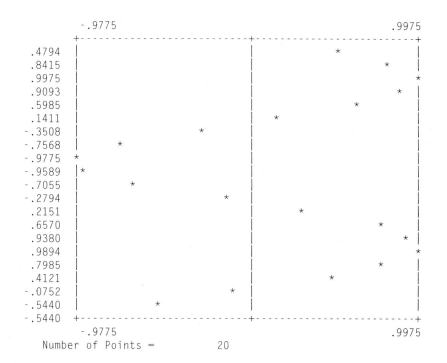

```
                 -.9775                                        .9975
                 +---------------------------+------------------------------+
        .4794    |                           |                  *           |
        .8415    |                           |                        *     |
        .9975    |                           |                             *|
        .9093    |                           |                      *       |
        .5985    |                           |                 *            |
        .1411    |                           |         *                    |
       -.3508    |               *           |                              |
       -.7568    |        *                  |                              |
       -.9775   *|                           |                              |
       -.9589    |*                          |                              |
       -.7055    |          *                |                              |
       -.2794    |                      *    |                              |
        .2151    |                           |      *                       |
        .6570    |                           |                    *         |
        .9380    |                           |                      * |     |
        .9894    |                           |                            * |
        .7985    |                           |                    *         |
        .4121    |                           |              *               |
       -.0752    |                      *    |                              |
       -.5440    |            *              |                              |
       -.5440    +---------------------------+------------------------------+
                 -.9775                                        .9975
              Number of Points =          20
```

PLOTXY

Purpose

Subroutine to print a line printer cross-plot of a set of (*x, y*) data points.

Usage

```
CALL PLOTXY ( X, Y, NPTS, MINX, MAXX, MINY, MAXY,
       *               NBINX, NBINY, DEFALT, LU )
```

Arguments

Name	Type	Dim	I/O	Description
X	R	NPTS	I	X values of points to plot
Y	R	NPTS	I	Y values of points to plot
NPTS	I		I	Number of points in input data set
MINX	R		I	Smallest X value to plot. The default value is the smallest number in the data set.
MAXX	R		I	Largest X value to plot. The default value is the largest number in the data set.
MINY	R		I	Smallest Y value to plot. The default value is the smallest number in the data set.
MAXY	R		I	Largest Y value to plot. The default value is the largest number in the data set.
NBINX	I		I	Number of lines over which to plot the X data. (Maximum = 65; if NBINX $\leq$ 0, 65 will be used.)
NBINY	I		I	Number of columns over which to plot the Y data. (Maximum = 65; if NBINY $\leq$ 0, 65 will be used.)
DEFALT	L		I	If TRUE, default the choice of MINX, MAXX, MINY, and MAXY.
LU	I		I	Logical unit to print plot on

Algorithm

This subroutine makes a line printer plot of an input data set consisting of NPTS pairs of (X,Y) values on the device specified by logical unit LU.

Example

This example plots the (X,Y) pairs formed by the functions $x(t) = \sin(t)$ and $y(t) = \sin(2t)$ for $t = 0$ to 2π in steps of $\pi/20$. Note that the values of MINX, MAXX, MINY, and MAXY are defaulted.

```
      INTEGER MINX, MINY, MAXX, MAXY, NPTS
      REAL X(40), Y(40), PI
      PARAMETER ( PI = 3.141592 )
      PARAMETER ( NPTS = 40 )
      DO 10 I = 1, NPTS
         X(I) = SIN(REAL(I)*(PI/20.))
         Y(I) = SIN(2.*REAL(I)*(PI/20.))
   10 CONTINUE
      CALL PLOTXY ( X, Y, NPTS, MINX, MAXX, MINY, MAXY,
     *                 41, 41, .TRUE., 6 )
```

Result:

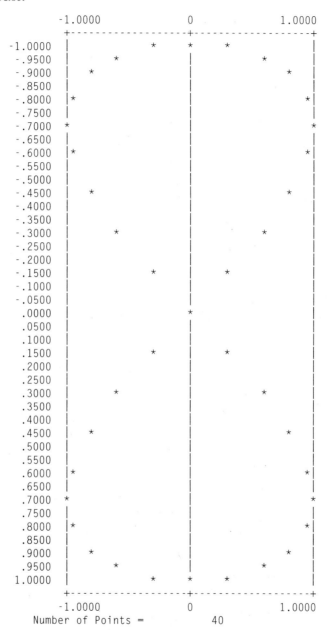

■ RE2CHR

Purpose

Function to convert a real value into a 12-character string, with the number printed in as readable a format as possible considering its range.

Usage

```
CALL RECT ( X, Y, R, THETA )
```

Arguments

Name	Type	Dim	I/O	Description
VALUE	R		I	Input floating-point number
RE2CHR	CHR*12		O	Function returns a 12-character string containing a representation of VALUE

Algorithm

This routine prints out the number according to the following rules:

1. VALUE > 9999999.   1PE12.5
2. VALUE < −999999.   1PE12.5
3. 0. < ABS(VALUE) < 0.01   1PE12.5
5. VALUE = 0.0   F12.4
6. Otherwise   F12.4

Example

This example uses RE2CHR to print out three real values.

```
      REAL X, Y, Z
      CHARACTER*12 RE2CHR
      DATA X, Y, Z / 0., 450000000., .025 /
      WRITE (*,1000) RE2CHR(X), RE2CHR(Y), RE2CHR(Z)
 1000 FORMAT (5X,A,5X,A,5X,A)
```

Result

```
     .0000      4.50000E+08           .0250
```

■ RMAX/RMIN

Purpose

To return the magnitude and location of the maximum (minimum) value in a real array.

Usage

```
CALL RMAX ( RA, N, MAXVAL, INDEX )
CALL RMIN ( RA, N, MINVAL, INDEX )
```

Arguments

Name	Type	Dim	I/O	Description
RA	R	N	I	Input array
N	I		I	Number of elements in array RA
MAXVAL	R		O	Maximum value in array RA
MINVAL	R		O	Minimum value in array RA
INDEX	I		O	Index of array element containing max value

Algorithm:

```
INDEX  ← 1                    INDEX  ← 1
MAXVAL ← RA(I)                MINVAL ← RA(I)
DO for I = 2 to N             DO for I = 2 to N
   IF RA(I) > MAXVAL Then        IF RA(I) < MINVAL Then
      MAXVAL ← RA(I)               MINVAL ← RA(I)
      INDEX  ← I                   INDEX  ← I
   END of IF                    END of IF
END of DO                     END of DO
```

Example

This example uses RMAX to find the maximum value in a 10-element array RA.

```
      REAL    RA(10), MAXVAL
      INTEGER N, INDEX
      DATA N /10/
      DATA RA /  1.01,  -5.35,  11.01, -17.06,  2.00,
     *          22.05, -11.02,   0.00,  11.17,  1.00 /
      CALL RMAX ( RA, N, MAXVAL, INDEX )
      WRITE (*,1000) INDEX, MAXVAL
1000 FORMAT (' RA(',I2,') = ',F10.4)
```

Result

```
 RA( 6) =    22.0500
```

RAN0/RAN1 (Subroutine/Real Function)

Purpose

These routines generate a sequence of uniformly distributed pseudorandom numbers in the range [0, 1). Both routines perform the same function: RAN0 is a subroutine, and RAN1 is a real function.

Usage

```
CALL RAN0 ( VALUE )
VALUE = RAN1()
```

Arguments

Name	Type	Dim	I/O	Description
VALUE	R		O	A value in the random number sequence
RAN1	R		O	Function: RAN1 returns a value in the random number sequence

Algorithm

Subroutine RAN0 and function RAN1 generate uniform pseudorandom number sequences in the range [0, 1). One value in the sequence is returned for each call to the routines. The numbers are generated using a linear congruential generator, and the sequence of numbers is the same every time a program is run with a given seed value. If it is important to vary the random sequence generated in different runs of a program, use subroutine SEED to change the starting value for the sequence.

Example

This example uses function RAN1 to generate 20 random numbers between 0 and 1.

```
        REAL RAN1
        WRITE (*,*) 'Uniform random number sequence:'
        DO 10 I = 1, 4
            WRITE (*,1000) RAN1(), RAN1(), RAN1(), RAN1(), RAN1()
1000        FORMAT (1X,5F10.6)
     10 CONTINUE
```

Result

```
Uniform random number sequence:
  .211300    .475440    .585012    .221498    .288601
  .245580    .440584    .443984    .381704    .268560
  .341588    .393383    .105424    .381416    .680617
  .351177    .963465    .643407    .405819    .487737
```

SEED

Purpose

Subroutine to set the starting point for the pseudorandom sequences generated by routines RAN0, RAN1, GRAN0, and GRAN1.

Usage

```
CALL SEED ( ISEED )
```

Arguments

Name	Type	Dim	I/O	Description
ISEED	I		I	An initial value for the random number generator

Algorithm

Subroutine SEED sets an initial value for the linear congruential generator used to generate pseudorandom numbers by routines RAN0, RAN1, GRAN0, and GRAN1. Each value of ISEED will produce a different sequence. If it is important to vary the random sequence generated in different runs of a program, subroutine SEED should be called with a different value of ISEED at the beginning of each run.

Example

This example illustrates the fact that the sequence generated by function RAN1 depends on the starting seed specified by the user. Whenever calls to RAN1 are made with the same seed, the sequence of numbers is the same. If a different seed is used, a different sequence of random numbers is generated.

```
     REAL RAN1
     WRITE (*,*) 'Uniform random number sequence with seed -2:'
     CALL SEED (-2)
     WRITE (*,1000) RAN1(), RAN1(), RAN1(), RAN1(), RAN1()
1000 FORMAT (1X,5F10.6)
     WRITE (*,*) 'Uniform random number sequence with seed 10011:'
     CALL SEED (10011)
     WRITE (*,1000) RAN1(), RAN1(), RAN1(), RAN1(), RAN1()
     WRITE (*,*) 'Uniform random number sequence with seed -2:'
     CALL SEED (-2)
     WRITE (*,1000) RAN1(), RAN1(), RAN1(), RAN1(), RAN1()
```

Result

```
     Uniform random number sequence with seed -2:
       .244897    .046321    .752436    .933613    .715778
     Uniform random number sequence with seed 10011:
       .379621    .018576    .125185    .714263    .022848
     Uniform random number sequence with seed -2:
       .244897    .046321    .752436    .933613    .715778
```

SIMUL/DSIMUL/CSIMUL (Single Precision/Double Precision/Complex)

Purpose

To solve a system of N simultaneous equations in N unknowns of the form AX = B, where A is an N × N matrix, and B is an N-dimensional column vector.

Usage

```
CALL SIMUL  ( RA, RB, NDIM, N, IERROR )
CALL DSIMUL ( DA, DB, NDIM, N, IERROR )
CALL CSIMUL ( CA, CB, NDIM, N, IERROR )
```

Arguments

Name	Type	Dim	I/O	Description
RA/DA/CA	R/D/C	NDIM × NDIM	I	Coefficients of X (Destroyed during solution)
RB/DB/CB	R/D/C	NDIM	I/O	Input: vector of constant terms Output: solution to the system of equations.
NDIM	I		I	Declared size of array RA/DA/CA
N	I		I	Order of the system of equations.
IERROR	I		O	Error flag: 0 = no error 1 = singular equations

Algorithm

These subroutines use the Gauss-Jordan method with maximum pivots for finding the solution to a system of simultaneous equations.

Example

This example calculates the solution to a 2 × 2 set of equations, and prints the results. The arrays are declared large enough for a 4 × 4 set of equations, but only a part of each array is used in this problem.

```
      REAL RA(4,4), RB(4)
      DATA RA(1,1), RA(1,2), RA(2,1), RA(2,2) / 1., 4., 2., -3. /
      DATA RB(1), RB(2) / 5., 2. /
      CALL SIMUL ( RA, RB, 4, 2, IERROR )
      WRITE (*,1000) RB(1), RB(2)
 1000 FORMAT (' The solution is X(1) = ', F10.4, ' and X(2) = ', F10.4)
```

Result

```
      The solution is X(1) =     2.0909 and X(2) =       .7273
```

SINC

Purpose

To calculate the sinc function: sinc (x) = sin (x) / x.

Usage

```
RESULT = SINC(X)
```

Arguments

Name	Type	Dim	I/O	Description
X	R		I	Value for which to calculate the sinc function
SINC	R		O	Function name: returns sinc (x)

Algorithm

This function calculates the function $sinc\ (x) = \sin\ (x)/x$, with special handling of the computation near $x = 0$.

Example

This example calculates sinc (x) for an arbitrary value of x, and prints the results.

```
      REAL SINC, X
      WRITE (*,*) 'Enter value of X:'
      READ (*,*) X
      WRITE (*,1000) X, SINC(X)
 1000 FORMAT (1X,' SINC(',F10.4,') = ', F10.4)
```

Result

```
Enter value of X:
1.0
 SINC(    1.0000) =        .8415
```

SSORTI/SSORTR/SSORTC (INTEGER/REAL/CHARACTER)

Purpose

To sort an array into ascending order using the selection sort algorithm

Usage

```
      CALL SSORTI ( IARRAY, N )
      CALL SSORTR ( RARRAY, N )
      CALL SSORTC ( CARRAY, N )
```

Arguments

Name	Type	Dim	I/O	Description
IARRAY	I	N	I/O	Integer array
RARRAY	R	N	I/O	Real array
CARRAY	CHAR	N	I/O	Character array
N	I		I	Number of elements in array

Algorithm

These subroutines sort arrays into ascending order using the selection sort algorithm. This algorithm is very inefficient, and is included here only for comparison to the better heapsort algorithm. Use the heapsort algorithm instead of this one.

Example

This example declares an integer array IARRAY and initializes with 15 values. It uses subroutine SSORTI to sort the array into ascending order.

```
      INTEGER IARRAY(15), N
      DATA N / 15 /
      DATA IARRAY / -100,    0,  -20,    1,  -20,
     *               90, -123,  602,    5,   17,
     *               91,   -4,    0,   37,  -11 /
      WRITE (*,*) ' IARRAY before sorting: '
      WRITE (*,1000) IARRAY
 1000 FORMAT (3X,5I6)
      CALL SSORTI ( IARRAY, N )
      WRITE (*,*) ' IARRAY after sorting: '
      WRITE (*,1000) IARRAY
```

Result

```
IARRAY before sorting:
  -100      0    -20      1    -20
    90   -123    602      5     17
    91     -4      0     37    -11
IARRAY after sorting:
  -123   -100    -20    -20    -11
    -4      0      0      1      5
    17     37     90     91    602
```

UCASE

Purpose

Subroutine shift a character string to uppercase.

Usage

```
CALL UCASE ( STRING )
```

Arguments

Name	Type	Dim	I/O	Description
STRING	**CHAR**		**I/O**	Input: input character string Output: character string shifted to uppercase

Algorithm

Subroutine UCASE shifts all lowercase letters in an input character string to uppercase, and leaves all other letters unchanged. It works for both ASCII and EBCDIC collating sequences.

Example

```
CHARACTER*30 STRING
STRING = 'This is a Test: 12345%!?.'
WRITE (*,'(A,A)') ' Before UCASE: ', STRING
CALL UCASE ( STRING )
WRITE (*,'(A,A)') ' After UCASE:  ', STRING
```

Result:

```
Before UCASE: This is a Test: 12345%!?.
After UCASE:  THIS IS A TEST: 12345%!?.
```

APPENDIX

E

Answers to Quizzes

Quiz 1-1

1. (a) 11011_2 (b) 1011_2 (c) 100011_2 (d) 1111111_2
2. (a) 14_{10} (b) 85_{10} (c) 9_{10}
3. (a) 162655_8 or $E5AD_{16}$ (b) 1675_8 or $3BD_{16}$ (c) 113477_8 or $973F_{16}$
4. $131_{10} = 10000011_2$, so the fourth bit is a zero
5. (a) ASCII: M; EBCDIC: ((b) ASCII: {; EBCDIC: # (c) ASCII: (unused); EBCDIC: 9
6. (a) -32768 (b) 32767
7. Yes, a 4-byte variable of the real data type can be used to store larger numbers than a 4-byte variable of the integer data type. The 8 bits of exponent in a real variable can represent values as large as 10^{38}. A 4-byte integer can only represent values as large as 2,147,483,647 (about 10^9). To do this, the real variable is restricted to 6 or 7 decimal digits of precision, while the integer variable has 9 or 10 decimal digits of precision.

Quiz 2-1

1. Valid real constant
2. Invalid—commas not permitted within constants
3. Invalid—real constants must have a decimal point
4. Invalid—single quotes must be doubled within a character string
5. Valid integer constant
6. Valid character constant
7. Valid real constant
8. Valid logical constant
9. Valid character constant
10. Invalid—character constants must be enclosed by single quotes
11. Valid real constant
12. Valid real constant
13. Invalid—logical constants must be surrounded by periods
14. Valid real constant

15. Same
16. Different
17. Different
18. Different
19. Valid program name
20. Invalid—program name must be ≤ 6 characters long
21. Invalid—program name must begin with a letter
22. Valid integer
23. Invalid—more than six characters
24. Invalid—underscore character illegal
25. Invalid—name must begin with a letter
26. Valid real
27. Valid real
28. Valid real
29. Invalid—no parentheses present
30. Invalid—character data in integer parameter
31. Valid

Quiz 2-2

1. The order is (1) exponentials, working from right to left; (2) multiplications and divisions, working from left to right; (3) additions and subtractions, working from left to right; (4) relational operators (**.EQ., .NE., .GT., .GE., .LT., .LE.**), working from left to right; (5) **.NOT.** operators, (6) **.AND.** operators, working from left to right; (7) **.OR.** operators, working from left to right; (8) **.EQV.** and **.NEQV.** operators, working from left to right. Parentheses modify this order—terms in parentheses are evaluated first, starting from the innermost parentheses and working outward.
2. (*a*) legal: result = 12   (*b*) legal: result = 42   (*c*) legal: result = 2   (*d*) legal: result = 2   (*e*) illegal: division by 0   (*f*) legal: result = 40.5   (*g*) illegal: two adjacent operators
3. (*a*) 8   (*b*) 8   (*c*) 8   (*d*) 8.66667   (*e*) 8.0   (*f*) 8.66667
4. (*a*) 7   (*b*) -21 (*c*) 7   (*d*) 9   (*e*) -13
5. (*a*) legal: result = 256.0   (*b*) illegal: real value raised to negative real power   (*c*) legal: result = 4
 (*d*) legal: result = 4.0
6. The statements are illegal, since they try to assign a value to parameter K.
7. RESULT = 44.16667
8. A = 3.0; N = 3

Quiz 2-3

1. `REQ = R1 + R2 + R3 + R4`
2. `REQ = 1. / ( 1./R1 + 1./R2 + 1./R3 + 1./R4 )`
3. `T = 2. * PI * SQRT ( L / G )`
4. `V = VMAX * EXP( - ALPHA * T ) * COS ( OMEGA * T )`
5. dist $= \frac{1}{2} at^2 + v_0 t + x_0$

6. freq $= \dfrac{1}{2\pi\sqrt{\mathrm{LC}}}$

7. Energy $= \frac{1}{2} L i^2$
8. The results are

```
126    5.000000E-02 T
```

Make sure that you can explain why **A** is equal to 0.05!

9. (*a*) legal: result = FALSE   (*b*) illegal: .NOT. only works with logical values   (*c*) legal: result =
TRUE   (*d*) legal: result = TRUE   (*e*) legal: result = TRUE   (*f*) legal: result = TRUE
(*g*) legal: result = TRUE   (*h*) Illegal: .OR. only works with logical values

10. 1   3   180   2.000000   30.000000   3.489839E-02

Quiz 3-1

```
1. IF ( X .GE. 0. ) THEN
      SQRTX = SQRT ( X )
      WRITE (*,*) 'The square root of X is ', SQRTX
   ELSE
      WRITE (*,*) 'Error-X < 0!'
      SQRTX = 0.
   END IF
2. IF ( ABS(DEN) .LT. 1.0E-10 ) THEN
      WRITE (*,*) 'Divide by zero error!'
   ELSE
      FUN = NUM / DEN
      WRITE (*,*) 'FUN = ', FUN
   END IF
3. IF ( DIST .GT. 300. ) THEN
      COST = 110. + 0.20 * ( DIST - 300. )
   ELSE IF ( DIST .GT. 100. ) THEN
      COST = 50. + 0.30 * ( DIST - 100. )
   ELSE
      COST = 0.50 * DIST
   END IF
   AVCOST = COST / DIST
```

4. These statements are incorrect. There is no **ELSE** in front of **IF (VOLTS .LT. 105.)**.

5. These statements are incorrect. A parameter is declared after the first executable statement of the program.

6. These statements are correct. Since $C < \sqrt{|A| + |B|}$, the tests will fail, and the program will print 'Tests failed...'.

7. These statements are incorrect. It is illegal to use a relational operator with logical data.

8. These statements are technically correct, but they are unlikely to do what the user intended. If the temperature is greater than $100°C$, then the user probably wants 'Boiling point of water exceeded' to be printed out. Instead, the message 'Human body temperature exceeded' will be be printed out, since the **IF** structure executes the first true branch that it comes to. If the temperature is greater than $100°C$, it is also greater than $37°$.

Quiz 3-2

1. 4
2. 0
3. 1
4. 7
5. 9
6. 0
```
7. IRES = 10
8. IRES = 55
9. IRES = 0
```

10. IRES = 100
11. IRES = 55
12. Invalid: These statements redefine **DO** loop index I within the loop.
13. Valid
14. Illegal: **DO** loops overlap.
15. Illegal: two different **DO** loops terminate on two different **CONTINUE** statements having the same statement label.

Quiz 4-1

Note: There is more than one way to write the **FORMAT** statements in this quiz. Each of the answers shown below represents one of many possible correct answers to the question.

1.
```
      WRITE (*,100)
  100 FORMAT ('1',24X,'This is a test!')
```
2.
```
      WRITE (*,110) I, J, DATA1
  100 FORMAT ('0',2I10,F10.2)
```
3.
```
      WRITE (*,110) RESULT
  110 FORMAT (' ',T13,'The result is ',1PE12.4)
```
4.
```
   -.0001**********     3.1416
----|----|----|----|----|----|
    5    10   15   20   25   30
```
5.
```
     .000    .602E+24      3.14159
----|----|----|----|----|----|
    5    10   15   20   25   30
```
6.
```
-.0001 .60E+24   3.142
----|----|----|----|----|----|
    5    10   15   20   25   30
```
7.
```
********** 6.0200E+23   31.4159
----|----|----|----|----|----|
    5    10   15   20   25   30
```
8.
```
2767

   24
****
----|----|----|----|----|----|
    5    10   15   20   25   30
```
9.
```
   32767  00000024  -1010101
----|----|----|----|----|----|
    5    10   15   20   25   30
```
10.
```
ABCDEFGHIJ     12345
----|----|----|----|----|----|
    5    10   15   20   25   30
```
11.
```
                    ABC12345IJ
----|----|----|----|----|----|
    5    10   15   20   25   30
```
12.
```
 ABCDEFGHIJ12345
----|----|----|----|----|----|
    5    10   15   20   25   30
```
13.
```
ABCDE  12345
----|----|----|----|----|----|
    5    10   15   20   25   30
```
14. Correct—all format descriptors match variable types.
15. Probably incorrect. All format descriptors match the types of the variables, but it is likely that user does not intend the **1P** scale factor to be applied to the **F10.4** descriptor.

16. Correct—all format descriptors match variable types.

17. Incorrect. Format descriptors do not match variable types for TEST and IERROR.

18. This program skips to the top of a page, and writes the following data.

```
                 Output Data
                 ===========


POINT( 1) =      1.200000      2.400000
POINT( 2) =      2.400000      4.800000
----|----|----|----|----|----|----|----|
    5   10   15   20   25   30   35   40
```

19. This program skips to the top of a page, and writes the following data.

```
****************************************************************************
*                                                                        *
*                                                                        *
*                         This is a title box!                           *
*                                                                        *
****************************************************************************
----|----|----|----|----|----|----|----|----|----|----|----|----|----|----|----|
    5   10   15   20   25   30   35   40   45   50   55   60   65   70   75   80
```

20. This program writes the following data on the next line (no skipping).

```
   -171.0010E+08 1000.0000        0
----|----|----|----|----|----|----|----|--
    5   10   15   20   25   30   35   40
```

21. This program writes the following data starting on the first line of the next page.

```
                    Grade List




DOE             JOHN              Q    88.0   B





                 End of Grade List
----|----|----|----|----|----|----|----|----|----|----|
    5   10   15   20   25   30   35   40   45   50   55
```

22. This program skips three lines, and writes the line 'This is a test!'. Then it skips to the next page and writes 'This too!'. Finally, it skips two more lines and writes out the data as shown below.

```
   This is a test!
```

```
   This too!


   ***             3.142         1.414          *****          12

   -32767          3.142E+00        14.142       9.300E+07         12
   *                .314E+01         1.414       93000000.0
----|----|----|----|----|----|----|----|----|----|----|----|----|----|----|
    5   10   15   20   25   30   35   40   45   50   55   60   65   70   75
```

Quiz 4-2

Note: There is more than one way to write the **FORMAT** statements in this quiz. Each of the answers shown below represents one of many possible correct answers to the question.

1.
```
      READ (*,100) AMP, COUNT, IDENT
  100 FORMAT (9X,F11.2,T30,I6,T60,A13)
```
2.
```
      READ (*,110) TITLE, I1, I2, I3, I4, I5
  110 FORMAT (T10,A25,/(4X,I8))
```
3.
```
      READ (*,120) STRING, NUMBER
  120 FORMAT (T11,A10,///,T11,I10)
```
4. $A = 1.65 \times 10^{-10}$, B = 17., C = −11.7
5. A = −3.141593, B = 2.718282, C = 37.55
6. A = 1.024, B = 1.024, C = 1.024
7. I = −35, J = 6705, K = 3687
8. Problem 4: no change.

   Problem 5: no change.

   Problem 6: A = 1024.0, B = 1.024, C = 10240.0

   Problem 7: I = −3500, J = 6705, K = 36870
9. STR1 = 'FGHIJ', STR2 = 'KLMNOPQRST', STR3 = 'UVWXYZ0123   ', STR4 = ' _TEST_ 1'
10. Correct.
11. Correct. These statements read integer JUNK from columns 60–74 of one line, and then read real variable SCRATCH from columns 1–15 of the next line.
12. Incorrect. Real variable EL will be read with an I6 format descriptor.
13. TITLE = Measurement Summary, INDEX1 = 1, X1 = −230.3, Y1 = 0.121221, INDEX2 = 2, X2 = 87.6, Y2 = −11.352. The value stored in Y1 may not be what the user intended due to the assumption that there are six decimal places in the number. Also, the value in X2 is not correct because a part of the number was outside the field of the format descriptor.
14. $X1 = 3.141593 \times 10^{10}$, X2 = 3141593., X3 = 31415.93, X4 = 141592.7, TITLE = 'TEST DATA', A = −1.26, B = 16.2. Logical variable VALID produces an error, since there is no value within the L5 field.

Quiz 4-3

Note: There is more than one way to write the **FORMAT** statements in this quiz. Each of the answers shown below represents one of many possible correct answers to the question.

1.
```
      OPEN (UNIT=25, FILE='IN052691', IOSTAT=ISTAT)
      IF ( ISTAT .NE. 0 ) THEN
          WRITE (*,100) 'Open error on FILE.  IOSTAT = ', ISTAT
  100     FORMAT (1X,A,I6)
      ELSE
          ...
      END IF
```
2.
```
      OPEN (UNIT=4, FILE=OUTNAM, STATUS='NEW',IOSTAT=ISTAT)
```
3.
```
      CLOSE (UNIT=24)
```
4.
```
      READ (8,*,IOSTAT=ISTAT) FIRST, LAST
      IF ( ISTAT .LT. 0 ) THEN
          WRITE (*,*) 'End of file encountered on LU 8.'
      END IF
```

5.
```
      DO 10 I = 1, 8
         BACKSPACE (13)
   10 CONTINUE
```
6. These statements could work. However, if we are reading from the file, it would be better to use **STATUS='OLD'**.

7. Incorrect. You cannot specify a file name with a scratch file.

8. Incorrect. You cannot use a real value as an LU number.

9. Correct.

10. Incorrect for two reasons. The statements open LU9 and try to close LU8. Also, the close statement attempts to use a real value as an LU number.

Quiz 5-1

1. 15

2. 256

3. 41

4. Valid. The array is initialized with the values in the **DATA** statement.

5. Invalid. PHASE(0) is not a legal array element.

6. Invalid. Cannot assign a value to an array.

7. Valid. The values in array INDEX will be printed out.

8. Mostly valid. The values in array error will be printed out. However, since ERROR(0) was never initialized, we don't know what will be printed out, or even whether printing that array element will cause an I/O error.

9. Valid. A table of numbers and their squares will be printed for all integers between 1 and 10.

10. Probably invalid. These statements will compile correctly, but they probably do *not* do what the programmer intended. A 10-element integer array MYDATA will be created. Each **READ** statement reads values into the entire array, so array MYDATA will be initialized 10 times over (using up 100 input values!). The user probably intended for each array element to be initialized only once.

11. Valid. A 6-element integer array INPUT will be created and initialized with **READ** statements.

12. Valid. First, the **DO** loop and **WRITE** statement will write out each value in array STRING, with one value per line. Next, the second **WRITE** statement will write out each value in array STRING, with two values per line.

Quiz 5-2

1. 231 elements. The valid range is IRES(-10,0) to IRES(10,10).

2. 645 elements. The valid range is DATAIN(-64,0) to DATAIN(64,4).

3. 210 elements. The valid range is FILENM(1,1) to FILENM(3,70).

4. 294 elements. The valid range is IN(-3,-3,1) to IN(3,3,6).

5. Valid. DIST will be initialized with the values in the **DATA** statement.

6. Valid. TEMP(1,1) through TEMP(1,10) will be initialized with the value 33.0. All other values in array TEMP remain uninitialized.

7. These statements are valid. They set the elements of KDELTA to TRUE if I = J, and to FALSE otherwise. Then they print out the values of array KDELTA.

8. These statements are valid. They declare a 77-element array INDEX, and then initialize the array by reading values from file INPUT.

9. The data on the first three lines would be read into array input. However, the data is read in column order, so MYDATA(1,1) = 11.2, MYDATA(2,1) = 16.5, MYDATA(3,1) = 31.3, etc. MYDATA(2,4) = 10.0

10. The data on the first three lines would be read into array input. This time, the data is read in row order, so MYDATA(1,1) = 11.2, MYDATA(1,2) = 16.5, MYDATA(1,3) = 31.3, etc. MYDATA(2,4) = 11.0
11. The results of these statements are identical to those in problem 10.
12. DIST(6,2) = 9.0
13. 7

Quiz 6-1

1. The call to SUB1 is incorrect. The first argument in the calling sequence is an array and the second one is a scalar. The first argument in the subroutine itself is an array and the second argument is a scalar.
2. The call to AVESD is incorrect. The second parameter is declared as an integer in the calling program, but it is as a real value within the subroutine.
3. These statements are incorrect. Subroutine SUB3 uses 30 elements in array IARRAY, but there are only 25 values in the array passed from the calling program.

Quiz 6-2

1. The **SAVE** statement should be used in any subprogram that depends on local data values being unchanged between calls to the subprogram. All local variables that must remain constant between calls should be declared as **SAVE** variables.
2. A subroutine using a **COMMON** block to pass data can only work with the values in the **COMMON** block. A subroutine using an argument list to pass data can be called over and over with different data by changing the calling arguments.
3. This program will work on many computers, but it has two potentially serious problems. First, the value of variable **ISUM** is never initialized. Second, it is not **SAVED** between calls to SUB1. If this program works, it will print out the values I = 1, I = 2, etc.
4. There is a **COMMON** mismatch between the calling program TEST2 and subroutine SUB2. In program TEST2, a 10-element array is first in the common block. In subroutine SUB2, the 10-element array is second in the common block. As a result, data is mismatched, and X(5) = 6.0 in the subroutine instead of 5.0.
5. These statements are wrong. There can be no executable statements in a **BLOCK DATA** subprogram.

Quiz 6-3

1.
```
      REAL FUNCTION F1 ( X )
      IMPLICIT NONE
      REAL X
      F1 = X**2 -1.
      RETURN
      END
```
2.
```
      REAL FUNCTION F2 ( X )
      IMPLICIT NONE
      REAL X
      F2 = (X - 1.) / (X + 1.)
      RETURN
      END
```

3.
```
        REAL FUNCTION TANH ( X )
        IMPLICIT NONE
        REAL X
        TANH = (EXP(X)-EXP(-X)) / (EXP(X)+EXP(-X))
        RETURN
        END
```
4.
```
        INTEGER FUNCTION FACT ( N )
        IMPLICIT NONE
        INTEGER N, I
        FACT = 1.
        DO 10 I = N, 1, -1
           FACT = FACT * I
     10 CONTINUE
        RETURN
        END
```
5.
```
        LOGICAL FUNCTION COMPAR (X,Y)
        IMPLICIT NONE
        REAL X, Y
        COMPAR = X**2 + X**2 .GT. 1.0
        RETURN
        END
```
6. This function is incorrect because SUM is never initialized. The correct version of the function is
```
        FUNCTION AVE ( X, N )
        IMPLICIT NONE
        INTEGER N, J
        REAL X(N), SUM
     C
        SUM = 0.
        DO 10 J = 1, N
           SUM = SUM + X(J)
     10    CONTINUE
        AVE = SUM / N
        RETURN
        END
```
7. There are no errors in this function.

Quiz 7-1

1. This expression is FALSE for ASCII, and TRUE for EBCDIC.
2. This expression is FALSE for both ASCII, and EBCDIC.
3. This expression is FALSE.
4. The substring STRING(I:J) is illegal, since I > J. (Also, both I and J are beyond the maximum number of characters in the string.)
5. These statements are legal.
6. Variable NAME will contain the string
```
    'JOHNSON            ,JAMES              R'
```
7. A = '123'; B = 'ABCD23 IJKL'

8. ASCII: B = `'A1 <= A2'`, C = `'A1 LLE A2'`
   EBCDIC: B = `'A1>A2'`, C = `'A1 LLE A2'`
9. I = 4, J = 12
10. IPOS1 = 17, IPOS2 = 0, IPOS3 = 14

Quiz 7-2

1. Incorrect. There is a format descriptor mismatch here.
2. The statements are valid, and the result is

```
OUTPUT:
 -1234
```

Note that BUFF1(20:20) = `'T'`.
3. Incorrect. List-directed I/O does not work with internal files.
4. The statements are valid. IVAL1 = 456789, IVAL2 = 234, IVAL3 = 5678.90

Quiz 8-1

1.
```
                    2           100         6.40
----|----|----|----|----|----|----|----|----|----|----|----|
    5    10   15   20   25   30   35   40   45   50   55   60
```
2.
```
    4096.1  4096.07  .40961E+04  4096.1      4096.
----|----|----|----|----|----|----|----|----|----|----|----|
    5    10   15   20   25   30   35   40   45   50   55   60
```
3.
```
          DATA1(  1) =   -17.2000,       DATA1(  2) =      4.0000,
          DATA1(  3) =     4.0000,       DATA1(  4) =       .3000,
          DATA1(  5) =    -2.2200
----|----|----|----|----|----|----|----|----|----|----|----|----|----|
    5    10   15   20   25   30   35   40   45   50   55   60   65   70
```
4. I =
```
      I =      250000 J =        25
----|----|----|----|----|----|----|----|----|----|----|----|
    5    10   15   20   25   30   35   40   45   50   55   60
```
5.
```
      I =       -2002 J =      1776 K =       -3
----|----|----|----|----|----|----|----|----|----|----|----|
    5    10   15   20   25   30   35   40   45   50   55   60
```
6.
```
      I =       -2002 J =      -1001 K =      -3
----|----|----|----|----|----|----|----|----|----|----|----|
    5    10   15   20   25   30   35   40   45   50   55   60
```

Quiz 8-2

1. Invalid. It is illegal to use a file name with a scratch file.
2. Invalid. The **RECL**= clause must be specified when opening a direct access file.
3. Invalid. By default, direct access files are opened unformatted. Formatted I/O cannot be performed to unformatted files.
4. Invalid. Scratch files are empty when they are opened, so an attempt to read from a newly opened scratch file will fail.
5. Invalid. By default, sequential access files are opened formatted. Unformatted I/O cannot be performed to formatted files. (Note that this example tried to use both formatted and unformatted I/O to the same file. That will *always* fail, regardless of the formatting option with which the file is opened.)
6. Invalid. Either a file name or an LU may be specified in an INQUIRE statement, but not both.

Quiz 9-1

1. The result is **DOUBLE PRECISION**, with about 16 significant digits of accuracy.
2. The result is **REAL**.
3. The result is **INTEGER**.
4. The result is **COMPLEX**.
5. The result is **DOUBLE PRECISION**, but with only about seven significant digits of accuracy.

6.
```
      PROGRAM PRECIS
C
C  Purpose:
C    To calculate the number of significant digits available on a
C    computer.
C
      IMPLICIT NONE
C
      REAL    VALUE
      INTEGER NDIG
C
C    Add smaller and smaller numbers to 1.0 until the sum is no
C    longer different than the original number.
C
      VALUE = 1.0
      NDIG  = 0
    5 IF ( (1.0 + VALUE) .NE. 1.0 ) THEN
         NDIG  = NDIG + 1
         VALUE = VALUE / 10.
         GO TO 5
      END IF
C
C    When we get here, we have exceeded our limit.  Back off by 1 digit.
C
      WRITE (*,'(A,I3,A)') ' There are ', NDIG-1, ' significant digits.'
C
      END
```

7.
```
      (-1.980198E-02,-1.980198E-01)
   ----|----|----|----|----|----|----|----|----|----|----|----|
       5   10   15   20   25   30   35   40   45   50   55   60
```

8.
```
      PROGRAM CMPMTH
C
C  Purpose:
C    To perform the complex calculation:
C        D = ( A + B ) / C
C    where A = ( 1., -1.)
C          B = (-1., -1.)
C          C = (10.,  1.)
C
      IMPLICIT NONE
C
      REAL AR, AI, BR, BI, CR, CI, DR, DI, TEMPR, TEMPI
C
      DATA AR, AI / 1., -1. /
      DATA BR, BI / -1., -1. /
      DATA CR, CI / 10., 1. /
C
```

```
        CALL CMPADD ( AR, AI, BR, BI, TEMPR, TEMPI )
        CALL CMPDIV ( TEMPR, TEMPI, CR, CI, DR, DI )
C
        WRITE (*,100) DR, DI
  100 FORMAT (1X,'D = (',F10.5,',',F10.5,')' )
C
        END
        SUBROUTINE CMPADD ( A1, B1, A2, B2, A3, B3 )
C
C  Purpose:
C    Subroutine to add two complex numbers (A1, B1) and
C    (A2, B2), and store the result in (A3, B3).
C
        IMPLICIT NONE
C
        REAL A1, B1, A2, B2, A3, B3
C
        A3 = A1 + A2
        B3 = B1 + B2
C
        RETURN
        END
        SUBROUTINE CMPDIV ( A1, B1, A2, B2, A3, B3 )
C
C  Purpose:
C    Subroutine to divide two complex numbers (A1, B1) and
C    (A2, B2), and store the result in (A3, B3).
C
        IMPLICIT NONE
C
        REAL A1, B1, A2, B2, A3, B3, DENOM
C
        DENOM = A2**2 + B2**2
        A3 = (A1 * A2 + B1 * B2) / DENOM
        B3 = (B1 * A2 - A1 * B2) / DENOM
C
        RETURN
        END
```

It is much easier to use the complex data type to solve the problem than it is to use the definitions of complex operations and real numbers.

9.
```
        1.000000          (2.000000,3.000000E+00)      4.000000
  ----|----|----|----|----|----|----|----|----|----|----|----|
     5   10   15   20   25   30   35   40   45   50   55   60
```

Quiz 11-1

3.
```
        PROGRAM DOTPRD
C
C  Purpose:
C    To take the dot product of two vectors A and B.
C
        IMPLICIT NONE
C
```

```
      INTEGER    NVALS
      PARAMETER ( NVALS = 4 )
C
      REAL A(NVALS), B(NVALS)
      REAL VDOT
      EXTERNAL VDOT
C
      DATA A / 10.,  -2., 40., 3. /
      DATA B /  7., -10., -4., 6. /
C
      WRITE (*,'(A,F10.4)') ' The dot product is ', VDOT (A, B, NVALS)
      END
```

The dot product of vectors A and B is −52.

Quiz 12-1

1. Incorrect. Statement function QUAD must be called with four arguments, for instance: QUAD(A1,B1,C1, -3.).
2. Incorrect. The letter C is implicitly declared to be both **DOUBLE PRECISION** and **COMPLEX**.
3. Incorrect. Statement functions must be declared before the first executable statement in a program.
4. Incorrect. Dummy arguments may not be equivalenced.
5. Correct. This program illustrates the use of alternate subroutine returns. It returns to alternate branch 3.
6. `KE(M,V) = 0.5 * M * V**2`
7. `PE(M,H) = M * G * H`
8. `AREA(R) = 3.141592 * R**2`

Quiz 12-2

1. Valid. Prints `'X = 13.'`
2. Incorrect. The assigned **GO TO** cannot use a character variable.
3. Incorrect. An invalid statement number (15) is assigned to the assigned **GO TO** statement.

Quiz 13-1

1. Valid.
2. Invalid. A hyphen may not be used in a program name.
3. Invalid. Program names must begin with a letter.
4. Valid real.
5. Invalid. Variable names must begin with a letter.
6. Vaild integer.
7. Valid integer.
8. `INTEGER (KIND=2) LOOP_COUNT`   The largest integer that can be stored in this variable is 32,767.
9. `INTEGER (KIND=3) INDEX`   The largest integer that can be stored in this variable is 2,147,483,647.
10. `INTEGER (KIND=LONG) MICROSECONDS` where **LONG** has been previously declared.

11.
```
      TYPE STATE_VECTOR
          REAL(KIND=LONG)  RANGE
          REAL(KIND=SHORT) RANGE_RATE
          REAL(KIND=SHORT) AZIMUTH
          REAL(KIND=SHORT) ELEVATION
          REAL(KIND=LONG)  TIME_OF_VALIDITY
      END TYPE PERSON
      TYPE (STATE_VECTOR) TARGET
```
12. `TARGET%RANGE = 40.0D6`
13. `START_TIME >= 0.`
14. `IF ( A1 == A2 ) CALL SUBROUTINE_1`

Quiz 13-2

1.
```
      INTEGER AVE
      CHARACTER(LEN=1) GRADE
      IF (AVE > = 95 ) THEN
          GRADE = 'A'
      ELSE IF (AVE > = 90 ) THEN
          GRADE = 'B'
      ELSE IF (AVE > = 80 ) THEN
          GRADE = 'C'
      ELSE IF (AVE > = 70 ) THEN
          GRADE = 'D'
      ELSE
          GRADE = 'F'
      END IF
```
2.
```
INTEGER AVE
CHARACTER(LEN=1) GRADE
LETTER_GRADE:  SELECT CASE ( AVE )
               CASE ( 95:100 )
                   GRADE = 'A'
               CASE ( 90: 94 )
                   GRADE = 'B'
               CASE ( 80:89 )
                   GRADE = 'C'
               CASE ( 70:79 )
                   GRADE = 'D'
               CASE ( 0:69 )
                   GRADE = 'F'
               END SELECT LETTER_GRADE
```
3.
```
SUM = 0.
LOOP1:  DO I = 1, 1000
            SUM = SUM + C(I)
        END DO LOOP1
```
4.
```
READ (LU,*,IOSTAT = ISTAT) DATA(I)
DO WHILE (ISTAT == 0 )
    I = I + 1
    READ (LU,*) DATA(I)
END DO
```
5.
```
WHERE ( COVARIANCE > 0. )
    COVARIANCE = SQRT(COVARIANCE)
END WHERE
```

6. PROGRAM MATRIX_SUBTRACTION

```
!  Purpose:
!    To read in two matrices from a disk file and subtract them.  (This quick-
!    and-dirty program lacks some of the error checking that a production
!    program should include.)

!  Record of revisions:
!     Date        Programmer          Description of change
!     ====        ==========          =====================
!    10/15/93    S. J. Chapman        Original code

IMPLICIT NONE

!  Declare parameters.

INTEGER, PARAMETER :: SHORT  = 1     ! Single precision is KIND=1 on this machine
INTEGER, PARAMETER :: INT32  = 3     ! 32-bit integers are KIND=3 on this machine
INTEGER, PARAMETER :: MAXROW = 4     ! Maximum number of rows
INTEGER, PARAMETER :: MAXCOL = 4     ! Maximum number of columns


!  Declare the variables used in this program.

REAL (KIND=SHORT) A(MAXROW,MAXCOL) ! Matrix A
REAL (KIND=SHORT) B(MAXROW,MAXCOL) ! Matrix B
REAL (KIND=SHORT) C(MAXROW,MAXCOL) ! Matrix C
INTEGER (KIND=INT32) I             ! Index variable
INTEGER (KIND=INT32) J             ! Index variable
INTEGER (KIND=INT32) M             ! Number of rows in matrices
INTEGER (KIND=INT32) N             ! Number of columns in matrices

! Get matrix size.

WRITE (*,*) 'Enter matrix size (N x M):'
READ (*,*) N, M

! Get matrix A.

DO I = 1, N
   DO J = 1, M
      WRITE (*,'(1X,A,I2,A,I2,A)') 'Enter A(', I, ',', J, '):'
      READ (*,*) A(I,J)
   END DO
END DO
! Get matrix B.

DO I = 1, N
   DO J = 1, M
      WRITE (*,'(1X,A,I2,A,I2,A)') 'Enter B(', I, ',', J, '):'
      READ (*,*) B(I,J)
   END DO
END DO

! Subtract matrices.
```

```
C = A - B

! Write out result.

WRITE (*,'(1X,A)') ' A - B = '
DO I = 1, N
   WRITE (*,'(4X,6(F7.2,2X))') ( C(I,J), J = 1, M )
END DO

END PROGRAM
```

Quiz 13-3

1. An internal subroutine can only be called from within the routine in which it is declared, while an external subroutine can be called from any routine.
2. Dynamic memory permits a FORTRAN program to allocate *only the memory that it will actually use* when solving a problem, instead of allocating the largest amount of memory that it will ever need to solve the problem. As a result, the same program can run on big computers and little computers, with large problems being solved on the big machines and smaller problems solved on the smaller ones. The main disadvantage of dynamic memory is that the programmer must remember to both allocate it before use and deallocate it after use.
3.

```
PROGRAM READ_NAMELIST

! Purpose:
!    To illustrate a NAMELIST-directed READ statement.

USE F90_KIND

IMPLICIT NONE

! Declare variables
INTEGER (KIND=INT32) I, J, K, L    ! Integer variables

! Declare namelist
NAMELIST /MYLIST/ I, J, K, L

! Initialize variables
DATA I, J, K, L / 1, 2, 3, 4 /

! Write NAMELIST before update
WRITE (UNIT=6, NML=MYLIST)

! Read NAMELIST update
READ (UNIT=5, NML=MYLIST)

! Write NAMELIST after update
WRITE (UNIT=6, NML=MYLIST)

END
```

APPENDIX

Answers to Selected Exercises

Many of these exercise answers consist of FORTRAN programs. There are many possible correct FORTRAN programs for any given problem. The programs given here are good examples, but they are not the only way to solve the exercises.

Chapter 1

1. (*a*) 1010_2 (*c*) 1001101_2
2. (*b*) 137_{10} (*d*) 5_{10}
5. Six significant digits of precision, and range is 10^{-78}–10^{78}.

Chapter 2

1. (*a*) Valid real constant   (*b*) Valid character constant
   (*c*) Invalid constant—numbers may not include commas
6. (*a*) Legal: result = 0.888889   (*b*) Legal: result = 30   (*c*) Illegal   (*d*) Legal: result = 0.002
12. The program will run, but it will produce wrong answers, because the sine and cosine functions expect their arguments to have units of radians, not degrees.
14.
```
          PROGRAM GETPAY
C
C  Purpose:
C    To calculate an hourly employee's weekly pay.
C
C  Record of revisions:
C      Date        Programmer          Description of change
C      ====        ==========          =====================
C    10/21/93 -- S. J. Chapman         Original code
C
C  List of variables:
C    HOURS  -- Number of hours worked in a week.
C    PAY    -- Total weekly pay.
C    PRATE  -- Employees pay rate in dollars per hour.
C
       IMPLICIT NONE
C
```

```
C  Declare the variables used in this program.
C
       REAL HOURS, PAY, PRATE
C
       WRITE (*,*) 'Enter employees pay rate in dollars per hour:'
       READ (*,*) PRATE
C
       WRITE (*,*) 'Enter number of hours worked:'
       READ (*,*) HOURS
C
       PAY = PRATE * HOURS
C
       WRITE (*,*) 'Employee''s pay is $', PAY
C
       END
```

23.
```
       PROGRAM COSHX
C
C  Purpose:
C    To calculate the hyperbolic cosine of a number.
C
C  Record of revisions:
C      Date          Programmer          Description of change
C      ====          ==========          =====================
C    10/21/93 -- S. J. Chapman          Original code
C
C  List of variables:
C      X       -- Number to calculate cosh() of.
C      RESULT -- COSH(X)
C
       IMPLICIT NONE
C
C  Declare the variables used in this program.
C
       REAL X, RESULT
C
       WRITE (*,*) 'Enter number to calculate cosh() of:'
       READ (*,*) X
C
       RESULT = ( EXP(X) + EXP(-X) ) / 2.
C
       WRITE (*,*) 'COSH(X) =', RESULT
C
       END
```

Chapter 3

1.
```
       REAL       DEG2RD
       PARAMETER ( DEG2RD = 0.0174533 )
       COSTH = COS ( THETA * DEG2RD )
       IF ( ABS(COSTH) .GE. 1.0E-20 ) THEN
          TANTH = SIN ( THETA * DEG2RD ) / COSTH
       ELSE
          WROTE (*,*) 'Error: cosine(theta) too small.'
       END IF
```

3.
```
      DO 10 I = 0, 50, 2
         WRITE (*,*) I, I**2
   10 CONTINUE
```
8. The program STAT2 modified to use a DO WHILE loop is
```
      PROGRAM STAT2
C
C  Purpose:
C    To calculate mean and the standard deviation of an input
C    data set containing an arbitrary number of input values.
C
C  Record of revisions:
C       Date       Programmer          Description of change
C       ====       ==========          ======================
C 0.  12/29/90   S. J. Chapman       Original code
C 1.  12/31/90   S. J. Chapman       Correct divide-by-0 error if
C                                    0 or 1 input values given.
C
C  List of variables:
C      N       -- The number of input samples.
C      S       -- The standard deviation of the input samples.
C      SUMX    -- The sum of the input values.
C      SUMX2   -- The sum of the squares of the input values.
C                 units of reciprocal years.
C      X       -- An input data value.
C      XBAR    -- The average of the input samples.
C
      IMPLICIT NONE
C
C    Declare the variables used in this program.
C
      INTEGER N
      REAL    X, SUMX, SUMX2
      REAL    XBAR, S
C
C    Initialize the sums to zero.
C
      N     = 0
      SUMX  = 0.
      SUMX2 = 0.
      X     = 0.
C
C    Get first number, and echo it back to the user.
C
      WRITE (*,*) 'Enter first number: '
      READ  (*,*) X
      WRITE (*,*) 'The number is ', X
C
C    Loop to read input values.
C
      DO WHILE ( X .GE. 0. )
C
```

```
C       Accumulate sums.
C
        N     = N + 1
        SUMX  = SUMX + X
        SUMX2 = SUMX2 + X**2
C
C       Get next number.
C
        WRITE (*,*) 'Enter next number: '
        READ  (*,*) X
        WRITE (*,*) 'The number is ', X
C
     END DO
C
C    Check to see if we have enough input data.
C
     IF ( N .LT. 2 ) THEN
C
C       Insufficient data.
C
        WRITE (*,*) ' At least 2 values must be entered.'
C
     ELSE
C
C       Calculate the mean and standard deviation
C
        XBAR = SUMX / REAL(N)
        S    = SQRT( (REAL(N) * SUMX2 - SUMX**2)
     *         / (REAL(N) * REAL(N-1)) )
C
C       Tell user.
C
        WRITE (*,*) ' The mean of this data set is:', XBAR
        WRITE (*,*) ' The standard deviation is:   ', S
        WRITE (*,*) ' The number of data points is:', N
C
     END IF
C
C    Finish up.
C
     END
     PROGRAM FUNCTN
```
11.
```
C
C Purpose:
C   To evaluate the function of exercise 11 in Chapter 3.
C
C Record of revisions:
C     Date        Programmer              Description of change
C     ====        ==========              =====================
C   10/22/93 -- S. J. Chapman             Original code
C
```

```
C   List of variables:
C      X         -- Input variable.
C      Y         -- Input variable.
C      FUN       -- Resulting function.
C
       IMPLICIT NONE
C
       REAL X, Y, FUN
C
C      Get X and Y.
C
       WRITE (*,*) 'Enter X and Y:'
       READ (*,*) X, Y
C
C      Evaluate function.
C
       IF ( X .GE. 0. ) THEN
          IF ( Y .GE. 0. ) THEN
             FUN = X + Y
          ELSE
             FUN = X + Y**2
          END IF
       ELSE
          IF ( Y .GE. 0. ) THEN
             FUN = X**2 + Y
          ELSE
             FUN = X**2 + Y**2
          END IF
       END IF
C
C      Write out answer.
C
       WRITE (*,*) 'The result of the function is :', FUN
C
       END
```

15. (*a*) IRES = 21   (*b*) IRES = 13   (*c*) IRES = 0

Chapter 4

2. (*a*) Advance to new page and print contents of buffer.
   (*b*) Advance one line and print contents of buffer.   (*c*) Advance two lines and print contents of buffer.
   (*d*) Do not advance (remain in current line) and print contents of buffer.   (*e*) Results undefined.

3. (*c*) The result is printed out on the next line. It is

```
A =    1.002000E+06 B =    1.000100E+06 SUM =    2.002100E+06 DIFF =    19000.000000
----|----|----|----|----|----|----|----|----|----|----|----|----|----|----|----|
     5   10   15   20   25   30   35   40   45   50   55   60   65   70   75   80
```

6. (*b*)

```
ITEM1 = -300,  ITEM2 = -250,  ITEM3 = -210,  ITEM4 = -160,  ITEM5 = -105,
ITEM6 = -70,  ITEM7 = -17,  ITEM8 = -55,  ITEM9 = 102,  ITEM10 = 165
```

   (*c*)

```
LAST = 'JOHNSON          ', FIRST = 'JAMES            ', MI = 'R', SEX = 'M',
AGE = 45,  SKILL = 'ELECTRICAL ENGR      '
```

15.
```
      PROGRAM HHMMSS
C
C Purpose:
C   To convert a time in seconds since the start of the day
C   into Hh:MM:SS format, using the 24 hour convention.
C
C Record of revisions:
C     Date        Programmer           Description of change
C     ====        ==========           =====================
C   10/25/93 -- S. J. Chapman          Original code
C
C List of parameters:
C   SECPHR -- Number of seconds per hour.
C   SECPMN -- Number of seconds per minute.
C
C List of variables:
C   IHOUR  - Number of hours.
C   IMIN   - Number of minutes.
C   ISEC   - Number of seconds.
C   REMAIN - Remaining seconds to account for.
C   SECNDS - Input number of seconds since start of day.
C
      IMPLICIT NONE
C
C Declare parameters.
C
      INTEGER SECPHR, SECPMN
      PARAMETER ( SECPHR = 3600. )
      PARAMETER ( SECPMN = 60.   )
C
C Declare the variables used in this program.
C
      INTEGER IHOUR, IMIN, ISEC
      REAL    REMAIN, SECNDS
C
      WRITE (*,*) 'Enter the number of seconds since the start of day:'
      READ (*,*) SECNDS
C
C   Calculate the number of hours, and the number of seconds left
C   over after the hours are calcluated.
C
      IHOUR  = INT ( SECNDS / SECPHR )
      REMAIN = SECNDS - REAL ( IHOUR ) * SECPHR
C
C   Calculate the number of minutes left, and the number of seconds
C   left over after the hours are calcluated.
C
      IMIN   = INT ( REMAIN / SECPMN )
      REMAIN = REMAIN - REAL ( IMIN ) * SECPMN
C
C   Get number of seconds left.
C
```

```
            ISEC = NINT ( REMAIN )
      C
      C     Write out result.
      C
            WRITE (*,100) SECNDS, IHOUR, IMIN, ISEC
        100 FORMAT (1X,F7.1,' seconds = ',I2,':',I2.2,':',I2.2)
      C
            END
```

19.
```
            PROGRAM EX0419
      C
      C  Purpose:
      C    To open two files, and copy all positive values from file
      C    1 into file 2.
      C
      C  Record of revisions:
      C      Date        Programmer          Description of change
      C      ====        ==========          =====================
      C    10/25/93 -- S. J. Chapman         Original code
      C
      C  List of variables:
      C     ISTAT  -- I/O Status of READs.
      C     ISTAT1 -- I/O Status of input file OPEN.
      C     ISTAT2 -- I/O Status of output file OPEN.
      C     VALUE  -- Value read from input file.
      C
            IMPLICIT NONE
      C
      C     Declare the variables used in this program.
      C
            INTEGER ISTAT1, ISTAT2, ISTAT
            REAL    VALUE
      C
      C     Open files.
      C
            OPEN ( 98, FILE='INPUT.DAT', STATUS='OLD', IOSTAT=ISTAT1 )
            OPEN ( 99, FILE='NEWOUT.DAT', STATUS='NEW', IOSTAT=ISTAT2 )
      C
      C     Process data if both files opened correctly.
      C
            IF ( ( ISTAT1 .EQ. 0 ) .AND. ( ISTAT2 .EQ. 0 ) ) THEN
               READ (98, *, IOSTAT=ISTAT ) VALUE
      C
      C        While loop over successful READs.
      C
         1     IF ( ISTAT .EQ. 0. ) THEN
                  IF ( VALUE .GT. 0. ) THEN
                     WRITE (99,*) VALUE
                  END IF
                  READ (98, *, IOSTAT=ISTAT ) VALUE
                  GO TO 1
               END IF
      C
```

```
C        Close files.
C
         CLOSE (98)
         CLOSE (99)
      END IF
C
      END
```

Chapter 5

4. (*a*) 80 elements; valid subscript range is 1–60.   (*c*) 225 elements; valid subscript range is 32–256.
(*e*) 161,051 elements; valid subscript range is $(-5:-5:-5:-5:-5)$ to $(5:5:5:5:5)$.

5. (*a*) Invalid. ICOUNT is an array, and arrays cannot be used as index elements. (*Array elements* such as ICOUNT(1) could have been used, however.)

(*b*) Invalid. This code tries to assign values to nonexistent array elements.

(*c*) Valid. The statements print out the words 'VALUE = ' at the top of a new page, and then the 10 values in the array, with one value per line. The value are printed out in the following order: 5.00, 10.00, 4.00, 9.00, 3.00, 8.00, 2.00, 7.00, 1.00, 6.00.

(*d*) These statements print out the values in array ARRAY, with 10 values printed per line.

```
9.    PROGRAM RECT1
C
C  Purpose:
C     To read in a two-dimensional vector in magnitude & angle form,
C     and convert it into rectangluar form.
C
C  Record of revisions:
C      Date         Programmer             Description of change
C      ====         ==========             =====================
C     10/25/93 -- S. J. Chapman            Original code
C
C  List of parameters:
C     DEG2RD -- Convert degrees to radians
C
C  List of variables:
C     ISTAT   -- I/O Status of READs.
C     ISTAT1  -- I/O Status of input file OPEN.
C     POLAR   -- Array containing the magnitude and angle of the vector
C                POLAR(1) contains magnitude
C                POLAR(2) contains angle in degrees
C     RECT    -- Array containing the rectangular components of the vector.
C
      IMPLICIT NONE
C
C     Parameters.
C
      REAL         DEG2RD
      PARAMETER ( DEG2RD =  0.0174533 )
C
C     Declare the variables used in this program.
C
```

```
        REAL    POLAR(2), RECT(2)
C
C     Get vector in polar form.
C
        WRITE (*,100) 'Enter the magnitude and angle (in degrees)',
     *                ' of the vector:'
  100 FORMAT (1X,A,A)
        READ (*,*) POLAR
C
C     Convert to rectangular form.
C
        RECT(1) = POLAR(1) * COS ( DEG2RD * POLAR(2) )
        RECT(2) = POLAR(1) * SIN ( DEG2RD * POLAR(2) )
C
C     Write out result.
C
        WRITE (*,110) RECT
  110 FORMAT (1X,'The rectangular form of the vector is',
     *          F9.5,'i + ',F9.5,'j')
C
        END
```

13.
```
        DO 10 I = -50, 50, 5
            WRITE (*,100) I, VALUES(I)
  100       FORMAT (7X,'VALUES(',I3,') = ',F8.4)
   10 CONTINUE
```

14.
```
        PROGRAM EX0514
C
C  Purpose:
C    To read in a array, and find the sums of all rows and
C    columns in the array.
C
C  Record of revisions:
C     Date        Programmer          Description of change
C     ====        ==========          =====================
C   10/25/93   S. J. Chapman          Original code
C
C  List of parameters:
C     MAXSIZ -- Maximum size of array.
C
C  List of variables:
C     A       -- Array.
C     I       -- Index variable.
C     ISTAT   -- I/O status.
C     J       -- Index variable.
C     NCOL    -- Number of cols actually used in array A
C     NROW    -- Number of rows actually used in array A
C     SUMCOL  -- Sum of each column in array A
C     SUMROW  -- Sum of each row in array A
C
        IMPLICIT NONE
C
        INTEGER    MAXSIZ
        PARAMETER ( MAXSIZ = 10 )
C
```

```
      INTEGER   I, J, NCOL, NROW, ISTAT
      REAL      A(MAXSIZ,MAXSIZ), SUMROW(MAXSIZ), SUMCOL(MAXSIZ)
      CHARACTER FILENM*20
C
C     Get the name of the disk file containing the array.
C
      WRITE (*,1000)
 1000 FORMAT (' Enter the file name containing the array: ')
      READ (*,1010) FILENM
 1010 FORMAT ( A20 )
C
C     Open input data file.  Status is OLD because the input data must
C     already exist.
C
      OPEN ( UNIT=1, FILE=FILENM, STATUS='OLD', IOSTAT=ISTAT )
C
C     Was the OPEN successful?
C
      IF ( ISTAT .EQ. 0 ) THEN
C
C         The file was opened successfully, so read the size of array A.
C
          READ (1,*) NROW, NCOL
C
C         If the sizes are <= MAXSIZ, read A in and process it.
C
          IF ( (NROW .LE. MAXSIZ ) .AND. (NCOL .LE. MAXSIZ ) ) THEN
             DO 10 I = 1, NROW
                 READ (1,*) (A(I,J), J=1,NCOL)
   10        CONTINUE
C
C            Clear the sum arrays.
C
             DO 20 I = 1, NROW
                SUMROW(I) = 0.
   20        CONTINUE
             DO 30 J = 1, NCOL
                SUMCOL(J) = 0.
   30        CONTINUE
C
C            Sum the rows and columns.
C
             DO 50 I = 1, NROW
                SUMROW(I) = 0.
                DO 40 J = 1, NCOL
                   SUMROW(I) = SUMROW(I) + A(I,J)
                   SUMCOL(J) = SUMCOL(J) + A(I,J)
   40           CONTINUE
   50        CONTINUE
C
C            Write results.
C
```

```
                DO 60 I = 1, NROW
                    WRITE (*,100) I, SUMROW(I)
      100           FORMAT (1X,'Sum of row ',I2,' = ',F12.4)
       60       CONTINUE
                DO 70 J = 1, NCOL
                    WRITE (*,110) J, SUMCOL(J)
      110           FORMAT (1X,'Sum of col ',I2,' = ',F12.4)
       70       CONTINUE
C
            END IF
        END IF
C
        END
```

17.
```
        PROGRAM DTPRDN
C
C Purpose:
C   To read in two N-dimensional vectors and calculate the
C   dot product of the two vectors.
C
C Record of revisions:
C     Date        Programmer          Description of change
C     ====        ==========          =====================
C   10/25/93    S. J. Chapman         Original code
C
C List of parameters:
C   MAXSIZ -- Maximum size of vectors.
C
C List of variables:
C   DPROD   -- Dot product of vectors V1 and V2.
C   I       -- Index variable.
C   NDIM    -- Dimension of vectors V1 and V2.
C   V1      -- First vector.
C   V2      -- Second vector.
C
        IMPLICIT NONE
C
        INTEGER    MAXSIZ
        PARAMETER ( MAXSIZ = 10 )
C
        INTEGER    I, NDIM
        REAL       DPROD, V1(MAXSIZ), V2(MAXSIZ)
C
C Get dimesnion of vectors V1 and V2.
C
        WRITE (*,*) 'Enter dimension of vectors V1 and V2:'
        READ (*,*) NDIM
C
C Is NDIM <= MAXSIZ?
C
        IF ( NDIM .LE. MAXSIZ ) THEN
C
C       Yes.  Get vector V1.
C
```

```
            WRITE (*,*) 'Enter vector V1:'
            READ (*,*) (V1(I), I = 1, NDIM)

C
C         Get vector V2.
C
            WRITE (*,*) 'Enter vector V2:'
            READ (*,*) (V2(I), I = 1, NDIM)
C
C         Calculate dot product.
C
            DPROD = 0.
            DO 10 I = 1, NDIM
               DPROD = DPROD + V1(I) * V2(I)
   10       CONTINUE
C
C         Write out result.
C
            WRITE (*,110) DPROD
  110       FORMAT (1X,'The dot product of V1 and V2 is ',F12.6)
C
         ELSE
C
C         No.  NDIM > MAXSIZ.
C
            WRITE (*,120) NDIM, MAXSIZ
  120       FORMAT (1X,'Too many dimensions: ', I3, ' > ', I3 )
C
         END IF
C
         END
24.      PROGRAM MATADD
C
C   Purpose:
C     To read in two matrices and add them if they are of compatible
C     sizes.
C
C   Record of revisions:
C      Date        Programmer           Description of change
C      ====        ==========           =====================
C    10/25/93   S. J. Chapman           Original code
C
C   List of parameters:
C     MAXSIZ -- Maximum size of arrays.
C
C   List of variables:
C     A      -- First array to add.
C     B      -- Second array to add.
C     C      -- First array to add.
C     FILEN1 -- Name of file containing array A.
C     FILEN2 -- Name of file containing array B.
C     I      -- Index variable.
C     ISTAT1 -- I/O status on file containing array A.
C     ISTAT2 -- I/O status on file containing array B.
```

```
C      J       -- Index variable.
C      NCOL1   -- Number of cols actually used in array A
C      NROW1   -- Number of rows actually used in array A
C      NCOL2   -- Number of cols actually used in array B
C      NROW2   -- Number of rows actually used in array B
C
       IMPLICIT NONE
C
       INTEGER   MAXSIZ
       PARAMETER ( MAXSIZ = 20 )
C
       INTEGER   I, J, NCOL1, NROW1, ISTAT1, NCOL2, NROW2, ISTAT2
       REAL      A(MAXSIZ,MAXSIZ), B(MAXSIZ,MAXSIZ), C(MAXSIZ,MAXSIZ)
       CHARACTER FILEN1*20, FILEN2*20
C
C      Get the name of the disk file containing array A.
C
       WRITE (*,1000)
 1000  FORMAT (' Enter the file name containing array A: ')
       READ (*,1010) FILEN1
 1010  FORMAT ( A20 )
C
C      Get the name of the disk file containing array B.
C
       WRITE (*,1020)
 1020  FORMAT (' Enter the file name containing array B: ')
       READ (*,1010) FILEN2
C
C      Open input data files.  Status is OLD because the input data
C      must already exist.
C
       OPEN ( UNIT=1, FILE=FILEN1, STATUS='OLD', IOSTAT=ISTAT1 )
       OPEN ( UNIT=2, FILE=FILEN2, STATUS='OLD', IOSTAT=ISTAT2 )
C
C      Were the OPENs successful?
C
       IF ( (ISTAT1 .EQ. 0) .AND. (ISTAT2 .EQ. 0) ) THEN
C
C         The files were opened successfully.  Read the size of array A.
C
          READ (1,*) NROW1, NCOL1
C
C         Read the size of array B.
C
          READ (2,*) NROW2, NCOL2
C
C         If any dimension exceeds MAXSIZ, tell user and quit.
C
          IF ( (NROW1.GT.MAXSIZ) .OR. (NCOL1 .GT. MAXSIZ) .OR.
     *         (NROW2.GT.MAXSIZ) .OR. (NCOL2 .GT. MAXSIZ) ) THEN
C
C            Error.
C
```

```
            WRITE (*,1030) MAXSIZ
 1030       FORMAT (1X,'Error—An array dimension exceeds MAXSIZ:',I6)
C
C       If NROW1 <> NROW2 or NCOL1 <> NCOL2, tell user and quit.
C
        ELSE IF ( (NROW1 .NE. NROW2) .OR. (NCOL1 .NE. NCOL2) ) THEN
C
C           Error.
C
            WRITE (*,1040) NROW1, NCOL1, NROW2, NCOL2
 1040       FORMAT (1X,'Error—Incompatible sizes: A is ',I2, ' x ',
     *              I2,', and B is ', I2, ' x ', I2,'.')
        ELSE
C
C           Read matrices A and B.
C
            DO 10 I = 1, NROW1
               READ (1,*) (A(I,J), J=1,NCOL1)
               READ (2,*) (B(I,J), J=1,NCOL1)
   10       CONTINUE
C
C           Add the arrays together.
C
            DO 30 I = 1, NROW1
               DO 20 J = 1, NCOL1
                  C(I,J) = A(I,J) + B(I,J)
   20          CONTINUE
   30       CONTINUE
C
C           Write out the result.
C
            WRITE (*,*) 'The resulting matrix C is:'
            DO 40 I = 1, NROW1
               WRITE (*,1050) (C(I,J), J=1,NCOL1)
 1050          FORMAT (1X,8(F9.2,1X))
   40       CONTINUE
C
        END IF
C
C       Close files
C
        CLOSE (1)
        CLOSE (2)
C
     ELSE
C
C       If we get here, there was an error opening one of the files.
C       Tell user, and quit.
C
        IF ( ISTAT1 .NE. 0 ) THEN
           WRITE (*,1060) FILEN1, ISTAT1
 1060      FORMAT (1X,'Error opening file ',A,': IOSTAT = ',I6)
        END IF
```

```
                    IF ( ISTAT2 .NE. 0 ) THEN
                       WRITE (*,1060) FILEN2, ISTAT2
                    END IF
                 END IF
      C
                 END
```

Chapter 6

7. (*a*) Correct.   (*b*) Incorrect. Function FACT is recursive—it calls itself.
   (*c*) Incorrect. The array is type **REAL** in the main program and type **INTEGER** in the subroutine. Also, variable I is used but not declared in the subroutine.

9. The variables in common block DATA1 are declared differently in the main program and the subroutine. *This is bad programming practice.* Here, L corresponds to A and M(2) corresponds to B(2), but because of the different lengths, N(2) corresponds to C(4). Therefore, the output from this program is

   1.000000   3.000000   3.000000

13.

```
          SUBROUTINE RAN2 ( VAL )
      C
      C  Purpose:
      C    To generate uniform random numbers in the range [-1., 1.)
      C    using subroutine RAN0.
      C
      C  Record of revisions:
      C      Date          Programmer          Description of change
      C      ====          ==========          =====================
      C    10/30/93 -- S. J. Chapman          Original code
      C
      C  List of calling arguments:
      C     NAME    I/O  TYPE          DESCRIPTION
      C     ====    ===  ====          ===========
      C     VAL      O   REAL          Random number.
      C
      C  List of local variables:
      C     None.
      C
              IMPLICIT NONE
      C
      C     Declare variables.
      C
              REAL VAL
      C
      C     Call RAN0.
      C
              CALL RAN0 ( VAL )
      C
      C     Map to the proper output range.
      C
              VAL = 2.0 * VAL - 1.0
      C
              RETURN
              END
```

16. The function to calculate sinh (*x*) is shown below:

```
      FUNCTION SINH1 ( X )
C
C  Purpose:
C    To calculate the hyperbolic sine function.
C
C  Record of revisions:
C     Date        Programmer          Description of change
C     ====        ==========          =====================
C    10/30/93 -- S. J. Chapman        Original code
C
C  List of calling arguments:
C     NAME     I/O  TYPE         DESCRIPTION
C     ====     ===  ====         ===========
C     X        I    REAL         Input value.
C     SINH1    O    REAL         sinh(x)
C
C  List of local variables:
C     None.
C
      IMPLICIT NONE
C
C     Declare variables.
C
      REAL SINH1, X
C
C     Calculate the hyperbolic sine function.
C
      SINH1 = ( EXP(X) - EXP(-X) ) / 2.
C
      RETURN
      END
```

30.
```
      FUNCTION DETER3 ( A )
C
C  Purpose:
C    To calculate the determinant of a 3 x 3 matrix.
C
C  Record of revisions:
C     Date        Programmer          Description of change
C     ====        ==========          =====================
C    10/30/93 -- S. J. Chapman        Original code
C
C  List of calling arguments:
C     NAME     I/O  TYPE         DESCRIPTION
C     ====     ===  ====         ===========
C     A        I    REAL ARR     Input 3 x 3 matrix.
C     DETER3   O    REAL         Determinant of the matrix A
C
C  List of local variables:
C     None.
C
      IMPLICIT NONE
C
C     Declare variables.
C
```

```
      REAL A(3,3), DETER3
C
C     Calculate the determinant.
C
      DETER3 = A(1,1)*A(2,2)*A(3,3) + A(1,2)*A(2,3)*A(3,1)
     *       + A(1,3)*A(2,1)*A(3,2) - A(3,1)*A(2,2)*A(1,3)
     *       - A(3,2)*A(2,3)*A(1,1) - A(3,3)*A(2,1)*A(1,2)
C
      RETURN
      END
```

33.
```
      FUNCTION EXP1 ( X )
C
C  Purpose:
C    To calculate EXP(X) using an infinite series.
C
C  Record of revisions:
C      Date        Programmer           Description of change
C      ====        ==========           =====================
C    10/30/93 -- S. J. Chapman          Original code
C
C  List of calling arguments:
C     NAME    I/O  TYPE          DESCRIPTION
C     ====    ===  ====          ===========
C     X       I    REAL          Input value.
C     EXP1    O    REAL          EXP(X)
C
C  List of local variables:
C     I        - DO loop index.
C     IFACT    - I!, or 1*2*...*I
C     XI       - X**I, X to the Ith power
C
      IMPLICIT NONE
C
C     Declare variables.
C
      INTEGER I, IFACT
      REAL    X, EXP1, XI
C
C     Calculate the first term of the series:
C     X**0 / 0! = 1.0
C
      EXP1 = 1.
C
C     Calculate the next 11 terms of EXP(X).
C
      XI    = 1.
      IFACT = 1
      Do 10 I = 1, 11
         XI    = XI * X
         IFACT = IFACT * I
         EXP1  = EXP1 + XI / REAL(IFACT)
   10 CONTINUE
C
      RETURN
      END
```

Chapter 7

1. A = '1234567890123456', B = 'ABCDEFGHIJKLMNOP', C = '678   IJK   '

6. STR1 = 'ABCDEFGHI', STR2 = 'ABCDEFGHIfghi   ', TEMP = 'fghi '. These values will be the same on computers with either ASCII or EBCDIC collating sequences. In ASCII machines, BASE1 = 64 and BASE2 = 96. On EBCDIC machines, BASE1 = 192 and BASE2 = 128.

17.

```
      SUBROUTINE UCASE ( STRING )
C
C  Purpose:
C    To shift a character string to UPPER case (ASCII or
C    EBCDIC).
C
C  Record of revisions:
C      Date         Programmer          Description of change
C      ====         ==========          =====================
C    10/31/93     S. J. Chapman         Original code
C
C  List of calling arguments:
C    NAME    I/O  TYPE          DESCRIPTION
C    ====    ===  ====          ===========
C    STRING  IO   CHARACTER     Input/output character string
C
C  List of local variables:
C    I       -- Index variable.
C    DELTA   -- Difference between upper case and lower case
C    LBASE   -- Base of lower-case letters
C    LENGTH  -- Length of STRING
C    S       -- Converted character.
C    UBASE   -- Base of upper-case letters.
C
      IMPLICIT NONE
C
C    Declare calling parameters
C
      CHARACTER*(*)  STRING
C
C    Declare local variables
C
      INTEGER    DELTA, I, LBASE, LENGTH, UBASE
      CHARACTER*1 S
C
C    Get the length of the input STRING.
C
      LENGTH = LEN ( STRING )
C
C    Get the bases of the Upper Case and Lower Case alphabets.
C
      UBASE = ICHAR ( 'A' ) - 1
      LBASE = ICHAR ( 'a' ) - 1
      DELTA = UBASE - LBASE
C
```

```
C       Now shift lower case letters to upper case.  There will be
C       several tests here to avoid the gaps in the EBCDIC collating
C       sequence.
C
        DO 10 I = 1, LENGTH
           IF ( (STRING(I:I).GE.'a') .AND. (STRING(I:I).LE.'i') .OR.
     *          (STRING(I:I).GE.'j') .AND. (STRING(I:I).LE.'r') .OR.
     *          (STRING(I:I).GE.'s') .AND. (STRING(I:I).LE.'z') ) THEN
              S = CHAR ( ICHAR ( STRING(I:I) ) + DELTA )
              STRING(I:I) = S
           END IF
     10 CONTINUE
C
        RETURN
        END
```

27.
```
        PROGRAM FCOPY
C
C  Purpose:
C    To read FORTRAN source code from an input file and copy it to
C    an output file, stripping out any comment lines in program.
C
C  Record of revisions:
C     Date        Programmer          Description of change
C     ====        ==========          =====================
C    10/31/93    S. J. Chapman         Original code
C
C  List of variables:
C     FILEN1 -- Name of input data file to read.
C     FILEN2 -- Name of output data file to read.
C     ISTAT  -- I/O status variable:  0 for success
C     ISTAT1 -- File open status variable:  0 for success
C     ISTAT2 -- File open status variable:  0 for success
C     LINE   -- Line of source code
C
        IMPLICIT NONE
C
C    Declare the variables used in this program.
C
        INTEGER      ISTAT, ISTAT1, ISTAT2
        CHARACTER*36 FILEN1, FILEN2, LINE*72
C
C    Get the name of the file containing the input data.
C
        WRITE (*,*) 'FCOPY -- Source file copy program'
        WRITE (*,1000)
   1000 FORMAT (' Enter the input file name: ')
        READ (*,1010) FILEN1
C
C    Get the name of the file to write the output data to.
C
```

```
 1010 FORMAT ( A36 )
      WRITE (*,1020)
 1020 FORMAT (' Enter the output file name: ')
      READ (*,1010) FILEN2
C
C     Open input data file.  Status is OLD because the input data
C     must already exist.
C
      OPEN ( UNIT=8, FILE=FILEN1, STATUS='OLD', IOSTAT=ISTAT1 )
C
C     Open output data file.  Status is NEW so that we don't overwrite
C     existing data.
C
      OPEN ( UNIT=9, FILE=FILEN2, STATUS='NEW', IOSTAT=ISTAT2 )
C
C     Was the OPEN successful?
C
      IF ( ( ISTAT1 .EQ. 0 ) .AND. ( ISTAT2 .EQ. 0 ) ) THEN
C
C        The files were opened successfully, so read the data from
C        the input file and put it into the output file if it is
C        not a comment line.
C
         READ (8, 1030, IOSTAT=ISTAT) LINE
 1030    FORMAT (A72)
C
C        Begin WHILE loop.  Did we read the value successfully?
C
   10    IF ( ISTAT .EQ. 0 ) THEN
C
C           Yes.  If not a comment, write out this line.
C
            IF ( ( LINE(1:1) .NE. 'C' ) .AND.
     *           ( LINE(1:1) .NE. 'c' ) .AND.
     *           ( LINE(1:1) .NE. '*' ) ) THEN
               WRITE (9, 1030, IOSTAT=ISTAT) LINE
            END IF
C
C           Read next line.
C
            READ (8, 1030, IOSTAT=ISTAT) LINE
            GO TO 10
C
C           End of WHILE Loop
C
         END IF
      END IF
C
C     Handle file open errors.
C
      IF ( ISTAT1 .NE. 0 ) THEN
         WRITE (*,1040) ISTAT1
 1040    FORMAT (1X,'Open error on input file: ISTAT = ', I6)
      END IF
C
```

```
        IF ( ISTAT2 .NE. 0 ) THEN
           WRITE (*,1050) ISTAT2
  1050    FORMAT (1X,'Open error on output file: ISTAT = ', I6)
        END IF
C
        END
```

Chapter 8

5. A possible program to generate and display the random numbers is shown below.

```
        PROGRAM EX0805
C
C  Purpose:
C    To generate 9 random numbers in the range [-100000,
C    100000), and display them using the G11.5 and SP
C    format descriptors.
C
        IMPLICIT NONE
C
C     Declare the variables used in this program.
C
        INTEGER I
        REAL    VALUE(9)
        CALL SEED ( 10101 )
C
C     Get the numbers.
C
        DO 10 I = 1, 9
           CALL RANO ( VALUE(I) )
           VALUE(I) = 200000. * VALUE(I) - 100000.
   10 CONTINUE
C
C     Display the numbers.
C
        WRITE (*,1000) VALUE
 1000 FORMAT (1X,'VALUE = ',/,(5X,SP,G11.5))
C
        END
```

When this program is executed, a typical result is

```
VALUE =
    -27516.
    +82003.
    +10979.
    +512.64
    +72487.
    -11277.
    +25156.
    -1525.1
    -85090.
```

7. (*a*) $-.6388E+11$ (*b*) -638.8 (*c*) $-.6388$ (*d*) 2346.

11. The status of the file is **'UNKNOWN'**. It is a formatted file opened for sequential access. Blanks will be interpreted as nulls in the file. The length of each record is variable. If the file is not found, a new file will be created. If there is an error in the open process, the program containing this statement will abort.

16.

```
      PROGRAM BLKRM2
C
C  Purpose:
C    To read FORTRAN source code from an input file and copy it to
C    an output file, stripping out trailing blanks.  This program
C    uses the INQUIRE statement to ensure that the input file
C    already exists, and that the output file does not already
C    exit. If the output file does exist, the program asks the
C    user whether or not to overwrite it.
C
C  Record of revisions:
C      Date       Programmer         Description of change
C      ====       ==========         =====================
C    10/31/93    S. J. Chapman       Original code
C 1.  1/25/94    S. J. Chapman       Formats changed
C
C  List of variables:
C    EXIST1 -- File 1 exists.
C    EXIST2 -- File 2 exists.
C    FILEN1 -- Name of input data file to read.
C    FILEN2 -- Name of output data file to read.
C    ISTAT  -- I/O status variable:  0 for success
C    ISTAT1 -- File open status variable:  0 for success
C    ISTAT2 -- File open status variable:  0 for success
C    LINE   -- Line of source code
C    YN     -- Yes / No response
C
      IMPLICIT NONE
C
C    Declare the variables used in this program.
C
      INTEGER      ISTAT, ISTAT1, ISTAT2, LASTC
      LOGICAL      EXIST1, EXIST2
      CHARACTER*20 FILEN1, FILEN2, LINE*80, YN*1
C
C    Get the name of the file containing the input data.
C
      WRITE (*,*) 'BLKREM — Copy removing trailing blanks'
      WRITE (*,*) 'Enter the input file name: '
      READ (*,'(A20)') FILEN1
C
C    Get the name of the file to write the output data to.
C
      WRITE (*,*) 'Enter the output file name: '
      READ (*,'(A20)') FILEN2
C
C    Does the input file exist?
C
```

```
          INQUIRE (FILE=FILEN1,EXIST=EXIST1)
C
C     If so, does output file exist?
C
      IF ( EXIST1 ) THEN
          INQUIRE (FILE=FILEN2,EXIST=EXIST2)
C
C         If output file exists, do we overwrite it?
C
          IF ( EXIST2 ) THEN
              WRITE (*,1010) FILEN2(1:LASTC(FILEN2))
 1010         FORMAT (1X,'File ',A, ' exists.  Overwrite it? (Y/N)')
              READ (*,'(A)') YN
          END IF
          IF ( (.NOT. EXIST2) .OR. ( YN .EQ. 'Y' ) .OR.
     *         ( YN .EQ. 'y' ) ) THEN
C
C             Open input data file.  Status is OLD because the input data
C             must already exist.
C
              OPEN (UNIT=8,FILE=FILEN1,STATUS='OLD',IOSTAT=ISTAT1)
C
C             Open output data file.  Status is UNKNOWN since we want to
C             overwrite a file if it exists.
C
              OPEN (UNIT=9,FILE=FILEN2,STATUS='UNKNOWN',IOSTAT=ISTAT2)
C
C             Was the OPEN successful?
C
              IF ( ( ISTAT1 .EQ. 0 ) .AND. ( ISTAT2 .EQ. 0 ) ) THEN
C
C                 The files were opened successfully, so read the data from
C                 the input file and put it into the output file without
C                 trailing blanks.
C
                  READ (8, '(A72)', IOSTAT=ISTAT) LINE
C
C                 Begin WHILE loop.  Did we read the value successfully?
C
   10             IF ( ISTAT .EQ. 0 ) THEN
                      WRITE (9, '(A)', IOSTAT=ISTAT) LINE(1:LASTC(LINE))
C
C                     Read next line.
C
                      READ (8, '(A72)', IOSTAT=ISTAT) LINE
                      GO TO 10
                  END IF
C
C                 End of WHILE Loop
C
              END IF
C
```

```
C               Do you want to delete input file?
C
                WRITE (*,*) 'Delete input file? (Y/N)'
                READ (*,'(A)') YN
                IF ( ( YN .EQ. 'Y' ) .OR. ( YN .EQ. 'y' ) ) THEN
                   CLOSE ( 8, STATUS='DELETE')
                ELSE
                   CLOSE ( 8, STATUS='KEEP')
                END IF
                CLOSE ( 9 )
             END IF
C
C         Handle file open errors.
C
             IF ( ISTAT1 .NE. 0 ) THEN
                WRITE (*,1020) ISTAT1
   1020         FORMAT (1X,'Open error on input file: ISTAT = ', I6)
             END IF
C
             IF ( ISTAT2 .NE. 0 ) THEN
                WRITE (*,1030) ISTAT2
   1030         FORMAT (1X,'Open error on output file: ISTAT = ', I6)
             END IF
          END IF
C
          END
```

Chapter 9

3. The final type of the expression is COMPLEX. The final precision is about seven significant digits.

5. (*a*) Double-precision, with 16 significant digits.   (*b*) Integer, with about 3 significant digits.

  (*c*) Complex, with seven significant digits.

6.
```
          SUBROUTINE DDERIV ( F, X0, DX, DFDX, ERROR )
C
C   Purpose:
C     To take the derivative of function F(X) at point X0
C     using step size DX.  This subroutine expects the
C     function F(X) to be passed as a calling argument.
C
C   Record of revisions:
C       Date        Programmer          Description of change
C       ====        ==========          =====================
C     05/02/93    S. J. Chapman         Original code
C
```

```
C   List of calling arguments:
C      NAME    I/O  TYPE      DIM      DESCRIPTION
C      ====    ===  ====      ===      ===========
C      F       I    DBLE FUN           Function to differentiate.
C      X0      I    DBLE              Location to take derivative.
C      DX      I    REAL              Desired step size.
C      DFDX    O    DBLE              Derivative.
C      ERROR   O    INT               Error flag:
C                                     0 - No error.
C                                     1 - DX < \ <> 0.
C   List of local variables:
C      none

      IMPLICIT NONE
C
C     Declare the dummy arguments for this subroutine.
C
      INTEGER  ERROR
      DOUBLE PRECISION F, X0, DX, DFDX
      EXTERNAL F
C
C     If DX < \ <> = 0., this is an error.
C
      IF ( DX .LE. 0. ) THEN
         ERROR = 1
         RETURN
C
C     IF DX is specified, then calculate derivative using the
C     specified DX.
C
      ELSE IF ( DX .GT. 0. ) THEN
         DFDX = (F(X0 + DX) - F(X0) ) / DX
         ERROR = 0
      END IF
C
      RETURN
      END
```

8.
```
      SUBROUTINE CSIMUL ( A, B, NDIM, N, ERROR )
C
C   Purpose:
C     Subroutine to solve a set of N complex linear equations
C     in N unknowns using Gaussian elimination and the maximum
C     pivot technique.
C
C   Record of revisions:
C        Date       Programmer          Description of change
C        ====       ==========          =====================
C 0. 06/11/91   S. J. Chapman       Original code for subr SIMUL
C    11/12/92   S. J. Chapman       Modified for complex coefficients
C
```

```
C  List of calling arguments:
C     NAME    I/O  TYPE       DIM      DESCRIPTION
C     ====    ===  ====       ===      ===========
C     A        I   CMPLX ARR NDIMxNDIM Array of coefficients (N x N).
C                                      This array is of size NDIM x
C                                      NDIM, but only N x N of the
C                                      coefficients are being used.
C                                      The declared dimension NDIM
C                                      must be passed to the sub, or
C                                      it won't be able to interpret
C                                      subscripts correctly.  (This
C                                      array is destroyed during
C                                      processing.)
C     B        IO  CMPLX ARR  NDIM     Input: Right-hand side of eqns.
C                                      Output: Solution vector.
C     N        I   INTEGER             Number of equations to solve.
C     ERROR    O   INTEGER             Error flag:
C                                      0 — No error
C                                      1 — Singular equations
C
C  List of local parameters:
C     EPSLON -- A "small" number for comparison when determining that
C               a matrix is singular.
C
C  List of local variables:
C     FACTOR -- Factor to multiply eqn IROW by before adding to
C               eqn JROW
C     IROW   -- Number of equation currently being processed
C     IPEAK  -- Pointer to equation containing maximum pivot value
C     JROW   -- Number of equation compared to current equation
C     KCOL   -- Index over all columns of equation
C     TEMP   -- Scratch real variable
C
       IMPLICIT NONE
C
C      Calling arguments.
C
       INTEGER NDIM, N, ERROR
       COMPLEX A(NDIM,NDIM), B(NDIM)
C
C      Parameters.
C
       REAL        EPSLON
       PARAMETER ( EPSLON = 1.0E-6 )
C
C      Local variables.
C
```

```fortran
          INTEGER IROW, JROW, KCOL, IPEAK
          COMPLEX FACTOR, TEMP
C
C     Process N times to get all equations...
C
          DO 50 IROW = 1, N
C
C         Find peak pivot for column IROW in rows I to N
C
              IPEAK = IROW
              DO 10 JROW = IROW+1, N
                  IF (ABS(A(JROW,IROW)) .GT. ABS(A(IPEAK,IROW))) THEN
                      IPEAK = JROW
                  END IF
   10         CONTINUE
C
C         Check for singular equations.
C
              IF ( ABS(A(IPEAK,IROW)) .LT. EPSLON ) THEN
                  ERROR = 1
                  RETURN
              END IF
C
C         Otherwise, if IPEAK<> IROW, swap equations IROW & IPEAK
C
              IF ( IPEAK .NE. IROW ) THEN
                  DO 20 KCOL = 1, N
                      TEMP           = A(IPEAK,KCOL)
                      A(IPEAK,KCOL) = A(IROW,KCOL)
                      A(IROW,KCOL)  = TEMP
   20             CONTINUE
                  TEMP      = B(IPEAK)
                  B(IPEAK) = B(IROW)
                  B(IROW)  = TEMP
              END IF
C
C         Multiply equation IROW by -A(JROW,IROW)/A(IROW,IROW), and
C         add it to Eqn JROW (for all eqns except IROW itself).
C
              DO 40 JROW = 1, N
                  IF ( JROW .NE. IROW ) THEN
                      FACTOR = -A(JROW,IROW)/A(IROW,IROW)
                      DO 30 KCOL = 1, N
                          A(JROW,KCOL) = A(IROW,KCOL)*FACTOR + A(JROW,KCOL)
   30                 CONTINUE
                      B(JROW) = B(IROW)*FACTOR + B(JROW)
                  END IF
   40         CONTINUE
   50 CONTINUE
C
```

```
C     End of main loop over all equations.  All off-diagonal
C     terms are now zero.  To get the final answer, we must
C     divide each equation by the coefficient of its on-diagonal
C     term.
C
      DO 60 IROW = 1, N
         B(IROW)     = B(IROW) / A (IROW,IROW)
         A(IROW,IROW) = 1.
   60 CONTINUE
C
C     Set error flag to 0 and return.
C
      ERROR = 0
      RETURN
      END
```

Chapter 10

6.
```
      SUBROUTINE LSQFT ( X, Y, NVALS, ORDER, C, IERROR )
C
C  Purpose:
C    To perform a least-squares fit of an input data set
C    to the polynomial
C      Y(X) = C(0) + C(1)*X + C(2)*X**2 + C(3)*X**3 + ...
C    and print out the resulting coeffficients.  The fit
C    can be to any polynomial of first through ninth order.
C    The input data set consists of NVALS (X,Y) pairs contained
C    in  arrays X and Y.  The output coefficients of the
C    polynomial fit are placed in array C.
C
C  Record of revisions:
C     Date        Programmer          Description of change
C     ====        ==========          =====================
C    08/01/93   S. J. Chapman        Original code
C
C  List of calling arguments:
C    NAME    I/O  TYPE      DIM     DESCRIPTION
C    ====    ===  ====      ===     ===========
C    X       I    REAL ARR  N       Array of X data values.
C    Y       I    REAL ARR  N       Array of Y data values.
C    NVALS   I    INT               Number of values in arrays
C                                   X and Y.
C    ORDER   I    INT               Order of the fit to perform
C    C       O    REAL ARR  0:ORDER Coefficients C0, C1, C2, ...
C    IERROR  O    INT               Error flag:
C                                   0 - No error.
C                                   1 - Singular equations
C                                   2 - Not enough input values
C                                   3 - Illegal order specified
C
```

```
C   List of local parameters:
C      MAXORD -- Maximum order of fit
C
C   List of local variables:
C      A       -- Array of coefficients of C
C      B       -- Right side of coefficient equations
C      I       -- Index variable
C      J       -- Index variable
C      SUMXN   -- The sum of all input X**N values where
C                 N = 0, 1, ..., 2*ORDER
C      SUMXNY  -- The sum of all X**N*Y values where
C                 N = 0, 1, ..., 2*ORDER
C
       IMPLICIT NONE
C
C   Declare the dummy arguments for this subroutine.
C
       INTEGER NVALS, ORDER, IERROR
       REAL    X(NVALS), Y(NVALS), C(0:ORDER)
C
C   Declare parameters.
C
       INTEGER    MAXORD
       PARAMETER ( MAXORD = 9 )
C
C   Declare local variables.
C
       INTEGER I, J
       REAL    SUMXN(0:2*MAXORD)
       REAL    SUMXNY(0:MAXORD)
       REAL    A(0:MAXORD,0:MAXORD), B(0:MAXORD)
C
C   First, check to make sure that we have enough input data.
C
       IF ( NVALS .LT. ORDER+1 ) THEN
C
C      Insufficient data.  Set IERROR = 2, and get out.
C
          IERROR = 2
C
       ELSE IF ( (ORDER .LT. 1) .OR. (ORDER .GT. MAXORD) ) THEN
C
C      Illegal equation order.  Set IERROR = 3, and get out.
C
          IERROR = 3
       ELSE
C
C      Zero the sums used to build the equations.
C
```

```
            DO 10 I = 0, 2*ORDER
               SUMXN(I) = 0.
     10     CONTINUE
C
            DO 20 I = 0, ORDER
               SUMXNY(I) = 0.
     20     CONTINUE
C
C          Build the sums required to solve the equations.
C
            DO 50 I = 1, NVALS
               DO 30 J = 0, 2*ORDER
                  SUMXN(J) = SUMXN(J) + X(I)**J
     30        CONTINUE
C
               DO 40 J = 0, ORDER
                  SUMXNY(J) = SUMXNY(J) + X(I)**J * Y(I)
     40        CONTINUE
     50     CONTINUE
C
C          Set up the coefficients of the equations.
C
            DO 80 I = 0, ORDER
               DO 70 J = 0, ORDER
                  A(I,J) = SUMXN(I+J)
     70        CONTINUE
     80     CONTINUE
C
            DO 90 I=0, ORDER
               B(I) = SUMXNY(I)
     90     CONTINUE
C
C          Solve for the LSQFIT coefficients.  They will
C          be returned in array B if IERROR = 0.
C
            CALL SIMUL ( A, B, MAXORD+1, ORDER+1, IERROR )
C
C          If IERROR = 0, return the coefficients to the
C          user.
C
            IF ( IERROR .EQ. 0 ) THEN
               DO 100 I = 0, ORDER
                  C(I) = B(I)
    100        CONTINUE
            ELSE
               DO 110 I = 0, ORDER
                  C(I) = 0.0
    110        CONTINUE
            END IF
         END IF
C
         RETURN
         END
```

Chapter 11

6.
```
      PROGRAM PLTSNC
C
C  Purpose:
C    To plot the sinc and the derivative of the sinc function
C    between -2*PI and 2*PI.
C
C  Record of revisions:
C      Date        Programmer          Description of change
C      ====        ==========          =====================
C    10/31/93    S. J. Chapman         Original code
C
C  List of externals:
C      DERIV  -- Calculates derivative of a function at a point.
C      PLOTXY -- Plot (X,Y) pairs of points.
C      SINC   -- Function SINC(X)
C
C  List of variables:
C      DSINC1 -- The derivative of the sinc function.
C      DX     -- Step size for evaluating derivative
C      I      -- DO loop index
C      IERROR -- Error flag
C      MAXX   -- Dummy variable
C      MAXY   -- Dummy variable
C      MINX   -- Dummy variable
C      MINY   -- Dummy variable
C      SINC1  -- The sinc function.
C      STEP   -- Increment between successive points X(I)
C      X      -- Points at which to evaluate SINC(X) and DSINC(X)
C
      IMPLICIT NONE
C
C    Declare parameters.
C
      INTEGER    LU
      REAL       TWOPI
      PARAMETER ( LU    =  6        )
      PARAMETER ( TWOPI =  6.283185 )
C
C    Declare external functions.
C
      REAL     SINC
      EXTERNAL SINC
C
C    Declare the variables used in this program.
C
      INTEGER I, IERROR
      REAL    X(41), SINC1(41), DSINC1(41), STEP, DX
      REAL    MINX, MINY, MAXX, MAXY
C
```

```
C      Get step size for plots.
C
       STEP = 2. * TWOPI / 41.
C
C      Get the values of the SINC(X) function at points X(I).
C
       DO 10 I = 1, 41
          X(I)     = REAL(I-1) * STEP - TWOPI
          SINC1(I) = SINC(X(I))
   10 CONTINUE
C
C      Get the values of the derivative of the SINC function at
C      the same points X(I).
C
       DO 20 I = 1, 41
          DX = 0.
          CALL DERIV ( SINC, X(I), DX, DSINC1(I), IERROR )
   20 CONTINUE
C
C      Plot the SINC function.
C
       CALL PLOTXY ( X, SINC1, 41, MINX, MAXX, MINY, MAXY,
      *              41, 0, .TRUE., LU )
C
C      Plot the derivative of the SINC function.
C
       CALL PLOTXY ( X, DSINC1, 41, MINX, MAXX, MINY, MAXY,
      *              41, 0, .TRUE., LU )
C
       END
```

13.
```
       PROGRAM DISTRB
C
C  Purpose:
C    To generate a histogram of the noise distributions
C    produced by subroutines RANO and GRANO.
C
C  Record of revisions:
C     Date        Programmer          Description of change
C     ====        ==========          =====================
C    10/31/93    S. J. Chapman        Original code
C
C  List of externals:
C     HIST   -- Generate and plot histograms.
C     GRANO  -- Generate zero-mean gaussian random variables.
C     RANO   -- Generate uniform random variables.
C
C  List of parameters:
C     LU     -- Output LU.
C     NVALS  -- Number of random samples to process.
C
```

```
C  List of variables:
C      DSINC1 -- The derivative of the sinc function.
C      DX      -- Step size for evaluating derivative
C      GAUSS  -- Array of Gaussian distributed noise data.
C      I       -- DO loop index
C      IERROR -- Error flag
C      UNIF    -- Array of uniformly distributed noise data.
C
       IMPLICIT NONE
C
C      Declare parameters.
C
       INTEGER    LU
       INTEGER    NVALS
       PARAMETER ( LU     = 6     )
       PARAMETER ( NVALS = 10000 )
C
C      Declare the variables used in this program.
C
       INTEGER I, IERROR
       REAL    UNIF(NVALS), GAUSS(NVALS)
C
C      Get arrays of uniformly-distributed random values and
C      Gaussian-distributed random values.
C
       DO 10 I = 1, NVALS
          CALL RANO ( UNIF(I) )
          CALL GRANO ( GAUSS(I) )
    10 CONTINUE
C
C      Generate and plot histogram of uniformly-distributed data.
C
       WRITE (LU,1000) 'Histogram of Uniformly Distributed Data'
  1000 FORMAT (//,T30,A)
       CALL HIST (UNIF, NVALS, 21, 0., 1., .FALSE., LU, IERROR)
C
C      Generate and plot histogram of Gaussian-distributed data.
C
       WRITE (LU,1000) 'Histogram of Gaussian Distributed Data'
       CALL HIST (GAUSS, NVALS, 21, -4., 4., .FALSE., LU, IERROR)
C
       END
```

Chapter 12

7. (a) POWER(VOLTS,AMPS,THETA) = VOLTS * AMPS * COS(THETA)
   (b) AREA(BASE,HEIGHT) = 0.5 * BASE * HEIGHT
   (c) THETA(A,B,C) = ACOS ((A**2+B**C**2) / (2.*A*B))

Chapter 13

3. (*a*) Legal. (*b*) Illegal: ampersand is an illegal character.
(*c*) Illegal: question mark is an illegal character. (*d*) Illegal: must begin with a letter.

7. The subroutine shown below shifts lowercase characters to uppercase using a **SELECT CASE** structure.

```
SUBROUTINE UCASE ( STRING )
!
!   Purpose:
!     To shift a character string to UPPER case (ASCII only).
!
!   Record of revisions:
!       Date        Programmer            Description of change
!       ====        ==========            =====================
!     11/01/92     S. J. Chapman          Original code
!
!   List of calling arguments:
!       NAME    I/O  TYPE            DESCRIPTION
!       ====    ===  ====            ===========
!       STRING  IO   CHARACTER       Input/output character string
!
!   List of local variables:
!       I        -- Index variable.
!       LENGTH -- Length of STRING
!       S        -- Converted character.
!
!   Declare calling parameters
!
CHARACTER(LEN=*) STRING
!
!   Declare local variables
!
INTEGER     I, LENGTH
CHARACTER*1 S

!   Get the length of the input STRING.

LENGTH = LEN ( STRING )

!   Now shift lower case letters to upper case.

DO I = 1, LENGTH
   SELECT CASE ( STRING(I:I) )
   CASE ('a':'z')
      S = CHAR ( ICHAR ( STRING(I:I) ) - 32 )
      STRING(I:I) = S
   END SELECT
END DO

RETURN
END
```

Index